Baedeker's
GREECE

A SPECTRUM BOOK

PRENTICE-HALL, Inc., Englewood Cliffs, New Jersey 07632

Cover picture: Temple of Poseidon, Cape Soúnion

169 colour photographs
65 maps and plans
1 large road map

Text:
Dr Otto Gärtner (Glossary of Technical Terms,
Greece from A to Z)
Gerald Sawade (Climate)

Editorial work:
Baedeker Stuttgart
English language: Alec Court

Cartography:
Ingenieurbüro für Kartographie
Huber & Oberländer, Munich

Design and layout:
Creativ + Druck GmbH
Ulrich Kolb, Stuttgart

Conception and general direction:
Dr Peter Baumgarten,
Baedeker Stuttgart

English translation:
James Hogarth

© Baedeker Stuttgart
Original German edition

© The Automobile Association
United Kingdom and Ireland

© Jarrold and Sons Ltd
English Language edition Worldwide

Licensed user:
Mairs Geographischer Verlag GmbH & Co.,
Ostfildern-Kemnat bei Stuttgart

Reproductions:
Gölz Repro-Service GmbH,
Ludwigsburg

The name *Baedeker* is a registered trademark

Source of illustrations:

Many of the coloured photographs were supplied by
the National Tourist Organisation of Greece in Athens
and Frankfurt am Main (through the Frankfurter
Werbe- und Verlagsgesellschaft).

Others:
Allianz-Archiv (p. 262)
Assimakopouli, Athens (pp. 31, 37; 43, left; 56, 98,
110; 176, left; 184, right; 193, 213; 218, left; 268)
Hans Baedeker, Stuttgart (pp. 114, 123, 124, 126;
190, top left; 204, foot)
Erdmann Baier, Mainz (pp. 132, left; 142, 202; 204,
top; 238, 244; 250, right; 279, top)
Bavaria-Verlag, Gauting (pp. 224, top; 231; 250,
bottom left)
Delta, Athens (pp. 38, 63, 66, 113; 138, top; 150, 163,
182, 197, 215; 224, foot; 225; 229, both; 236, 261)
Dr Otto Gärtner, Giessen (pp. 48, bottom right; 68, 88,
90; 91, top; 92, top; 93, 94)
Hannibal (Tryfides), Athens (pp. 27; 32, both; 40; 43,
top; 128, 179, 187, 207; 208, both; 210, both; 222,
242)
Olympic (Decopoulos), Athens (pp. 7, 23; 24, both;
25, 28, 44; 48, left and top right; 51, 67, 70, 72, 76, 78,
79; 91, right; 92, left; 101, both; 102, both; 104, 109;
111, both; 115; 118, both; 121, 131; 132, right; 141;
145, both; 146, 161, 162, 175; 176, right; 177, 188;
190, bottom right; 191; 199, foot; 206, 214, 217, 235;
241, both; 282)
Aris Spyropoulos, Athens (pp. 138, foot; 140; 184,
left; 185; 199, top; 211, top; 219, 232, 240, 245, 249,
274; 279, foot)
Zentrale Farbbild Agentur GmbH (ZEFA), Düsseldorf
(cover picture; p. 264)

The panorama of Athens on pp. 80–81 was drawn by
Werner Gölitzer, Stuttgart; the drawings of Sappho
(p. 172) and the Venus de Milo (p. 180) are by Katja
Ungerer, Stuttgart.

How to Use this Guide

The principal towns and areas of tourist interest are
described in alphabetical order. The names of other
places referred to under these main headings can be
found in the Index.

Following the tradition established by Karl Baedeker
in 1844, sights of particular interest and hotels and
restaurants of particular quality are distinguished by
either one or two asterisks.

In the lists of hotels b.=beds. Hotels are classified in
the categories shown on p. 273.

A glossary of technical terms in the fields of art, history
and mythology is given on p. 44.

The symbol ⓘ at the beginning of an entry or on a
town plan indicates the local tourist office or other
organisation from which further information can be
obtained. The post-horn symbol on a town plan
indicates a post office.

Only a selection of hotels and restaurants can be
given: no reflection is implied, therefore, on establishments not included.

In a time of rapid change it is difficult to ensure that all
information given in a guidebook is entirely accurate
and up to date, and the possibility of error can never be
completely eliminated. The publishers are always
grateful, therefore, for corrections and suggestions for
improvement.

Printed in Great Britain by Jarrold & Sons Ltd,
Norwich

ISBN 0-13-056002-2 paperback
ISBN 0-13-056010-3 hard cover

This guidebook forms part of a completely new series of the world-famous Baedeker Guides to Europe.

Each volume is the result of long and careful preparation and, true to the traditions of Baedeker, is designed in every respect to meet the needs and expectations of the modern traveller.

The name of Baedeker has long been identified in the field of guidebooks with reliable, comprehensive and up-to-date information, prepared by expert writers who work from detailed, first-hand knowledge of the country concerned. Following a tradition that goes back over 150 years to the date when Karl Baedeker published the first of his handbooks for travellers, these guides have been planned to give the tourist all the essential information about the country and its inhabitants: where to go, how to get there and what to see. Baedeker's account of a country was always based on his personal observation and experience during his travels in that country. This tradition of writing a guidebook in the field rather than at an office desk has been maintained by Baedeker ever since.

Lavishly illustrated with superb colour photographs and numerous specially drawn maps and street plans of the major towns, the new Baedeker Guides concentrate on making available to the modern traveller all the information he needs in a format that is both attractive and easy to follow. For every place that appears in the gazetteer, the principal features of architectural, artistic and historic interest are described, as are its main areas of scenic beauty. Selected hotels and restaurants are also included. Features of exceptional merit are indicated by either one or two asterisks.

A special section at the end of each book contains practical information, details of leisure activities and useful addresses. The separate road map will prove an invaluable aid to planning your route and your travel within the country.

Contents

Greece from A to Z

Aegina · Agrinion · Aiyion · Alexandroupolis · Alonnisos · Amfissa · Amorgos · Amphiareion · Amphipolis · Anafi · Andros · Arakhova · Arcadia · Argolid · Argos · Argo-Saronic Islands · Arkhanes · Arta · Astypalaia · Athens · Athos · Attica · Attic Riviera · Ayia Triada · Ayios Efstratios · Ayios Nikolaos · Bassai · Boeotia · Brauron · Chaironeia · Chalcidice · Chios · Corfu · Corinth · Crete · Cyclades · Dafni · Delos · Delphi · Dodecanese · Dodona · Drama · Edessa · Eleusis · Epidauros · Epirus · Euboea · Farsala · Florina · Folegandros · Fourni · Fyli · Geraki · Gla · Gortys · Gournia · Gythion · Hydra · Hymettos · Ialysos · Ierapetra · Igoumenitsa · Ikaria · Ioannina · Ionian Islands · Ios · Iraklion · Isthmia · Itea · Ithaca · Ithomi · Kaiafas · Kalamata · Kalambaka · Kalavryta · Kalymnos · Kamena Vourla · Kamiros · Karditsa · Karpathos · Karytaina · Kasos · Kastelli Kisamou · Kastoria · Kato Zakros · Kavala · Kea · Kefallinia · Khania · Khersonisos · Kimolos · Knossos · Koroni · Kos · Kyllini · Kyparissia · Kythira · Kythnos · Lamia · Larisa · Lasithi · Lefkas · Lemnos · Leros · Lesbos · Levadia · Lindos · Litokhoro · Loutraki · Macedonia · Malia · Mani · Mantineia · Marathon · Megalopolis · Melos · Mesolongi · Mesopotamos · Meteora · Methoni · Metsovo · Mistra · Monemvasia · Mycenae · Mykonos · Nafpaktos · Nafplion · Naxos · Nemea · Nikopolis · Nisyros · Northern and Eastern Aegean Islands · Olympia · Mount Olympus · Olynthos · Orkhomenos · Oropos · Osios Loukas · Parga · Mount Parnassus · Mount Parnis · Mount Parnon · Paros · Patmos · Patras · Paxi and Antipaxi · Mount Pelion · Pella · Peloponnese · Mount Pentelikon · Perakhora · Phaistos · Philippi · Pindos · Piraeus · Plataiai · Poros · Porto Kheli · Porto Rafti · Porto Yermeno · Preveza · Pylos · Pyrgos · Rethymnon · Rhamnous · Rhodes · Rion · Salamis · Salonica · Samaria Gorge · Samos · Samothrace · Santorin · Saronic Gulf · Serifos · Serrai · Servia · Sifnos · Sikinos · Sitia · Skiathos · Skopelos · Skyros · Sounion · Sparta · Spetsai · Sporades · Symi · Syros · Taygetos · Tegea · Tempe · Thasos · Thebes · Thermaic Gulf · Thermopylai · Thessaly · Thrace · Tilos · Tinos · Tiryns · Tolon · Trikala · Tripolis · Troizen · Vergina · Veria · Volos · Vonitsa · Xylokastro · Zakynthos

Introduction to Greece

There is no generally accepted system for the transliteration of modern Greek place-names and personal names into the Latin alphabet, and the visitor to Greece will find much diversity and inconsistency of spelling, for example on signposts and in guidebooks and other literature in English. The situation is still further complicated by changes in pronunciation which have taken place since ancient times, so that many familiar old classical names look very different in modern Greek: thus the ancient Hymettus or Hymettos may appear as Imittós.

In this Guide modern Greek place-names and personal names are transliterated in a form approximating to their pronunciation. Classical names are given in their "Greek" rather than their "Latin" form (e.g. Polykleitos rather than Polyclitus), except where there is an accepted English form (Athens, Piraeus) or where the name is so familiar in its Latin form that it would be pedantic to insist on the Greek spelling (e.g. Thucydides, not Thoukydides).

Windmill on Mýkonos

Greece
(Hellenic Republic)

Boundaries of
geographical regions

Boundaries of nomoi

Greece, with an area of just under 132,000 sq. km (50,965 sq. miles) and a population of rather more than 9 million, is divided into 10 geographical **regions**, which in turn are subdivided into 51 **nomoi** (*nomí*) (administrative units). The nomoi are made up of 147 *eparchies* (rural districts), with 264 *municipalities* (*demoi, dími*), 5762 *rural communes* (*koinotetes, kinótites*) and 11,691 *settlements* (*oikismoi, ikismí*). The monastic republic of **Athos** has its own independent administration.

Since the fall of the military dictatorship in 1974 and the referendum on the monarchy, in which the great majority of the population voted for the abdication of the exiled king, Greece has been a democratic **Republic**. The new constitution of 1975 gives wide authority to the President, who is elected by Parliament by a two-thirds majority for a term of five years. He appoints and dismisses the head of the government, can dissolve Parliament in certain specified circumstances and in a situation of national emergency has the power to legislate.

Parliament, elected for a four-year term (most recently in 1977) has 300 members. The most important political parties are the New Democracy (Néa Dimokratía) party and the Pan-Hellenic Socialist Movement. The Union of the Centre, the Communist Party and the National Movement are confined in present circumstances to a subordinate role.

An associate member of the European Community since 1962, Greece became a full member on 1 January 1980. It is also a member of the United Nations, NATO and numerous other international organisations.

Administrative Units (Nomoi)

	Nomos and Chief town	Area in sq. km (sq. miles)	Population	Pop. per sq. km (sq. mile)
1	Evros (Alexandroúpolis)	4242 (1638)	140,000	33 (85)
2	Rhodope	2543 (982)	110,000	42 (112)
3	Xanthi	1793 (692)	85,000	46 (122)
4	Kavála	2109 (814)	125,000	58 (153)
5	Drama	3468 (1339)	92,000	26 (69)
7	Kilkis	2614 (1009)	85,000	32 (84)
8	Salonica	3560 (1375)	720,000	200 (523)
9	Lésbos (Mytilini)	2154 (832)	115,000	53 (138)
10	Chalcidice (Poliyiros)	2945 (1137)	75,000	25 (66)
11	Pieria (Katerini)	1506 (581)	92,000	61 (158)
12	Imathia (Véria)	1712 (661)	120,000	69 (182)
13	Pélla (Edessa)	2506 (968)	130,000	50 (134)
14	Flórina	1863 (719)	52,000	51 (72)
15	Kastoriá	1685 (651)	46,000	27 (71)
16	Kozani	3565 (1376)	140,000	38 (102)
17	Grevena	2838 (1096)	35,000	15 (32)
18	Ioánnina	4990 (1927)	135,000	27 (70)
19	Thesprotia (Igoumenitsa)	1514 (585)	42,000	27 (72)
20	Préveza	1086 (419)	60,000	52 (143)
21	Arta	1613 (623)	80,000	49 (128)
22	Tríkala	3367 (1300)	135,000	39 (104)
23	Kardítsa	2576 (995)	135,000	52 (136)
24	Lárisa	5350 (2066)	232,000	43 (112)
25	Magnesia (Vólos)	2636 (1018)	165,000	61 (162)
26	Evritania (Karpenision)	2045 (790)	30,000	14 (38)
27	Aetolia and Acarnania (Agrinion)	5447 (2103)	230,000	42 (109)
28	Phthiotis (Lamía)	4368 (1686)	155,000	35 (92)
29	Phocis (Amfissa)	2121 (819)	41,000	20 (50)
30	Euboea (Khalkis)	3908 (1509)	165,000	42 (109)
31	Boeotia (Levádia)	3211 (1240)	115,000	36 (93)
32	Attica (Athens)	3380 (1305)	260,000	76 (199)
33	Corinth	2289 (884)	115,000	49 (130)
34	Achaia (Pátras)	3209 (1239)	245,000	75 (198)
35	Elis (Pýrgos)	2681 (1035)	165,000	62 (159)
36	Arcadia (Trípolis)	4419 (1706)	111,000	25 (65)
37	Argolid (Nauplia)	2214 (855)	90,000	40 (105)
38	Messenia (Kalamáta)	2991 (1155)	175,000	58 (152)
39	Laconia (Sparta)	3636 (1404)	96,000	26 (68)
40	Corfu (Kérkyra)	641 (247)	95,000	145 (385)
41	Lefkás	325 (125)	25,000	76 (200)
42	Kefallinía (Argostoli)	935 (361)	37,000	39 (102)
43	Zákynthos	406 (157)	30,000	74 (191)
44	Khaniá	2376 (917)	120,000	50 (131)
45	Réthymnon	1496 (578)	61,000	41 (106)
46	Iráklion	2641 (1020)	215,000	79 (211)
47	Lasíthi (Ayios Nikólaos)	1823 (704)	66,000	36 (94)
48	Dodecanese (Rhodes)	2705 (1044)	121,000	45 (116)
49	Cyclades (Ermoupolis)	2572 (993)	86,000	34 (87)
50	Sámos (Vathy)	778 (300)	42,000	54 (140)
51	Chios	904 (349)	55,000	60 (158)
	Greater Athens	428 (165)	2,550,000	5958 (15,455)
	Athos	336 (130)	1700	5 (13)

Greece, the cradle of Western culture, has long attracted scholars and travellers interested in its classical past; but in recent years it has also been discovered by a wider public who have come to appreciate its many other attractions. The visitors who are now drawn to Greece in such large numbers do not go only to see its ancient sites and recall the contribution it has made to European cultural and intellectual life, but to enjoy the extraordinary beauty of its scenery, the Mediterranean charm of its islands, still largely unspoiled, the ready hospitality of its people and its beautiful beaches – all combining to form a marvellously seductive holiday land.

No other country is so characteristic of the Mediterranean world as Greece. Slender and intricately articulated, surrounded by a multitude of islands of all shapes and sizes, it pulls away from the more solid structure of south-eastern Europe, reaching far out into the sea to Europe's most southerly outpost, the long island of Crete. It is a land of mountains, deeply penetrated by the ubiquitous sea and wrapped in the mantle of a climate which is everywhere the same. Greek land and the Greek seas – the Ionian Sea in the W, the Aegean in the E – are parts of an indivisible whole, one of which cannot be conceived without the other. No part of the Peloponnese or central Greece is much more than 50 km (31 miles) from the sea, and even in northern Greece the maximum distance from the sea is not much more than 100 km (62 miles).

Greece is a relatively small country, with a land mass of only 131,900 sq. km (50,926 sq. miles), but the area of sea which it occupies is something like 400,000 sq. km (154,440 sq. miles). About a fifth of its land area (25,166 sq. km – 9717 sq. miles) is accounted for by islands. The sea cuts deeply into the land from the W in the Gulf of Corinth and carves the eastern and southern coasts into a complex pattern of promontories and inlets, peninsulas and bays, linking them up with the scatter of islands to the S and E. Of the country's total coastline of 15,021 km (9334 miles)

The Principal Mountains of Greece

ome 11,000 km (6835 miles) are contri-ɔuted by the 2000 islands. Greece's land frontiers amount to only 1171 km (727 miles) (247 km (153 miles) with Albania, 246 km (153 miles) with Yugoslavia, 475 km (295 miles) with Bulgaria and 203 km (126 miles) with Turkey).

Mainland Greece, bounded by mountainous regions on the W, has an open seaboard on the E, with coastal plains and natural harbours. The *mountains* rise for the most part above 1000 m (3281 ft), frequently exceeding 2000 m (6562 ft), reaching their highest point in Olympus (2917 m – 9571 ft). They appear even higher than they are, rising directly out of the sea and in many rugged coastal areas rearing up in sheer cliffs to the summit. They are very different from the Alps, however, since they have been shaped not by glaciers but by weathering and water erosion. There are no jagged peaks or arêtes; the hills are predominantly of gentle rounded form, characterised more by horizontal than by vertical lines. There are few areas of lower hills, and the mountains are always visible in the background; low-lying land is the exception. There are, it is true, many areas of plain; but they are small, frequently at a high altitude and always framed by hills. Many of them are connected with basins which frequently have no drainage to the exterior and are occupied by lakes and bogs. Others lie on the sea or are washed by the sea which penetrates far inland in deeply indented gulfs and inlets.

It is these *plain basins* that provide the people of Greece with their main lebensraum. They are cut off from one another, linked only by routes running through inhospitable mountains or over difficult passes (though the road system is constantly being developed). Access is therefore frequently easier by sea. The extent of these plain areas increases from S to N; the only plains of any size are in the N (Thessaly, Macedonia) and in Laconia. In ancient times this fragmentation of Greek territory led to the formation of many small independent states, consisting of the *polis* (city) and its immediately surrounding area.

Rivers of any considerable length are found only in the N (Thessaly, Macedonia, Thrace) – the Pinios, the Axios, the Strymon, the Nestos, the Evros. They give

Greece a series of fertile flood plains in which agriculture has made substantial progress in recent years. In the rest of the country the rivers mostly dry up in summer but during the rainy season swell into raging torrents.

The intricate coastal topography of mainland Greece has its counterpart in the multitude of **islands** scattered in the Aegean to the E and the Ionian Sea to the W, which in ancient times developed the seafaring skills of the Greeks and made them at an early stage the economic and cultural mediators between the three continents of the ancient world. – The most thickly clustered islands are those in the Aegean, between the Greek mainland and the Turkish coast. *Euboea* (*Evvia*), the largest of the central Greek islands is, like the *Northern Sporades* to the NE, a continuation of the Othrys range on the mainland and was considered in ancient times as a detached part of Boeotia. The *Cyclades*, lying around Delos, which fill the southern Aegean, are the most south-easterly extension of Euboea and Attica. *Kýthira* (*Cythera*), SE of the Peloponnese, is a stepping-stone on the way to *Crete*, the largest of the Greek islands (apart from the independent island of Cyprus), which closes off the Aegean on the south; straggling from E to W, it is a continuation of the mountain ranges of Anatolia.

Off the SW coast of Asia Minor, between *Rhodes* and *Sámos*, extends a string of islands, the *Southern Sporades*, most of them belonging to the Dodecanese. Widely dispersed in the north-eastern Aegean are the large islands of *Chios*, *Lésbos*, *Lemnos*, *Samothrace* and *Thásos*. – Off the W coast of Greece lie the *Ionian Islands*, the central group of which is ethnologically and historically associated with the nearby mainland of central Greece.

Geology. – The mountain ranges and massifs of Greece form a pattern of great intricacy and variety. In the W they are comprehended under the term Hellenides (Dinarides), which in the Greek peninsula run from NW to SE and extend in a wide arc by way of Crete and Rhodes to Asia Minor. They are folded mountains of Alpine structure, formed fairly late in geological time and consisting mostly of Mesozoic and Tertiary rocks, in particular limestones, sandstones, marls and con-glomerates. Apart from this folding the territory of Greece has been subjected to violent upthrusting and downfaulting at various periods in the earth's history, continuing into quite recent times. In the Peloponnese late Tertiary deposits laid down by the sea are found at an altitude of 1800 m (5906 ft).

Quite different formations occur in the eastern part of the peninsula and in the Aegean. In early geological times the Aegean basin was occupied by a folded range of ancient mountains, mostly of crystalline and metamorphic rocks, whose eroded remains survive in Thrace and Macedonia (the Rhodope massif), the Cyclades and the southern Peloponnese (the Pelagonian massif) and whose peaks emerge from the sea in the form of islands.

In the Mesozoic era these ancient hills were covered by the Tethys Sea, which left massive deposits of slates, sandstones and limestones. During the Pleistocene, after the withdrawal of the sea, they formed a land link between Greece and Asia Minor. Then in the Quaternary period three large depressions were formed in this area – the northern Aegean basin (up to 1950 m (6398 ft) deep), to the N of an imaginary line from the Magnesian peninsula by way of Lemnos to the Gallipoli peninsula (the Dardanelles being a drowned river valley); the central Aegean basin (up to 4850 m (15,913 ft) deep) between Euboea, the Cyclades, Samos and Chios; and the southern Aegean basin (up to 4453 m (14,610 ft) deep), north of a line from Kýthira by way of Santorin to Rhodes. These depressions are separated by ridges around 500 m (1641 ft) deep, and are marked off from the south-eastern Mediterranean by a shelf some 800 m (2625 ft) deep.

It is a reflection of this highly unstable structure that the territory of Greece, even more markedly than the rest of the Mediterranean area, is fragmented by countless faults and fractures, to an extent found hardly anywhere else on the earth. The faults affected both the folded rocks and the ancient basement, producing a mosaic of hills of varying height and countless little basins and plain areas, forming deep bays, long promontories and peninsulas, a scatter of islands, rugged cliffs and a fantastically patterned coastline. In the fault zones there was violent volcanic activity, decreasing in more recent times, with its accompani-ment of earth tremors and thermal springs. The folding and faulting of limestones has produced the karstic formations to be seen all over Greece and on the islands, particularly in the Ionian Sea.

Major Earthquakes in Greece	
c. 1400 B.C.	Devastation of Minoan civilisation
464 B.C.	Devastation in Eurotas valley; destruction of Sparta (20,000 killed?)
6th c. A.D.	Destruction of Olympia
1856	Crete
1886	Devastation of three towns and 123 villages in Messenia
1926	Rhodes
1928	Destruction of Corinth
1944	West coast of Máni devastated
1953	Ionian Islands
1975	Severe tremors in Aetolia and Acarnania
1978	Northern Greece; much damage in Salonica

Climate

Greece reaches out from the Balkan land mass far into the eastern Mediterranean, with numerous peninsulas, islands and islets. Its climate depends on a corresponding variety of influences.

Mainland Greece has in the N, in some inland basins and in the higher mountain areas a climate partly determined by continental influences, with wide temperature variations between day and night and between summer and winter (Kavála annual average 10·8 °C (51 °F), January 1° (34°), July 21·5° (71°); Salonica annual average 15·9° (61°), January 6° (43°), July 26° (79°), min. over year −9·5° (15°), max. 41·6° (107°); Ioánnina, alt. 520 m (1706 ft) annual average 14·4° (58°), January 6° (18°), August 24° (75°)).

Elsewhere, including the *islands*, Greece has a **Mediterranean climate**, with high winter and summer temperatures and rain mainly in winter. – The average annual temperature on the mainland at sea level is over 16 °C (61°) rising towards the S to 18·7° (66°) (Lárisa 16·1° (61°), Vólos 16·9° (62°), Athens 17·4° (64°), Náfplion 18·1° (65°), Kalamáta 18·7° (66°)). On the islands it increases from 17·7° (64°) (Corfu, Ándros) to 18·5° (66°) (Zákynthos, Náxos, Iráklion); Santorin is rather cooler (17·1° – 63°). The January average ranges on the mainland from 6° (42°) (Lárisa) to 7·5° (44°) (Vólos, Lamía), 9·3° (48°) (Athens), 11° (52°) (Pátras, Náfplion) and 11·5° (52°) (Kalamáta), on the islands from 10° (50°) (Corfu) to 11° (52°) (Ándros, Santorin), 12° (53°) (Zákynthos; Khaniá and Iráklion on Crete) and 13° (55°) (Náxos). The summer maximum (usually in July but at some places in August) is almost everywhere around 26·5° (79°) (exceptions being Santorin 24° (76°), Náxos 25° (77°) and Sparta 27·5° (80°)). The lowest and highest recorded temperatures are −5·5° (22°) and 43° (109°) at Athens, −2·8° (27°) and 41° (106°) on Corfu and 0·1° (32°) and 45·7° (113°) on Crete.

Sea temperatures (measured on the surface) in January and August are 11·5° (53°) and 25·6 (78°) at Salonica, 14·8° (58°) and 25·6° (78°) at Athens, 15·5° (60°) and 26·8° (80°) on Corfu and 15·2° (58°) and 25·6° (78°) on Crete.

The amount and annual distribution of **rainfall** is conditioned by the mountainous topography and the prevailing winds. The west winds which blow in winter cause heavy rainfall in western Greece, decreasing in intensity towards the S (December rainfall on Corfu 180 mm (7 in.), at Ioánnina and Árta 160 mm (6 in.), at Mesolóngi 130 mm (5 in.). Still farther S, particularly in the Peloponnese and on Crete, a high winter rainfall is produced by warm, moist and frequently very stormy winds from the SW and S (December figures for Zákynthos 230 mm (9 in.), Kyparissía, Sparta and Khaniá in Crete 160 mm (6¼ in.), Anoyia, on the northern slopes of the Mt Ida range, 250 mm (8¾ in.)). In the rain shadow of the west winds the winter maxima are considerably lower (Kavála February 82 mm (3¼ in.), Salonica November 64 mm (2¼ in.), Vólos November 74 mm (3 in.), Athens December 68 mm (2¾ in.). Salonica and Lárisa have also a maximum in May (each 52 mm (2 in.)). On the Cyclades, S of Athens, the influence of the moist *sirocco* is felt more strongly in winter (Ándros December 130 mm (5 in.), Sýros January 100 mm (4 in.), Náxos January 80 mm (3 in.), Santorin December and January each 77 mm (3 in.)).

In summer the weather is determined by the *etesian winds*, dry winds from the N and NE, often blowing with considerable force. The summer becomes increasingly dry towards the S (Salonica 24 mm (0·9 in.) in August, Lárisa 19 mm (0·7 in.) in August, Corfu 6 mm (0·2 in.) in July, Athens 5 mm (0·2 in.) in July, Náxos, Santorin and Khaniá on Crete 1 mm (0·04 in.) in July and August). Typical also is the *meltemi*, a sharp dry wind which blows from the NW between May and September, rising to considerable violence in the early afternoon and falling again towards evening, which may create difficulties for shipping. In the mountainous inland regions the summer rainfall is rather higher, with frequent thunder showers (Sparta 12 mm (0·5 in.) in July).

While the winter maxima on the whole decrease only gradually from N to S, the **summer drought** is much more marked towards the S. This is reflected not only in the figures of minimum rainfall, but still more strikingly in the number of dry months. In northern Greece there are 3 to 4 months which can be called dry (i.e. with evaporation exceeding rainfall), but in central Greece there are 4 or 5, in southern Greece and the Aegean 5 or 6, on Santorin 7. In the south of Greece there are 3 or 4 months which are practically rainless.

The longer period of summer drought explains the fact that places with a much higher winter maximum (Zákynthos 230 mm (9 in.), Corfu 180 mm (7 in.); Khaniá 160 mm (6¼ in.) nevertheless have lower annual figures (Zákynthos 1115 mm (44 in.), Corfu 1172 mm (46 in.); Khaniá 707 mm (27¾ in.)). Eastern Greece, with comparable winter maxima, also shows notably lower annual figures (Kavála annual 642 mm (25¼ in.), February 82 mm (3¼ in.); Salonica annual 486 mm (19 in.), November 64 mm (2½ in.); Athens annual 384 mm (15 in.), December 68 mm (2¾ in.); Santorin annual 357 mm (14 in.), December 77 mm (3 in.)).

The dry air and high rate of evaporation make the heat of summer relatively tolerable. During the winter, which particularly in the S is wet and mild, the sky may be heavily overcast, but the sun keeps breaking through, and few indeed are the days without any sunshine. All over Greece the rain may be heavy but it seldom lasts long. Snow is rare at sea level, but lies for a long time on mountains above 1000 m (3280 ft), the climate in the mountain regions being closer to the Central European pattern. The contrast between summer and winter is accentuated by the fact that Greece has a very short spring and no autumn, summer being immediately followed by the onset of the rainy season.

Thus Greece has only **three seasons** – the period when nature comes to life and vegetation grows and ripens (March to June), the period of drought (June or July to October) and the rainy season (October to March or April).

Flora and Fauna

The **flora** of Greece is of typically Mediterranean character with leathery-leaved evergreens and succulents; the trees never exceed a very moderate height. In the fertile depressions and coastal regions, up to a height of about 800 m (2625 ft), mixed forests of oaks, planes, Aleppo pines, carob-trees, etc., alternate with a macchia (Greek *longos*) of holm-oaks, kermes-oaks, arbutus, mastic-bushes, laurel, broom, oleander and wild olives. In the wetter regions of western Greece the macchia is found higher up (800–2000 m – 2625–6562 ft), in the drier SE at lesser heights, becoming increasingly sparser and merging into the type of dry macchia known as *frigana*, with semi-shrub-like plants, junipers, heaths and spurges, which provides meagre grazing for sheep and goats. Mixed deciduous forests of beech, chestnut, plane, maple and elm are found up to heights of over 1500 m (4922 ft), particularly in the mountains of northern and central Greece, coniferous forests to heights of over 1700 m (5578 ft). Above this height, up to 2000 m (6562 ft), only the Apollo fir is found. Beyond the tree line are scanty Alpine meadows – in so far as the karstic formations of the limestone hills permit the growth of any vegetation at all.

The natural landscape of Greece is characterised not by the luxuriance of the S but by tracts of bare and barren countryside. Since ancient times the natural cover of trees and macchia has been largely destroyed by the extension of arable land and animal grazing. At best it has given place to olive-groves, fig plantations and vineyards; at worst it has reverted to wasteland. In recent years, however, efforts have been made to halt this latter trend by reafforestation. – Additions to the native flora of Greece have been the agave and prickly pear from Central America and the date-palm from Africa, originally introduced as an ornamental tree but also found growing wild.

The extensive devastation of the flora has considerably reduced the habitats, and consequently the variety of species, of the **fauna** of Greece. Deer and wild boar live in the mountains, and bears and wolves occasionally come in from the Balkans. There are numerous reptiles, the Greek tortoise being particularly common; and countless species of birds pass through Greece on their southward migration. A popular sport among Greeks, and one sometimes offered to visitors, is the shooting of rabbits and birds (particularly quails).

Sea-caves provide a refuge for seals, a species threatened with extinction. – Apart from the various species of fish to be found all over the Mediterranean, octopuses, shellfish, lobsters and spiny lobsters are caught round the coasts. – The sponge-fishing which was formerly practised all over the Aegean is now concentrated in the waters off the North African coast.

Population

The Greek population of something over 9 million is confined to a relatively small area of cultivable land, which shows the high density of 219 people to a sq. kilometre (84 to a sq. mile) compared with the overall density of 66 to the sq. kilometre (25 to a sq. mile).

Just under half the population live in the country, mostly in villages of closely packed houses. The determining factor in the siting of a village is the availability of drinking water, and the well is usually the hub of the village's life. Isolated farms and hamlets are rare. – Towns feature less prominently in the total picture, though they are now increasing rapidly in number and size; they are to be found mainly in the eastern half of mainland Greece and are mostly of small or medium size, showing the same closely huddled pattern as the villages. There are only four towns with a population over 100,000 – Athens, the capital, and the adjoining port town of Piraeus, which together with their suburbs make up an urban area of $2\frac{1}{2}$ million people; Salonica, chief town of northern Greece, with a population of some 500,000 including suburbs; and Pátras (pop. 112,000), chief town of the Peloponnese. In contrast to the mainland towns, most of the islands show a steady decline in population, and several (e.g. Kastellorízo) are faced with total depopulation. The poor quality of the soil and the fragmentation of holdings by inheritance have so reduced the standard of living that many young people prefer to seek a better livelihood in mainland Greece, the industrialised countries of Western Europe or the United States. The consequence is a steady ageing of the island population and the neglect or abandonment of farms which the older generation are no longer able to run.

The Greek people are of mixed origin, with Slav, Albanian and other European elements, but their consciousness of national identity, based on a common language and a common religion, has down the centuries shown an astonishing persistence and an astonishing power of assimilation. They withstood 400 years of Turkish rule, with the drain of so many of their boys into the Turkish service and other oppressions of all kinds, without yielding and without giving up hope. Although when the new kingdom of

The Regions of Greece

Geographical region	Area in sq. km (sq. miles)	Population	Pop. per sq. km (sq. mile)
Thrace	8578 (3312)	335,000	38 (101)
Macedonia	34,177 (13,196)	1,917,000	55 (145)
Epirus	9203 (3553)	317,000	34 (89)
Thessaly	13,929 (5378)	667,000	47 (124)
Ionian Islands	2307 (891)	187,000	80 (210)
Central Greece and Euboea	24,480 (9452)	996,000	41 (105)
Greater Athens	428 (165)	2,550,000	5958 (15,455)
Peloponnese	21,439 (8278)	997,000	46 (120)
Aegean Islands	9113 (3519)	419,000	46 (119)
Crete	8336 (3219)	462,000	55 (144)

Greece was established in 1830 it was necessary to set up two courts in Athens, one for Greeks and one for Albanians, since the population of Attica was predominantly Albanian, this duality has long ceased to be a problem; and during the struggle for freedom from Turkish rule the Albanians in Greece, particularly on the islands of Hýdra and Spétsai, were among the most ardent and energetic of Greek patriots. This sense of national unity was reinforced by events after the First World War, when $1\frac{1}{2}$ million Greek refugees came in from Asia Minor and 518,000 Turks and 92,000 Bulgarians left Greece. There are now only small minorities of some 120,000 Turks in Thrace and on Rhodes and Cos, 80,000 Slavs in Macedonia and 18,000 nomadic Koutsovlachs (Arumans) in Thessaly. – An imprint was also left on the Dodecanese by the long period of Turkish and later Italian rule, and on the Ionian Islands by the British protectorate during the 19th c., which gave these islands an enduring link with Western European culture.

In spite of all modern developments the *family* and the habit of living harmoniously together which it fosters are still determining factors in Greek life. The great majority of the population are country-folk, and even in large towns many districts preserve the atmosphere of country life. It remains true, nevertheless, that in recent years the large towns have grown with alarming rapidity at the expense of the country areas, creating both social problems and problems of infrastructure.

Religion. – In spite of regional differences resulting from the circumstances of history and of the country's extreme geographical fragmentation, the Greeks have preserved a deep national awareness. One great unifying force, particularly in times of trouble, has been the *Orthodox Church*, which has preserved its full authority in both private and public life. Since 1833 the Greek Church has been autonomous, since 1850 it has been recognised by the Oecumenical Patriarchate in Constantinople (Istanbul) as autocephalous (i.e. as being governed by its own synod and having power to appoint its own patriarch), and since 1864 it has been the established State church; its supreme head is the archbishop of Athens. Only the Dodecanese, which were united with Greece only in 1912–13, and the monastic republic of Athos are still subject to the jurisdiction of the patriarchate of Constantinople, while Crete occupies a special position as a semi-autonomous province of the church. – Some 94% of the population profess the Greek Orthodox faith; the rest are Mohammedans, Jews, Roman Catholics (a relic of the Venetian occupation of the Cyclades) and Protestants.

History

Neither in ancient times nor in later centuries was it possible to think in terms of a general history of Greece: the history of the country was made up of a series of individual histories of particular cities or regions. The efforts to achieve a unified Greek policy which are associated with the name of Perikles were of a purely ephemeral nature; and the amphictyonies (associations of cities) were of much greater religious than political importance. The attempts of the Macedonian dynasty to win the leadership of Greece had only a superficial appearance of success within Greece itself, and led in the end to the intervention of Rome and the end of the league of Greek states. It was only in the 19th c. that the Greeks were able to recover their independence and found a unified state.

From the earliest times to the Persian wars (3rd millennium to *c.* 500 B.C.). – During the 3rd millennium B.C. the SESKLO CULTURE and later the DIMINI CULTURE flourished in mainland Greece, while on the Aegean islands the CYCLADIC CULTURE emerged and on Crete the MINOAN CULTURE, which reached its peak about 2000 B.C. and was economically and culturally dominant until its sudden collapse in the 15th c. B.C.

2600–2200 Early Minoan (Pre-Palatial periods I, II, and III).

About 2000 Beginning of the Indo-European migration from the Balkans into Greece. These early Greeks (ACHAEANS) develop around 1580 the Mycenean government and economic system, whose trading activities extend to Sicily in one direction and the eastern Mediterranean countries in the other. On the Acropolis in Athens, in Argolid (Mycenae, Tiryns) and in other parts of Greece (Thebes, Pýlos) local ruling princes erect citadels, usually surrounded by Cyclopean walls, which show the influence of Minoan civilisation.

2000–1600 Middle Minoan, also with three periods. I (*c.* 1900): first palaces at Knossos and Phaistós on Crete. II (*c.* 1800): the heyday of Minoan culture (Kamares ware). III (*c.* 1700): rebuilding, after earlier destruction, of the (second) palaces of Knossos (the "Labyrinth") and Phaistós; building of the palace of Ayía Triáda.

1600–1400 Late Minoan. Collapse of the Minoan empire *c* 1400, perhaps as the result of an earthquake; further rebuilding of the (third) palace of Knossos by MYCENAEAN GREEKS.

1400–1000 Sub-Minoan period. *Dorian migration*; the Cyclades and Euboea remain Ionian.

About 1200 Further incursion by northern tribes (the Sea Peoples). The Achaean Greeks (AEOLIANS and IONIANS) withdraw eastward and around 1000 B.C. found colonies on the W coast of Asia Minor and the islands of the eastern Aegean.

In subsequent centuries there develop the little states, each confined to its own small territory, which make up the map of Greece until the Macedonian period.

1194–1184 *Trojan War.*

1104 The DORIANS, led by the *Heraclidae,* occupy the Peloponnese.

1000–700 Period of the geometric style in pottery.

About 950 Foundation of **Sparta.**

About 820 Legislation of *Lycurgus* (Lykourgos) in Athens.

About 800 Homer and the Homerids.

776 Traditional date of foundation of the **Olympic Games**; starting point of Greek reckoning of dates by olympiads (periods of four years).
In the course of the 8th c. the Greek states, frequently directed by the oracle at Delphi, found colonies all over the Mediterranean.

740–720 Sparta's attempt to conquer Messenia leads to the *First Messenian War*; the Achaeans are driven out of Achaea and settle in the Ionian Islands.

734 Foundation of Syracuse (Sicily) by the CORINTHIANS.

707 Foundation of Taras (Tarentum) by the SPARTANS.

About 700 End of the Dorian migration. Aeolians now begin to settle in the eastern Aegean (Lesbos) and on Cyprus, Ionians in the Northern Sporades, Euboea, the Cyclades (round a central cult site on Delos) Chios, Sámos and Ikaría, and Dorians on Crete, Melos, Thera (Santorin), Anaphe, the Dodecanese, Rhodes and the Ionian Islands.

650–630 *Second Messenian War*; period of the poet Tyrtaios (war songs).

632 Rising led by *Kylon* in Athens. Killing of Kylon; banishment of Alcmaeonidae.

621 Legislation of *Draco* in Athens.

About 600 The poetess *Sappho* and the poet *Alcaeus* (Alkaios) on Lésbos; flowering of sculpture and architecture on Náxos, Delos and Sámos; invention of hollow casting of bronze.

600–590 The *Sacred War*: Athens and Sikyon make war on, and destroy, Krisa and Kirrha.

594 *Solon* gives Athens a constitution.

About 570 The philosopher *Pythagoras* born on Samos (d. 497–496 at Metapontion in southern Italy).

560–510 Athens ruled by *Peisistratos* and his sons *Hippias* and *Hipparchos.* The Greek colonies in Asia Minor fall under the control of PERSIA.

After 550 Náxos flourishes under the tyrant *Lygdamis*, Sámos under *Polykrates*.

532 Introduction of the cult of Dionysos at Athens; first performance of a tragedy.

528 Death of Peisistratos.

514 Hipparchos murdered by Harmodios and Aristogeiton.

After 512 Northern coast of the Aegean occupied by the Persians.

510 Hippias driven out of Athens (d. 490). Reform of the Solonic constitution by the Alcmaeonid *Kleisthenes.*

From the Persian wars to Alexander the Great (*c.* 500 to 338 B.C.)

500–494 Rising of the Ionian Greeks, led by *Histiaios* of Miletus and *Aristagoras*, against the Persians.

492 *First Persian campaign* against Greece. Aegina submits to *Mardonios*, and is then laid waste by Sparta and Athens under *Miltiades*. Persian fleet wrecked on Athos.

490 *Second Persian campaign.* Battle of *Marathon*: Persian army led by Datis and Artaphernes defeated by the Athenians under Miltiades.

489   Unsuccessful expedition against Páros led by Miltiades; his death.

480   *Third Persian campaign*, led by Xerxes. Battle of Thermopylai (Leonidas), followed by naval battle of Artemision and Greek victory, under the leadership of Sparta and Themistokles of Athens, over the Persian fleet at *Salamis*.

This great victory arouses the Greeks' consciousness of their common identity as an ethnic and cultural community, in spite of their political fragmentation into a large number of small city states (*poleis*, singular *polis*).

Hymns of *Pindar*. Tragedies of *Aeschylus* (Aiskhylos: d. 456).

479   Fighting continues against the Persians who are still in Greece. Battle of Plataiai (Plataea: Pausanias of Sparta, Aristeides of Athens). Naval battle of Mykale (Leotychides of Sparta, Xanthippos of Athens).

478–477   Athens takes over the leadership of the Greek cities. Formation of an alliance of Hellenic states, the **Confederacy of Delos**.

465   The Athenian general *Kimon* defeats the Persians on land and sea in the battle of the River Eurymedon. Conquest of the Chersonese.

462   *Themistokles* is exiled (d. 448).

About 460   *Hippokrates*, the great Greek physician, is born on Kos (d. 375 in Larisa).

459–450   *Third Messenian War*. Athenian auxiliaries sent back by the Spartans; Athenian alliance with the Argives (457).

456–450   Unsuccessful Athenian expedition to Egypt.

456   Athenians defeated in the Argolid, but victorious at sea over the allied fleet of Corinth, Epidauros and Aegina.

455   *Kimon* exiled from Athens.

455–451   *War between the Athenians and the Spartans and Boeotians*. The Athenians are defeated by the Spartans at Tanagra (455), but defeat the Boeotians at Oinophyta in the same year. Conquest of Aegina. Kimon is recalled (452). Armistice between Athens and Sparta (449).

After 450   Laws of Gortyn (Crete).

449   Naval war against the Persians. Kimon dies during the siege of Kition (Cyprus), but his fleet defeats the Persians at Salamís (Cyprus). End of the Persian wars.

442–429   The **golden age of Athens** under *Perikles*: work on Acropolis by *Pheidias, Iktinos* and *Mnesikles*.
Polygnotos (painter).
Tragedies of *Sophocles* (d. 405).
"Histories" of *Herodotus*.

433   The victory of Korkyra, with Athenian help, over Corinth in the Sybota islands leads to the Peloponnesian War.

431–404   *Peloponnesian War*, which is interrupted by the Peace of Nikias (421) but ends in the defeat of Athens. The Spartans appoint 30 tyrants to rule Athens.
Thucydides (historian); tragedies of *Euripides* (d. 406); comedies of *Aristophanes*; *Hippokrates* (physician); *Polykleitos* (sculptor); *Socrates* and the sophists.

431   Attack on Plataiai (Platea) by the Thebans. The Spartans invade Attica.

430   Plague in Athens.

429   Death of Perikles.

428–427   The island of Lésbos defects from the Athenian cause but is reconquered.

427   The philospher *Plato* born in Athens (d. in Athens 347). Fall of Plataiai. Successful expedition into Acarnania led by *Demosthenes*. Reconquest of Lésbos.

425   Demosthenes lands in Messenia and fortifies Pylos. The Spartan general *Brasidas* occupies Sphakteria, which falls to the Athenian *Kleon*. Kýthira occupied by the Athenians; raid into Boeotia. Athenians defeated at Delion.

422   Battle of Amphipolis: Brasidas victorious, but dies of wounds. Kleon killed while fleeing.

421   Peace of Nikias.

418   Battle of Mantineia: Athenians and Argives defeated by the Spartans.

416   Island of Melos captured by the Athenians.

415–413   The *Sicilian expedition* of the Athenians, led by *Alkibiades, Nikias* and *Lamachos*. Alkibiades is accused of sacrilege and flees to the Spartans. Annihilation of the Athenian army and fleet at Syracuse (413).

413   On the advice of Alkibiades the Spartans occupy Dekeleia and make an alliance with the Persians against Athens. Athens is abandoned by its allies.

412   Athenian naval victory at Miletus.

411   Overthrow of the Athenian constitution. Alkibiades recalled. Athenian naval victories at Abydos.

410   Alkibiades defeats the Spartan fleet at Kyzikos (Cyzicus). Athens recovers control of the sea.

407   The Spartan *Lysander* defeats the Athenian fleet at Notion. Alkibiades dismissed (d. 404).

406   Athens victorious in naval battle of Arginousai.

405   Lysander destroys Athenian naval power in the battle of Aigospotamoi.

404   Athens surrenders to Lysander: the Thirty tyrants.

403   Thrasyboulos restores democracy.

401   Campaign of *Cyrus* the younger against his brother *Artaxerxes Mnemon*. Battle of Cunaxa. Retreat of the Ten Thousand led by *Xenophon*.

400   Flowering of painting (*Zeuxis, Parrhasios*).

399   The philospher **Socrates** (b. 470) is condemned to death, and dies by drinking hemlock.

396–394   *War of Spartans against Persians. Agesilaos* of Sparta victorious in Asia (396).

395–387   *Corinthian War*: Athens, Corinth and Thebes against Sparta.

395   Battle of Haliartos. The Spartan leader Lysander killed.

394   Battle of Knidos: the Spartan fleet is defeated by the Athenian general Konon and the Persian *Pharnabazos*. Battle of Koroneia: Agesilaos defeats the allies.

387   The Spartan leader *Antalkidas* makes peace with the Persians.

379–362 *War between Sparta and Thebes. Pelopidas* frees Thebes.

377 Establishment of the Second Athenian Confederacy by the Athenian generals *Chabrias, Iphikrates* and *Timotheus.*

371 The Theban leader *Epameinondas* defeats Sparta at Leuktra and establishes the **hegemony of Thebes.**

370 The Thebans in the Peloponnese. Messenia independent; Megalopolis capital of Arcadia.

364 Battle of Kynoskephalai: *Pelopidas* victorious, but killed in the battle.

362 Battle of Mantineia: Epameinondas victorious, but killed in the battle.

359 *Philip II* becomes king of Macedonia. Agesilaos goes to Egypt to support rebels, but dies on the voyage home (358). *Praxiteles* (sculptor).

357–355 *War of the Allies against Athens.* Battle of Amphipolis: the Athenians against Philip.

355–346 *Sacred War against Phocis.*

352 Philip victorious in Thessaly, but halted by the Athenians at Thermopylai.

348 Olynthos destroyed by Philip.

346 Peace between Philip and Athens. – *Aeschines.*

343 Philip summons the philosopher *Aristotle* (b. Stageira in Macedonia 384, d. Chalcis on Euboea 322) to be tutor to his son Alexander (b. 356).

340 Philip conquers Thrace and besieges Byzantium. Athens declares war and compels him to raise the siege.

339–338 *Sacred War against Amfissa.*

338 The MACEDONIANS defeat the Athenians and Thebans in the battle of Chaironeia. Philip becomes a commander-in-chief of the Greeks for the Persian war.

From Alexander the Great to the destruction of Corinth (336–146 B.C.).

336 *Alexander the Great* succeeds his murdered father, destroys Thebes (335) and thereafter founds the **Macedonian world empire.** *Diogenes* (philosopher); *Lysippos* (sculptor); *Apelles* and *Protogenes* (painters).

335 Alexander destroys Thebes.

334 Alexander in Asia. Battle of the Granikos. Chios and Lésbos temporarily in Persian hands.

333 Battle of Issos.

332 Siege of Tyre. Foundation of Alexandria.

331 Battle of Arbela.

330 *Darius Codomannus* murdered. Spartan rising: King *Agis II* killed at Megalopolis.

327 Alexander's expedition to India.

323 After Alexander's death the struggles between the *Diadochi* begin.

323–322 *Lamian War.*

321 *Perdikkas* murdered.

319 Death of *Antipater.*

306 *Antigonos* and *Demetrios Poliorketes* assume the title of king.

301 Battle of Ipsos: Antigonos killed. **Aetolian League.**

300 *Epicurus* and *Zeno* (philosophers); comedies of *Menander.*

296 Death of *Kassandros.*

287–275 King *Pyrrhos* of Epirus in Italy. The GAULS invade Macedonia and Greece.

280 **Achaean League.**

278 *Antigonos Gonatas* king of Macedon.

251 *Aratos,* general of the Achaean League, frees Sicyon.

241 King *Agis IV* of Sparta seeks to reform the state.

255 King *Kleomenes III* of Sparta overthrows the ephors.

221 Battle of Sellasia: the Achaeans and Macedonians defeat *Kleomenes* (d. 219).

From 220 Rome steadily increasing in strength.

220–217 War between the Aetolian and Achaean Leagues.

215 Philip V of Macedon makes an alliance with *Hannibal,* the Aetolian League allies itself with ROME: *First Macedonian War.*

207 *Philopoimen,* a general of the Achaean League (the "last of the Greeks"), defeats the Spartans at Mantineia.

206 Peace between Philip V and the Aetolian League.

200 Philip V at war with Rome: *Second Macedonian War.*

197 The Roman consul *Flaminius* defeats the Macedonians at Cynoscephalae. Greece remains independent.

190 Battle of Magnesia: the Romans defeat *Antiochus* of Syria. End of the Aetolian League.

171–168 *Third Macedonian War: Perseus* of Macedon against Rome.

168 *Aemilius Paulus* defeats Perseus at Pydna.

148 War between the Achaean League and Rome: Roman victory at Scarphea.

146 The Romans destroy Corinth. End of the Achaean League. Greece and Macedon become the Roman province of MACEDONIA.

Greece under Roman and Byzantine rule (2nd–1st c. B.C. to A.D. 1453).

About 133 Slave revolts in Attica.

88–87 The Greeks take part in the *Mithridatic War.*

85 *Sulla* wins the battle of Orkhomenós.

48 *Julius Caesar* defeats Pompey at Pharsalos.

42 *Antony* and *Octavian* defeat Caesar's murderers, *Brutus* and *Cassius,* at Philippi.

31 Octavian (Augustus) defeats Antony at Actium (Aktion) in Epirus.

31 B.C.–A.D. **14** Augustus sole ruler of Rome. Greece becomes the Roman province of ACHAEA. Revival of local confederacies of Greek cities.

A.D. **49–54** The Apostle *Paul* preaches **Christianity in Thessalonica, Athens and Corinth.**

117–138 Much building in Greece in the time of the Emperor *Hadrian*. The sophist *Herodes Atticus* in Athens.

About 170 *Pausanias* writes his famous "Description of Greece".

249–251 *Decius* Emperor. First appearance of the GOTHS on the frontiers of Greece.

260–268 Gothic incursions into Greece. Defence of Athens by Dexippos.

323–337 Under *Constantine the Great* **Byzantium** becomes capital of the Roman Empire and Christianity is victorious.

361–363 The Emperor *Julian* favours the Greeks. Unsuccessful attempt to restore paganism.

379–395 *Theodosius I* emperor.

393 Last Olympic Games of antiquity.

395 Division of the Roman Empire. The Goths, led by *Alaric*, destroy Eleusis, storm Athens and devastate the Peloponnese.

467–477 Incursions of the VANDALS into Greece.

527–565 *Justinian I* emperor.

529 The school of philosophy in Athens is closed.

540 Slave invasion of Greece.

End of 6th c. The SLAVS and AVARS advance through Greece and into the Peloponnese.

717–741 *Leo III* emperor.

727 Greek rising; unsuccessful naval expedition to Constantinople.

746–747 Plague in Greece. The Slavs spread over the Peloponnese.

About 805 The Slavs defeated at Patras.

867–886 *Basil I* emperor of Byzantium. – The Slavs in the Peloponnese are converted to Christianity. *Photius* patriarch: beginning of the schism between the Greek and Latin churches, which was to be formally declared in 1054.

1019 The Emperor *Basil II* defeats the BULGARS at Thermopylai and Athens; first appearance of ALBANIANS in Greece.

1040 Norwegian VARANGIANS, led by Harald Hardrade, in Athens.

1084–85 The Normans in Thessaly (Salonica); successful defence of Lárisa.

1194 The ITALIAN *Orsini* seizes the islands of Kefallinía, Ithaca and Zákynthos.

Beginning of 13th c. The VENETIANS occupy Crete, Kythira and the southern tip of the Peloponnese.

1204 The **Crusaders** take Constantinople and found the Latin Empire. *Boniface de Montferrat*, king of Salonica, conquers Boeotia and Attica (d. 1207). *Othon de la Roche* is granted the fiefs of Athens and Boeotia, and in 1205 becomes "Megaskyr" (Grand Duke) of Athens. *Geoffroy de Villehardouin* conquers the W coast of the Peloponnese with the help of Guillaume de Champlitte, who in 1205 becomes first prince of the Morea (Peloponnese).

1207 The Ventian *Marco Sanudo* conquers Náxos and founds the duchy of Náxos or the Dodecanese.

1207–22 *Demetrius* king of Salonica.

1210 Geoffroy de Villehardouin becomes second prince of the Morea. Conquest of Corinth.

1211–12 Conquest of Náfplion and Argos.

1218 After Geoffroy de Villehardouin's death his son *Geoffroy II* (d. 1245) becomes third prince of the Morea, and is recognised by the Latin Emperor *Pierre de Courtenay* as duke of Achaea.

1222 *Theodore Angelus Comnenus* conquers Salonica and is crowned emperor.

1245 *Guillaume II de Villehardouin* succeeds his brother Geoffroy as prince of the Morea (d. 1278).

1246 Emperor *Vatatzes* of Nicea reunites Salonica with Byzantium.

1248 Monemvasia conquered by Guillaume II.

1258 *Guy I* becomes duke of Athens.

1259–82 *Michael VIII Palaeologus* Byzantine emperor.

1261 Michael VIII conquers Constantinople. End of the Latin Empire.

1262 Guillaume II de Villehardouin is compelled to cede to Byzantium the fortresses of Mistra, Monemvasía and Maina in the Peloponnese. Beginning of the Byzantine reconquest of the peninsula, followed by the intellectual and artistic flowering of **Mistra**.

1267 *Baldwin II*, the last Latin emperor, cedes to *Charles of Anjou* his feudal superiority over the principality of Achaea.

1308 The duchy of Athens passes to *Gautier de Brienne*.

1311 Defeat of army of French knights by Catalan mercenaries; Gautier is killed.

1312 *Roger Deslaur* duke of Athens.

1364 Death of *Robert of Tarentum*, last prince of Achaea.

1380 Robert's nephew *Jacques des Baux* conquers the Morea (d. 1383).

1389 The Venetians occupy Náfplion and extend their rule over the whole of Greece and the islands.

1394 *Rainerio Acciaiuoli*, ruler of Corinth, becomes duke of Athens. – Argos occupied by the Venetians.

1395 *Theodore I Palaeologus* (1383–1407) recovers Corinth.

1386 *Pierre Bordeaux de Saint-Supéran* recognised by King Ladislas of Naples as prince of the Morea (d. 1402).

1404 *Centurione Zaccaria*, a Genoese, prince of the Morea (d. 1432).

1430 Morea recovered by the Palaeologi.

1435 Thebes occupied by the TURKS.

29 May 1453 Mehmet II conquers Constantinople: end of the Eastern Roman Empire.

Greece under the Turks (*c*. 1450 to 1828).

1456 The Turks besiege Athens: beginning of almost 400 years of Turkish rule in Greece.

1460 The Turks conquer the Peloponnese, with the exception of the Venetian possessions.

1463 Argos conquered by the Turks, but retaken by the Venetians.

1464 The Venetian general *Capello* occupies Euboea.

1470 Euboea recaptured by the Turks.

1499–1501 Sultan *Bayezit II* captures Lepanto, Methóni, Koróni and Navarino, but fails to take Náfplion and Monemvasía.

1503 Peace between Turkey and Venice.

1540 Náfplion and Monemvasía taken by the Turks.

16th c. As a Turkish province, the Dodecanese is granted extensive autonomy in domestic affairs.

1573 Peace treaty between Venice and Turkey, leaving the whole of Greece in Turkish hands.

1579 The Venetian duchy of Náxos falls to the Turks.

1645–69 Unsuccessful war by Venice against the Turks.

1685–99 Conquest of the Peloponnese (Morea) by the Venetians.

1715 Morea recaptured by the Turks.

1718 Peace of Passarowitz, confirming the Turks in possession of Morea.

1770 Unsuccessful *Greek rising*, supported by Russian forces under *Orlov*. Many Albanians flee to the islands.

1779 *Hassan Pasha* defeats the Albanian rebels at Trípolis.

1815 BRITISH protectorate over the Ionian Islands.

1821–28 *War of Greek Liberation*.

1821 *Alexander Ypsilanti* (d. 1828 in Vienna), leading the forces of the Hetairia, crosses the River Prut and calls on the Greeks to fight for their freedom. Successful rising in the Peloponnese.

1822 *Dramalis* defeated by *Kolokotronis* and *Nikitas*. *Kurshid Pasha* defeats a Greek army at Peta. Athens occupied by the Greeks.

1823 *Omer Vriones* defeated by the Greeks at Karpenísi.

1825 Ibrahim Pasha recovers the Peloponnese.

1826 Fall of Mesolongi. The Turks recapture Athens.

1827 *John Kapodistrias* chosen as Regent. Naval battle in Navarino Bay.

1828 Ibrahim Pasha abandons the Peloponnese. Landing of a FRENCH expeditionary force.

The Kingdom of Greece (1830–1974).

1829 First London Protocol: Greece a hereditary monarchy, but required to pay tribute to Turkey.

1830 Second London Protocol: Greece a **sovereign kingdom**.

1831 Kapodistrias murdered; his brother *Augustine* becomes President (abdicates 1832).

1832 Prince Otto of Bavaria proclaimed king of the Hellenes as *Otto I*.

1833 Otto arrives in Greece, not yet of age (Regency); residence at first in Náfplion.

1834 Residence transferred to Athens, which thereafter acquires many buildings in neo-classical style, mostly designed by German architects.

1835 Otto I comes of age.

1843 Rising in Athens. First Greek constitution of modern times.

1850 Piraeus blockaded by the British navy.

1854 French forces seize Piraeus and the Greek fleet (until 1857), since Greece supports Russia in the Crimean War.

1856 Catastrophic earthquake on Crete.

1862 After a number of risings King Otto I leaves the country.

1863 A Danish prince, William of Sonderburg-Glücksburg, becomes king as *George I*.

1864 Britain cedes the Ionian Islands to Greece. – New constitution.

1881 Greece acquires Thessaly and part of Epirus.

1886 Blockade of Piraeus by the European powers.

1897 After the Turkish *occupation of Crete*, unsuccessful war against Turkey. Treaty of Constantinople: high indemnity payment, cession of strategic points on borders of Thessaly and Macedonia, establishment of an international commission to control Greek finances.

1898 Crete is granted self-government under Turkish suzerainty.

1908 Crete united with Greece.

1910 *Venizelos*, a Cretan, becomes Greek prime minister.

1912 ITALIAN forces occupy most of the Dodecanese.

1912–13 *Balkan Wars:* Greece acquires the northern part of the country and the islands of Thásos, Imbros, Tenedos, Lésbos and Sámos.

1913 After the murder of King George I he is succeeded by his son *Constantine I*.

1917 Prince *Alexander*, as Regent, breaks with the Central Powers.

1919–20 Under the treaties of Paris and Sèvres Greece receives southern Albania, western Thrace (from Bulgaria) and eastern Thrace and a mandate over Smyrna (from Turkey).

1920 King Constantine I recalled to Greece.

1920–22 The *Greco-Turkish War* ends in the defeat of Greece. Constantine abdicates in favour of his son *George II*. Under the treaty of Lausanne the Greeks lose the territories in Asia Minor which had been occupied by Greek settlers since ancient times, together with the islands of Imbros and Tenedos. Over 1½ million refugees flee to Greece.

1923 Turkey cedes the Dodecanese to Italy

1 May 1924 Declaration of **Republic**. Much unrest, frequent changes of government.

1926 A severe earthquake devastates the W coast of Rhodes.

1928–32 Venizelos again in power.

1930 Treaty of Ankara, settling differences with Turkey.

1935 Restoration of the **monarchy**; return of King *George II*.

1936 Coup d'état by General *Metaxas*: establishment of **dictatorship**.

Territorial Development of Modern Greece

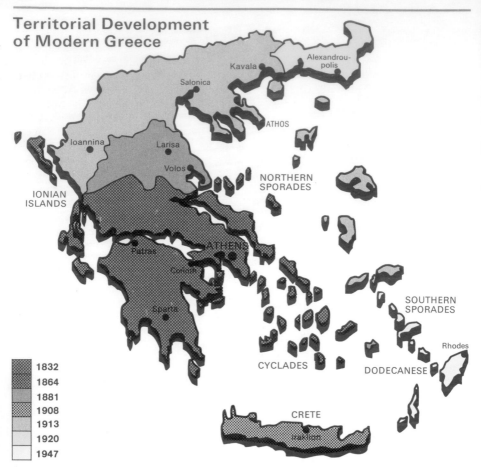

Kavala

Alexandrou-polis

Salonica

ATHOS

Ioannina

Larisa

Volos

IONIAN ISLANDS

NORTHERN SPORADES

Patras

ATHENS

Corinth

Sparta

SOUTHERN SPORADES

Rhodes

CYCLADES

DODECANESE

1832
1864
1881
1908
1913
1920
1947

CRETE

Iraklion

1940   After occupying Albania the Italians march into Greece but are driven back and lose part of Albania to Greece.

1941–44   *German and Italian occupation* (mainland and Crete). The king goes into exile in London.

1944   Archbishop *Damaskinos* Regent.

1945–49   *Civil War* between government forces and Communists.

1946   King George II returns to Athens, but dies in the following year.

1947   George's brother *Paul I* becomes king. The Dodecanese returns to Greece.

1949   Decisive victory of government forces over the Communists.

1952–53   New constitution. – Greece becomes a member of NATO.

1953   Devastating earthquake in the Ionian Islands.

1962   Greece becomes an associate member of the European Economic Community.

1964   Death of King Paul; he is succeeded by his son *Constantine II*.

1967   Coup d'état by Colonel *Papadopoulos*, followed by **military dictatorship**. After an unsuccessful attempt at a counter-coup the king flees to Rome; General *Zoitakis* becomes Regent.

1969   Greece leaves the Council of Europe and withdraws from the International Convention on Human Rights.

1972   Zoitakis relieved of his office as Regent; Colonel Papadopoulos becomes chief of state.

1973   Greece establishes diplomatic relations with the German Democratic Republic. After an unsuccessful attempt at a putsch in the Greek navy there is a mutiny on the destroyer "Volos" in Italian waters. Abolition of the monarchy and proclamation of a **Republic** (a parliamentary presidential democracy). The change is confirmed in a government-managed referendum. Papadopoulos becomes President; new constitution; civilian government headed by *Markezinis*. Bloody rioting by left-wing students in Athens, followed by military revolt led by General *Ioannidis*. General *Gizikis* becomes the new head of state.

The Republic of Greece (since 1974).

1974   Tensions with Turkey (Aegean oilfields, Cyprus). Democratic civilian government, with *Karamanlis* as Prime Minister. Greece withdraws troops from NATO. General election: Karamanlis's "New Democracy" party gains an absolute majority. Greece rejoins the Council of Europe. Referendum in favour of a democratic Republic.

1975   New constitution.

1977   Defence agreement with the United States (US bases).

1978   Severe earthquake in northern Greece (particularly Salonica).

1979   Treaty on Greece's entry into the European Economic Community signed in Athens on 26 June; to come into effect, after ratification by the parliaments of the ten states concerned, on 1 January 1981.

Art

Prehistoric period. – No other pre-historic discoveries have aroused so much excitement as the royal graves of Mycenae and the palaces of Crete. Much more modest, but much older, are the finds of *Neolithic* material in Thessaly and Boeotia, on Samos and Crete and in Chalcidice and the Peloponnese. In contrast to the rather meagre Palaeolothic material so far discovered, these point to the existence of substantial settlements with a consider-able level of cultural achievement. It is not yet possible, however, to say much about the people who occupied Greece in the centuries after 3500 B.C. The layouts of their houses show a predominance of straight lines, with an attempt, usually successful, to achieve rectangular structures.

On the basis of the finds of pottery it is possible to distinguish two geographical areas – one in the SE, taking in Crete, the Dodecanese, the Cyclades and Samos (museums of Iráklion, Rhodes and Pytha-górion), and the other in central and northern Greece, the area of the **Sesklo culture**, named after the type-site in Thessaly (museums of Vólos and Chai-roneia). The pots are elegantly shaped, at first burnished red and black ware, occasionally with incised designs, later with painted decoration. A variety of decorative techniques are used – red designs on a light ground or white designs on a dark ground. Pottery or, more rarely, stone idols with strongly em-phasised female sexual characteristics, found in settlement levels but not in burials.

In the **Dimini culture** of Thessaly, which begins after 2900 B.C. and has close relationships with the Danube area, spiral motifs appear in the pottery decoration and curved lines occasionally occur in the plans of buildings. The lines of the pots are less finely articulated than in the Sesklo culture. The vessels become roun-der and fuller in other parts of Greece as well during the 3rd millennium B.C. (Archaeological Museum, Salonica). More organic forms find their best ex-pression in zoomorphic vases, with rather abstract variants in the so-called "sauce-boats", duck-shaped vessels and beaked jugs (Náfplion and Tegéa museums). The source of these types is to be found in NW Anatolia. The islands lying off the coasts of Asia Minor were so closely bound up with the eastern cultural sphere during this period that they have been quite appropriately called Western Anatolia. – Another distinctive local style was de-veloped in the **Cyclades**, where vessels and utensils were made from the local marble as well as from clay. The marble idols of the Cyclades (National Ar-chaeological Museum, Athens) were exported to other parts of Greece. – The finest flowering of prehistoric culture, however, was achieved on Crete.

North entrance to Palace of Knossos (Crete)

Crete. – In the *Early Minoan* period (before about 2000 B.C.) there were numerous small flourishing settlements in the Górtys plain, on the Gulf of Morabello and on the little islands of Mochlos and Psira. Grave goods, sometimes of great richness, were buried with the dead. The large palaces of *Knossos* and *Phaistós* were built in a later period and enlarged between 1900 and 1800 B.C.; they contain numerous rooms of different shapes and sizes laid out round interior courtyards, with a complex system of staircases and light shafts and with unusually shaped columns tapering towards the base. Here and at *Mália* open-air theatres were used for ceremonies and acrobatic perfor-mances. Large rooms alternate with smaller ones, and there are a variety of cult rooms, bathrooms (sometimes with a terracotta bath), lavatories, store-rooms and cellars. Similar, though on a rather smaller scale, is the palace at *Ayía Triáda*, the last to be built; but here are to be seen the oldest fresco paintings, and it was only at Ayía Triáda that new buildings of any size were erected after the destruction of the Cretan palaces around 1400 B.C.. The inhabitants of Knossos and Phaistós were content with makeshift accom-modation rigged up in the ruins of the old palaces. Apart from the palaces the

The "Harvesters Vase" from Ayía Triáda (Crete)

remains of other houses have been preserved; and at *Gourniá* in eastern Crete the layout of a whole town has been recovered, with the foundations of houses and the street pattern so clearly visible that it takes little imagination to visualise the life of this little Minoan town of the 2nd millennium B.C..

The development of *Minoan culture* can be charted with the help of dated Egyptian imports, and a relative chronology can be established on the basis of the rich finds of pottery (Iráklion Museum). The Kamares style (named after a cave on the slopes of Mt Ida) was dominant in the first quarter of the 2nd millennium B.C.. The contours are compact and clear, and the vases are decorated with brightly coloured and freely drawn patterns of spirals, stylised flowers, stairs, etc. – In the Late Minoan "Palace style" the forms become slenderer and more elegant, with flowing lines and handle forms which at times take on a Baroque exuberance, and the vases are strikingly decorated with floral patterns and double-axe motifs.

The finest artistic achievements of Late Minoan Crete are the wall paintings, sometimes preserved only in fragments (Iráklion Museum). Natural though this painting appears, it cannot be described as naturalistic. It reproduces sensuous movement in forms and colours; it is based on observation of nature, but

conveys that observation in the form of impressions, without seeking to impose any preconceived structure on the material.

Paintings of this kind have also been found in the Minoan settlement at Fylakopí on the island of **Melos**. This island had long been of importance as the source of the obsidian used in making knives and arrowheads; for although the men of the 3rd millennium had copper they knew nothing of bronze. It was not until the beginning of the 2nd millennium that the technique of adding tin to copper to produce bronze came into use throughout the eastern Mediterranean.

Mycenae. – While the Cretan empire was at the peak of its power the Peloponnese, and in particular the Argolid, was pursuing its own course of development. The Mycenaean culture certainly developed out of a close contact with Crete, but the Argolid was never a Cretan cultural province in the same way as Melos and Thera. From about 1600 B.C. Mycenae was the dominant power in the Peloponnese; but here, as at Tiryns, a short distance away to the SE, the buildings are not palaces but strongholds designed with an eye to defence. Mycenae occupies a commanding situation surrounded by massive walls within which

The Snake Goddess from Knossos (Crete)

Gold cup from a tomb at Vaphió

Michael Ventris, who showed the language to be Greek, although written in a script which was certainly not devised for Greek. The 600 tablets found here, now under study in the National Archaeological Museum in Athens, were merely administrative records, but nevertheless can be made to yield valuable information about the political and social structure of the period and, even more significantly, about its religious conceptions: there are references in the texts to Dionysos and Paian (Apollo).

the buildings are fitted closely together. In contrast to the irregular layout of the Cretan palaces, there seems at Mycenae to be an attempt to achieve some degree of symmetry. Here, too, in the later phases, large wall paintings are found. The artists may well have been Cretans, but they had to adapt themselves to the requirements of their patrons, both in the themes (including battle and hunting scenes which are not found in Crete) and in the composition, which shows a stronger tectonic sense and sometimes a certain rigidity. The valuable grave goods found in the shaft graves (14th c. B.C.) bear witness to the power of the ruling family; they included almost 14 kg (31 lb) of gold in the form of ornaments and utensils. A characteristic feature is the presence of large numbers of weapons; for this is a very different world from the peaceful Cretan empire, which no doubt relied on a powerful fleet for protection but needed no other defences. The most striking examples of the monumental architecture of the later Mycenaean period are the Lion Gate and the "Treasury of Atreus", a beehive-shaped (*tholos*) tomb still to be seen in situ. Tombs of this type are found at many other places in the Peloponnese (e.g. at Vaphio, famous for the two gold cups discovered there and for the earliest use of iron) and in mainland Greece.

Important light has been thrown on the history of the second half of the 2nd millennium by material discovered at the settlement of *Ano Englianos* (Messenia), which has been thought to be the Homeric Pýlos, home of Nestor. This evidence takes the form of inscribed clay tablets, excellently preserved by being baked in the fire which destroyed the building in which they were found. The script, known as Linear B, was deciphered after the last war by the English architect

This material, and the prospect of finding and interpreting similar texts at Mycenae and on Crete, raise the problem of the original *population* of Greece on to a new plane. The script and language of the tablets have made it possible to confirm earlier hypotheses. The literary tradition of the settlement of the Greek islands by Carians can be related in time to the 3rd millennium and the introduction of Anatolian pottery types. From about 2000 B.C. the Carians were caught between two other population groups. On the one hand there were the Cretans, like the Carians a non-Greek people, whose Minoan culture cannot have originated in Greece or any of the neighbouring countries. Comparisons have been made with the early Indus culture (Mohenjo Daro); although the similarities are unlikely to reflect any actual movement of peoples, but may perhaps be the result of influences from the village cultures of the Taurus and Iran, moving both E and W. The other peoples from the mainland of Greece and the Peloponnese who pushed back the Carians in the Bronze Age, however, were Greek. The dead who were buried in the shaft graves of Mycenae were still honoured as heroes in the period of the tholos tombs: there had, therefore, been no change of dynasty. These kings of the Argolid must have been heroes of the kind celebrated in the "Iliad". And the Linear B tablets now tell us that not only was Greek spoken throughout the Peloponnese but that it was used in those parts of Crete in which the palaces were destroyed around 1400 B.C.

The *pottery*, with its astonishing abundance and wide distribution, gives evidence of the development and expansion of Mycenaean culture. The pottery is often decorated with patterns of Cretan origin but, unlike the vessels of precious metal, is locally made, and does not match the quality of the best Cretan products. Like the wall paintings of the Argolid, it shows a stronger tectonic structure and uses only a selection from the range of Cretan motifs. The vessel forms include both imitations of Cretan vessels and specifically indigenous types. This ware was exported to Asia Minor (Troy), Cyprus, Syria, Palestine, Egypt, Sicily and probably also Spain. From about 1300 B.C. signs of decadence begin to appear in the vase decoration; the style becomes steadily more schematic, and finally degenerates completely. Although in the final stages new subjects begin to appear (human figures, horses, domestic animals) the artists have no longer the skill to give them convincing expression.

Geometric style. – Although after the collapse of the Minoan and Mycenaean civilisations some historical memories and religious conceptions were handed on, together with certain technical skills, Greek art – the development of which was indirectly affected by the Dorian migration (*c.* 1200 B.C.) – made a fresh start. The achievements of the civilisations of previous centuries were abandoned, and ritual and political forms, customs and practices underwent radical change. A new conception of the world was given expression in the simplest form. The buildings now erected were small, and at first of perishable materials; the vessels and utensils used were modest, though produced with great care; the pottery cinerary urns and grave goods had only the most limited decoration. This new decorative style, with its lines and circles, is known as the Geometric style. The characteristic motif is the meander, though this does not appear in the first ("Proto-Geometric") phase. In later stages we find more valuable metal utensils (votive offerings), small sculpture in pottery, ivory and metal, and jewellery. The Geometric period extended over some four centuries. To this period belong the remains of a temple on Samos which date from about 800 B.C.

Geographical differences can be recognised in the development of the Geometric style. The best pottery was produced in Athens, and only in the final phases was Athenian ware surpassed in quality by Corinthian. The vessel forms are precise, clearly articulated and of simple lines; so too are the figures of humans and animals which begin to appear in the decoration about 900 B.C. The themes, sometimes involving numerous figures, include mourning for the dead, funeral biers and funeral processions, battles on land and sea, gymnastic and musical performances, dances, birds and other animals. The development of the style can be seen in the serried ranks of vases in the Kerameikos Museum, from the cemetery outside the double gate in the old town walls of Athens. Some of the amphoras which were used as funerary monuments were over 1·5 m (5 ft) high (National Archaeological Museum, Athens). The artists who painted the vases were less concerned with the purely optical impression than with the idea which they wanted to convey – e.g. the human figure may show the head and lower part of the body in profile, the torso frontally – and individual characteristics are of less importance than what is felt to be typical. The main principles of composition are symmetry and arrangement in regular rows; and when both these principles are combined they produce a dense centralised composition.

Although the Near Eastern countries had shown the way, and Syria in particular had produced some notable small sculpture, all this work was surpassed by the Greek achievement, introducing a whole new repertoire of forms. In the statuettes now produced the limbs are clearly detached from one another, but the figures cannot stand by themselves: except where they formed part of a larger whole, as a member of a group or an attachment to some implement or utensil, they must either have been leaned up against something or merely laid down. While the figures in vase paintings remain within the upper and lower margins of a frieze or are strictly confined within a rectangular frame, the small sculpture makes a freer use of space: their outlines are not of the same geometric precision, the impetuous vigour of their bearing and their glance is not always subjected to the discipline of form (man with helmet, with legs wide apart: National Archaeological Museum, Athens). This freer treatment is most notable in representations of the human figure. In this respect such items as the hundreds of little bronze horses to be seen in the museum at Olympia are less different from their counterparts on vases than are the bronzes and terracottas of human figures from the warriors and mourning women depicted on vases. The leading bronze foundries were evidently in the Peloponnese and Athens.

Archaic period (*c*. 670–490 B.C.). – Considerable as were the originality and the artistic achievement of the Geometric period, the immediately following period was no less remarkable. Its most important contribution to Greek art – and to Western culture as a whole – was a new conception of the life-size statue. Large sculpture had long been produced in the East, and particularly in Egypt; and the Greeks had now reached a stage in their own development, a moment of maturity, when they were ready to follow these earlier examples. But here again they remained largely independent. In comparison with Egyptian work the earliest Greek statues may at first sight appear rather primitive. They are not direct copies – certainly not copies of the cult images which stood in the temples and were frequently no more than large statuettes, though sometimes reaching a height of 2 m (7 ft). These divine images were either not shaped by human hand at all or only very crudely hewn into the likeness of man – sacred objects which were supposed to have fallen from heaven or been found in marvellous circumstances in some wild part of the country. The men of the Geometric period had conceived their divinities in the form of such images,

Archaic stele with relief carving

which later Greek writers referred to as "unhewn blocks of wood". The images were clad in cloth garments and on the occasion of ritual festivals were bathed and anointed. They were thus treated as having a real existence, as being natural beings. In contrast to these images, the oldest large marble figure which has come down to us (*c*. 660 B.C.: National Archaeological Museum) is a deliberately created artistic form. An inscription on this statue of the goddess Artemis, Apollo's sister, records that it was dedicated by one Nikandre of Náxos. It was found in the Temple of Artemis on the island of Delos, and is identified as the goddess herself by the holes bored in her hand, presumably for her bronze bow and arrows. This earliest example of Greek monumental sculpture shows not only great sureness of touch in the individual forms – still visible in spite of the weathering of the surface and the loss of the original colours – but also an exact proportion between the parts and the whole. The structure of this whole is admittedly conceived only from the front, and the figure is flatter than the Geometric bronzes and terracottas; but it shows the unified composition and the single dominating rhythm which had previously been found only in vase paintings and not in small sculpture. One consequence, however, was the loss of the earlier dynamic expressiveness, the free extension of the body in space; for the monumentality of large statuary could at first be achieved only by using the simplest forms. The oldest marble statues show less of the overflowing creative power found in earlier statuettes; and the sculpture of the 7th c. has none of the luxuriance of Oriental imagery found in the vase paintings of the same period. Nevertheless the fact that in the very beginnings of large sculpture those types were created which influenced the whole development of ancient sculpture, and indeed have continued to influence sculptors down to our own day, demonstrates the intensity of final effect produced by this deliberate limitation.

Alongside the draped figures of women there now appears the type of the *kouros*, the figure of a young man represented unclothed. The earliest examples of this type are fragments found at the same site and made of the same material as the figure dedicated by Nikandre (Delos

Museum). They can be reconstructed on the basis of a well-preserved bronze statuette with a tiered hair-style and a wide belt in the Delphi Museum. The fact that these figures wear a belt on their otherwise naked body indicates that their nakedness did not reflect the way they went about in everyday life but was a stylistic form deliberately selected on ethical and artistic grounds. Slightly later are the *kouroi* found on the island of Santorin (Thera), which have a more elaborate hair-style but no belt. These figures, unfortunately in a poor state of preservation, are the earliest examples of over-life-size figures in Greek sculpture.

Even allowing for the chances of preservation, the figures found in the *Cyclades* mark these islands out as one of the centres of Greek sculpture of the earliest period. The flowering of sculpture in the Cyclades was undoubtedly promoted by the excellent stone which was available there: the marble quarries of Naxos are inexhaustible, and the marble of Paros was famed as the finest material for the sculptor. It is perhaps no mere chance, therefore, that the earliest sculptor whose name is recorded, *Euthykartides*, describes himself as a Naxian (Delos Museum: triangular base with inscription, ram and Gorgons' heads, about 620 B.C.; only feet of statue preserved). The name suggests a man of noble family; the inscription refers to him as both the donor and the sculptor of the statue.

The forms created in the Cyclades, however, became the model for the whole of Greece only through the work of the great creative artists of Athens. The name of the leading master of his day, a contemporary of Euthykartides, is not known to us. His principal work was a statue 2·5 m (8 ft) high which stood on a tomb outside the Dipylon in Athens. The head (National Archaeological Museum, Athens), hands, shoulder and knee (Agora Museum) have been preserved. There is another statue by the same sculptor – smaller but still more than life-size – in the Metropolitan Museum in New York. In the vigour of their lines, the clear structure of the planes on all four sides and the rendering of detail, the perfection of which is almost reminiscent of the regularity of mineralogical forms, these figures are quite without peer. Later stages in the development of the kouros type are represented by the colossal figure

from Cape Soúnion (*c.* 600 B.C.: National Archaeological Museum, Athens), the figures of Kleobis and Biton (*c.* 590 B.C.: Delphi Museum), the torso from Megara (*c.* 570–560 B.C.: National Archaeological Museum), the kouros from Tenea (*c.* 560 B.C.: Munich) and the funerary statues of Kroisos (*c.* 530 B.C.: National Archaeological Museum) and Aristodikos (*c.* 510 B.C.: National Archaeological Museum). From about 640 B.C., too, the draped figures of women (half life-size statue from Auxerre, now in the Louvre, Paris) gain increased plastic fullness and spatial quality without losing their tectonic structure and precision. In the headless statue of Hera from Samos (Louvre, Paris) the flat planes and four-square structure of the earlier examples are merged into a more unified, almost columnar, composition. The delicate modelling of the surface (almost entirely covered with an intricate pattern of

Archaic kore

pleats) betrays the hand of a master – whose name is unknown, for the inscription mentions only the donor, *Cheramyes* (who appears on at least two other votive inscriptions). Roughly contemporary with this statue (*c.* 560 B.C.) is a group of four (originally six) figures on a large base, with an inscription naming the persons represented and also the sculptor, *Geneleos* (Vathy Museum). Among later examples of the same type, the *kore*, one figure returns to the simpler angular forms of the 7th c. but shows a feeling of individuality in the taut features and intense glance (Acropolis Museum). Others enrich the tradition by still more elegantly draped robes and the dreamy beauty of the lowered eyelids (Acropolis Museum). The 5th c. kore dedicated by *Euthydikos* (Acropolis Museum) has, unlike her predecessors, a serious and indeed melancholy expression.

The *temple* achieved monumentality not in the 7th c. like the sculpture but some 70 years later, in the early 6th c. On the island of *Corfu* (Korkyra), within the Corinthian sphere of influence, there was built about 590 B.C. a temple of Artemis which already shows the canonical forms of Doric architecture. Particularly notable is the well-preserved sculpture from the W pediment (Kérkyra Museum), which has figures of Medusa and her sons Chrysaor and Pegasos, framed by wild beasts, in the centre, a scene from the destruction of Troy to the left and Zeus fighting giants to the right. Some 20 years later, almost contemporary with one another, are the Doric temple built to house the old image of Athena on the Acropolis in *Athens* and the huge Temple of Hera on *Samos*, with no fewer than 134 columns, built by Rhoikos and Theodoros. In spite of the difference between their absolute dimensions (the one 44 m (144 ft) long, the other 105 m (344 ft)) the proportion of breadth to length is about the same (1:2) in both temples. The earlier temples had been much longer in proportion to their breadth (1:4, 1:5). While the Temple of Athena has in all essentials the proportions of the canonical temple *in antis* surrounded by columns, the Temple of Hera is typical of the colossal temples of the Ionic order in its size, its magnificence and the multiple ranks of columns enclosing the cella. From this temple there is a direct line leading to Hadrian's completion of the Temple of Zeus in Athens in the Corinthian order.

The plan of Rhoikos' temple on Samos is known to us, but only from the robber trenches dug by later stone-robbers. The only column still standing belongs to a more recent temple completed centuries later. This later structure, however, gives a striking impression of the size of the early temple, for its dimensions and proportions, as seen from the well-preserved foundations, correspond exactly to those of Rhoikos' temple, although the later temple was moved some 40 m (131 ft) W. – The foundations of the old temple of Athena on the Acropolis are still easily distinguishable, and there are many fragments of the superstructure, including some of the sculpture from the pediments, in the Acropolis Museum (front pediment – lion, IX; rear pediment – Herakles, VA, Typhon, VE). The temple was pulled down when the Erechtheion was built to replace it a little to the N. The use of the Doric order in the middle of the 6th c., however, can be seen in the Temple of Apollo in Corinth. The columns, firmly based on the three-tier substructure, rear massively up, the very incarnation in stone of static forces, topped by the capitals which seem flattened by the weight of the roof structure, now represented only by a few blocks of the architrave.

In the *painted pottery* of the early Archaic period four groups of workshops stand out sharply from one another. – The leading place in number of workshops and quality of work was taken by *Corinth*. The material used was the local clay, yellowish white to light green in colour. Most of the vessels are small, designed to contain oil for cosmetic purposes. They are frequently decorated with tiny friezes of animals, and sometimes also with mythological scenes, which are mainly found on the larger vases (examples in Corinth and Aegina museums; outstanding pieces are a jug formerly in the Chigi collection, now in Rome, and a mixing jar with the banquet of Eurytios, now in the Louvre). In these workshops the technique of black-figure decoration was invented, the figures standing out in black on a clay-coloured ground and the details being incised with a hard point. – The second group of workshops was in the eastern Aegean islands, the largest quantity of material having been found on *Rhodes*. Animal friezes predominate in the decoration, and the general effect is more Oriental, more "carpet-like", than in the rest of Greece (examples in Rhodes

Museum; outstanding piece a jug formerly in the Lévy collection, now in the Louvre). – The third group was in the *Cyclades* (Náxos, Páros, Melos). Here individual human figures or animals (lions, horses) were drawn with great care. Pairs of figures and individual heads are found which in their flatness, their contours and their proportions are reminiscent of the earliest examples of large sculpture (Mýkonos Museum; National Archaeological Museum, Athens; Náxos Museum). – Finally there was *Athens*, which evolved a distinctive form of dramatic narrative decoration on vases which were sometimes of very considerable size. Even the animal friezes and the individual figures seem to be there for their contribution to the subject-matter rather than on artistic or formal grounds, and this gives expression to the idea behind the decoration more strongly than in the work of the other groups. This expressive tendency can be seen as looking forward to the later achievements of Attic painting. In the 6th c. this style dominated the field: the only new development was the Spartan school of vase painting, which was mainly confined to drinking-cups. By the end of the 6th c. all the other workshops had been driven out of business by the Attic potters' competition. Slightly earlier, between 550 and 525 B.C., an Attic potter and painter, still practising the black-figure technique, had reached one of the summits of Greek painting. This was *Exekias*, nine signed examples of whose work have been preserved (examples: Geryoneus and Herakles, in the Louvre; Leda and her sons, in the Vatican Museums, Rome). But already as he was painting his latest works a new technique of red-figure decoration was developing. This method, specifically Attic, uses the same kind of colour contrasts as in the mature black-figure style, but in reverse. The ground is now painted black, and it is the figures which retain the reddish colouring of the clay. The details are no longer incised but painted in brilliant black or in thin matt lines. The figures now gain in plastic quality as compared with the silhouette figures of the black-figure technique.

Severe style (*c.* 490–450 B.C.). – The "Severe" style is the very apt name given to a distinct and characteristic phase of Greek art. The term, applied in the first place to *sculpture*, is not to be understood in contrast to the preceding Archaic

period but as the first phase in the development of mature classical art. The later phases of classical art are sometimes, less aptly, described as the "rich", the "beautiful" or the "free" style; in contrast to these the Severe style reflects an awareness of the serious, and indeed the tragic, quality of human existence. There is an anticipation of this in the melancholy expression of the kore of Euthydikos, although her posture is still typical of the korai of the Archaic period. Figures of men and youths evidently broke free at an earlier stage than figures of korai from the old axial and symmetrical canons of composition. A group by *Antenor* glorifying the liberation of Athens from tyranny (510 B.C.) may already have shown freer and livelier forms of the Severe style; but we know it only from copies of a version dating from 476 B.C. A chronological reference point is given by the Persian capture of the Acropolis of Athens in 480 B.C., when many votive offerings were damaged, including a statue of the highest quality of a youth, of which at least two fragments have been preserved (Acropolis Museum, Athens: lower part of body). We know the names of some of the leading sculptors of this period – *Kritios*, *Nesiotes*, *Kalamis*, *Dionysios*, *Onatas*, *Pythagoras* and *Myron*. A group of Athena and Marsyas and a statue of a discus-thrower can be confidently ascribed to Myron.

The "Critian Boy" in the Acropolis Museum shows clearly the change in posture which now came into vogue. The weight of the body is no longer borne equally on both legs: a clear distinction is made between the leg which supports the body and the one which remains free, and this difference is reflected in the whole muscular structure of the figure right up to the shoulders. The most notable feature is that the front of the torso and the face are no longer in the same plane, the head being turned to the right.

The discovery of man as an individual and his own personal responsibility within the bonds of religion and the community now found expression in art, and the thousand-year-old representational conventions which remained predominant in Egypt and the ancient East were now cast off by the contemporaries of Herakleitos. This new conception of man's dignity as man and this new severity of artistic

The Charioteer, Delphi

expression were displayed in the votive gift of a four-horse chariot presented to the sanctuary of Apollo at Delphi by the ruler of Syracuse, of which the charioteer has survived (Delphi Museum: also a good example of the technical skills of the period, with inset eyes and eyelashes). But this period also saw the beginnings of a consistent practice of differentiating between the representations of gods and of men. The marble torso of a Spartan warrior (Sparta Museum) may be a representation of Leonidas, the hero of Thermopylai; but the bronze statue of an unclothed bearded man (National Archaeological Museum, Athens) which shows a similar liveliness of representation, depicts a figure from an altogether different sphere. The effortless power of the arm, drawn back to hurl a weapon (no doubt Poseidon's trident), and the tranquil majesty of the features can belong only to a god.

Hardly a single example of this later sculpture has survived, and none of the most famous works of the period. The precious metal and bronze was subsequently melted down, the marble broken up and used in building or burned to produce limestone. But the originals at any rate survived into the Roman period, when numerous reproductions of them were made, and many of these works,

therefore, are known to us in copies, and sometimes in numerous copies. Examples of such copies of works in the Severe style are a marble statue of Apollo found in the Theatre of Dionysos in Athens (National Archaeological Museum) and five bronze clothed statues from Herculaneum, reduced to six-sevenths the size of the originals (National Museum, Naples). There are, however, very numerous pieces of *small sculpture* – thousands of bronze statuettes, various articles incorporating figural decoration, including in particular stands for circular metal mirrors, and terracottas. The high quality and craftsmanship of these small items reflects the increased national confidence which followed the defeat of the Persians, high artistic dedication and an intimate fusion of art and technical skill; and their survival is at least some compensation for the loss of the larger works. The figure which served to support a hemispherical bronze bowl (National Archaeological Museum, Athens) can stand beside the finest works on a similar theme; the figure, a consummate example of the mature Severe style, is not only perfectly conceived to perform its function as a support but can stand on its own as an independent work of art.

The *painting* of this period was of equally notable artistic quality. Its greatest master was *Polygnotos* of Thásos, whose best-known works were in Athens (of which he was made a citizen) and in an assembly hall at Delphi. He used fresco technique, painting his works on prepared wall surfaces or wooden panels. Although we have detailed descriptions of his paintings, particularly those at Delphi, the most vivid impression of his composition and draughtsmanship is to be had from a number of vase paintings which are evidently based on monumental paintings (Louvre, Paris). The scale and the focal point of all such paintings, even those with 70 or more figures, was determined by the individual human figure. Some degree of perspective effect was contrived for the purpose of representing movement by foreshortening of the limbs and emphasis on weapons and accoutrements like shields. There was, however, no sense of perspective in the composition as a whole: the individual figures were not seen from a common viewpoint but were depicted in a single plane surface. Those vase painters who were not directly basing their work on mural or panel

Spartan warrior (Leonidas?)

place of a free-standing statue on a tomb; and the tradition of the funerary relief was continued in the Severe style (Palazzo dei Conservatori, Rome; National Archaeological Museum, Athens; Archaeological Museum, Salonica). When two figures were represented they were now not always merely set behind one another facing in the same direction but were related to one another (Louvre, Paris). This opened up new compositional possibilities and challenges. The same features are found in votive reliefs, such as the figure of a boy (formerly with a gilded bronze garland) found at Soúnion (National Archaeological Museum, Athens) or a relief showing Athena in front of an inscribed stone (Acropolis Museum). The finest examples of relief carving in the Severe style, however, are to be found in architectural sculpture – the sculpture in full relief on the pediments of temples.

Temples. – The *Temple of Aphaia* near the E coast of Aegina was built about 500 B.C., but some of the figures in the battle scene in the E pediment were damaged and renewed, probably before 480 B.C.; and the transition from the Archaic to the Severe style took place between the carving of the original sculpture on both pediments and the renewal of the E pediment (Glyptothek, Munich). The earlier work forces the figures into a schematic composition of parallel lines,

paintings perfected their art within the framework of the genre. The remark already made about the small sculpture of the period is equally true of the vase painting: at no other time in the history of Greek art was such perfection of individual forms combined with such harmony between form and function. An incomparable example of this relationship between the vase and the vase painting is provided by a drinking bowl now in Würzburg bearing the signature of *Brygos*. It is significant that consummate effects of this kind are achieved even with the simplest subjects, indicating that the artists were catering for a large clientele of education and taste.

The Greek art of *relief sculpture* – including the fully rounded figures in temple pediments – is a genre closer to painting than to free-standing sculpture. Reliefs and paintings, however different in other respects, have a common feature in the background which links together the separate elements in the scene depicted on it or in front of it. Already in the Archaic period a narrow slab of stone with a representation in low relief or painting within incised lines sometimes took the

Temple of Aphaia, Aegina

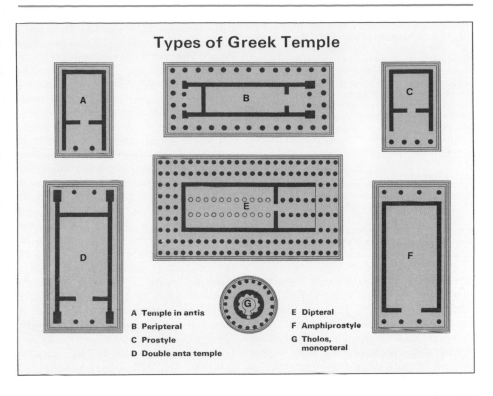

Types of Greek Temple

A Temple in antis
B Peripteral
C Prostyle
D Double anta temple

E Dipteral
F Amphiprostyle
G Tholos, monopteral

while the later work from the E pediment shows a unified and organic composition with a feeling of movement. The *Temple of Zeus at Olympia* (completed in 456 B.C.) still resembles the Temple of Aphaia in detailed architectural form; for although it was not so squat as earlier recon structions suggested, it must un doubtedly have had a certain heaviness of effect. The column drums of muschelkalk limestone still cover a considerable area on the site of this temple, the largest in the Peloponnese. The roof and the sculp tured decoration were of Parian marble (Museum, Olympia). In addition to the pediment sculpture there were 12 metopes with relief decoration (fragments in Louvre, Paris) on the front and rear end of the cella, depicting the 12 labours of Herakles. Athena frequently appears in these scenes as the hero's divine patron and helper. In addition to "action" scenes (e.g. the cleansing of the Augean stables) in a diagonal compositional pattern there are quieter and more static scenes (e.g. Atlas with the apples of the Hesperides) of a type particularly characteristic of the Severe style. The E pediment represents a legend featuring Zeus as a judge, Oino maos (a mythical king of Elis) and Pelops (a hero particularly revered at Olympia), and recalling the foundation of the Olympic chariot races. The W pediment depicts the fight between Greek heroes and centaurs at a wedding feast, with Apollo standing majestically between the contestants – the counterpart to the figure of Zeus on the E pediment. The imposing figures of the gods have the same visionary character as the statue of Poseidon already referred to. The statue of Zeus carved by Pheidias for the cella was probably set up some 25 years after the completion of the temple.

The Greek temple

The temple ranks with the theatre as one of the supreme achievements of Greek architecture. It was not designed as a meeting-place of the faithful, but as the home of the cult image, and thus of divinity itself. The form was derived from the megaron of a residential building, as seen in fully developed form, for example, in the throne-rooms of Mycenaean palaces.

The simplest type is the **temple in antis**, in which the *naos* (cella) is preceded by a *pronaos* (porch or antechamber) flanked by forward projections (*antae*) of its side walls. Between the antae are two columns supporting the pediment (Treasury of the Athenians, Delphi). There might on occasion be antae at both ends of the temple.

Where another row of columns stands in front of the antae, supporting the projecting pediment (one column in front of each of the antae, with two or four between) the temple is known as **prostyle** (E temple in the Erechtheion, Athens). If there is a similar row of columns on the rear end of the temple it is known as *amphiprostyle* (Temple of Nike, Acropolis).

From the second half of the 7th c. B.C. the classical form was the **peripteral** temple, in which the cella was surrounded on all four sides by a colonnade (*peristasis*). At one end was the entrance, preceded by a pronaos; at the other end was a rear chamber, the *opisthodomos*. In the 6th c. an elongated ground-plan was favoured, with six columns at the ends and 16 along the sides (Temple of Hera, Olympia; Temple of Apollo, Delphi, with 6×15 columns). In the 5th c. the classical proportions of the temple were developed, with *x* columns at the end and 2*x*+1 along the sides (Temple of Zeus, Olympia, 6×13 columns; Parthenon, Athens, 8×17).

If the temple has a double row of columns on all four sides it is known as **dipteral** (Olympieion, Athens). If the inner row of columns is omitted to leave room for a wider cella the temple is known as pseudo-dipteral (Temple of Artemis, Magnesia on the Maeander). – A further type of temple is the **tholos**, on a circular ground-plan (Epidauros, Delphi).

Pheidias and Polykleitos. – These two names mark the high point of Greek art. Both were sculptors, although Pheidias also painted in his earlier days. They differed, however, in the subjects they chose: Pheidias owed his fame to his statues of gods, while Polykleitos mainly devoted himself to human figures. This difference was merely the external reflection of their personal and profoundly different conceptions of the function of art; but seen from our later point in time and against the whole background of the development of art they move closer together, with their diverse aspects complementing one another to form a single culminating point in the history of the art of antiquity.

Pheidias was born in Athens, probably at the beginning of the 5th c. B.C. He inscribed his name, and that of his father, on the base of what was probably his last work, the statue of Zeus at Olympia. This statue was completed about 430 B.C., and Pheidias is believed to have died soon afterwards, perhaps in 428. There are divergent traditions about the teacher from whom Pheidias learnt his art. At a later stage in his career he worked in collaboration with the painter *Parrhasios*, and it has recently been suggested that Pheidias may have been a pupil of *Euenor* of Ephesus, Parrhasios' father. This theory is based on the possibility that a column bearing Euenor's signature which was set up on the Acropolis of Athens about 475 B.C. bore a small statue of Athena by the youthful Pheidias. The statue has been preserved and is now in the Acropolis Museum; and in fact it has the appearance of an early forerunner of the statues of

Athena carved by the mature Pheidias. It is a work of notable quality, and in various details (the left hand resting on the hip) anticipates the full classical style. The figure as a whole, of course, still bears the marks of the Severe style; but Pheidias must have been at work during that period, even though his principal works belong to a later period. The two large votive offerings which the Athenians commissioned from Pheidias after their victory at Marathon in 490 B.C. – a bronze group at Delhi and a bronze figure of Athena Promachos, 16·5 m (54 ft) high, on the Acropolis – were probably not produced until between 460 and 450; but thereafter a whole series of works, known to us only from copies and descriptions, followed in quick succession. On the Acropolis were a bronze figure of Apollo Parnopios (statue in Kassel; head in National Archaeological Museum, Athens) and a bronze figure of Athena Lemnia (probably 448–447 B.C.: statue in Dresden, head in Bologna), in Ephesus a bronze Amazon (Vatican Museums, Rome). In 447 B.C. work began on the building of the Parthenon, one of Perikles' undertakings the supreme direction of which was entrusted to Pheidias, as Plutarch tells us. Two architects were responsible for the construction of the temple, and numerous sculptors worked on the relief decoration of the metopes (before 442–441 B.C.), the best preserved of which are those depicting fights with centaurs (British Museum, London), the frieze (Acropolis Museum, Athens; British Museum, London) and the pediment sculpture (438–432 B.C.: Acropolis Museum, British Museum). The chryselephantine cult image (438 B.C.) was the work of Pheidias himself. When Pheidias later created the chryselephantine statue of Zeus at Olympia he was clearly following up the experience he had gained in setting up the image of Athena Parthenos in Athens.

Although Pheidias maintained, and indeed enhanced, the visionary aspect of the divine images in the Severe style, he departed from the earlier pattern of representation. It has been well observed of the statue of Apollo in Kassel that scant attention is paid to the proper distribution of weight, since although the supporting leg shows an outward curve the free leg is not correspondingly concave (Chr. Karusos). As a result the side with the supporting leg conveys an impression of movement, while the other side is vertical, as if rooted to the ground; and the almost mincing posture suggests a certain instability. The unity of the figure does not reside in its physical structure: the god is superior to the laws of gravity, and both the body and the face show that this is a divine and transcendent being. This is also the case with the Dresden figure of Athena, who is depicted presenting weapons to a warlike group of settlers setting out for Lemnos. The face of the Bologna head shows that the figure forms part of something very different from the ordinary genre scene. The statues from the Parthenon and the temples at Olympia not only reach out beyond all accustomed degrees of grandeur and splendour but are seeking to achieve entirely new effects. An important factor in this respect is the space which these statues occupied within the temple, taking up its full height and breadth, almost bursting out of its confines. And the wealth of attributes and the detail of the carving are beyond all numbering here.

This transcendental, superhuman vitality of the gods is no less evident in the Parthenon pediments (E pediment, birth of Athena; W pediment, contest between Athena and Poseidon for possession of Attica); but the frieze takes us into a different world. It represents the procession at the Panathenaic festival which took Athena's new robe to the Acropolis, where the assembled divinities of Olympus awaited it. Here the sculptors give expression to all the beauty of the human body and all the grace of youth. We are at once reminded of the finest of the funerary reliefs of Attica, the sculptors of which no doubt also worked on the Parthenon – to the magnificent figure of a youth in the act of releasing a bird from a cage, as the soul is released from the body (National Archaeological Museum, Athens), or the intimately associated figures of the two women on the grave stele of Hegeso (also in the National Museum), in an almost circular composition of consummate harmony. The stele of Dexileos (394 B.C.: Kerameikos Museum, Athens) still shows the influence of such works by Pheidias as the relief of a horseman in the Villa Albani in Rome.

In this context, too, we must consider the lekythoi (oil-flasks), with scenes painted or drawn in colour on a white ground, which were used only as grave goods to accompany the dead (National Archaeological Museum and Kerameikos Museum, Athens). On these we see representations of the tomb monument, the dead persons, their relations and friends, the life of this world and the next, often indiscriminately mingled.

The designs for the carving on the shield of Athena Promachos were drawn by *Parrhasios*, but of this work nothing has survived, even in the form of copies. We have in fact none of the work of Parrhasios or of any of the other famous Greek painters; but we have such excellent descriptions of his style and draughtsmanship that it has been possible to show that some of the vases with decoration on a white ground were influenced by him, including some original works. The Acropolis Museum contains a work by *Alkamenes*, a sculptor of rather conservative bent, depicting a woman with a small boy snuggling against her; and we have also a fragment and parts of the base of a statue of the goddess of retribution (Nemesis) carved by the more impulsive *Agorakritos* for the town of Rhamnous in Attica (British Museum, London; National Archaeological Museum, Athens).

In addition to altering the strict rules of construction in sculpture Pheidias also presided over a mingling and modification of the canonical orders of architecture. The shaping of the interior of the Parthenon was determined by the form and intended effect of the cult statue: the temple was, as it were, made to measure for the statue. The number and proportions of the columns were unusual, and the frieze was an element from the Ionic order which did not properly belong to the Doric order. The continuation of the interior row of columns around the back of the cult image must be seen as reflecting the special status of the image: the effect aimed at is that of a total work of art. A similar tendency is seen in the later work on the Parthenon by *Iktinos* and in the Temple of Apollo at Bassai, in which Corinthian capitals were used for the first time. The Propylaia of the Acropolis, built by *Mnesikles* in the time of Pheidias, have both Doric and Ionic columns. But during the period of building activity which began with the Parthenon even purely Ionic forms were modified in a specifically Attic way (Temple of Nike, Erechtheion), while Doric buildings like the splendidly preserved Hephaisteion in Athens or the Temple of Poseidon on Cape Soúnion are barely conceivable without the model provided by the Parthenon.

Polykleitos of Argos was some 15 years younger than Pheidias. We have only copies of his statues, but some of the original bases and inscriptions have been preserved (Kyniskos, Pythokles, Xenokles: Olympia Museum). His earliest work was the "Diskobolos" (Vatican Museums, Rome), the style of which is better preserved in a head with the addition of small wings (Pergamon Museum, East Berlin) than in complete statues. An Amazon now in Rome (Capitoline Museum) and the "Westmacott Athlete" (British Museum), probably belonging to the Kyniskos base, both date from the middle of the 5th c. A much more famous work was the "Doryphoros" (Spear-Carrier), of which more than 30 copies are known (4th c. relief, with addition of horse: National Archaeological Museum, Rome). A Herakles now in Rome (Museo Baracco) and a youth tying a ribbon round his head (National Archaeological Museum, Athens) are probably late works. The originals of all these statues were in bronze, but Polykleitos also worked in the chryselephantine technique. His last work, a statue of Hera for the temple at Argos, which was burned down in 423 B.C. and had to be rebuilt, was in the same technique as Pheidias' temple statues, and according to Strabo was in no way inferior to them in magnificence and grandeur.

Polykleitos' statues were governed by strict rules, both in respect of the form of the body and the facial features. The marks of the feet on the surviving statue bases, and the copies of the statues themselves, show that even more markedly than in the "Critian Boy", one leg bore most of the weight. To an even greater extent than in the Critian Boy, too, the whole body was governed by a system of correspondences: to the free leg corresponded the arm which was in active movement, to the supporting leg the arm which hung quietly by the figure's side. This resulted in a completely balanced and harmonious composition, extending to every detail of the figure, including the face, which have none of the spiritualisation of Pheidias' gods. Polykleitos' statues achieve their artistic unity by a precise observance of the laws of structure and mathematical proportion. At the same time the creative process depended in the last analysis on an element of the irrational, as Polykleitos himself emphasised in a theoretical treatise. It is not surprising, however, that he was criticised for the uniformity of his figures, which were in fact merely variations on the same general scheme. That may be true, but the criticism is misconceived; for it is precisely this that makes Polykleitos a supreme representative of Greek art, which from its very beginnings showed both the will and the ability to create types. In this respect the artist of the high classical period proves himself the heir to the art of the Archaic period. In his statues of youths Polykleitos gives expression to the same ideas, though at a higher stage of development, as another sculptor from Argos had expressed a century and a half earlier in his statues of Kleobis and Biton.

Late classical art (c. 390–330 B.C.). – While in the Severe style even the paintings of Polygnotos and the work of the vase painters had sought to achieve a plastic effect, the development of the classical school after Pheidias and Polykleitos showed a painterly trend. During the last decades of the 5th c. B.C. large-scale painting was already seeking to contrive new effects by the use of light and shade on garments and male bodies. The painters were now not merely producing frescoes and panel paintings but also decorating rooms in private houses and painting architectural scenes as stage settings. Once again we see a reflection of this work in vase painting, which achieves more colourful effects by the use of white ground-colour, gilding and even relief moulding of certain parts. The themes become light, gentle, sentimental.

In the earlier reliefs the figures had been related to one another either by the action or by the mood of the scene. In the numerous Attic *funerary reliefs* of the 4th c. B.C. (National Archaeological Museum, Athens: forbidden by sumptuary legislation about 310 B.C.) the mere existence of the figures is sufficient. To an increasing extent they become isolated from one another, standing out like individual statues against the relief background. This does not mean, however, that the figures themselves are given greater plasticity:

instead the architectural framework of the scene gains in importance, so that the figures are set within a niche. The artistic theme of these reliefs thus became the relationship between the figures and the frame within which they were enclosed. The figures, moulded in the round though they were, could now be seen from only one viewpoint – that of the spectator face to face with the relief background.

This is true also of the statues of the most celebrated creator of divine images after Pheidias, **Praxiteles**. They too are designed to be seen from only one viewpoint, and they too are spatial compositions which, like the reliefs, seek to achieve a picture-like effect by the use of highlights, deep shadows and transitional nuances. At the same time there was a more vivid use of colour than had previously been usual. It is significant that Praxiteles believed his finest statues to be those which had been painted by the contemporary painter *Nikias*. We can get some idea of the nature of the colouring from those of the little terracotta figures

The Hermes of Praxiteles, Olympia

from Tanagra which preserved their surface coating of clay and their painting (National Archaeological Museum, Athens; Thebes Museum). In the interpretation of his themes Praxiteles showed a very individual approach. He represented Apollo as a youthful figure barely beyond adolescence and still with the interests of a boy – leaning against a tree in a relaxed posture and reaching out with his right hand to catch a lizard which is climbing up the trunk (marble copy of a bronze original: Vatican Museums, Rome). In his Aphrodite of Knidos (50 copies in many museums) he ventured for the first time in Greece to depict a goddess completely naked. A similar conception of the weightless being of the gods is expressed in a late work, not quite finished, representing Hermes with the infant Dionysos, the original of which was found at Olympia (Museum, Olympia). Three original reliefs by Praxiteles from the bases of statues by him at Mantineia (National Archaeological Museum, Athens) depict clothed figures – Apollo with six Muses, Marsyas challenging Apollo to a musical contest and the flaying of the defeated Marsyas.

Other examples of the painter's treatment of relief are provided by the frieze on the gigantic funerary monument (the "Mausoleum") of King Mausolos of Caria (d. 352 B.C.), the best-preserved fragments of which, depicting a fight with Amazons, are in the British Museum. Attempts have been made to distinguish four different groups within the considerable amount of material that survives, corresponding to the four famous contemporaries of Praxiteles – Timotheos, Skopas, Leochares and Bryaxis – who were traditionally supposed to have carved the sculptured decoration on each of the sides of the monument, which was almost square in plan.

Timotheos also worked on the pediments of the Temple of Asklepios at Epidauros (*c.* 375 B.C.: National Archaeological Museum, Athens). A statue of Leda by him is preserved in a poor copy (Capitoline Museum, Rome), and an Artemis by him is represented together with a figure of Apollo in a long robe playing the lyre on a statue base found in Italy (Sorrento Museum). Both statues were set up in the Temple of Apollo on the Palatine in Rome in the time of Augustus; they probably stood originally in a temple at Rhamnous.

Skopas was an architect as well as a sculptor, and was responsible for the rebuilding, probably around 340 B.C., of the Temple of Athena Alea at Tegea which had been destroyed by fire in 395 B.C. The sculpture from the pediments of the temple (National Archaeological Museum, Athens) was probably also by Skopas, or at least produced in his workshop and under his direction. In concentrated power of movement, the passionate facial expressions and the high quality of the marble-working this surpasses even the best parts of the frieze from the Mausoleum. The E pediment depicted the hunt of the Calydonian boar by Meleager, the W front probably a warlike encounter between Herakles and Achilles.

Tholos at Delphi (Marmariá)

Leochares and Bryaxis were also noted for their figures of gods. The bronze original of the Apollo Belvedere (Vatican Museums, Rome) was probably by *Leochares. Bryaxis* – who was, to judge from his name, of Carian origin – was in his younger days, when he worked on the Mausoleum, a pioneer of a modern style with a diagonal compositional axis; towards the end of his life, which extended into the 3rd c., he might stand as a representative of the final phase of the late classical style. – In spite of their diversity of individual temperament, origin and technique, however, all these artists are at one as representatives of a particular stage in the development of art in which painterly tendencies constantly recur. In sculpture external forms are depicted by the effects of light and shade in the treatment of the surfaces and by the disposition of the composition within a flat area of space.

The clearest example of the dissonant elements in the late classical style, which are combined to form a work of art only through the achievement of a painterly or picturesque effect, both in spatial and atmospheric terms, is the *grave relief from the Ilissos* now in the National Archaeological Museum, which shows affinities with the style of Skopas. The figure of the dead youth is typical of one composed in a flat area of space. He stands in a relaxed pose, leaning back and looking at the spectator with an almost indifferent glance, while his aged father, sharply drawn in profile, stands leaning on his staff, with his left hand raised to his chin, and gazes at his son, deep in thought, but receives no answering glance. The diagonally composed steps and the pillar on which the young man has laid his cloak represent the tomb. Associated with him, both formally and personally, are the small servant who sits sleeping on the steps and the dog sniffing about on the ground: they are both now lost and abandoned. To questions about the meaning of death or of life there is no answer but the beauty created by art.

A characteristic feature of the architecture of the late classical period was the *rotunda*. The earliest example of the type was the round temple in the precinct of Athena Pronaia at *Delphi* (Marmariá), followed by the Thymele at *Epidauros*. In both of these buildings, as in the earlier temple of Apollo at Bassai and the later temple of Athena Alea at Tegéa, the Doric order was used on the exterior and the Corinthian in the interior. A magnificent Corinthian capital found at Epidauros probably served as the model for all the others on that site. The Philippeion (second half of 4th c. B.C.) at *Olympia* has Ionic columns on the exterior and Corinthian half-columns in the interior. A small rotunda in Athens, the choregic monument of Lysikrates (333 B.C.), has only Corinthian half-columns, now used on the exterior; on this monument, too, relief decoration reappears (a Dionysiac frieze). The occasion for the erection of this monument (the victory of a choir financed by Lysikrates in a dramatic competition) and the decorative themes (Dionysos and satyrs, the transformation of Tyrrhenian pirates into dolphins) bring us back to the theatre; and this period saw the first monumental *theatres* – the theatre at *Epidauros*, finely designed as a total work of art, and the rebuilding of the theatre at *Athens* (completed 330 B.C.). Both of these are masterly achievements in terms of both architecture and acoustics.

Apelles and Lysippos. – It is difficult to assess the quality and the influence of works of art which have not survived even in copies and have not even left any mark on other artistic genres. While we can see some reflection of the wall paintings of Polygnotos or Parrhasios in contemporary vase painting, and have excellent ancient copies of paintings by contemporaries of Apelles ("Perseus and Andromeda" by Nikias, "Alexander's Battle" by Philoxenos: National Museum, Naples), we have no evidence of this kind about the work of Apelles himself. The remains of his work, indeed, are in inverse proportion to his fame. But the subjects of his paintings, his virtuoso-like mastery of his craft, his position as a contemporary of the great events of Alexander's reign and his friendship with Alexander himself all make it necessary to mention his name here.

Apelles (*c.* 370–310 B.C.) was born in the Ionian city of Kolophon in Asia Minor, learnt his craft in the painting school at Sikyon in the Peloponnese, later lived on the island of Kos and perhaps died there. He was one of a group of three artists who had a kind of monopoly of portraying Alexander the Great. There are references in classical literature to at least 18 portraits by him, including five portraits of Alexander, two of which were taken to Rome and set up in the Forum by Augustus. We know the measurements of these pictures (2·65 by 2·35 m (9 by 8 ft)), since the positions they occupied are still visible. The quality of these portraits must have lain both in the fidelity of the likeness and in their magnificent expression of the "imperial idea" which led Augustus to display them in the most prominent position in Imperial Rome. In each of these portraits Alexander was shown with the attributes and insignia of his power – on horseback, with a thunderbolt, with the Dioskouroi, in a chariot – in the role known to the Romans as "Triumphator". But Apelles was also the first artist who is known to have painted a self-portrait, no doubt showing the same truth to life and the same spiritual interpretation of the physical features as his other portraits. This was the first self-portrait only in the sense that the artist now became the subject of the picture without any attempt

at disguise; for earlier artists had no doubt created a projection of their own ego in the legendary figures they portrayed.

A notable feature of Apelles' other paintings was that he rarely depicted actions or events: scenes from the old myths and legends are absent from his work. The gods and heroes were depicted either as individual figures or surrounded by other mythological personages. His most famous picture was one of Aphrodite rising out of the sea which later found its way to Rome. Like all his work so far as we know, it was a panel picture, not a wall painting, and used only the colours black, white, yellow and red. Although we have insufficient information about the style and composition of his pictures to be able to assert that he marked the culmination of the picturesque tendencies of the late classical period and in his use of spatial and aerial perspective prepared the way for Hellenistic art, it is clear at any rate from the literary evidence that his importance at a turning-point in the history of art was at least as great as that of Lysippos.

Lysippos (*c.* 395–300 B.C.), a native of Sikyon, worked even more exclusively than Polykleitos in bronze; but he was not confined to the Peloponnesian tradition of the great masters of Argos. Although he spoke of Polykleitos' Doryphoros as his model, he is also said to have declared that he was no man's pupil: artists must follow nature, not their predecessors. He was credited with producing some 1500 statues, and he was Alexander the Great's favourite sculptor, as Apelles was his favourite painter. His work is poorly represented, however, among the surviving copies: his works were not "classical" enough and therefore were not popular during the great age of copying. Among the many works of sculpture representing Alexander which are preserved in copies or in variants the official portraits by Lysippos (Louvre, Paris; Archaeological Museum, Istanbul) do not take a high place. Of the four statues of Zeus by Lysippos which are referred to in the literary sources we can form no conception, while his other portrayals of gods and heroes may be represented by a number of statues of Herakles, including the late work, best known in a copy (National Archaeological Museum, Athens) which belonged to the Farnese

Lion-Hunt mosaic, Pélla (Macedonia)

collection, and in another copy (Palazzo Pitti, Florence) has an inscription ascribing it to Lysippos. As with Polykleitos, we also have some of the original bases for statues by Lysippos, including one (Poulydamas: Museum, Olympia) which preserves remains of carving.

We do not know, however, whether his most famous statue – an athlete scraping himself with a strigil (preserved in a single copy: Vatican Museums, Rome) – may have come from one of these bases, although it is very characteristic of Lysippos' style. Departing from the canon of rather thickset figures, it shows slenderer proportions: the head is smaller in relation to the rest of the figure, and the supporting and the free leg are more sharply distinguished than in Polykleitos' statues. This difference between the two legs, however, no longer determines the structure of the figure. The stance is now almost labile: it appears as if the weight might be transferred at any moment to the free leg. The object is to achieve a posture which has been aptly called the "pendulum position". The transitory effect is produced not only by this latent possibility of a change of position but also by the smoothly flowing contours and above all by the slight turn of the body on its axis – as if inviting the spectator to walk round the statue without taking his eyes off it. The figure is designed to be seen not merely from a single viewpoint but from all round, and thus achieves a new kind of spatial effect. But the matter goes farther than this: an element of space is caught up into the statue itself. The wide stance, the reaching-out movement of the arms involve the immediately surrounding

space so intimately with the figure that the plastic surfaces no longer mark the boundaries of the artistic composition. The statue now stands within an area of space which in a sense is shaped and influenced by its form. These innovations seem to have brought Lysippos to the very frontiers of his art, and to mark the end of an epoch. In the words of J. G. Droysen, "the name of Alexander marks the end of an era in world history and the beginning of a new one"; and this is true also of art. Lysippos marked not only the culmination of one phase of Greek art but the first intimation of a new and final phase.

Hellenistic period. – The Hellenistic period in art lasted from the death of Alexander (323 B.C.) to the establishment of the Roman province of Achaea (27 B.C.), which marked the end of Greece as an independent political and cultural organism. During these three centuries there came into being – alongside the old artistic centres in the Peloponnese, Athens and its dependent territories, and the old-established Greek colonies on the coast of Asia Minor – the new capitals of the independent kingdoms which had been carved out of Alexander's empire, chief among them Alexandria and ·Pergamon.

In *sculpture* it might appear that in the early years of the period the achievements of Lysippos were not followed up. Numerous works of art of the late 4th c. B.C. still continue late classical traditions. One masterpiece of this period survives only in a fragment – a female head found on the southern slopes of the Acropolis in

Athens and now in the National Archaeological Museum. The passionate mouth and the fiercely yearning glance have led to its identification as Ariadne. What makes this head particularly notable is not only the rarity of surviving examples of original free-standing sculpture of the highest quality but also the opportunity it gives us of comparing the fire and delicacy of the original with the sentimental trivialisation of a copy which also survives (Berlin). It is clear, therefore, that the Ariadne was a celebrated work of sculpture, an *opus nobile*. Its creator had close affinities with the sculptor who produced the large group of Niobe and her children (copies in Uffizi, Florence), probably originally set up in the open air, which connoisseurs of the Imperial period ascribed to either Praxiteles or Skopas. The figures of Ariadne and the Niobids do indeed show a development of the style of these two great sculptors; but they were created at a time when Praxiteles and Skopas were both dead.

It would be natural to suppose that the introduction of new impulses by Lysippos would lead to the dying out of the older tradition; but it is remarkable that in fact post-Lysippan sculpture in purely Hellenistic style appears resistant to his conception of the statue and his use of space. Numbers of works produced in the first half of the 3rd c. B.C. are clearly not designed to be seen from a variety of viewpoints: cf., for example, a figure of a divinity like the statue of Themis by *Chairestratos* (original: National Archaeological Museum, Athens), which stood in a temple at Rhamnous, or a portrait statue like the figure of Demosthenes by *Polyeuktos* (Vatican Museum, Rome). But the classical appearance of these works is deceptive: the sculptured surfaces are instinct with the mobility of the Lysippan manner, apparently only just under control, and the figure of Demosthenes expresses a spiritual tension richer in contrast and in complexity than is found in any portrait of the classical period. It is not surprising, therefore, that towards the end of the century the Hellenistic feeling for space, which is present in these works, as it were, in repressed form, achieves full and powerful expression.

This trend can be detected in the "Barberini Faun" (Munich), depicted asleep but on the point of awakening. It is seen in fully developed form in such over-life-size works as the great monument erected by *Attalos I* of Pergamon to commemorate a victory over the Galatians in 230 B.C. (base with inscription and copies of principal figures: Rome) and the famous *Victory of Samothrace* (original: Louvre, Paris). The Victory (Nike), dated to the beginning of the 2nd c., probably commemorates a Rhodian victory over Antiochos III of Syria in 190 B.C. When compared with the vigour and panache of this work even the liveliest figures of the classical period appear subdued. And yet the vehement movement which carries the winged goddess on to meet the wind does not seem overdone, and the passionate intensity with which every fold in her robe and every feather in her wings is delineated appears, both in total effect and in detail, entirely unforced and free of empty rhetoric.

This cannot perhaps be said of every detail of the carving on the monumental *Altar of Zeus from Pergamon* (Pergamon Museum, East Berlin); but nevertheless in terms of richness of composition and power of execution the frieze depicting a fight between gods and giants, dating from the reign of Eumenes II (197–159 B.C.), need fear no comparisons. The smaller frieze depicting the mythological genealogy of the ruling family of Pergamon, executed during the reign of Attalos II (159–138 B.C.), shows a quieter, almost idyllic, trend. It is notable that the first deliberate copies of earlier work were made at Pergamon. The city apparently had cultural links with Athens, and reproductions of Attic figures of divinities were set up in its temples. They are distinguished from later copies by the enthusiasm of their assimilation, which militated against the fidelity of the reproduction.

This trend, however, reflected a gradual decline in creative force. After such works as the *Aphrodite of Melos* (Venus de Milo: Louvre, Paris) and the Poseidon also found on Melos (National Archaeological Museum, Athens), both of which are dated to about the middle of the 2nd c. B.C., all art forms become forced, imitative, academic – characteristics quite alien to the natural and unconstrained quality of Greek art. But that even in these circumstances great artists could still produce notable work is demonstrated by the fragments of groups of gods by *Damophon* of Messene (after 150 B.C.: National Archaeological Museum, Athens, and Lykosoura Museum) and the famous Laokoon group by *Hegesandros, Polydoros* and *Athenodoros* (Vatican Museums, Rome), a work of the late Hellenistic period shortly before its end.

In *architecture* the Ionic order was predominant during the Hellenistic period. In addition to temples – and the great temples of eastern Greece were all rebuilt or renovated in late classical and Hellenistic times – changed political and social conditions called for a variety of other buildings, including council chambers, stoas and imposing and luxurious residences. The stoa, a long hall with one or more rows of columns along its open side, was a feature particularly characteristic of Hellenistic architecture, found in sacred precincts and in the market-places which were the main centres of public life. Notable examples can be seen in the cities of Asia Minor and, since the excavations of the last few decades, in the Agora of Athens. The stoa built in the Athenian Agora by Attalos II of Pergamon was rebuilt by the American excavators and now houses a museum of material found in the Agora.

Painting still clung to the traditions of the preceding period; but the use of perspective was developed, and the figures had the proportions established by Lysippos. Among notable surviving examples of the work of this period are numerous painted grave stelae from Pagasai (Vólos Museum) and monumental dome frescoes at Kazanlǎk in Bulgaria. The art of vase painting had completely disappeared.

Roman period. – When the Roman general Aemilius Paulus defeated King Perseus of Macedon in 168 B.C. he set up a monument celebrating his victory in the sanctuary at Delphi, with a frieze depicting the decisive battle of Pydna which is purely Hellenistic in style. By about 100 B.C., however, a distinctive style had been evolved on Delos for the portrait statues commissioned by Italian patrons (National Archaeological Museum, Athens). The bodies were based on earlier models (statues of gods or heroes), almost unchanged; but while in Greek sculpture,

even in portrait statues, the figure was conceived and depicted as a whole, in Roman work the head took on a special importance of its own. Actual likenesses of individuals now became possible for the first time, whether in the form of statues, busts or herm portraits. Whereas in Greek representations of human beings the general always predominated over the individual, the Romans sought to depict the distinctive characteristics of the sitter. The individual personality was now mirrored with uncompromising fidelity in Roman portraits. This basic difference from the Greek portrait was maintained even in the neo-classical work of the Augustan period, when the aim, particularly in portraits of members of the Imperial house (Pythagórion Museum, Sámos), was to achieve a kind of tranquil simplicity in detail as well as in general effect. And although all the portraits produced in Greece during the Roman period still show a last dying touch of Hellenistic grace this does not obscure the fact that they are quite different from earlier Greek work.

The *architecture* of the Roman provinces, making much use of the arch and the vault, surpassed Hellenistic architecture in scale and boldness of construction. In *Athens*, however, the buildings erected at the beginning of the period were still relatively modest, like the Tower of the Winds, which was equipped with a water-clock and sundial by a certain Andronikos. The neo-classical style of the early Empire is represented by the remains of the circular Temple of Rome and Augustus to the E of the Parthenon, some of the ornament of which was painstakingly copied from the Erechtheion. The reliefs on the stage of the Theatre of Dionysos reproduce classical types of divine figures. The Monument of Philopappos (grandson of the last ruler of Commagene), on the hill SW of the Acropolis (c. A.D. 115), is also in neo-classical style. A new Roman market was built near the old Agora about A.D. 5, and in the reign of Hadrian a whole new district was built. The Arch of Hadrian has an inscription referring to the older city to the W as the city of Theseus and the new area to the E, which included the Temple of Zeus, as the city of Hadrian. The Odeon of Herodes Atticus, named after the wealthy private citizen who built it, also dates from the time of Hadrian.

In spite of its splendour this architecture of the late period has a rather contrived and stereotyped air. Greece was now a mere Roman province, and as such was exposed to Rome's glorification of its own history. The *historical relief*, familiar on the triumphal arches of Italy and on the columns of Trajan and Marcus Aurelius, now came to Macedonia, and the Arch of Galerius in Salonica (*c.* A.D. 300) depicts victorious Roman armies, battle and marching scenes, the Roman general among his legionaries, and the goddess Fortuna, ruler of the world: a greater contrast to the frieze depicting the battle of Pydna can hardly be imagined. The composition is no longer related to the human figure with its established proportions, and the crowded scenes lack any sense of plastic form. The details of costume and weapons, standards, exotic animals and a variety of accessories are meticulously depicted; but exact delineation of the scene and the action, of the various arms and the various ranks, is lost in the overcrowded and formless profusion of the whole. Within this whole the proliferation of circumstantial detail becomes a stylistic element of subordinate importance, and the total effect is almost of an abstract pattern in a single plane.

Ceiling fresco in Perívleptos monastery, Mistra

There was a great flowering of *mosaics* in the Hellenistic period. The earliest examples, in the 5th and early 4th c. B.C. (Athens, Olynthos), were pebble mosaics, which reached their highest point of achievement at *Pélla* in the time of Alexander. In the 3rd c. coloured tesserae came into use (e.g. in houses on Delos).

In **Byzantine art**, particularly in mosaics and paintings, the individual figure again came into its own, but this time in the new setting of Christianity. The Byzantine monuments in which Athens and the rest of Greece are so rich owe nothing to Greek art: they belong to a new phase of history and of art which must be seen in the wider framework involving not only Byzantium itself but Ravenna and the whole of Roman/Christian art.

In the 4th c. A.D. a strictly frontal pose came into favour in relief sculpture (carving on base of the obelisk in the Hippodrome, Constantinople), and this also became predominant in many aspects of Byzantine art, particularly in *icons*. In this new Christian art sculpture in the round gave place to relief carving for the transcendental representation of sacred figures, and a prominent place was occupied by painting, including mosaic work. Byzantine art was above all a religious art, which sought to create buildings in the image of the divine cosmos. Of central importance in this respect is the cruciform ground-plan of Byzantine churches, represented by the domed cruciform church which in the Middle Byzantine period (9th–12th c.) replaced the older basilican form; and equally significant is the decoration of the churches with figures of Christ Pantokrator (Ruler of All), the Mother of God, saints and church festivals, to be seen notably in the two 11th c. monastic churches of *Ósios Loukás* and *Dafní*, the churches at *Mistra* dating from the late Byzantine period (1261–1453) and the early Byzantine mosaics of *Salonica*. The Byzantine Museum in Athens offers a general survey of Byzantine art in Greece. – The traditions of Byzantine art were carried on during the Turkish period, for example in the monasteries of *Metéora* (16th c.) and *Athos* and the numerous churches of *Kastoriá*.

After the liberation of Greece in the 19th c. Byzantine art still served as a model in

Cathedral of St Demetrius, Mistra

Academy, Athens

such buildings as the Ophthalmic Clinic and the New Mitrópolis in Athens; but the great bulk of the buildings now erected looked back to the art of antiquity, in the work of such architects as *Christian Hansen, Theophil Hansen, Friedrich von Gärtner, Schaubert* and *Kleanthes*. Examples of this neo-classical architecture in Athens include the University, the Academy, the National Library, the Royal Palace and the Stadion, re-erected in marble in its original form.

Glossary of Technical Terms (Art, History, Mythology)

Abacus:
The upper part of the capital of a Doric column, a square slab above the echinus. See diagram, p. 49.

Abaton:
The innermost sanctuary of a temple, to which only priests were admitted.

Acanthus:
A spiny-leaved plant used in the decoration of Corinthian and Byzantine (Justinianic) capitals.

Acropolis:
The highest part of a Greek city; the Citadel.

Acroterion:
A figure or ornament on a roof ridge or the top of a pediment.

Adyton:
See Abaton.

Aegis:
The cuirass worn by the goddess Athena with the head of the Gorgon Medusa (Gorgoneion).

Agora:
The market-place of a Greek city, the main centre of public life.

Alabastron:
An oil-flask without base or handles.

Altis:
The sacred grove at Olympia.

Amazonomachia:
A fight between Greeks and Amazons.

Amphiprostyle:
(Temple) with columned portico at both ends.

Amphora:
Two-handled jar of bulbous form.

Anathema:
Votive offering.

Annulus:
A ring round the shaft of a Doric column below the echinus.

Anta:
Pillar-like projection at the end of the side wall of the cella of a temple. *Temple in antis*, a temple with antae at one end, with columns between them.

Aphesis:
Starting-line on the running track of a stadion.

Apotheosis:
Deification of a human being.

Apse:
A projection, usually semicircular, at the end of a temple cella or church.

Archaic art:
Art of the 7th and 6th c. B.C. in Greece.

Architrave:
A horizontal stone lintel resting on the columns of a temple, etc. See diagram, p. 49.

Archon:
The highest official of a Greek city.

Aryballos:
Spherical oil-flask

Astragal:
Knucklebone; applied to the beaded moulding of the Ionic order.

Basileus:
King.

Basilica:
1. Originally a royal hall (*stoa basilike*), usually divided into aisles, used for commercial or judicial purposes.
2. The standard form of Christian church developed in the 4th c., with three or five aisles.

Bema:
1. Platform used by orators.
2. Chancel of a Christian church.

Bomos:
Square altar.

Bothros:
Pit for offerings.

Bouleuterion:
Council chamber; the meeting-place of the council (*boule*) of a Greek city.

Capital:
The top of a column or pillar.

Caryatid:
A female figure supporting an entablature.

Cavea:
The auditorium (seating) of a theatre.

Cella:
The enclosed chamber of a temple.

Cenotaph:
Funerary monument not containing a body.

Centauromachia:
Fight between Lapiths and centaurs.

Chiton:
A pleated linen garment worn with a belt, mostly in Ionia.

Chlamys:
A short cloak.

Choregos:
"Choir-leader": a person who financed the choir performing in a tragedy.

Chryselephantine:
(Sculpture) of gold and ivory on a wooden core.

Chthonian:
(Divinities) of the earth.

Classical art:
Art of the period from 480 to 330 B.C. *Early classical*, 480–460; *high classical*, 460–430; *late classical*, 430–400; *post-classical*, 4th c.

Corinthian order:
See Orders, below.

Crepidoma:
Three-stepped platform of a temple. See diagram, p. 49.

Cycladic culture:
Culture of the 3rd millennium B.C. in the Cyclades.

Cyclopean:
(Walls) of large irregular blocks, ascribed in antiquity to the Cyclopes.

Cyma:
Wave moulding with double curvature.

Demos:
People, community; popular assembly; settlement.

Diakonikon:
The right-hand lateral apse of a Byzantine church.

Diazoma:
Gangway between tiers of seating in a theatre.

Dimini culture:
A Greek mainland culture of the first half of the 3rd millennium B.C., named after the type site near Vólos.

Dipteral:
(Temple) surrounded by a double row of columns.

Dipylon:
Double gateway.

Doric order:
See Orders, below.

Double anta temple:
Temple with antae at both ends.

Dromos:
Passage; specifically, passage leading into a Mycenaean tholos tomb.

Echinus:
Convex moulding under the abacus of a Doric capital. See diagram, p. 49.

Ekphora:
Solemn funeral procession.

Entablature:
The superstructure carried by columns.

Entasis:
Swelling in the lower part of a column.

Ephebe:
A youth who is not yet a full citizen.

Epigonoi:
Descendants of the Seven against Thebes.

Epiphany:
Apparition of a divinity.

Epistyle:
See Architrave.

Eschara:
Altar for burnt offerings.

Esonarthex:
Inner porch of a church.

Euthynteria:
The top course of the foundations of a temple, used for levelling purposes.

Exedra:
A recess or projection, usually semicircular, containing benches.

Exonarthex:
Outer porch of a church.

Frieze:
Decorative band above the architrave of a temple; in the Doric order made up of metopes and triglyphs, in the Ionic order plain or with continuous carved decoration. See diagram, p. 49.

Geison:
Cornice of a temple. See diagram, p. 49.

Geometric style:
Style using geometric ornament, in favour between 1050 and 700 B.C. *Proto-Geometric*, 1050–925; *early Geometric*, 925–850; *severe Geometric*, 850–775; *mature Geometric*, 775–750; *late Geometric*, 750–700.

Gigantomachia:
Fight between gods and giants.

Gorgoneion:
Gorgon's head on the aegis of Athena.

Gymnasion:
A school for physical training or general education (from *gymnos*, "naked"), consisting of a square or rectangular courtyard surrounded by colonnades and rooms of varying size and function.

Hekatompedon:
A temple 100 feet (30 m) long.

Helladic culture:
Greek mainland culture of 2600–1150 B.C. *Early Helladic*, from 2600; *Middle Helladic*, from 2000; *Late Helladic* (Mycenaean), from 1580.

Hellenistic period:
From Alexander the Great to Augustus (330–30 B.C.).

Heraion:
Temple or sanctuary of Hera.

Herm:
A square pillar with a head of Hermes or some other god; later with a portrait head.

Heroon:
Shrine of a hero.

Hieron:
Sanctuary.

Hierophant:
Priest of the mysteries (e.g. at Eleusis and on Samothrace).

Himation:
Cloak worn over the chiton.

Hippodamian:
(Town layout) with regular grid of streets intersecting at right angles; named after Hippodamos of Miletus.

Hippodrome:
Elliptical course for chariot races.

Hoplite:
Heavily armed foot soldier.

Hydria:
Water jar.

Hypocaust:
Under-floor heating system for baths, etc.

Hypostyle:
Having a roof supported by columns.

Iconostasis:
Screen in a Byzantine church between the sanctuary and the main part of the church, bearing tiers of icons.

Intercolumnium:
Space between two columns.

Ionic order:
See Orders, below.

Isodomic:
Horizontally coursed (masonry).

Kabeiroi:
Non-Hellenic divinities, whose worship was centred particularly on Samothrace.

Kantharos:
A drinking-cup with two handles and a high foot.

Kastro:
Castle, usually Byzantine or Venetian.

Kathedra:
Bishop's throne.

Katholikon:
Principal church of a monastery.

Kerameikos:
Potters' quarter of Athens.

Kerykeion:
Staff of Hermes or of a herald.

Kithara:
A stringed instrument, Apollo's lyre.

Klepsydra:
Well-house, cistern; water-clock.

Klerouchia:
Attic military colony.

Kline:
Couch, bed.

Koilon:
See Cavea.

Kore (plural **korai**):
Maiden, girl; statue of a girl; name given to Persephone.

Kouros (plural **kouroi**):
Youth; statue of a naked youth.

Krater:
Two-handled jar for mixing water and wine.

Kylix:
Shallow drinking-cup with horizontal handles.

Lapiths:
A legendary people in Thessaly.

Lekythos:
Narrow-necked oil-flask.

Lesche:
Assembly room, club-house.

Loutrophoros:
A large two-handled vessel used to fetch water for the bridal bath; often depicted on the tombs of those who died unmarried.

Maeander:
A continuous fret or key pattern, named after the River Maeander (Büyük Menderes) in Asia Minor.

Magoula:
Prehistoric settlement hill in Thessaly.

Megaron (plural **megara**):
The principal room in a Mycenaean palace; perhaps the basic form of the Greek temple.

Metope:
Rectangular panel between the triglyphs in the frieze of a Doric temple, either plain or with relief decoration.

Metroon:
Sanctuary of the Great Mother.

Minoan culture:
Culture on the island of Crete, 2600–1100 B.C.

Monopteral:
(Temple) without a cella, usually circular.

Mycenaean:
Greek mainland culture (=Late Helladic), 1580–1150 B.C.

Naiskos:
Small temple.

Naos:
Cella of temple.

Narthex:
Porch of a Byzantine church.

Necropolis:
Cemetery ("city of the dead").

Nekromanteion, nekyomanteion:
Oracle of the dead.

Nomos:
Administrative district.

Nymphaeum:
Shrine of the nymphs; fountain-house.

Odeon:
Hall (usually roofed) for musical performances.

Oinochoe:
Wine-jug.

Olympieion:
Sanctuary of Olympian Zeus.

Opisthodomos:
Chamber at the rear end of a temple.

Orchestra:
Circular or semicircular area between the stage and the auditorium of a theatre in which the chorus danced.

Orders:
1. *Doric:* column without base; shaft with (usually 20) sharp-edged flutings; capital consisting of echinus and abacus; entablature with metope frieze.
2. *Ionic:* column on base of Ionic type (either Anatolian or Attic) with 20 flutings separated by ridges; capital with two spiral volutes.
3. *Corinthian:* base and column as in Ionic order; capital consisting of calyx (kalathos) surrounded by two rows of acanthus leaves.
4. *Composite:* capital developed in Roman times, combining Ionic and Corinthian features.

Orthostat:
Large block of stone, set vertically, in the bottom course of a temple wall.

Ostracism:
A system of voting on potsherds (ostraka) for the banishment of a citizen.

Palaistra:
Training school for physical exercises (wrestling, etc.).

Palladion:
Archaic wooden figure of Pallas Athene; the protective image of a city.

Panayia:
"All Holy"; the Mother of God.

Pantokrator:
"Ruler of All"; Christ.

Parekklisia:
Subsidiary church, chapel.

Parados:
Side entrance to the orchestra of a theatre.

Pediment:
Triangular termination of a ridged roof.

Pegasos:
A winged horse ridden by the Corinthian hero Bellerophon; later used to refer to the inspiration of a poet.

Pelopion:
Sanctuary of Pelops.

Pendentive:
A triangular section of vaulting forming the transition from a square base to a circular dome.

Peplos:
A woollen cloak worn by women.

Peribolos:
Enclosure wall of a sacred precinct.

Peripteral:
(Temple) surrounded by a peristyle.

Peristasis:
See Peristyle.

Peristyle:
Colonnade surrounding a building.

Petasos:
Broad-brimmed hat.

Pinax:
Painted tablet of wood, terracotta or stone.

Pithos:
Large storage jar.

Polemarch(os):
Military leader.

Polygonal:
(Masonry) of irregularly shaped stones.

Polythyron:
Minoan hall with several doors on two sides.

Poros:
A kind of limestone.

Prohedria:
Seat of honour in theatre or stadion.

Pronaos:
Entrance portico of temple.

Propylaia:
Monumental form of propylon.

Propylon:
Gateway.

Proskenion:
Fore-stage.

Prostyle:
(Temple) with columned portico in front.

Prothesis:
Left-hand lateral apse of a Byzantine church.

Protome:
Human torso or forequarters of animal as a decorative feature on a building or vase.

Prytaneion:
Office of the *prytanes* (city councillors).

Pyrgos:
Tower, bastion.

Pyxis:
Cylindrical vase.

Rhyton:
Drinking vessel, often in the form of an animal's head.

Sesklo culture:
Greek mainland culture of 3500–2900 B.C., named after the type site near Vólos.

Sima:
Gutter of building, with lion's-head water-spouts.

Skene:
Stage building of theatre.

Skyphos:
Drinking-cup with two horizontal handles.

Sphendone:
Rounded end of a stadion

Spira:
Rounded base of cella wall.

Stadion:
1. Measure of length, 600 feet (*c.* 183 m); a stade.
2. Running track 600 feet long.
3. Stadium, including running track and embankments or benches for spectators.

Stele:
Upright stone slab (often a tombstone), usually with an inscription and frequently with relief carving.

Stoa:
Portico; hall with pillars along front.

Strigil:
Curved blade used to scrape dust and oil off the body after exercise.

Stylobate:
The uppermost step of a temple. See diagram, p. 49.

Synthronon:
Stone benches for clergy in apse of a Byzantine church.

Temenos:
Sacred precinct.

Templon:
Chancel screen in Byzantine church. Cf. Iconostasis.

Terma:
Finishing line in stadion.

Tessera:
Small cube of stone, glass, etc., used in mosaic-work.

Tetrastyle:
(Temple) with four columns on façade.

Thesauros:
Treasury.

Tholos:
Circular building, rotunda; domed Mycenaean tomb.

Thymele:
Altar in orchestra of theatre.

Thyrsos:
Staff entwined with ivy and vines, an attribute of Dionysos.

Toreutics:
The art of ornamental metal-work.

Torus:
Convex moulding of semicircular profile. See diagram, p. 49.

Triglyph:
Projecting member, with two vertical channels, between the metopes of the Doric order. See diagram, p. 49.

Trochilus:
Convex moulding. See diagram, p. 49.

Tropaion:
Trophy; votive or victory monument.

Tympanon:
Rear wall of temple pediment. See diagram, p. 49.

Volute:
Spiral scroll of Ionic capital.

Xoanon:
Archaic wooden cult image.

Zophoros:
Frieze of human figures and animals. See diagram, p. 49.

Temple of Nike, Athens (Ionic)

Temple of Hera, Olympia (Doric)

The Classical Orders

In the **Doric order** the shaft of the column, which tapers towards the top and has between 16 and 20 flutings, stands directly, without a base, on the stylobate above the three-stepped substructure. A characteristic feature is the *entasis* (swelling) of the columns, which along with the frequently applied curvature of the steps of the substructure relieves the austerity of the building. The capital consists of the echinus, curving up from the shaft, and the square abacus. It carries the architrave with its frieze of triglyphs and metopes, which may be either plain or with relief ornament. Between and below the triglyphs are the drop-like guttae. The tympanon is enclosed by the horizontal cornice (geison) and the oblique mouldings which form an angle with it, and usually contains the pediment figures. The sculptured decoration normally consists of the carving on the metopes and the pediment figures, but may extend also to the front of the pronaos. Where limestone and

not marble was used it was faced with a coat of stucco. The surface was not left in its natural colour but was painted, the dominant colours being blue, red and white.

The **Ionic order** has slenderer and gentler forms than the Doric, the "male" order. The flutings of the columns are separated by narrow ridges. The column stands on a base, which may be either of the Anatolian type (with several concave mouldings) or the Attic type (with an alternation between the convex torus and the concave trochilus). The characteristic feature of the capital is the spiral volute on either side. The architrave is not straight, but made up of three sections, each projecting over the one below. The frieze is continuous, without triglyphs to divide it up. The Ionic temple, originating in the territories occupied by the Ionian Greeks, was well suited to the construction of large structures, like the gigantic temples of Ephesus, Sardis and Didyma in Asia Minor.

The **Corinthian order** is similar to the Ionic except in the form of the capital. The characteristic feature of this is the acanthus leaves which enclose the circular body of the capital, with tendrils reaching up to the concave architrave. – The Corinthian order was particularly popular under the Roman Empire, which also evolved the "composite" capital out of a marriage of the Ionic and Corinthian forms and developed ever more elaborate decorative schemes.

Corinthian capital in the Agora, Athens

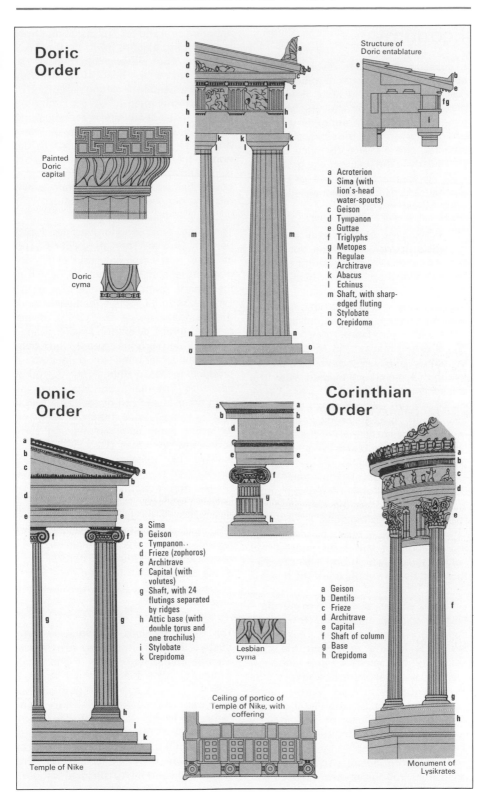

Doric Order

Painted Doric capital

Doric cyma

a Acroterion
b Sima (with lion's-head water-spouts)
c Geison
d Tympanon
e Guttae
f Triglyphs
g Metopes
h Regulae
i Architrave
k Abacus
l Echinus
m Shaft, with sharp-edged fluting
n Stylobate
o Crepidoma

Structure of Doric entablature

Ionic Order

a Sima
b Geison
c Tympanon
d Frieze (zophoros)
e Architrave
f Capital (with volutes)
g Shaft, with 24 flutings separated by ridges
h Attic base (with double torus and one trochilus)
i Stylobate
k Crepidoma

Temple of Nike

Lesbian cyma

Ceiling of portico of Temple of Nike, with coffering

Corinthian Order

a Geison
b Dentils
c Frieze
d Architrave
e Capital
f Shaft of column
g Base
h Crepidoma

Monument of Lysikrates

Economy

In consequence of its relatively unfavourable geological and geographical structure Greece is barely able, now as in ancient times, to produce sufficient food for its population. In antiquity this was one of the reasons for the establishment of colonies, and it still leads many Greeks, particularly in the younger age groups, to emigrate to the New World or to seek employment in the industrialised countries of Western Europe.

The broad base of the Greek economy is **agriculture**. Its main products, sometimes grown on carefully built-up terraced fields, are corn (wheat, maize, barley), wine (and also table grapes, raisins, currants and sultanas), tobacco, cotton, fruit (including southern species), figs and early vegetables (tomatoes, etc.). The olive-tree makes a major contribution in the form of olives and olive oil. Stock-farming is mainly concerned with the smaller animals (sheep and goats). Greek agriculture has still difficulty, however, in meeting the country's needs, as a result of the poor quality of much of the land, the lack of trained workers and structural problems which stand in the way of improved methods of cultivation. Some 80% of all agricultural holdings are under 12 acres and still use old-fashioned and inefficient farming methods. – *Fishing* is unproductive as a result of inadequate regeneration of the food supply and continual over-fishing, and it is necessary to import fish to supply domestic needs.

Greece is well supplied with **minerals** – bauxite, pyrites, magnesite, iron, chromium, zinc, lead and other ores – but money is lacking to import the coal necessary for smelting, and although there are some deposits of lignite, this is an inadequate substitute. Marble, much used in building, is quarried in many places. – The pattern of **industry** is conditioned by the agricultural sector, the most important branches by far being the production of foodstuffs (canned foods, dried fruit, fruit juices, fresh vegetables) and textiles (carpets, clothing), leather goods and tobacco goods. Any further development of industry is hampered by the *shortage of power supplies*. Fully 80% of the country's requirements of electric power are supplied by thermal power stations using locally mined lignite and imported coal and oil. The rest comes from hydroelectric stations (e.g. on the River Akheloos), but although the capacity of these stations has been increased they produce a steadily declining proportion of national requirements. – At the beginning of 1974 considerable reserves of *oil* and *natural gas* were found by underwater drilling off the island of Thasos in the northern Aegean; but these reserves are also claimed by Turkey, and their discovery has added a further strain to the relations between the two countries.

The *islands* are among the least developed parts of Greece. There is practically no industry, and commerce and craft production depend on agriculture, which is the islands' principal source of income. (With 1,349,693 acres of cultivable land, the islands account for 13·4% of the national total.) While the smaller islands can do little more than supply their own needs, the larger ones export agricultural produce to the mainland and to other countries. The main products since ancient times have been olives (both for oil and for eating), wine, honey or wax, and in recent times also melons and early vegetables, tomatoes (Cyclades) for the making of tomato purée, sultanas, almonds and groundnuts (Crete), table grapes and currants (Ionian Islands), cotton, tobacco, mastic (Chios), and peaches, apricots, apples and pears (canning factory on Crete). – Sheep and goats are still, as in the past, the main suppliers of milk and meat. The poor roads on most of the islands mean that the mule is still indispensable as a draught animal and beast of burden.

The island fisheries are no more productive than in the rest of Greece. Sponge-diving, once one of the major sources of income in the eastern Aegean, is declining as a result of competition from synthetic sponges, and is now concentrated in the waters off the North African coast. The Greek sponge-fishing fleet is traditionally based in the Dodecanese, where there are small boatyards which build and repair the local caiques.

The working of minerals in the islands (by small and medium-sized undertakings with a maximum of 400 workers) is confined to small deposits of iron, manganese, nickel, chromium, zinc, lead and molybdenum (Euboea and Melos).

Sunset in the Aegean

World-famous marble has been worked since ancient times on Tinos, Chios, Náxos and Páros. Pozzolana, a volcanic earth found on Santorin and Melos, was already valued in ancient times as mortar in the construction of harbour installations. – Craft production is based on the local supplies of clay (pottery, ceramics) and the rearing of sheep and goats (woollen carpets, textiles, leatherworking).

Commerce and transport. – In this economic situation there is always a heavy balance of payments deficit which causes the government great concern. A contribution towards meeting the deficit is made by remittances from Greeks working abroad, the earnings of the Greek merchant navy and the tourist trade. Since 1962 Greece has been an associate member of the EEC and in 1981 became a full member – a development which is leading to the removal of customs and commercial barriers to trade.

Given the interpenetration of land and sea in the geography of Greece, it is not surprising that *shipping* plays a predominant part in the country's economy. After suffering heavy losses in two world wars Greece still has the fifth largest tonnage in the world (27,000,000 GRT). In addition to carrying on an active coastal traffic and serving Greece's innumerable islands the Greek merchant shipping fleet also plays a considerable part in international shipping. There are large shipyards in the port of Piraeus and in the Bay of Eleusis. – Greece has always had a relatively small *railway* network (at present 2543 km (1580 miles)); but in this

hilly country it is difficult to contemplate any further development. There is, however, a connection with central and northern Europe via Salonica and Belgrade; and the main lines from Athens via Salonica to Idomeni and from Athens to Corinth and Pátras are due to be electrified. – A more effective contribution to meeting present-day transport needs has been made by the development of a system of good *roads*; and it is now possible to drive to every part of the Greek mainland, including the hilly areas, without difficulty. There are almost 38,000 km (23,613 miles) of roads, including 9000 km (5593 miles) of well surfaced national highways. Increasing attention has been given to the construction of motorways, and the road from Salonica (good connection with the Yugoslav frontier) via Lárisa to Athens and on to Pátras is now the country's most important traffic artery.

An element of major importance on the economy of Greece is **tourism**, which in 1978 brought more than $4\frac{1}{2}$ million foreigners (including 634,000 from the USA, 520,000 from Germany and 514,000 from Britain) into the country – roughly half its normal population. The needs of these visitors have been catered for by the provision of additional hotel and other accommodation and the construction of new roads; but the government is also very conscious of the possible drawbacks which this steadily increasing influx of tourists may bring with it. Nevertheless it must be expected that with its unique remains of one of the world's great civilisations, its beautiful climate and its magnificent scenery Greece will continue in the coming years to attract increasing numbers of visitors.

Greece
A to Z

Lion Gate, Mycenae

Aegina

ΑΙΓΙΝΑ

(Aíyina)

Nomos (administrative district): Piraeus. – Dialling code: 02 97.
Area: 83 sq. km (32 sq. miles). – Population: 9550.
ⓘ Tourist Police,
   Vasiléos Yeoryíou B;
   tel. 2 23 91.

TRANSPORTATION. – Frequent boat services between Piraeus and the town of Aegina or Ayía Marína. – Bus from quay at Aegina to Temple of Aphaia and Ayía Marína on the E coast, to Pérdika in the S of Vayiá on the N coast. – Boat trips to the small neighbouring island of Angístri and Palaiá Epídavros.

HOTELS. – TOWN OF AEGINA: *Nausikaa Bungalows*, B, 66 b.; *Areti*, C, 39 b.; *Avra*, C, 57 b.; *Brown*, C, 48 b.; *Danae*, C, 100 b.; *Pharos*, C, 72 b.; *Klonos*, C, 84 b. – AYÍA MARÍNA: *Apollo*, B, 203 b.; *Aegli*, C, 14 b.; *Akti*, C, 44 b.; *Ammudia*, C, 26 b.; *Aphaia*, C, 32 b.; *Argo*, C, 116 b.; *Blue Horizon*, C, 28 b.; *Galini*, C, 67 b.; *Kalliopi*, C, 25 b.; *Karyatides*, C, 36 b.; *Kyriakis*, C, 57 b.; *Magda*, C, 40 b.; *Marina*, C, 56 b.; *Nuremberg*, C, 24 b.; *Oasis*, C, 30 b.; *Pantelaros*, C, 50 b.; *Saronis*, C, 20 b. – MÉSAGROS (near Ayía Marína, alt. 80 m (262 ft)): *Posidon*, C, 36 b. – PÉRDIKA: *Moondy Bay Bungalows*, B, 144 b.; *Aegina Maris*, B, 184 b. – SOUVÁLA AND VÁTA: *Ephi*, C, 59 b.; *Saronikos*, D, 33 b.; *Xeni*, C, 14 b. – ISLAND OF ANGÍSTRI: *Keryphalia*, C, 16 b.

Aegina, an island in the Saronic Gulf within easy reach of Athens, is a popular resort with both Athenians and foreigners. It combines the attractions of its agreeable setting of fields, macchia and forests with its great tourist attraction, the Temple of Aphaia, extensive beaches and facilities for all kinds of water sports.

HISTORY. – The earliest settlement of the island dates back to the 4th millennium B.C., and by 2500 B.C. there was a fortified trading post on the W coast carrying on trade between the mainland, the Cyclades and Crete. Dorian immigrants who arrived about 1000 B.C. continued this tradition, and by the 7th c. the island's trading connections reached as far afield as Egypt and Spain. About 650 B.C. Aegina minted the first coins in Europe. In the 5th c. there was increasing conflict with Aegina's near neighbour Athens, which in 459 B.C. compelled the island to surrender and destroyed its economic power. – In 1826 Aegina was the seat of the first Greek government, headed by Kapodistrias.

SIGHTS. – The chief town, **Aíyina** (pop. 6100), recalls this later period in its history with its neo-classical houses. Notable features of the town are the *chapel of St Nicholas* on the N breakwater of the harbour, the remains of a *temple of Apollo* on the site of the *ancient city* (where new excavations are being carried out) on the N side of the town, and the *museum* (pottery from the 3rd millennium on, material from the temples of Apollo and Aphaia, a marble sphinx, etc.) near the *Mitrópolis church.*

The road to the Temple of Aphaia passes the old medieval capital of the island, which was abandoned about 1800, *Palaiokhóra* (8 km – 5 miles). Scattered

Temple of Aphaia, Aegina

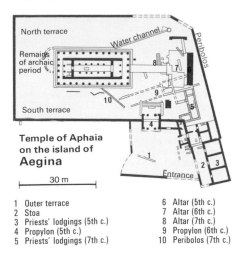

Temple of Aphaia
on the island of
Aegina
|— 30 m —|

1 Outer terrace
2 Stoa
3 Priests' lodgings (5th c.)
4 Propylon (5th c.)
5 Priests' lodgings (7th c.)
6 Altar (5th c.)
7 Altar (6th c.)
8 Altar (7th c.)
9 Propylon (6th c.)
10 Peribolos (7th c.)

among the ruins are more than 20 white-washed churches and chapels, mostly dating from the 13th and 14th c., some containing frescoes.

The *Temple of Aphaia stands in a commanding situation above the E coast, 12 km (7 miles) from the town. The marble figures from the pediments were acquired by King Ludwig I of Bavaria at the beginning of the 19th c. and are now in Munich. German excavations in 1901 brought to light a dedicatory inscription to the goddess of fertility from an earlier temple of about 580 B.C. which preceded the present one (erected about 510). In the later temple the old goddess Aphaia was probably joined by Athena.

The entrance to the sacred precinct, on the S side, leads past the *propylon*, with priests' lodgings behind it, to the main complex, which consists of the temple itself, the altar to the E of the temple and the ramp which links the two. The **Doric temple**, "the most polished building of the late Archaic period" (Gruben), is built of limestone, originally faced with stucco. The *pediment figures*, depicting the Trojan War, and the roof were of marble. Well preserved and extensively restored, the temple is of imposing effect. The *cella*, with three aisles separated by rows of columns in two tiers, is surrounded by a colonnade (6×12 columns). The cult image stood between the last pair of columns in the cella. On the W side of the temple, where further excavations are at present in progress, the foundations of the building can be seen.

In clear weather the view from the temple extends to the Acropolis in Athens.

From the temple it is only a short distance on foot (25 minutes) or by car to the bay of **Ayía Marína**, where a much-frequented little resort has grown up in the last twenty years. Many boats do not put

in to the town of Aíyina but anchor off Ayía Marína, providing a shorter means of access to the temple.

Also worth seeing are the hill of *Profítis Ilías* (524 m – 326 miles), on which there was a sanctuary of Zeus Hellanios (bus to Marathón on the W coast); the convent (nunnery) of *Panayía Khrysoleóndissa*; and the *Ómorfi Ekklisía* ("beautiful church"), between Aíyina and Palaio-khóra, which dates from 1289 (frescoes).

Agrinion
ΑΓΡΙΝΙΟΝ
(Agrínion)

Nomos: Aetolia. – Dialling code: 06 41.
Altitude: 90 m (295 ft). – Population: 24,800.
ⓘ Tourist Police,
    Papakósta 25;
    tel. 2 33 81.

TRANSPORTATION. – Air and bus connections with Athens.

HOTELS. – *Esperia*, B, 42 b.; *Galaxy*, B, 51 b.; *Soumelis*, B, 36 b.; *Acropole*, C, 41 b.; *Alice*, C, 50 b.; *Leto*, C, 63 b.; *Tourist*, C, 54 b.

CAMPING SITE.

Agrinion is the chief town of the nomos of Aetolia and Acarnania and a centre of the local tobacco trade. It lies a short distance NW of Lake Trikhonis.

SURROUNDINGS. – 27 km (17 miles) E, on the N shore of Lake Trikhonis, is the **sanctuary of Apollo** of *Thérmos* The present temple was erected about 625 B.C. on the site of an earlier temple of the 10th–9th c., built in close proximity to a Helladic megaron.

Aiyion
ΑΙΓΙΟΝ
(Aíyion)

Nomos: Achaea.
Altitude: 15 m (49 ft). – Population: 18,000.

TRANSPORTATION. – Railway station on the Corinth–Pátras line. Bus connections with Corinth and Pátras.

HOTELS. – *Anglias*, E, 14 b.; *Chelmos*, E, 17 b. – ALSO IN SURROUNDING AREA, ON COAST: TO W: SELIANITIKÁ: *Kanelli*, C, 78 b.– LÓNGOS: *Long Beach*, B, 211 b.; *Spey Beach*, C, 72 b. – LAMBIRI (13 km – 8 miles):

Avra, C, 27 b.; *Galini*, C, 23 b. – TO E: VALIMITIKÁ (5 km – 3 miles): *Eliki Beach*, C, 278 b. – NIKOLEÍKA (10 km – 6 miles): *Poseidon Beach*, B, 170 b.

CAMPING SITE.

The town of Aíyion lies on the S coast of the Gulf of Corinth, 35 km (22 miles) E of Pátras. It is situated on a rocky plateau above the beach, with springs at the foot which were already frequented in ancient times. The ancient city of Aigion was a member of the Achaean League. During the medieval period, under the name of Vostitsa, it was for a time the centre of a Latin barony.

SURROUNDINGS. – Diákofto, 15 km (9 miles) E (hotels: Panorea, D, 10 b.; Chelmos, D, 15 b.), a station on the Pátras–Corinth railway line. From here there is a rack railway to Kalávryta (see p. 150): at *Megaspíleon*, on this line (45 minutes from station), is a **cave monastery** founded in the 5th c.

Komotini (alt. 45 m (148 ft), pop. 28,000; hotels: Orpheus, B, 150 b.; Xenia, B, 56 b.; Astoria, C, 27 b.; Democritus, C, 96 b.), a station on the Salonica–Istanbul railway line 98 km (61 miles) W of Alexandroúpolis, lies in a wide plain (tobacco-growing) below the Rhodope hills (1483 m – 4866 ft).

Xanthi (alt. 80 m (262 ft), pop. 26,500; hotels: Xenia, B, 48 b.; Democritus, C, 69 b.; Sissi, C, 31 b.), a station on the Salonica–Istanbul line 50 km (31 miles) W of Komotini, lies in a tobacco-growing area on the southern slopes of the Karaóglou hills. – 27 km (17 miles) S is the site of the ancient city of **Abdera** (mod. Greek Avdíra), a port town founded in 656 B.C. by Klazomenai (near Smyrna), which flourished in the 6th and 5th c. thanks to its fertile soil and its trade with the hinterland. It was the home of Protagoras (c. 485–c. 415), one of the earliest sophists, and Demokritos (c. 460–c. 380), founder of the atomist theory. Excavations directed by Lazarides from 1950 onwards on a tongue of land flanking a good natural harbour, now surrounded by fields, brought to light part of the ancient city, including the foundations of houses, a section of the town wall on the inland side and traces of a theatre.

Alexandroupolis

ΑΛΕΞΑΝΔΡΟΥΠΟΛΙΣ
(Alexandhroupolis)

Nomos: Evros. – Dialling code: 05 51.
Altitude: 10 m (33 ft). – Population: 24,000.
ⓘ **Tourist Police,**
Karaiskáki 6;
tel. 2 62 11.

TRANSPORTATION. – Air connections with Athens and Salonica; station on Salonica–Istanbul railway line; boat connections with Samothrace and Piraeus.

HOTELS. – *Motel Astir*, A, 54 b.; *Egnatia*, B, 180 b.; *Alex*, C, 52 b.; *Aphroditi*, C, 36 b.; *Dionysos*, C, 46 b.; *Galaxias*, C, 47 b.; *Olympion*, C, 22 b.; *Park*, C, 42 b.

CAMPING SITE. – BATHING BEACH.

Alexandroúpolis (Alexandrople) is the most easterly town on the coast of Thrace, near the frontier with Turkey on the River Evros. It was founded by the Turks under the name of Dedeagach ("grandfather's tree"), and became Greek in 1912. Now a centre of the local tobacco trade, the town has no features of particular tourist interest.

SURROUNDINGS. – Alexandroúpolis is a good base from which to visit the island of **Samothrace** (see p. 233: 5–7 boats weekly).

It is also a centre from which to explore **Thrace**, which has a Turkish and Islamic minority. Two towns are of particular interest:

Alonnisos

ΑΛΟΝΝΗΣΟΣ
(Alónnisos)

Nomos: Magnesia.
Area: 64 sq. km (25 sq. miles). – Population: 1425.

TRANSPORTATION. – Boat connections with Vólos, Skiáthos, Skópelos and Skýros.

HOTELS. – *Galaxy*, C, 58 b.; *Marpunta*, C, 200 b.

SWIMMING. – Khrýsi Miliá and Kókkino Kástro, N of Patitíri.

The island of Alónnisos lies in the Northern Sporades, in the middle of the chain of islands which begins with Skiáthos in the W.

The villages on this long narrow island are in the SW, opposite Skópelos. Among them are the chief place, **Alónissos** (pop. 500), situated on a hill, and the little harbour town of *Patitíri*, on the S coast, which offers the best prospect of finding accommodation. From here there are boat trips E to the neighbouring island of *Peristéra* (area 14 sq. km (5 sq. miles), pop. 65) and NE to the islands of *Kyrá Panayiá* (or Pélagos: area 25 sq. km (10 sq. miles), pop. 70: monastery), *Ghioúra* (area 11 sq. km (4 sq. miles): ruined monastery, wild goats with goatherds) and *Pipéri* (area 7 sq. km (3 sq. miles)).

Amfissa
ΑΜΦΙΣΣΑ
(Ámfissa)

Nomos: Phocis.
Altitude: 180 m (591 ft). – Population: 5500.

HOTELS. – *Stalion*, C, 45 b.; *Apollon*, D, 52 b.

Amfissa, a country town in Phocis, lies on a hill 14 km (9 miles) NW of Itéa on the road to Lamía, surrounded by olive-groves. In ancient times it was the capital of the Locrians, and its medieval castle – dating from the time when the town, then known as Salona, was held by Frankish knights – is built on the polygonal walls of the ancient acropolis.

Amorgos
ΑΜΟΡΓΟΣ
(Amorghós)

Nomos: Cyclades.
Area: 121 sq. km (47 sq. miles). – Population: 1800.

TRANSPORTATION. – Boat connections with Piraeus, Páros, Náxos and Santorin in the Cyclades, and Rhodes (once weekly to each island).

HOTELS. – KATÁPOLA: *Mavros*, B, 20 b. – AIYIÁLI: *Mike*, B, 19b.

The island of Amorgós, lying SE of Náxos in the Cyclades, is 32 km (20 miles) long and between 2 and 6 km (1 and 4 miles) across. A ridge of hills runs along the island, falling steeply down to the SE coast; there are a number of bays along the NW coast.

There were three ancient settlements on the island, now represented by the villages of *Arkesíni* in the S, **Katápola**, the principal harbour, in the centre and *Aiyiáli* in the N.

The principal place on the island is **Amorgós** or *Khóra* (pop. 460), 4 km (2 miles) from Katápola (bus), with a *castle* which belonged to the dukes of Náxos. From here it is 20 minutes on a track which is fairly steep in the final section to the ***monastery** of *Panayía Khozoviótissa*, founded in 1088, whose

whitewashed buildings cling to the rock in a fantastic situation above the rugged coast. The chapel on the topmost level contains a *miraculous icon* and numerous silver lamps presented by worshippers. From the terrace in front of the chapel there are wide-ranging views.

From Aiyiáli the hill of **Kríkelas** (761 m – 2497 ft) can be climbed: wide views from the top.

Land improvement and other development projects are being carried out on Amorgós by Hellenic Societies in Germany.

Amphiareion
ΑΜΦΙΑΡΕΙΟΝ
(Amfiárion)

Region and nomos: Attica.

The Amphiareion is an ancient sanctuary, the home of an oracle, beautifully situated in a quiet wooded

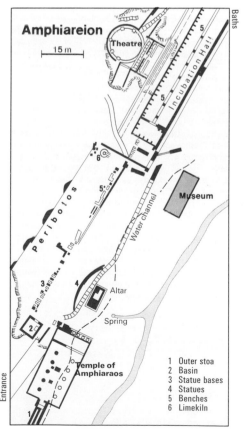

Amphiareion

15 m

Baths

Incubation Hall

Theatre

Museum

Water channel

Peribolos

Altar

Spring

Temple of
Amphiaraos

Entrance

1 Outer stoa
2 Basin
3 Statue bases
4 Statues
5 Benches
6 Limekiln

valley in northern Attica, SE of Oropós.

The site is reached from Athens by taking the national highway exit for Kapandríti (30 km – 19 miles) and continuing via Kapandríti and Kálamos in the direction of Oropós. The entrance to the site is on the right after a bend to the right 4 km (2 miles) beyond Kálamos (49 km (30 miles) from Athens).

MYTH and HISTORY. – *Amphiaraos* was a mythical king of Argos who had the gift of clairvoyance. On his way to Boeotia during the expedition of the Seven against Thebes he was victorious in a contest at Neméa (see p. 195) during the funeral ceremony of the young prince Opheltes. During the battle for Thebes he was snatched away by Zeus and disappeared into a cleft in the earth, but later re-emerged on the borders of Attica and Boeotia and was revered in a sanctuary, built round a sacred spring, as a seer and a hero who brought salvation and healing.

The sanctuary and the cult of Amphiaraos have much in common with the Asklepieion at Epidauros (see p. 130). – The site was excavated by Leonardos and Petrakos.

A path runs downhill from the entrance. Immediately on the right is the **temple** (4th or 3rd c. B.C.). This had six Doric columns along the front between antae (pilasters). The interior is divided into three aisles by two rows of five columns. A porch built on to the rear of the temple contained a second door leading to the *priests' lodgings*. Against the rear wall of the cella can be seen the *base for the cult image*; in the centre is an *offerings table*.

In front of the temple, beside the sacred spring, stands an **altar**, which according to Pausanias was dedicated to Amphiaraos and numerous other divinities. – Beyond this, on the left, are *statue bases* of the Roman period. Farther along in the **incubation hall** worshippers seeking a cure slept, wrapped in the skin of a ram which they had previously sacrificed at the altar. The hall (4th c. B.C.) is 110 m (361 ft) long and divided into two aisles by a row of 17 Ionic columns, with 41 Doric columns along the exterior. The two rooms at the ends were probably intended for women. Behind the incubation hall is the **theatre**, with five marble *seats of honour* round the orchestra and a well-preserved *stage building*. In this theatre musical contests were held every five years from 332 B.C. onwards. – Farther down are remains of *Roman baths*. On the other side of the stream are a *klepsydra* (water-clock) and *remains of houses*. – The small **museum** contains interesting local finds.

Amphipolis
ΑΜΦΙΠΟΛΙΣ
(Amfípolis)

Region: Macedonia. – Nomos: Sérrai.

ACCOMMODATION IN STAVRÓS, 27 km (17 miles) SW on the coast to the S of the main road: *Aristoteles*, C, 30 b.; *Athos*, C, 48 b.; *Posidonion*, C, 14 b.; *Avra Strymonikou*, E, 19 b.

CAMPING SITE: Aspróvalta, 17 km (11 miles) SW.

An ancient city in Macedonia, 60 km (37 miles) W of Kavála near the mouth of the River Strymon. Amphipolis was a major Greek stronghold and in Roman times an important station on the Via Egnatia, the main road from Byzantium to the Adriatic.

Excavations by Greek archaeologists have revealed parts of the *town walls*. The most striking monument is a majestic stone *lion which stands immediately W of the bridge over the Strymon, outside the bounds of the ancient city. The lion, restored from fragments in 1936 by Oscar Broneer, is very similar to the lion of Chaironeia (see p. 106).

Anafi
ΑΝΑΦΗ
(Anáfi)

Nomos: Cyclades.
Area: 35 sq. km (14 miles). – Population: 450.

TRANSPORTATION. – Boat services Piraeus–Páros–Santorin–Anáfi–Náxos–Piraeus.

A hilly little island in the Cyclades 20 km (12 miles) E of Santorin.

The small open harbour lies on the S coast. Above it, at an altitude of 220 m (722 ft), is the island's only village, **Khóra**, under a medieval *castle* which belonged to the dukes of Náxos. The ancient city of *Anaphe* lay to the E, on a hill 300 m (984 ft) high. From here a road with ancient paving leads to the *Panayía monastery* at the eastern tip of the island, with another medieval castle, *Gigitróli*, on a steeply scarped hill.

There is a sandy beach on the S coast at *Kalimátia*, the site of the ancient harbour.

Andros
ΑΝΔΡΟΣ
(Ándhros)

Nomos: Cyclades.
Area: 380 sq. km (147 sq. miles). – Population: 10,450.

TRANSPORTATION. – Boat connections with Rafína (on the E coast of Attica 24 km (15 miles) from Athens) and Tínos. Buses from Ándros to Gávrion and to Apikiá.

Arákhova

HOTELS. – ÁNDROS: *Paradisos*, B, 76 b.; *Xenia*, B, 44 b.; *Aegli*, C, 27 b. – APIKIÁ: *Helena*, B, C, 13 b.; *Pighi*, C, 20 b. – BATSÍ: *Lykion* (pension), B, 28 b.; *Chrysi Akti*, C, 72 b. – GÁVRION: *Aphrodite*, B, 43 b. – KÓRTHION: *Korthion*, C, 27 b.

BATHING BEACHES. – Batsí, Gávrion, etc.

Ándros is the most northerly of the Cyclades, lying only 11 km (7 miles) from Euboea and 1200 m (1312 yards) from Tínos. Characteristic features of the landscape are the many large *dovecots (also found on Tínos).

The chief town, **Ándros** (pop. 2450), lies in the middle of the E coast. In the newer part of the town is the *Zoodókhos Piyí church*, with a carved iconostasis of 1717. From the oldest part of the town a bridge leads to the ruins of the medieval *castle*.

From Ándros (commonly known as Khóra) a road runs S to the second harbour on the E coast, **Órmos**, and the little village of *Kórthion*, situated amid lemon-groves. NW of Ándros is *Apikiá*, with a mineral spring, and beyond this the *Áyios Nikólaos monastery*, founded in 1560.

A road runs from Ándros to the W coast, by way of *Mesariá* (5 km (3 miles): church of 1158) and *Palaiópolis* (11 km – 7 miles), on the site of the ancient capital of the island, to the harbours of **Batsí** (8 km – 5 miles) and **Gávrion** (8 km – 5 miles).

Arakhova
ΑΡΑΧΩΒΑ
(Arákhova)

Nomos: Boeotia.
Altitude: 950 m (3117 ft). – Population: 3000.

TRANSPORTATION. – Bus connections with Athens.

HOTELS. – *Anemolia*, B, 70 b.; *Xenia*, B, 88 b.

Arákhova, a mountain village in Phocis, 9 km (6 miles) E of Delphi, is noted for its magnificent *situation in the wild country on the southern slopes of Parnassus, its colourful textiles in traditional patterns and its red wine.

On the western outskirts of the village an asphalted road branches off the road to Delphi and climbs into the Parnassus range.

Arcadia
ΑΡΚΑΔΙΑ
(Arkadhía)

The upland region of Arcadia, in the centre of the Peloponnese, reaches its highest points in the N: Erýman-thos (2224 m – 7297 ft), Khelmós (2355 m – 7727 ft) and Kyllíni (2376 m – 7796 ft). The few areas of plain are concentrated round Trípolis and Megalópolis. The most important river is the Alfíos (Alpheus), with its tributaries; other areas have no drainage to the sea, leading to the formation of bogs.

HISTORY. – In the 2nd millennium B.C. this inaccessible region was occupied by the Arcadians, and their possession of the territory was not contested by the Dorians moving into the Peloponnese. There was an ancient Arcadian shrine dedicated to Zeus on Mt Lykaion. For long the people of Arcadia maintained their simple peasant way of life, and the earliest city states grew up on the fringes of the region (e.g. Tegéa, Mantineia). In the 5th c. B.C. and again in 250 B.C. the Arcadians formed themselves into a league. According to Strabo the region was derelict and almost depopulated in the early imperial period (when it had already become the setting for pastoral poetry).

In the crusading period (13th c.) many Frankish barons built their castles on the hills of Arcadia – e.g. at Níkli (near Tegéa), Veligósti (Megalopólis), Karýtaina (above the River Alpheus) and Ákova (on the River Ládon). – During the Turkish period Tripolitsa (now Trípolis) was founded as the residence of the Pasha of the Morea.

Only within recent years has Arcadia become less isolated as a result of an extensive programme of road-building, but away from the main roads it has preserved much of its original sequestered character. Although this may appeal to the tourist, however, it has led many of the younger generation of Arcadians to drift away from the land into the towns.

Argolid
ΑΡΓΟΛΙΣ
(Argolís)

The Argolid, in the north-western Peloponnese, played a central part in the history of Greece. Already settled in Neolithic times, it was occupied by the Archaeans around 2000–1900 B.C., and during the Mycenaean period (1580–1100 B.C.) was the most densely populated part of Greece. Mycenae, Tiryns and Argos, as well as such lesser cities as Midea and Prosymna, were centres of power, of economic activity and of a rich culture. The excavations carried out by Heinrich Schliemann from 1874 onwards led to the rediscovery of this forgotten world.

MYTH and HISTORY. – Many of the Greek myths were associated with this region, and the role played by Argos in these myths foreshadowed its later development. Akrisios, king of Argos in succession to Danaos and Lynkeus, drove out his twin brother Proitos, who fled to nearby Tiryns, followed by his son Megapenthes, and had the town fortified by Cyclopes from Asia Minor. Akrisios had a daughter named Danaë, who was visited by Zeus in a shower of gold. Their son *Perseus* killed the Gorgon, freed *Andromeda*, accidentally killed his father while throwing the discus, handed over Argos to his cousin Megapenthes in exchange for Tiryns, surrounded Mycenae and Midea with walls and incorporated them into his dominions. Sthenelos, son of Perseus and Andromeda, married Nikippe, daughter of Pelops, and his son Eurystheus was the last of the Perseids. It was in his service that *Herakles* performed his famous labours. Eurystheus later drove out the sons of Herakles, whose descendants in the fourth generation returned in the time of Oxylos.

The intervening period was filled by the descendants of Pelops, the Pelopids or Atreids, among whom, at the time of the Trojan War, were *Agamemnon*, his wife *Klytaimnestra* and their children *Orestes*, *Iphigeneia* and *Elektra*. Orestes' son Tisamenos was the last

Mycenaean king of Sparta; and after him came the "return of the Heraclids" – i.e. the migration of the Dorians into the Peloponnese, the claim to descent from Herakles giving the newcomers an honourable ancestry.

If the mythological tradition is considered in relation to the archaeological evidence and the historical course of events, the Perseid dynasty can be dated to about 1600 B.C. (shaft graves, Mycenae), the Pelopids to about 1400 B.C. (tholos tombs, Mycenae) and the Heraclids to the time of the Dorian migration (12th c. B.C.).

In the Dorian period Argos became the most powerful city in the region, and the Heraion of Argos acquired increasing importance as its central shrine. There was also an important shrine dedicated to Zeus at Neméa in the north-western Argolid.

During the period of Venetian rule Nauplia (Náfplion), known to the Venetians as Napoli di Levante ("Naples of the East"), became a powerful stronghold, taking in the hills of Acronauplia and Palamidi.

Nowadays the coastal resorts of **Náfplion** and **Tolón**, together with resorts farther E like **Ermióni** and **Porto Khéli** and the offshore islands of **Spétsai** and **Hýdra**, are major centres of the tourist trade. The ancient sites still exert their fascination, however, on visitors interested in the past of this beautiful part of Greece.

Argos
ΑΡΓΟΣ
(Árgos)

Nomos: Argolid.
Altitude: 15 m (49 ft). – Population: 16,700.

TRANSPORTATION. – Station on Corinth–Trípolis railway line; bus connections with Náfplion and Palaiá Epídavros.

HOTELS. – *Mycenae*, C, 42 b.; *Telessila*, C, 45 b.

In ancient times Argos was the centre of the Argolid, to which it gave its name. It is now a country town situated in a fertile plain near the Gulf of Náfplion, at the foot of the hill topped by its acropolis (Lárisa, 289 m (948 ft)) and the low dome of Aspís (the "Shield", 80 m (262 ft)).

HISTORY. – The site of Argos was occupied in pre-Greek times, and during the Mycenaean period it became the seat of the *Danaid* dynasty. After the coming of the Dorians, in the 1st millennium B.C., it grew into a place of considerable importance, although during the 7th and 6th c. it exhausted itself in strife with Sparta. In the 5th c. the Argos school of sculptors produced the great *Polykleitos*, who perfected the canon (the ideal human figure) of Doric sculpture. In 146 B.C. the city became Roman. In A.D. 267 and 305 it was plundered by the Goths. During the Middle Ages and the early modern period it belonged to the Venetians (1388–1463, 1686–1715) and Turks (1463–1686, 1715–1826). National assemblies were held in the ancient theatre in 1821 and 1829.

SIGHTS. – In the *Platía* in the centre of the town stand the **church of St Peter** and the **Archaeological Museum**, the most notable exhibits in which, apart from the pottery and mosaics, are the items from Lerna (in basement). On the road to Trípolis are the excavated remains of the *Agora*. Opposite, on the lower slopes of Lárisa, are the **Theatre** and remains of *Roman baths*. The ancient town walls took in both Aspís and Lárisa. The latter hill can be climbed in 45 minutes: half way up is the *Panayía monastery*, and on the top is a medieval *castle* (view). In the lower ground between the two hills *temples of Apollo and Athena* and *Mycenaean graves* were found.

SURROUNDINGS. – **Mycenae** (17 km – 11 miles): see p. 188. – **Tiryns** (7 km – 4 miles): see p. 251. – **Náfplion** (12 km – 7 miles): see p. 192. – The Argive *Heraion, 11 km (7 miles) NE of Argos, is reached by way of the village of *Khónika*. From Mycenaean times onwards it was the principal Argive sanctuary; the sanctuary in its present form, laid out on terraces on the slopes of a hill 600 m (1969 ft) high, dates from the 8th–5th c. B.C. On the S side a broad ancient staircase leads up to a *portico* and the foundations of the 5th c. *Temple of Hera* which contained a chryselephantine statue of Hera by Polykleitos. On the next terrace stood the older (7th c.) *temple* which was destroyed by fire in 423 B.C. Adjoining this were porticoes and pillared halls. The impressiveness of the site is due not so much to the meagre remains as to its grandiose and solitary situation.

The road from Khónika to Náfplion runs past the village of **Mérbaka**, named after a 13th c. Roman Catholic bishop of Corinth, William of Moerbeke. In the churchyard is one of the most beautiful churches in the region.

5 km (3 miles) S of Argos on the road to Trípolis a minor road (signposted) branches off to the village of **Kefalári**, with a large plane-tree. A spring which emerges from the rock here was believed by Strabo to be the outflow of the Stymphalian Lake. Here, where once Pan and the nymphs were worshipped, there now stands a *chapel* dedicated to the Mother of God as *Zoodókhos Piyí* ("Life-Giving Spring"). Nearby is the *"Pyramid"* (actually the stump of a pyramid) of Kefalári, which is frequently interpreted as a mausoleum but in fact was certainly part of a military control system of the 4th c. B.C.

Just beyond the village of *Mýli* on the road to Trípolis, on the left close to the sea, can be seen the roofed-over American excavations at **Lerna**, a site occupied from Neolithic times onwards. Here a double line of defensive walls of the Early Helladic period was found built over a Neolithic dwelling of the 4th millennium B.C. In the centre of the site is an *Early Helladic palace*, known as the "House of the Tiles", which was built about 2200 B.C. and burned down about 2000 B.C. Measuring 24 by 11 m (79 by 36 ft), it is the largest building of the pre-Greek period in Greece. After its destruction it was buried under a mound of earth enclosed by a large circle of stones. Two Mycenaean shaft graves provide evidence of Mycenaean occupation of the site about 1600 B.C. Immediately N of the site is the *Spring of the Hydra*, which is associated with one of the labours of Herakles.

Argo-Saronic Islands
ΝΗΣΟΙ ΑΡΓΟΣΑΡΩΝΙΚΟΥ
(Nísi Argosaronikoú)

HOTELS. – ON MÉTHANA: *Ghionis*, B, 100 b.; *Pigae*, B, 47 b.; *Saronis*, B, 44 b.; *American*, C, 49 b.; *Dima*, C, 38 b.; *Methanien*, C, 57 b.

This name is now applied to the islands within easy reach of Athens,

Sunset over the island of Hýdra

from Salamís by way of Aegina to Póros, Hýdra and Spétsai.

Salamís can be reached from Athens by the ferry from Pérama. Connections with the other islands (hydrofoils as well as ordinary boats) are provided by the Argosaronikos Service from Piraeus, which also serves the peninsulas of Méthana and Ermióni on the E coast of the Peloponnese.

Méthana, linked with the Peloponnese by a narrow strip of land, is a spa (sulphureous springs) recommended for rheumatism, arthritis, gynaecological conditions and skin diseases.

Museum in Iráklion: see p. 142). The skull of a slaughtered bull found in one female grave indicated that the occupant was a woman of high rank, probably a priestess-queen.

SURROUNDINGS. – W of Arkhánes is **Mt loúktas** (811 m (2661 ft): motor road, 1 hour on foot), which from Iráklion (particularly well seen from Kazantzakis' grave) looks like the recumbent profile of the sleeping Zeus. In ancient times the tomb of Zeus (who was believed to have been brought up in Crete) was honoured on the summit of the hill, and excavation has revealed a *Minoan hilltop sanctuary*. The top of the hill is now occupied by a chapel of the Transfiguration (Metamórfosis) and a recently built radio station.

S of Mt loúktas are the remains of the ancient settlement of **Lýkastos**, which sent warriors under Idomeneus to the siege of Troy.

Arkhanes
ΑΡΧΑΝΕΣ
(Arkhánes)

Island: Crete. – Nomos: Iráklion.
Altitude: 360 m (1181 ft). – Population: 4000.

TRANSPORTATION. – Bus connection with Iráklion.

HOTEL. – *Dias*, B, 55 b.

A little country town noted for its *rozakí* grapes and its wine.

The road from Iráklion runs SE past Knossos, bears right after a viaduct built in 1830 (12 km – 7 miles) and reaches Arkhánes in another 3 km (2 miles).

SIGHTS. – Two churches with 14th c. frescoes, **Ayía Triáda** and, outside the town, **Áyii Asómati** (with an inscription of 1315 attributing the paintings to Michael Patsidiotis).

The village is built over a **Minoan settlement**, making excavation of the site difficult. Recently, however, Sakellarakis has achieved notable results in the investigation of a complex consisting of a *palace, sanctuary* and *necropolis*. Excavations on the hill of Fourní above the village (1964 onwards) were particularly productive. The **necropolis** found here contained numerous skeletons as well as grave goods; among the tombs were a *temple tomb* of a type found at Knossos and a *tholos tomb* of purely Mycenaean type dating from the 14th c. B.C. (finds now in Room VI in the Archaeological

Arta
ΑΡΤΑ
(Árta)

Nomos: Árta. – Telephone dialling code: 0681.
Altitude: 30 m (98 ft). – Population: 19,000.
ⓘ **Tourist Police,**
Stamatelopoúlou 12;
tel. 2 75 80.

TRANSPORTATION. – Bus services to Athens and places in Epirus.

HOTELS. – *Xenia*, B, 40 b.; *Amvrakia*, C, 110 b.; *Anessis*, C, 48 b.; *Kronos*, C, 102 b.

Árta, chief town of a nomos in Epirus, is situated on the left bank of the River Árakhthos and occupies the site of ancient Ambrakia, which gave its name to the Ambracian Gulf.

HISTORY. – Founded in the 7th c. B.C. by settlers from Corinth, Ambrakia became in 297 the capital of *Pyrrhos*, king of the Molossians of Epirus. In 31 B.C. the population of the town was transferred to the newly founded city of Nikopolis. Then in the 13th c. the town, now known as Árta, became capital of the Despotate of Epirus, the rulers of which were related to the Imperial house of the Angeloi and for a time, during the occupation of Constantinople by the "Franks", themselves bore the title of emperor. This period left its mark on Árta in the form of the castle built on the site of the ancient acropolis (now occupied by the Xenia Hotel), a number of churches in the town and monasteries in the surrounding area. In 1318 Árta fell into the hands of the Norman lordship of Kefallinía; in 1340 it returned briefly to Byzantine control; in 1348 it became part of the Serbian principality of Ioánnina; in 1449 it was occupied by the Turks; and in 1881 it was united with Greece.

SIGHTS. – On a hill on the N side of the town, to the left of the road, is the church of *Panayía Parigorítissa (Mother of God the Swiftly Consoling), built by Despot Nikifóros in 1290: a two-storey cube-shaped structure of palatial effect, with three superimposed tiers of columns supporting the 24 m (79 ft) high dome. The material for this boldly conceived building came in part from the ruins of Nikopolis. *Mosaics* (the Pantocrator) have been exposed in the dome; on the iconostasis is an image of the Mother of God as Consoler.

The church of *Ayía Theodóra also dates from the 13th c. It was enlarged by the mother of Despot Nikifóros, Theodóra (later recognised as a saint), after the murder of her husband Michael II (1271). In the narthex is her *sarcophagus*, the front of which has fine relief carving showing Theodóra and her small son. Her dual role as ruler and saint is expressed by her dress, with a nun's veil over her state robes, and her attitude, with her right hand holding a sceptre and her left raised in the gesture of blessing.

Other features of interest are the church of Áyios Vasílios (14th c.), with brick and tile decoration on the exterior, and a gracefully arched *Turkish bridge* over the Árakhthos.

Round the town are numerous churches and monasteries, notable among them the Káto Panayía to the N and the Vlakhernai monastery to the NE (both 13th c.).

Astypalaia
ΑΣΤΥΠΑΛΑΙΑ
(Astipálaia)

Nomos: Dodecanese.
Area: 96 sq. km (37 sq. miles). – Population: 1500.

HOTELS. – *Astynea*, D, 39 b.; *Paradisos*, D, 19 b.

Astypálaia is the most south-easterly island in the Cyclades, but is associated administratively with the Dodecanese, whose destinies it shared for many centuries.

The SW and NE ends of the island are linked by an isthmus 7 km (4 miles) long and only 100 m (328 ft) across in places. On this isthmus the chief place on the island, Astypálaia (pop. 1200), has numerous *chapels* and an imposingly situated Venetian castle.

There are bathing beaches on both sides of the isthmus.

Athens
ΑΘΗΝΑΙ
(Athinai)

Nomos: Attica. – Telephone dialling code: 01.
Altitude: 40–150 m (131–492 ft). – Population: 1·9 million.
ⓘ **Greek National Tourist Organisation (EOT)**,
Amerikis 2 (between Stadíou and Panepistimíou, near Sýntagma);
tel. 3 22 31 11.
Information Bureau Sýntagma,
Karageórgi Sérvias 2;
tel. 3 22 25 45.
Information Bureau, Eastern Airport,
tel. 9 79 95 00.
Tourist Police,
Leofóros Sýngrou 7;
tel. 1 71.

USEFUL ADDRESSES. – Department of Antiquities and Restoration, Ministry of Culture, Aristídou 14, tel. 3 24 30 56. – Greek Automobile and Touring Club (ELPA), Mesolóngi 2, tel. 7 79 16 15 (information on road conditions). First Aid Station, tel. 1 66. – KAT (Accident and Orthopaedic Hospital), Kifissiá road, tel. 8 01 44 41. – *British School of Archaeology*, Souidias 52. – *American School of Classical Studies*, Souidias 54.

EMBASSIES. – *United Kingdom:* Ploutárkhou 1. – *United States of America:* Leofóros Vasílissis Sofías. – *Canada:* Ioannou Gennadiou.

RAIL SERVICES. – Trains to Salonica and Alexandroúpolis leave from the Central Station (Stathmós Larísis); trains to Corinth and the Peloponnese (Kalamáta) from the nearby Peloponnese Station.

AIR SERVICES. – Athens has two airports at Ellinikó: the Eastern Airport for international flights, the National or Western Airport for domestic and international flights by Olympic Airways.

BUS SERVICES. – Within Athens and its suburbs there are yellow trolleybuses and green buses. There are also country bus services to towns all over Greece. Many services leave from Sýntagma Square, Akadimías Street and Káningos Square (near Omónia Square). There are also bus services run by the municipal transport authorities: information and timetables at Karólou 1–3 (near Omónia Square) and at Peloponnese Station.

METRO. – This runs (partly underground) from Piraeus through the city centre to Kifissiá in the N, and is known as the *Ilektrikós*. Important stations within

The Parthenon floodlit

the city are Thísion (NW of the Agora), Monastiráki, Omónia, Viktória (W of the Pedion Areos) and Attikís (NE of the Central Station).

HOTELS. – ROUND SÝNTAGMA: *Amalia, Leofóros Amalías 10, L, 188 b.; *Athénée Palace, Kolokotróni 1, L, 176 b.; *Athens Hilton, Leofóros Vasílissis Sofías, L, 960 b.; *Caravel, Leofóros Vasiléos Alexándrou 2, L, 841 b.; *Grande Bretagne, Sýntagma, L, 662 b.; *King George, Sýntagma, L, 223 b.; *King's Palace, Panepistimíou 4, L, 396 b.; *St George Lycabettus, Platía Dexaménis, L, 278 b.; Astor, Karageórgi Sérvias 16, A, 234 b.; Attika Palace, Karageórgi Sérvias 6, A, 147 b.; Electra, Ermoú 5, A, 180 b.; Electra Palace, Nikodímou 18, A, 196 b.; Esperia Palace, Stadíou 22, A, 338 b.; Olympic Palace, Filellínon 16, A, 168 b.; Adrian, Adrianoú 74, B, 44 b.; Arethusa, Mitropóleos 6–8, B, 158 b.; Athens Gate, Leofóros Sýngrou 10, B, 202 b.; Athinais, Vasílissis Sofías 99, B, 162 b.; Christina, Kalliróis 15, B, 173 b.; Galaxy, Akadimías 22, B, 192 b.; Metropol, Stadíou 55, B, 100 b.; Minerva, Stadíou 3, B, 86 b.; Omiros, Apóllonos 15, B, 60 b.; Palladion, Panepistimíou 54, B, 115 b.; Pan, Mitropóleos 11, B, 92 b.; Plaka, Kapnikáreas 7, B, 123 b.; Titania, Panepistimíou 52–54, B, 754 b.; Aphrodite, Apóllonos 21, C, 162 b.; Carolina, Kolokotróni 55, C, 57 b.; Caryatis, Nikodímou 31, C, 50 b.; Hermes, Apóllonos 19, C, 85 b.; Imperial, Mitropóleos 46, C, 33 b.; Royal, Mitropóleos 44, C, 35 b.; etc.

ROUND OMÓNIA SQUARE: Ambassadeurs, Sokrátous 67, A, 370 b.; King Minos, Pireós 1, A, 287 b.; Academos, Akadimías 58, B, 220 b.; Achillion, Agíou Konstantínou 32, B, 980 b.; Alfa, Khalkokondýli 17, B, 167 b.; Arcadia, Márni 46, B, 154 b.; Athens Center, Sofokléous 26, B, 259 b.; Cairo City, Márni 42, B, 140 b.; Candia, Deliyánni 40, B, 252 b.; Delphi, Platía Ayíou Konstantínou 1, B, 93 b.; Dorian Inn, Pireós 15–19, B, 287 b.; El Greco, Athinás 65, B, 167 b.; Eretria, Khalkondýli 12, B, 119 b.; Grand Hotel, Veranzérou 10, B, 190 b.; Ilion, Ayíou Konstantínou 7, B, 166 b.; Ionis, Khalkondýli 41, B, 194 b.; Marathon, Karólou 23, B, 174 b.; Marmara, Khalkondýli 14, B, 252 b.; Minoa, Karólou 12, B, 80 b.; Alcestis, Platía Theátrou 18, C, 224 b.; Amaryllis, Veranzérou 45, C, 98 b.; Ares, Pireós 7, C, 71 b.; Arias, Karólou 20, C, 79 b.; Aristides, Sokrátous 50, C, 158 b.; Artemis, Veranzérou 20, C, 79 b.; Aspasia, Satovriándou 26, C, 65 b.; Astra, Deliyánni 46, C, 48 b.; Asty, Pireós 2, C, 224 b.; Atlas, Sofokléous 30, C, 33 b.; Attalos, Athinás 29, C, 155 b.; Banghion, Omónia 18B, C, 93 b.; Capitol, Omónia, C, 168 b.; Carlton, Omónia 7, C, 60

b.; Diros, Ayíou Konstantínou 21, C, 84 b.; Elite, Pireós 23, C, 80 b.; Europa, Satovriándou 7, C, 67 b.; Euripides, Evripídou 79, C, 119 b.; Mediterranean, Veranzérou 28, C, 82 b.; Nausicaa, Karólou 21, C, 73 b.; Nestor, Ayíou Konstantínou 58, C, 95 b.; Odeon, Pireós 42, C, 98 b.; Olympia, Pireós 25, C, 74 b.; Orpheus, Khalkondýli 58, C, 71 b.; Oscar, Samoú 25, C, 151 b.; Parnon, Trítis Septemvríou 20, C, 88 b.; Pythagorian, Ayíou Konstantínou 28, C, 106 b.; Vienne, Pireós 20, C, 104 b.; etc.

NEAR NATIONAL MUSEUM: Acropole Palace, 28 Oktovríou 51, L, 173 b.; Park, Leofóros Alexándras 10, L, 279 b.; Divani-Zafolia, Leofóros Alexándras 87–89, A, 353 b.; Atlantic, Solomoú 60, B, 275 b.; Plaza, Akharnón 78, B, 239 b.; Xenophon, Akharnón 340, B, 310 b.; Aristoteles, Akharnón 15, C, 102 b.; Morpheus, Aristotélous 3, C, 35 b.; Museum, Bouboulínas and Tósitsa, C, 108 b.; Paradise Rock, Akharnón 50, C, 97 b.; etc.

AMAROÚSSION: Anagenisis, C, 18 b.

KIFISSIÁ: *Pentelikon, Deliyánni 66, L, 112 b.; Apergi, Deliyánni 59, A, 183 b.; Attikon, Pentélis 12, A, 41 b.; Cecil, Xenías 7, A, 150 b.; Cóstis Dimitracópoulos, Deliyánni, A, 54 b.; Grand Chalet, Kokkinára 38, A, 38 b.; Palace, Kolokotróni 1, A, 150 b.; Semiramis, Khariláou Trikoúpi 36, A, 78 b.; Theoxenia, Filádelfos 2, A, 120 b.; Nausicaa, Péllis 6, B, 30 b.; and several hotels in categories C, D and E.

PÁRNIS: *Casino Mont Parnes, L, 212 b. (alt. 1050 m (3445 ft)); Xenia, B, 300 b.; Kyklamina, C, 30 b.

PENTÉLIKON: Achillion, Pálea Pentéli, C, 21 b.

ACCOMMODATION FOR YOUNG PEOPLE. – XAN (YMCA), Omírou 28, tel. 3 62 69 70. – XEN (YWCA), Amerikís 11, tel. 3 62 42 91. – Students' Residence, Ippokrátous 15.

CAMPING SITES. – ATHENS: Leofóros Athinón 198, tel. 5 71 53 26. – DAFNÍ: Ierá Odós, tel. 5 90 95 27 (10 km (6 miles) W of city centre). – NÉO EVROPAIKÓN: in Néa Kifissiá, on Athens–Lamía road, tel. 8 01 54 02. – NÉA KIFISSIÁ: on Athens–Lamía road, 16 km (10 miles) N of city centre, tel. 8 01 64 35. – PATÍTSIA: in Káto Kifissiá, on Athens–Lamía road, tel. 8 00 17 05.

CASINO. – In Hotel Mont Parnes (outside the city, to the NE).

EVENTS. – *Athens Festival* in Odeon of Herodes Atticus, July–Sept. (drama, opera, music, ballet); folk dancing in open-air theatre on Philópappos Hill, May–Sept.
Son et Lumière on Pnyx, April–Oct.

ENTERTAINMENT. – Most places of entertainment are in the picturesque old **Plaka** district, a favourite haunt of tourists, well provided with restaurants, cafés, tavernas with bouzouki music, discotheques, luxurious bars and night-clubs. Other night spots are to be found on the main coast road to Glyfáda.

Eight *theatres* offer a wide choice of entertainment to visitors who have some knowledge of modern Greek. There are numerous *cinemas*, including many open-air cinemas. Foreign films are frequently shown in the original version with Greek subtitles.

SWIMMING and WATER SPORTS. – See under *Attic Riviera* (Coast of Apollo).

SHOPPING. – Most of the shops selling *folk art* are in the neighbourhood of Monastiráki Square, where there is also a flea market on Sundays.
An excellent display of craft products can be seen in the showrooms of the National Organisation of Greek Handicrafts at Mitropóleos 9 (tel. 3 22 10 17); the articles on show are not for sale, but prospective purchasers can be put in touch with the producers.
There are showrooms for the display and sale of *textiles* and *carpets* at Leofóros Alexándrou 91. Craft goods are also displayed and sold in the showrooms of the Greek Craftsmen's Cooperative at Leofóros Amalías 56.

Gold and silver jewelry of excellent quality can be seen in jewellers' shops, most of them to the N of Sýntagma Square.
Reproductions of ancient jewelry and ornaments in gold and silver can be bought in the National Archaeological Museum, which also sells reproductions of other museum exhibits.
Visitors should think twice before purchasing any *antiques*, since the export of works of art of this kind is, in general, prohibited.

Good buys in Athens are precious stones, leather goods, furs and gramophone records (particularly folk music and contemporary light music). The most fashionable shopping district is between Sýntagma and Kolonáki Square, to the S of Lykabettós.

The political centre of Attica since the unification (synoecism) attributed to Theseus and the capital of Greece since 1834, ** Athens has long been the largest and most important city in Greece. It has a university and a College of Technology, it is the seat of the archbishop of Athens and of Greece, and it is the economic, commercial and banking centre of the country. Its historic buildings and its museums hold incalculable treasures. With its international and domestic airports, its bus services to every corner of Greece, its two railway systems and its shipping lines based on Piraeus, it is the natural starting-point of any journey in Greece; and its importance as a tourist centre is matched by the steadily increasing hotel resources within the city and its suburbs and down the coast of Attica towards Soúnion, the construction and improvement of the road system and the development of the coastal strip along the bay of Fáliron into an attractively laid-out and excellently equipped holiday region.

Athens lies in the wide coastal plain on a site which provided its early inhabitants with a sufficiency of agricultural land, an easily defensible hill and good harbours within easy reach, but yet was far enough away from the sea to give security from surprise attack. The plain is surrounded by hills which form natural frontiers marking off Attica from the rest of Greece. To the W are Korydallos (468 m – 1536 ft) and Aigaleos (453 m – 1486 ft); to the N Parnes (modern Greek Párnis, 1413 m (4636 ft)) and Pentelikon (Pentéli, 1109 m (3639 ft)), which was and is famous for its marble; and to the E the broad ridge of Hymettós (Imittós, 1027 m (3370 ft)). Between the various ranges gaps and passes facilitate communications with the interior of Greece.

A number of lower hills rise out of the plain of Attica, among them Lykabettós (modern Lykavittós, 277 m (909 ft)), now crowned by a chapel dedicated to St George, and Tourkovoúnia (the "Turkish Hills": the ancient Anchesmos, 338 m (1109 ft)), both of which lay outside the ancient city and have only been included within the built-up area in recent times. The hill of most importance in the history of Athens, however, was the Acropolis (156 m – 512 ft)), which was built on as early as Mycenaean times and was ideally suited to be the site of a fortress, with its

The resort of Lagosini, SE of Athens

Monument of Philopappos, Hill of the Muses

Kekrops, part man and part serpent, who was credited with the first numbering of the people, the first laws and the introduction of monogamy and the alphabet. His reign saw the conflict between Poseidon and Athena for the land of Attica from which Athena emerged victorious. The tomb of Kekrops was incorporated in the Erechtheion, the shrine of a later king, Erechtheus, and now lies under the Porch of the Caryatids. Close by is an olive-tree, marking the spot where Athena is said to have planted the first olive-tree in Attica.

Kekrops was succeeded by Kranaos, who ruled at the time of the great Flood of Greek mythology and was deposed by Amphiktyon. After ruling for 12 years Amphiktyon was in turn displaced by Erichthonios, son of Hephaistos and Athena or the Earth Mother, who, like Kekrops, had the form of a serpent. Erichthonios set up a wooden cult image of the goddess and initiated the Panathenaic festival. He was succeeded by his son Pandion, and Pandion was followed by his son *Erechtheus*, whose "mighty stronghold" is referred to by Homer (*Iliad*, 2, 547). His twin brother Boutes was a priest of Athena and Poseidon, whose cult was later celebrated in the Erechtheion. Erechtheus was succeeded by his descendants Kekrops II and Pandion II, the latter of whom was deposed and fled to Megara. His son *Aigeus* returned to Athens, and it is from him that the Aegean takes its name. Legend has it that he flung himself into the sea when he saw ships with black sails returning from Crete and believed that his son Theseus had failed in his mission.

This *Theseus*, who was believed to have united all the inhabitants of Attica under the leadership of Athens (the "synoecism"), was the tenth of the mythical kings and the great hero of Athens. He destroyed Prokroustes and other robbers who infested the road between Troezen, where he had been brought up, and Athens; he killed the Minotaur and ended the tribute paid by Athens to King Minos of Crete; with his friend Peirithoos he fought the centaurs and with Herakles the Amazons; and he abducted the youthful Helen from Sparta and brought her to Aphidna in Attica. He was killed on the island of Skyros by his host, King Lykomedes; and his remains were brought from there to Athens by Kimon about 475 B.C. and the Theseion erected in his honour.

The last king of Theseus' line was Thymoites, who, in gratitude for military help, assigned the crown to Melanthos, who had been driven out of Pylos by the invading Dorians. From Melanthos the throne passed to his son Kodros, who sacrificed his life in 1068 B.C. to save Athens from the Dorians. According to some traditions Kodros was the last of the kings; according to others he was succeeded by his son Medon, while other sons led Greek settlement on the W coast of Asia Minor. Thus *Neleus* was credited with the foundation of Miletus, *Androklos* with that of Ephesus.

moderate height, sufficient area and natural access on the W. To the S of the Acropolis, a short distance away, are the Hill of the Nymphs (105 m – 345 ft), with the Observatory, the Pnyx (110 m – 361 ft), meeting-place of the Assembly in ancient Athens, and the Hill of the Muses (147 m – 482 ft), crowned by the monument commemorating Philopappos, prince of Commagene.

The area of Athens is ill provided with natural watercourses, and since they are now largely built over they play little part in the pattern of the city. The ancient city was traversed by the Eridanos, which rises on Lykabettós, leaves the city precincts near the Sacred Gate in the Kerameikos, where it can still be seen, and flows W to join the Ilissos. The Ilissos itself rises on the SW slopes of Hymettós and flows westward between the Olympieion and the Stadion to join Athens' principal river, the Kephissos, which, rising at Kifissiá on the slopes of Pentelikon, flows S, to the W of the ancient city, to reach the sea in the bay of Fáliron.

History

The mythical origins. – The early days of Athens were associated with the names of a series of mythical kings. According to the traditions recorded by Apollodorus and others the first king of Athens was

Early history. – These mythical traditions reflect the history of Athens from the early Mycenaean period to the turn of the 2nd–1st millennium. In fact, however, the history of the city goes much farther back. Finds on the S slope of the Acropolis and in the Agora area show that the site of Athens was already occupied in the Neolithic period, about 3000 B.C. After the arrival of the early Greek peoples Athens participated in the development of the Mycenaean world. About 1400 B.C. the Acropolis became the site of a royal fortress (Kekrops) and surrounded by a cyclopean wall, the whole course of which has been established; part of this wall, the Pelargikon, is still preserved near the Temple of Nike. The palace was on the N side of the Acropolis, where, near the old temple of Athena, the stone bases of two timber columns can be seen, protected by gratings.

The Acropolis, which then covered an area of 35,000 sq. m (41,860 sq. yd) (Mycenae 30,000 sq. m (35,880 sq. yd), Tiryns 20,000 sq. m (23,920 sq. yd)), no doubt served as a place of refuge for the inhabitants of the settlements on the Agora, the Dipylon, the Hill of the Muses and the Areopagos. The Dorian migration of the 12th c. passed Attica by (cf. the myth of Kodros), and accordingly the Athenians regarded themselves in historical times as the indigenous inhabitants. The city did, however, give asylum to refugees from the Peloponnese, and the resultant population pressure led to the colonisation of western Asia Minor and its offshore islands. The historian Thucydides saw the activities of Theseus as historical facts, and regarded the synoecism by which Theseus established the unity of Attica as a state as the foundation of Athens' later greatness. Nevertheless the history of the period of kingly rule is wholly obscure: all that is known is that after the end of the monarchy the functions of the kings passed to the archons, who changed every year. Thereafter there came into being, probably in the 8th c. B.C, an aristocratic state whose great families supplied the nine annually appointed members of the government – the *archon* who gave his name to the year (archon eponymos), the *basileus* who performed the cult functions of the earlier kings, the *polemarchos* or military commander and six *thesmothetai* (lawgivers). The Areopagos (lawcourt) was made up of former archons; the name came from its meeting-place on the Hill of Ares (*Areios pagos*). The popular Assembly met in the Agora.

From Solon to Perikles. – In the 7th c. B.C. there were severe social tensions in Athens, since the nobility possessed almost all the land, while the mass of the population, their tenants, fell into debt and sank to the condition of serfs. This situation was remedied by the first Attic legislators, *Drakon* (c. 624 B.C.) and *Solon*, scion of the old royal family of the Medontids, who was elected archon and arbiter, with full powers, in 594–593 B.C. Solon's reform wiped out all public and private debts and abolished the practice, previously common, of selling debtors into slavery. He also limited individual holdings of property and reformed the system of weights and measures and coinage. The population was divided into four classes according to their taxable income. The highest class consisted of the archons; the second and third (knights and yeomen) occupied the other government posts and were responsible for defence; while the fourth, the *thetes*, were members of the popular Assembly (Ekklesia) and Court (Heliaia). The Council of 400 was established alongside the Areopagos.

After the time of Solon further tensions arose between the inhabitants of the different parts of Attica – in the Kephissos valley, in the coastal areas and among the small farmers of the interior. This last group, the poorest, found a leader in *Peisistratos*, a noble from Brauron, who occupied the Acropolis with his bodyguard in 561–560 B.C. and made himself sole ruler (*tyrannos*) of Athens. He was compelled to flee from the city on more than one occasion, but from 546 until his death in 528–527 he ruled with absolute power. His reign was one of the most brilliant periods in the history of Athens. Democratic rather than tyrannical, in the judgment of Aristotle, he erected fine

new buildings in Athens and Eleusis, including the temple of Athena Polias, built on the site of the old royal palace on the Acropolis. He also re-instituted the Panathenaic festival, introduced the cult of Dionysos and with it the performance of tragedy, and caused the Homeric poems to be collected.

After the death of Peisistratos his sons Hippias and Hipparchos took over the government. In 514 B.C. Hipparchos was murdered in an act of private revenge, and although Harmodios and Aristogeiton were later honoured as the tyrant-killers who had cast off the yoke of tyranny Hippias in fact continued to rule as a particularly ruthless tyrant until 510, when he was overthrown and expelled from Athens by the Alcmaeonids.

The leading representative of the Alcmaeonids was *Kleisthenes*, who reformed the constitution of Athens in 508–507 B.C. and introduced democracy. The basis of the system was the organisation of the population into *phylai* (tribes). Attica was divided into three parts – the city, the coast and the interior – and each of these parts into ten *trittyes*. The ten tribes were then formed by taking one *trittys* from each of the three regions. Each tribe sent 50 representatives to the Council of 500, which met in the Bouleuterion in the Agora. As a further precaution against excessive political ambition and influence Kleisthenes in troduced the system of "ostracism", an effective weapon in the hands of the Assembly which brought down many prominent politicians.

The following decades were dominated by the struggle with Persia. On the advice of Hippias, who had fled to Persia, Persian forces landed in the bay of Marathón in 490 B.C. but were defeated by the Athenians with the assistance of Plataiai; the Spartans arrived too late. The following years were used by *Themistokles* to build up a strong fleet. When the Persians returned in 480 the Athenians were compelled to abandon Attica and evacuate the population, but the Athenian fleet was victorious in a naval battle at **Salamís**, which, with the battles of Plataiai and Mykale (479 B.C.), put an end to the danger from Persia. As a protection against further attacks Athens was surrounded by the "Themistoclean walls", still to be seen in the Kerameikos area (as strengthened by Konon in the 4th c.).

The Persian wars had so strengthened the position of Athens within the Greek world that it became leader of the Delian League established in 478 B.C. In 454 the League's treasury was transferred from the island of Delos to Athens, where it was used by Perikles to finance the construction of the Parthenon and other buildings on the Acropolis – the most splendid artistic achievement of Athens in its great age, the 5th c.

Perikles, who succeeded Kimon as the dominant figure in Athens in 461 B.C., maintained his position, in spite of much opposition, until his death in 429. Seeing Sparta and Persia as the main enemies, he strengthened the naval alliance, which the island of Aegina and other states were compelled to join. The buildings on the Acropolis, which was no longer a stronghold of the city's rulers but a citadel of the gods, still bear witness to the spiritual and artistic power of the age of Perikles.

Later antiquity. – This great flowering of art, to which artists from all over Greece contributed, was ended by the **Peloponnesian War** (431–404), a conflict between Athens and Sparta which fatally weakened all the participants. The Athenian empire fell to pieces, and Athens itself fell under the rule of terror of the Thirty Tyrants. In 403, however, democracy was restored. The conflict with Sparta revived in the 4th c., and in 377 Athens founded the second Attic maritime league, seeking to maintain its position by changes in its alliances. But now a new power was rising in the north, the **Macedonia** of **Philip II**, which began by capturing Attic possessions in the N including Amphipolis (357) and in the battle of Chaironeia (338) established its dominance over the whole of Greece. The age of the democratic city state, the *polis*, was at an end.

The reign of Philip's son *Alexander the Great* marked the beginning of an age of peace and prosperity for Athens, interrupted by periods of occupation. Alexander respected Athens for its intellectual achievement, and thet retained theputation during the subsequent period, when it was a place of no great political importance and declined into a small country town until embellished by Hellenistic rulers with imposing buildings such as the Stoa of Attalos and the Stoa of Eumenes. Its nadir came in 86 B.C., when it was sacked by Roman troops under *Sulla*. Under the Empire the city enjoyed a further period of prosperity. The Roman Agora dates from the time of Augustus, but a major contribution to the development of Athens was made by *Hadrian*, who built the "city of Hadrian" round the Olympieion, which he completed, with a gateway between his city and the "city of Theseus". In this period too *Herodes Atticus*, a native of Marathón, erected other fine buildings (Odeon, Stadion). The city's schools of rhetoric now became famous.

In A.D. 267 Athens was captured and plundered by the Heruli, an East Germanic people, and thereafter it was surrounded by defensive walls enclosing a much smaller area. The walls ran N from the Propylaia to the Stoa of Attalos, then E across Hadrian's Market and finally S to the E site of the Acropolis. Much stone from buildings in the Agora was used in the construction of the walls.

The schools of Athens maintained their importance in subsequent periods, and about 400 a large new Gymnasion was built in the Agora – the home of the University of Athens.

Medieval and modern times. – Athens now gradually declined into a provincial town in the Byzantine Empire. Christianity had long been established in the city, and in 426 the great pagan temples were closed. In 529 the university and the Platonic Academy were also closed down. The first Christian church in Athens was built in Hadrian's Market (the "Library of Hadrian") in the 5th c., and in the 5th or 6th c. the Parthenon, the Erechtheion and the Temple of Hephaistos were also given over to Christian worship. The town was now remote from the centre of events and was visited only once by an emperor – Basil II in 1085, a few years after the foundation of the monastic church of Dafní by an imperial official (*c.* 1080).

After the 4th Crusade (1203–04) Athens became the capital of a Frankish duke, who built his palace in the Propylaia on the Acropolis, now once again a fortress. In 1456, three years after the fall of Constantinople, the town was taken by Mehmet II, and it remained in Turkish hands until the liberation of Greece in the 19th c. The Parthenon, long a Christian church and since 1204 a Roman Catholic cathedral, now became a mosque. The Turkish commandant resided in the

Changing the guard, President's Palace

Propylaia, and his harem was accommodated in the Erechtheion. In 1775 the fortress had a population of 3000 Turks, some 5000 Greeks lived in the area N of the late Roman walls (the "Valerian Walls") and there were some 1000 Albanians of the Christian faith in the Plaka, under the N side of the Acropolis. (This compares with Attica's estimated population in the time of Perikles of 170,000 citizens, 30,000 *metoikoi* or foreign settlers and 115,000 slaves.) Only two of the mosques of the Turkish period have been preserved (without their minarets) – Syntrivani in Monastiráki Square and Fetiye Camii near the Tower of the Winds. During the 17th c. a number of Europeans visited Athens, and to their accounts we owe our knowledge of the condition of the Parthenon before its destruction by a Venetian grenade in 1687.

During the 19th c. wars of liberation Athens was the object of bitter fighting. In 1821–22 it was taken by the Greeks, but in 1826 the town and in 1827 the fortress were recaptured by the Turks, who were not finally expelled until 12 April 1833. A new period of development began when King Otto I made Athens the **capital** of the new kingdom of Greece on 1 January 1834. After independence the population of Athens increased by leaps and bounds, from 8000 in 1823 to 42,000 in 1860, 105,000 in 1889 and 600,000 in 1928. Extensive new quarters were built when, after the catastrophe in Asia Minor in 1923, 300,000 refugees flooded into Athens and Piraeus, creating a problem which it took decades to solve. Athens and Piraeus have long formed a single large urban area in which modern buildings are totally dominant. Greater Athens, with nine city wards and 38 associated communes extending in a vast sea of houses over the plain of Attica between the sea and Pentelikon, now has a population of more than 2·5 million and is the undisputed economic as well as political capital of Greece.

Pausanias, the "Baedeker of antiquity". – An invaluable guide to the topography of ancient Athens, supplementing the evidence provided by the surviving remains, is contained in Book I of the "Description of Greece" written by Pausanias in the 2nd c. A.D. This work, justly famed as the "Baedeker of antiquity", has proved of great value in guiding excavation and interpreting its results.

Pausanias, coming from Soúnion, arrived in Piraeus and entered Athens, after passing the tombs outside the walls, by the Dipylon (Double Gate) in the Kerameikos area. From there he went along the Panathenaic processional way to the Agora, of which he gives a detailed though not complete account, also covering the hill to the W with the Temple of Hephaistos. His next section is devoted to the area around the Olympieion and the Ilissos, where he mentions numerous temples and the Gymnasion of Kynosarges, home of the philosophical school of the Cynics founded by Antisthenes, the approximate situation of which on the left bank of the Ilissos has now been established.

Pausanias also refers to another school of philosophers, the Lykeion (Lyceum) in which Aristotle once taught, situated in the area of what is now Sýntagma Square. Then, after the Stadion, he turns his attention to the Acropolis. Going along the street called the Tripods (in which he fails to mention the Monument of Lysikrates, still visible today), he comes to the Theatre of Dionysos and then finds his way up the southern slope of the hill, passing the sanctuary of Asklepios, to the Acropolis. From the Propylaia he makes for the sanctuary of Artemis Brauronia and then for the altar of Zeus Polieus on the highest point of the hill, the Parthenon and the Erechtheion. Then follows a description of the courts of Athens, the Areopagos and the Heliaia (which has been identified at the SW corner of the Agora). Finally Pausanias describes numerous tombs on the road to the oldest philosophical school in Athens, Plato's Academy, the Academy itself, the Kolonos Hippios on which Oedipus died and the Sacred Way to Eleusis.

A translation of Pausanias' guide by Peter Levi has been published by Penguin Books. This edition, with helpful footnotes, will be found invaluable by those who want to get the feel of ancient Athens (or of other ancient sites in Greece).

Museums, Galleries and Archaeological Sites

Acropolis
Mon. and Wed.–Sat. 7.30 a.m to 7.30 p.m.;
Sun. and pub. hol. 10–6;
at full moon also 9–11.45 p.m.,
closed Tues.

Acropolis Museum
Wed.–Mon. 9–4.30;
closed Tues.

Agora
Mon. and Wed.–Sat. 7.30 a.m. to 7.30 p.m.;
Sun. and pub. hol. 10–6;
closed Tues.

Agora Museum (*Stoa of Attalos*)
Mon. and Wed.–Sun. 9.30–4.30;
closed Tues.

Argo Gallery
Merlin 8;
pictures.

Art Centre
Glykonos 4;
art exhibitions.

Astor Gallery
Karageórgis Sérvias 16;
pictures.

Attalos, Stoa of
See Agora Museum.

Benaki Museum
Koumbari 1;
Mon. and Wed.–Sat. 8.30–2;
Sun. and pub. hol. 10–6;
closed Tues.

Byzantine Museum
Vasílissis Sofías 22;
Tues.–Sat. 9–6;
Sun. and pub. hol. 10–6;
closed Mon.

Desmos Art Gallery
Akadímías 28;
art exhibitions.

Desmos Gallery
Syngrou 4;
art exhibitions.

Diogenes Gallery
Diogenou 12;
pictures and sculpture.

Diogenes Gallery
Tsakalof 10;
pictures.

Fine Art Centre
Zaimis 18;
special exhibitions.

Folk Art Museum
Kydathinaion 17;
Tues.–Sun. 9–1;
closed Mon.

Greek Women's Lyceum
Dimokritou 17;
special exhibitions.

Iolas Zoumboulakis Gallery
Kolonaki 20;
pictures.

Jewish Museum
Melidoni 5;
Wed. 1–6 and Sun. 9–1.

Kerameikos
Mon. and Wed.–Sat. 7.30 a.m. to 7.30 p.m.;
Sun. and pub. hol. 10–6;
closed Tues.

Kerameikos Museum
Ermoú 148;
Mon. and Wed.–Sat. 9–3.30;
Sun. and pub. hol. 10–4.30;
closed Tues.

National Archaeological Museum
Corner of Patission and Tositsa;
Tues.–Sat. 9–6;
Sun. and pub. hol. 10–2.30;
closed Mon.

National Gallery
Mikhalakopoulou 1;
Tues.–Sat. 9–4;
Sun. 10–2;
closed Mon.

National Historical Museum
Stadíou 13;
Tues.–Sun. 9–1;
closed Mon.

Ora Cultural Centre
Xenophontos 7;
pictures.

Rotonda Gallery
Skoufa 20;
pictures.

Stoa Tekhnis
Solonos 13;
pictures by Greek artists.

Tholos Gallery
Filellinon 20;
pictures.

Zappion
Special exhibitions.

Zygos Art Gallery
Iofontos 33;
special exhibitions.

Archaeological sites and national museums are closed on 1 January, 25 March, Good Friday, Easter Day and Christmas Day.

The Acropolis

Sightseeing in Athens

Ancient Athens

The Acropolis

The limestone plateau of the Acropolis, situated in the middle of the plain of Attica, was a site well suited for the fortified "upper city", originally a royal fortress and a precinct enclosing the most sacred shrines of Athens, later the exclusive stronghold of the gods. This religious centre of ancient Athens, given its classical form in the age of Perikles, thus became a monument to the Greek sense of human values, reflecting standards which have remained valid down to our own day. In spite of the destruction they have suffered down the centuries – not least the devastating explosion in 1687, when a Venetian grenade blew up the Turkish powder magazine in the Parthenon and brought it down in ruin – these buildings still convey something of the splendour of the Periclean period, in which Athens stood at the centre of the Greek world in intellectual and artistic as well as in political terms.

The 19th and early 20th c. did a great deal, by the removal of later buildings and restoration of the ancient ones, to restore the structures on the Acropolis to their original 5th c. state. The work began in 1836, immediately after the liberation of Greece from the Turks, with the re-erection (by Ludwig Ross, a member of King Otto's staff) of the Temple of Athena Nike, which had been incorporated in a Turkish bastion, and culminated in the re-erection of the columns along the N side of the Parthenon in the twenties of the present century.

But our own century has also done more damage to the Acropolis within a few decades than the previous two millennia and more. As a result of the waste gases and exhaust fumes produced by a huge modern city, the taking off and landing of thousands of aircraft (which are now prohibited from overflying the Acropolis) and the tramping of the 3 million visitors who climb up to the Acropolis every year, the rock surface and the marble facing are being worn away, the Pentelic marble is breaking down into gypsum, the surviving pieces of classical sculpture (e.g. on the W frieze of the Parthenon) are flaking off, and altogether destruction is proceeding at an alarming rate and on an alarming scale. Accordingly a 15 million dollar programme for saving the Parthenon was initiated by UNESCO. The first visible results were that the central passage of the Propylaia was covered with a wooden floor, a protective roof was built over the Porch of the Caryatids and visitors were excluded from the interior of the Parthenon. It remains an open question, however, how far the various measures taken or planned will succeed in preserving this incomparable monument of antiquity from the devastating effects of modern technological civilisation.

Excellent views of the Acropolis – offering a valuable preliminary to a visit or an informative general impression for visitors with little time at their disposal – are to be enjoyed from various points in the city. The N side can be seen from the Agora, the SE side from the Olympieion and the W side (in particular the monumental Propylaia) from the Pnyx. The **Pnyx** was the meeting-place of the popular Assembly after the reform carried out by Kleisthenes in 507 B.C., the place where statesmen, including Themistokles and Perikles, appeared before the people of Athens. Visitors can still see the rock-hewn *tribune* from which the orators spoke, the *altar of Zeus* (*c.* 400 B.C.) and the retaining wall of the auditorium, constructed of gigantic blocks of stone about 330 B.C. Here too can be seen some remains of the shorter circuit of town walls (*diateichisma*) built in 337 B.C.

The finest view of the Acropolis, however, is the view of its S side from the *Hill of the Muses. From the car park on the far side of the hill we go E along the rocky ridge towards the conspicuous Monument of Philopappos, commemorating a prince of Commagene (SE Anatolia) who was exiled to Athens by the Romans and died there in A.D. 116. In gratitude for his munificence the Athenians allowed his tomb to be erected on this exceptional site – an honour, it has been remarked, that was not granted in the great days of Athens even to such a man as Perikles. On the frieze round the base Philopappos is shown as a Roman consul driving in a chariot and accompanied by lictors. Above this are seated figures of the dead man and (to the left) Antiochos IV, Philopappos' grandfather, the last king of Commagene (until A.D. 72). – On the way to this monument of the personality cult under the Roman Empire we pass various cisterns and rock-cut chambers, one of them misnamed the "Prison of Socrates". Along the way, too, there are attractive and constantly changing views of the Acropolis, with the various buildings clearly visible – on the Acropolis itself the Propylaia, the Erechtheion and the Parthenon, on its southern slopes the Odeon of Herodes Atticus, the Stoa of Eumenes, the Theatre of Dionysos and the columns of the Monument of Thrasyllos. In the background is the pointed summit of Lykabettós. – The hill is a popular resort in the warm afternoon light; but it is also well worth coming here in the early morning.

The rocky crag of the **Acropolis measures 320 m (1050 ft) from W to E and 156 m (512 ft) from N to S, and is 156·20 m (512 ft) high at its highest point. It falls down precipitously on the N, E and S sides, so that the access from the earliest times was always from the W.

In the Mycenaean period the cyclopean walls of the fortress followed the lie of the land closely. On the N side were two small gates leading to the Klepsydra spring and to the caves in the N face of the rock. On the site later occupied by the older temple of Athena stood the royal palace, and to the E of the Erechtheion were other dwellings. There are remains of at least ten buildings dating from the archaic period (7th and 6th c.) as well as the remains of two temples. One of these,

the early 6th c. Temple of Athena was built on the site of the Mycenaean megaron (great hall), which was 100 feet long by 50 feet across (32·80 by 16·40 m) and was accordingly known as the Hekatompedon; it had no colonnade round the cella. The large pediment of poros limestone now in the Acropolis Museum probably belonged to this temple: in the centre bulls attacked by lions, to the left Herakles and Triton, to the right a figure with three bodies (Nereus?). About 520 B.C. Peisistratos built a temple with a colonnade of 6×12 columns – either a reconstruction of the Hekatompedon or a new building – in which marble was used for the first time in the figures on the pediment (Athena and a battle with giants). This "Old Temple" succeeded the Hekatompedon as the sanctuary of Athena Polias and housed the old wooden cult statue. Its ground-plan can be identified immediately S of the Erechtheion.

All the buildings of the Archaic period were destroyed by the Persians in 480 B.C. The remains of the Old Temple were razed to the ground in 406, after the removal of the cult image (*xoanon*) to the new temple of Athena in the eastern part of the Erechtheion. In the rebuilding by Themistokles immediately after the destruction column drums and fragments from the entablature were used, as can still be seen in the N wall. Some time later, after 467, the line of the defences on the S side of the Acropolis was altered by Kimon, who built the present straight wall. The ground level behind the walls built both by Themistokles and Kimon was raised, using debris from the buildings and sculpture destroyed by the Persians; and excavations in this rubble carried out in 1885–86 under the direction of Panayiotis Kavvadias yielded numerous pieces of sculpture and architectural fragments, including the many figures of *korai* (maidens) which are now among the principal treasures of the Acropolis Museum.

Within the fortified area as extended by Kimon the great building and rebuilding programme of the classical period was carried out by Perikles. The Parthenon was built between 447 and 438, the Propylaia between 437 and 432, the Temple of Athena Nike between 432 and 421, the Erechtheion between 421 and 406.

The only structure dating from a later period of which remains are still to be seen is a round temple of Rome and Augustus, dating from the early Empire, below the E end of the Parthenon.

The Acropolis is now entered by the Beulé Gate, built after the Herulian raid in A.D. 267, using stone from destroyed buildings, among them the Dorian monument of Nikias from the southern slope of the Acropolis. Tickets are sold here.

Immediately in front rear up the *Propylaia, built by Mnesikles in 437–432 B.C. He had conceived a monumental and symmetrical structure consisting of three wings, but the daring original plan had to be modified to take account of the old temple of Athena Nike on the projecting spur of rock to the right (the "Pyrgos of Nike"). Traces of the earlier *Propylon* of the 6th c. B.C. can still be seen.

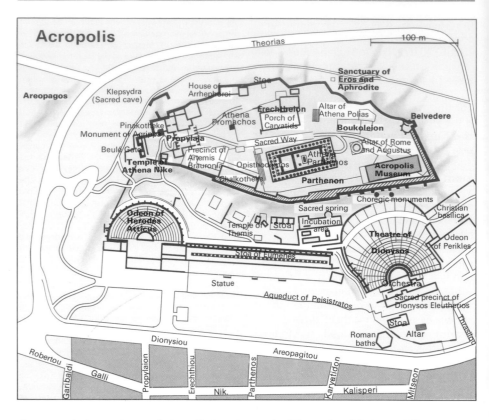

Acropolis

Theorias

100 m

Areopagos

Klepsydra
(Sacred cave)

House of
Arrhephoroi

Stoa

Sanctuary of
Eros and
Aphrodite

Athena
Promachos

Erechtheion
Porch of
Caryatids

Altar of
Athena Polias

Belvedere

Pinakotheke
Monument of Agrippa

Propylaia

Boukoleion

Beulé Gate

Precinct of
Artemis
Brauronia

Sacred Way

Altar of Rome
and Augustus

Temple of
Athena Nike

Opisthodomos

Athena
Parthenos

Acropolis
Museum

Chalkotheke

Parthenon

Choregic monuments

Odeon of
Herodes
Atticus

Temple of
Themis

Stoa

Sacred spring

Incubation
area

Theatre of
Dionysos

Christian
basilica

Odeon
of Perikles

Stoa of Eumenes

Orchestra

Statue

Aqueduct of Peisistratos

Sacred precinct of
Dionysos Eleuthereos

Stoa

Robertou

Dionysiou

Areopagitou

Roman
baths

Altar

Garibaldi

Galli

Propylaion

Erechthiou

Nik.

Parthenos

Karyatidon

Kalisperi

Mitseon

On top of the native rock is a flight of steps, the lowest step being of grey Eleusinian marble and the rest of Pentelic marble. The central structure of the Propylaia consists of a portal with five gateways, increasing in width and height towards the centre. The architrave of the central gateway is extended by the addition of a metope – a device used here for the first time but which later became common. In front of the portal is a deep vestibule, the central carriageway of which is flanked by three Ionic columns on each side; the front pediment is supported by six Doric columns. While this western portico makes an imposing entrance, the corresponding portico at the E end, also with Doric columns, is shorter and lower; seen from the top of the Acropolis it appears small and modest, subordinate to the more important cult buildings.

The W portico is flanked by side wings. To the left is the *Pinakotheke*, which housed a collection of pictures, and to the W of this is the high base of the *Monument of Agrippa* (Augustus' son-in-law), erected in 27 B.C. It was originally planned to have a building similar to the Pinakotheke on the S side, but this was reduced to a narrow passage or vestibule giving access

to the ***Temple of Athena Nike**, Athena who brings victory. The temple was built between 432 and 421 B.C. with four Ionic columns at each end. This type of column was then already old-fashioned, leading Carpenter to suggest that in this temple built after the time of Perikles an older design by Kallikrates was used (see the account of the architectural history of the Parthenon, below). In front of the little temple the remains of an *altar* can be identified, and opposite this a fragment of the Mycenaean defensive walls, the *Pelargikon*. Under the 5th c. paving within the temple can be seen remains of earlier structures. The temple platform was originally surrounded by a parapet. Finds from the site are in the Acropolis Museum.

The present state of the Propylaia and the Temple of Nike is the result of 19th and 20th c. restoration, for both buildings had been damaged and disfigured from the 13th c. onwards by their use as the residence of Frankish dukes and Turkish commandants and for the purposes of defence.

Beyond the Propylaia the bare rock of the Acropolis, worn smooth by the feet of countless visitors, rises in a gentle slope.

Numerous cuttings in the rock mark the positions of the cult images and votive monuments which once stood here, many of them mentioned by Pausanias. Among them was a figure of Athena Hygieia (semicircular base for a bronze statue against the most southerly column of the E portico of the Propylaia, together with an altar, still visible). Exactly on the axis of the central roadway of the Propylaia stood a bronze statue of Athena Promachos, a celebrated work by Pheidias which was later carried off to Constantinople and was destroyed in 1203 during the Crusaders' siege of the city. The goddess, whose lance was visible far and wide, stood on a marble base, part of which, with huge egg-and-dart moulding, has survived in situ.

Immediately to the right (S) of the Propylaia are the remains of the *Brauronion*, the cult precinct of Artemis of Brauron, which was brought to Athens by Peisistratos, and the *Chalkotheke*, in which works of art in bronze were kept. Beyond this a broad flight of steps hewn from the rock leads up to the higher level on which the Parthenon stands. The ancient processional way ran along the N side of the temple (opposite the seventh column a rock-cut dedication to Ge, the Earth Mother) to the entrance at the E end.

The **Parthenon**, the temple of the Maiden Athena (Athena Parthenos), was built between 447 and 438 B.C. (sculpture completed 432), the master-work of the architect Iktinos and of Pheidias, to whom Perikles had entrusted the overall direction of the building work on the Acropolis.

ARCHITECTURAL HISTORY. – This has been established, with a high degree of probability, by the work of Hill, Dinsmoor and Carpenter. In 490 B.C. or soon afterwards the foundations for the first Parthenon, consisting of 22 courses of masonry with a height of up to 10·75 m (35 ft), were built and the lower drums of the columns were laid, but the building, designed to have 6×16 columns, was still unfinished at the time of the Persian invasion in 480, and the column drums were damaged by fire. – In 468 Kimon continued the work, with Kallikrates as architect, but the construction of this "Pre-Parthenon" was halted on Kimon's death in 450. – In 447, under Perikles, the new master of Athens, the erection of the present Parthenon was begun. Kallikrates was replaced by Iktinos, who used the column drums and metopes already available in his altered plan. The foundations were adapted to accommodate the new and wider ground-plan; the older foundations, extending farther to the E, can be clearly distinguished on the S side.

Standing on a substructure with steps 52 cm (20 in.) high, the temple now had eight columns along the ends and 17 along the sides (compared with the previous 6×16). The Doric columns stand 10·43 m (34 ft) high, with a diameter at the base of 1·90 m (6 ft) and at the top of 1·48 m (5 ft). They have 20 flutings and show a distinct swelling in the middle (the feature known as entasis). Similarly the substructure shows a gentle curve, rising towards the middle (best seen on the uppermost step, the stylobate). These features (entasis and curvature), together with the slight inward inclination of the columns (the corner columns leaning diagonally inward), were deliberately contrived to avoid any impression of heaviness or rigidity and to create the effect of an organically evolved structure.

The building was roofed with slabs of marble. The lions' heads at the corners of the roof were not pierced to serve as water-spouts but were purely ornamental; the water simply ran off at the corners without any channel. On the architrave at the E end are dowel holes marking the place where shields captured by Alexander the Great at the battle of the Granikos in 334 B.C. were suspended.

The INTERIOR (now closed to visitors) is in two parts. At the W end is a square chamber, with remains of painting dating from the time when it was used as a Christian church, leading into the Parthenon proper, the roof of which was borne on four Ionic columns. At the E end the pronaos leads into the cella in which stood the chryselephantine statue of Athena, known to us only from descriptions and later copies. The cavity for the base on which it stood can be seen in the floor of the cella. The statue, completed in 438 B.C., stood some 12 m (39 ft) high; the face and hands were of ivory, the garments of gold (weighing, we are told, over 1000 kg (2205 lb)). The statue was later taken to Constantinople and destroyed there. Marks in the floor show that a two-tier Doric colonnade ran along the sides and to the rear of the statue – an entirely new conception of the interior of a temple. It has been supposed that the broader ground-plan of the temple, with eight instead of six columns along the ends, was necessary to accommodate this conception: the earliest example of a temple in which the overall plan was determined by the form of the interior.

No less famous than the statue of Athena was the sculpture on the exterior of the Parthenon – the E and W pediments, the Doric metopes and the Ionic frieze along the top of the cella wall. Some of the sculpture is in the Acropolis Museum and some in the Louvre, but most of it is in the British Museum (the "Elgin marbles", brought to London by Lord Elgin in 1801).

The *pediments*, completed in 432 B.C., depicted the birth of Athena from Zeus' head (E pediment) and the contest between Athena and Poseidon for the possession of Attica. In the E pediment are copies of

Dionysos and the heads of the Sun god's and Moon goddess's horses at each end, in the W pediment King Kekrops and one of his daughters (original). The 92 *metopes* depicted a gigantomachia (battle of giants: E end), a fight with centaurs (S side: the best preserved), fighting with Persians (or Amazons: W end), and the Trojan War (N side).

The *frieze* which runs along the outer wall of the cella is 1 m (3 ft) high and 160 m (525 ft) long. It depicts not a mythical or historical theme but an occasion in the life of Athens in the classical period, the great Panathenaic procession which took place every four years, making its way from the Gymnasion through the Dipylon and over the Agora to the Acropolis. The procession begins at the SW corner and runs along the W end, where the slabs are still in situ, and the N side to the E end, where it met the other half of the procession running along the S side.

Outside the E end of the Parthenon is the little **Temple of Rome and Augustus**, dating from the early Imperial period, the decorative forms of which were modelled on the Erechtheion. To the N of the temple, on the highest point of the Acropolis, are cuttings in the rock which mark the position of the Temple of Zeus Polieus. A short distance E is the **Belvedere*, from which there are extensive views of the city.

Porch of Caryatids, Erechtheion

The****Erechtheion**, on the N side of the Acropolis, was built between 421 and 406 B.C. It has a complex ground-plan, since it had to be accommodated to a number of earlier shrines on the site. At the E end was the temple which housed the old wooden cult image of Athena Polias, patroness of Athens; at the W end were the tomb of Erechtheus, the tomb of Kekrops – below the Porch of the Caryatids which projects on the S side, its entablature borne by six figures of maidens – and, in the floor of the N porch, the marks left by Poseidon's trident. On the cella wall, above a band of elegant palmette ornament, is a frieze of grey Eleusinian marble on which white marble figures were applied. – Immediately S of

the Erechtheion can be seen the foundations of the *Old Temple of Athena* (6th c.), which was destroyed in 480 B.C., and two column bases, protected by gratings, probably belonging to the megaron (central hall) of the Mycenaean palace.

To the W of the Erechtheion is an olive-tree which commemorates the first olive-tree planted by Athena. In this area was the *Pandrosion*, the temple of the dew goddess Pandrosos. To the NW can be seen the remains of the *House of the Arrhephoroi*, in which during the four years between Panathenaic festivals four girls between the age of seven and 11 lived as temple servants and assistants to the priestess of Athena. It was one of their tasks to make the peplos (robe) in which the image of Athena was arrayed for the festival. From the courtyard beside the House of the Arrhephoroi a staircase leads down through an opening in the Acropolis walls to a *sanctuary of Eros and Aphrodite*, from which the arrhephoroi brought up certain secret objects (hence their name: "bearers of that which must not be spoken of"). Farther W, built against the Acropolis walls, are the remains of a building which is presumed to have been the dwelling of the priestess of Athena.

The ****Acropolis Museum**, built between 1949 and 1953 and inconspicuously sited low down at the SE corner of the Acropolis, contains one of the world's finest collections of Greek sculpture.

The E end of the museum contains material dating from the Archaic period (6th c.) recovered from the rubble left by the Persian destruction: pediments of temples and treasuries, votive statues and – extending into the W end – figures from the marble pediment of the Old Temple (Rooms I–V). The other rooms to the W (VI–IX) are mainly devoted to sculpture of the classical period (5th c.).

The *Vestibule* is dominated by a huge marble owl, the emblem of Athena (No. 1347: beginning of 5th c.), and also contains a ***marble statue of Athena** from the Propylaia (No. 1336: end of 5th c.), a ***marble base** with a *relief* of a dancing soldier (No. 1338: 4th c.) and a marble ***funerary lekythos** (No. 6407: end of 4th c.). We now turn left to enter *Room I*, which contains material of the early 6th c. To the left is a ***pediment** of painted poros limestone (No. 1: *c.* 600 B.C.) depicting Herakles and the Hydra, the charioteer Iolaos and a crab which bit Herakles' foot. Opposite the entrance doorway is a lioness tearing apart a young bull, from a large ***pediment** of poros limestone (No. 4: *c.* 490). To the right is a *Gorgon* (No. 701: early 6th c.).

Section of the Parthenon frieze

The "Rampin Horseman", Acropolis Museum

Room II contains two halves of the *"**Red Pediment**", the right-hand half with the introduction of Herakles into Olympus (No. 9+55: *c.* 580), the left-hand half with the fight between Herakles and Triton (No. 2: *c.* 560); the *"**Pediment of the Olive-Tree**", probably depicting the story of Troilos; an interesting model of a temple, beside a figure of a *water-carrier* (No. 52: *c.* 570); and two parts of a *pediment of poros limestone, probably from the Hekatompedon, with Herakles and Triton to the left and a figure with three bodies, now identified as Nereus, to the right (No. 35: 580–570). The central part of the pediment was probably the group displayed in Room III depicting two lions rending a bull (No. 3). Also in Room II are the famous **Moschophoros**, the figure of a man carrying a calf in Hymettian marble, a votive offering by one Rhombos (No. 624: *c.* 570), and the earliest of the *korai*, votive offerings to Athena, which were set up in large numbers on the Acropolis; this Attic work shows the maiden holding a pomegranate in one hand and a garland in the other (No. 593: early 6th c.).

Room III contains, in addition to the fragment of a pediment already mentioned, the torsos of two *korai*, probably from Náxos or Samos (Nos. 619 and 677: 580–550).

Room IV, a long hall, contains a whole series of master works. First there are four or five works ascribed to the same sculptor, Phaidimos. The earliest is the *"**Rampin Horseman**" (the head is a cast: original in the Louvre), part of the oldest-known equestrian group

in Greece, the other horseman in the group being represented only by fragments. It has been supposed that the group depicted the sons of Peisistratos, Hippias and Hipparchos, or alternatively the Dioscuri (No. 590: *c.* 550). The ***Peplos Kore**, named after the Dorian peplos she wears, is a mature work by the same sculptor (No. 679: *c.* 530). A *lion-head spout* from the Old Temple of Athena (No. 61: *c.* 525) and a *hound* from the Brauronion (No. 143: *c.* 520) are also attributed to Phaidimos. Another *equestrian statue* of a figure wearing Persian or Scythian dress probably represents Miltiades (No. 606: *c.* 520).

The central features of the last section of Room IV are the *korai, figures of girls wearing a peplos and in the later examples a more richly decorated chiton, over which they usually wear a cloak (himation). As a rule one hand gathers up the peplos, while the other holds an offering. The figures, usually rather larger than life-size, stood in the open air, and many of them show evidence of the crescent-shaped iron cover which was let into their head to protect them from bird droppings. They were originally painted, and some traces of colouring can still be seen, particularly on their garments.

We first note a *kore with a serious expression*, in Ionian costume (No. 673: 520–510), an elegant *kore from Chios*, with a beautifully draped painted chiton (No. 675: *c.* 510) and a magnificent *head of a kore* (No. 643: *c.* 510). Then, in a large semicircle, come (from left to right) a large kore from *Chios* (No. 682: *c.* 520), a finely modelled kore, probably from the Peloponnese (No. 684: *c.* 490), the enigmatic *"**Kore with the Sphinx's Eyes**" (No. 674: *c.* 500) and a kore clad only in a chiton (No. 670: *c.* 510). A large seated *figure of Athena* in the middle of the group, a work by Endoios (No. 625: *c.* 530), is followed by the clothed *figure of a young man* (No. 633: late 6th c.), the *"**Severe Kore**", the only one not gathering up her garment (No. 685: *c.* 500), a *kore from the Ionian Islands*, preserved almost intact (No. 680: *c.* 520) and a large kore which has also survived almost undamaged (No. 671: *c.* 520).

In *Room V* are the 2 m (7 ft) high *Kore of Antenor*, with a base bearing the names of the donor, Nearchos, and the sculptor, Antenor (Nos. 681 and 681A: *c.* 525), and *figures* from the pediment of the Peisistratid Old Temple representing Athena in a battle with giants (No. 631: *c.* 525). In the alcove to the left is a collection of fine pottery ranging in date from the Geometric to the late classical period.

Room VI brings us to the early 5th c. B.C., the beginnings of classical art, the earliest examples of which date from before the fateful year 480, the year of the Persian conquest. It includes also works in the Severe style. Of particular interest are the *"Sulky Kore*", dedicated by Euthydikos (Nos. 686 and 609: *c.* 490), the "Kore of the Propylaia", set up shortly before the Persian attack (No. 688: *c.* 480), a *figure of Athena* (No. 140: 480–470), the *relief of a potter* (No. 1332: *c.* 500), the *head of a youth* from the workshop of Pheidias and the *forequarters of a horse* (No. 697: a noble work of 490–480). Famous works of the early classical period are the *"**Fair-Haired Youth**", a figure of unusual melancholy beauty (No. 689: shortly before 480), a relief of *"Mourning Athena*" (No. 695: 460–450) and the oldest of this group, the *Critian Boy*, ascribed to Kritios or his workshop (No. 698: 485). The torso and the head of this figure were found separately in 1865 and 1888. It is the earliest statue known to us in which the archaic posture with each leg bearing an equal weight gives place to the classical pose with one leg bearing the weight and the other hanging free. In this respect Kritios was a forerunner of the art of the classical period.

The following rooms are devoted to the buildings of the classical period on the Acropolis. *Room VII* contains plaster reproductions of the *Parthenon pediments*, a *metope* from the S side (centaur and Lapith: No. 705), a *torso of Poseidon* from the W pediment (No. 885) and two *horses' heads* from Poseidon's team (Nos. 882 and 884).

Room VIII contains large sections of the *Parthenon frieze* (1 m (3 ft) high, 160 m (525 ft) long) depicting the Panathenaic procession and giving a vivid impression of life in Athens in the Periclean period. The N frieze shows horsemen, *apobatai* (who jump on and off moving chariots), marshals, musicians, youths carrying hydrias and sacrificial animals; the last slab (No. 857) is undoubtedly the work of Pheidias himself. From the S frieze there are figures of horsemen; from the E frieze Poseidon, Apollo and Artemis, probably by Alkamenes, a pupil of Pheidias.

On the projecting wall which divides the room into two are parts of the *Erechtheion frieze*, carved some decades after the Parthenon frieze, between 409 and 405 B.C. The reconstruction shows the technique used, the figures in light-coloured Pentelic marble being attached to the background of darker Eleusinian marble with metal pegs. The significance of the figures is unclear.

Finally there are a series of slabs from the *parapet* round the Temple of Nike, which are dated to about 410 B.C. They show Athena enthroned on a rock (No. 989) with a series of goddesses of victory, including the famous *Nike loosing her sandal* (No. 973).

Room IX contains a large *mask of a deity* (No. 6461), a *bas-relief* of an Attic trireme (No. 1339) and an idealised *portrait of the young Alexander* (No. 1331), probably carved by Leochares or Euphranor after Alexander's visit to Athens about 335 B.C.

The Areopagos and the Slopes of the Acropolis

The Acropolis rock was circled in ancient times by a footpath, known from inscriptions to have been called the *Peripatos*, which can still be followed for much of the way. If we turn right at the foot of the road leading down from the Acropolis we come, before reaching the path along the N side, to the **Areopagos** (Areios pagos, Hill of Ares), with rock-cut steps leading up to the top. This rocky hill, 115 m (378 ft) high, was the seat of the supreme court of ancient Athens. Here in Mycenaean times, as Aeschylus relates in his tragedy "The Eumenides", Orestes was called to account for the murder of his mother Klytaimnestra. The goddess Athena herself secured his acquittal, whereupon the Erinnyes or Furies who had been relentlessly pursuing him – and who had a cave sanctuary on the Areopagos – turned into the Eumenides or "Kindly Ones". The occasion was commemorated by an altar dedicated to Athena Areia by Orestes to which Pausanias refers. Of this and of other buildings on the site nothing now remains. – Chapter 17 of the Acts of the Apostles records the address which the Apostle Paul gave to the "men of Athens" on this ancient sacred site in the year 50, referring to Christ as the "unknown god" to whom one of the many altars on the hill was dedicated. A modern bronze tablet (to the right of the steps up the hill) is inscribed with this text, and on the northern slopes of the Areopagos are the remains of a *basilica* dedicated to Dionysios, a member of the Areopagos, who was Paul's first convert in Athens.

The remains on the lower slopes of the Areopagos are more easily visible than those on the hill itself. On the N side are *Mycenaean chamber tombs* with long entrance passages, no doubt the graves of the kings who resided on the Acropolis,

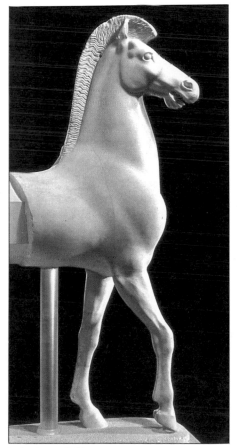

In the Acropolis Museum

Panoramic view of Athens

and to the SW, at the foot of the hill, a residential quarter (seen from Apostolou Pávlou Street) has been excavated. At one of the street corners can be seen the trapezoid *Amyneion*, the shrine of an ancient local healing god, Amynos.

Although the smoothness of the rock does not make for easy walking, it is well worth while climbing the Areopagos for its magnificent view of the Propylaia and the excellent general view which it affords of the Agora. This *view of the Agora* can also be enjoyed from the modern path which runs E, roughly on the line of the ancient Peripatos. On the right-hand side of this path can be seen, on the northern slope of the Acropolis, the masonry of the **Klepsydra**, the spring which supplied the Acropolis with water from the most ancient times. Above it are two prominent **caves**, the *Cave of Apollo Pythios* (below the Pinakotheke) and to the left of this the *Cave of Pan*. The old shepherd god Pan was particularly honoured in Athens after the Persian wars, since the Athenian victory at Marathón in 490 B.C. was believed to be due to his help. Farther along, below the House of the Arrhephoroi, is the *Cave of Aglauros*, and NE of this, below the Erechtheion, a sanctuary of Eros and Aphrodite.

The remains on the S side of the Acropolis are more abundant and more important,

extending from prehistoric times to the 2nd c. A.D., and indeed into the early Christian period.

In the 6th c. B.C. Peisistratos transferred the cult of Dionysos from Eleutherai in the Kithairon hills (on the road to Thebes) to Athens, where accordingly the god was known as Dionysos Eleuthereus, and a temple was built to house the old cult image from Eleutherai. In association with the cult of Dionysos – the god of drunkenness, of transformation, of ecstasy and the mask – the *Theatre of Dionysos* was built in a natural hollow on the slopes of the Acropolis. Nine building phases have been distinguished by Travlos, the first two dating from the 6th and 5th c. The theatre and the temple precinct were separated about 420 B.C. when a pillared hall facing S was built, involving the transfer of the temple to another site. The breccia foundations of this later temple, for which Alkamenes made a chryselephantine cult image, can be seen to the S of the remains of the hall. About 330 B.C. the theatre's present stone tiers of seating were built; they rise up to directly under the rock of the Acropolis, where there is a cave (now occupied by the chapel of Panayía Spiliótissa) and above this two columns of a monument erected by Thrasyllos in 320–319 B.C. The 67 tiers of seating, which could accommodate some 17,000 spectators, are

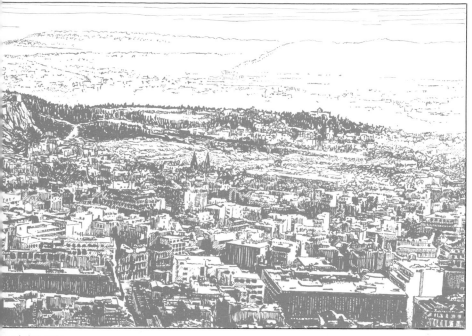

om Lykabettós

divided into three sections by transverse gangways, and the lowest section is divided vertically into 13 wedges separated by stairways. In the front row are *seats of honour* inscribed with the names of the occupants; in the centre is the seat reserved for the priest of Dionysos Eleuthereus, decorated with reliefs, with postholes in the ground pointing to the existence of a canopy. Behind the priest's seat is the *throne* of the Emperor Hadrian. The *orchestra* is paved with marble slabs and is surrounded by a marble barrier to provide protection from the wild beasts who took part in shows during the Roman period. The *stage buildings* on the S side were several times rebuilt. Here there are striking *reliefs* of Dionysiac scenes, which according to the most recent theory were re-used in an orators' tribune of the 5th c. A.D.

The importance of the Theatre of Dionysos – of which there is a fine general view from the S wall of the Acropolis – is that it was constructed at the time that tragedy was being introduced, and indeed created, in Athens. The first drama was performed in 534 B.C., probably in the Agora, by Thespis, who is said to have travelled about in a waggon as a strolling player. This early form, in which a single actor performed along with a chorus, was the beginning of a development which led in the 5th c. B.C. – the period of pride and confidence after the Persian wars – to the brilliant flowering of Greek tragedy. The works of the three great Attic tragedians were first performed in the Theatre of Dionysos in celebration of the Dionysiac cult; and here Aeschylus – who had fought at Marathón as a hoplite and was proud to have this recorded on his tombstone – Sophocles and Euripides appeared in person. Thus the Theatre of Dionysos became the place of origin of the European theatre. – To the E of the Theatre stood the square Odeon, built at the expense of Perikles.

Adjoining the Theatre of Dionysos on the W is the 163 m (535 ft) long **Stoa of Eumenes**, built by King Eumenes II of Pergamon (197–159 B.C.), who not only erected magnificent buildings in his own city (Great Altar of Pergamon) but sought to do honour to Athens by the erection of this stoa. His example was followed by his brother and successor Attalos II (159–138 B.C.), who built the Stoa of Attalos in the Agora, probably using the same architect.

The Stoa of Eumenes differed from the Stoa of Attalos in having no rooms behind the double-aisled colonnade. It was thus not designed for the purposes of business but was merely a spacious promenade for visitors to the Temple and Theatre of Dionysos. It was two-storeyed, with

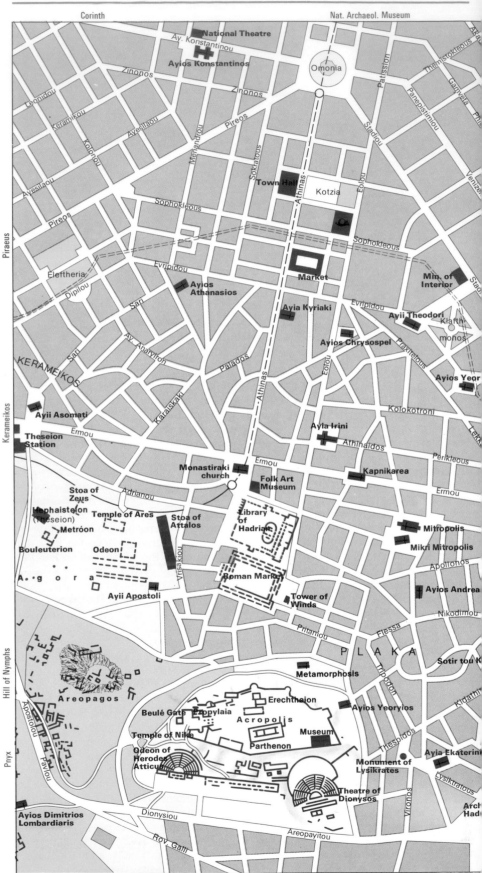

Corinth   Nat. Archaeol. Museum

===== Presumed line of ancient walls   Airport, Sou

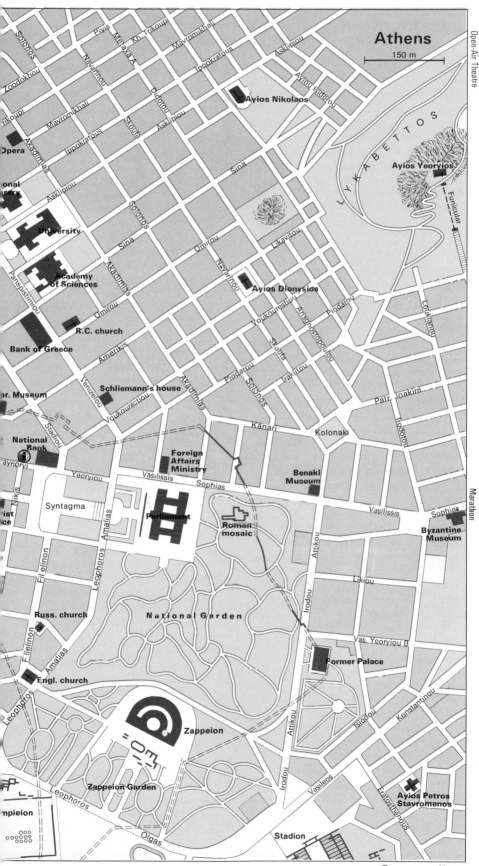

Athens

150 m

Doric columns on the exterior, Ionic columns in the interior on the ground floor and capitals of Pergamene type on the upper floor. Since the stoa was built against the slope of the hill, it was protected by a retaining wall supported by pillars and round arches; the *arcades*, originally faced with marble, can still be seen. In front of the E end of the stoa are the foundations of the *Monument of Nikias*, erected by Nikias in 320 B.C. to commemorate his victory as *choregos*; material from this monument was built into the Beulé Gate of the Acropolis after 267 B.C.

Immediately W of the Stoa of Eumenes is the *Odeon of Herodes Atticus, built by the great art patron of that name, a native of Marathón (A.D. 101–177), after the death of his wife Regilla in 161. Its proximity to the Theatre of Dionysos provides a convenient demonstration of the difference between the Greek and the Roman theatre. The Greek theatre fitted its auditorium into a natural hollow, and the rows of seating extended round more than a semicircle. The orchestra was originally exactly circular, and the low stage structure (*skene*) lay close to it on one side, only loosely connected with it. Between the auditorium and the stage were the open passages for the entrance of the choir (*parodoi*). The principles of Roman theatre construction were quite different. The auditorium (*cavea*) was exactly semicircular, the side entrances were vaulted over and the stage, which in the later period was raised, was backed by an elaborate stage wall (*scenae frons*) of several tiers, lavishly decked with columns and statues, which rose to the same height as the top rows of seats or the enclosure wall of the auditorium. The auditorium and the stage thus formed an architectural unity, and the theatre became a totally enclosed space. The theatre was open to the sky, but an odeon, intended for musical performances, would be roofed. The 32 steeply raked rows of seating in the Odeon of Herodes Atticus could accommodate 5000 spectators, and were faced with marble (recently restored). The theatre, which was incorporated in the defences of the medieval castle, is in such an excellent state of preservation that it is used during the Athens Festival every summer for dramatic performances and concerts by leading European artistes.

Returning along the Stoa of Eumenes to the Theatre of Dionysos, we come to a path leading up to the terrace above the stoa. Here we see the remains of the **Asklepieion**, the shrine of the healing god Asklepios which was established here, beside a sacred spring, in 420 B.C., when the cult of Asklepios was brought to Athens from Epidauros. Within the rectangular precinct, just under the Acropolis rock, here hewn into a vertical face, is a *stoa* 50 m (164 ft) long, originally two-storeyed, which was erected in the 4th c. B.C. to accommodate the sick who came here to seek cure. Associated with it is a cave containing the sacred spring. The spring is still credited with healing powers, and accordingly the cave is now used as a chapel.

Parallel to this stoa another similar building, of which some remains are still to be seen, was erected in Roman times along the S side of the sacred precinct. Both of these buildings faced towards the centre of the precinct, in which stood the *temple*. This was oriented to the E and had four columns along the front (prostyle, tetrastyle). The foundations of the temple and the altar which stood in front of it can still be distinguished. In early Christian times a basilica was built over the remains of the temple and the altar, and some architectural fragments bearing Christian crosses can be seen lying about the site.

At the NW corner of the sacred precinct is a *bothros*, a round pit for offerings, originally surrounded by columns bearing a canopy. To the W of this are the foundations of another stoa and of a small *temple* lying at an angle to the other buildings – perhaps the first temple of Asklepios, dating from the late 5th c. B.C.

Farther along the path, which leads to the entrance to the Acropolis, can be seen traces of the prehistoric settlement which lay on the southern slopes of the Acropolis.

The Agora

To the N of the Acropolis lay a number of large open squares, the Agora, the Roman Market and the Library of Hadrian.

A good general *view of the Agora, the market square of ancient Athens, can be obtained from the N wall of the Acropolis, the Areopagos hill, the path which runs E from the Areopagos along the N slopes of the Acropolis or from the path along the foot of the Areopagos. It is also a help towards understanding the site to approach it from the N entrance, just off Hadrian Street (Adrianoú) near St Philip's church, where a layout plan is displayed.

The *Agora was excavated and studied by American archaeologists in 1931–41 and 1946–60 after the demolition of a whole quarter of the city, and the remains have been incorporated in an attractive park. In recent years further excavations have been carried out N of the Piraeus railway, which previously marked the boundary of the excavation site, and to the E of the Agora, where, under a modern road, excavation revealed the ancient road linking the Agora with the Roman Market, together with the buildings which flanked the road.

From the Mycenaean period until the end of the 7th c. B.C. this was a cemetery area. It began to be used as an agora in the early 6th c., in the time of Solon, and the oldest buildings were erected at the W end of the site, under the Agora hill. Thereafter it remained for many centuries the centre of the city's public life, each century erected new buildings, frequently at the expense of earlier ones.

To the time of Peisistratos (c. 600–528 B.C.) belong the Altar of the Twelve Gods, the tyrant's house at the SW corner and the Enneakrounos fountain at the SE corner. After Kleisthenes' reform (508 B.C.) there was much new construction – the courthouse of the Heliaia (on the site of an earlier Solonic building), the large drainage channel on the W side of the site, the old Bouleuterion for the Council of 400 and a small temple dedicated to the Mothers, the Metroon. After the destruction by the Persians (480–479 B.C.), in the time of Kimon, the circular Tholos was built. Other buildings erected in the course of the 5th c. included the Temple of Hephaistos, the Stoa of Zeus and the South Stoa. The temples of Apollo Patroos, Zeus Phratrios and Athena Phratria were built in the period after 350 B.C. The 2nd c. contributed large new stoas on the S side of the Agora, the Stoa of Attalos and a new Metroon. Sulla's campaign in 86 B.C. caused much destruction in the Agora. Later, around 20 B.C., the open space in the middle of the Agora was built up for the first time, with the erection of the Odeon of Agrippa and near this a new temple of Ares. The 2nd c. A.D. saw the erection of the Library of Pantainos. In the following century, however, the Herulian invasion (267) brought a further catastrophe, and thereafter the Stoa of Attalos was incorporated in the late Roman walls which enclosed the reduced city area. For more than a hundred years the Agora, lying outside the walls, lay empty and abandoned; then, about 400, there was a fresh burst of building activity. The Tholos was restored, a Gymnasion was built to house the University of Athens and the Temple of Hephaistos became a Christian church. This was the last phase in the long history of the Agora: by about A.D. 550 it was abandoned, and it was

not reoccupied until the 11th c., when it began to develop into the populous quarter which was pulled down to permit the American excavations.

From the N entrance there is a general view of the spacious rectangular area of the Agora, bounded on the E (left) by the Stoa of Attalos and on the W by the Agora hill with the well-preserved temple of Hephaistos. The *Panathenaic Way*, still retaining some of its original paving, cuts diagonally across the area. This was the road followed by the Panathenaic procession on its way from Kerameikos to the Acropolis. – Turning left, we come to the **Stoa of Attalos**, in front of which are the remains of a small building and a circular fountain-house (at the N end) and of an orator's tribune (*bema*) and the base for a statue of Attalos (half way along). The stoa, 116 m (381 ft) long, was built by King Attalos II of Pergamon (159–138 B.C.), brother and successor of Eumenes II, who built the Stoa of Eumenes on the S side of the Acropolis. It was (and is, since the faithful reconstruction of the original building in 1953–56) two-storeyed, with Doric columns fronting the lower floor and Ionic columns on the upper floor. The stoa proper, which is backed by a series of rooms (originally 21) to the rear, is divided by Ionic columns into two aisles. The reconstruction has restored the impressive spatial effect of the long pillared hall.

The purpose of the rebuilding was to provide an appropriate home for the *Agora Museum.

The display of sculpture in the *portico* begins at the S end with a colossal *statue of Apollo Patroos (S2154: 4th c. B.C.), which Pausanias ascribed to the sculptor Euphranor. Then follow two *statues (opposite the 2nd column) representing the Iliad and the Odyssey (S2038 and 2039: early 2nd c. A.D.); a *priestess (opposite the 4th column: S1016: 4th c. B.C.), flanked by two *herms*, the one on the right bearing a child (S33 and S198: Roman); a *marble stele inscribed with a law against tyranny and a relief depicting Democracy crowning the people of Athens (at the 5th column: I 6524: 336 B.C.); *sculpture* from the Temple of Hephaistos (opposite the 11th column); and *acroteria* from the Stoa of Zeus (at the N end of the portico: S312 and S373: c. 410 B.C.).

To the rear of the portico, at the S end, are four small rooms containing two *Ionic columns* from an unknown building of the 5th c. B.C., a sales counter and a collection of *wine amphoras*.

The long *main hall* displays in chronological order a large collection of material, most of which is notable not for its artistic quality but for the evidence it gives on life in ancient Athens. The collection begins with the Neolithic period (3rd millennium B.C.). The Mycenaean period (1500–1100 B.C.) is represented by vases and grave goods, including two *ivory caskets carved with griffins and nautiluses (case 5: Bl 511 and 513). From the early Iron Age (11th–8th c. B.C.) date 9th c. *tombs with their grave goods, and also Proto-Geometric and Geometric *vases (cases 11, 17 and 18). Then come vases in Orientalising style, a *mould for casting a bronze statue* dating from the Archaic period (6th c.) and a beautiful 6th c. terracotta *figure of a kneeling boy (P1231). There are numerous items illustrating the everyday life of the classical period (5th c.) – inscriptions, a *machine for the selection of public officials by lot* (I 3967), *sherds used in the process of ostracism (including one with the name of Themistokles, case 38), a terracotta child's commode, domestic utensils, etc. On either side of the exit are cases 61 (finds from a well, ranging in date from the 1st to the 10th c. A.D.) and 63 (material of the Byzantine and Turkish periods).

Proceeding SE from the Stoa of Attalos along the Panathenaic Way, we see on the left the *Library of Pantainos* (2nd c. A.D.). In front of it are remains of the late Roman *town walls* (after A.D. 267), with many re-used fragments from earlier buildings. Outside the Agora enclosure, on the left of the ancient road, are remains of the *sanctuary of the gods of Eleusis*.

Turning right at this point, we come to the **Church of the Holy Apostles**, the only surviving church in this quarter. The church, built in the 11th c. over a semicircular nymphaeum, was sub-sequently much altered but has now been restored to its original state. The dome is borne on four columns; semicircular apse and transepts; good *frescoes* in the interior. In the narthex are wall paintings (*c.* 1700) from the nearby church of St Spyridon, demolished in 1939. Im-mediately S of the church there once stood the Athenian Mint and the Enneakrounos fountain.

To the W of the church are the remains of the *second South Stoa*, the *Middle Stoa*, running parallel to it on the N, and the *East Stoa* linking the two (all 2nd c. B.C.). Adjoining the W end of the South Stoa is the square building of the *Heliaia* (5th c. B.C.), on the N side of which was a water-clock of about 350 B.C.

A well-preserved Corinthian capital of considerable size marks the position of the *Odeon of Agrippa*, lying N of the Middle Stoa in the centre of the Agora. Built about 20 B.C. by the Roman general Agrippa, it was a square building with a stage and 18 rows of seats which could accommodate an audience of 1000 (some remains preserved). In the 2nd c. A.D. a new entrance was constructed on the N side, with three tritons and three giants supporting the roof of the portico; three of these figures are still erect. After the destruction of the original building by the Herulians in A.D. 267 the site was used about A.D. 400 for the erection of a Gymnasion to house the University of Athens, which was closed down by the Emperor Justinian in A.D. 529; the foun-dations of this building can still be seen.

Going W from here, we see on a lower level a *boundary stone* (*horos*) dating from about 500 B.C., cross the large drainage channel and come to the build-ings on the W side of the site.

The first of these is the circular *Tholos* (diameter 18·30 m (60 ft), which once housed the sacred hearth and was the meeting-place of the 50 *prytaneis* (*c.* 465 B.C.). To the N of this is the **Metroon**, with the **Bouleuterion** (5th c. B.C.) to its rear. In the 2nd c. B.C. a colonnade was built in front of the vestibule of the Bouleuterion and the Metroon in order to unify the façade facing the Agora. The present floor surface of the Metroon belongs to a Christian church installed in the ancient building in the 5th c. The next building – also surviving only in the form of foundations – is the *Temple of Apollo Patroos* (4th c. B.C.), the cult image from which is now in the Stoa of Attalos. In an annex to the temple the earliest popu-lation register of Athens was kept. Im-mediately beyond the temple, extending to the Piraeus railway line (the con-struction of which destroyed its N end), is the **Stoa of Zeus Eleutherios** (Zeus who maintains the freedom of the city). The stoa, originally 46·55 m (153 ft) long, with projecting wings at each end, was built about 430 B.C., probably by Mnes-ikles, the architect of the Propylaia. In front of it, on a round base, stood a statue of Zeus Eleutherios. During the Roman period a square annex was built on to the rear of the stoa, perhaps for the purposes of the Imperial cult. Pausanias tells us that the Stoa of Zeus contained pictures, including representations of the Twelve Gods, Theseus and the battle of Man-tineia.

It used to be thought that the Stoa of Zeus was the same as the Royal Stoa (Stoa Basileios), but this has now been identified in the excavation area beyond the

Piraeus railway line. Built soon after 480 B.C., the Royal Stoa resembled the Stoa of Zeus in having projecting wings at the ends but was considerably smaller (18 m (59 ft) long, 6·20 m (20 ft) wide). It was the seat of the Archon Basileus, who took over the cultic functions of the kings. Among those functions was the trial of offenders accused of *asebeia* (impiety, godlessness); and accordingly this stoa may have been the scene of Socrates' trial in 399 B.C., when he was condemned to death by drinking hemlock, after defending himself against charges of impiety and the corruption of youth in the "Apology" recorded by his pupil Plato.

Another of Plato's dialogues, the "Death of Socrates", is set in the **Prison**, in which Socrates spent his last days in the company of his pupils. This prison, which had traditionally but erroneously been located on the Hill of the Muses, has now been identified by an American archaeologist, E. Vanderpool, in a building situated under the W side of the Areopagos, 100 m (328 ft) from the SW corner of the Agora in the direction of the Pnyx (20 m (66 ft) S of the modern path which runs along the northern slopes of the Areopagos from Apostolou Pávlou Street). The building, dating from the middle of the 5th c. B.C., measured 37·50 by 16·50 m (123 by 54 ft) and had an open passage down the middle, flanked by cells and a bath-house. The entrance was at the N end, and the S end was occupied by a courtyard. Among the finds were 13 vessels only 4 cm (2 in.) high – just big enough to contain a fatal dose of hemlock – and a statuette of Socrates.

In front of the buildings along the W side of the Agora are numerous **monuments** – a long *base* which once supported statues of the eponymous heroes of the ten Athenian tribes (second half of 4th c. B.C.); the *altar of Zeus Agoraios*; a *statue of the Emperor Hadrian* (2nd c. A.D.); the *Temple of Ares*, a large rectangular structure originally built on another site about 440 B.C. and moved here in the Augustan period; and finally, close to the railway line, one corner of the *Altar of the Twelve Gods* (6th c. B.C.).

From the Tholos an attractive path runs up the Agora hill (Kolonos Agoraios) to the Temple of Hephaistos. The erroneous name of Theseion still stubbornly persists (and is perpetuated by the name of the nearby station of the Piraeus railway); but the actual situation of the real Theseion, in which the remains of the Attic hero Theseus were deposited after being brought back from the island of Skyros in 475 B.C., remains unknown.

The ****Hephaisteion**, lying near the smiths' and craftsmen's quarter of Athens, was dedicated to the divinities of the smiths and the arts, Hephaistos and Athena. It is one of the best preserved of surviving Greek temples, thanks to the conversion into a Christian church which saved it from destruction.

This Doric temple, with the classical ground-plan of 6×13 columns, was built about the same time as the Parthenon but is considerably smaller (columns 5·71 m (19 ft) high, Parthenon 10·43 m (34 ft)). In general it is more austere and conservative than the Parthenon, but has certain features (e.g. Ionic friezes instead of Doric triglyphs on the façades of the pronaos and opisthodomos) which appear to be modelled on the Parthenon. The explanation is that building began, probably under the direction of Kallikrates, before 449 B.C. but was suspended to allow concentration of effort on Perikles' great building programme on the Acropolis and resumed only during the Peace of Nikias (421–415 B.C.), after Perikles' death. This late date explains the more recent aspect of the E end, with the entrance to the temple. Here the portico, the *coffered ceiling of which is completely preserved, is three bays deep (compared with one and a half at the W end), and is tied in to the axis of the third columns; the pronaos frieze is carried across to the N and S peristyles; and the metopes have carved decoration, while elsewhere they are plain. All these are innovations which give greater emphasis to the E end, departing from the earlier principle of a balance between the two ends.

The damaged *pronaos frieze* depicts battle scenes, the *W frieze* fighting between Lapiths and centaurs (in the middle the invulnerable Lapith Kaineus being driven into the ground by centaurs). In spite of its small size the cella had columns round three sides framing the cult images of Hephaistos and Athena by Alkamenes which were set up in the temple about 420 B.C.; again an imitation of the Parthenon. The cella walls were roughened and covered with paintings.

When the temple was converted into a Christian church dedicated to St George in the 5th c. it became necessary to construct a chancel at the E end in place of the previous entrance. A new entrance (still preserved) was therefore broken through the W wall of the cella, and the old E entrance wall was removed, along with the two columns of the pronaos, and replaced by an apse. At the same time the

Reliefs on the Tower of the Winds, Roman Market

timber roof normal in Greek temples was replaced by the barrel vaulting which still survives. When King Otto entered the new capital of Greece in 1834 a solemn service was held in St George's Church (depicted in a picture by Peter von Hess in the Neue Pinakothek, Munich). Thereafter it became a museum and continued to serve this purpose into the present century.

The Roman Market and Hadrian's Library

Between the Stoa of Attalos and the Library of Pantainos is the beginning of an ancient road leading to the **Roman Market**. While the Greek Agora grew and developed over the centuries, this later market was laid out on a unified plan within a rectangular area measuring 112 by 96 m (367 by 315 ft). It has two gates: at the W end a *Doric gateway* built between 12 B.C. and A.D. 2 and at the E end an *Ionic propylon* probably dating from the reign of Hadrian in the 2nd c. A.D. It was surrounded by *colonnades*, off which opened shops and offices, and on the S side was a *fountain*. During the Turkish period a **mosque**, the Fetiye Camii, was built on the N side of the market; this now serves as an archaeological store.

The entrance to the Roman Market is at the E end, near the **Tower of the Winds**. This octagonal structure, 12 m (39 ft) high, was built about 40 B.C. and housed a water-clock. It owes its present name to the carved representations of the eight wind gods below the cornice. Under these figures are *sundials*. – To the S is a building with the remains of arches, the function of which is not known (offices of the market police? Caesareum?). At the entrance to this excavation area is a marble *latrine* with almost 70 seats (1st c. A.D.).

Parallel to the Roman Market, only 16 m (52 ft) away, is another complex of similar character but different function – **Hadrian's Library**, founded by the emperor of that name in A.D. 132. This was a colonnaded court measuring 122 by 82 m (400 by 269 ft), with exedrae (semicircular recesses) in the external walls. Part of the W end, with Corinthian columns and a propylon of four columns, has been preserved. The present entrance, however, is at the E end (Eolou Street). The central room in the E range of buildings, much of which is still standing, was a library, with niches for bookshelves. The rest of the building probably served similar purposes; the courtyard was laid out as a garden, with a central pool.

The columns and other architectural elements now to be seen in the courtyard came from the 5th c. *Megáli Panayía church*.

Kerameikos – the Cemetery on the Eridanos

Bordering the Agora on the NW was the POTTERS' QUARTER of ancient Athens, extending W to the Academy. Known as Kerameikos – after Keramos, the patron of potters – this area where the Attic potters produced their magnificent work has, appropriately, given its name to the art and craft of ceramics. After 479 B.C., when Themistokles enclosed the city within walls following the Persian invasion, part of the area lay within the walls and part outside them.

Only part of the old Kerameikos quarter has been excavated – the area lying in the angle between Ermoú and Pireos Streets, beside the Ayía Triáda church. In this area there were two gates: the Sacred Gate by the Eridanos, through which the Sacred Way passed on its way to Eleusis, with a road to Piraeus branching off on the left within the excavated area; and the larger *Dipylon* (Double Gate), starting-point of the ancient road, 39 m (128 ft) wide, which ran 1·5 km (1 mile) NW to the Academy.

From the 11th c. onwards this area, on both sides of the Eridanos, was used for burial, and a continuous sequence of tombs can be traced from the sub-Mycenaean period to late antiquity. The monumental funerary amphoras ("Dipylon vases") of the 8th c. B.C., the starting-point from which we can follow the development of Attic art, are now in the National Archaeological Museum, and the remains now visible on the site are predominantly of the 5th and 4th c. B.C.

Within the excavated area are many different types of tomb, either the originals or copies – individual tombs, family burial plots or funerary precincts, terraces of tombs. This is the most thoroughly excavated of all Athenian cemeteries – by Greek archaeologists from 1863, by German archaeologists from 1907. Still little affected by mass tourism, it is quiet and full of atmosphere.

The entrance is in Hermes Street (Ermoú), beside the *Museum, which displays the more recent finds. Of particular interest is the large collection of *pottery*, which allows the visitor to follow the history of the area and the development of Greek pottery. The first room contains sculpture from tombs. Immediately on the right is the *stele of Ampharete*, showing the dead woman with her infant grandchild (*c.* 410 B.C.), and opposite this is an *equestrian relief* of Dexilos, killed in a skirmish at Corinth in 394 B.C. Other items of interest are the archaic *stele of Eupheros* (*c.* 500 B.C.), a *sphinx* as a tomb guardian, an *equestrian statue* and *statue bases* with carved decoration (procession of horsemen, wild boar fighting a lion).

Going N from the museum on an ancient road, we pass on the left the *tomb of two sisters, Demetria and Pamphile* (*c.* 350 B.C.) and come to the **Street of Tombs**, which led to Piraeus; the tombs are of the 5th and 4th c. (those of the 4th c. being more numerous). Turning left (W) along this road, we pass the equestrian monument of Dexileos (original in the museum), the *tomb of Agathon and Sosikrates* of Herakleia in Pontos (with three stelae), the *tomb of*

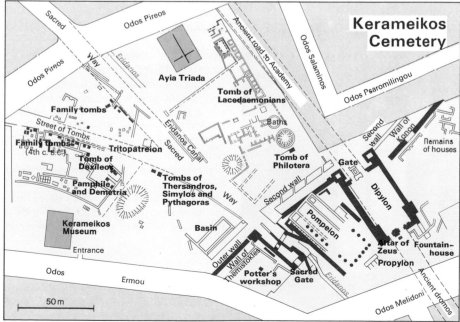

Kerameikos Cemetery

Dionysios of Kollytos, topped by a bull, and the *burial plot of Archon Lysimachides* of Acharnai, built of polygonal blocks, guarded by a Molossian hound and decorated with reliefs (Charon, a funeral meal). Beyond this is a crudely constructed *altar* belonging to the cult precinct of Hekate. – If we now return along the same road we see on the left two interesting family burial plots – first that belonging to the family of Eubios (stele of Bion) and then that of the family of Koroibos, with the *funerary stele* in the middle, a *relief of Hegeso* (*c.* 410 B.C.: cast) on the left and a *loutrophoros* (a large water jar for the bridal bath, set over the tomb of a person who died unmarried) on the right. Then, in front of the small trapezoid *sanctuary of the Tritopatreis* (ancestor gods), with inscribed boundary stones at the NE and SE corners, is a large round *tumulus* of the mid 6th c., constructed for one of the great families of that period, perhaps that of Solon. Beyond this, on the right, we see the simple tombs of ambassadors from Korkyra (*c.* 375 B.C.) and Pythagoras of Selymbria (*c.* 450 B.C.).

Here the Street of Tombs meets the **Sacred Way** to Eleusis. Along this road to the left (away from the city) are the *tombs of Antidosis and Aristomache* and beyond this the very handsome *loutrophoros of Olympichos*. In the other direction, towards the city, the Sacred Way runs alongside the Eridanos to the Sacred Gate in the town walls, which were built in great haste by Themistokles in 479 B.C., using stones from numerous earlier tombs, and reinforced in the 4th c. by the construction of an outer wall and a ditch. Turning left along the walls, we come to the **Dipylon**, which consists of *two towers* at the outer end, a rectangular *court* flanked by parallel walls and a *double gate* at the SE (inner) end. Immediately inside the gate are an *altar* dedicated to Zeus, Hermes and Akamas and a *fountain-house*.

On either side of the Dipylon, set against the town walls, are boundary-stones (*horoi*) marking the width (39 m – 128 ft) of the road to the Academy, which begins here. Along this road men who had fallen in war were buried in common graves, which were regarded with special honour. It was on one such occasion, at the beginning of the Peloponnesian War (431 B.C.) that Perikles gave the famous funeral

oration recorded by Thucydides. One such tomb has been excavated – the *state tomb of the Lacedaemonians* (i.e. the Spartan officers who died in 403 B.C. fighting the Thirty Tyrants of Athens), on the S side of the road at the second boundary-stone. Just at the edge of the excavated area are the remains of another tomb (anonymous). Pausanias refers to other tombs of special honour on the road to the Academy, including that of Harmodios and Aristogeiton, murderers of the tyrant Hipparchos.

Between the walls, the Sacred Gate and the Dipylon is the **Pompeion**, named after the procession (*pompē*) to the Acropolis which formed up here during the Panathenaic festival. There are remains of two buildings, one overlying the other. The earlier one, dating from about 400 B.C., consisted of a court surrounded by columns (6×13): i.e. it was a *gymnasion*. Objects used in the Panathenaic festival were found here. Wheel-ruts in the propylon show that the court was entered by wheeled vehicles. The rooms on the N side, which have preserved some remains of pebble mosaic paving, were probably the scene of the ceremonial banquet at the end of the Panathenaic festival; and Hoepfner suggests that the Panathenaic vases which were the prizes for victors in the contests may have been presented here.

This earlier building was destroyed by Sulla in 86 B.C., and much later, in the 2nd c. A.D., was replaced by a three-aisled hall, which in turn was destroyed by the Herulians in A.D. 267. The plans of both buildings can be seen most clearly from outside the site in Melidoni Street (turn left along Ermoú when leaving the site and then immediately left again).

On the way out it is well worth while looking at the collection of modest little *funerary colonnettes* (kioniskoi) which have been brought together in the pine-grove beside the museum. These simple monuments were erected after a sumptuary law of 317 B.C. banning the lavish tombs produced by the funerary art which had developed over the course of 400 years.

The broad road from the Dipylon led to the **Academy**, 1·5 km (1 mile) away, the meeting-place from 387 B.C. of Plato and his pupils, the first institution of its kind in the world. Excavations in Kimon Street, beyond the railway line, have yielded valuable results. Among the buildings found were a square *hall* (between Euclid and Tripolis Streets) and immediately N of this a small *temple*, possibly dedicated to the hero Akademos. There is also a large building laid out round an inner courtyard dating from the Imperial period. Of particular interest is a building measuring 8·50 by 4·50 m (28 by 15 ft) (now covered with a protective roof) which dates from the early Bronze Age (2300–2100 B.C.) – the oldest building so far discovered in Athens.

From the Academy site Tripolis Street (Tripóleos) runs NW to the **Kolonos Hippios**, the hill which gave its name to the deme of Kolonos, the home district of

Tomb of Dionysios of Kollytos, Kerameikos

The Olympieion

Sophocles (*c*. 496–406 B.C.). This was the setting of "Oedipus on Kolonos", written when Sophocles was 90. The hill now lies in a rather poor district of the city. On it are the tombs of two archaeologists, Carl Otfried Müller (1797–1840) and François Lenormant (1837–83).

The Olympieion and Surrounding Area

When Syngros Street (Odós Sýngrou), the road from Piraeus and Fáliron, was constructed during the 19th c. it was aligned on two massive columns belonging to the *Olympieion, which still dominates the area E of the Acropolis.

A temple to the supreme god of the Greek pantheon, who had previously been worshipped in the open air, was built on this site by Peisistratos at some time before 550 B.C. – a hundred years before the erection of the Temple of Zeus at Olympia. It measured 30 by 60 m (98 by 197 ft) – rather smaller than the later Parthenon. Peisistratos' sons Hippias and Hipparchos resolved to replace it by a gigantic temple with a double colonnade (*dipteros*) measuring 41 by 107·75 m (135 by 354 ft), comparable with the temple built by Polykrates on the island of Samos. Work on this building, which was to have 8×21 columns, was suspended after the expulsion of Hippias in 510 B.C., and it lay unfinished for almost 350 years until about 175 B.C., when the Syrian king Antiochos IV commissioned a Roman architect, Cossutius, to complete it. The new temple was designed to have a double colonnade of 8×20 Corinthian columns, 17 m (56 ft) high, of Pentelic marble; but this temple too remained unfinished, and it was not completed for another 300 years, until about A.D. 130, when Hadrian had it finished in accordance with Cossutius' plan. Its building had thus taken altogether 700 years.

Reflecting the tastes of the period of the tyrants, a Syrian king and a Roman emperor, this temple of Olympian Zeus was alien to the Attic sense of measure, and has always been overshadowed by the Parthenon, although its architectural qualities merit more attention than they have received. The cella, which contained

a statue of Hadrian as well as the cult image of Zeus, has disappeared, as have most of the 104 columns, to the making of which went no less than 15,500 tons of marble. The surviving remains, however – the group of 13 columns, with part of the entablature, at the SE corner, two isolated columns on the S side and another column which collapsed in 1852 – are still of imposing grandeur. It is not certain whether the 13 SE columns belong to the Hellenistic building and the three on the S side to the Roman one, or whether they are all of Roman date.

The entrance to the site is in Leofóros Ólgas. Near the entrance, in the old defensive ditch of Athens, are a number of *column drums* from the temple of the Peisistratid period. Farther W are the remains of *Roman baths* and other buildings. Through the partly reconstructed *propylon* we enter the large rectangular *temenos* in which the temple stands. From the S wall of the temenos we look down into an excavated area on a lower level in which, among other structures, the foundations of the Temple of Apollo Delphinios and the large rectangle of the Panhellenion can be distinguished. They are among the many temples and shrines on the banks of the Ilissos, which flows through this area; others include the Temple of Aphrodite in the gardens on the right bank of the stream, the Metroon and the shrine of Artemis Agrotera on the left bank. In Christian times a **basilica** was built here by the spring of *Kallirhoe*.

To the W of the Olympieion enclosure, on the edge of the very busy Leofóros Amalías, stands the **Arch of Hadrian** (A.D. 131–132), which marks the boundary between the ancient city of Athens and the Roman extension of the city – between the "city of Theseus" and the "city of Hadrian", as an inscription on the arch records.

Immediately opposite is Lysikrates Street, at the far end of which is the **Monument of Lysikrates**, a rotunda 6·50 m (21 ft) high surrounded by Corinthian columns. The *frieze* round the top depicts scenes from the life of Dionysos (the transformation of the pirates, who captured

The Stadion – a bird's eye view

Dionysos, into dolphins). The stone acanthus flower on the roof originally bore a bronze tripod and cauldron, the prize received by Lysikrates when the choir he had financed as choregos was victorious in the tragedy competition in 334 B.C. Later incorporated in a Capuchin convent and used as a library – when it was known as the "Lantern of Diogenes" – this is the only surviving example of the numerous choregic monuments in the ancient Street of the Tripods. Other choregic monuments in Athens are the Monument of Nikias between the Theatre of Dionysos and the Stoa of Eumenes and the Monument of Thrasyllos above the Theatre of Dionysos.

Schliemann's house in Athens

NE of the Olympieion, between two hills, is the *Stadion. Although this large marble structure, with seating for 70,000 spectators, is modern it has the same form and occupies the same site as its ancient predecessor, in which the Panathenaic games were held. It was provided with new marble seating in A.D. 140–144 by Herodes Atticus, whose tomb was on the hill to the N.

Herodes Atticus, who was born in Marathón in A.D. 101 and died there in 177, was one of the great art patrons of antiquity, who rose to high office under Hadrian and Antoninus Pius, becoming archon, chief priest, consul and tutor to future emperors, though later he was charged with various offences in the Imperial court. He had a great reputation as a rhetor, but his writings did not outlive his own day. He was famous for his munificence, financing the Stadion and the Odeon named after him in Athens, the renovation of the Stadion at Delphi, the provision of a water supply and the building of a nymphaeum at Delphi and the renovation of the spring of Peirene at Corinth.

When the Stadion was rebuilt for the first Olympic Games of modern times in 1896 it was financed, as in the days of Herodes Atticus, by a wealthy private citizen, Yeoryios Averof, who thus – like other

modern Greeks, particularly those who have made their money abroad – continued the ancient tradition of the *euergetes* ("benefactor").

Modern Athens

The modern city of Athens dates from the reign of King Otto I (1834–62), a scion of the Bavarian house of Wittelsbach. The plan which was to convert a sleepy little town into the new capital of Greece was the work of a number of Germans, two Danes, a Frenchman and a Greek. The general lines of the new town to be built N of the old city were laid down by a German from Breslau, Schaubart, and his Greek friend Kleanthes in 1832–33, while the Greek government was still based at Náfplion.

From **Omónia Square** (Platía Omonías, Square of Concord), originally conceived as the site of the royal palace, three streets fan out towards the S – Athena Street (Athínas), which runs due S to Monastiráki Square, with a vista of the Acropolis; Piraeus Street (Pireós), to the SW; and Stadion Street (Stadíou) to the SE, with Venizelos Street or University Street (Venizélou, Panepistimíou) running parallel to it.

Along the foot of the triangle formed by Athena and Stadion streets runs Hermes Street (Ermoú), laid out by Leo von Klenze in 1834. During the construction of this street the Kapnikaréa church was preserved from demolition by the intervention of the king and his father King Ludwig I of Bavaria. At its E end, where it meets Stadion Street, Hermes Street runs into another large square, known since

Omónia Square from the air

the 1843 revolution as **Sýntagma** (Platía Syntágmatos, Constitution Square). On the higher E side of the square, which is now surrounded by hotels, airline offices, etc., stands the former royal palace (by Friedrich von Gärtner, 1834–38), now the **Parliament Building**, with the *Tomb of the Unknown Soldier*, guarded by evzones, in front of it.

To the S and E of the palace Queen Amalia laid out the Royal Gardens, now known as the **National Garden**, in an area of former wasteland. One of the city's relatively few open spaces, this is now a popular place of recreation and relaxation. Adjoining it on the S, in the direction of the Olympieion, is the **Zappion Park**, with the Zappion, an exhibition hall designed by Ernst Ziller and built at the expense of the Zappas brothers.

A general impression of the modern city and of the efforts made in the reigns of Otto I and George I to dignify the new capital with imposing neo-classical architecture can be gained by walking along Venizelos Street (University Street) from Sýntagma Square. On the right, fronted by loggias, is the *Iliou Mélathron*, built by Ernst Ziller as a residence for Heinrich Schliemann and his Greek wife Sophia and now occupied by the Supreme Court (Areios Pagos). Then follow the Byzantine-style *Ophthalmic Clinic* and Leo von Klenze's *church of St Dionysius* (Roman Catholic: King Otto did not adopt the Orthodox faith). A dominant position, farther along the street, is occupied by the **University** (by the Danish architect Christian Hansen; begun 1837), flanked by two grandiose buildings by Hansen's younger brother Theophil, the *Academy of Art* (1859–85) on the right and the *National Library* (begun 1887) on the left. In front of the academy are two columns bearing statues of Athena and Apollo, and the steps leading up to the building are flanked by seated figures of Plato and Socrates. In front of the university are statues of Kapodistrias, who as Governor of Greece (1827–31) had proclaimed the establishment of the university, and the writer and scholar Adamantios Korais; King Otto, who initiated the building of the university, appears in a painting above the entrance, surrounded by the Muses. – The rest of Venizelos Street is made up of modern shops and offices, with occasional remnants of the two-storey neo-classical

buildings of the 19th c. It ends in Omónia Square, a busy traffic intersection with an elaborate fountain in the centre. Under the square is a station on the Athens Underground.

Returning along Stadion Street (Stadíou), we come, half way along – just down from the university – to *Klafthmon Square* (Platía Kláfthmonos), at the NW corner of which is the *Church of SS. Theodore*. The next prominent building is the *Old Parliament* (by the French architect Boulanger, 1871), now occupied by the National Historical Museum. In front of it stands an equestrian statue of *Theodóros Kolokotrónis*, the great fighter for the freedom of Greece. Venizelos Street then runs into Sýntagma Square.

For another walk starting from Sýntagma we go along Leofóros Vasílissis Sofías, to the left of the Parliament Building, and continue to the end of the National Garden. Here we can either turn right along Herodes Atticus Street (Iródou tou Attikoú), passing on the left the former *Crown Prince's Palace* (by Ziller, 1890–98), later the royal palace, or turn left to reach *Kolonáki Square* and from there climb to the top of **Lykabettós** (277 m – 909 ft), which can also be reached by funicular from the end of Plutarch Street (Ploutárkhou). On top of the hill are a *chapel* dedicated to St George and a restaurant (view).

Monastiráki Square

Those who want to see something of the busy shops and markets of Athens should walk S from Omónia Square along Athena Street (Athínas) and its side streets to Monastiráki Square, at the junction with Hermes Street (Ermoú). Here Hephaistos Street (Iféstou) goes off to the right and Pandrosos Street (Pandrósou) to the left, lined with shops of every kind and bustling with activity. In Monastiráki

Square is the former *Syntrivani Mosque*, and behind it can be seen the pillared front of **Hadrian's Library**.

This is the beginning of the **PLAKA**, the old district lying between the N side of the Acropolis and Hermes Street and extending eastward almost to Leofóros Amalías. In the narrow lanes and little squares of the Plaka, visitors will encounter a number of small churches and modest houses in neo-classical style; but, like the old tavernas, they are steadily becoming rarer as the district is increasingly taken over by the showier and noisier establishments which cater for the tourist trade.

The Churches of Athens

In the Christian period Athens was, politically and culturally, an unimportant provincial town within the Byzantine Empire. The buildings of this period, therefore, cannot compare with those to be seen in the capital, Constantinople, or the Empire's second largest city, Salonica. Nevertheless they are of considerable interest.

In the 5th and 6th c. the Parthenon was converted into the church of the *Panayía Athiniótissa* (remains of painting on outer wall of opisthodomos) and the Temple of Hephaistos into the church of St George, and the *Megáli Panayía* (Great Church). Finds from other buildings of this period are preserved in the Byzantine Museum. The surviving churches mostly date from the Middle Byzantine period (10th–12th c.) and are predominantly of the domed cruciform type. The ground-plan is in the form of a Greek cross with four arms of equal length, and the church has a central dome (and sometimes smaller subsidiary domes over the arms).

Going S from Sýntagma Square along Leofóros Amalías, we pass in the third street on the right the *church of St Nicodemus* (1045), which has been a Russian Orthodox church since 1852, when the church (which had been damaged during the wars of liberation) was purchased by the Tsar of Russia. The paintings in the interior, by Ludwig Thiersch, date from the subsequent restoration. – Farther along Leofóros Amalías is the neo-Gothic *St Paul's Church* (Church of England), designed by Kleanthes in the mid 19th c.

A short distance SW, in Kidathinéon Street, is the 13th c. *church of Sotíra Kottáki*, originally a domed cruciform church, later altered into a basilica. Turning left into Farmáki Street, we come to *St Catherine's Church* (Ayía Ekateríni), situated in a spacious palm-shaded courtyard behind the remains of a colonnade of the Roman Imperial period. Although later enlarged, the church preserves its 13th c. dome and apses. Close by is the Monument of Lysikrates. Going N from this along Tripods Street (Tripódon) and then turning left up Epikhármou, we come to *Áyios Nikólaos Rangavá*, built in the 11th c. within the precincts of the palace of the important Rangava family and later altered. Continuing along Tripods Street and then by way of Erotokrítou into Erechtheus Street (Erekhtheos), a stepped lane, we reach the beautiful domed cruciform church of *Áyios Ioánnis Theológos* (13th c.), restored some years ago. At the top of the steps on the right is the entrance to a complex belonging to the monastery of the Holy Sepulchre in Jerusalem, in which is the *church of the Anárgyri*, with a 17th c. Baroque interior. Higher up the hill is a settlement of immigrants from the island of Anáfi (Anafiotiká), with the little *church of St Simeon* (1847). To the W of this is the *church of the Metamórfosis*, a small domed cruciform church (14th c.), with an altar made out of an Early Christian capital. Going downhill from here past the Tower of the Winds to the E entrance of Hadrian's Library, we can see the remains of the 5th c. *Megáli Ekklisía*. From here Pandrosos Street, to the left, leads to Monastiráki Square, in which, on a lower level, is the *Pantánassa church*, of basilican type. Going W from here along Hephaistos Street (Iféstou) and turning into the second little street on the left, we pass the *church of St Philip* and come to the entrance to the Agora, near which is

Kapnikaréa church

the 11th c. *church of the Holy Apostles*. Returning to Hermes Street and going W, we come to the recently restored 11th c. *church of the Áyii Asómati* (Ayii Asomati=Incorporeal Spirits, i.e. angels). From here Sarri Street runs NE towards Euripides Street (Evripídou), in which is the tiny *chapel of Áyios Ioánnis Kolóna*, named after a Roman column which rises above its roof; the assistance of St John the Baptist is invoked here for the cure of ailments affecting the head. At the E end of Euripides Street is Klafthmon Square, in which stands the *church of the Áyii Theódori* (SS. Theodore), a handsome 11th c. church built of stone and brick, with a belfry.

Going S from here by way of Márkou and Kalamióti streets, we come back to Hermes Street, just at the *Kapnikaréa church*. This 11th c. domed cruciform church, a very fine example of the type, was later enlarged by the addition of a porch and a chapel on the N side. The paintings cover the complete icono-graphic programme as developed in the Middle Byzantine period. – A short distance SE is Mitrópolis Square, in which are the old and new **Mitrópolis churches**. The *New Mitrópolis* (1842–62) was designed by Schaubert, with the needs of the court and the capital in mind. In the crypt (entrance to the left of the doorway) are the remains of Patriarch Gregory V, who was hanged in Constantinople by the Turks (1821) and is honoured as a neomartyr. The *Little Mitrópolis, dedicated to the Panayia Gorgoepíkoos and Áyios Eleftherios, is a 12th c. building of the greatest interest. The builder incorporated in the structure a variety of ancient and medieval fragments of architectural ornament and sculpture, including two parts of an ancient calendar frieze (arranged in the wrong order) above the entrance, pilaster capitals, pediments from funerary aediculae, figural reliefs, etc. – all of the most charming effect. – From here we return to Sýntagma Square along Mitrópolis Street (Mitropóleos), passing on the right the tiny church of *Ayía Dýnamis*, carefully preserved under the corner of a large modern office block which has been built over it.

It is well worth taking a trip through the suburb of Kaisariani to the *monastery of Kaisarianí*, situated in a valley on the reafforested slopes of Mt Hymettós. – The name comes from a spring close to a shrine of Aphrodite from which the Emperor Hadrian caused an aqueduct to be built to Athens: thereafter the spring was known as *kaisariane*, Imperial. It was (and is) credited with healing powers, particularly for women who desire to bear a child. The water of the spring still flows from an archaic ram's head in the courtyard of the monastery.

During the Turkish period the monastery was renowned for its library and for a number of learned abbots. Among the students of the seminary which flourished here for many years – one of the few in existence during that period – was the future Patriarch Gregory V, martyred in 1821. The last abbot died in 1855, and thereafter the monastery was abandoned and fell into decay. At last, in 1952, it was carefully restored at private expense. This restoration, combined with the reafforestation of the surrounding area, has made Kaisarianí one of the most attractive spots in the neighbourhood of Athens – an ancient monastery set among trees, a spring of clear water and an antique column from a temple of Aphrodite set in a shady courtyard, all combining to make a haven of peace, a place for contemplation and repose.

The monastery church is of the domed cruciform type. It was erected around 1000 on the site of an earlier church, and is therefore rather older than the buildings of this type in Athens itself. The dome is borne not on the walls but on four columns with Ionic capitals, giving the interior an air of lightness. A templon formed of marble screens separates the chancel (*bema*) from the rest of the church. The painting is much later than the church, having been done in the 16th c., during the Turkish period, probably by a monk from Athos. It is in strict accordance with the rules for the hierarchical disposition of the various themes – Christ Pantokrator in the dome, with the Prophets below him and the four Evangelists in the pendentives; the Mother of God enthroned in the apse, with angels, the Communion of the Apostles and the Fathers of the Church below her; and on the barrel vaulting of the arms of the cross the various church festivals. In the porch is a fine representation of the Trinity. The porch, like the S chapel dedicated to St Antony, was added in the late 17th c., as was the bell-cote.

There are considerable remains of the conventual buildings. Entering by the main entrance, to the E, we see on the left a building which was originally a bath-house and later housed oil-presses. Beyond this, set back a little, are a two-storeyed range of cells and a tower house belonging to the Venizelos family of Athens, who were great benefactors of the monastery. In the right-hand corner are the kitchen and refectory, now housing a small museum.

On the hills outside the W gateway of the monastery (20 minutes' walk) are other *remains of churches* dating back to the 6th c., beside the *monks' cemetery*. From here too there are wide views of Athens and the sea, with Kaisarianí lying below in its peace and seclusion.

After visiting the ancient tombs of Athens in the Kerameikos some visitors may be interested in seeing a more recent cemetery, the principal **Cemetery of Athens**. It is reached by going up the Odos Anapáfseos (Street of Repose), which branches off Ardettos Street (Ardítou), a major traffic artery to the S of the

Olympieion. Beside a chapel to the left of the entrance are the *graves of archbishops of Athens*, and beyond these the elaborate *tomb of Yeoryios Averof*, who financed the building of the Stadion. Higher up the slope is the temple-like *mausoleum of Schliemann* (designed by Ziller), and near this the *tomb of Kanaris*. On the left of the central avenue which leads down to the second church is the *tomb of Kolokotronis*. Apart from such individual tombs this beautifully laid-out cemetery is highly informative on Greek attitudes to death and burial in the 19th and early 20th c.

The Museums of Athens

Acropolis Museum: see p. 76.

Agora Museum: see p. 85.

The **Benáki Museum**, in Leofóros Vasílissis Sofías, grew out of the private collection assembled by Antonios Benakis. On its three floors it displays material illustrating the Greek struggle for liberation (1821), relics and mementoes of kings Otto I and George I, Byron and various heroes of the wars of liberation, manuscripts, icons (including two ascribed to the young El Greco), costumes from the different parts of Greece, ancient pottery and Islamic and East Asian material.

The *Byzantine Museum, also in Leofóros Vasílissis Sofías, is housed in a palace built for the duchesse de Plaisance by Kleanthes in 1840, on a site which was then in open country. It contains a valuable collection of Byzantine art from Greece and Asia Minor.

In the *courtyard* are *architectural fragments* from Early Christian basilicas and Byzantine churches (5th–15th c.) and a reproduction of a fountain depicted in a mosaic at Dafní. – The *left-hand wing* contains a large collection of *icons, arranged partly in chronological order and partly according to iconographic types. – The *right-hand wing* supplements this survey of the art of icon-painting.

MAIN BUILDING. – The rooms on the *ground floor* illustrate the development of the church interior. *Room 1* contains a scaled-down *reconstruction of an Early Christian basilica* (5th–6th c.), showing the templon which separates the chancel (bema), with the altar and the seats of the priests (synthronon), from the rest of the church. The pulpit is copied from the one in Áyios Minás in Salonica. In *Room 3* is a typical *Middle Byzantine domed cruciform church* (10th–11th c.), with a sculptured *eagle* on the floor, marking the omphalos (navel). *Room 4* shows a

post-Byzantine church with a carved and gilded *iconostasis* (17th–18th c.) and a *bishop's throne* from Asia Minor (18th c.). There are also some individual works of great interest, among them sculptured representations of the *Good Shepherd* (No. 92), in which the old type of the lamb-carrier, as seen in the Acropolis Museum, is applied to Christ, and *Orpheus* (No. 93), and also (*Room 2*) some rare *Byzantine reliefs*. – On the *upper floor* large numbers of icons are displayed, including a fine *mosaic icon* of the Mother of God Episkepsis (No. 145: 14th c.), together with Gospel books, historical documents (e.g. a *chrysobull* of the Emperor Andronikos II dated 1301: Room 1), *gold jewelery* from Lésbos (Room 2) and *liturgical vestments and utensils*, particularly notable among these being an *epitaphios* from Salonica (an embroidered cloth used in the representation of the Holy Sepulchre on Good Friday: 14th c.) in Room 4.

The **Folk Art Museum** at Kidathinéon 17 gives some impression of the richness, variety and distinctive characteristics of Greek folk art, the inheritor of Byzantine traditions, and will appeal particularly to those interested in embroidery, woodcarving, folk painting, etc.

The **Kanellópoulos Collection** was presented to the State in 1972 by Pavlos and Alexandra Kanellópoulos and opened as a museum in a neo-classical house on the upper edge of the Plaka (corner of

National Archaeological Museum

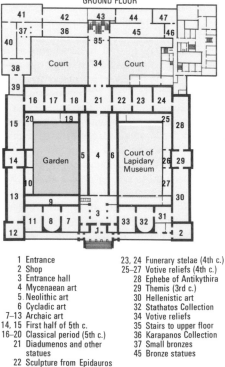

GROUND FLOOR

1	Entrance	23, 24	Funerary stelae (4th c.)
2	Shop	25–27	Votive reliefs (4th c.)
3	Entrance hall	28	Ephebe of Antikythira
4	Mycenaean art	29	Themis (3rd c.)
5	Neolithic art	30	Hellenistic art
6	Cycladic art	32	Stathatos Collection
7–13	Archaic art	34	Votive reliefs
14, 15	First half of 5th c.	35	Stairs to upper floor
16–20	Classical period (5th c.)	36	Karapanos Collection
21	Diadumenos and other statues	37	Small bronzes
22	Sculpture from Epidauros	45	Bronze statues

Rooms not listed are not at present open to the public

Theorías and Pánou) in 1976. The exhibits (sculpture, pottery, icons) range in date from prehistoric times to the 19th c.

Kerameikos Museum: see p. 89.

The richly stocked **National Archaeological Museum** in Patission Street, built by Ludwig Lange in 1860 and considerably enlarged since then, is the finest collection of Greek art in the world. It would take repeated visits to get anything approaching a complete idea of its full range and richness: here we can do no more than refer to a selection of the outstanding exhibits.

The entrance hall (sale of tickets, slides, books) leads straight into the *Mycenaean Hall* (Room 4), with material excavated by Heinrich Schliemann and others at Mycenae and other Mycenaean sites, illustrating the richness of the Mycenaean culture which combined the nobility and monumentality of Achaean Greek art with the refinement of Minoan Crete (1600–1150 B.C.).

The exhibits are not arranged chronologically but according to sites or types of material. The front part of the hall is occupied by material from Mycenae itself, including the famous *gold mask of a king from Shaft Grave V (253: c. 1580 B.C.), together with gold cups, vases, carved ivories, richly decorated daggers, boar's-tusk helmets*, the *"Warrior Vase"* (1426: c. 1200 B.C.) and two *pillars* from the entrance to the "Treasury of Atreus". – Particularly notable items in the rear part of the hall are the two famous *gold cups* (1758 and 1759) from Vaphió, S of Sparta, which date from the 15th c. B.C.

To the left is the *Neolithic Hall* (Room 5), with material from the Greek mainland, including objects from Dímini (4th millennium B.C.), Sésklo (3rd millennium B.C.) and Orchomenós (3rd–2nd millennium B.C.). – To the right is the *Cycladic Hall* (Room 6), with material of the 3rd and 2nd millennia B.C. from the Cyclades. Characteristic of the highly developed art of this insular culture are the *"Cycladic idols"*, the *"Cycladic frying-pans"*, the *Harp-Player* (3908) and the *flying-fish frescoes* from Fylakopí on the island of Melos (5844: 16th c. B.C.).

Returning to the entrance hall, we continue clockwise through the chronologically arranged collections, beginning with the Geometric period (9th–8th c. B.C.) and continuing through the Archaic (7th–6th c.) and Classical (5th–4th c.) to the Hellenistic (3rd–1st c.) and Roman periods.

Room 7. In the centre is the *Dipylon Vase* from the Kerameikos cemetery, a monumental sepulchral vase in Geometric style with a representation of the lament for the dead, dating from the time of Homer (V804: c. 750 B.C.). On the right-hand wall is a flat, almost board-like, *relief* from the island of Delos, dedicated by Nikandre (1: c. 650 B.C.). Metopes from the Archaic Temple of Athena in Mycenae (2702, 2869, 2870, 4471: c. 620 B.C.).

Room 8 is dominated by two *kouroi* from Soúnion, some 3 m (10 ft) high (2720, 3645: 626–600 B.C.).

When Greek artists began to produce large sculpture around 600 B.C. they achieved monumental expression in over-life-size figures of naked youths (*kouroi*). Characteristic features of these figures are the rigidly frontal pose and the equal distribution of weight on both legs, with the left foot always in front of the right. Originally the hands were held close to the thighs, with clenched fists; later the arms hung free. – Also in this room are the *head and hand of a kouros* from Kerameikos (the "Dipylon Head", 3372: c. 600 B.C.).

Room 9 (to right) contains a *winged Nike* from Delos (21: c. 500 B.C.) and, to the right of this, a slim *kouros from Melos* (1558: c. 550 B.C.). Of particular interest is the excellently preserved *kore* holding a lotus flower in her left hand, with an inscription giving her name as Phrasikleia (4889). This figure was found by Mastrokostas in 1972 at Merénda near Markópoulo (Attica), along with the *kouros* (4890) in Room 10, adjoining. Stylistic comparisons suggest that the figure of Phrasikleia was carved about 530 B.C. by Aristion, a sculptor from Páros working in Attica who was also responsible for the *kouros of Anávyssos* in Room 13 (see below). In Andrew Stewart's view the kore of Merénda and the Theseus and Antiope group from Erétria (Khalkís Museum) are also by Aristion or his school.

Returning to Room 8, we pass into *Room 11*, which contains the *stele of Aristion*, by Aristokles (29: c. 510 B.C.), and a kouros from the island of Kéa (3686: c. 530 B.C.). In *Room 12*, to the left, are a *relief of a running hoplite* from Athens (1959: c. 510 B.C.) and heads from the first E pediment of the Temple of Aphaia on Aegina (c. 500 B.C.).

In *Room 13*, a long hall, are more kouroi, including a late Archaic figure with arms akimbo from the Ptoion (127: c. 510 B.C.) and the massive *kouros of Anávyssos* by Aristion of Páros (3851: 540–530 B.C.), with an inscription on the base: "Stop and weep at his grave for the dead Kroisos, destroyed by wrathful Ares while fighting among the warriors in the forefront of the battle."

In *Room 14* we move from Archaic to Classical art: *relief of Aphrodite* (?) from Melos (3990: 470–460 B.C.); *relief of a youth* with a garland (originally a metal attachment) from Soúnion (3344: c. 470 B.C.).

Room 15. – On left an *Eleusinian votive relief* depicting Demeter giving the first ear of corn to the boy Triptolemos, with her daughter Persephone or Kore (126: c. 440). In the centre of the room is an over-life-size *bronze statue* of a god (15161) found in the sea off Cape Artemision (northern Euboea), previously identified as Zeus but now generally recognised as representing Poseidon. The latest research indicates that it was made after the battle of Plataiai (479 B.C.) as an offering to the sanctuary of Poseidon on the Isthmus or to a sanctuary on Cape Artemision (Kleine).

Room 16 contains tomb monuments, including the large *marble lekythos* of Myrrhine (4485: c. 420 B.C.). In *Room 17* are a *votive relief* from Piraeus depicting Dionysos with actors (1500: c. 400 B.C.) and a *head of Hera* from the Argive Heraion. To the right of this room is the L-shaped *Room 19–20*, which contains a small Roman copy of Pheidias' Athena Parthenos, the *"Varvakion statuette"* (129: 2nd–3rd c. A.D.). From here we can enter one of the four inner courtyards of the museum.

Returning to Room 17, we continue into *Room 18*, with the most celebrated monument from Kerameikos, the *stele of Hegeso, with a relief of Hegeso and her maid (3624: *c.* 410 B.C.). *Room 21* contains the *Diadumenos*, a Roman marble copy of a lost bronze original by Polykleitos (1826: *c.* 440 B.C.), and the *Hermes of Andros*, a Roman copy of an original from the school of Praxiteles (218: 4th c. B.C.) – two works which exemplify the change from the vigorous but controlled physical representations of the 5th c. to the spiritualised approach of the 4th. Also in this room is the *boy rider*, who has recently been mounted on a bronze horse (15177: 2nd c. B.C.).

Room 22: sculpture from Epidauros. *Rooms 23 and 24*: funerary *stelae* of the 4th c. B.C., including the *Ilissos Stele*, perhaps by Skopas (578: *c.* 350 B.C.). An adjoining side room, *Room 25*, contains *statues* and *votive offerings* dedicated to Amynos and Asklepios.

Room 28 contains the *Ephebe of Antikythira*, an original work in bronze (Br 13396: 340 B.C.) of *Hygieia*, probably by Skopas (3602: *c.* 360 B.C.), and a *head of Asklepios* from the island of Amorgós (4th c. B.C.). – *Room 30*: a figure of Poseidon from Melos (235: 2nd c. B.C.) and *bronze heads* of a boxer from Olympia (Br 6439: *c.* 350 B.C.), a philosopher (Br 13400: 3rd c. B.C.) and a man from Delos (Br 14612: *c.* 100 B.C.). – *Room 32* contains the Helene Stathatos collection.

From Room 21 we pass between two columns to enter the next section of the museum. *Room 34* contains *votive offerings* to Pan and the Nymphs. To the left, at the foot of the staircase leading to the upper floor, are *Rooms 36 and 37*, which contain the **Karapanos Collection**, with numerous small bronzes of the Archaic and Classical periods, including a *horseman* from Dodona (16547: *c.* 550 B.C.), a *goddess with a dove* (Aphrodite or Dione) from the Pindos (460 B.C.), the famous *Zeus hurling a thunderbolt* from Dodóna (16546: 450 B.C.), an *Athena Promachos* from the Acropolis (6446: *c.* 500 B.C.) and a *head of Zeus* from Olympia (6440: *c.* 500

B.C.). In the adjoining *Room 41* are a number of large bronzes found by chance in Piraeus in 1959, including an *Apollo* (*c.* 510 B.C.) and an *Artemis* (4th c. B.C.), and the *Ephebe of Marathon*, probably by Praxiteles or his school, which was recovered from the sea in 1925 (*c.* 350 B.C.).

On the *upper floor* are three collections which are well worth seeing if time permits – the very comprehensive *collection of vases* (best seen with the aid of the guide by Varvara Philippaki which can be bought in the entrance hall); the sensational finds, including in particular *wall paintings* of about 1500 B.C., which have been made at Akrotíri on the island of Santorin since 1967; and *material from the Cyprus Museum* in Nikosia.

The **National Gallery**, opposite the Hilton Hotel, contains a collection of Greek painting of the 19th and 20th c., including works by Gisi, Volonkakis and Yakovidi.

The **National Historical Museum**, in the Old Parliament Building in Stadion Street (Stadíou), is devoted to the history of Greece in the 18th and 19th c. The main emphasis is on the period of the struggle for the liberation of Greece (1821). Among the relics of this period are *Byron's helmet and sword*.

SURROUNDINGS of Athens. – Popular places of resort, particularly in summer, are two suburbs of Athens which lie up in the hills and accordingly have a very agreeable climate – **Amaroússion** (alt. 230 m (755 ft)), which features in Henry Miller's "Colossus of Maroussi", and the even more attractive **Kifissiá** (alt. 267 m (876 ft); pop. 14,200). Other pleasant places to stay are the hills of **Párnis**, N of Athens, and **Pentélikon**, to the NE.

The monastery of Dionysíou, Athos

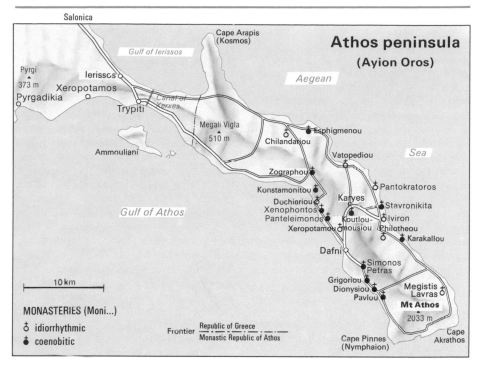

Athos/Ayion Oros

ΑΘΩΣ / ΑΓΙΟΝ ΟΡΟΣ

(Áthos/Áyion Óros)

Region. Chalcidice. – Autonomous monastic republic.
Area: 321 sq. km (124 sq. miles). – Population: 1700.

TRANSPORTATION. – Boats from Tripití and Ouranópolis to Dafní.

The Holy Mountain (Áyion Óros) of Athos, an autonomous region within Greece and for more than a thousand years a centre of Orthodox monasticism, is the most easterly of the three "fingers" of the Chalcidice peninsula. This "garden of the Mother of God", as it is known to the monks, is of great natural beauty, with its hilly landscape and great expanses of forest washed by the waters of the Aegean, and of extraordinary interest with its 20 great monasteries and its host of lesser monastic houses and hermitages scattered about the peninsula – a corner of Byzantium that has survived into modern times.

The first settlers on this finger of land up to 5 km (3 miles) wide which extends SE for some 45 km (28 miles) and rises to a height of 2033 m (6670 ft) in Mt Athos, were a few isolated hermits; then in A.D. 963

Athanasios, a monk from Trapezus (Trebizond), established, with the support of the Emperor Nikephoros Phokas, the first monastery, the Megísti Lávra, which is still the largest. This was followed by numerous other foundations, which were governed in accordance with a constitution (Typikon) laid down by the Emperor John Tsimisces (969–976). The pattern of monastic life was coenobitic (communal), with prayer in common, meals in common and an abbot elected for life to rule each monastery. With the mystical movement known as hesychasm (from *hesuchos*, "tranquil, quiet") which developed in the 14th c. a new form of monastic life known as idiorrhythmic emerged. Under this system, apart from prayers in common, each monk was left free to choose his own pattern ("rhythm") of life and to practise his own form of asceticism, each monastery being governed by three trustees with a restricted term of office. In time most of the monasteries adopted the idiorrhythmic pattern.

In recent years there has been a tendency to return to the coenobitic rule. At a recent count 12 of the 20 monasteries were coenobitic – Esphigménou, Stavronikíta and Karakalloú on the NE coast, Zográphou, Xenophontos, Koutloumousíou, Konstamonítou, Panteleímonos, Símonos Pétra, Grigoríou, Dionysíou and Pávlou on the SW coast. The other eight were idiorrhythmic – Chilandári, Vatopédi, Pantokrátoros, Ivíron, Philotheoú and the Megísti Lávra (Great Lavra) on the NE coast, Dochiaríou and Xeropotámou on the SW coast. In addition to the 20 great monasteries there are numerous lesser establishments – 12 *sketai*, some of them of considerable size, *kellia* occupied by "families" of three or more monks, smaller isolated houses and hermitages (found particularly on the steep S coast of the peninsula). Most of the monks are Greek, but even in the changed conditions of today the other Orthodox nations are also represented – Russians in Panteleímonos, Bulgarians in Zográphou, Yugoslavs in Chilandári. Although political circumstances have led to a decline in the Russian monastery there has been an influx of young monks into some of the other houses in recent years. The affairs of the monastic republic as a whole are managed by a Sacred Council (lera Epistasía) which meets in the village of Karyés, and is made up of representatives of each of the 20 monasteries who are appointed for a year at a time.

Athos is very different from the normal tourist area, and visitors must learn to fit in with the ways of this monastic republic. No women or "beardless boys" are admitted. Foreign visitors (who are limited to a quota of ten per day) should obtain a letter of recommendation from their embassy or consulate, which must then be taken to the Ministry of Foreign Affairs in Athens or the Ministry for Northern Greece in Salonica. There they will obtain an authorisation for presentation to the authorities on Athos. From the landing-stage at Dafní they travel by bus to **Karyés**, where they must first register with the police and then proceed to the Epistasía, where they receive the *diamonitirion*, the document which entitles them to receive hospitality (free of charge) in the monasteries. In each monastery there is a guest wing (*arkhondaríkion*), with a guest-master (*arkhondáris*) who is responsible for looking after visitors. The use of tape-recorders and ciné-cameras is prohibited, but cameras are permitted.

From Karyés the various monasteries can be visited on foot, or it may be possible to hire a mule or, from Karyés to Ivíron, get a lift on some form of motor transport. Depending on weather conditions, and on the rather irregular boat services, many of the monasteries can also be reached by sea. The mule-tracks and footpaths leading to the monasteries are of variable quality and frequently strenuous. The ascent of **Mt Athos** (2033 m (6670 ft): about 7 hours from the Great Lavra),

which is the scene of an annual procession to the *chapel of the Transfiguration* on the summit, is for experienced climbers only.

The monasteries are surrounded by massive walls, against which are built the monks' and guests' quarters and the tower housing the library. The principal church (Katholikón) stands in the middle of the courtyard, usually with the fountain (*fyáli*) and refectory (*trápeza*) in close proximity. Many of the churches and refectories contain fine wall paintings, and the libraries and treasuries of the monasteries hold many valuable books and precious objects. A visit to Athos, for those who approach it in the right spirit, will altogether be a memorable experience.

Attica
ATTIKH
(Attikí)

Attica, the most easterly region of central Greece, is bounded on the S and E by the sea, on the N by Boeotia and on the W by the ancient territory of Megaris. With an area of 3350 sq. km (1293 sq. miles), it is broken up by ranges of hills, between which lie four plains – the one around the city of Athens, the Thriasian plain around Eleusis to the W, the Mesóyia ("Central Plain") between Hymettós and the W coast and the plain of Marathón to the NE.

Attica has been settled by man since the Neolithic period, and it contains numerous fortified sites dating from pre-Greek and Mycenaean times. Tholos tombs have been found at Thorikós, Marathón and Meníndi, pointing to the existence of independent principalities which were abolished in Theseus' "synoecism" (see Athens, History, p. 68). Although sanctuaries like Eleusis with its mysteries and the Temple of Poseidon on Cape Soúnion maintained their importance throughout antiquity, Athens increasingly developed into the political, cultural and economic centre of Attica, helped by the proximity of the ideal natural harbour of Piraeus.

Cape Soúnion, the southernmost tip of Attica

Since Greece achieved its independence and Athens became its capital in 1834 a huge modern metropolis has spread far out over the central plain, and the olive-groves which once lay between Athens and Piraeus have long since disappeared. The plain of Eleusis has been disfigured by industrial installations, but the Marathón and Mesóyia plains have largely preserved their agricultural character. The coastal strips have been developed, and a whole string of seaside resorts has grown up between Athens and Soúnion – the **Attic Riviera** (see below) or "Coast of Apollo". The E coast to the S of Marathón has also become a popular holiday area (see p. 178).

Costumes of Attica

Attic Riviera

This is the name given to the stretch of *coast between Athens and Cape Soúnion, also known as the "Coast of Apollo". A number of important ancient sites have been found here – for example at Áyios Kósmas and Anaflystos, near Anávyssos – but in modern times the area was sparsely populated until the influx of refugees from Asia Minor after 1922 (the theme of Ilias Venesis's novel "Galini"). The S coast of Attica has been transformed by the development of mass tourism since the end of the last war, and a whole series of popular resorts have sprung up.

The resorts are listed below going S from Athens.

Pálaion Fáliron: *Coral*, B, 160 b.; *Edem*, B, 20 b.; *Posion*, B, 162 b.; *Avra*, C, 70 b.; *Ephi*, C, 35 b.; *Phryne*, C, 23 b. – **Kalamáki:** *Saronis*, A, 74 b.; *Albatros*, B, 152 b.; *Rex*, B, 53 b.; *Venus*, B, 54 b.; *Alkyon*, C, 26 b.; *Attica*, C, 62 b.; *Blue Sea*, C, 138 b.; *Galaxy*, C, 83 b.; *Hellinikon*, C, 96 b.; *Tropical*, C, 88 b. – **Ellinikó:** *Christina Maria*, C, 21 b.; *Kyma*, C, 10 b. – **Glyfáda:** **Astir Bungalows*, L, 156 b.; *Atrium*, A, 104 b.; *Congo Palace*, A, 160 b.; *Philissia*, A, 39 b.; *Phoebe*, A, 22 b.; *Hekabe*, A, 26 b.; *Oasis*, A, 140 b.; *Olivia House*, A, 38 b.; *Palace*, A, 140 b.; *Palmyra Beach*, A, 95 b.; *Villa Krini*, A, 21 b.; *Antonopoulos*, B, 84 b.; *Delphini*, B, 73 b.; *Phenix*, B, 265 b.; *Florida*, B, 159 b.; *Four Seasons*, B, 146 b.; *Gripsholm*, B, 107 b.; *Ideal*, B, 74 b.; *Kreoli*, B, 92 b.; *London*, B, 142 b.; *Miranda*, B, 64 b.; *Niki*, B, 113 b.; *Regina Maris*, B,

The resort of Glyfáda on the Attic Riviera

135 b.; *Riviera*, B, 151 b.; *Sea View*, B, 141 b.; *Sivylla*, B, 71 b.; *Triton*, B, 71 b.; *Villa Helena*, B, 24 b.; *Villa Katerina*, B, 47 b.; *Zina*, B, 36 b.; *Adonis*, C, 85 b.; *Arion*, C, 56 b.; *Avra*, C, 71 b.; *Blue Rivage*, C, 156 b.; *Blue Sky*, C, 36 b.; *Glyphada*, C, 100 b.; *Ilion*, C, 56 b.; *Oceanis*, C, 135 b.; *Perla*, C, 112 b.; *Rial*, C, 67 b.; *Themis*, C, 84 b. – **Voúla:** *Voula Beach*, A, 106 b.; *Aktaion*, B, 31 b.; *Atlantis*, B, 27 b.; *Castello Beach*, B, 64 b.; *Galinie*, B, 38 b.; *Plaza*, B, 31 b.; *Kabera*, C, 17 b.; *Nufara*, C, 42 b.; *Orion*, C, 49 b.; *Palma*, C, 70 b.; *Rondo*, C, 84 b. – **Kavoúri:** *Apollon Palace*, L, 530 b.; *Cavouri*, A, 198 b.; *Pelikina*, A, 40 b.; *Pine Hill*, B, 158 b.; *Maro*, C, 15 b. – **Vouliagméni:** *Astir Palace*, L, 462 b.; *Electra*, A, 20 b.; *Greek Coast*, A, 103 b.; *Lilly*, A, 34 b.; *Margi House*, A, 147 b.; *Blue Spell*, B, 71 b.; *Strand*, B, 134 b. – **Várkitsa:** *Glaros*, A, 81 b.; *Haris House*, A, 24 b.; *Varkiza*, B, 55 b.; *Holidays*, C, 65 b. – **Lagonísi:** *Xenia Lagonisi*, L, 711 b.; *Var*, B, 38 b. – **Anávyssos:** *Alexander Beach*, A, 194 b.; *Apollon Beach*, B, 168 b.; *Calypso*, B, 85 b.; *Eden Beach*, B, 568 b.; *Silver Beach*, C, 54 b. – **Legrená:** *Amphitrite*, B, 62 b.; *Minos*, B, 72 b. – **Soúnion:** see p. 241.

CAMPING SITES: Voúla and Legrená.

Ayia Triada
ΑΓΙΑ ΤΡΙΑΔΑ
(Ayía Triáda)

Island: Crete. – Nomos: Iráklion.

*Ayía Triáda, 2 km (1 mile) W of Phaistós in southern Crete, is the site of a royal villa of the Minoan period.

From the custodian's house, below the entrance to the site, there is an excellent

general view of the remains. The northern range of buildings and beyond this to the left the western range can be clearly distinguished. Along the northern range, from E to W, is a *flight of steps* leading to

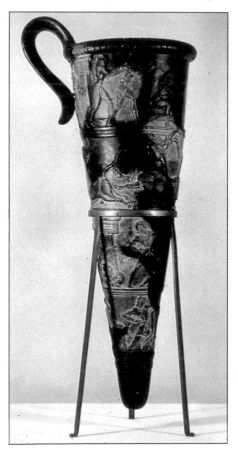

Rhyton with boxing scenes from Ayía Triáda

the old road to Phaistós, *residential quarters* and *store-rooms*, with large *pithoi* decorated in relief still standing in situ. In the store-rooms were found 19 bronze ingots and the "Harvesters Vase" now in Iráklion Museum. These structures are partly overlaid by a Mycenaean **megaron** (between 1375 and 1100 B.C.). In the western part of this range of buildings are a handsome *polythyron* overlooking the coastal plain, and the *archive rooms*. – In the western range of buildings there are more store-rooms.

Below the northern range of buildings is the town area, with the *market*, in which are a row of eight shops fronted by a pillared **portico**, all dating from the Late Minoan period.

The little *chapel* in the angle between the two wings of the villa is dedicated to St George. Farther W is the **chapel of the Holy Trinity** (Ayía Triáda) after which the site is named.

Ayios Efstratios
ΑΓΙΟΣ ΕΥΣΤΡΑΤΙΟΣ
(Áyios Efstrátios)

Nomos: Leshos.
Area: 43 sq. km. (17 sq. miles) – Population: 1000.

TRANSPORTATION. – Weekly boat service (Piraeus–Áyios Efstrátios–Lemnos–Samothrace–Alexandroúpolis).

The little island of Áyios Efstrátios (highest point 295 m (968 ft)) lies in the northern Aegean 30 km (19 miles) S of Lemnos. On the largest bay on the W coast is the village of the same name, with a castle and windmills on the hillside above it.

The island, known as *Halonesos* in antiquity, protected the sea route from Athens to the islands of Lemnos and Imbros and the Hellespont.

Ayios Nikolaos
ΑΓΙΟΣ ΝΙΚΟΛΑΟΣ
(Áyios Nikólaos)

Island: Crete. – Nomos: Lasíthi.
Telephone dialling code: 0841.
Altitude: 10 m. (33 ft) – Population: 3700.
ⓘ Tourist Organisation,
   Omírou 7;
   tel. 2 23 21.
   Tourist Police,
   Omírou.

TRANSPORTATION. – Bus services to Iráklion, Psykhró (Lasíthi) and Ierápetra. – Boat services to Piraeus and to Kárpathos and Rhodes. – Boat trips to the island of Psirá.

Hotels. – *Minos Beach*, L, 233 b.; *Mirabello Bungalows*, L, 244 b.; *Mirabello*, A, 322 b.; *Hermes*, A, 379 b.; *Ariadne Beach*, B, 142 b.; *Coral*, B, 257 b.; *Akratos*, C, 60 b.; *Alkistis*, C, 30 b.; *Creta*, C, 50 b.; *Cronos*, C, 68 b.; *Delta*, C, 19 b.; *Du Lac*, C, 74 b.; *Rhea*, C, 214 b. – YOUTH HOSTEL.

SWIMMING: Minos Beach; bays to S of town.

Áyios Nikólaos, chief town of the nomos of Lasíthi, lies on the W side of the Gulf of Mirabello, with a picturesque little fishing harbour which is linked with the small inland lake of Voulisméni. Situated in a fertile region, it is an attractive town which grew up after 1850 through the settlement of families from Sfakía and Kritsá.

The *Museum* contains finds from the surrounding area. Recently 20 tombs were discovered under a bridge in Áyios Nikólaos by Kostis Davares, director of the museum; in one of them were the remains of a boy of 13 or 14, with an almost completely preserved victor's garland round his head and an oil-flask and strigil by his side.

SURROUNDINGS. – On a hillside 11 km (7 miles) S is **Kritsá**, one of the largest villages in Crete (pop. 2500). From the coffee-houses on the valley side of the main street there is a view extending to the sea.

Just before the village, on the right, stands a fine 13th c. church, the *Panayía Kyrá*, a gleaming white building with three apses, one at the end of each of its three aisles (the one on the S side being the oldest). The church contains notable 14th c. frescoes (life of the Mother of God, Evangelists, saints).

On the near side of Kritsá a dirt road goes off on the right to the remains of the Doric city of **Lató** (suitable for cars; on foot 45 minutes' walk through beautiful scenery).

Lató, a fortified town built on terraces, is typical of a Dorian settlement. It was founded in the 7th c. B.C., but the structures now visible probably date from the 5th c. The town has a magnificent situation on a hill saddle, with its buildings climbing up the northern slope. From the W gate of the town a stepped lane runs up to the Agora, passing between the town walls (with towers) on the left and a dense huddle of houses on the right. In the Agora are the rectangular foundations of a small *temple*, probably dedicated to the vegetation goddess Lato who gave her name to the town. On the N side of the square is a *grand staircase* of Minoan type, beyond which are two structures which have been identified as a *council chamber* and a *refectory*. If we continue up between the remains of the northern part of the town we come to the top of the hill, from which there is a superb *view extending to the Gulf of Mirabello.

21 km SE of Áyios Nikólaos is the Minoan site of **Goúrnia** (see p. 137). – 14 km (9 miles) from Goúrnia, on the S coast, is **Ierápetra** (see p. 139).

14 km (9 miles) NW of Áyios Nikólaos is the little country town of **Neápolis** (pop. 4000; Hotel Neapolis, D, 20 b.), with a local museum.

12 km (7 miles) N of Áyios Nikólaos, at the point where the *Spinalónga peninsula* joins the mainland, is **Eloúnda** (hotels: Elounda Beach, L, 578 b.; Astir Palace, L, 224 b.; Aristea, C, 70 b.) This was the site of an ancient city, but most of the remains have been submerged by the sea. On the isthmus the *mosaic pavement* of an Early Christian basilica can be seen. At the N end of the offshore islet of *Spinalónga* is a *Venetian fortress* (1526), later used as a leper colony.

Bassai
ΒΑΣΣΑΙ
(Vássai)

Region: Peloponnese. – Nomos: Elis.

The **Temple of Apollo Epikourios stands on a remote site (alt. 1130 m (3708 ft)) on the slopes of Mt Lykaion, 14 km (9 miles) from the village of Andrítsaina, from which a road runs up to within a short distance of the site. Rediscovered in 1763, the temple has since then largely been re-erected. According to Pausanias, who regarded it as second only to the temple at Tegéa for the beauty of its stone and its exact proportions, it was built by Iktinos, the architect of the Parthenon, as a thank-offering by the city of Phigaleia for being spared from the plague of 429 B.C. to which Perikles fell a victim in Athens.

The temple shows some unusual features. The column ratio (6×15) follows the

Bassai
Temple of Apollo Epikourios

Temple of Apollo, Bassai

Archaic pattern rather than the classical norm of 6×13, and the temple is oriented not to the E but to the N, though it has a doorway in the E wall of the cella. While the external columns are Doric the cella has two rows of Ionic columns – not free-standing but set close to the walls and engaged in projecting buttresses. A frieze (now in the British Museum) ran round the walls of the cella above the columns, a departure from the previously normal practice of having the frieze on the external walls. Iktinos thus created a fully developed internal Ionic peristasis and showed himself "a leader of the avant-garde in architecture" (Gruben), carrying a stage farther the trend towards increased emphasis on the interior of the temple which is already evident in the Parthenon.

At the far end of the cella, at the entrance to the adyton in which the cult image of the god was housed, there originally stood a column with a Corinthian capital – the earliest known use of this type. The temple thus made use of all three of the Greek orders. The Corinthian capital was present when the temple was examined by Haller von Hallerstein in 1811 but subsequently disappeared and is known to us only from his drawing.

The adyton must have served some unknown cult purpose. With this separate holy of holies within the cella, with its elongated ground-plan and its 6×15 columns, the Temple of Apollo at Bassai is reminiscent of the temple in the central sanctuary of Apollo at Delphi, which Iktinos reproduced here, reducing it in size by exactly a third.

The best way to reach Bassai from Trípolis is by way of *Megalópolis* (see p. 179) and *Karýtaina* (see p. 153). An alternative approach is from Pýrgos, on the W coast of the Peloponnese, by way of Kréstena, to the S of the River Alpheios, and Andrítsaina.

SURROUNDINGS. – It is a 2½ hours' walk from Bassai to **Figalía**, with the remains of ancient *Phigaleia*, continuing to the Neda gorge. – Accommodation can be found in **Andrítsaina**, a hill village of wooden houses (alt. 765 m (2510 ft); hotels: Theoxinia, B, 30 b.; Pan, C, 12 b.).

Boeotia
BOIΩTIA
(Viotía)

Boeotia occupies an area of 3000 sq. km (1158 sq. miles) in central Greece, between the gulfs of Corinth and Euboea and between Phocis and Attica. The plains around its capital, Thebes, and in the Asopos valley – supplemented in modern times by the land won by the drainage of Lake Kopais – have made Boeotia an agricultural region since ancient times; and its inhabitants were traditionally regarded as rather uncouth rustics, in spite of the fact that it was the birthplace of Hesiod, Pindar and Plutarch. In the field of art, however, it produced only the sculptor Kalamis.

HISTORY. – In Mycenaean times Boeotia possessed important fortified towns, among them Thebes, Orchomenós and Gla. In the historical period a league of cities was formed, of which Thebes became the leader in the time of Epameinondas (371–361 B.C.). The town of Thebes was destroyed on several occasions, e.g. by Alexander the Great in 335 B.C. and by Catalan mercenaries in the 13th c., and did not recover its position until the 19th c. During the Turkish period the capital of the region was Levádia.

Although most visitors only pass through Boeotia on the way to somewhere else, it has a number of sites and monuments which are well worth seeing. The Mycenaean period is represented by **Orkhomenós** (see p. 201) and **Gla** (p. 136), the 1st millennium B.C. by **Chaironeia** (p. 106) and the Kabirion of Thebes, and the Christian era by the churches of **Skripoú**, one of which can be seen when visiting Ósios Loukás.

Brauron
BPAYPΩNA
(Vravróna)

Region and nomos: Attica.

At Brauron on the E coast of Attica, 8 km (5 miles) NE of Markópoulo, Papadimitríou excavated between 1948 and 1963 a *sanctuary of Artemis which has been excellently restored and is now a most impressive and interesting site.

HISTORY. – The site was occupied from Neolithic times. Remains of Middle Helladic buildings (2000–1600 B.C.) were found on the acropolis hill, and there was evidence of dense occupation in the Late Helladic (Mycenaean) period (1600–1100 B.C.). After a period of abandonment the site was resettled in the 9th c. B.C. Brauron's heyday was in the 5th and 4th c., but after 300 B.C. the land became waterlogged and was again abandoned. – The cult of Artemis Brauronia was transferred from Brauron to the Acropolis of Athens in the 6th c. by Peisistratos, himself a native of Brauron.

In Mycenaean times the goddess Artemis was known here as Artemis Iphigeneia; and according to Euripides Iphigeneia, daughter of king Agamemnon of Mycenae, was a priestess at Brauron after her return from the Tauric Chersonesos until her death. In the classical period Athenian girls served in the sanctuary between the ages of five and 10. They were known as "little bears" *(arktoi)* from the saffron-coloured garments they wore, recalling a she-bear sacred to Artemis.

At the foot of a hill near a 12th c. chapel of St George is a small *shrine*, behind which are the *Cave of Iphigeneia* (now roofless) and a "*sacred house*". To the N are the rock-cut footings of the Temple of Artemis which replaced an earlier building in the first half of the 5th c. B.C. Beyond this is a **stoa** built round three sides of a courtyard (430–420 B.C.), with the entrance on the W side, where there is an ancient bridge. The Doric columns of the stoa, which were of limestone, had marble capitals. Six rooms in the N wing and three in the W wing each contained 11 wooden beds for the "little bears".

The **Museum** contains finds from the site – in Rooms 1–3 material from the sanctuary of Artemis, in Room 5 pottery from the acropolis (Early to Late Helladic). Room 4 and the Atrium also display material from the Merénda necropolis (vases of the 9th–4th c. B.C., tomb stelae), Room 5 pottery from Anávyssos and the Peráti necropolis.

SURROUNDINGS. – 500 m (1641 ft) inland are the excavated remains of an early Byzantine **basilica** and baptistery (6th c.). – 9 km (6 miles) S is the picturesque little port of *Porto Ráfti* (see p. 218).

Chaironeia
XAIPΩNEIA
(Khairónia)

Region and nomos: Boeotia.

The monumental *Lion of Chaironeia rears up against a backdrop of cypress trees by the roadside 14 km (9 miles) N of Levádia (see p. 174). It commemorates a battle in 338 B.C. in which the allied Greek city states were defeated by Philip II of Macedon and his 18-year-old son Alexander.

The battle marked the end of the independent Greek *polis* and the beginning of the Macedonian domination of Greece. The fallen Macedonians were buried in an earth mound on the battlefield (2 km (1 mile) E of the Lion monument), the ashes of the Athenian dead were sent to Athens by Philip, and Thebes raised a tomb for the dead soldiers of its Sacred Band which was enclosed by a low wall and marked by the figure of the lion, standing 5·50 m (18 ft) high on its stone base. – In 86 B.C. Sulla's Roman army defeated the troops of Mithridates of Pontos on the same battlefield.

Of the ancient city of **Chaironeia** (1·5 km (1 mile) W) there remains only a small rock-cut theatre on the slopes of the acropolis hill (now known as Petrakhos hill). It was the birthplace of the philosopher and biographer Plutarch, a priest of Apollo at Delphi (A.D. *c.* 45–*c.* 120), who returned to Chaironeia in his old age.

Chalcidice
ΞΑΛΚΙΔΙΚΗ
(Khalkidikí)

Area: 3000 sq. km (1158 sq. miles).
ⓘ Tourist Police, Néa Moudánia,
    28 Oktovríou 31;
    tel. (0373) 2 13 70.

TRANSPORTATION. – Chalcidice is traversed by two roads running from W to E, Salonica–Rentína–Kavála and Salonica–Polýgyros–Ierissós, from which side roads branch off and run S. Bus connections with Salonica. – Boat services between Ouranópolis and Dafní, the port of Athos.

HOTELS. – KASSÁNDRA PENINSULA. – NÉA MOUDÁNIA: *Kouvraki*, C, 37 b. – SÁNI: *Kassandra Sani*, A, 436 b.; camping site. – KALÁNDRA: *Mendi*, A, 311 b. – AYIA PARASKEVI: *Aphrodite*, B, 44 b. – PALOÚRI: *Xenia*, B, 144 b. – KHANIÓTIS: *Hermes*, C, 52 b.; *Khaniotis*, 58 b.; *Plaza*, C, 36 b.; *Strand*, C, 85 b. – KALLITHÉA: *Athos Palace*, A, 132 b.; *Pallini Beach*, A, 938 b.; *Ammon Zeus*, B, 208 b.; *Vassos*, B, 171 b.; *Kallithea*, C, 65 b.; *Kentrikon*, C, 50 b.; *Toronaion*, C, 18 b.

BETWEEN KASSÁNDRA AND SITHONÍA: *Gerakini Beach*, B, 560 b.

SITHONÍA PENINSULA. – ORKYLIÁ: *Sermili*, B, 231 b. – METAMÓRFOSIS: *Golden Beach*, C, 82 b. – NÉOS MARMÁRAS: *Village Inn*, B, 161 b.

ATHOS PENINSULA. – IERISSÓS: *Mount Athos*, B, 75 b. – OURANÓPOLIS: *Eagles' Palace*, A, 302 b.; *Xenia*, B, 84 b.

EAST COAST. – ASPRÓVALTA: camping site. – STAVRÓS: *Athos*, C, 48 b.

The peninsula of Chalcidice, a hilly and well-wooded region, lies SE of Salonica, with three finger-like sub-peninsulas reaching out into the sea – to the W Kassándra, in the middle Sithonía (or Lóngos), to the E Athos. The name of the peninsula recalls that the Euboean city of Chalkis (see p. 132) founded 32 cities here, including Olynthos (p. 201).

In recent years Chalcidice, with its magnificent long sandy beaches, has become a rapidly developing holiday region, and there are now numerous resorts excellently equipped to cater for tourists.

Chios
ΞΙΟΣ
(Khios)

Nomos: Chios.
Telephone dialling code: 0271 (Chios), 0272 (Kardámyla).
Area: 842 sq. km (325 sq. miles). – Population: 52,500.
ⓘ Tourist Police,
    Neorion;
    tel. 2 65 55.
    Olympic Airways,
    Rodokanáki 17.

TRANSPORTATION. – Air services from Athens, boat services from Piraeus. Local connections with the

Chios

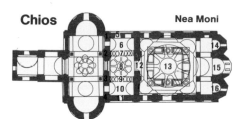

Nea Moni

ICONOGRAPHY

1 Symeon Stylites
2 Stylite, Isaiah, Jeremiah
3 Daniel, Ezechiel, Symeon Stylites
4 Daniel Stylites
5 Washing of the Feet
6 Before the Washing of the Feet, Entry into Jerusalem
7 Stephen the Yr, Ephraim, Arsenius, Nicetas, Antony, Maximus, John Calybites
8 Joachim, Anna, Stephen, Panteleimon, Theodore Stratelates, Bacchus, Orestes, Mardarius, Eugenius, Auxentius, Eustratius, Sergius, Mary
9 John Studites, Theodosius, Euthymius, Menas,

Pachomius, Sabbas, John Climacus
10 Pentecost
11 Gethsemane, Betrayal
12 Pantocrator
13 Nativity, Presentation in Temple, Baptism, Transfiguration, Crucifixion, Descent from Cross, Descent into Hell, Annunciation, Cherubim, John the Theologian, Andrew, Luke, Bartholomew, Seraphim, Philip, Mark, Matthew, Angels, Pantocrator
14 Archangel Michael
15 Mother of God Orans
16 Archangel Gabriel

neighbouring islands of Inoúsai (area 14 sq. km (5 sq. miles); pop. 170; school of seamanship), to the NE, and *Psará*, to the NW (boats from Vólyssos).

HOTELS. – CHIOS: *Chandris Chios*, B, 294 b.; *Xenia*, B, 50 b.; *Aktaeon*, C, 53 b.; *Kyma*, C, 82 b. – KARDÁMYLA: *Kardamyla*, B, 60 b. – INOÚSAI: *Prasonisia*, D, 11 b.

In some of the fortified medieval houses in the village of Mésta are holiday apartments fitted out by the Greek Tourist Organisation.

SWIMMING. – N of the town of Chios: Vrondádes (6 km (4 miles), pebbles), Langáda (15 km (9 miles), pebbles), Kardámyla (27 km (17 miles), sand). S of the town: Karfás (6 km (4 miles), sand), etc.

Chios lies just off the peninsula of Çeşme in Turkey, which forms the S side of the Gulf of Smyrna, and at the narrowest point in the gulf is only 8 km (5 miles) from the Turkish mainland. The island is traversed from N to S by a range of limestone hills rising to 1297 m (4255 ft). The chief town is on the E side, facing the Anatolian coast.

HISTORY. – About 1000 B.C. settlers from Ionia established themselves on the island, which later – together with some other places – claimed to be the homeland of Homer. In the 6th c. B.C. an important school of sculptors was active on Chios. From 512 to 479 the island was under Persian rule, and thereafter became a member of the Attic maritime league, but was able to maintain its independence – as it did in the Hellenistic period and under the Romans, with whom it sided as early as 190 B.C. Held from 1204 to 1304 by the Venetians and later by the Genoese, it became Turkish in 1566. The popularity of mastic (the resin of the lentisk tree which grows on the island) and of the sweets made with it in the Sultan's harem gave Chios

a special status, but no Greek was allowed to live within the Citadel. In 1822 Chios was the scene of the bloody massacres depicted in the picture by Delacroix. Severe devastation was caused by an earthquake in 1881. Chios became a part of Greece in 1912, but as a result of the First World War it lost its economic hinterland on the mainland of Turkey and thereafter had to give asylum to many of the Greeks expelled from Asia Minor.

SIGHTS. – The town of **Chios** (pop. 24,050), which is the island's principal port, lies on the E coast. In a former mosque in *Platía Vounákis* is the **Archaeological Museum**, which contains pottery dating from prehistoric times onwards, coins and some sculpture. On the N side of the square is the entrance to the Genoese *Citadel*, within which only Turks were allowed to live between 1566 and 1912. The enlarged *Folk Museum* and the completely renovated **Korais Library** were reopened in 1978. The library, the third largest in Greece (140,000 volumes), is named after the Chios-born scholar Adamantio Korais (1748–1833), who later worked in Paris.

In the fertile Kampos to the S of the town is the **mansion of the Argentis family**, now open to the public. The house with its marble fountains and painted water wheels, set in a large orange-grove, provides a picture of the way of life of the Genoese and native aristocracy.

*Convent of Néa Moni. – From the town of Chios a road runs W through the colourful village of *Karyés* (5 km – 3 miles) and over a pass to the Néa Moní, a straggling complex of buildings in a verdant setting now occupied only by a few nuns. The convent, founded by the Emperor Constantine IX Monomachos (1042–55), is notable for its magnificent **mosaics* on a gold ground, which rank with those at Dafní near Athens (see p. 117) and Ósios Loukás (p. 202) among the finest surviving examples of 11th c. religious art.

The DOME of the convent church is borne, like the one at Dafní, on eight piers and spans the full width of the church, not merely the central aisle. The walls still have their original facing of red marble. The mosaics were partly destroyed by the 1881 earthquake; in particular those on the dome, which collapsed, were lost. In subsequent restoration work the dome was rebuilt and the surviving mosaics made safe. Among the principal scenes are the Baptism of Christ, the Crucifixion, the Descent from the Cross and the Descent into Limbo. In the main apse is the Mother of God, flanked by the archangels Michael and Gabriel in the lateral apses. There are also fine mosaics in the esonarthex – the Washing of the Feet, the Mother of

God with local saints, the Betrayal. All these mosaics date from the period of foundation of the convent (c. 1050) and are thus rather later than those at Ósios Loukás and rather older than those at Dafní. The frescoes in the exonarthex (among them a Last Judgment) date from the late Byzantine period (14th c.). The other conventual buildings were damaged during a Turkish punitive expedition in 1822 against Chios, which was sympathetic to the cause of liberation, and many of them are now in a state of some dilapidation, as are the hostels for pilgrims round the convent. By the gateway of the convent is a *chapel* commemorating those who were killed in 1822. Other notable features are the old *refectory* (trápeza) and a large *cistern* a few paces to the right of the main gateway. From the terrace of the new refectory, the one now used by the nuns, there is a very beautiful view.

Going N from Chios, we pass through the villa suburb of **Vrondádes** (6 km (4 miles); pop. 4700). At the N end of the little town, near the sea, are the Pasha's Spring (Basávrysi) and a large block of dressed stone which was probably a *shrine of Cybele*. This is popularly known as the Daskalópetra (Teacher's Stone) or the Skholí Omírou (School of Homer) – recalling the island's claim to be the birthplace of Homer. – Continuing along the coast, we come to **Langáda** (15 km – 9 miles), near which are the excavated remains of *Delphinion*, a site fortified by the Athenians in 412 B.C. At *Kardámyla* (27 km (17 miles); pop. 1300) a road goes off on the right to the little port of **Mármaron** (25 km (16 miles); pop. 2400; sandy beach). Beyond Kardámyla the main road continues round the N of the island, passing through Víki and the picturesque village of **Kéramos** to reach **Ayion Gála** (50 km – 31 miles).

Another road leads NW from Chios along the northern slopes of Mt *Aipos* to **Vólyssos** (40 km – 25 miles) and its harbour at Límnia. From Límnia there is a motorboat service to the island of **Psará** (area 40 sq. km (15 sq. miles); pop. 600), 18 sea-miles away, the birthplace of Kanaris, the fighter for Greek liberation. After being depopulated by pirate raids Psará was resettled by Albanians in the 16th c. Like Hydra, it took an active part in the wars of liberation, and 4000 out of the island's 6000 inhabitants were killed in Turkish reprisals. The survivors then left the island and settled on Euboea (Néa Psará=Erétria) and Sýros. Later Psará was again resettled from Chios. The only village on the island is in a bay on the S coast, below a medieval castle. On the N coast is the monastery of the Dormition (Kímisis Theotókou), on the W coast are sandy beaches.

30 km (19 miles) S of Chios, in the centre of the villages which produce mastic (*mastikhokhoriá*), is **Pyrgí**, a picturesque little place dominated by a Genoese *castle*. The 12th c. *church of the Áyii Apóstoli* (frescoes) follows the pattern of the Néa Moní, which also served as a model for other churches on the island. Many of the houses have attractive sgraffito decoration.

8 km (5 miles) SW of Pyrgí is the archaeological site of **Káto Fáno**, with remains of a *temple of Apollo*; 7 km (4 miles) SE is the site of **Emborió**. A road runs NW from Pyrgí to the port of **Ayía Anastasía** or *Basalimáni* (43 km (27 miles) from Chios), from which we can return to Chios by way of **Eláta** and the medieval village of **Vésa**.

Corfu
KEPKYPA
(Kérkira)

Nomos: Corfu. – Telephone dialling code: 0661.
Area: 593 sq. km. – Population: 89,600.
ⓘ EOT,
   Arseníou 35;
   tel. 3 05 20.
   Olympic Airways,
   Zavitsianoú 18.

TRANSPORTATION. – Air services from Athens and London; boat services from Venice, Ancona, Brindisi and Piraeus; ferry services from Igoumenítsa and Pátras.

Rocky coastal scenery, Corfu

HOTELS. – TOWN OF KÉRKYRA: *Corfu Palace, L, 195 b.; Cavalieri, A, 91 b.; Astron, A, 63 b.; King Alkinoos, B, 102 b.; Olympiakon, B, 90 b.; Arcadion, C, 95 b.; Atlantis, C, 112 b.; Bretagne, C, 38 b.; Calypso, C, 34 b.; Dalia, C, 32 b.; Hermes, C, 62 b.; Ionion, C, 163 b.; Splendid, C, 30 b.; Suisse, C, 58 b.; and many in categories D and E. – IN ANEMÓMYLOS AND KANÓNI: *Corfu Hilton, L, 515 b.; Corfu Canoni, A, 306 b.; Ariti, A, 312 b.; Arion, B, 199 b.; Marina, B, 192 b.; Royal, C, 147 b.; Salvos, C, 176 b.

S OF KÉRKYRA. – ALYKÉS (3 km – 2 miles): Kerkyra Golf, A, 444 b. – PÉRAMA (7 km – 4 miles): Steyia, A, 138 b.; Aeolos Beach, B, 451 b.; Akti, B, 117 b.; Aegli, C, 71 b.; Argo, C, 28 b.; Oasis, C, 128 b. – GASTOÚRI (10 km – 6 miles): Achillion, C, 27 b. – BENÍTSES (12·5 km – 8 miles): Potamaki, B, 216 b.; Benitses Inn, C, 44 b. – ÁYIOS IOÁNNIS PERISTERÓN: *Marbella Beach, L, 538 b.; Marbella Beach Apartments, A, 152 b. – MORAITIKÁ (20 km – 12 miles): *Miramare Beach, L, 285 b.; Delfinia, A, 151 b.; Messoghi Beach, B, 977 b.; Sea Bird, C, 25 b. – MESÓYI (22 km – 14 miles): Rossis, C, 40 b.; Rulis, C, 30 b. – KOUSPÁDES (33 km – 21 miles): Boukari, C, 20 b.

N OF KÉRKYRA. – KONTOKÁLI (6 km – 4 miles): Kontokali Palace, A, 467 b. – GOUVIÁ (8 km – 5 miles): *Astir Palace Corfu, L, 590 b.; Corcyra Beach, A, 452 b.; Galaxias, C, 51 b. – DAFNÍLA (11 km – 7 miles): *Eva Palace, L, 219 b.; Robinson Club, A, 342 b. – DASIÁ (12 km – 7 miles): *Castello, L, 132 b., Chandris Corfu, A, 544 b.; Chandris Dasia, A, 467 b.; Dasia, C, 102 b. – ÝPSOS (14 km – 9 miles): Ypsos Beach, B, 85 b.; Mega, C, 61 b. – NISÁKI (22 km – 14 miles): Nisaki Beach, A, 444 b.

ON W COAST (FROM N TO S). – ARÍLLAS (45 km – 28 miles): Arilla Beach, C, 25 b.; Marina, C, 29 b. – PALAIOKASTRÍTSA (20–25 km – 12–16 miles): Akrotiri Beach, A, 230 b.; Oceanis, B, 123 b.; Paleokastritsa, B, 267 b.; Pavillon Xenia, B, 14 b.; Odysseus, C, 64 b.; Zephyros, D, 20 b. – LIAPÁDES (22 km – 14 miles): Chrysi Akti, C, 34 b. – ERMÓNES (14 km – 9 miles): Ermónes Beach, A, 504 b.; Ariti, A, 312 b. – GLYFÁDA (16 km – 10 miles): Grand Hotel Glyphada Beach, A, 417 b. – ÁYIOS GÓRDIOS (16 km – 10 miles): Ayios Gordios, A, 364 b.; Chrysses Folies, C, 33 b. – ANÓ PAVLIÁNA (19 km – 12 miles): Iliovasilevma, D, 16 b.

CAMPING SITES. – Kontokáli, Dassiá, Ýpsos, Pyrgí.

RESTAURANTS. – There are numerous restaurants on the island. In the town of Kérkyra the following are to be recommended – Aigli and Aktaion on the Esplanade, Ragnatella on the town walls and Rex, Chrysomallis, Pantheon and Nafplion.

*Corfu, the most northerly of the Ionian Islands and their adminis-trative centre, offers a varied range of attractions to visitors – its mild climate, its pleasant scenery and its many excellent beaches – and is well equipped with tourist facilities and amenities.

SIGHTS. – The town of Kérkyra (pop. 26,900) occupies the site of the ancient city of Korkyra, founded by settlers from Corinth in 734 B.C. The modern town displays a combination of Greek, Venetian

A glimpse of St Spyridon's church, Kérkyra

and British features. – Starting from the Harbour, which has been considerably developed in the last 20 years or so, we go past the New Fortress (1576–89) into the picturesque OLD TOWN, in which are the Venetian *Theatre (1663–93) and the *church of St Spyrídon. In the sacristy of the church, to the right of the chancel, is a *silver sarcophagus containing the remains of St Spyridon, archbishop of Cyprus in the 4th c. His relics were taken to Constantinople and brought to Corfu after the fall of the city; since then he has been the island's patron saint.

From the church we continue to the Esplanade, a large park-like area between the old town and the Old Fortress (built 1386, strengthened 1500). From here there are fine *views extending to Mt Pantokrator and the mainland of Greece. To the left of the entrance to the fortress is a monument to Count Matthias von der Schulenburg, who commanded the stub-born defence of the island against the Turks in 1716. Venice did him the rare honour of erecting a monument to him during his lifetime ("adhuc viventi"), and on his death granted him the further distinction of burial in the Arsenal in Venice.

Along the W side of the Esplanade are colonnaded houses dating from the period of British rule. Another reminder of

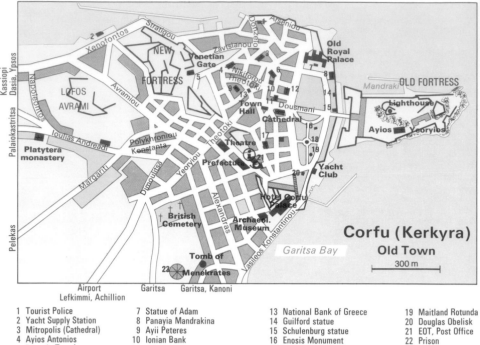

Airport   Garitsa   Garitsa, Kanoni
Lefkimmi, Achillion

1 Tourist Police	7 Statue of Adam	13 National Bank of Greece	19 Maitland Rotunda
2 Yacht Supply Station	8 Panayia Mandrakina	14 Guilford statue	20 Douglas Obelisk
3 Mitropolis (Cathedral)	9 Ayii Peteres	15 Schulenburg statue	21 EOT, Post Office
4 Ayios Antonios	10 Ionian Bank	16 Enosis Monument	22 Prison
5 Panayia Tenedou	11 Ayios Ioannis	17 Anglican church	
6 Ayios Spyridon	12 Panayia ton Xenon	18 Bandstand	

that period is a small round temple in neo-classical style in the gardens to the S. On the N side of the Esplanade is the former residence of the British Governor, erected in 1816, which later (from 1864) became the Royal Palace and now houses the *Museum of Asiatic Art, founded in 1975 to house the large collection of Japanese and Chinese art assembled by Ambassador Manos, to which was added in 1976 the collection of Ambassador Khadzivasiliou, consisting of 450 items from India, Tibet, Nepal, Thailand, Korea and Japan.

The *Archaeological Museum is in King Constantine Street (Vasiléos Konstantínou).

The finest exhibit in the museum is the *Gorgon Pediment from the W front of a temple of Artemis of about 600 B.C. The central figure in this is the Gorgon Medusa, represented as mistress of the beasts and accompanied by her children Pegasos and Chrysaor. Other items of interest are Gorgon antefixes, statuettes of Artemis found near the temple, portrait heads of the historian Thucydides and the dramatist Menander and an archaic lioness from the tomb of Menekrates (c. 600 B.C.). 200 m (220 yards) beyond the museum, on the road out of town, a side road on the right leads to the tomb of Menekrates, of which the circular substructure is preserved.

The Vlakhernai monastery and Mouse Island, Corfu

The seafront promenade runs S through the suburb of Garitsa and past the former royal summer residence, Mon Repos, to the peninsula of **Palaiópolis**. Opposite the park gate stands *Palaiópolis church*, on the site of an ancient temple. To the right is a road leading to the site of the *Temple of Artemis*, discovered in 1911.

At the end of the peninsula (4·5 km – 3 miles) is **Kanóni**, a tree-shaded terrace affording a magnificent *view of the bay and well equipped with cafés and restaurants. Immediately in front are two small islets: on the nearer one (linked with the mainland by a causeway) is the small *monastery of Vlakhernai*; to the rear, reached by boat, is **Pontikonísi** ("Mouse Island"), with a large clump of trees. Pontikonísi is claimed to be the Phaeacian ship which brought Odysseus back from Scheria to Ithaca and was turned to stone by Poseidon. The scenery of Kanóni and its situation near the ancient city have led some to suppose that the meeting between Odysseus and Nausikaa took place here; another claimant is Palaiokastrítsa.

Near Sidari, on the north coast of Corfu

up to the castle is a parking place with a small restaurant which affords the finest *view of Palaiokastrítsa and the surrounding area.

The best return route to Kerkyra is by way of **Glyfáda** and the crag of *Pélekas* (*view).

South of the island. – A favourite outing from Kérkyra is to the *Villa Akhillion (Achilleion, 10 km (6 miles)), built for the Empress Elizabeth of Austria in 1890, acquired by Kaiser Wilhelm II in 1907 and now occupied by a gambling casino. The road to **Mesóyi** (22 km – 14 miles) passes numerous beaches and then leaves the coast, reaching the sea again at **Kávos** (47 km – 29 miles), at the southernmost tip of the island.

Palaiokastrítsa, Corfu

North of the island. – The road runs NW from Kérkyra and comes to the **Platytéra monastery** on the outskirts of the town, which contains the tomb of Kapodistrias, first President of Greece, who was murdered at Nauplia in 1831. The road then continues up the E coast and after passing through the resorts of **Kontokáli** and **Gouviá** (8 km – 5 miles) comes to a fork, where one road continues along the coast to **Kassiópi** (37 km – 23 miles), at the N end of the island, while the other cuts across to **Palaiokastrítsa** (25 km – 16 miles) on the NW coast. Some archaeologists believe this to be the site of the city and palace of the Phaeacian king Alkinoos. There is excellent swimming from the local beaches. Near here are the *Palaiokastrítsa monastery*, situated on a promontory, and the castle of *Angelokastro* (alt. 329 m (1079 feet)). Half way

Corinth
ΚΟΡΙΝΘΟΣ
(Kórinthos)

Nomos: Corinth. – Telephone dialling code: 0741.
Altitude: at sea level. – Population: 21,000.
ⓘ **Tourist Police,**
    Koliátsou 33;
    tel. 2 32 83.

TRANSPORTATION. – On the Peloponnese Railway; lines to Athens and Piraeus, Pátras–Kalamáta, Argos–Kalamáta. – Ferry service to Brindisi (Italy) from the recently modernised harbour.

HOTELS. – CORINTH: *Kypselos*, B, 36 b.; *Akropolis*, C, 28 b.; *Bellevue*, C, 31 b.; *Ephira*, C, 85 b.; *Akti*, D, 35 b.; *Apollon*, D, 34 b.; *Byron*, D, 13 b.; *Heraeum*, D, 12 b. – OLD CORINTH: *Xenia*, A, 3 b. – LECHAION: *Corinthian Beach*, C, 108 b.

*Corinth was transferred to a new site in 1858 after a severe earthquake and rebuilt after a further earthquake in 1928 and a great fire in 1933. The site of ancient Corinth, which has been excavated since 1896 by

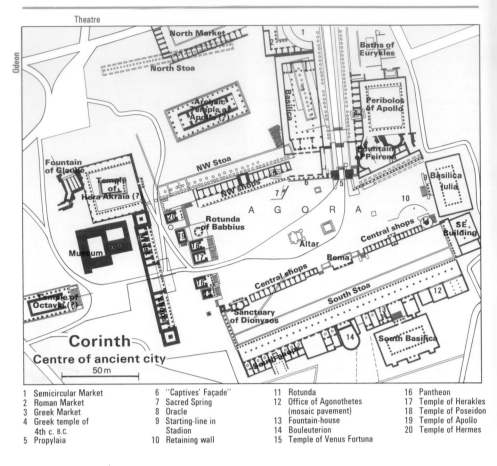

Corinth
Centre of ancient city
50 m

1 Semicircular Market	6 "Captives' Façade"	11 Rotunda	16 Pantheon
2 Roman Market	7 Sacred Spring	12 Office of Agonothetes	17 Temple of Herakles
3 Greek Market	8 Oracle	(mosaic pavement)	18 Temple of Poseidon
4 Greek temple of	9 Starting-line in	13 Fountain-house	19 Temple of Apollo
4th c. B.C.	Stadion	14 Bouleuterion	20 Temple of Hermes
5 Propylaia	10 Retaining wall	15 Temple of Venus Fortuna	

the American School, lies 7 km (4 miles) SW in a beautiful setting at the foot of the hill of Acrocorinth (Akrokorinthos). There are extensive remains, mostly dating from the Roman period, dominated by the imposing ruins of the Archaic Temple of Apollo.

HISTORY. – Corinth owed its great importance in ancient times to its situation. The hill of Acrocorinth provided a strong acropolis; and it was said that it and Ithome were the two horns of the Greek bull, and that whoever held them possessed the Peloponnese. The town controlled the 6 km (4 miles) wide Isthmus, the only land route into the Peloponnese, and with its two harbours, Lechaion in the Gulf of Corinth and Kenchreai in the Saronic Gulf, also controlled the movement of goods between the two gulfs.

The site of Corinth – the name of which is pre-Greek – was already occupied in Neolithic times. In historical times it attributed its foundation to *Korinthos*, son of Marathon, and to Sisyphos. About 1000 B.C. Doric settlers established themselves here beside a Phoenician trading post. Under the Bacchiad dynasty (from 747 B.C.) the city enjoyed a period of prosperity, founding colonies on Corfu and at Syracuse. In 657 B.C. (?) the Bacchiads were succeeded by Kypselos, who ruled for 30 years as a tyrant and was followed by his more notable son *Periandros*, an absolute ruler for 40 years, from about 628 B.C. He ranked as one of the Seven Sages, and during his reign the Archaic culture

of Corinth reached its apogee, the city's political and economic power being matched by its cultural achievement. Here the Doric temple reached its classical form, and the typical "Corinthian roof" of flat tiles was developed. Corinthian bronzes and pottery were disseminated throughout the entire Greek world; and during this period, according to Vitruvius, the Corinthian capital was invented by Kallimachos.

In 196 B.C. Corinth became the headquarters of the Achaean League. In 146 it was plundered and destroyed by a Roman general, Mummius, and remained in a state of ruin until Caesar rebuilt it in 44 B.C. In A.D. 51–52 the Apostle Paul lived and taught in Corinth. In the 2nd c. the city was embellished by the Emperor Hadrian and Herodes Atticus. In A.D. 521 Corinth was destroyed by a severe earthquake, and thereafter only Acrocorinth remained inhabited, until a settlement grew up in the 10th c. in the area of the ancient Agora. Neither under the Franks (from 1210) nor under Turkish rule was Corinth able to recover its former importance; nor indeed has it done so in modern times.

Ancient Corinth. – The best plan is to enter the site from the ancient Lechaion road, on the N side of the excavated area.

From here there is a general view of most of the site. Climbing up on an ancient paved road – as travellers arriving in the Lechaion harbour would have done – we come to the *propylon* at the entrance to the Agora. To the right of the road, here 7·50 m (25 ft) wide, is the **Basilica** (1st–2nd c.); on the left there follow in succession the Roman *Baths of Eurykles*, a public *latrine* with 20 seats (2nd c. A.D.), the *Peribolos of Apollo* and the *****Fountain of Peirene**. The fountain was magnificently rebuilt in marble by Herodes Atticus in the 2nd c. A.D., with three apses enclosing a square court, and a new façade with six round-arched openings was erected in front of the old fountain-house, probably dating from the time of Periandros, the old front walls of which can still be seen. (The water has now been diverted for the use of the village.)

A shallow flight of steps leads to the N propylon of the **Agora**, measuring 255 by 127 m (837 by 417 ft), a large colonnaded area which was the hub of the city's political and economic life. At the lower E end the paving of the Greek period has been preserved, but otherwise the remains are almost entirely Roman. Along the S side runs the **South Stoa**, 165 m (541 ft) long, with 33 shops. The third room from the E, which is covered with a protective roof, contains a Roman *mosaic pavement* and is at present used as a store for the tiled roof structure of a cult building. Beyond the South Stoa is the **South Basilica**, at the E end of which are the *South-East Building* and the **Basilica Iulia**, built by the Emperor Claudius about

A.D. 45. – Parallel to the South Stoa, running from end to end of the Agora, are the **Central Shops**, and half way along the row is the *****Bema* from which speakers addressed the people. Here in A.D. 52 the Apostle Paul appeared before the Roman governor Gallio, a brother of Seneca's; and there is some evidence on the Bema of the Christian church which was later built here.

Along the W end of the Agora are a number of Roman *****temples** set on podia – from S to N the *Temple of Venus*, the *Pantheon* and the *temples of Poseidon, Hercules and Apollo*. In front of the Temple of Apollo is the Corinthian **Rotunda of Babbius**. To the W of this row of temples are the **West Shops**, between which a broad flight of steps leads up to the higher level on which stands *Temple E* (probably built for Augustus' sister Octavia), by the entrance to the museum. New excavations in the area to the S have revealed several occupation levels and brought to light a *mosaic pavement* dating from about 500 B.C.

There is also a row of shops along the N side of the Agora, at any rate towards the W end, near the propylon and the "Captives' Façade". In front of the row of shops is the *****Sacred Spring**, in a Greek fountain-house (5th c. B.C.) in the form of

Remains of the Temple of Apollo, Corinth

In the Agora, Corinth

a Doric triglyph; seven steps lead down to the chamber containing the spring.

From here we climb the low hill on which stands the conspicuous *Temple of Apollo. Of the original temple there survive seven columns, part of the entablature, the rock-cut footings and part of the foundations. There were originally 6×15 massive monolithic columns. The cella was divided into two chambers, each of which had two rows of columns. The remains are sufficient to reveal the austere monumentality of the temple, a magnificent example of early Doric architecture, which was built about 540 B.C. on the site of an earlier 7th c. temple.

Other notable remains are the **Fountain-House of Glauke** (to the W of the Temple of Apollo), the *Odeon* and *Theatre* (NW of the museum, outside the enclosed area) and the *Asklepieion* (600 m (656 yards) N of the museum).

The *Museum gives a comprehensive view of the art of Corinth.

Room I contains Neolithic and Helladic material (4th–2nd millennium B.C.). In *Room II*, opposite Room I, are items ranging in date from the Proto-Geometric period (11th c. B.C.) to Hellenistic times. Of particular importance is the *pottery collection, arranged in chronological order in a clockwise direction, which gives a complete picture of the development of Corinthian pottery from the 11th c. onwards. *Room III* contains Roman, Byzantine and Frankish material, including statues of *Augustus* and his grandson *Lucius Caesar* (opposite the entrance) and of other Roman emperors, a 2nd c. *mosaic pavement* (on the left-hand long wall) and *figures in Phrygian dress, 2·57 m (8 ft) high, from the "Captives' Façade". There are also numerous exhibits in the inner courtyard and its galleries. A separate room is devoted to votive offerings from the Asklepieion.

The ascent to **Acrocorinth** (Akrokórinthos, 575 m (1887 ft)) is facilitated by a road which climbs to a point near the lowest gate on the W side. This commanding site was fortified in ancient times, and its defences were maintained and developed during the Byzantine, Frankish, Turkish and Venetian periods. After a moat (alt. 380 m (1247 ft)) constructed by the Venetians there follow the first gate, built in the Frankish period (14th c.) and the first wall 15th c.); then come the second and third walls (Byzantine: on the right, in front of the third gate, a Hellenistic tower). Within the fortress we follow a path running NE to the remains of a mosque (16th c.) and then turn S until we join a path leading up to the eastern summit, on which there once stood the famous Temple of Aphrodite, worshipped here after the Eastern fashion (views of the hills of the Peloponnese and of the Isthmus).

The old harbour of **Lechaion** lies N of ancient Corinth, 4 km (2 miles) W of the modern town. It is now completely silted up, but the outlines of the harbour basin can still be distinguished. On its W side Greek archaeologists found remains of a 5th c. Christian basilica in 1956–61. It is the largest in Greece (220 m (722 ft) long). Its octagonal baptistery was still in use when the basilica was destroyed by an earthquake in 551.

The Isthmus of Corinth is cut by the *Corinth Canal, constructed between 1882 and 1893. Involving an excavation of up to 80 m (262 ft) in depth, the canal is 6·3 km (4 miles) long, 23 m (75 ft) wide and 8 m (26 ft) deep, and can take ships of up to 10,000 tons. It follows much the same line as a canal planned by the Emperor Nero, but this early project, like other later ones, was never carried through. The best view of the canal is from the bridge which carries the road over it. – In order to avoid the long passage round the Peloponnese the *Diolkos* was constructed in ancient times – a slipway on which small vessels could be transported across the Isthmus on carts. Remains of this can be seen at the W end of the canal.

Crete
KPHTH
(Kríti)

Four nomoi: Iráklion, Khaniá, Réthymnon and Lasíthi.
Area: 8259 sq. km (3189 sq. miles). – Population: 465,500.

ACCESS. – There are frequent ferry services from Piraeus and air services from Athens to Khaniá, Athens to Iráklion and Rhodes to Iráklion. – As in other parts of Greece, there are numerous local bus services.

**Crete, the largest of the Greek islands and the fifth largest in the Mediterranean (after Cyprus, Sicily, Sardinia and Corsica), is a world of its own and a place of unique fascination, with its magnificent and very varied scenery, the distinctive character of its people and the striking remains of Europe's first advanced civilisation.

Crete measures 260 km (162 miles) from W to E and between 14 and 60 km (9 and 37 miles) from N to S, forming a massive barrier along the S side of the Aegean. It is dominated by lofty limestone mountains, part of the mountain system which runs down through mainland Greece (Píndos, Taýgetos), turns towards Crete and extends by way of Kárpathos and Rhodes into Asia Minor. At the W end of the island are the **White Mountains** (*Léfka Óri*, 2452 m (8045 ft)), in the centre **Ida** or Psilorítis (2456 m – 8058 ft), with the *Kamáres Cave*, and to the E **Díkti** (2148 m – 7048 ft), with the *Dictaean Cave*. In these various mountain ranges there are

numerous cave systems and rugged gorges.

There are fertile plains on the N coast and the Lasíthi plateau, but the largest cultivated area on the island is the Mesará plain half way along the S coast, with access to the Libyan Sea at the port of Tymbáki. Elsewhere the S coast is rocky, with only a few small harbours. The major towns and ports, therefore, are on the N coast, including **Iráklion** (see p. 142) and **Khaniá** (p. 158). The climate of the N coast is Mediterranean, of the S coast sub-tropical.

The early history of Crete was rediscovered by Sir Arthur Evans, who excavated and restored the palace of Knossos from 1900 onwards. Since then archaeology has filled out our picture of the history and civilisation of Crete in these early centuries.

MYTHOLOGY and HISTORY. – The Greek myth tells us that Zeus in the form of a bull carried off Europa, daughter of the king of Tyre, from Phoenicia to Crete, where he himself had been born to Rhea in a cave, and by her had three sons – Minos, Rhadamanthys, judge of the dead, and Sarpedon, king of Lycia in Asia Minor. Pasiphaë, Minos' wife, persuaded Daidalos, an artist who had fled from Athens, to construct a wooden cow, in which she concealed herself and was impregnated by a bull belonging to Minos with the Minotaur. Thereupon Minos commissioned Daidalos to construct the Labyrinth to house this bull-headed monster; and Athens was required to send an annual tribute of youths and maidens to Crete, where they were killed by the Minotaur. Finally Theseus sailed from Athens with his companions and killed the Minotaur, with the help of Minos' daughter Ariadne, who gave him a skein of wool which enabled him to find his way out of the inextricable tangle of passages in the Labyrinth. Ariadne then fled with Theseus but was abandoned by him on Náxos, where the god Dionysos made her his wife. Daidalos and his son Ikaros escaped with the help of wings which he had contrived. Ikaros fell into the sea but Daidalos made good his escape and was pursued by Minos to Sicily, where he died.

These mythical tales reflect Greek memories of the Cretan world with which Greece had many contacts during the Mycenaean period (e.g. the tribute payable by Athens which was ended by Theseus). In that world the bull played an important part, reflected in the bull-leaping games of religious significance and the cult symbol of a bull's horns. It was a world of very different religious conceptions from those of the Greeks, a world of refined courtly culture with a centrally directed economy.

About 2600 B.C. the island, then occupied by a Neolithic population which seems to have had African connections, was settled by incomers, perhaps from Asia Minor, who created the Minoan Copper and Bronze Age culture (2600–1100 B.C.). Evans divided this into three periods – Early Minoan (2600–2000 B.C.), Middle Minoan (2000–1550 B.C.) and Late

A Cretan in his local costume

Áyios Nikólaos, Crete

Minoan (1550–1100 B.C.). With the advance of knowledge a division into four periods has come into favour – Pre-Palatial (2600–2000 B.C.), Proto-Palatial (2000–1700 B.C.), Neo-Palatial (1700–1400 B.C.) and Post-Palatial (1400–1100 B.C.).

About 2000 B.C. or soon after that date the Old Palaces were built – royal residences and at the same time the religious, administrative and economic centres of Minoan Crete. Repeated rebuildings indicate that they were damaged on various occasions, no doubt by earthquakes or fires. About 1700 B.C. they were destroyed, and about 1600 a further period of building activity began, in which the New Palaces were erected. These in turn were destroyed in the 15th c. B.C.: the previously accepted date was about 1450, but recently a good case has been made for 1375 B.C. as the date of destruction of Knossos. Spyridon Marinatos suggested that the sudden collapse of Minoan civilisation was caused by a tidal wave and earthquakes associated with a volcanic explosion on the island of Santorin, and this theory was rapidly accepted by the learned world. Wolfgang Schiering, however, has criticised this theory and suggested that the catastrophe was due to a regional tectonic movement which in consequence of the complex geological stratification of Crete did not affect Knossos – as was the case in a similar earthquake in 1926. This would explain the continued existence of this settlement, which survived, much reduced in size, into the final period of Minoan culture.

In the 15th c. B.C. Achaean Greeks settled on the island, particularly at Knossos – perhaps Mycenaean princes marrying into the ruling families, accompanied by a train of followers. This was followed after 1100 B.C. by the arrival of large numbers of Dorians,

changing the whole face of the island. The Minoans, thereafter known as Eteocretans ("true Cretans"), fled to the E of the island, and a series of new towns were founded, among them Lató, Dréros, Priniás and Górtys. In 67 B.C. the Romans arrived in Crete and made Górtys the capital of the island and of the North African territory of Cyrenaica. After the division of the Empire in A.D. 395 Crete was ruled from Byzantium. In 824 it was occupied by the Arabs, who founded the town of Rabd-el-Kandak, later known as Candia and now as Iráklion, but was recovered in 961 by Nikephoros Phokas, later emperor. In 1204 the island fell to Venice, which held it for 450 years. In 1669 the Turks occupied the capital after a siege of 22 years. In 1898 the island was granted autonomy under a Greek ruler, Prince George, and in 1913 it became part of Greece.

The province of Crete is now divided into four *nomoi* – from W to E Khaniá, Réthymnon, Iráklion and Lasíthi. The chief town was Khaniá until 1971, when the centre of administration was moved to Iráklion, the largest town on the island.

Crete has many remains of the past, dating from all the different periods of its history. Minoan culture is represented by the palaces of Knossos, Mália, Phaistós, Ayia Tríada and Káto Zákros, the large houses at Týlisos, Ámnisos and Nírou Kháni, the town of Gourniá and the new excavations at Arkhánes, as well as by the material in the National Archaeological Museum in Iráklion. Outstanding among Greek and Roman sites are Górtys and Lató. Among important Byzantine churches are St Titos at Górtys (6th c.) and the Panayía Kerá at Kritsá (12th c.; frescoes 14th c.). The Venetian period is represented by fortifications, arsenals and the Morosini Fountain in Iráklion, numerous strongholds on the N and S coasts and a number of churches. Relatively little has survived from the Turkish period: the main features are a number of mosques.

Not least among the attractions of Crete is its scenery – the Lasíthi plateau (see p. 169) with its windmills, the Samariá gorge, the mountains with their caves, long stretches of beautiful coast and much else besides.

There are good beaches on the N coast – in the Gulf of Mirabello, near Iráklion (Karterós, 6 km (3 miles) E; Stómion, 5 km (3 miles) W), E of Réthymnon and at Khaniá. The towns and villages on the S coast such as Ierápetra, situated at the mouths of valleys, have smaller beaches.

Cyclades
ΚΥΚΛΑΔΕΣ
(Kikládhes)

The Cyclades are the numerous islands in the southern Aegean which lie between the Greek mainland and the Peloponnese in the W, Crete in the S and the islands off the Anatolian coast in the E. They are so named because to the ancient Greeks they lay in a circle (kyklos) round the little island of Delos, the birthplace of Apollo.

Geologically the islands are a continuation of the hills of Attica and Euboea, so that two chains of islands can be distinguished: to the W, linking up with Attica, are the islands of Kéa, Kýthnos, Sérifos, Sífnos, Kímolos, Mílos (Melos) and Folégandros; to the E, linked with Euboea, are Ándros, Tínos, Mýkonos, Delos and Rinía. Between these two chains is a central group of numerous islands, including Sýros, Páros, Náxos, Íos, Amorgós, Santorin, Anáfi and Astypálaia. Melos and Santorin are of volcanic

origin; the other islands are formed from crystalline rocks, schists and limestones.

HISTORY. – The Cyclades were of great importance on the early shipping routes between Greece and Asia Minor. In the 3rd millennium B.C. they developed the culture known as Cycladic. In the 2nd millennium Minoan and Mycenaean influence became predominant. After the Dorian migrations most of the islands were inhabited by Ionians, those to the S by Dorians. In the 7th c. B.C. the island of Naxos was predominant; in the 6th c. the Cyclades fell under Athenian control; in the Hellenistic period they formed the Nesiotic League. During the Byzantine period the islands were exposed to piracy by the Arabs and others. After the 4th Crusade (1203–04) the Italian duchy of the Archipelago or of Náxos was established. In 1566 the islands were occupied by the Turks. Finally in 1830 they became part of the kingdom of Greece.

Common to all these islands are their poor soil and the typical "Cycladic architecture", derived from very early architectural forms – cube-shaped whitewashed houses with flat roofs, and churches built up from simple formal elements (the cube, the cylinder, barrel vaulting, spherical vaulting). The Cyclades are rich in evidence of 4500 years of history: to the 3rd millennium B.C. belong the Cycladic idols found on Náxos, to the 2nd millennium the excavated sites of Akrotíri (Santorin), Fylakopí (Melos) and Ayía Iríni (Kéa), to the 1st millennium such sites as Delos, Thera and Melos, to the Byzantine centuries the church at Ekatontapyliani on Páros, to the Frankish period in the Middle Ages numerous castles (Náxos, Amorgós, Anáfi, Folégandros, etc.). Nor should the fantastic natural scenery of the volcanic caldera of Santorin be forgotten. Several of these islands, in particular Mýkonos (see p. 190), are now popular and well-equipped holiday resorts.

Dafni
ΔΑΦΝΙ
(Dhafní)

Region and nomos: Attica.

A monastery situated 10 km (6 miles) W of central Athens on the road to Eleusis, famed for its 11th c. *mosaics.

HISTORY. – The name refers to a shrine of Apollo, to whom the laurel (*daphne*) was sacred, which once stood on the site. It was succeeded by an Early Christian monastery, which gave place to the present

The monastery of Dafní

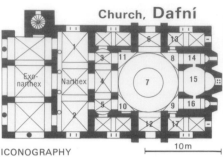

Church, **Dafní**

10m

ICONOGRAPHY

1 Last Supper, Washing of the Feet, Betrayal
2 Presentation of the Virgin, Blessing of the Priests, Joachim and Anna
3 Elpidophorus, Pegasius, Bacchus, Aphthonius
4 Dormition
5 Orestes, Mardarius, Sergius, Auxentius
6 Andronicus, Tarachus, Probus; Crucifixion, Raising of Lazarus, Entry into Jerusalem
7 Pantocrator and Prophets
8 Annunciation
9 Nativity
10 Baptism of Christ
11 Transfiguration
12 Samonas, Guriel, Abibus; Descent into Hell, Incredulity of Thomas, Christ in the Temple
13 Nativity of the Virgin
14 John the Baptist, Silvester, Aaron, Stephen, Zacharias, Anthimus
15 Mary, Michael, Preparation of the Throne, Resurrection, Gabriel
16 Nicholas, Eleutherius, Gregory the Wonderworker, Lawrence, Avercius, Gregory of Agrigento
17 Magi

building in 1080. The monastery was dedicated to the Dormition (*koimesis*, mod. Greek *kímisis*) of the Mother of God. In 1205, after the Frankish occupation of Athens, it was handed over to Cistercian monks and became the burial place of the Frankish lords (later dukes) of Athens. From this period date the battle-mented defensive walls and a number of sarcophagi. At the beginning of the Turkish period the monastery was reoccupied by Orthodox monks. During the 19th c. war of liberation Dafní suffered damage and was abandoned. A thorough restoration in 1955–57 saved the buildings from further decay and ensured the preservation of the structure and the surviving mosaics.

The picturesque and attractive *courtyard* of the monastery is bounded on the W by one side of the cloister, on the N by the S wall of the church and on the W by other monastic buildings. From the W entrance to the church we pass through the *Gothic exonarthex*, dating from the period of Cistercian occupation, and the narthex into the church, which ranks with Ósios Loukás near Delphi (see p. 202) and the Néa Moní on Chios (p. 106) as one of the three finest 11th c. churches in Greece. The *naos*, on a Greek cross plan, is dominated – as in these other two churches – by a large central dome which spans both the central aisle and the two lateral aisles. From the dome the grave and majestic figure of Christ Pantokrator looks down. In the pendentives under the dome are four of the major themes of Orthodox iconography – the Annunciation (NE), the Nativity (SE), the

The Betrayal: a mosaic in the church at Dafní

Baptism of Christ (SW) and the Trans-figuration (NW).

Numerous other mosaics have been preserved in the rest of the church. In the N arm of the cross are the Raising of Lazarus, the Entry into Jerusalem (NW), the Nativity of the Virgin and the Crucifixion (NE), in the S arm the Magi, the Resurrection (SE), the Presentation in the Temple and the Doubting of Thomas (SW). In the *chancel* are the Resurrection and Mary between the archangels Michael and Gabriel, in the *prothesis* (to the left) John the Baptist and in the *diakonikon* (to the right) St Nicholas; above the door of the *naos* is the Dormition, in the *narthex* the prayer of Joachim and Anna, the Washing of the Feet and the Last Supper. All these scenes show the mosaic art of the 11th c. at its peak, in a fascinating combination of the Greek sense of beauty and Christian spiritualisation.

From July to September the Tourist Pavilion at Dafní is the scene of a Wine Festival, with free wine-tasting, Greek culinary specialities, music and dancing

Delos
ΔΗΛΟΣ
(Dhílos)

Nomos: Cyclades. – Area: 3·6 sq. km (1·4 sq. miles).

HOTEL. – *Xenia*, B, 7 b.

TRANSPORTATION. – Boats from Mýkonos.

Although it is one of the smallest of the Cyclades, and much the smallest of the group formed by Mýkonos, Delos and Rinía, **Delos was a place of such importance in ancient times that the surrounding islands were known as the Cyclades, since it was thought that they lay in a circle (kyklos) round the island on which the god Apollo was born. The extensive area of remains (excavated from 1873 onwards by French archaeologists) is one of the most important archaeological sites in Greece. Delos leaves an unforgettable impression on visitors, whether they see it in spring, when it is gay with an abundance of flowers, or in autumn, when the austere lines of

this granite island are revealed in their nakedness.

HISTORY. – The myth relates that Leto, pursued by Hera, found refuge on a floating rocky island, which Poseidon then anchored to the sea bottom with pillars of granite. Here, under a palm, she bore to Zeus the twins Apollo and Artemis, attended by Arge and Opis, two maidens from the hyperborean regions of the N, which the god was required to visit annually in winter.

The cult of Apollo was introduced by Ionian Greeks, while the cult of Artemis can be traced back to the cult of the Great Goddess revered by the pre-Greek population. Towards the end of the 3rd millennium B.C. this earlier population established a settlement on the hill of Kýnthos (113 m – 371 ft), followed in the 2nd millennium by another settlement in the area of the later sacred precinct. The oldest cult buildings (Sanctuary of Artemis, tomb of the "Hyperborean Maidens") date from Mycenaean, if not from pre-Greek, times. From the 7th c. Delos was under the influence of the large neighbouring island of Náxos, which promoted the development of the sanctuary. Later Athens won a predominant position, basing itself on the tradition that on his way back from Crete Theseus had visited Delos, danced the sacred crane dance and established the Delian Festival. In the 6th c. B.C. Peisistratos carried out a "purification" of the island, with the removal of all tombs (apart from that of the two hyperborean maidens) from Delos to the neighbouring island of Rheneia. In the 5th c. B.C. Delos became the headquarters of the Delian Confederacy, a maritime league under the leadership of Athens, but in 454 B.C. the Athenians carried off the treasury of the league and deposited it on the Acropolis. A second purification of the island was carried out in 426–425 B.C., after which it was forbidden for anyone to be born or to die on it. In 314 B.C. Delos broke away from Athens to become independent, and thereafter enjoyed a period of great prosperity. In 166 B.C. the Romans declared Delos a free port, which promoted its development as a trading centre – dealing, among other things, in slaves – and led to the growth of a considerable commercial town to the S of the sacred area. The end came after the island was plundered by Mithridates IX of Pontos in 88 B.C., followed by a further plundering in 69 B.C. Thereafter the island was almost uninhabited, and when Pausanias visited it in the 2nd c. A.D. he saw only the custodians of the deserted sanctuary. A fresh settlement was established in Christian times, but this did not last long.

SIGHTS. – The tour of the site, taking in remains of various periods from the 2nd millennium B.C. to Roman times, begins on the W side of the island, in the area of the ancient harbour, where visitors land at a mole built up of excavation debris. From the Agora of the Competaliasts (Freedmen) we follow a broad paved way (on left) which runs N to the entrance to the *Sacred Precinct. It is flanked by two stoas, the *Stoa of Philip V* of Macedon (*c.* 210 B.C.) and the *South Stoa* (*c.* 180 B.C.), behind which are the remains of the *South Agora*. Climbing the three marble steps of the **Propylon**, worn by the feet of countless pilgrims, we enter the **Hieron**

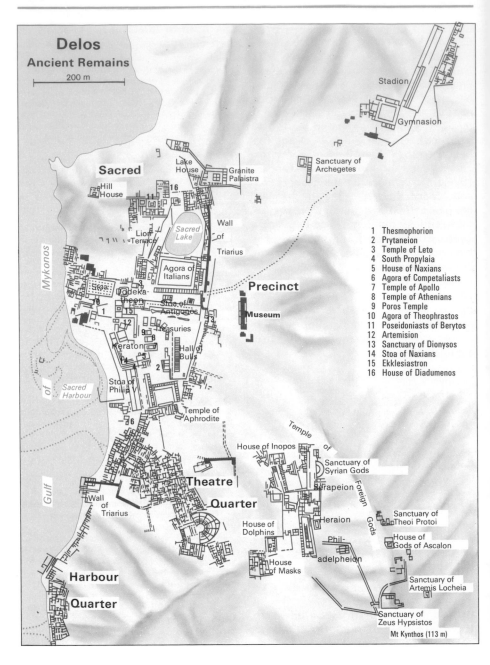

Delos
Ancient Remains

200 m

Stadion

Gymnasion

Sanctuary of
Archegetes

Sacred

Lake
House

Granite
Palaistra

Hill
House

16

11

Lion
Terrace

Sacred
Lake

Wall
of

Triarius

Agora of
Italians

Precinct

Stoa
Dodeka-
theon

Stoa of
Antigonos

Museum

Mykonos

Treasuries

Keraton

Hall of
Bulls

Stoa of
Philip V

Sacred
Harbour

of

Temple of
Aphrodite

6

Temple of

House of Inopos

Sanctuary of
Syrian Gods

Serapeion

Theatre

Wall
of
Triarius

Quarter

Heraion

House of
Dolphins

Phil-
adelpheion

House
of Masks

Foreign Gods

Sanctuary of
Theoi Protoi

House of
Gods of Ascalon

Gulf

Harbour

Quarter

Sanctuary of
Artemis Locheia

Sanctuary of
Zeus Hypsistos

Mt Kynthos (113 m)

1   Thesmophorion
2   Prytaneion
3   Temple of Leto
4   South Propylaia
5   House of Naxians
6   Agora of Competaliasts
7   Temple of Apollo
8   Temple of Athenians
9   Poros Temple
10   Agora of Theophrastos
11   Poseidoniasts of Berytos
12   Artemision
13   Sanctuary of Dionysos
14   Stoa of Naxians
15   Ekklesiastron
16   House of Diadumenos

of Apollo, which extends northward to the *Stoa of Antigonos* and eastward to the Hellenistic wall beyond the *Ship Hall* (see below). Immediately adjoining the Propylon, to the right, is the **House of the Naxians** (beginning of 6th c. B.C.), on the N side of which is the base (5·10 by 3·50 m (17 by 11 ft), 70 cm (28 in.) high) of a marble statue of Apollo erected by the Naxians about 600 B.C. Part of the trunk and the thighs of this colossal figure, which originally stood some 9 m (30 ft) high, can be seen to the NW of the precinct, which was bounded on the S and W by a *stoa* erected by the Naxians.

Here the excavators found a large building, almost square in plan, identified as the *Keraton* in which the old horned altar of Apollo once stood. Immediately adjoining to the N is the badly ruined Precinct of Artemis, which centred on the Temple of Artemis, built in the 2nd c. B.C. on the site of an older 7th c. building.

In the centre of the Sacred Precinct are three *temples of Apollo*, of which only the substructures remain. The oldest and smallest, the most northerly of the three, dates from the first half of the 6th c. B.C. It was built of poros limestone and housed an 8 m (26 ft) high bronze statue of Apollo cast by Tektaios and Angelion of Aegina. The second temple, the most southerly, was the largest of the three and the only one to be surrounded by columns (6×13). It was begun in the 5th c. B.C. but was apparently not completed until the 3rd. Between these two temples is the third and latest of the three, the Temple of the Athenians (after 426 B.C.). – To the N of the temples, set in a semicircle, are the *treasuries*, from which we continue to the so-called *Prytaneion* and farther E to a long building of the 3rd c. B.C. (9 by 67 m – 30 by 220 ft) which is known as the **Hall of the Bulls** after its bull's-head capitals or as the Ship Hall after a ship which was set up here in thanksgiving for a Macedonian naval victory.

We now proceed to the **Sanctuary of Dionysos**, on the E side of the Hieron of Apollo, in which are several *marble phalluses*. On one of the bases are carvings of scenes from the cult of Dionysos (*c.* 300 B.C.). From here we turn W along the **Stoa of Antigonos**, with *bull's-head metopes* on the entablature, which was built by king Antigonos Gonates of Macedon about 250 B.C. Rather less than half way along this is a semicircular structure dating from Mycenaean times, the *tomb of the Hyperborean Maidens* who attended Leto at the birth of the divine twins.

At the W end of the Stoa of Antigonos we leave the Hieron of Apollo, continue past the *Agora of Theophrastos* (126 B.C.) and a *hypostyle hall* (208 B.C.) on the left, and

then pass the *Temple of the Twelve Gods* to reach the *Temple of Leto* (on the right of the path). This was built about 550 B.C. and preserves some courses of marble, with a bench running round the exterior, on gneiss and granite foundations. To the right, E of the temple, is the *Agora of the Italians* (end of 2nd c. B.C.), the largest of a number of similar structures built to house foreign merchants. From here, passing between the Temple of Leto and a long granite building, we follow the processional way, flanked by a number of *lions in Naxian marble dating from the 7th c. B.C. – the earliest monumental figures of animals in Greek art. They look out over the Sacred Lake, which was filled in in 1925–26 on account of the danger of malaria. In the lake is a palm-tree, recalling the palm under which Leto gave birth to Apollo and Artemis. Other remains in the northern part of the site are the *Establishment of the Poseidoniasts of Berytos* (built for the accommodation of merchants from Beirut), the *Granite Palaistra* and the *Lake Palaistra*. – We now return to the Agora of the Italians and continue past the *Fountain of Minoa* (to which a flight of steps leads down) to the museum.

The ***Museum** contains a fine collection of material from the site, although some of the best items found here, such as the relief of Nikandre, are now in the National Archaeological Museum in Athens.

In the two central rooms are works of Archaic art, including (on left) a *marble tripod base* with a ram's head and Gorgons (7th c. B.C.), a *sphinx*, several *kouroi* and *korai* (6th c. B.C.), a *hand of the Naxian*

The Lion Terrace, Delos

Apollo (on right) and three *seated figures of women* (7th c. B.C.). The room to the left of the entrance contains fragments from the Temple of the Athenians (*acroteria* and *figures from the pediment*), herms, funerary stelae, small sculpture, terracottas and pottery. The room to the right contains *votive offerings from the Temple of Artemis*, fragments of sculpture and inscriptions.

Adjoining the museum is a restaurant, which also has a number of bedrooms. From here we can look round the area to the NE, in which are the *Gymnasion*, the *Stadion* and a *residential quarter* near the sea, with a synagogue.

The next section of our tour leads from the museum to Mt Kýnthos. We come first to the *Terrace of the Syrian and Egyptian Gods (2nd c. B.C.), with the Sanctuary of Hadad and Atargatis, which includes a small *theatre*, and the *Sanctuary of Serapis and Isis* (façade of temple re-erected). Here too is a temple of Hera (5th c. B.C.), oriented to the S, from which a flight of steps climbs the slopes of Mt Kýnthos. On top of the hill are remains of a 3rd c. *temple* dedicated to Zeus Kynthios and Athena Kynthia, who were worshipped here from the 7th c. B.C. A mosaic pavement with an inscription which was still visible some years ago has now disappeared. From the hilltop there are wide views. On the way down we can see, on the W side of the hill, a *grotto* roofed with massive stone slabs containing the base of a statue (not, as it is frequently claimed to be, a grotto sacred to Apollo).

We now come to the site of the ancient city of Delos, which has been called the "Greek Pompeii". A typical example of a house of the Hellenistic period is the one known as the *House of the Dolphins*. The entrance leads into the peristyle, with the mosaic pavement which gives the house its name, and adjoining this are a large room and several smaller apartments, with a kitchen at the SE corner. Opposite it is the larger *House of the Masks*, the peristyle of which has been re-erected (masks and mosaics of Dionysos). The badly ruined *theatre*, with seating for some 5000 spectators, dates from the 3rd c. B.C. Behind the stage is a large cistern with nine chambers in which rain-water flowing down from the auditorium was collected. There are a number of other notable buildings on the "Theatre Road" which brings us back to the harbour, including (on right) the *House of the*

Trident and the *House of Dionysos*, both named after their mosaics, and (on left) the *House of Cleopatra*, named after the statues of Kleopatra and her husband Dioskourides which were found here.

Immediately W of Delos is the island of Rínia, the ancient *Rheneia* (area 14 sq. km (5 sq. miles); pop. 45). A narrow isthmus, with a sandy beach, links the northern part of the island with its southern part, in which numerous ancient tombs, sarcophagi and funerary altars have been found.

Delphi
ΔΕΛΦΟΙ
(Dhelfí)

Region and nomos: Phocis.
Altitude: 520–620 m (1706–2034 ft). – Population: 1200.
Telephone dialling code: 0265.
ⓘ Tourist Police,
   Fridirikis 27;
   tel. 8 22 20.

TRANSPORTATION. – Bus service from Athens.

HOTELS. – *Amalia*, A, 334 b.; *Vouzas*, A, 112 b.; *Xenia*, A, 82 b.; *Europa*, B, 92 b.; *Kastalia*, B, 37 b.; *Greca*, C, 26 b.; *Hermes*, C, 44 b.; *Inichos*, C, 32 b.; *Leto*, C, 30 b.; *Mantion*, C, 24 b.; *Pan*, C, 20 b.; *Parnassos*, C, 38 b.; *Phaethon*, C, 35 b.; *Pythia*, C, 50 b.; *Stadion*, C, 45 b.

YOUTH HOSTEL. – CAMPING SITES: 4 km (2 miles) away on the Itéa road; 19 km (12 miles) away at Kírra, near Itéa.

RECREATION and SPORT. – The Delphi area offers plenty of scope for walkers and climbers and also for winter sports, particularly on Parnassus (2457 m (8061 ft): see p. 204). – BATHING BEACHES at Itéa, Kírra and Galaxídi. Yacht supply station at Itéa.

Delphi, lying on the slopes of Mt Parnassus high above the Gulf of Corinth, is one of the most famous cult sites in Greece, renowned throughout the ancient Greek world and beyond as the sanctuary of Apollo and the seat of his oracle. The site ranks along with the Acropolis in Athens, Olympia and the island of Delos among the most important sites of the classical period of Greece; and the wealth of ancient remains combines with its magnificent mountain setting to make Delphi one of the high points of any visit to Greece.

Delphi, home of the oracle, magnificently situated on the slopes of Parnassus

The village of Delphi has developed in recent years into a busy little town, well equipped with hotels and shops to cater for the swarms of visitors who come here. It is a very young settlement, established in 1892, when the little village of Kastrí which had grown up on the site of the Temple of Apollo was moved to its present position, 1 km (1 mile) W of the ancient site and separated from it by a projecting ridge of hill, to allow excavation by French archaeologists to proceed.

HISTORY. – The two crags known as the Phaidriades ("the Resplendent Ones"), Phlemboukos ("Flaming") and Rhodini ("Rose-Pink"), enclose a rocky gorge containing the Castalian spring, from which the ravine of the River Pleistos, densely planted with olive-trees, runs down to Itéa Bay. At the foot of the Phaidriades, close to the Castalian spring, there was in early times a shrine of the Earth Mother, Ge, guarded by the dragon known as Python. The myth relates that the sun god Apollo killed Python and, after an act of expiation in the valley of Tempe in Thessaly, became lord of the sanctuary as Apollo Pythios. His temple was built over a cleft in the rock from which issued vapours promoting the gift of prophecy. But although a male deity had thus displaced the older goddess, a woman still played a central role in the cult of the oracle in the sanctuary of Delphi, which ranked along with Olympia as the principal pan-Hellenic shrine. This was the *Pythia*, who sat on a tripod above the cleft in the rock and whose stammered oracular utterances were conveyed by priests and prophets to those seeking the oracle's advice.

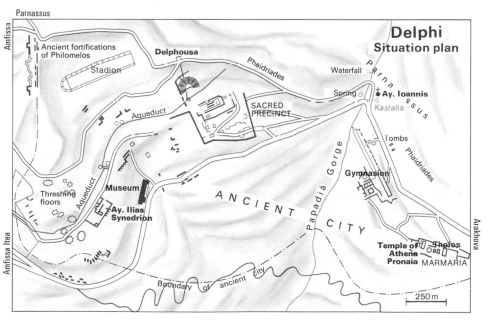

Many of the oracle's prophecies are known, dating back to the Mycenaean period (2nd millennium B.C.). In those early days Orestes was told by the oracle that he could expiate the murder of his mother by fetching the cult image of Artemis from Tauris in Scythia. Around 680 B.C. the oracle guided settlers from Megara to found the city of Byzantion on the Bosporus, later to become Constantinople. In 547 B.C. it told Kroisos (Croesus), king of Lydia in Asia Minor, that if he crossed a certain river he would destroy a great kingdom: whereupon Kroisos crossed the River Halys and was defeated by the Persians, so destroying his own kingdom. In 480 B.C. the oracle declared that Athens, then threatened by the Persians, would be invincible behind a wooden rampart – and so it proved when the fleet built by Themistokles defeated the Persians in the battle of Salamis. The Delphic oracle, which reached the peak of its influence in the 7th and 6th c. B.C., thus played a part in directing the establishment of Greek colonies and in reaching political decisions; and no less significant was the influence of Apollo, the god who granted expiation and made laws, on the development of Greek ethics and law.

The recipients of the oracle's advice expressed their thanks in votive offerings, which brought great wealth to Delphi, much of it stored in treasuries built by individual cities. Most of this has been lost, but some important items can still be seen in the Delphi Museum, and the bronze serpent column set up at Delphi in 479 B.C. after the Athenian victory over the Persians at Plataiai still stands in the Hippodrome in Istanbul.

Delphi enjoyed a final period of prosperity in the reign of Hadrian (2nd c. A.D.), but its day was ended by earthquake damage and the edict by Theodosius I A.D. 392 closing down all pagan shrines. Later the modest little village of Kastrí was built amid the ruins of the temple. The site was rediscovered by a German archaeologist, Ulrichs, and excavation has been carried on since 1892 by French archaeologists.

TOUR OF THE SITE. – A visit to Delphi falls into three parts: the Sanctuary of Apollo, with the Stadion; the Castalian spring and the Sanctuary of Athena at Marmariá; and the museum.

The *Sanctuary of Apollo lies above the modern road and is approached from the museum by a footpath parallel to the road which runs past remains of a mosaic pavement belonging to an Early Christian basilica to the main entrance to the site. By way of the Roman Market we come to the SE gateway of the sacred precinct, which in the classical period was roughly trapezoid in shape, measuring 200 m (656 ft) from N to S and 130 m (427 ft) from E to W and surrounded by a plain enclosure wall. From the gateway the Sacred Way runs uphill, first going W, then bending sharply NE and finally bearing N to end in front of the entrance to the Temple of Apollo.

The Sacred Way was lined with votive monuments erected by various Greek cities, reflecting the diversity of the political pattern of ancient Greece. The monuments themselves have disappeared, but many of their bases have survived. The series begins on the left-hand side of the Sacred Way with the long narrow base of the monument dedicated by the Athenians in gratitude for their victory over the Persians at Marathón (which had sculpture by Pheidias). Then follow monuments dedicated by Argos – the Seven against Thebes, the Trojan horse and an exedra with figures of the Epigonoi – and others by Taras in southern Italy. On the right-hand side was a bronze bull dedicated by Korkyra (*c.* 480 B.C.), followed by a colonnade built by the Spartans after their defeat of Athens in the naval battle of Aigospotamoi in 405 B.C., standing opposite the Athenian monument in honour of Marathón. In front of the Spartan colonnade was a monument erected by the Arcadians to commemorate their victory over the Spartans at Leuktra in 371 B.C. Beyond it was a semicircular monument erected – like the one on the opposite side of the Sacred Way – by Argos, with figures of kings of Argos.

Treasury of the Athenians, Delphi

Along the next section of the Sacred Way, on the left, are the first of the more than 20 treasuries in which votive offerings were preserved from the weather and from theft – the Doric treasury of Sikyon (*c.* 500 B.C.), in the foundations of which can be seen an earlier circular structure, and the Ionic treasury of the island of Siphnos (525 B.C.), considerable remains of which can be seen in the museum. At the point where the Sacred Way bends NE stands an *omphalos stone* set up here some years ago, reflecting the ancient belief that Delphi was the central point, the navel (omphalos), of the world, established at the place where two eagles sent out by Zeus from the ends of the earth met one

Sacred Precinct   **Delphi**

1 Main gate (entrance)
2 Votive monument of
   Korkyra
3 Votive monument of
   Athenians
4 Votive monument of
   Spartans
5 Votive monument of Argos
6 Votive monument of Taras
7 Treasury of Sikyon

8 Treasury of Siphnos
9 Treasury of Megara
10 Treasury of Thebes
11 Treasury of Boeotia
12 Treasury of Potidaia (?)
13 Treasury of Athenians
14 Treasury of Cnidians
15 Bouleuterion
16 Asklepieion

17 Rock of Sibyl
18 Column of Naxians
19 Treasury of Corinthians
20 Treasury of Cyrene
21 Prytaneion
22 Tripod of Plataiai
23 Votive monument of
   Rhodians
24 Altar of Chios

26 Votive monument of
   Syracusans
28 Treasury of Akanthians
27 Temenos of
   Neoptolemos (?)
28 Votive monument of
   Thessalians
29 Alexander's Lion-Hunt
30 Dionysion

another. Then follows the *Treasury of the Athenians* (built in or shortly after 510 B.C. and re-erected in 1903–06), in the form of a Doric temple in antis. The metopes (copies: originals in the Museum) depict themes from the myths of Theseus and Herakles. Immediately beyond the treasury is the retaining wall, with shallow recesses for votive inscriptions, below the *Bouleuterion*.

We now come to the oldest part of the sacred precinct. Between the Sacred Way, just before it crosses the *Halos* ("Threshing-Floor"), the scene of cult ceremonies, and the Temple of Apollo stand side by side the *Rock of the Sibyl*, the *Shrine of Ge* and the site of a tall Ionic column bearing the figure of a sphinx erected by the Naxians about 550 B.C. To

the rear is a *polygonal wall* of the 6th c. B.C., covered with ancient inscriptions, supporting the platform on which the temple stands. Against it is built the 28 m (92 ft) long **Stoa of the Athenians** (after 479 B.C.). Just before the Sacred Way bears N, on the right, are the remains of the Treasury of the Corinthians, which also contained offerings from King Midas of Phrygia and kings Gyges and Kroisos of Lydia (although these had long since disappeared by the time Pausanias visited Delphi in the 2nd c. A.D.).

Alongside the next part of the Sacred Way, which runs N in a series of steps, were other votive monuments. The surviving remains include the circular base of the "Serpent Column" of 479 B.C., formed of three intertwined snakes, and, on the esplanade in front of the Temple of Apollo, the tripods erected by the Deinomids of Syracuse and the pillar which bore a statue of King Prusias II of Bithynia. The esplanade is dominated by an *altar* (partly re-erected) dedicated by the island of Chios and by the six re-erected columns of the *Temple of Apollo, with a ramp leading up to the entrance, at the E end.

The present temple is the third on the site. The first temple, erected in the 7th c., was burned down in 548 B.C. The second was built by the Alcmaeonids in 531 B.C. after their expulsion from Athens by Peisistratos. In Archaic style, with 6×15 Doric columns and sculpture depicting Apollo's arrival in Delphi on the E pediment, it collapsed in 373 (fragments in museum). The third temple, built between 346 and 320 B.C., preserved the elongated ground-plan of the Archaic temple and re-used the old column drums, but the detailing has the cool harmony of the late classical period. Of the main structure only the foundations are left, but we know that the portico contained inscriptions with the sayings of the Seven Sages (including the famous Apollonian imperative *Gnothi seauton*, "Know thyself") and that at the W end of the cella was an adyton in which the Pythia sat.

The water of the Kassotis spring probably played some part in the cult of the oracle: according to Pausanias it "brought the women in the adyton of the god into a condition in which they could prophesy." With this Georges Roux associates the **spring chamber** on the terrace between the temple and the polygonal wall, to which a flight of 12 steps leads down. From the spring a channel runs into the foundations of the temple, and an outflow hole can be seen in the polygonal wall. This Kassotis spring or Spring of the Muses belonged to the second temple, but was removed during the building of the third temple in 346 B.C. in order to strengthen the foundations. On the slope of the hill above the temple stood the figure of the "Charioteer", now in the museum, which was buried under a mass of earth brought down by an earthquake in 373 B.C. and thus preserved from later metal-thieves. Close by is a large niche which once housed a sculptured representation of Alexander the Great's lion-hunt. – A flight of steps leads up to the *Theatre* (4th c. B.C., with later rebuilding down to the Roman period), which could accommodate 5000 spectators. It lay within the sacred precinct, as did the *Lesche* (Assembly Hall) *of the Cnidians*, built against the N wall of the precinct. From the theatre there is a very fine view of the sacred precinct, extending down to Marmariá below.

Continuing uphill, we come 30 m (98 ft) higher up, under a vertical rock face, to the **Stadion**, which received its final form in Roman times. Of this structure there survive the tiers of seating and the seats of honour on the N side, the rounded W end (*sphendone*) and part of the entrance at the E end. The presence of the Theatre and the Stadion is a reminder that the Pythian Games were held at Delphi from 590 B.C. onwards – musical and athletic contests, which included also chariot races run in the Hippodrome in the valley below.

Castalian spring, Delphi

To the E of the Sacred Precinct, in a gorge between the Phaidriades, is the **Castalian Spring**, with recesses for votive offerings in the rock. Here the faithful purified themselves before making their way to the temple on a path now barred by the enclosure fence. On the opposite side of the road is a path leading down to the **Gymnasion**, which consisted of a 180 m (197 yards) long covered running track and a palaistra (training area), with a circular *bath* 10 m (33 ft) in diameter.

Continuing down the path, we come to the *Marmariá* precinct, with the *Sanctuary of Athena Pronaia ("Athena in front of the temple" – i.e. the Temple of Apollo). The *later Temple of Athena* (4th c. B.C.) is followed by the circular **Tholos** (soon after 400 B.C.), which had Doric columns round the outside and Corinthian columns in the interior (partly re-erected), the Ionic *Treasury of Massilia*

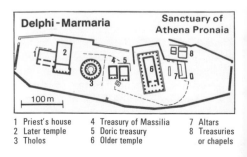

Delphi-Marmaria	Sanctuary of Athena Pronaia

100 m

1 Priest's house	4 Treasury of Massilia	7 Altars
2 Later temple	5 Doric treasury	8 Treasuries
3 Tholos	6 Older temple	or chapels

(Marseilles), with a beautifully profiled base (c. 530 B.C.), a *Doric treasury* (5th c. B.C.) and the old *Temple of Athena*, built about 510 B.C. on the site of a still older building of the early 6th c., later destroyed by a rock fall and damaged by a further rock fall in 1905. The Doric capitals of the earlier building, with their fine echinus mouldings, can still be seen, as can the capitals and columns, still standing, of the late Archaic temple. To the E of this temple, which, like the other Marmariá buildings, is oriented to the S, are a number of *altars*, extending towards the E gate of the precinct, which can still be identified. Further excavations are now under way, directed towards the investigation of the southern part of the precinct.

The *Museum, between the excavated area and the village, contains a fascinating collection of finds from the site, only a selection of which can be mentioned here. On the landing of the steps leading up to the entrance is an *omphalos stone* of the Roman period, carved with a net-like pattern.

Room I. – In the centre of the room are the *Sphinx of the Naxians* (c. 550 B.C.) and a *caryatid* from the Treasury of the Siphnians (c. 525 B.C.), the *frieze from which is displayed on the walls: to the left the pediment (Herakles stealing the Pythia's tripod) and the E frieze (assembly of the gods and Trojan War), to the right the N frieze (Gigantomachia) and W frieze (Judgment of Paris).

Room II. – *Kleobis and Biton, sons of the priestess of Hera at Argos, two massive figures by a Peloponnesian sculptor (c. 600 B.C.: 2·16 m (7 ft) high).

From here we enter the new room, opened in 1978, with *votive offerings* of the 7th–5th c. B.C. found under the Sacred Way N of the Treasury of the Corinthians, including a life-size *bull of silver and gold, *carved ivories and impressive fragments of *chryselephantine statues* of Apollo and his sister Artemis (6th c. B.C.). These new finds, offerings from eastern Greece and Asia Minor, are of particular importance since they include the only examples so far discovered of chryselephantine sculpture. Previously all such figures, including such famous works as those of Pheidias in the Parthenon and the Temple of Zeus at Olympia, had been lost and were known only from literature.

Room III. – *Metopes* from the Treasury of the Athenians, including Theseus and Antiope, Herakles and the Arcadian hind.

Rooms IV–V. – Remains of the Archaic Temple of Apollo, in particular (Room V) the E pediment, depicting the god's coming to Delphi. To the right of this is an *acroterion* from the temple in the form of a winged Victory.

Room VI. – *Stele* from Marmariá depicting an athlete and his attendant (460 B.C.); *circular altar* with the figure of a girl (c. 310 B.C.); head of Dionysos (4th c. B.C.).

Room VII (to right). – Architectural fragments from the Tholos in the Sanctuary of Athena Pronaia, including part of the entablature with carved metopes and semi-columns from the interior with Corinthian capitals (soon after 400 B.C.).

Room VIII. – *Statue of Agias* (c. 350 B.C.; by Lysippos?); *acanthus column* with three korai or Thyades (c. 350 B.C.); *head of a philosopher* (c. 280 B.C.).

Room IX. – The *Charioteer, the famous bronze statue of Sotades of Thespiai, dedicated by the Sicilian tyrant Polyzalos to commemorate a victory in the chariot race at the Pythian Games in 478 or 474 B.C. In adjoining cases are fragments of the chariot and horses.

Room X. – Bronzes; *marble statue of Antinoos, the Emperor Hadrian's favourite (2nd c. A.D.).

SURROUNDINGS. – 9 km E is the village of Arákhova (see p. 61). – Parnassus: see p. 204. – 19 km (12 miles) S is the port of Itéa (see p. 148). – 17 km (11 miles) from Itéa is Galaxídi, on the Gulf of Corinth (castle, monastery, small museum). – 14 km (9 miles) NW of Itéa is Ámfissa (p. 59).

Dodecanese
ΔΩΔΕΚΑΝΗΣΑ
(Dhodhekanísa)

The Dodecanese ("Twelve Islands") are the group of islands extending from Pátmos to Rhodes, together with the Kárpathos group and the island of Meyísti (Kastellórizo) which lie respectively SW and E of Rhodes.

Together with Sámos and its neighbouring islands they form the Southern Sporades. The largest of these islands, with an area of 13,989 sq. km (5401 sq. miles), is Rhodes (see p. 222), which was frequently also a place of some historical importance. The islands were first considered as a group when the Knights of St John moved from Cyprus to Rhodes in 1309, and until their further move to Malta in 1522 were also known as the Knights of Rhodes. In modern times the name of Dodecanese was applied to the group of islands which were ceded to Italy by Turkey in 1912 and at the end of the Second World War passed to Greece.

A fisherman on the island of Pátmos (Dodecanese)

Ancient sites in the Dodecanese include the Asklepieion on Kos (see p. 164) and, on Rhodes, the acropolises of Rhodes and Lindos (pp. 222, 174) and the town of Kámiros (p. 151). The Knights of John have left their mark on Rhodes, Kos, Kálymnos (p. 151) and Sými (p. 244). Pátmos has important Christian remains (the monastery of St John, the Cave of St Anne).

The excellent climate and the infrastructure built up during the period of Italian occupation have promoted the development of some of the islands, in particular Rhodes, into major tourist centres.

Dodona
ΔΩΔΩΝΗ
(Dhodhoni)

Region: Epirus. – Nomos: Ioánnina.

RESTAURANT. – There is a tourist pavilion at the entrance to the site.

The sanctuary of Zeus at Dodóna, home of a noted ancient oracle, lies in a beautiful setting at the foot of Mt Tómaros in Epirus, 18 km (11 miles) SW of Ioánnina.

The road to Dodóna branches off the main road 5 km (3 miles) S of Ioánnina (on right: signpost) and comes in another 16 km (10 miles) to the entrance to the site.

HISTORY. – The oracle of Dodóna developed in a region which was inhabited from 2000 B.C. by Thresprotians and from 1200 B.C. by Molossians, and was served by priests called *helloi* or *selloi*, believed to be of pre-Indo-European, Pelasgic origin. After 1200 B.C. the source goddess Naia, who had previously been worshipped here and continued to be honoured under the name of Dione, was joined by the weather god Zeus Naios. The god was worshipped in a sacred oak-tree, his oracle being expressed in the rustling of its leaves, which was then interpreted by the priests. The earliest evidence of votive offerings dates back to the 7th c. B.C. The sanctuary, munificently supported by Pyrrhos of Epirus (297–273 B.C.) and Philip V of Macedon (219 B.C.), was destroyed in A.D. 391; but in the 5th and 6th c. Dodóna was still the see of a bishop.

SIGHTS. – The **shrine of the oracle** is marked by an oak-tree planted on the site of the original oak and by the foundations of the temenos of Zeus. Features that can be identified include the precinct wall, the *Sacred House* beside the oak-tree (early 4th c. B.C.), with various 3rd c. additions and alterations, and three small *temples* dedicated to Dione, Herakles and Aphrodite lying to the E of the precinct and a *hypostyle hall* to the W, all dating from the 3rd c. B.C.

On the way from the entrance to the site to these remains we come to the largest building at Dodóna, the *Theatre (3rd c. B.C.), which was excavated in 1959, with the massive supporting walls of the auditorium. With a diameter of 122 m (400 ft) and 21 tiers of seating in three sections, this is one of the largest theatres in Greece. The orchestra was converted during the Augustan period into an arena for wild beast shows, and the changes then made can be clearly distinguished. – Behind the theatre are the **town walls** with their *towers*, and in front of it can be seen the tiers of stone seating of the **Stadion**. The remains of an episcopal church erected in the Christian period can be seen to the E of the sacred precinct.

Near the Metropolitan's (Archbishop's) Palace, from which there is a magnificent prospect of the plain, is the **Church of the Dormition** (Kímisis tis Panayías), built on the site of a pagan temple, with *frescoes*. Until the finds at Vérgina (see p. 253) Édessa was thought to be the site of the ancient city of Aigai, capital of the kings of Macedon before the foundation of Pella about 400 B.C.

Drama
ΔΡΑΜΑ
(Dhráma)

Nomos: Dráma.
Altitude: 110 m (361 ft). – Population: 33,000.

TRANSPORTATION. – Dráma is on the Salonica–Alexandroúpolis railway line.

HOTELS. – *Xenia*, B, 44 b.; *Apollo*, C, 75 b.; *Exborikon*, C, 108 b.

The town of Dráma, 36 km (22 miles) NW of Kavála in eastern Macedonia, lies at the foot of Mt Falakron (2194 m (7199 ft)) on a river which is harnessed to drive oil-mills. The area is well watered and fertile, producing cotton, rice and tobacco which are processed in the town.

Edessa
ΕΔΕΣΣΑ
(Édhessa)

Nomos: Pélla. – Telephone dialling code: 0381.
Altitude: 320 m (1050 ft). – Population: 1600.
ⓘ **Tourist Police**,
Leofóros Filíppou 31;
tel. 2 33 55 (summer only).

TRANSPORTATION. – Édessa is on the Salonica–Flórina road (bus service).

HOTELS. – *Xenia*, B, 40 b.; *Alfa*, D, 60 b.; *Olympion*, D, 72 b.; *Pella*, D, 54 b.

The Macedonian town of Édessa, formerly also known as Vódena, lies 68 km (42 miles) W of Salonica on a terrace in the foothills of Mt Vérmion, above the Macedonian plain. With its abundant supply of water (falls on the River Voda) it is a popular summer resort.

Eleusis
ΕΛΕΥΣΙΣ
(Elefsís)

Region and nomos: Attica.
Altitude: 8 m (26 miles). – Population: 15,500.

TRANSPORTATION. – On the Athens–Corinth railway line; bus service from Athens.

HOTELS. – *Melissa*, C, 31 b.; *Steghi*, D, 27 b. – YOUTH HOSTEL.

Within the present-day industrial town of Elefsís, on the coast 22 km (14 miles) W of central Athens, is the site of ancient *Eleusis, home of the Eleusinian mysteries, an important sanctuary dating back to Mycenaean times.

HISTORY. – The Eleusinian cult arose out of the myth of the goddess Demeter, who lamented at the Kallikhoros well here the loss of her daughter Persephone, abducted by Hades; and no corn grew on the earth until Zeus commanded that Persephone should be allowed to return above ground annually in spring. Demeter thereupon established the Eleusinian mysteries, in which she was honoured as the granter of fertility and Persephone (also known as Kore, the Maiden) as an annually returning vegetation goddess. The initiates of the mysteries, who were admitted in two stages to the Lesser and the Greater Eleusinia, appear to have been given the promise not only of the annual renewal of nature but also of a resurrection.

TOUR OF THE SITE. – From the entrance we walk past remains dating from the Roman period (temple of Artemis, triumphal arch) to the *Greater Propylaia* (2nd c. A.D.), to the left of which is the round opening of the *Kallikhoros well*. Beyond this are the *Lesser Propylaia* (54 B.C.), from which the *Ploutonion*, a cave sacred to Pluto, can be seen in the side of the hill (to right) on which the ancient city lay.

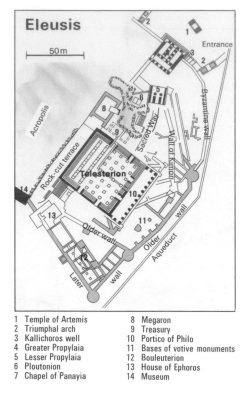

Eleusis

⊢ 50m ⊣

Entrance

Acropolis

Sacred Way

Byzantine wall

Wall of Kimon

Telesterion

Rock-cut terrace

Older wall

Older Aqueduct

Later wall

1 Temple of Artemis	8 Megaron
2 Triumphal arch	9 Treasury
3 Kallichoros well	10 Portico of Philo
4 Greater Propylaia	11 Bases of votive monuments
5 Lesser Propylaia	12 Bouleuterion
6 Ploutonion	13 House of Ephoros
7 Chapel of Panayia	14 Museum

The central feature of the site is the **Telesterion**, the hall in which the mysteries were celebrated. The Solonic Telesterion was erected about 600 B.C. on the site of a small Mycenaean temple of the 14th c. B.C., with an Anaktoron (holy of holies) which remained until Roman times the central element in the structure. Various additions and alterations were carried out in the 6th and 5th c. B.C., and in its final form the Telesterion measured 54 by 52 m (177 by 170 ft), with seven rows of six columns. Between 330 and 310 B.C. the *Portico of Philo* was added. Round the hall ran tiers of seating, those hewn from the rocky hillside being still preserved. Recent Greek excavations have identified the position of the Anaktoron, the centre of the ceremonies conducted by the hierophants.

From here rock-cut steps lead up to the *Museum, in the forecourt of which are statues and a sarcophagus with a representation of the Calydonian boar-hunt.

In the entrance hall are a Demeter by Agorakritos (c. 420 B.C.) and a cast of the votive relief of Demeter, Persephone and the boy Triptolemos (440 B.C.: original in the National Archaeological Museum, Athens). – Room I: sculpture from the pediment of the Archaic Telesterion; statuette of Persephone (c. 480

B.C.); two Archaic kouroi (540 and 530 B.C.); Proto-Attic amphora with the blinded Polyphemos, Perseus and Medusa (7th c. B.C.). – Room II: Archaic kore and ephebe (4th c. B.C.; by Lysippos?); Asklepios (3rd c. B.C.). – Room III: statues of the Roman period. – Room IV: caryatid from the Lesser Propylaia; Corinthian vase with chimaera (7th c. B.C.); terracotta sarcophagus with the skeleton of a child. – Room VI: pottery from Eleusis, bronze vases, etc.

Epidauros
ΕΠΙΔΑΥΡΟΣ
(Epídhavros)

Region: Peloponnese. – Nomos: Argolid.
Altitude: 90 m (295 ft).

TRANSPORTATION. – Epidauros is reached from Náfplion (41 km – 25 miles) or by the new road from Corinth via Néa Epídavros (63 km – 39 miles).

HOTELS. – EPIDAUROS: Xenia II Bungalows, B, 48 b. – NÉA EPÍDAVROS: Epidaurus, C, 13 b. – PALAIÁ EPÍ-DAVROS: Aktis, C, 16 b.; Koronis, C, 13 b.; Maronika, C, 19 b.; Plaza, C, 17 b.; Posidon, C, 18 b.

EVENTS. – Performances in the ancient theatre annually in July and August.

**Epidauros, the most widely famed sanctuary of Asklepios, the god of healing, lies in a quietly beautiful setting in the Argolid.

HISTORY. – In pre-Greek times the god of Maleas (Maleatas) was worshipped on the hill of Kynortion (above the theatre, outside the enclosure), and the Greeks equated this earlier divinity with their god Apollo. Then, at a time that has not been established, Apollo was joined by his son Asklepios, who had grown up at Trikka in Thessaly. Every four years games were held in honour of the god, and from 395 B.C. there was also a dramatic festival. From the end of

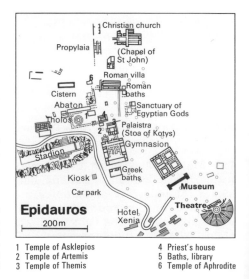

Epidauros

⊢ 200m ⊣

Christian church

Propylaia

(Chapel of St John)

Roman villa

Roman baths

Cistern

Abaton

Sanctuary of Egyptian Gods

Tholos

Palaistra (Stoa of Kotys)

Gymnasion

Stadion

Greek baths

Kiosk

Car park

Hotel Xenia

Museum

Theatre

1 Temple of Asklepios	4 Priest's house
2 Temple of Artemis	5 Baths, library
3 Temple of Themis	6 Temple of Aphrodite

The ancient theatre, Epidauros

the 5th c. B.C. the cult of Asklepios spread widely throughout the ancient world, reaching Athens in 420 B.C. and Rome (under the name of Aesculapius) in 293 B.C. To cater for the crowds of pilgrims who travelled to Epidauros in quest of healing much new building was carried out at the site in the 4th and 3rd c. On the evidence of the votive inscriptions the priest-doctors were already practising psycho-therapeutic methods of treatment. A thermal spring was also used, and surgical instruments have been found on the site. Theatrical performances, which were thought to bring about the purgation or purification of the spectator (katharsis) by inspiring pity and fear, also played a part in treatment. – The sanctuary continued to flourish into the late Roman period, but was closed down about A.D. 400, during the reign of Theodosius I. In the 6th c. Justinian built a fortress in the ruins.

TOUR OF THE SITE. – Before reaching the present entrance to the site we pass on the right the *Stadion* with its tiers of stone seating. The *Theatre, built against the lower slopes of the hill, is remarkable for its excellent state of preservation and for its acoustics.

A. von Gerkan's investigations have shown that the theatre does not date from the 4th c. B.C., as had been supposed on the basis of Pausanias' account. The lower part up to the semicircular gangway, with its tiers of seats divided by staircases into 12 wedge-shaped sections, was built in the early 3rd c. and the upper part added in the 2nd c., giving the theatre a total capacity of 14,000 seats. In the centre is the circular orchestra (diameter 9·77 m (32 ft)). Of the stage buildings (skene) only scanty remains survive; on either side were ramps leading up to the roof of the proskenion, which was used as a raised part of the stage. The entrances for the chorus (parodoi), which are situated between the stage and the supporting walls of the auditorium, lead into the theatre through ceremonial doorways.

From the theatre we walk past the museum to the remains of a large hostel (katagogion) measuring 76·30 m (250 ft) each way, which had 160 rooms on two floors. 100 m (328 ft) W of this are baths and, just to the N, a Gymnasion (76 m (249 ft) square) which was converted into an Odeon in Roman times. In the centre of the site, approached from the N by a sacred way which passes through propylaia, are the principal buildings of the sanctuary, surrounded by stoas in which pilgrims slept while awaiting cure – the Doric Temple of Asklepios (380–375 B.C.) and the circular Tholos (360–330 B.C.), built by Polykleitos the Younger. Of the Tholos only the foundations survive, with a system of concentric passages in which the snakes sacred to Asklepios may have been kept. A clearer impression of this building, which was notable for its lavish decoration, can be found in the Museum, in the last room of which there is a partial reconstruction. The circular cella was surrounded by 26 Doric columns and had 14 Corinthian columns around its internal wall. In the centre of the floor, decorated in two colours, was an opening leading down to the basement. The elaborate nature of the decoration can be judged from the coffered ceiling, the high quality of the work by the Corinthian *capital, carved by Polykleitos himself. – The other rooms of the museum contain inscriptions, surgical instruments, statues of Asklepios (some of them casts) and architectural fragments from the propylaia and the Temple of Asklepios.

SURROUNDINGS. – The little harbour towns of Néa and Palaiá Epídavros (each 19 km (12 miles): bathing beaches) can be reached by way of Ligourió.

Epirus
ΗΠΕΙΡΟΣ
(Ípiros)

Local costumes, Epirus

Epirus (i.e. the "Mainland", as opposed to the offshore islands) covers an area of 9200 sq. km (3552 sq. miles) in NW Greece, between the Albanian frontier and the Ambracian Gulf, the Ionian Sea and the Pindos mountains. Historically the territory of Epirus extended into southern Albania.

It is a hilly region with an abundance of rain which favours the development of agriculture and particularly of stock-farming. In ancient times it was regarded as a rather backward area; but the oracle of Acheron, the river of the underworld, was known to Homer, and the oracle of Zeus at Dodóna was widely famed. The most notable historical figure produced by Epirus was the Molossian king Pyrrhos (319–272 B.C.), who was praised by Hannibal as the greatest general after Alexander the Great. In later centuries the region was settled by incoming Slavs and Albanians, and in the 13th c. it again achieved some importance under the Byzantine Despot of Árta. The Turkish occupation which began in 1449 lasted until 1914, when it was ended by a demarcation of the much-disputed frontier between Greece and Albania. The

chief town is Ioánnina (see p. 140), which has a recently founded university.

The principal ancient sites in Epirus are Dodóna, the nekyomanteion of Mesopótamos and the city of Nikópolis, founded by Augustus. The medieval period is represented by the churches of Árta; and evidence of the Turkish occupation is preserved in Ioánnina, which was ruled by Ali Pasha as a semi-independent principality from 1788 to 1822. Párga (see p. 203), situated in a picturesque bay with one of the few harbours on this rocky coast, has developed into a holiday resort of some consequence.

Euboea
ΕΥΒΟΙΑ
(Évvia)

Nomos: Euboea.
Area: 3658 sq. km (1412 sq. miles). – Population: 163,000.
ⓘ Tourist Police, Khalkís,
Kótsou 2;
tel. (0221) 2 46 62.
Tourist Police, Aidipsós (summer only),
Okeanídon 3;
tel. (0226) 2 35 25.

TRANSPORTATION. – Rail and bus services from Athens (1½ hours in each case); ferries from Rafína to Marmári and Kárystos, from Oropós to Erétria, from Glýfa to Ayiókambos, from Arkítsa to Aidipsós, from Kými to the Sporades.

HOTELS. – KHALKÍS: Lucy, A, 156 b.; Hilda, B, 223 b.; John's, B, 98 b.; Palirria, B, 214 b.; Chara, C, 73 b.; Kentrikon, C, 35 b.; Manica, C, 48 b. – NEAR THE TOWN: St Minas Beach, A, 185 b.

NORTH OF KHALKÍS. – NÉA ARTÁKI (8 km – 5 miles): Bel Air, B, 82 b.; Angela, C, 78 b.; Telemachus, C, 48 b. –

Párga, on the W coast of Epirus

PROKÓPION (52 km – 32 miles): *Anessis*, E, 13 b. – AYÍA ANNA (77 km – 48 miles): *Aigli*, D, 10 b. – LIMNI (86 km – 53 miles): *Avra*, C, 11 b.; *Plaza*, C, 12 b. – ISTIÁIA (129 km – 80 miles): *Hermes*, D, 16 b.; *Neopn*, E, 19 b. – NÉOS PÝRGOS (135 km – 84 miles): *Akroyiali*, D, 28 b.; *Oasis*, D, 36 b. – AIDIPSÓS (Loutra, 151 km – 94 miles): *Aigli*, A, 154 b.; *Avra*, A, 133 b.; *Petit Palais*, A, 17 b.; *Adonis*, B, 47 b.; *Galaxias*, A, 64 b.; *Chara*, B, 65 b.; *Hermes*, B, 78 b.; *Herakleon*, B, 69 b.; *Kentrikon*, B, 56 b.; *Thermae Syla*, B, 115 b.; *Anessis Batis*, C, 90 b.; *Artemision*, C, 27 b.; *Atlantis*, C, 38 b.; *Galini*, C, 68 b.; *Ilion*, C, 34 b.; *Irene*, C, 55 b.; *Istiaia*, C, 61 b.; *Knossos*, C, 71 b.; *Leto*, C, 65 b.; *Mikra Epavlis*, C, 33 b.; *Minos*, C, 41 b.; *Mitho*, C, 40 b.; *Nefeli*, C, 71 b. – GREGO-LÍMANO (Likhas, 181 km – 112 miles): *Gregolimano – Roi Soleil*, A, 340 b.

SOUTH OF KHALKÍS. – LEFKÁNTI: *Lefkanti*, C, 79 b. – *Malakónta* (3 km – 2 miles): *Eretria Beach*, A, 453 b.; *Malakonta Beach*, B, 298 b. – ERÉTRIA (22 km – 14 miles): *Holidays in Evia*, B, 639 b.; *Periyiali Eretrias*, B, 68 b.; *Elfis*, C, 168 b. – AMÁRYNTHOS (31 km – 19 miles): *Blue Beach*, B, 400 b.; *Stefania*, B, 88 b.; *Amarynthos*, C, 70 b. – *Almyropótamos* (77 km – 48 miles): *Galazio Delfini*, C, 20 b. – NÉA STÝRA (96 km – 60 miles): *Aiyilion*, C, 51 b.; *Aktaion*, C, 75 b.; *Delfini*, C, 39 b.; *Marmari*, C, 156 b. – KÁRYSTOS (124 km – 77 miles): *Apollon Resort*, B, 150 b.; *Als*, C, 62 b.; *Galaxi*, C, 136 b.; *Karystion*, C, 75 b.; *Louloudi*, C, 48 b.; *Plaza*, C, 68 b.

INTERIOR AND NE COAST. – KÝMI (93 km – 58 miles): *Betis*, C, 60 b.; *Aktaion*, D, 23 b. – STENÍ (32 km – 20 miles): *Dirfys*, C, 52 b.; *Steni*, C, 70 b.

SWIMMING. – At Paganítsa and Kourénti (to the N) and Vasilikó (S of town).

In the harbour, Khalkís (Euboea)

island's chief town, Khalkís, is connected with the mainland by a swing bridge. Compressed into this narrow channel, the tides – elsewhere in Greek waters barely perceptible – show a marked variation between ebb and flow, a phenomenon which created a hazard for ancient shipping and is still a danger to small modern boats. The landscape pattern of Euboea is set by its ranges of hills and mountains, reaching a height of 1398 m (4587 feet) in **Ókhi**, to the S, and 1743 m (5719 feet) in **Dírfys**, in the centre of the island, and by the alternation between its rich vegetation cover and areas of forest in the N, the sparser growth of the S and the barren upland regions.

HISTORY. – In ancient times the rival cities of Chalkis and Erétria vied with one another for control of the island, until finally Athens established its authority. In 338 B.C. Euboea became Macedonian, in 194 B.C. Roman. After the 4th Crusade it fell into the hands of Boniface of Montferrat, who divided it into three territories and assigned them to Italian *terzieri*. In 1306 Venice gained control of the island, now known as Negroponte. Occupied by the Turks in 1470, it became part of Greece in 1830. The present division into the eparchies of Istiáia, Khalkís and Kárystos corresponds to the medieval division into three territories.

Coastal scenery on Euboea

Euboea, whose coastal towns and villages have increasingly developed into tourist resorts, is the largest Greek island after Crete, larger than Lésbos and Corfu. It seems more like part of the mainland than an island, however, since it is separated only by a narrow strip of sea from the E coasts of Boeotia and Attica, with which it runs parallel for some 175 km (109 miles), varying in breadth between 6 and 50 km (4 and 31 miles).

At its narrowest point the strait between Euboea and the mainland, **Evripos**, is only 60 m (197 feet) wide, and the

SIGHTS. – The capital of the island, **Khalkís** (alt. 10 m (33 feet), pop. 36,000), situated at the point where Evripos is only 60 m (197 feet) wide, was in ancient times a thriving city which established numerous colonies, and is still the administrative and economic centre of Euboea. The **Archaeological Museum** in Aristotle Street contains fine fragments of the *frieze of the Temple of Apollo* in Erétria, including a metope depicting Theseus and Antiope (*c.* 510 B.C.). The *Historical Museum*, containing medieval material, is housed in a former mosque (Platía Pesónton Oplitón). The church of *Ayía Paraskeví* was the Roman Catholic cathedral during the period of Crusader occupation. A Turkish fortress occupies the site of the ancient acropolis. – On the mainland opposite Khalkís is the **Bay of Aulis**, where Iphigeneia was sacrificed at the beginning of the Trojan War. – On the way from Khalkís to *Stení* (33 km (21 miles) NE; pop. 770; bus) it is possible to climb **Dírfys** (1743 m (5719 feet); about 6 hours), from the summit of which there are extensive views.

The attractive village of **Prokópion** (pop. 760), formerly known as Akhmet Aga, 58 km (36 miles) from Khalkís in the N of the island, is noted for its handicrafts and for the *church of St John the Russian*. – **Límni** (86 km – 53 miles) lies on the W coast between two wooded hills. – **Artemísion** (117 km (73 miles); pop. 500) has the remains of a sanctuary of Artemis (10 minutes N). Off Cape Artemision there was a naval battle between Greeks and Persians in 480 B.C. The large bronze statue of Zeus now in the National Archaeological Museum in Athens was found here in 1926–28. – **Loutrá Aidipsoú** (151 km (94 miles): pop. 1900) is a well-known spa recommended for the treatment of rheumatism, arthritis, sciatica and gynaecological conditions. A short distance N of the town is the little harbour of **Ayiókampos**, from which there is a ferry service to **Glýfa** on the coast of Thessaly.

In **Erétria** (Néa Psará: pop. 1900), 22 km (14 miles) from Khalkís in the S of the island, there are substantial ancient remains, including a *theatre* (built *c.* 430 B.C., altered after 330 and *c.* 200 B.C.), to the E of the theatre a *gymnasion* and the *walls of the acropolis*. The site of a temple of Apollo (*c.* 510 B.C.) has also been located NE of the gymnasion.

In 1975 Swiss archaeologists found the intersection of the main N–S and E–W streets of the ancient city. The tombs of the founder of the city and his family, with a shrine for the cult of the dead built over them, were found to the S of the W gate. Nearby were a Heroon (7th c. B.C., later moved to another site) and a palace belonging to a family closely connected with the cult practised in it (5th c. B.C.).

On the site of the ancient Agora is a *museum* containing local finds.

Amárynthos (31 km (19 miles); pop. 2400) is an attractive fishing port. – Green marble has been worked since ancient times at **Stýra** (42 km (26 miles); pop. 550) and **Kárystos** (124 km (77 miles); alt. 20 m (66 feet); pop. 3350). The

present town of **Kárystos** was founded in 1833 in a bay near the site of the ancient city, now known as Palaiokhóra, where there is a Venetian castle. To the SE of the site are ancient marble quarries.

The little town of **Kými** (alt. 200 m (656 feet); pop. 3200) lies above the harbour of **Paralía Kýmis** (sandy beach).

Farsala
ΦΑΡΣΑΛΑ
(Fársala)

Nomos: Larisa.
Altitude: 180 m (591 feet). – Population: 6500.

TRANSPORTATION. – Station on the Athens–Salonica railway line (13 km (8 miles) W); bus service from Athens.

HOTEL. – *Akhillion*, D, 28 b.

The Thessalian town of Fársala, on a site which has been continuously occupied since Neolithic times, was destroyed by an earthquake in 1954 and thereafter rebuilt in modern style.

The only evidence of its long past is an Archaic tomb on the western outskirts of the town, a circular structure surrounded by large slabs of stone.

HISTORY. – Fársala is notable mainly as the scene of the battle of Pharsalos in the summer of 48 B.C., in which Caesar defeated Pompey. This was the first of three battles fought in Greece in the 1st c. B.C. which had decisive effects on the history of Rome; the others were Philippi in 42 B.C. (see p. 214) and Aktion (Actium) in 31 B.C. (see p. 195).

From the hill (348 m – 1142 feet) above the town there is a view of the battlefield in the Enipefs valley to the N.

Florina
ΦΛΩΡΙΝΑ
(Flórina)

Nomos: Flórina.
Altitude: 660 m (217 feet). – Population: 12,000.

HOTELS. – *Lyngos*, B, 76 b.; *Tottis*, B, 63 b.

Flórina lies on a plateau to the N of the Verna hills, 16 km (10 miles) from the frontier crossing into Yugoslavia (Bitola). Situated in a well-cultivated farming region, it has an agricultural college and a well-known fruit market.

There is a trunk road from here via Édessa and Pélla to Salonica (160 km – 99 miles).

Folegandros
ΦΟΛΕΓΑΝΔΡΟΣ
(Folégandhros)

Nomos: Cyclades.
Area: 34 sq. km (13 sq. miles). – Population: 7000.

TRANSPORTATION. – Folégandros is served by boats which make the round trip Piraeus–Páros–Santorin–Folégandros–Síkinos–Íos–Náxos–Piraeus.

HOTEL. – *Danassis*, E, 27 b.

The long, narrow island of Folégandros, lying between Melos and Santorin in the Cyclades, has, like the neighbouring island of Síkinos, played little part in history and, again like Síkinos, lies off the beaten track of modern tourism. The E end of the island, edged by cliffs and rising to a height of 414 m (136 feet) in the centre, is dry and inhospitable, but the W end has a water supply from springs and a milder climate which have promoted the development of terraced cultivation.

In the western part of the island is Anó Meriá (alt. 260 m (853 feet); pop. 380). The little harbour of Karavostásis (alt. 10 m (33 feet); pop. 30) lies on the N coast of the eastern half. The chief place, Folégandros, is 3 km (2 miles) away on a plateau in the centre of the island. Nearby is a medieval castle (Palaiókastro).

Fourni
ΦΟΥΡΝΟΙ
(Fúrni)

Nomos: Samos.
Area: 30 sq. km (12 sq. miles). – Population: 1000.

Foúrni is an island, surrounded by several smaller islets, with an irregular and much-indented coastline. Most of the inhabitants live in the village of the same name on the W coast, from which there are regular boat services to the neighbouring islands of Ikaría and Sámos.

Fyli
ΦΥΛΗ
(Filí)

Region and nomos: Attica.

Although it is only a few kilometres outside Athens, Fylí lies in the heart of the countryside of Attica, with an old monastery and one of the ancient Athenian fortresses defending the frontiers of Attica.

Leaving Athens on the Liosía road past the Lárisa Station, we come to Anó Liosía (13 km – 8 miles), the village of Fylí (18 km (11 miles): bus from Athens to this point) and the lonely monastery of Panayía ton Klistón (22 km – 14 miles). The name of the monastery (Mother of God of the Gorges) refers to its situation on the rock face above the defile of the River Goúras, on the slopes of Mt Párnis. The monastery is believed to have been founded in the 14th c., but both the church and the monks' quarters were later rebuilt and enlarged. Upstream is an ancient *grotto of the god Pan*, the setting of Menander's comedy "Dyskolos".

A few kilometres farther on we see on the left the walls of the ancient fortress of Phyle, to which we must climb up on foot.

HISTORY. – After the Peloponnesian War Athens built a ring of frontier fortresses designed to protect Attica against attack from the Megarid and Boeotia to the W. Beginning with the fortified city of Eleusis on the coast, this defensive system continued with the fortress of Ánakton and the town of Oinoe on Mt Kithairon (NW of Eleusis) and then ran E via Phyle, Dekeleia and Áphidna to Rhamnoús on the E coast of Attica. – The construction of the fortress of Ánakton led Mégara to erect a counter-fortification at Aigósthena, the most northerly point in its territory (see p. 219).

Phyle stands on a rectangular plateau (alt. 683 m (2241 feet)) at the pass carrying the road from Athens to Tánagra in Boeotia under the western slopes of Mt Párnis. The site had probably been occupied by an earlier fortress in which Thrasyboulos assembled his supporters in 403 B.C. for the attack on the Thirty Tyrants. The W and SW parts of the 4th c. **fortress** (which was excavated by Skias in 1900) have collapsed into the gorge, but considerable stretches of the *walls* of dressed stone, with four towers and two gates, have been preserved to the level of the wall-walk. The stones, measuring 2·75 m by 38 cm (9 feet by 15 inches), stand between six and 20 courses high. At some later period the interior of the fortress was infilled to the height of the walls.

SURROUNDINGS. – On the way back to Athens we can turn off in Anó Liosía into a road on the left which comes in 3 km (2 miles) to **Akhárnai**, on the road to Mt Párnis (p. 204). The site was occupied from Mycenaean times, and in the classical period it was a place of some consequence; it was the setting of Aristophanes' "Acharnians". 3 km (2 miles) before the village, near a Mycenaean tholos tomb, remains of the later fortifications can be seen on the hill to the left of the road.

Geraki
ΓΕΡΑΚΙ
(Yeráki)

Region: Peloponnese. – Nomos: Laconia.
Population: 2000.
No accommodation available.

Geráki, a quiet little place occupying the site of the ancient Geronthrai, lies in an impressive setting in a high valley in the Párnon range, 41 km (25 miles) SE of Sparta.

From its heyday in Byzantine times, under the rule of the Despots of Mistra, Geráki preserves many churches and chapels, the most notable of which is **Áyios Ioánnis**. On the way up to the Frankish castle (1 hour's walk: first SE, then to the left beyond the cemetery) are a number of other churches, including the 12th c. **Ayía Paraskeví**.

Geráki Castle, one of the numerous Crusader castles in the Peloponnese, was built by Guy de Nivellet in 1234 on a ridge of Mt Párnon to protect the area from attack by the Tsaconians. A vaulted passage leads through the battlemented walls into the castle. The *chapel*, a three-aisled basilica, is very well preserved. The altar bears Guy de Nivellet's coat of arms. On the iconostasis is an icon of the church's patron, St George, on whose feast-day a service is still celebrated here.

SURROUNDINGS. – From Geráki there are fairly mediocre roads to two places on the E coast of the Peloponnese, the little ports of **Leonídi** (50 km (31 miles) NE) and **Monemvasía** (67 km (42 miles): see p. 187).

Gla
ΓΛΑ
(Gla)

Region and nomos: Boeotia.

This Mycenaean fortress lies at the NE end of the Kopais plain, formerly Lake Kopais.

26 km (16 miles) from Thebes on the main road to Lamía the hill on which Gla lies can be seen rising out of the plain on the right of the road, 1 km (about a ½ mile) away. To reach it, turn off left to the village of Kástro and use the underpass. The narrow access road encircles the hill, which rises to 70 m (230 feet) at the N end. The massive **walls**, 5·70 m (19 feet) thick and still standing 3 m (10 feet) high, enclose the whole area of the hill; they are 3 km (2 miles) long (cf. Mycenae, 900 m (2953 feet)) and take in an area of 200,000 sq. m (77,220 sq. miles), making this the largest stronghold of its period. From the N gate we continue up to the highest point on the hill, with the remains of the *palace*, the two wings of which are set at a right angle. To the S, in the direction of the S gate, are the remains of other residential buildings. There was a double gateway on the E side.

Gortys
ΓΟΡΤΥΣ
(Górtis)

Island: Crete. – Nomos: Iráklion.

Górtys or Gortyn was an important Dorian settlement in southern

Crete, 45 km (28 miles) from Iráklion on the road to Phaistós, which in Roman times (67 B.C. to A.D. 395) became capital of Crete and the North African province of Cyrenaica. The remains, mainly dating from the Roman period, were excavated by Italian archaeologists.

The most important structures are immediately right of the road, beginning with the church of St Titos (a disciple of the Apostle Paul who evangelised Crete and became its first bishop). The church, a three-aisled pillared basilica, dates from the 6th c.; the three *apses* have been preserved, and the N apse now serves as a modest *chapel*. – NW of the church is the *Odeon, a circular structure of Roman date, in the semicircular ambulatory of which is the *Code of Gortyn*, a legal code in the Doric dialect dating from about 500 B.C. The text is written "boustrophedon" (i.e. as the ox ploughs, with alternate lines running left to right and right to left). – Beyond the bed of a stream, on the slopes of the acropolis hill, are the remains of a theatre.

On the other side of the road, some 250 m (820 feet) farther E, a narrow path leads S through an olive-grove to the *Temple of the Egyptian Gods* (100 m – 328 feet) and beyond this the Temple of Apollo (6th c. B.C.), to which a marble-clad apse was added in Roman times. Immediately SW are the ruins of a theatre, and 100 m (328 feet) farther E the remains of the *Praetorium* (the residence of the Roman governor) and a *nymphaeum*.

SURROUNDINGS. – At Platanós, 6·5 km (4 miles) S of the village of Áyii Déka, which is only a short distance from Górtys, is the largest tholos tomb in Crete (interior diameter 13 m (43 feet)), dating from the 3rd millennium B.C. – From Áyii Déka a road goes to Léntas (27 km – 17 miles), on the S coast. Near here is the Asklepieion of *Lebéna*, founded at a thermal spring by Górtys in the 4th c. B.C. To the N of an 11th c. chapel dedicated to St John can be seen remains of a temple, a mosaic pavement, etc.

Gournia
ΓΟΥΡΝΙΑ
(Gurniá)

Island: Crete. – Nomos: Lasíthi.

Gourniá is a Minoan site on the N coast of Crete, 19 km (12 miles) E of Ayios Nikoláos near the Gulf of Mirabello. It is the only Minoan town which has been completely excavated, usefully supplementing the evidence derived from the Minoan palaces and country houses.

The custodian conducts visitors from the road on the E side of the site along the lanes between the remains of houses, which give an impression of the life of a city of the 16th c. B.C., particularly since a number of everyday objects (e.g. grinding stones) have been left in situ. On top of the hill are the remains of a small palace in which the ruler of the town, or perhaps the governor, lived. From the palace a flight of steps in the corner leads into the Agora. If we follow a narrow street westwards from this square and then turn N we come to a small *shrine* dating from the last phase of the town, which was destroyed about 1450 B.C. and thereafter fell into oblivion. Finds from the site are in Iráklion Museum.

Gythion
ΓΥΘΕΙΟΝ
(Yíthion)

Nomos: Láconia.
Altitude: 10 m (33 feet). – Population: 7500.

TRANSPORTATION. – Boat services to Piraeus, Kýthira and Monemvasía; bus services to Sparta and Areópolis (Máni). Yacht supply station.

HOTELS. – *Lakonis*, A, 148 b.; *Belle Hélène* (12 km (7 miles) from town), B, 180 b.; *Laryssion*, C, 150 b.; *Pantheon*, C, 99 b.

SWIMMING: NW of the town.

Gýthion is a port on the Gulf of Laconia, 46 km (29 miles) S of Sparta and 24 km (15 miles) W of the mouth of the Eurotas.

The island of Marathonísi, connected with the mainland by a causeway, was the ancient Kranai, on which tradition had it that the Trojan prince Paris married Helen, whom he had carried off from Sparta. Near the barracks is a Roman theatre.

SURROUNDINGS. – Gýthion is a good base from which to visit the Máni peninsula (26 km– 16 miles), Sparta (46 km – 29 miles), Mistra (51 km – 32 miles) and Monemvasía (60 km – 37 miles). See the entries for these places.

Coastal scenery, Hýdra

Hydra
ΥΔΡΑ
(Ídhra)

Nomos: Attica. – Telephone dialling code: 0298.
Area: 50 sq. km (19 sq. miles). – Population: 2550.
ⓘ Tourist Police (summer only),
Navárkhou Vótsi;
tel. 5 22 05.

TRANSPORTATION. – The Argosaronikos service links Hýdra with Piraeus and with the islands of Aegina, Póros and Spétsai.

HOTELS. – *Miramare*, A, 50 b.; *Miranda*, A, 30 b.; *Delfini*, B, 20 b.; *Hydrousa*, B, 72 b.; *Xenon Dimitras*, B, 17 b.; *Hydra*, C, 23 b.; *Leto*, C, 74 b.

SWIMMING: immediately W of the harbour (rock, with concreted surfaces) and in Mandráki Bay (pebbles and rock).

The long rocky island of *Hýdra, lying off the NE tip of the Peloponnese, is now a popular summer holiday resort.

The town of Ídra (Hýdra) rises in an amphitheatre above its sheltered harbour. A number of handsome mansions belonging to ship-owning families, among them the houses of the Tsamádos and Kountouriótis families, recall the powerful support given to the Greek struggle for

The harbour, Ídra (Hýdra)

freedom by the wealthy ship-owners of Hýdra. Other features of interest on the island are the Church of the Dormition (Kímisis Theotókou, 18th c.) in a former monastery by the harbour; the 15th c. *Profítis Ilías monastery* (an hour's walk from the town); and the 16th c. *Zourvás monastery* at the E end of the island (3 hours' walk; also accessible by boat).

Hymettos
ΥΜΕΤΤΟΣ
(Imittós)

Region and nomos: Attica.

The plain of Attica is bounded on the E by the long ridge of Hymettos (1027 m – 3370 feet), made up of the bluish-grey Hymettian marble, overlying Pentelic marble, which was worked in ancient times. The hills were then covered with forest, and the honey of the region was renowned.

In recent decades efforts have been made to replant trees on the long deforested slopes of the hill, particularly around Kaisarianí monastery. The monastery has an abundant spring, one of the many once found on Hymettos.

On the summit plateau there was a sanctuary of Zeus Ombrios, who was invoked with prayers for rain. Other shrines on Hymettos were the *precinct of Apollo Proopsios* and, at the southern end of the range, the *Grotto of the Nymphs* (3 km (2 miles) N of Vári).

There is now a road which runs from the suburb of Kaisarianí, on the E side of Athens, to Kaisarianí monastery and continues to Astéri monastery, with a domed cruciform *church* (frescoes), ending on the summit plateau (military area, closed to the public).

Below the N end of Hymettos stands the monastery of Áyios Ioánnis Kynigós, which has a small early 13th c. *church* with later additions. It is reached from the Athens–Markópoulo road (2 km (1 mile) before Stavrós).

Ialysos

ΙΑΛΥΣΟΣ

(Ialisós)

Island: Rhodes. – Nomos: Dodecanese.

Ialysós ranks with Líndos and Kámeiros as one of the three ancient cities on the island of Rhodes. It lies 15 km (9 miles) SW of the town of Rhodes in a grove of pines and cypresses above the coastal plain of Triánta, at an altitude of 267 m (876 feet), with views extending to the coast of Asia Minor.

The hill has been occupied by a succession of strongholds from Mycenaean times (c. 1400 B.C.) onwards. In 1308 it was used by the Knights of St John as a base for their attack on Rhodes, and in 1522 it served the same purpose for the Turks. An attractive broad stepped footpath leads up to the acropolis.

On the plateau can be seen the foundations of a temple of Athena, built in the 3rd c. B.C. on the site of an earlier temple, which in early Christian times was in turn replaced by a church; a cruciform font, sunk into the ground, can still be seen. There are also a small chapel with 15th c. frescoes and the church and cloister of the Filérimos monastery, restored during the period of Italian occupation. A stepped path leads down to a Doric fountainhouse (4th c. B.C.) on the hillside.

Ierapetra

ΙΕΡΑΠΕΤΡΑ

(Ierápetra)

Island: Crete. – Nomos: Lasíthi.
Altitude: 5 m (16 feet). – Population: 6500.

TRANSPORTATION. – Bus services from Áyios Nikólaos and Sitía.

HOTELS. – Atlantis, C, 134 b.; Creta, C, 49 b.; Lygia, C. 29 b.; Myrtos, C, 18 b.

Ierápetra is a small port on the S coast of Crete, occupying the site of the ancient city of Hierapytna, with a handsome Venetian castle on an adjoining promontory and an interesting little museum in the town

hall. It has a beach of fine sand, shaded by tamarisks, with a number of tavernas and bathing cabins.

The road from Áyios Nikólaos runs E to Pakhyámmos (long sandy beach) and then turns S to cross the island at its narrowest point (total distance 35 km (22 miles)).

An interesting return route is provided by the road which runs W from Ierápetra via Anó Viánnos, Arkalokhóri and Knossos to Iráklion (100 km – 62 miles).

Igoumenitsa

ΗΓΟΥΜΕΝΙΤΣΑ

(Igumenítsa)

Nomos: Thesprotia. – Telephone dialling code. 0665.
Altitude: 10 m (33 feet). – Population: 4000.
ⓘ Tourist Police,
Dangli 17;
tel. 2 23 02.

TRANSPORTATION. – Ferry services from Italy, Kérkyra and Pátras.

HOTELS. – Xenia, B, 72 b.; Tourist, C, 40 b.; and hotels in categories D and E.

This little town in Epirus is of importance as a ferry terminal and the starting-point of a tour of western Greece or through the Pindos mountains into Thessaly.

Ikaria

ΙΚΑΡΙΑ

(Ikaría)

Nomos: Samos. – Telephone dialling code: 0275.
Area: 255 sq. km (98 sq. miles). – Population: 7700.
ⓘ Tourist Police (summer only);
tel. 2 12 22.

TRANSPORTATION. – Ikaría is served by boats sailing from Piraeus to Mýkonos, Ikaría and Sámos.

HOTELS. – ÁYIOS KÝRIKOS (Thérma Lefkádos): Toula, A, 288 b.; Anna (pension), C. 16 b. – THÉRMAI: Apollon, C, 62 b. – ÉVDILOS: Georgios, E, 13 b.

Ikaría, lying W of Sámos, owes its name to Ikaros, who flew from Crete with his father Daidalos but plunged into the Icarian Sea which also bears his name.

The island is traversed by an upland ridge rising to 1000 m (3281 feet), with bare and treeless summits but slopes covered with macchia and forest. At the foot of the steep SE slope is the little port of **Áyios Kýrikos**, which in recent years has developed into something of a tourist centre. From here a road runs 4 km (2 miles) NE to **Thérmai**, on the site of the ancient city of the same name, with medicinal springs (recommended for rheumatism, arthritis and neuritis), continuing to the villages of Karavostámon, Évdilos and Armenísti on the N coast.

Ioannina
IΩANNINA
(Ioánnina, Iánnina)

Nomos: Ioánnina. – Telephone dialling code: 0651.
Altitude: 520 m (1706 feet). – Population: 40,000.
ⓘ **Greek National Tourist Organisation (EOT),**
Napoleóndos Sérva 2;
tel. 2 50 86.
Tourist Police,
Kaloúdi 10;
tel. 2 56 73.

TRANSPORTATION. – Air services from Athens and Salonica; bus connections with Athens and towns in the surrounding area.

HOTELS. – *Acropole*, B, 58 b.; *Palladion*, B, 242 b.; *Xenia*, B. 100 b.; *Alexios*, C, 156 b.; *Astoria*, C, 30 b.; *Dioni*, C, 74 b.; *Egnatia*, C, 96 b.; *Esperia*, C, 59 b.; *Galaxy*, C. 72 b.; *King Pyrrhos*, C, 40 b.; *Metropolis*, C,

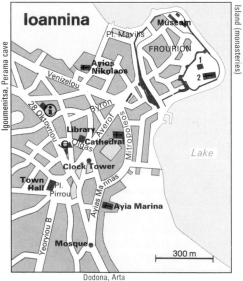

1 Tomb of Ali Pasha   2 Church of Ayii Anaryiri

33 b.; *Olympic*, C, 84 b.; *Tourist*, C, 55 b.; *Vyzantion*, C, 200 b.

CAMPING SITE.

Ioánnina, on the W side of the Lake of Ioánnina, is capital of the province of Epirus and has a university established in 1965. It is noted for its silversmiths' work. The old parts of the town have preserved something of the atmosphere of the Turkish period.

Lake of Ioánnina

HISTORY. – Ioánnina grew up in the Middle Ages on the site of a monastery of St John. In 1085 it was fortified by the Normans, and in 1345 became the seat of Serbian princes. From 1430 to 1913 it was in Turkish hands. The town's heyday was between 1788 and 1822, when it was the residence of Ali Pasha (1741–1822), nominally subject to the Sublime Porte but in fact enjoying almost absolute independence.

SIGHTS. – The **Fortress** (*Frourion*), with the *Aslan Aga Mosque* (1619), which now houses a Folk Museum, is of interest for its associations with the reign of Ali Pasha, but also affords beautiful views of the lake and the Pindos mountains beyond. Visitors will also enjoy strolling about the old town or along the lakeside promenade with its tavernas, among them the "Kyrá Frosýni", named after one of a number of Greek women who were drowned in the lake by Ali Pasha. Another interesting trip is by boat to the island in the lake with its seven monasteries. Ali Pasha took refuge in the monastery of St Panteleimon when he was being pursued by Turkish troops and was shot through the ceiling of the room to which he had retreated; he was then aged 81. There is a memorial room. His modest tomb is outside the Fethiye Mosque, at the SE corner of the fortress.

SURROUNDINGS. – 23 km (14 miles) S is **Dodóna**, seat of the oracle of Zeus (see p. 128). – 30 km (19 miles) W, to the N of the main road to Igoumenítsa, is **Zítsa**, with the commandingly situated monastery of St Elias, celebrated by Byron in "Childe Harold". – 4 km (2 miles) NE is the stalactitic cave of **Pérama**. – A trip northward in the direction of the Albanian frontier can be recommended for its magnificent scenery. In this area are the **Zagorokhoriá**, the villages in the Zagória mountains which were semi-autonomous even in the Turkish period. 16 km (10 miles) along the road to Kónitsa a road goes off on the right to Vítsa and Monodéndri (37 km (23 miles) from Ioánnina), near the Víkos gorge, with the River Voidomatis flowing through it far below. Here are the grazing grounds of the nomadic Sarakatsans, who regard themselves – unlike the Koutsovlachs and Aromunians – as descendants of ancient Greek tribes.

Ionian Islands
IONIOI NHΣOI
(Iónii Nísi)

Glyfáda beach, Corfu (Kérkyra)

The Ionian Islands, also known as the Eptánisos ("Seven Islands"), are strung out along the W coast of Greece, extending from the Albanian frontier to the Peloponnese. In this westerly situation, with more rain than most other parts of Greece, the islands have a mild climate and a lush growth of vegetation, with the exception of Kýthira, which lies apart from the others off the southern tip of the Peloponnese.

The Ionian Sea, which was equated by ancient authors with the Adriatic and is now seen as its southern continuation, and the Ionian Islands owe their name, according to Aeschylus, to the wanderings of Io, and according to later sources to the Illyrian hero Ionios (spelled with omicron, the short *o*). They thus have no connection with the Ionian Greeks (derived from Ion with an omega, the long *o*), who left Greece in the 11th and 10th c. and settled on the Anatolian coast, giving this eastern Greek territory its name of Ionia.

Evidence of settlement dating back to Mycenaean times has been found on the islands, but their first emergence into the light of history was in 734 B.C., when Corinth founded the city of Korkyra, later Kérkyra. In the 5th c. B.C. the islands came under Athenian influence, and in the 2nd c. B.C. all of them, including Kýthira, became Roman. Later they came under Byzantine rule, and in 1085 were conquered by the Normans; then in 1203–04 the 4th Crusade brought another change of masters. The islands now fell into the hands of Italian rulers, and then, one after the other, came under Venetian control – Kýthira in 1363, Kérkyra (thereafter known as Corfu) in 1386, Zákynthos in 1479, Kefallinía in 1500 (after a 21-year period of Turkish rule) and finally Lefkás (which had been Turkish since 1467) in 1684.

Venetian rule lasted until the fall of the Republic of St Mark in 1797. During this period the islands provided a refuge for many Greeks fleeing from the Turks, including artists from Crete who founded a school of their own here; and throughout these centuries they enjoyed a richer cultural life than the rest of Greece.

After an interlude of French rule the young "Republic of the Seven Islands" became a British protectorate in 1815; and in 1864 Britain returned the islands to Greece.

Ios
IOΣ
(Íos)

Nomos: Cyclades.
Area: 108 sq. km (42 sq. miles). – Population: 1270.

TRANSPORTATION. – Íos is served by boats sailing from Piraeus to Páros, Íos and Santorin. Island bus from Órmos Íou to Khóra.

Íos

Iráklion
HPAKΛION
(Iráklion)

Island: Crete. – Nomos: Iráklion.
Telephone dialling code: 081.
Altitude: 30 m (98 feet). – Population: 70,000.
(i) Greek National Tourist Organisation (EOT)
Xanthoudidoú 1;
tel. 28 20 96.
Tourist Police
(also office of Olympic Airways),
25 Avgoústou.
(Offices of shipping lines also in this street).

HOTELS. – Khrysi Akti, B, 19 b.; Armodoros, C, 60 b.;
Sea Breeze, C, 26 b.

YOUTH HOSTEL.

TRANSPORTATION. – Boat services from Piraeus. –
Air services from Athens and Rhodes. – Bus services
all over island: to Knossos from Platía Kornárou; to
eastern Crete from Platía Eleftherías; to the S
(Phaistós, Tymbáki) from the Khaniá or Panígra Gate;
to the SE (Arkhánes, Kastélli) from the Kainoúria Gate;
to western Crete from El Greco Park.

**Íos – recently discovered by holi-
daymakers wanting to "get away
from it all" – lies in the Cyclades,
half way between Páros and Santorin. According to an ancient tradition Homer died here, and his grave
is said to be somewhere in the NE of
the island.**

The little port of Órmos Íou (alt. 5 m (16
feet), pop. 110) lies in a sheltered bay on
the W coast (sandy beach). As the boat
approaches the harbour the eye is caught
by the dazzlingly white church of Ayía
Iríni on the S side of the bay (10 minutes'
walk from the harbour). 2 km (1 mile)
away, on the hillside above the island's
principal valley, is Khóra (alt. 100 m (328
feet), pop. 1100), on the site of an ancient
settlement, with a very typical row of
windmills. Overlooking the charming little
village is a chapel with an attractive
terrace, above which, on the summit of
the hill, is another chapel (view).

From Khóra excursions can be made to
Yialó beach, Kálamos monastery and
Plakotó Cave on the N coast. There are
also possible boat trips to the sandy bays
in the S and SW of the island and to the
neighbouring islands of Síkinos (see p.
239), to the W, and Iráklion, to the N.

Iráklion (area 18 sq. km (7 sq. miles), pop. 150), along
with Kéros (area 15 sq. km (6 sq. miles), pop. 8), Káto
and Anó Koufonísi (area 13 sq. km (5 sq. miles), pop.
250) and Skhinoúsa (area 10 sq. km (4 sq. miles),
pop. 188) belong to the Erimonísia, the group of
"Lonely Islands" between Íos and Náxos.

HOTELS. – Arina Sand (2 km (1 mile) away), A, 452
b.; Astir, A, 72 b.; Astoria, A, 273 b.; Atlantis, A, 294 b.;
Knossos Beach, Kháni Kókkini, A, 194 b.; Xenia, A,
156 b.; Kosmopolit, B, 59 b.; Esperia, B, 94 b.; Kastro,
B, 63 b.; Mediterranean, B, 105 b.; Akti, Kháni
Kókkini, C, 36 b.; Daedalos, C, 115 b.; Domenico, C,
73 b.; El Greco, C, 157 b.; Galini, C, 66 b.; Heraclion,
C, 72 b.; Knossos, C, 46 b.; Mirabello, C, 42 b.;
Mykonos, C, 18 b.; Olympic, C, 135 b.; Park, C, 51 b.;
Pasiphae, C, 31 b.; Phaedra, C, 43 b.; Poseidon, C,
49 b.; Prince, C, 50 b.; Selena, C, 52 b.

YOUTH HOSTEL.

BATHING BEACHES. – Karterós (6 km (4 miles) E),
Stómion (5 km (3 miles) W).

***Iráklion, the largest town in Crete
and since 1971 once again its administrative centre, lies half way along
the N coast of the island. It was
founded by the Arabs in A.D. 824
under the name of Rabd el-Kandak
and reconquered by Byzantium in
941. In 1204 it passed to Venice and –
now known as Candia – was developed into a powerful stronghold
which withstood a Turkish siege for
22 years (1647–69) but was finally
taken. When Crete became part of
Greece in 1913 the town was re-
named Iráklion (Herakleion) after
the ancient port of that name which
lay in this area.**

Iráklion suffered damage in an earthquake
in 1926 and during the Second World
War, but shows no signs of this and has all
the bustle and activity of a busy Greek
town. The life of the town still centres on
the old part of Iráklion within the circuit of

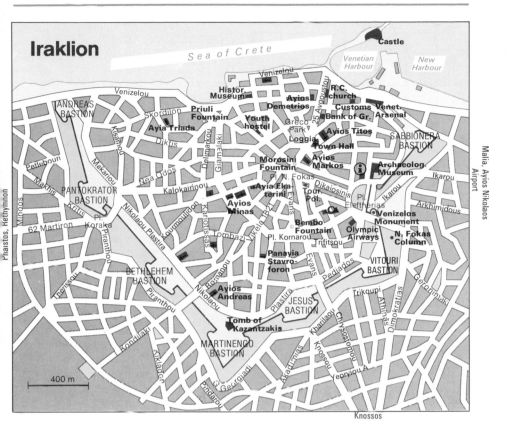

Iraklion

Sea of Crete

Venetian walls, still preserved for most of their length.

SIGHTS. – The **New Harbour** or **Commercial Harbour**, to the E of the old **Venetian Harbour**, has been considerably developed in recent years. The entrance is commanded by the Venetian *Castle*, with the lion of St Mark. The old Venetian Arsenals were partly demolished some years ago during the construction of new access roads to the harbour, but although the façades have been removed the barrel-vaulted roofs are still impressive.

From the harbour 25th August Street (25 Avgoústou), lined with shops, offices and shipping agencies, goes up into the **town centre**. On the left are the *church of St Titos* (first bishop of Crete: the church possesses a reliquary containing his skull which was removed to Venice in 1669 but returned in 1965), the **Town Hall**, the Venetian **Loggia** (1627; damaged in the Second World War but since restored) and the **church of St Mark**, now a museum of religious art. Off the street to the right is the little *El Greco Park*. After crossing a little square with the **Morosini Fountain** (1628, with a 14th c. lion)

25th August Street ends in *Nikephoros Phokas Square* (Platía Nikifórou Foká), named after the Byzantine general (later emperor) who recovered Crete from the Arabs. Bearing right from this square is Kalokairinos Street (Kalokairinoú), one of the town's busiest shopping streets, and straight ahead are 1821 Street and 1866 Street, bustling on weekdays with the crowded activity of the market. 1966 Street leads into Platía Kornárou, with the **Bembo Fountain** (1558), from which Odós Karteroú (to the right) leads to the 19th c. **Cathedral of Áyios Minás**, in the S aisle of which are *icons by the Cretan painter Michael Damaskinos. In the same square are the smaller churches of *Ayía Ekateríni* (16th c.) and *Áyios Minás* (18th c.).

Farther S we come to the **Venetian walls**, begun in 1538 by the famous military engineer Sanmichele. At their most southerly point, on the Martinengo Bastion, a simple wooden cross marks the *tomb of Nikos Kazantzakis*, Crete's greatest writer, who was born in Iráklion in 1882 and died in Freiburg in Germany in 1957. On his grave is the inscription: "I hope for nothing, I fear nothing: I am free." From here there is a fine *view of Mt

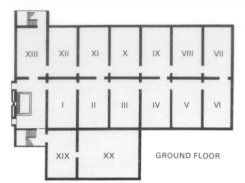

GROUND FLOOR

I   Neolithic and Pre-Palatial (2500–2000 B.C.)
II   Proto-Palatial: Knossós, Mália (2000–1700 B.C.)
III   Proto-Palatial: Phaistós (2000–1700 B.C.)
IV   Neo-Palatial: Knossós, Phaistós, Mália (1700–1450 B.C.)
V   Late Neo-Palatial: Knossós (1450–1400 B.C.)
VI   Neo-Palatial and Post-Palatial: Knossós, Phaistós (1400–1350 B.C.)
VII   Neo-Palatial: central Crete
VIII   Neo-Palatial: Káto Zákros (1700–1450 B.C.)
IX   Neo-Palatial: eastern Crete
X   Post-Palatial (1400–1100 B.C.)
XI   Sub-Minoan and Early Geometric (1100–800 B.C.)
XII   Late Geometric and Orientalising (800–650 B.C.)
XIII   Sarcophagi
XIX   Archaic period (7th–6th c. B.C.)
XX   Classical and late (5th c. B.C.–4th c. A.D.)

Iraklion Archaeological Museum

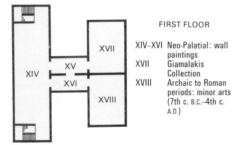

FIRST FLOOR

XIV–XVI   Neo-Palatial: wall paintings
XVII   Giamalakis Collection
XVIII   Archaic to Roman periods: minor arts (7th c. B.C.–4th c. A.D.)

Iouktas and of long stretches of the walls, which enclose the landward side of the town for a total distance of 5 km (3 miles), with strongly defended gates like the Panígra or Khaniá Gate on the W side.

If, starting from Nikephoros Phokas Square, we go SE along Constantine Street, we pass on the right a block of government offices, on the site of Venetian barracks. In a square off the street to the right is a *monument to Daskaloyannis*, a Greek freedom fighter who was executed by the Turks in 1771. Constantine Street ends in the spacious *Freedom Square* (Platía Eleftherías), a popular promenade and meeting-place in the evenings.

On the N side of the square is Iráklion's most important single tourist attraction, the **Archaeological Museum**. This

occupies a modern building, earthquake-proof, erected in 1937 on the site of an earlier Franciscan friary, restored after war damage in 1951 and extended by the construction of four additional rooms in 1964. It contains the largest and finest collection of Cretan antiquities, of which only a selection can be mentioned here. To get any real impression of the treasures it contains not one but several visits are required.

Room I (Neolithic and Pre-Palatial periods, 2500–2000 B.C.). – Case 1: *idols and pottery vessels* from houses under the palace at Knossos and from the Cave of Eileithyia. Case 3: *pottery* in the Pýrgos and Áyios Onoúfrios styles. Case 6: *pottery* in the Vasilikí style. Case 7: *stone vessels* from the island of Mókhlos, including the *lid of a pyxis* (jewellery casket) in the form of a recumbent dog. Case 9: *vessels from tholos tombs* in the Mesará, including vases with barbotine decoration. Case 10: *pottery* from Palaíkastro (eastern Crete), including a *votive bowl* depicting a shepherd and his sheep and a *four-wheeled cart*, the oldest of its kind. Case 13: *marble idol* of a goddess, *ivory statuettes*, *stone utensils*. Case 15: *material from tombs* in the Mesará, including a *vessel in the form of a bull* with an acrobat clinging to its horns. Case 17: *gold jewellery* from the Mesará and the island of Mókhlos.

Room II (Proto-Palatial period, 2000–1700 B.C.: Knossos, Mália, hilltop shrines). – Case 19: *pottery* from Mália, including vases in the Vasilikí style, a jug with an engraved figure of the goddess of fertility, and moulds for the casting of double axes. Case 20: material from the votive deposit at Goúrnes, near Iráklion, and from Týlisos: *idols* in the form of the horned masks worn by priests at certain religious ceremonies. Case 21: finds from hilltop shrines, including *votive vessels* in the form of bulls. Cases 22 and 23: *vases in Kamáres style* from Knossos, including *eggshell ware*. Case 24: material from hilltop shrines, including *votive terracotta figures* of men and women praying and a *model shrine* with three columns. Case 25: the *"Town Mosaic"* (pottery plaques representing house fronts); *gold-handled dagger* from Mália. Case 28: *seals* from Knossos and Mália. Case 29: polychrome *vases* from Knossos dating from the end of the Proto-Palatial period.

Room III (Proto-Palatial period, 2000–1700 B.C.: Phaistós). – Cases 3–38: polychrome *vases* from the palace at Phaistós and from the Kamáres Cave on Mt Ida, after which this pottery is named. Case 39: large vessels, including a superb *amphora* (No. 1680). Case 40: *clay sealings* with ornamental patterns and figures of men and animals. Case 41: the famous *Phaistós Disc*, a pottery disc stamped on both sides with hieroglyphic characters (photograph, p. 214). The text has not been deciphered, but it may be a religious hymn. Case 42: *cult utensils*, including offering tables and "fruit-stands". Case 43: particularly fine *vessels* from the palace at Phaistós, including a large *"fruit-stand"* with an ornamental rim and polychrome decoration.

Room IV (Neo-Palatial period, 1700–1450 B.C.: Knossos, Phaistós, Mália). – Cases 44–46 : *pottery* from Knossos. Cases 47–48: utensils of stone, bronze

Libation jug from a tomb at Katsabás

and clay from Mália, including a Marine style *jug decorated with nautiluses, starfish, etc. Case 49: pottery from Phaistós, including a rhyton in Marine style, with a nautilus, the *figure of a goddess or priestess, offering tables and jugs. Case 50: objects from the underground repository of the principal temple at Knossos, including the famous *statuettes of the snake goddess. Case 51: **cult vessel of steatito in the form of a bull's head, with an eye of rock crystal, a jasper pupil and the nostrils formed from a large tridacna shell. The right-hand side of this magnificent piece from the Little Palace at Knossos is original; the rest is restored. Case 52: *sword from Mália with a gold-plated hilt and a pommel of rock crystal; fragments of a group from Knossos showing a man making an offering in a hilltop shrine. Case 55: objects found along with the snake goddesses at Knossos. Case 56: *ivory statuette of a bull-jumper in the act of leaping over a bull, from Knossos. Case 57: *gaming-board of ivory and rock crystal from Knossos.

Room V (late Neo-Palatial period, 1450–1400 B.C.: Knossos). – Case 60: pottery in vegetable style; *alabaster amphora. Case 61: *bull's head from the Little Palace; bronze statuettes. Case 65: seals from various sites. Case 66: stone libation vessels from the throne-room at Knossos, in use at a religious ceremony immediately before the destruction of the palace. Case 69: tablets with inscriptions in Minoan Linear A script from various sites.

Room VI (Neo-Palatial and Post-Palatial periods, 1400–1350 B.C.; cemeteries of Knossos and Phaistós). – Case 74: ivory *jewel-case depicting the capture of a wild bull in a rocky landscape. Case 78: *boar's-tusk helmet (of a type found on the Greek mainland in the Mycenaean period) from a grave at Záfer Papoúra, near Knossos. Case 81: *jewellery from a grave at Knossos, including a *scarab of Pharaoh Amenophis III of ivory jewel-cases, lids of ivory and rock crystal; bronze mirrors, razors, combs and small weights for weighing the souls of the dead. Case 82: grave goods

from Katsabás, the port of Knossos, including an *amphora with representations of boar's-tusk helmets an *alabaster amphora with the cartouche of Pharaoh Tuthmosis III. Case 83: "Palace-style" amphoras from Knossos. Case 85: *bronze helmet with cheek-pieces. Case 86: *jewellery from the royal tombs at Kalývia Pyrgiótissa, Phaistós. Case 87: *gold jewellery from various sites. Case 88: grave goods from Mycenaean tombs at Arkhánes.

Room VII (Neo-Palatial period: megara and villas in central Crete). – On the N wall are three large *double axes from Nírou Khaní and *double horns from the same site. Case 89: bronze statuettes of male worshippers, an obsidian *rhyton from Týlisos, vases and stone lamps from Nírou. Case 92: bronze statuettes of worshippers, small votive animals. Case 93: pottery from the villa at Ayía Triáda. Case 94: the famous **Harvesters Vase from Ayía Triáda, with relief decoration showing the men returning from the fields with their implements, singing as they go. Case 95: the *'"Chieftain's Cup", also from Ayía Triáda, showing a helmeted man with his sword held on his shoulder appearing before a king or prince holding a sceptre. Case 96: *rhyton with carvings of athletic games, boxing and bull-leaping, from Ayía Triáda. Cases 97 and 98: bronze swords and double axes from the cave sanctuary at Arkalokhóri. Case 99: copper talents (currency ingots), each weighing 30 kg (66 lb), from Ayía Triáda. Case 101: *jewellery from various sites, including two *bees depositing a drop of honey in a comb.

Room VIII (Neo-Palatial period, 1700–1450 B.C. Káto Zákros). – Case 105: vessels and utensils, including a bronze *incense-burner decorated with ivy leaves. Case 108: pottery and stone vessels; one of the few surviving examples of the *stone capitals which topped timber columns. Case 109: a unique **libation vase of rock crystal with rock-crystal beads in a gold setting round the neck and handle. Case 111: stone *rhyton, originally cased in gold, with a relief depicting a Minoan hilltop shrine. Case 113: copper

Bull's-head rhyton from Knossos

Detail from the Dolphin Fresco, Knossos

talents and elephant tusks, probably from Syria. Case 115: a large bronze saw and other implements. Case 116: *bull's-head rhyton. Case 118: cult vessels from the treasury, found intact, of the shrine at Káto Zákros.

Room IX (Neo-Palatial period: eastern Crete). – Cases 119 and 120: material from Palaíkastro. Case 121: pottery from Gourniá. Case 128: seals from central and eastern Crete.

Room X (Post-Palatial period, 1400–1100 B.C.). – Case 132: *group of dancers from Palaíkastro. Case 133: rigidly stylised figurines of goddesses with symbols like birds and poppies on their heads. Case 135: votive statuettes and cult utensils, including a stone altar in the form of a column. Case 140: cult objects from Knossos, including a model of a circular shrine. Case 143: *man on a swing, model of a sacred ship.

Room XI is devoted to the sub-Minoan and early Geometric periods, when Dorian Greeks had already established themselves in Crete (1100–800 B.C.). During this period the old cults still survived in certain places, for example in the Cave of Eileithyia (the goddess of childbirth and fertility) at Ínatos on the S coast, as is shown by the clay models of double axes (Case 149) found in association with statuettes. Iron weapons and implements indicate that iron was in use on Crete at the beginning of the 1st millennium B.C. (Case 153).

Room XII (late Geometric and Orientalising period, 800–650 B.C.). – Case 163 contains a fine *oinochoe depicting a pair of lovers, perhaps Theseus and Ariadne. The same theme is found on an urn (No. 6391) in Case 167 and a bronze cauldron in Case 169. Case 168 contains an interesting example of the "Daedalic" style, a *two-handled vessel of the 7th c. B.C. depicting a fertility goddess standing between two water birds and holding a sacred tree in each hand. The scene is painted, only the head with its ceremonial hair-style being moulded in relief (partly flaked off).

Room XIII contains a collection of terracotta sarcophagi of the "chest" and "bath-tub" types, in which the dead were buried in a crouching position.

We now go up to the first floor and enter Room XIV, a long hall with large numbers of wall paintings from palaces and villas. Going left from the landing and continuing in a clockwise direction, we come first to part of the group of *rhyton-bearers from the processional fresco at Knossos which originally contained some 500 figures. Beyond this are *griffins from the Knossos throne-room, figures of praying women and goddesses, and several *processional frescoes from Ayía Triáda. In front of the E wall is a *stucco floor from Ayía Triáda depicting dolphins and fishes. On the S side are a *fresco of figure-of-eight shields, the *"Prince with the Feathered Crown" from the processional corridor at Knossos, a *carved bull's head from the N gateway of Knossos, the *"Ladies in Blue", the *Dolphin Fresco from the Queen's Megaron, the *Partridge Frieze from the Caravanserai at Knossos and the *Lily Frescoes from the villa at Ámnisos. In the middle of the room is the famous limestone **sarcophagus from Ayía Triáda, a masterpiece of the 14th c. B.C. which depicts scenes from the cult of the dead enacted in the open air (Case 171).

In the adjoining Rooms XV and XVI are further wall paintings of the Neo-Palatial period (1600–1400 B.C.), including *dancing scenes in the palace courtyard in front of a tripartite shrine (painted in the miniature style) and the ever-popular *"Parisienne".

Beyond these rooms are Rooms XVII and XVIII. Room XVII contains the Giamalakis Collection (in Case 181, model of a circular shrine in which stands a goddess, with two men cowering on the roof). Room XVIII contains examples of the minor arts of the Archaic, Classical, Hellenistic and Roman periods (7th–4th c. B.C.).

Returning to the ground floor, we come to two rooms containing Greek and Roman work. Room XIX is devoted to the monumental art of the Archaic period (7th–6th c. B.C.), including the great *frieze from a temple at Priniás, the *doorway of the same temple, with figures of goddesses, the *divine triad from the Delphinion at Dreros (Case 210) and a *stele with the famous Cretan hymn to Zeus (Case 209).

Room XX contains sculpture ranging in date from the classical period to late antiquity (5th c. B.C. to 4th c. A.D.). The few Greek works, which include a *metope from a temple at Knossos with a scene from the exploits of Herakles (No. 363) and the *funerary stele of a young archer (No. 145), are outnumbered by the numerous Roman works, mostly from Górtys, then capital of the island. Among them are an over-life-size *Apollo Pythios (No. 326), *Pluto and Persephone (No. 260), a copy of the Doryphoros of Polykleitos (No. 343), a copy of Pheidias' Athena Parthenos, portrait statues and heads of the Emperors Hadrian (No. 5), Marcus Aurelius (No. 230) and Trajan (No. 317), a *mosaic pavement from Roman Knossos, signed with the Latin name of the artist, Apollinaris, written in Greek characters (2nd c. A.D.), and a large *sarcophagus from Mália (No. 387: 3rd c. A.D.).

Going W from the harbour on the seafront promenade, we come, behind the Xenia Hotel, to the *Historical and Ethnographic Museum, which contains material dating from early Christian times to the present day.

In the basement are tombstones and inscriptions of the Venetian period, frescoes from a Turkish house and Turkish tombstones, items from the church of St Titos at Górtys and a rose window from the church of San Francesco in Iráklion. The ground floor is mainly devoted to religious art (icons, iconostases, vestments, liturgical utensils), together with jewellery and coins, maps and documents. – On the *first floor* are more *maps* and *manuscripts*, a *reconstruction of a peasant house* and – perhaps the most important exhibit – the *study of Nikos Kazantzakis*, with his desk, part of his library and editions of his works. His "Odyssey" lies open on the desk.

SURROUNDINGS. – TO THE W AND SW. – **Amoudára** (11 km (7 miles); Hotel Creta Beach, A, 249 b.). – **Fódele** (26 km – 16 miles), a village situated in a valley planted with orange-groves which is believed to be the birthplace of the painter El Greco ("the Greek"), who was born as Kyriakos Theotokopoulos about 1545 and died at Toledo in 1614. – **Tylisos** (14 km (9 miles): bus), with three Minoan villas built about 1550 B.C. on top of earlier buildings. From the entrance we come first to House B, with the larger House A beyond it. To the N is House C, with the remains of a Mycenaean megaron adjoining it.

TO THE SE. – **Knossós** (5 km – 3 miles): see p. 160. – **Arkhánes** (15 km – 9 miles): see p. 64. – **Vathýpetro** (21 km (13 miles): bus to Arkhánes), with a Minoan villa of the 16th c. B.C., magnificently situated on a hill. To the W is the residential block, to the S the workshop wing; on the outside of the W wall is a cult niche, and in the E courtyard, opposite a columned hall, is a tripartite shrine. Oil and wine presses, still in situ, are a reminder of the agricultural activities carried on by the owners of the villa.

TO THE E. – 9 km (6 miles) from Iráklion, beyond the airport is **Karterós** (Hotel Amnisos, B. 108 b.; Motel Xenia, B, 84 b.), in a bay called Florida Beach which offers good bathing. – **Ámnisos**, 1 km (about a ½ mile) beyond Karterós, was a Minoan port. On the E side of Palaiokhóra hill are the remains of a villa which yielded the Lily Frescoes (c. 1600 B.C.) now in Iráklion Museum.

S of Ámnisos on the road to Episkopí (signpost) is the **Cave of Eileithyia** (63 m (226 feet) long, up to 12 m (39 feet) wide), a shrine of the goddess of childbirth and fertility Eileithyia, who was venerated here from the 3rd millennium B.C. until late antiquity through all changes of population, culture and religion. A flashlight should be taken.

12 km (7 miles) from Iráklion is **Kháni Kókkini**, a hotel colony situated close to the beach (Hotel Knossos Beach, A, 194 b.; Akti, C, 36 b.). – 13 km (8 miles) from Iráklion is **Nírou Kháni**, with a well-preserved Minoan villa of about 1500 B.C. which yielded the largest-known bronze double axes. Near here is *Goúrnes* (Hotel America, B, 84 b.).

Isthmia
ΙΣΘΜΙΑ
(Isthmía)

Nomos: Corinth. – Altitude: 10 m (33 feet).

HOTELS. – ISTHMÍA: *King Saron*, A, 280 b.; *Isthmía*, B, 140 b. – PÁLAION KALAMÁKI: *Kalamaki Beach*, B, 141 b. – LOUTRÓ ELÉNIS: *Polit*, B, 48 b.; *Kakanakos*, C, 30 b.

The village of Isthmía, to the S of the eastern end of the Corinth Canal, is of interest for the remains of the ancient sanctuary of Poseidon (1 km (about a ½ mile) S of the canal) which have been excavated since 1952 by American archaeologists. This was the scene of the Isthmian Games which were held every second year from 582 B.C. onwards, the victor's prize being a crown of wild celery or spruce.

SIGHTS. – The ground-plan of the *Temple of Poseidon*, built in 460 B.C. as successor to an earlier temple of the 7th c. B.C., can be observed: it was a Doric peripteral temple with the classical proportions of 6×13 columns. It was damaged by fire in 394 B.C. and thereafter rebuilt. NE of the temple was the theatre, to the SE the stadion, built in the 4th c.

The ancient buildings were destroyed in the 6th c. A.D., during the reign of Justinian, when the stones were used in the construction of a *Byzantine fortress* (remains E of theatre), part of the defences built across the Isthmus, and constantly renewed in later centuries, to protect the Peloponnese from attackers coming from the N. The wall ran roughly parallel to the present canal and was 6 Roman miles long (1 Roman mile=1000 paces=1618 yards) – as the name of the village of Examília still indicates. Remains dating from the Mycenaean period (13th c. B.C.) have been found S and SE of the Temple of Poseidon. There are substantial remains of a defensive wall built in 480–479 B.C. and restored in 297 B.C. and A.D. 253. This was followed by the work carried out in Justinian's reign (c. A.D. 540); and there are references to further repair and strengthening of the wall in late Byzantine times and during the Venetian period.

SURROUNDINGS. – 2 km (1 mile) S of the Temple of Poseidon is the village of *Kekhriás*, which marks the site of the ancient Corinthian port of **Kenchreai**. Part of the old harbour works still lies under the water. N of the harbour, near the Kalamaki Beach Hotel, the site of a temple of the classical period has been identified.

2 km (1 mile) S of the harbour of Kenchreai is a spring with an abundant flow of water which has been known since the time of Pausanias (II, 2, 3) as Helen's Bath, *Loutró Elénis*.

Itea

ITEA

(Itéa)

Nomos: Phocis.
Altitude: 5 m (16 feet). – Population: 2500.

HOTELS. – *Galini*, B, 60 b.; *Kalofali*, B, 39 b.; *Xenia*, B, 36 b.; *Akti*, C, 40 b.; *Parnassos*, C, 13 b.

CAMPING SITE.

Itéa is a little port in a bay on the Gulf of Corinth, 19 km (12 miles) from Delphi. The ancient port of Kirrha lay E of the town.

Ithaca

ΙΘΑΚΗ

(Itháki)

Nomos: Kefallinía.
Area 94 sq. km (36 sq. miles). – Population: 4150.

TRANSPORTATION. – Boat services from Kérkyra, Kefallinía and Pátras. Island bus from Vathý to Stavrós in the N of the island.

HOTELS. – *Mentor*, B, 68 b.; *Odysseus*, B, 17 b.

Ithaca, home of Odysseus

Ithaca, one of the Ionian Islands, separated from the much larger Kefallinía by a channel 2 km (1 mile) wide, has been renowned since ancient times as the home of Odysseus. It consists of a northern and a southern part linked by an isthmus only 600 m (1969 feet) wide. The chief place of the island and its principal port, Vathý, lies in a sheltered situation in a long inlet which cuts inland from the NE.

Excavators from the time of Heinrich Schliemann (1868) have sought to identify places in the kingdom of Odysseus mentioned by Homer. The remains of buildings found by Schliemann on the 669 m (2195 feet) high hill of Aetós, 5 km (3 miles) from Vathý, which commands the isthmus, belong to the post-Mycenaean settlement of Alalkomenai. Mycenaean walls and pottery of the right date for Odysseus were found by British archaeologists from 1932 onwards near the northern village of Stavrós, on Pelikáta hill (1 km (about a $\frac{1}{2}$ mile) N, with views of a number of bays) and below the village on Pólis Bay. These were presumably the sites of the palace and the city. Finds from here are in the museums in Vathý and Stavrós. The Stavrós Museum contains a shard bearing the name Odysseus (8th c. B.C.) and an Attic lekythos depicting Athena, Odysseus and Telemachos (5th c. B.C.).

SIGHTS. – The chief place on the island, Vathý (rebuilt after an earthquake in 1953), has a very beautiful situation. The *Museum* contains a collection of Mycenaean vases. The village lies in an agricultural region (olives, wine), and Homer's "island of goats" still has numerous goats. An attractive run over the isthmus brings us to Stavrós (18 km (11 miles): bus), in the northern part of the island. Farther N is *Exoyí* (old church), and to the NE is the beautiful Fríkes Bay, beyond which is the village of Kióni. A taxi can be hired in Stavrós to drive up through rugged scenery to the monastery of Katharón (alt. 600 m (1969 feet)), from which there are magnificent *views of Vathý Bay.

Other interesting trips from Vathý (on foot) are to the nearby Cave of the Nymphs and the *Fountain of Arethusa* at the S end of the island (guide advisable).

Ithomi
IΘΩMH
(Ithómi)

Region: Peloponnese. – Nomos: Messenia.

Ithómi is a commanding hill (798 m – 2618 feet) in Messenia, 30 km (19 miles) N of Kalamáta.

HISTORY. – During the three wars (740–720, 660 and 464–459 B.C.) in which Sparta, situated to the E beyond the Taÿgetos range, sought to conquer or control Messenia, Ithómi was the last refuge of the Messenians. In 455 B.C. Athens gave the surviving defenders of the hill a new home at Naupaktos (see p. 191) on the Gulf of Corinth. After his victory over Sparta at Leuktra the Theban leader Epameinondas founded the town of Messene on the western and southern slopes of the hill in 369 B.C, with the idea that the existence of this town, along with Mantinela (see p. 178) and Megalópolis (p. 179), would prevent Sparta from reasserting its authority. The new town and its land were ringed by a wall 9 km (6 miles) long. The site is now occupied by the tiny village of Mavromáti (alt. 420 m (1378 feet)).

SIGHTS. – To the E of **Mavromáti**, beyond a hill saddle, is the fortress-like **monastery of Voúrkano** (17th c.). From the saddle a winding path leads up to the summit of Ithómi, with a ruined monastery on the site of the acropolis; the climb takes an hour.

From the E end of the village a path descends to a rectangular open space, formerly known as the Agora. In the centre of the area recent excavations have brought to light a Doric **temple of Asklepios** with 6×12 columns dating from the Hellenistic period. To the E are a small *theatre*, a *propylon* and a pillared hall, to the E a number of *cult buildings*, including a shrine of Artemis Orthia.

From the W side of this site a path to the N, passing the ancient theatre, joins the road from Mavromáti to the **Arcadian Gate** beside the local *museum*. Of this monumental N gate of the town nine courses of dressed stone remain. On the outside are two square towers flanking an outer courtyard, on the inside a circular *inner courtyard* 19·70 m (65 feet) in diameter. On either side, but particularly to the W, the **town walls** can be followed for considerable stretches through the hilly terrain.

Mavromáti is reached from Kalamáta by way of the modern town of Messíni (30 km – 19 miles); or, coming from the N, by turning off at Tsuleíka into a road on the right which runs via Lábena (19 km (12 miles) from Tsuleíka).

Kaiafas
KAIAΦAΣ
(Kaiáfas)

Region: Peloponnese. – Nomos: Elis. Altitude: 10 m (33 feet). – Population: 1000.

HOTELS. – *Jenny*, B, 16 b.; *Archaea Sami*, C, 46 b.; *Geranion*, C, 77 b.

Kaiáfas, 21 km (13 miles) S of Pýrgos on the W coast of the Peloponnese, has been renowned since ancient times for its medicinal springs (recommended in the treatment of arthritis, gynaecological conditions, skin complaints, gallstones and hepatitis). It has beautiful long sandy beaches.

SURROUNDINGS. – 5 km (3 miles) SE is the little coastal town of Zákharo (Hotel Rex, C, 26 b.; Nestor, D, 19 b.). 8 km (5 miles) beyond this is Tholon, where a road goes off on the left to **Káto Figalia** (14 km – 9 miles). From here there is a road via Petratóna to Andrítsaina and the Temple of Apollo at Bassai (see p. 104). – 40 km (25 miles) S of Kaiáfas is Kyparissía with its castle (see p. 167).

Kalamata
KAΛAMATA
(Kalamáta)

Nomos: Messenia. – Telephone dialling code: 0721. Altitude: 25 m (82 feet). – Population: 40,000.
ⓘ **Tourist Police,** Aristoménous 46; tel. 2 31 87.

TRANSPORTATION. – Air services from Athens; bus services from Athens and to local towns; terminus of the Peloponnese Railway line from Athens via Corinth; yacht supply station.

HOTELS. – KALAMÁTA: *Philoxenia*, B, 224 b.; *Rex*, B, 96 b.; *Achillion*, C, 27 b.; *America*, C, 38 b.; *Elite*, C, 94 b.; *Philisvos*, C, 26 b.; *Valassis*, C, 34 b.; and many hotels in categories D and E. – AKTÍ AYÍOU AVGOUSTÍNOU: *San Agostino Beach*, B, 613 b. – ALMYRON (7 km (4 miles) SE): *Messinian Bay*, B, 84 b. – MIKRÁ MANTINÍA (11 km (7 miles) SE): *Taygetos Beach*, C, 50 b.

CAMPING SITES. – Fáros and Áyios Síon (6 km – 4 miles).

TAVERNAS on coast. – BATHING BEACH to E of town.

Kalamáta or Kalámai, on the S coast of the Peloponnese to the W of Taýgetos, is capital of the province of Messenia and a port for the shipment of the agricultural produce of the region.

HISTORY. – Kalamáta occupies the site of the Mycenaean town of Pharai, in the kingdom of Menelaos. In 720 B.C., with the rest of Messenia, it fell into Spartan hands. From 1204 it became the residence, together with Andravída (p. 167), of the Villehardouins, who gave it its present name. After periods of Byzantine, Turkish and Venetian rule it was sacked by Ibrahim Pasha in 1825. It is now a thriving market town.

SIGHTS. – Above the town is the Villehardouin **castle**. At the foot of the hill on which it stands is the **convent of St Constantine**, the nuns in which produce hand-woven silk articles. In the Kyriákos House is a *museum* displaying items of local interest, mainly from the Venetian period and the struggle for liberation.

SURROUNDINGS. – 30 km (19 miles) NW is the site of ancient **Messene**, on Mt Ithómi (see p. 149). – 51 km (32 miles) SW, in Navarino Bay, is **Pýlos** (p. 220). – **Sparta** (p. 241) and **Mistra** (p. 185) are reached on a beautiful road through the Taýgetos range (60 km – 37 miles). – SE of the town extends the **Máni** (p. 177).

Kalambaka
ΚΑΛΑΜΠΑΚΑ
(Kalambáka)

Nomos: Tríkala. – Telephone dialling code: 0432.
Altitude: 220 m (722 feet). – Population: 4600.
ⓘ **Tourist Information,**
Rammidi 33;
tel. 2 21 09 (summer only).

TRANSPORTATION. – Kalambáka is the terminus of the Fársala–Kalambáka railway line.

HOTELS. – *Divani*, A, 206 b.; *Xenia*, A, 44 b.; *Aiolikos Astír*, C, 29 b.; *Odyssion*, C, 42 b.; *Olympia*, C, 27 b.

CAMPING SITES. – Metéora and Vrákhos, between Kastráki and Metéora.

Kalambáka is a little country town situated at the point where the River Piniós emerges from the Pindos range into the Thessalian plain. It makes a convenient base from which to visit the Metéora monasteries

View of Kalambáka

(see p. 182), or a starting-point for a trip through the Pindos mountains to Ioánnina.

SIGHTS. – Under the sheer rock face of the Metéora is the *Mitrópolis church dedicated to the Dormition of the Virgin (15 August). It is a basilica, rebuilt in 1309 by Andrónikos Palaiológos, and tradition ascribes its foundation to the Emperor Justinian. Some features of the church are consistent with this dating – the basilican plan, the unusual *ambo* in the nave and the semicircular *priests' bench* in the apse (the synthronon which was a regular feature of early Byzantine churches, 5th–6th c.). The apse has a mosaic pavement. The paintings in the nave date from the period after the rebuilding; they were the work (1573) of Neophytos, son of the Cretan artist, Theophanes, who painted the Áyios Nikólaos monastery in the nearby Metéora.

Kalavryta
ΚΑΛΑΒΡΥΤΑ
(Kalávrita)

Nomos: Achaia.
Altitude: 725 m (2379 feet). – Population: 2000.

TRANSPORTATION. – Terminus of the rack-railway (cog railway) from Diákofto on the Gulf of Corinth.

HOTELS. – *Chelmos*, B, 34 b.; *Maria*, C, 26 b.

Kalávryta lies in a region with good natural water resources at the foot of Mt Erýmanthos in the northern Peloponnese. Rebuilt after its destruction by German forces in 1943, it is a good base for walks and climbs in the hills.

SURROUNDINGS. – 7 km (4 miles) SW is the **Ayía Lávra**, a monastery founded in 961, where the Greek fight for independence from the Turks was proclaimed in 1821. – 7 km (4 miles) NE is the cave monastery of **Megaspíleon**, founded in the 6th c. and frequently restored after fires in later centuries. It can be reached either by an asphalted road or by the rack-railway to Zakhlórou (or Megaspíleon) and on foot (45 minutes) from there.

Kalymnos
ΚΑΛΥΜΝΟΣ
(Kálimnos)

Nomos: Dodecanese.
Area: 111 sq. km (43 sq. miles). – Population: 13,000.

TRANSPORTATION. – Kálymnos is served by boats sailing between Piraeus and Rhodes and between Sámos and Rhodes.

HOTELS. – KÁLYMNOS: *Olympic*, C, 81 b.; *Thermai*, C, 23 b. – PÁNORMOS: *Drosos*, C, 100 b.

Kálymnos is best known as the island of the sponge-fishers, who continue, in this age of synthetic sponges, to sail every year to the southern Mediterranean to dive for natural sponges. In the busy – and quite large – port town of Kálymnos visitors can see the establishments in which the sponges are processed. There is also a small museum.

There is a road from Kálymnos to **Vathý** (6 km (4 miles): bus), in a deep bay on the E coast. Another road runs W, passing a castle of the Knights of St John perched on a sheer crag on the left, to **Khorió** (3 km – 2 miles) and then down to **Pánormos** or **Liniariá** (9 km (6 miles): sandy beach, restaurants). From Khorió it is possible to continue to **Myrtiés** and **Emborió**, at the northern tip of the island, where a Mycenaean *tholos tomb* has been found. From Liniariá a boat trip can be made to the little island of **Télendos** (ancient remains, medieval castle, ruined monastery).

Kamena Vourla
ΚΑΜΕΝΑ ΒΟΥΡΛΑ
(Kaména Vúrla)

Nomos: Phthiotis.
Altitude: at sea level. – Population: 4000.

TRANSPORTATION. – On the national highway from Athens to Salonica.

HOTELS. – *Galini*, A, 109 b.; *Avra*, B, 45 b.; *Leto*, B, 46 b.; *Rhadion*, B, 94 b.; *Sissy*, B, 190 b.; *Sonia*, B, 35 b.; *Thronion*, B, 78 b.; *Violetta*, B, 50 b.; *Acropole*, C, 38 b.; *Akti*, C, 35 b.; *Alma*, C, 31 b.; *Anastasia*, C, 26 b.; *Argo*, C, 45 b.; *Armonia*, C, 43 b.; *Astir*, C, 64 b.; *Buca*, C, 38 b.; *Chloe*, C, 45 b.; *Corali*, C, 36 b.; *Delphini*, C, 42 b.; *Diana*, C, 34 b.; *Kypreos*, C, 74 b.; *Neon Astron*, C, 41 b.; *Oceanis*, C, 43 b.; *Palirria*, C, 28 b.; *Pringhipikon*, C, 49 b.; *Regina*, C, 29 b.; *Tsironi*, C, 29 b.; also hotels in category D and many pensions.

Kaména Voúrla is a small spa (recommended for rheumatism, arthritis and neuritis) attractively situated on a wooded promontory opposite the island of Euboea.

SURROUNDINGS. – 7 km (4 miles) from Kaména Voúrla on the road to Athens is **Áyios Konstantínos** (hotels: Levendi, A, 56 b.; Akroyiali, C, 28 b.; Astir, C, 58 b.), a pretty little fishing village. – Beyond this (26 km – 16 miles) is **Arkítsa** (Hotel Kalypso Bungalows, B, 340 b.), from which there is a ferry service to Aidipsós on Euboea. – Then (30 km – 19 miles) comes **Livanates** (Hotel Achillion, C, 43 b.), where a road branches off on the right to the villages of **Atalánti** (7 km – 4 miles) and **Kalápodi** (6 km – 4 miles), where, immediately N of the road is a site which was first reported by Wheler in the 17th c. but has only recently been excavated. The excavations brought to light the foundations of a temple of Artemis measuring 19 by 46 m (62 by 151 feet) which dates from the late 5th c. B.C., together with an altar which was found intact, complete with its votive offerings. The excavators (Felsch and Kienast) identified this as the sanctuary of Artemis Elaphebolia of *Hyampolis*.

Kamiros
ΚΑΜΕΙΡΟΣ
(Kámiros)

Island: Rhodes. – Nomos: Dodecanese.

Kámiros, situated on the NW coast of Rhodes 34 km (21 miles) from the town of Rhodes, is the third of the ancient cities on the island (the others being Líndos and Ialysós).

Kámiros is reached from the town of Rhodes by the coast road via Paradísi (17 km (11 miles), road on left through the Valley of Butterflies to Petaloúdes) and Kalavárda (30 km – 19 miles). The site of the ancient city, excavated by Italian archaeologists, lies at an altitude of 120 m (394 feet) near the coast, where there is a tourist pavilion. The remains extend from the valley up to the highest point on which the temple precinct lies.

Kámiros was founded by Dorians around 1000 B.C. and flourished particularly in the 7th and 6th c. The remains now visible date mainly from a much later period (3rd and 2nd c. B.C.), and thus present the picture of a town of the Hellenistic age.

From the entrance to the site we come first to the **Agora**, in which is a semicircular *exedra*. To the S is the walled **Sacred Precinct**, square in plan, with benches round the sides. In a second **temenos** to the E of the agora are a number of *altars*. On either side of the main street, which runs uphill from the agora, are houses, including (on left) a well-preserved *"peristyle house"* with re-erected columns. On top of the hill there was a pillared hall 200 m (656 feet) long (re-erected but blown down in a storm). Beyond it can be seen cavities marking ancient cisterns and the foundations of a Doric temple.

Karditsa
ΚΑΡΔΙΤΣΑ
(Kardhítsa)

Nomos: Kardítsa.
Altitude: 110 m (361 feet). – Population: 25,000.

TRANSPORTATION. – Station on the branch railway line from Fársala to Kalambáka.

HOTELS. – *Arni*, C, 60 b.; *Astron*, C, 78 b.; *Avra*, C, 41 b.

Karditsa, founded during the Turkish period, is an agricultural market town in the Thessalian plain, under the E side of the Pindos range.

SURROUNDINGS. – In the hills 10 km (6 miles) W is **Mitrópolis**, with remains of Roman fortifications. – 15 km (9 miles) NW is **Fanári** (pop. 2000), with a Byzantine castle on a rocky crag.

Karpathos
ΚΑΡΠΑΘΟΣ
(Kárpathos)

Nomos: Dodecanese.
Area: 301 sq. km (116 sq. miles). – Population: 5400.

TRANSPORTATION. – Kárpathos is served by boats sailing between Rhodes and Áyios Nikólaos in Crete; also air services from Rhodes.

HOTELS. – *Porphyris*, C, 41 b.; *Anessis*, D, 21 b.; *Karpathos*, D, 28 b.

SWIMMING. – In Kárpathos Bay and on the SE and SW coasts.

Kárpathos, an island of great scenic attraction in the Dodecanese SW of Rhodes, is 48 km (30 miles) long by some 5 km (3 miles) across, with mountains rising to 1215 m (3986 feet).

Chapel on the island of Kárpathos

The chief place, **Kárpathos** (or Pigádia: alt. 25 m (82 feet), pop. 1200), lies in a wide curving bay on the E coast at the point of transition between the mountains and the lower ground. It was built during the period of Italian occupation, from 1912 onwards, on the site of ancient *Poseidion*. The insecurity of life in the medieval period is reflected in the hilltop sites of the island's villages, which can be seen in a round trip from the port.

The route runs via **Menetés** (7 km (4 miles) from Kárpathos: alt. 350 m (1148 feet), pop. 700) to **Arkássai** on the W side of the island (6 km (4 miles): alt. 47 m (154 feet), pop. 450; Early Christian basilica), then turns N to **Pylí** (7 km (4 miles): alt. 320 m (1050 feet), pop. 300) and **Voláda** (5 km (3 miles): alt. 440, pop. 500), and finally returns via **Apérion** (2 km (1 mile): alt. 320 m (1050 feet), pop. 720) to the starting-point. Other villages in the N of the island (reached by a road from Pylí) are **Mesokhorió** (14 km (9 miles): alt. 130 m (427 feet)), **Spóa** (7 km (4 miles): alt. 350 m (1148 feet)), **Ólympos** (28 km (17 miles): alt. 114 m (374 feet)) and **Diafáni** (10 km (6 miles): alt. 30 m (98 feet)).

Karytaina
ΚΑΡΥΤΑΙΝΑ
(Karítena)

Region: Peloponnese. – Nomos: Arcadia.
Altitude: 380 m (1247 feet). – Population: 1050.

HOTEL. – *Trikolomion*, C, 15 b. (in Ypsoús, 16 km (10 miles) N).

This Arcadian village is impressively situated in the gorge of the Alfios (Alpheios) 16 km (10 miles) W of Megalópolis on the road to Andrítsaina and Bassai.

Above the village towers a Frankish castle (alt. 583 m (1913 feet)) built in the 13th c. by Hugues de Bruyère, baron of Karýtaina. A monument on the hillside commemorates Theódoros Kolokotrónis, hero of the war of liberation, who defended the castle against the Turks in 1821. From the castle gate can be seen a medieval bridge spanning the Alfios below the modern concrete bridge.

Kasos
ΚΑΣΟΣ
(Kásos)

Nomos: Dodecanese.
Area: 65 sq. km (25 sq. miles). – Population: 1400.

TRANSPORTATION. – The island is served by boats sailing between Rhodes and Áyios Nikólaos in Crete.

Kásos, a hilly island rising to 600 m (1969 feet), barren of vegetation apart from some fruit-orchards, lies in the Dodecanese SW of the larger island of Kárpathos.

The chief place, **Fry** (pop. 460), lies on the N coast to the E of another coastal village, **Ayía Marína** (alt. 120 m (394 feet), pop. 550). From there it is possible to reach **Arvanitokhorió** ("Albanian village") in the bare and hilly interior, in medieval times the chief place on the island.

Kastelli Kisamou
ΚΑΣΤΕΛΛΙ ΚΙΣΣΑΜΟΥ
(Kastélli Kisámu)

Island: Crete. – Nomos: Khaniá.
Altitude: 14 m (46 feet). – Population: 2000.

TRANSPORTATION. – Bus service from Khaniá. – Boats from Gýthion and Piraeus (weekly).

HOTELS. – *Kastro*, C, 21 b.; *Posidon*, D, 17 b.; *Morpheus*, E, 21 b.

This little country town lies in the Gulf of Kisamos on the N coast of western Crete. It occupies the site of ancient Kisamos and has remains of a theatre and temple, together with a church dating from the Venetian period. There is also a small museum.

SURROUNDINGS. – 6 km (4 miles) S, at an altitude of 300 m (984 feet), is the village of Anó Palaiókastro, on the site of **Polyrrhonia**, the oldest Dorian settlement in Crete (8th c. B.C.), with the remains of walls and temples and rock-cut tombs.

The Gulf of Kisamos is bounded by two peninsulas reaching out to sea like the horns of a bull. The one to the E, **Rodopoú** (with a village of the same name), is only 8 km (5 miles) wide and rises to a height of 750 m (2461 feet). At its NE end, near Cape Spátha, is the sanctuary of the nymph Diktynna, which was excavated by German archaeologists, with remains of a temple of the 2nd c. A.D. built over an earlier structure of the 7th c. B.C.

The western peninsula, **Gramvoúsa**, is difficult of access except for good walkers. At the base of the peninsula, on the W coast, is ancient *Phalasarna*, reached by way of Platanós (25 km – 16 miles). The remains include the quay of the ancient harbour, house walls and a rock-cut throne. As a result of an upthrust of the coastline in the 4th c. A.D. they now lie 30 m (98 feet) above sea level and 140 m (459 feet) from the coast.

Kastoria
ΚΑΣΤΟΡΙΑ
(Kastoriá)

Nomos: Kastoriá. – Telephone dialling code: 0467.
Altitude: 620–760 m (2034–2494 feet). – Population: 12,000.

Tourist Police,
Grammoú 24;
tel. 2 26 96.

TRANSPORTATION. – Air service from Athens; bus services from Athens and to places in the surrounding area.

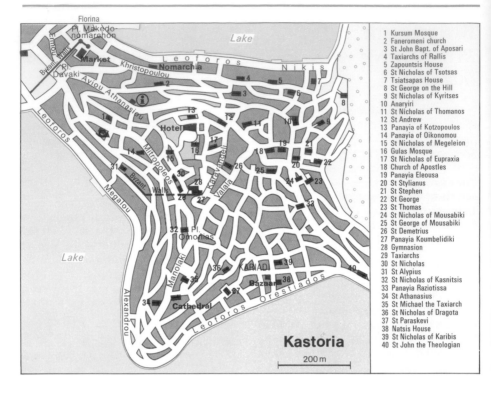

Kastoria

200 m

Florina

Lake

Lake

1 Kursum Mosque
2 Faneromeni church
3 St John Bapt. of Aposari
4 Taxiarchs of Rallis
5 Zapountsis House
6 St Nicholas of Tsotsas
7 Tsiatsapas House
8 St George on the Hill
9 St Nicholas of Kyritses
10 Anaryiri
11 St Nicholas of Thomanos
12 St Andrew
13 Panayia of Kotzopoulos
14 Panayia of Oikonomou
15 St Nicholas of Megeleion
16 Gulas Mosque
17 St Nicholas of Eupraxia
18 Church of Apostles
19 Panayia Eleousa
20 St Stylianus
21 St Stephen
22 St George
23 St Thomas
24 St Nicholas of Mousabiki
25 St George of Mousabiki
26 St Demetrius
27 Panayia Koumbelidiki
28 Gymnasion
29 Taxiarchs
30 St Nicholas
31 St Alypius
32 St Nicholas of Kasnitsis
33 Panayia Raziotissa
34 St Athanasius
35 St Michael the Taxiarch
36 St Nicholas of Dragota
37 St Paraskevi
38 Natsis House
39 St Nicholas of Karibis
40 St John the Theologian

HOTELS. – *Xenia du Lac*, A, 49 b.; *Acropolis*, C, 41 b.; *Anessis*, C, 38 b.; *Kastoria*, C, 20 b.; *Orestion*, C, 31 b.

The town of Kastoriá in western Macedonia, probably occupying the site of ancient Keletron, is charmingly situated on a peninsula in the lake of the same name. During the Turkish period it rose to prosperity as a centre of the fur trade.

SIGHTS. – There are no fewer than 72 churches and chapels in the town, many

A typical house in Kastoriá

of them with fine *wall paintings*. In the centre of the town, near the Gymnasion, are the **Church of the Taxiarchs** (11th–13th c.) and the **Panayía Koumbelidíki** (11th c.), the only church on a centralised plan. To the S, in Omónia Square, is the single-aisled **St Nicholas's Chapel** (*c.* 1000). On the highest part of the former citadel, near the Hotel Xenia du Lac, are the *Gulas Mosque*, the **Church of the Panayía** of Kotzópoulos and **St Nicholas's Chapel** of Eupraxia (11th–12th c.). In the N of the town are the **Church of the Anáryiri** (10th c., with 11th c. wall paintings) and *Ayios Stéfanos* (St Stephen), an 11th c. basilica with numerous wall paintings. There are a number of chapels of the Turkish period belonging to patrician mansions, some of which also survive.

Kato Zakros

ΚΑΤΩ ΖΑΚΡΟΣ

(Káto Zákros)

Island: Crete. – Nomos: Lasíthi.

A *palace and settlement of the Minoan period on the E coast of Crete, 115 km (71 miles) from Sitía and 25 km (16 miles) from Palaíkastro.

The palace, excavated by Nikolaos Platon from 1960 onwards, lies in a valley running down to the sea, in an area which on the evidence of the tombs in the "Valley of the Dead" was settled from about 2500 B.C. It dates mainly from the Neo-Palatial period and is estimated to have had some 200 rooms on three floors. After its destruction in a catastrophe about 1450 B.C. it was not reoccupied, and it was never plundered. The remains were thus left intact and yielded a rich harvest of finds, including more than 2000 vessels of clay, rock crystal, marble and slate coated with gold, many of them ranking among the finest and most valuable of their kind. These finds show that Káto Zákros was a centre of artistic production; but there is also evidence (e.g. six bronze ingots from Cyprus, ivory from Syria) that this port at the E end of Crete had far-reaching trade connections with other lands.

From the entrance to the site on the E side we come to the **central courtyard** of the palace, measuring 12 by 30 m (39 by 98 feet). To the N of the entrance are the main **residential apartments**, including a *polythyron* with a light-well. To the E of this is a circular basin. At the N end of the courtyard are the *kitchens*, with a *dining-room* beyond them. Along the W side are two large rooms, a basin and the palace *treasury*, which like everything else was found intact (contents in Archaeological Museum, Iráklion). At the SE corner a flight of eight steps leads down to a circular *fountain*.

Kavala
ΚΑΒΑΛΑ
(Kavála)

Nomos: Kavála. – Telephone dialling code: 051.
Altitude: 5–60 m (16–197 feet). – Population: 60,000.
ⓘ **Greek National Tourist Organisation (EOT),**
Platía Eleftherías;
tel. 2 24 25.
Tourist Police,
Eríthrou Stavroú 9;
tel. 2 29 05.

TRANSPORTATION. – Air service from Athens; bus service from Salonica; ferry to Thásos. Nearest railway station Dráma (32 km – 20 miles).

HOTELS. – KAVALA: *Tosca Beach*, A, 199 b.; *Galaxy*, D, 283 b.; *Oceanis*, B, 318 b.; *Philippi*, B, 83 b.; *Acropolis*, C, 28 b.; *Esperia*, C, 200 b.; *Nepheli*, C, 99 b.; *Panorama*, C, 95 b. – KALAMITSA (1·5 km (1 mile) W): *Lucy*, B, 291 b. – LOUTRA ELÉFTHERON (60 km (37 miles) W): *Panghaeon*, C, 48 b.

Kavála, the principal port in eastern Macedonia, is beautifully situated on the slopes of Mt Sýmvolon, rising from the spacious harbour to the Byzantine castle on the acropolis.

HISTORY. – The town was founded, probably in the 6th c. B.C., by settlers from the island of Paros, who named it Neapolis. It owed its rise to prosperity to the gold in the nearby Pángaion hills. In 168 B.C. it became Roman, and in 42 B.C. it served as a base for the fleet of Brutus and Cassius before their defeat at Philippi (see p. 214). In A.D. 50–51 the Apostle Paul landed here on his first journey into Europe. After the victory of Christianity the town became the seat of a bishopric subordinate to Philippi and took the name of Christópolis. Later the name Kavála came into use. From 1371 to 1912 the town was in Turkish hands. It is now a centre of the cotton trade and a port for the shipment of tobacco.

SIGHTS. – Fronting the town is the **Harbour**. Above it, occupying the site of the ancient acropolis, is the Byzantine

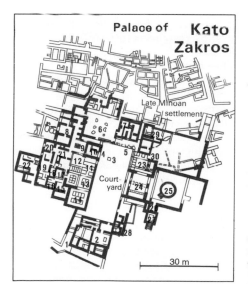

Palace of **Kato Zakros**

Late Minoan settlement

| 30 m |

1 S entrance	16 Treasury
2 Workshops	17 Lustral basin
3 Square foundation	18 Shrine
(for altar?)	19 Archives
4 Entrance to W wing	20–21 Rooms in which bronze
5 Pillared portico	ingots and elephants'
6 Kitchen and dining-room	tusks were found
7 Room with kitchen utensils	22 Dyer's workshop
8 Store-rooms	23 Queen's Megaron
9 Room with tiled floor	24 King's Megaron
10 Vestibule	25 Large circular basin
11 Large pillared hall	26 Square fountain
12 Light-well	27 Square basin
13 Square room	28 Circular fountain
14 Banqueting room	29 Lustral basin
15 Workshop	30 Entrance

Kavála – view over the harbour towards the Citadel

*Castle, within which was the birthplace of Khedive Mehmet Ali (b. 1769). The *aqueduct*, with two tiers of arches, carried water to the Citadel. The new **Archaeological Museum** contains material from Kavála (Neapolis) itself, Abdera, Amphipolis and Dráma.

SURROUNDINGS. – Within easy reach of Kavála are *Philippi* (15 km (9 miles): see p. 214); the **monastery of Ikosifínissis** on the NE slopes of the Pángaion hills (45 km (28 miles) via Eleftheroúpolis); the ancient site of *Amphipolis* (62 km (39 miles) W on the Salonica road: see p. 60) and the island of *Thásos* (p. 246).

Kea
KEA
(Kéa)

Nomos: Cyclades.
Area: 134 sq. km (52 sq. miles). – Population: 1660.

TRANSPORTATION. – Boat connections with Piraeus, Lávrion and Rafína in eastern Attica and the neighbouring islands of Euboea, Ándros, Tínos, Mýkonos and Sýros.

HOTELS. – KÉA: *Ioulis*, B, 21 b. – KORISSIÁ: *I Tsiamas*, B, 48 b.; *Kea Beach*, B, 150 b.; *Charthea*, C, 67 b.

BATHING. – Sandy beaches at Korissiá and Vourkári.

Kéa, one of the Cyclades lying close to the coast of Attica, was the birthplace of the lyric poets Simonides and Bacchylides (6th–5th c. B.C.).

The boat puts in at *Korissiá* (locally known also as *Livádi*) on the NW coast, which has recently begun to attract tourists. Across the bay lies the little village of *Vourkári* (20 minutes' walk), near which are the Ayía Iríni excavations. The chief place on the island, *Kéa*, lies 3 km (2 miles) inland, in an area of terraced fields.

SIGHTS. – On the small peninsula of **Ayía Iríni**, opposite the fishing village of *Vourkári* (10 minutes' walk), is a *Bronze Age settlement** (excavated by American archaeologists from 1960 onwards) which flourished between about 2000 and 1200 B.C.

Entering the excavation site by a modern staircase, near which is an ancient *fountain-house*, visitors can observe the various settlement levels, with walls standing to a considerable height, water channels, etc. The most notable features of the site are the*walls of the oldest temple found in Greece; *House A*, a large building with cellars, which may have served religious and administrative purposes; and the remains of a *tumulus tomb*. In the temple the altar, the doorway into the narrow cella and a bipartite adyton beyond the cella can be distinguished.

The chief place of the island, **Kéa**, on the site of ancient *Ioulis*, has a Venetian castle, now occupied by a hotel (views, extending over Attica). 2 km (1 mile) NE is an Archaic **lion*, hewn from a rock face. 6 km (4 miles) S of Kéa stands the monastery of **Ayía Triáda**, near which is an ancient tower.

Kefallinia
ΚΕΦΑΛΛΗΝΙΑ
(Kefallinía)

Nomos: Kefallinía.
Area: 781 sq. km (302 sq. miles). – Population: 31,800.

TRANSPORTATION. – Air services from Athens; boat connections with Kérkyra, Pátras and Piraeus; ferry between Argostóli and Lixoúri; island buses.

HOTELS. – ARGOSTÓLI: *Xenia*, B, 44 b.; *Aegli*, C, 17 b.; *Aenos*, C, 74 b.; *Ayios Gerasimos*, C, 28 b.; *Armonia*, C, 24 b.; *Dido*, C, 17 b.; *Phokas*, C, 18 b.; *Tourist*, C, 38 b.; and a number of hotels in category D.

SW OF ARGOSTÓLI. – LASSI (2 km – 1 mile): *Méditerranée*, A, 430 b. – PLATÝS YIALÓS (3 km (2 miles)): *White Rocks*, A, 190 b. – SVORONÁTA (10 km – 6 miles): *Irinna Hotel*, B, 321 b.

EAST COAST (FROM N TO S). – FISKÁRDO (53 km (33 miles) from Argostóli): *Panormos*, B, 10 b. – AYIA EVFIMÍA (9 km (6 miles) from Sámi): *Pylaros*, C, 17 b. – SÁMI (21 km (13 miles) from Argostóli): *Ionion*, C, 29 b.; *Kyma*, D, 16 b.; *Krinos*, E, 11 b.; *Samit*, E, 10 b. – PÓROS (26 km (16 miles) from Sámi): *Iraklis*, B, 12 b.; *Atrros Poros*, C, 18 b.

WEST. – LIXOÚRI: *Ionios Avra*, D, 22 b.; *Choropoula*, E, 22 b.

NW COAST. – ÁSSOS (34 km (21 miles) from Argostóli): *Myrto*, B, 10 b.

SWIMMING. – Beaches at Platýs Yialós, Myrtós and Sámi.

An idyllic bay on Kefallinía

Kefallinía (commonly pronounced **Kefalloniá**) is the largest of the Ionian Islands, separated from Ithaca by a channel 2 km (1 mile) wide. It is an island of hills, rising to 1628 m (5341 feet) in Mt Ainos, of fertile plains and of beautiful sandy beaches and long stretches of rocky coast. The Gulf of Argostóli cuts deep into the S side of the island, separating the western part from the main western part, which projects northwards to end in Cape Dafnoúdi.

HISTORY. – In Mycenaean times Kefallinía was part of the kingdom of Odysseus – although Homer does not mention the island's name, referring only to Same and Doulichion, which he believed to be two separate islands. In historical times Kefallinía shared the destinies of the neighbouring islands. In the medieval period it was conquered by the Norman leader Robert Guiscard, who died here in 1185 and is commemorated by the place-name Fiskárdo in the N of the island, and later was ruled by two Italian families, the Orsinis and the Tocchis. The island was occupied by the Turks for only 21 years, and was held by the Venetians from 1500 to 1797.

SIGHTS. – The chief place, **Argostóli** (pop. 8000), lies in a bay in the Gulf of Argostóli. Like other places on the island, it suffered earthquake damage in 1953 and was rebuilt in concrete. The **sea mills* at the northern tip of the peninsula on which the town stands (15 minutes' walk) were driven until 1953 by sea water surging along a rocky passage; but the earthquake led to a rise in the level of the coast, and the mills no longer work. – The **Museum* contains pottery of the Minoan, Mycenaean and later periods, Greek, Roman and Byzantine coins, and a bronze statue of the Emperor Hadrian found at Sámi in 1959.

SW of the town are the sandy beaches of Makrís Yialós and Platýs Yialós.

9 km (6 miles) S of Argostóli is the former capital of the island, **Áyios Yeóryios**, with a massive *castle* founded by the Byzantines and enlarged by the Venetians. In the plain below stands the convent of *Áyios Andréas*, with a **reliquary* containing the Apostle's foot. In the centre of the fertile Livathó plain are the picturesque villages of *Metaxáta* and *Lakíthra*. Between Argostóli and Lakíthra, to the left of the road, is the *Cave of St Gerasimos*, the island's patron saint, whose feast is celebrated on 16 August and 20 October (signpost).

The **monastery of Áyios Gerásimos** in a quiet valley E of Argostóli is reached by taking the Sámi road, turning right in 7 km (4 miles) and taking a road to the right beyond Frankáta. Continuing from Frankáta beyond the turning to Áyios Elefthérios and taking a road to the right we come to a mountain hut (1300 m – 4265 feet) on **Mt Ainos** (1628 m – 5341 feet): *views of Kefallinía and the neighbouring islands of Ithaca and Zákynthos.

The island's principal harbour, **Sámi** (pop. 1000), where the island boats call, lies in the only bay of any size on the E coast. Nearby are the remains of ancient *Same*. Immediately W of the village is an interesting *stalactitic cave*. To the N, on the way to the little coastal village of **Ayía Evfimía** (9 km (6 miles) from Sámi), a cave, the roof of which has fallen in, contains an *underground lake* notable for its beautiful colouring (Límni Melisáni).

In the N of the island is **Ássos** (34 km (21 miles) from Argostóli), with a Venetian *castle* built on a rocky peninsula. 17 km (11 miles) beyond this, on the northernmost tip of the island, lies the fishing village of **Fiskárdo**.

Khania

ΞΑΝΙΑ

(Khaniá)

Island: Crete. – Nomos: Khaniá.
Altitude: 20 m (66 feet). – Population: 40,000.
ⓘ **Greek National Tourist Organisation (EOT),**
Aktí Tombási;
tel. 2 64 26.
Tourist Police,
Karaiskáki 23;
tel. 2 44 77.

TRANSPORTATION. – Air service from Athens (office of Olympic Airways, Karaiskáki 34); bus connections with Iráklion, Kastélli, Palaiokhóra, Khóra Sfakíon, etc.; town buses.

HOTELS. – *Kydon*, A, 190 b.; *Doma*, B, 54 b.; *Lissos*, B, 68 b.; *Xenia*, B, 88 b.; *Porto Veneziano*, B, 120 b.; *Samaria*, B, 110 b.; *Canea*, C, 93 b.; *Diktynna*, C, 66 b.; *Elyros*, C, 14 b.; *Hellinis*, C, 28 b.; *Kriti*, C, 170 b.; *Kypros*, C, 36 b.; *Lucia*, C, 72 b.; *Plaza*, C, 17 b. – AT APTÉRA: *Aptera Beach*, C, 52 b.

TAVERNAS. – Mostly round the old harbour.

Khaniá, the second largest town on Crete and until 1971 its capital, is the economic centre of western Crete and administrative centre of its most westerly nomos (Khaniá), and the successor to a town which existed in Minoan times and was refounded by the Dorian invaders from Greece under the name of Kydonia (hence the name of the quince, melon kydonion, the "apple of Kydonia"). Passing in later centuries successively into Roman, Byzantine and Arab hands, it enjoyed a revival under Venetian rule from 1292 onwards. In 1645 it fell to the Turks. From 1898 to 1905 it was the residence of the Governor-General of Crete, Prince George of Greece. In 1941 it was captured by German forces, suffering severe damage in the process, but this has gradually been repaired.

SIGHTS. – The starting-point of our tour of the town is the *Venetian harbour*, on one side of which stands the **Janissaries' Mosque** (1645). Around the harbour is situated the older part of the town, within the Venetian *town walls*, considerable stretches of which still survive (e.g. on the W side of the town, where they end at a bastion near the sea). The old quarters of the town are Topanás and Evraikí, to the W of the harbour; Kastélli and Splánzia to the S; and Khiónes to the SE. In these quarters are to be found the remains of Khaniá's past.

In TOPANÁS (from Turkish *tophane*, "arsenal") are the remains of a number of Venetian palazzos, including a handsome *gateway* bearing the arms of the Renieri family (1608).

In EVRAIKÍ, once the Jewish quarter, is the *church of San Lorenzo*, the finest of Khaniá's 23 Venetian churches. During the Turkish period it became a mosque (fountain in inner courtyard), and it now houses the Archaeological Museum. This displays much material excavated by German archaeologists during the Second World War, including late Minoan sarcophagi and items from the Dorian and later periods, from Kydonia (Khaniá), Polyrrhenia, Aptera, the sanctuary of Diktynna on Cape Spátha and other sites in western Crete.

KASTÉLLI, the Venetian citadel, stands on the hill which was the original nucleus of the settlement. This has been confirmed by recent excavations which have brought to light in this quarter (Platía Merarkhías) a Minoan *palace* or *house*. Thus the earlier view that the Minoans settled only the central and eastern parts of the island has been disproved. – Other relics of the Venetian period are the Arcade of St Mark, the marble doorway of the Villa Zangarola and remains of arsenals (boat-houses) under the E side of the hill.

In addition to the Janissaries' Mosque beside the harbour the Turkish period is represented by a *minaret*, near the large **Market Hall**, which is modelled on the market of Marseilles. The minaret stands immediately S of the old town, in an area which is the heart of the town's business and commercial life. From here a long straight avenue, King Constantine Street, runs SE to the Nomarkhía (administrative headquarters of the nomos), which also houses a branch of the Greek National Tourist Organisation. From the Nomarkhía King George Street runs N to the outer district of Khalépas, in which are the former Governor's Palace and a house built by the statesman Eleftherios Venizelos.

SURROUNDINGS. – 6 km (4 miles) E of Khaniá on a road which crosses a fertile plain mainly occupied by orange-groves is **Soúda**, a harbour and naval base at the end of the 12 km (7 miles) long Soúda Bay, the largest natural harbour in the Mediterranean.

NE of Khaniá is the **Akrotíri** peninsula. An attractive short trip is to the *Profítis Ilías hill* (bus) for the sake of the view of Khaniá, Soúda Bay and the White Mountains which can be enjoyed from the tombs of the Cretan statesman Eleftherios Venizelos (1864–1936) and his son, near the chapel of St Elias (Elijah). – From here the road continues to the **Ayía Triáda monastery** (17 km (11 miles) from Khaniá), founded in 1632 by a member of the Venetian Zangarola family who had become a convert to the Orthodox faith, and accordingly also known as the Moní Tsangarólou. The monastery now houses a seminary for the training of priests. – From Ayía Triáda we can continue on foot (1 hour) to the other monastery on the peninsula, **Gouvernéto**, and the **cave church** of a hermit named John, situated above a rocky bay and notable for its Venetian doorway.

Khaniá is also a good base from which to visit a number of places of interest in western and south-western Crete:

Máleme (Hotel Maleme Beach, B, 426 b.) and **Goniás** (39 km – 24 miles). – Leaving Khaniá on the road which runs W along the N coast (numerous bathing beaches), we come in 18 km (11 miles) to

Máleme, where there is a large German military cemetery. 21 km (13 miles) beyond this is Kastélli Kisámou (p. 153). If we turn off the road to Kastélli in 8 km (5 miles) and take a side road on the right we come to the village of *Kolymbári*, with the fortress-like **Goniás monastery** and the Oecumenical Academy run by the autocephalous Church of Crete, the present director of which is Mr Papaderos.

Palaiokhóra (77 km – 48 miles). – Leaving Khaniá on the road to the W, we turn left at Tavronítis (19 km –12 miles) into a road which runs via *Voukoliés* (8 km (5 miles): Byzantine church dedicated to St Constantine) and Kándanos (31 km – 19 miles) to **Palaiokhóra** (pop. 1000), with a Venetian *castle* situated on a promontory. To the W of the town is a large sandy beach. From Palaiokhóra a trip can be made by boat to **Áyios Kýrikos Bay** (10 km (6 miles) E), the site of the Roman town of *Lissus*. There was a medicinal spring here and an associated sanctuary of Asklepios which has been excavated. **Soúyia**, on the next bay of any size, stands on the site of ancient *Syia*, and has a church containing an Early Christian mosaic pavement. – There is a boat service from Palaiokhóra to **Gávdos**, the most southerly Greek island.

Sfákia (73 km – 45 miles). – From Khaniá we go E to Vrýses (33 km – 21 miles) and then S by way of *Alikampos* (church of Panayía, with icons of 1315) and the Askýfou plain (730 m – 2395 feet) to **Khóra Sfakíon** on the S coast (Hotel Xenia, B, 23 b.), chief town of the Sfákia region, whose people have been known throughout history for their stubborn love of freedom. In earlier days, when trade with Africa was flourishing, the town had a population of 3000: today it has shrunk to a few hundreds. Notable among the town's churches, all built at private expense, is the Church of the Apostles. – In the vicinity of the town are a number of caves, one of which was occupied by Daskaloyannis, who was tortured to death by the Turks at Iráklion in 1770 after an unsuccessful rising. – 10 km (6 miles) E, above a sandy beach, we find the Venetian fortress of **Frangokástello** (1371), which can be reached either on foot or by boat. – To the W, also accessible by boat, is *Ayía Roúmeli*, at the end of the Samariá Gorge.

Samariá Gorge: see p. 231.

Khersonisos
ΧΕΡΣΟΝΗΣΟΣ
(Khersónisos)

Island: Crete. – Nomos: Iráklion.
Altitude: 20 m (66 feet). – Population: 620.

HOTELS. – *Belvedere*, A, 430 b.; *Creta Maris*, A, 1014 b.; *Nora*, B, 344 b.; *Avra*, C, 32 b.; *Eva*, C, 56 b.; *Glaros*, C, 81 b.; *Helena*, C, 24 b.

This village on the N coast of Crete, 26 km (16 miles) E of Iráklion, is named after a peninsula (Khersónisos) on which are the ruins of an Early Christian basilica with a partly preserved mosaic pavement.

Half way along the village on the road to the promontory is a Roman **fountain** with mosaic decoration. Ancient *Chersonesos* had a sanctuary of the goddess Britomartis; in Christian times it became the seat of a bishop. The village houses extend right down to the sandy beach, where there are a number of tavernas. A tourist centre has grown up in and around the village.

SURROUNDINGS. – 5 km (3 miles) E in the direction of Mália is **Stalída** (Hotel Anthousa Beach, A, 148 b.; Blue Sea, B, 286 b.), with a good beach.

8 km (5 miles) E of Khersónisos is **Mália** (see p. 177).

7 km (4 miles) W of Khersónisos (19 km (12 miles) E of Iráklion) is the village of **Goúves** (Hotel Candia Beach, A, 365 b.).

There are also interesting trips to be made to the S and SE of Khersónisos. – A narrow road runs S via **Kastélli Pediádos** (10 km (6 miles): Venetian castle) to **Panayía** (16 km – 10 miles), from which it is possible either to take a road to the right for **Arkalokhóri** (Minoan cult cave), or to continue S to **Anó Viánnos**, the chief place in the region (35 km (22 miles) from Panayía). Situated amid olive plantations, this occupies the site of ancient *Biennos*. Here can be seen the church of Ayía Pelayía (1360, with frescoes) and remains of the castle of Belvedere, originally built by the Genoese and later taken over by the Venetians. Near here a previously unsuspected sanctuary was recently discovered during road works; it had been frequented from Minoan into Roman times, and yielded votive offerings which were mostly addressed to Hermes and Aphrodite. – From Anó Viánnos a road runs E to Ierápetra (35 km – 22 miles).

To the **Lasíthi plateau**: see p. 169.

Kimolos
ΚΙΜΩΛΟΣ
(Kímolos)

Nomos: Cyclades.
Area: 36 sq. km (14 sq. miles). – Population: 1050.

TRANSPORTATION. – Kímolos is served by boats sailing between Piraeus and Melos. There are also boats between Kímolos and Apollónia on Melos.

The island of Kímolos, with its hills rising to 398 m (1306 feet) and its well-cultivated terraced fields, lies only 1 km (about a ½ mile) off the NE tip of Melos. In antiquity the chief place on the island was on the SW coast: today the only village is the one above the landing-place at *Psathí* on the E coast, with a

medieval castle from which there is a view of the neighbouring island of Polyaígos.

Knossos
ΚΝΩΣΟΣ
(Knosós)

Island: Crete. – Nomos: Iráklion.

TRANSPORTATION. – Bus from Iráklion (Platia Kornárou).

Knossos is the largest of the Minoan palaces and the most extensive excavation site in Crete. It lies 5 km (3 miles) SE of Iráklion on Kefalá, a hill sloping down towards the N, E and S.

The site of Knossos was discovered in 1878 by Minos Kalokairinos of Iráklion. Heinrich Schliemann tried to buy it, but the Turkish owner asked too much. It was, therefore, left to Sir Arthur Evans, whose name is indissolubly associated with Knossos, to acquire the site and begin its excavation at his own expense in 1900. The results of his work on this area of 20,000 sq. m (23,920 sq. yards) were sensational, bringing Minoan culture out of the darkness of oblivion and extending the historical picture back to about 2000 B.C., and indeed into the 3rd millennium.

Evans reconstructed considerable sections of the palace, using reinforced concrete for the sake of durability. His reconstructions have frequently been criticised, and his interpretation of the upper floor of the W wing is certainly questionable: for the rest, however, they are soundly based on the archaeological evidence. He also took care to distinguish the new work from the old. In the eastern range of buildings, with two storeys built into the hillside sloping down to the Kairatos valley, Evans's method was the only way of investigating the lower floors without destroying the upper ones. In the case of the grand staircase, for example, it was possible to replace the original timber columns, still identifiable in the rubble, first by timber supports and then by concrete columns of the same dimensions. In this way the excavated buildings gave a vivid impression of the original structures and gained in spatial effect.

The Palace of Knossos

Evans's practice of giving the various rooms names rather than numbers is, however, open to objection. Picturesque as they are, some of the designations he devised are wrong or misleading; but names like the "Queen's Megaron" or the "Hall of the Double Axes" are now so well established that they are retained in this account, with quotation marks as a reminder of their doubtful validity.

HISTORY. – The site of Knossos was occupied from Neolithic times onwards, and more than 7 m (23 feet) of occupation debris were found underneath the palace. Of the first palace of about 2000 B.C. a few remains are still visible, like the rounded corner N of the Throne-room. The later palace was built after 1700 B.C. as a royal residence, a cult centre and an economic centre. (The suggestion put forward some years ago that the site was a gigantic city of the dead, a necropolis, can be discounted.) The palace's four floors must have contained some 1300 rooms, of which roughly 800 can still be identified.

From 1450 B.C. Knossos was inhabited by Mycenaean Greeks, whose presence is reflected in the trend towards monumentality in the "Palace style" and also in the Linear B script deciphered by Ventris and Chadwick in 1953 – a Cretan script which was developed further for use by Mycenaean Greeks and was also employed in Mycenaean palaces in the Peloponnese. The destruction of the palace is dated on the basis of the latest research to about 1375 B.C.: thereafter only small numbers of people eked out a miserable existence in the ruins.

Like all the large Minoan palaces, the palace of Knossos is laid out round a rectangular central court aligned from N to S (53 by 25 m (174 by 82 feet)). The rooms are all rectangular and are arranged in accordance with a well-conceived plan – store-rooms along the W side, then cult rooms and public rooms, to the SE residential apartments, to the NE workshops and servants' quarters. In spite of this the layout of the palace is confusing, with its endless passages and countless rooms large and small. From its pre-Greek name of *labyrinthos* (probably "house of the labrys": i.e. of the double axe which had some cultic significance) the Greeks derived the concept of a labyrinth or maze which the word still possesses. The palace is built outward from the central court, and the exterior thus shows no uniformity or regularity. There were no defensive outer walls, indicating that the authority of the rulers of Knossos was securely established.

The tour of the palace begins in the *W Court*. To the left are three large circular pits, perhaps granaries; to the right a bust of Sir Arthur Evans. Through the W Porch, with a stone column base which once bore a wooden column, we enter a corridor which originally ran S for 24 m (26 yards) and then turned E towards the S Propylaion. The southern section has collapsed, so that we must now turn left through a doorway and pass through a number of rooms to reach the monumental *S Propylaion, from which we walk up a broad staircase to the upper floor or **piano nobile**. Beyond the Upper Propylaion is a hall with three columns

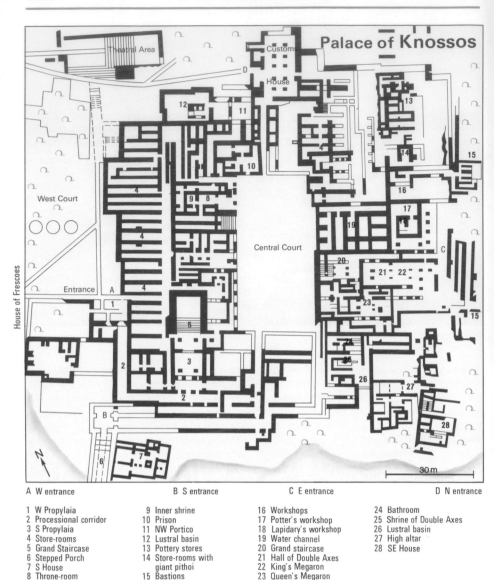

Palace of Knossos

Theatral Area

Customs

House

West Court

House of Frescoes

Entrance   A

Central Court

N

30 m

A	W entrance		B	S entrance		C	E entrance		D	N entrance

1	W Propylaia	9	Inner shrine	16	Workshops	24	Bathroom
2	Processional corridor	10	Prison	17	Potter's workshop	25	Shrine of Double Axes
3	S Propylaia	11	NW Portico	18	Lapidary's workshop	26	Lustral basin
4	Store-rooms	12	Lustral basin	19	Water channel	27	High altar
5	Grand Staircase	13	Pottery stores	20	Grand staircase	28	SE House
6	Stepped Porch	14	Store-rooms with	21	Hall of Double Axes		
7	S House		giant pithoi	22	King's Megaron		
8	Throne-room	15	Bastions	23	Queen's Megaron		

and three pillars, and beyond this again a staircase (on right) coming up from the Central Court. Looking down on the W side, we see some of the 22 **store-rooms**, with large, numbers of tall *pithoi* for storing oil, wine, corn, etc., still in situ. The store-rooms lie along a long corridor, at the N end of which was an archive room

Pithoi in the W store-rooms, Knossos

(no longer generally accessible) containing clay tablets with the palace accounts and records in Linear B script. – Continuing along the piano nobile, we come, beyond a corridor, to a large hall with two columns and the hall with six columns in which the painting of the "Parisienne" was found. In the restored rooms to the right (above the Throne-room) copies of wall paintings are displayed.

We now go down a narrow spiral staircase or the wide main staircase into the *Central Court*. Between the two staircases is the *Antechamber* to the Throne-room, with a porphyry basin which served some cult purpose. On the right-hand wall of the **Throne-room** is the original alabaster *"Throne of Minos"*, flanked by *paintings of griffins* above the benches which

The "Throne of Minos", Knossos

run round the room. This was not a royal reception room but a private apartment for the performance of some cult ceremony by the ruler, as is indicated by the *lustral basin* facing the throne. J. D. S. Pendlebury, who worked with Evans for some years, describes how when the Throne-room was excavated in April 1901 it was found in complete disorder: an overturned oil-jar lay in one corner, and the cult vessels had evidently been in use when the ceremony was interrupted by the final catastrophe.

From the Central Court we go S to the roofed-over remains of a tripartite shrine, beyond which are other **cult rooms**. From a vestibule we turn right into two small rooms, in one of which stands a finely decorated *pithos* some 2 m (7 feet) high; in the other the figure of the snake goddess was found. Straight ahead are the two **Pillar Crypts**, one beyond the other, in which sacrifices were offered (with depressions at the foot of the pillars for catching blood). In the rear crypt is a doorway (now closed) giving access to the store-room corridor. – Continuing S in the Central Court, we pass the site of a post-Minoan temple and come to the corridor along the S side of the court, with a copy of the "Priest-King" fresco which was found here. We now enter the *E Wing*

by way of the **Grand Staircase**. Going down one floor, we turn right immediately beyond the light-well, pass through a door and turn right again past the *Treasury* and then left to enter one of the *Queen's apartments*. To the S of the residential apartments, outside the main palace complex, are a number of rooms under a modern protective roof, the most important of which are a **bathroom** (*bath-tub* with reed decoration still in situ) and the adjoining "*Shrine of the Dove Goddess*". In this little shrine, only just over 1 m (3 feet) square, built in the final Minoan phase in the ruins of the destroyed palace, were found a series of cult utensils (dove goddesses, double axes, sacred horns, an offering table) just as they had been left by the worshippers, overtaken by some new catastrophe. – From here we can reach two buildings lying farther to the S, the "*House of the Chancel Screen*" and the "*House of the Chief Priest*".

Returning to the staircase, we now go down to the more important *second floor*. Passing a light-well, a guard-hall (?) and another light-well, we enter the "**Hall of the Double Axes**". This leads through four doorways into another hall (recently divided off by a wooden screen), a *polythyron*. As its name indicates, this second hall has "many doors" – three on the S side and four on the E side. It opens into a portico which is separated from another light-well by a row of columns. This part of the palace gives an excellent idea of the Minoan architects' skill in the planning of space and the provision of lighting. – From the S side of the main hall an angled corridor leads to the frescoed *"Queen's Megaron"*, which is lit by two light-wells and has a bath-tub in an adjoining room. To the left of the bathroom is a corridor which leads to the famous *lavatory*. Turning right beyond

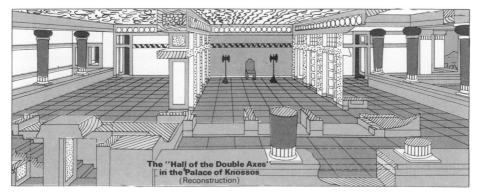

The "Hall of the Double Axes" in the Palace of Knossos (Reconstruction)

this, we pass an *archive room* and the place where the ivory figure of an acrobat was found and eventually come back to the grand staircase.

We now either go straight up into the Central Court and go down a staircase at its NE corner into the *N Wing* of the palace, or we reach this part of the palace ‹by passing through the royal apartments to the W–E corridor at the grand staircase and from there turn N towards the artists' and craftsmen's quarters. In this area can be seen the **workshops** of a potter and a lapidary, a room containing giant *pithoi over 2 m (7 feet) high, water channels and drains, and a staircase leading down to the E bastion.

We now return to the Central Court and go down a ramp at the N end, flanked by pillared halls (reconstruction of a relief of a bull in the left-hand hall), into the N Pillar Hall. To the left is the *Propylon*, at the end of the 230 m (252 yards) long sacred way from the Little Palace. Going along this, we come to the "**Theatral Area**", flanked on two sides by flights of shallow steps set at right angles to one another, which was probably the scene of religious ceremonies. From here we return over the W Court to the entrance to the site.

It is worth while taking time to see some of the other buildings round the palace. On the other side of the road is the *Little Palace, with a peristyle hall, a megaron and cult rooms. Following the road S for some 800 m (875 yards), we come to the *Temple Tomb, consisting of a court, an inner hall, a pillared crypt and the tomb chamber. On the way there we pass the "*Caravanserai*", which was connected with the palace by a bridge and probably served for the reception and accommodation of visitors coming to Knossos from the S. In the principal room was the "Partridge Fresco"; in the subsidiary rooms are foot-baths.

Koroni
ΚΟΡΩΝΗ
(Koróni)

Nomos: Laconia. – Telephone dialling code: 0725.
Altitude: 10 m (33 feet). – Population: 2300.

HOTEL. – *Phlisvos*, D, 15 b.

The little port of Koróni, 42 km (26 miles) SW of Kalamáta on the W side of the Gulf of Messenia, is noted for its castle. It occupies the site of ancient Asine, but in late antiquity was re-settled by the inhabitants of Korone (25 km (16 miles) N: now Petralídi) and took over the name of that town.

After the 4th Crusade the town was taken by Geoffroy de Villehardouin but was made over by him in 1206, together with Methóni, to the Venetians, who enlarged and strengthened the old Byzantine fortress. From 1560 to 1686 and from 1715 to 1828 the town was held by the Turks, who built further fortifications. Outside the walls on the E side of the town stands a monastery dedicated to St John the Baptist.

Kos
ΚΩΣ
(Kos)

Nomos: Dodecanese. – Telephone dialling code: 0242.
Area: 290 sq. km (112 sq. miles). – Population: 16,650.
ⓘ Greek National Tourist Organisation (EOT),
on the Quay;
tel. 25 09 19.
Olympic Airways,
Stefánou Kazoúli.

TRANSPORTATION. – Air service from Athens; served by boats sailing between Piraeus and Rhodes and between Rhodes and Sámos; island buses. A popular way of getting about is by hiring a bicycle.

HOTELS. – KOS: *Atlantis*, A, 380 b.; *Continental Palace*, A, 333 b.; *Ramira Beach* (3 km (2 miles) away), A, 224 b.; *Alexandra*, B, 150 b.; *Kos*, B, 132 b.; *Theoxenia*, B, 78 b.; *Acropole*, C, 10 b.; *Christina*, C, 39 b.; *Ekaterini*, C, 24 b.; *Elli*, C, 150 b.; *Elisabeth*, C, 32 b.; *Ibiscus*, C, 17 b.; *Koulias*, C, 57 b.; *Milva*, C, 99 b.; *Oscar*, C, 208 b.; *Veroniki*, C, 36 b.; *Zephyros*, C, 40 b. – LAMBÍ (2·5 km (2 miles) N): *Irene*, B, 33 b. – ÁYIOS FOKÁS (8 km (5 miles) SE): *Dimitra Beach*, B, 263 b. – KARDÁMENA (on S coast, 37 km (23 miles) from Kos): *Paralia*, D, 20 b. – KÉFALOS (on S coast, 46 km (29 miles) from Kos): *Sidney*, D, 40 b. – MARMARI (N coast): *Caravia*, A, 400 b., nude bathing beach.

BATHING BEACHES. – Immediately E and N of Kos; to the SE at Áyios Fokás; on the S coast at Kardámena aňd Kéfalos; on the NW coast at Tingáki and Mastikhári.

*Kos, the largest island in the Dodecanese after Rhodes, has become a popular holiday area, offering the attractions of its mild climate and beautiful scenery as well as an ancient sanctuary of Asklepios with extensive remains.

43 km (27 miles) long and between 2 and 11 km (1 and 7 miles) wide, the island lies close to the coast of Asia Minor in the Kerme Körfesi (the ancient Keramikos Kolpos), its north-eastern tip reaching to within 4 km (2 miles) of the Halikarnassos (Bodrum) peninsula in Turkey. The eastern part of the island is hilly, reaching a height of 846 m (2776 feet) in *Mt Díkaios* (the ancient *Oromedon*); the most fertile land lies on the northern slopes of the hill and in the plain round the capital, Kos. On the W side of the hill extends a plateau, and beyond the isthmus of Kéfalos, only 2 km (1 mile) wide, are the Látra hills (428 m – 1404 feet), made up of volcanic tuffs.

HISTORY. – The Achaean Greek inhabitants of the island were followed by Dorian incomers, who combined with Knidos, Halikarnassos and the three cities on Rhodes to form the Hexapolis (League of Six Cities). In 477 B.C. Kos joined the Attic maritime league. In the 5th c. the island's medical school enjoyed great reputation thanks to Hippokrates. In 412–411 B.C. an earthquake destroyed the old city of Astypálaia (near Kéfalos on the S coast), and in 366 B.C., in a "synoecism" following the example of Rhodes, the population was concentrated in the city of Kos.

In the Hellenistic period Kos supported the Egyptian Ptolemies (Ptolemy II Philadelphos was born on the island in 308 B.C.), and benefited from their patronage, as it did in a later period from that of the Roman emperors. In 431 it became the seat of a bishop, and thereafter shared the destinies of the other islands in the Dodecanese. Between 1309 and 1523 the island was held by the Knights of St John. During the period of Italian occupation (1912–47) the destruction caused by an earthquake in 1933 provided the opportunity for extensive archaeological excavations in the town of Kos.

SIGHTS. – The **town of Kos** has a population of 8900, including a number of Moslems. The **Harbour**, guarded by the *Castle of the Knights*, has modern port installations, various public offices dating from the Italian period and numerous tavernas. From here King Paul Street leads to the main square, in which we find coffee-houses, the Market, the *Defterdar Mosque* (18th c.) and the ***Archaeological Museum**.

The central hall, with roof lighting, is in the form of a peristyle. Its main feature is a ***mosaic pavement** depicting Hippokrates and Asklepios, the god of healing. Between the columns are Roman statues of draped figures, including Asklepios and Hygieia. In the side room on the right are two *statues of Artemis of Ephesus*, a *Marsyas* and a figure of **Hermes with a Ram* (with traces of painting). A narrow room devoted to the *minor arts* leads into a semicircular hall dominated by an over-life-size **statue of Hippokrates*. The last room contains a collection of *colossal statues* of the Roman period.

Going E from the museum, we pass the site of the *Agora* (2nd c. B.C.) and come to a square with a mosque of 1786 and the famous ****plane-tree**, many centuries old, its branches supported by props, including a small ancient circular altar. The tree is traditionally associated with the celebrated physician Hippokrates of Kos; but in fact the town of Kos was founded only after Hippokrates' death.

From the square with the plane-tree a bridge leads to the entrance of the mighty **Castle of the Knights**, above the gateway of which are the arms of the knights and an ancient frieze of masks. The original 14th c. castle was enlarged in 1457 and equipped with crenellated walls and bastions for cannon. Immediately beyond the entrance an *open-air museum* displays ancient column capitals, carved medieval coats of arms, Turkish prayer niches, etc. A ramp leads down to the original castle, in the building of which many fragments of ancient masonry were used, including the column shafts which can be seen in the roof of the entrance passage and (immediately beyond this, on left) an inscription in honour of Herodes Antipas (ruler of Palestine in the

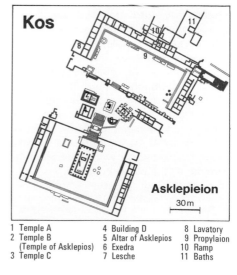

Kos

Asklepieion

30 m

1 Temple A	4 Building D	8 Lavatory
2 Temple B	5 Altar of Asklepios	9 Propylaion
(Temple of Asklepios)	6 Exedra	10 Ramp
3 Temple C	7 Lesche	11 Baths

Remains of the Asklepieion, Kos

S (uphill) side are a **fountain** (to the left of the steps leading up to the middle terrace) and (to the right of the steps) a *naiskos* donated by the Emperor Claudius' personal physician, C. Stertinius Xenophon of Kos. At the right-hand corner are another fountain and ablution facilities.

From this centre of treatment and healing we go up the steps to the cult centre on the *middle terrace*. Opposite the staircase is the *altar of the 4th c. B.C., sumptuously rebuilt in the 2nd c. on the model of the Great Altar at Pergamon. Oriented to face the altar is an Ionic **temple in antis**, two columns of which have been re-erected. To the left, beside the entrance to the cella, is a stone coffer in which the temple treasure was kept. Adjoining the temple on the S is a structure which has been identified as an *abaton*. At the E end of the terrace are the remains of a stoa open to the N. Between this, the altar and a semicircular exedra is a Corinthian *temple* of the 2nd c. A.D.

A broad **monumental staircase** leads to the *upper terrace*, 11 m (36 feet) higher, from which there are extensive *views. Like the lower terrace, this was surrounded by porticoes on three sides. It was dominated by a Doric peripteral temple (6×11 columns) built in 170–160 B.C., the culminating point in the axial disposition of the whole complex. Here the E–W orientation of the older temple of Asklepios gives place to a N–S orientation in which the effect is enhanced by the rise to successively higher levels.

time of Christ) recording his participation in games held in Kos.

In *Gregorios Street* (Grigoriou) is an excavation area of some size (Roman road and adjoining buildings; opposite this a reconstructed Roman villa and a small Roman Odeon). In the nearby Orthodox cemetery (beyond the Roman Catholic cemetery) is a *chapel of St John* (5th–6th c.). At the corner of Grigoriou and Pavlou are the excavated remains of a *temple of Dionysos*.

The *Asklepieion** (Sanctuary of Asklepios) lies 6 km (4 miles) SW of the town. The sacred precinct, discovered and excavated by R. Herzog in 1902 and further investigated by Italian archaeologists in 1928, extends over three terraces. The oldest of these is the middle terrace, on which an altar was erected to Asklepios, son of Apollo, about 350 B.C. in a grove of cypresses sacred to Apollo. Opposite there was built between 300 and 270 B.C. an Ionic temple in which the temple treasure was kept. The 2nd c. B.C. saw the addition of the lower terrace, with large stoas to accommodate the increasing numbers of visitors to the sanctuary, and the upper terrace, with a Doric temple dominating the whole complex.

We enter the Asklepieion on the N side, passing on the left **Roman baths** with well-preserved *hypocausts*. We then come to the *lower terrace* (93 by 47 m (305 by 29 feet)), which was surrounded on three sides by colonnades of 67 columns 3·70 m (12 feet) high, with treatment rooms and living quarters to the rear. On the

The road which runs W from Kos comes in 9 km (6 miles) to a road on the left which ascends to the hill village of **Asfendíou** with its medieval castle. 13 km (8 miles) from Kos another road on the left leads in 2 km (1 mile) to **Pylí** (Byzantine church with remains of frescoes, 15th c.), continuing to **Kardámena** (26 km – 16 miles), a little port on the S coast. The main road continues SW. At **Antimákhia** (24 km (15 miles): pop. 1500), with a castle of the Knights of St John, a road goes off on the right to **Mastikhári** (Early Christian church) on the N coast. The road passes the airport (27 km – 17 miles) and ends at **Kéfalos** (40 km (25 miles): pop. 1800), with another castle of the Knights. Nearby are the remains of ancient *Astypálaia*.

Kyllini
ΚΥΛΛΗΝΗ
(Killíni)

Region: Peloponnese. – Nomos: Elis.

TRANSPORTATION. – The nearest railway station is Gastoúni on the Pátras–Pýrgos line. – Ferry between Kyllíni and Zákynthos 2–3 times daily.

HOTELS. – KYLLÍNI: *Xenia*, A, 160b.; *Ionion*, C, 45 b.; *Xenia*, C, 150 b. – KÁSTRO KYLLÍNIS: *Kyllini Golden Beach*, A, 332 b.

TO THE SOUTH. – VARTHOLOMIÓ: *Fegarognevmata*, D, 17 b. – SKAFÍDIA: *Miramare Olympia Beach*, A, 665 b.

TO THE EAST. – AMALIÁS: *Amalia*, C, 28 b.; *Hellinis*, C, 27 b.

CAMPING SITES. – Kyllíni (Vartholomió), Kouroúta.

The Kyllíni peninsula – not to be confused with the hill of the same name in the northern Peloponnese – is the most westerly point in the Peloponnese. It ends in a ridge of hills which rises commandingly out of the wide coastal plain and is crowned by Khlemoutsí Castle. To the N of the hill is the little port of Kyllíni (known in the medieval period as Glaréntsa); in the middle is the village of Kástro and to the S is the spa of Loutrá Kyllínis, with large ˣsandy beaches which have made it a popular holiday centre.

HISTORY. – The area of alluvial land, partly flat and partly rolling, between the Kyllíni peninsula and Mt Erýmanthos was known in antiquity as *Elis*. Then as now it was a productive farming region, whose abundance of livestock is referred to by Homer ("Iliad", XI, 671 ff.; "Odyssey", IV, 635 ff.). In this region too were the Augean stables which Herakles had to cleanse. By capturing the territory of Pisatis on the River Alpheios and Triphylia, to the S of the river, Elis gained control of Olympia and the conduct of the Olympian Games. Its capital was the city of *Elis*, founded in 471 B.C.

After the 4th Crusade (1203–04) the territory fell into the hands of the Villehardouins, who built the town of Andréville (now Andravída) as their capital. Communications with Europe were maintained through the port of Glaréntsa, 15 km (9 miles) W on the N side of the Kyllíni peninsula, on which Geoffroy II de Villehardouin built in 1223 the mighty castle of Clairmont (now garbled into Khlemoutsí).

SIGHTS. – On the site of the ancient city of **Elis**, at the present-day village of *Boukhióti*, Austrian and Greek excavations have brought to light a *theatre* and the Hellenistic *agora*. The site lies 15 km (9 miles) E of the village of Gastoúni, on the Pátras–Pýrgos road, and is reached on a country road.

In **Andravída** the only relic of the medieval Frankish capital is the 13th c. *cathedral of St Sophia* with its fine Gothic vaulting. In the chancel is the carved tombstone of Agnes, daughter of Despot Geoffroy de Villehardouin. – **Khlemoutsí Castle** has recently been thoroughly restored. The main entrance, to the NW, leads into the spacious outer ward, beyond which is the inner ward, roughly elliptical in plan, with a series of

rooms and galleries – including a chapel – built against its high outer walls. From the upper platform there are views extending as far as the island of Zákynthos.

Kyparissia
ΚΥΠΑΡΙΣΣΙΑ
(Kiparissía)

Region: Peloponnese. – Nomos: Messenia.
Altitude: 160 m (525 feet). – Population: 5500.

HOTELS. – *Ionion*, C, 38 b.; *Artemis*, C, 41 b.

The Messenian town of Kyparissía, centre of the region of Triphylia, lies near the W coast of the Peloponnese on the slopes of Mt Psykhró (alt. 218 m (715 feet)).

In ancient times this was the port of Messene. During the Middle Ages it was known as *Arkadiá*, having provided a home for refugees from Slav-occupied Arcadia. Its **castle** has a history going back to ancient times, and in later centuries was enlarged and strengthened by the Byzantines and the Crusaders (who took it in 1204); it is commandingly situated, with far-ranging views. The town was destroyed by Ibrahim Pasha in 1825 during a punitive expedition against the rebellious Greeks.

SURROUNDINGS. – 14 km (9 miles) S on the coast road is **Filiátra** (Hotel Triphylia, C, 24 b.). The road then turns inland to **Gargaliani** (Hotel Ionian View, A, 12 b.; Astron, D, 26 b.) and continues via **Khóra** to **Pýlos** (see p. 220), 69 km (43 miles) from Kyparissía.

Kythira
ΚΥΘΗΡΑ
(Kíthira)

Nomos: Attica.
Area: 278 sq. km (107 sq. miles). – Population: 39,600.

TRANSPORTATION. – Boat services from Piraeus and Gýthion; island bus.

HOTEL. – AYÍA PELAYÍA: *Cytheria*, C, 15 b.

Kýthira (the ancient Kythera, Cythera) has long been regarded as one of the Ionian Islands, although it lies

well away from the rest of the group, 14 km (9 miles) S of the Peloponnese. Administratively, however, it is no longer subordinate to Kérkyra but to Athens. On this rocky island the Minoans established a settlement at Kástri, and later it was settled by Phoenicians. Kýthira vies with Cyprus in claiming to be the birthplace of Aphrodite.

SIGHTS. – Kýthira (pop. 850), the chief place of the island and one of the most attractive of the little island towns, lies above Kapsáli Bay, 3 km (2 miles) from its harbour. It has a small *museum* containing local finds. On a crag adjoining the town stands a Venetian *castle* (view), with two churches, the Myrtidiótissa and the Pantokrátor.

The island's other landing-place is at Ayía Pelayía, an open anchorage on the NE coast 4 km (2 miles) beyond Potamós (pop. 780). Other places of interest are Milopótamos (castle), on the W coast; the old medieval capital of Palaiokhóra, situated near the NE coast on a hill between two gorges, which was destroyed in 1536 by the Turkish admiral Khaireddin Barbarossa; and Palaiókastro, in Aviémona Bay on the E coast, with the remains of a temple of Aphrodite and of the island's ancient capital, *Skandeia*, which is mentioned by Homer.

Kythnos
ΚΥΘΝΟΣ
(Kíthnos)

Nomos: Cyclades.
Area: 99 sq. km (38 sq. miles). – Population: 1600.

TRANSPORTATION. – Kýthnos is served by boats sailing between Piraeus and Melos.

HOTELS. – LOUTRÁ: *Xenia Anagenisis*, C, 93 b. – MERÍKHAS: *Posidonion*, C, 158 b.

Kýthnos is a bare island in the western Cyclades.

The boats call at Loutrá, a small health resort on the E coast (recommended for rheumatism, arthritis and gynaecological conditions), from which there is a road to the chief place on the island, Kýthnos (5 km (3 miles) S: alt. 160 m, pop. 880),

with a church of 1613, and to Dryopís (6 km (4 miles): alt. 190 m, pop. 1100), with numerous windmills.

On the W coast is the fishing village of Meríkhas, with a bathing beach nearby at *Nisí*. On a hill between the two bays on the W coast stood the ancient city of Kýthnos, of which there are some remains at *Evraiókastro*. At the NW tip of the island is the medieval *castle* known as *Tis Oriaias to Kastro* ("Castle of the Fair Lady").

Lamia
ΛΑΜΙΑ
(Lamía)

Nomos: Phthiotis. – Telephone dialling code: 0231.
Altitude: 100 m (328 feet). – Population: 39,000.
ⓘ Tourist Police,
 Tsirimókou 5;
 tel. 2 32 81.

TRANSPORTATION. – On the motorway from Athens to Salonica.

HOTELS. – LAMÍA: *Apollonion*, C, 66 b.; *Emborikon*, C, 29 b.; *Delta*, C, 75 b.; *Helena*, C, 85 b.; *Leonideon*, C, 53 b.; *Samaras*, C, 124 b.; *Sonia*, C, 38 b.

YOUTH HOSTEL.

YPÁTI: *Oeta*, A, 63 b.; *Pigae*, A, 52 b.; *Xenia*, A, 143 b.; *Anessis*, B, 41 b.; *Anixis*, B, 28 b.; *Hellas*, B, 84 b.; *Lux*, B, 85 b.; *Pantheon*, B, 44 b.; *Rodon*, B, 32 b.; *Alfa*, C, 49 b.; *Astron*, C, 49 b.; *Lamia*, C, 54 b.; *Othrys*, C, 57 b.; *Phthiotis*, C, 22 b.; *To Neon*, C, 34 b.; *Ypati*, C, 48 b.

Lamía, chief town of the nomos of Phthiotis, which was claimed in ancient times to be the home of Achilles, lies near the Gulf of Lamía at the foot of Mt Othrys. The site of the acropolis is now occupied by a medieval castle.

SURROUNDINGS. – 25 km (16 miles) W, in the Sperkhiós valley, is the spa of Ypáti (recommended for cardiac conditions and circulatory disorders), with a 14th c. castle.

14 km (9 miles) SE is the pass of Thermopýlai (see p. 248).

A number of places on the coast near Lamia are now rising tourist resorts. 4 km (2 miles) NE of the town is Karavómylos (Hotel Stylis Beach. C, 297 b.).

Larisa
ΛΑΡΙΣΑ
(Lárisa)

Lasithi Plateau
ΟΡΟΠΕΔΙΟ ΛΑΣΙΘΙΟΥ
(Oropédhio Lasithíou)

Nomos: Lárisa. – Telephone dialling code: 041.
Altitude: 75 m (246 feet). – Population: 72,500.
ⓘ Tourist Police,
Vasílissis Sofías;
tel. 22 79 00.

TRANSPORTATION. – Air service from Athens; on Athens–Salonica and Lárisa–Vólos railway lines.

HOTELS. – *Divani Palace*, A, 144 b.; *Astoria*, B, 108 b.; *Melathron*, B, 69 b.; *Motel Xenia*, B, 60 b.; *Achillion*, C, 80 b.; *Acropole*, C, 88 b.; *Adonis*, C, 62 b.; *Ambassadeurs*, C, 158 b.; *Anessis*, C, 104 b.; *Dionysos*, C, 156 b.; *El Greco*, C, 172 b.; *Esperia*, C, 34 b.; *Galaxy*, C, 55 b.; *Helena*, C, 88 b. ; *Kentrikon*, C, 29 b.; *Metropole*, C, 169 b.; *Olympion*, C, 44 b.; *Doma*, C, 56 b. – *Edelweiss* (12 km (7 miles) S on the national highway), B, 30 b.

Lárisa, chief town of the province of Thessaly and the centre of an agricultural region, is situated at a bend in the River Piniós (Peneios) in the Thessalian plain to the S of Mt Olympus.

HISTORY. – Human settlement in this area dates back to the Palaeolithic period. In the 2nd millennium B.C. Lárisa (the "Citadel") was founded by Pelasgians. They were followed by Achaeans and later by Dorians, who established a number of principalities, including that of the Aleuadai in Lárisa. Among those whom they attracted to their court was the physician Hippokrates of Kos, who died here in 370 B.C. In 344 B.C. the town fell into Macedonian hands. During the Middle Ages it was a staging point for incomers and invaders (Goths, Slavs, Bulgars). In the 13th c. it came under the authority of the Despotate of Arta, and in 1389 it fell into the hands of the Turks, who held it until 1881.

SIGHTS. – In a small square in the centre of the town is a mosque which now houses the *Archaeological Museum, with material ranging from the Palaeolithic (implements from the Piniós valley) through the Mesolithic (Magoula of Gremmos) and the Neolithic to the classical and Christian periods. The classical material includes funerary stelae, while Early Christian art is represented by sculpture and altar screens.

SURROUNDINGS. – 25 km (16 miles) N is the Vale of Tempe (see p. 246). – 39 km (24 miles) E is Ayiá (alt. 200 m (656 feet)), the starting-point for the ascent of Mt Ossa (see p. 201). – Around Lárisa are a number of magoulas (settlement mounds), among them the Magoula of Gremmos (11 km (7 miles) NW), which was occupied from the Neolithic period into Roman Imperial times.

Island: Crete. – Nomos: Lasíthi.

TRANSPORTATION. – Bus from Áyios Nikólaos and Neápolis to Psykhró.

HOTELS. – PSYKHRÓ: *Zeus*, D, 14 b.; *Diktaion Andron*, E, 8 b.; *Heleni*, E. 18 b.

The *Lasíthi plateau, a large level expanse enclosed by the mountains of the Díkti range to the S of the Gulf of Mália, is noted for the innumerable white-sailed windmills which draw up water for irrigation, and for the Dictaean Cave at Psykhró.

23 km (14 miles) E of Iráklion and 3 km (2 miles) W of Limín Khersonísou a road (signposted) branches off the coast road and runs S via Potamiés (11 km (7 miles): church of Panayía Gouverniótissa, with 14th c. frescoes) and Avdoú (6 km (4 miles): three 15th c. churches with wall paintings) to a pass just beyond Kerá (10 km (6 miles): to the right, below the village, the Panayía monastery). From the top of the pass there is a view of the plateau, roughly 5 by 10 km (3 by 6 miles) in extent, which in all ages has been a place of refuge for Cretans in difficult days. The road continues via Tsermiádes (alt. 840 m (2756 feet), pop. 1200) to Psykhró (alt. 855 m (2805 feet), pop. 515), at the SW edge of the plain.

From here it takes about 40 minutes to reach the stalactitic *Dictaean Cave, which competes with another cave on Mt Ida for the honour of having been the birthplace of Zeus. The cave was a cult site for many centuries, and the material found here ranged in date from the Minoan period to Roman times. From the easily accessible upper cave (to the right of the entrance), in which are the remains of an altar, it is possible to descend in summer to the larger cave below (which in spring is filled with water); one large stalactite in the lower cave is known as the "mantle of Zeus". – Guides to the cave can be found in the village. Stout footwear, a warm pullover or jacket and a flashlight are essential.

From Psykhró it is possible to climb to the summit of **Mt Díkti** (2148 m – 7048 feet) in 6–8 hours.

The return from Psykhró can be either by the same route as on the outward journey or by a road which branches off on the right at Tsermiádes and runs NE to Neápolis (31 km – 19 miles), from which it is another 14 km (9 miles) to Áyios Nikólaos.

Lefkas
ΛΕΥΚΑΣ
(Lefkás)

Nomos: Lefkás.
Area: 299 sq. km (115 sq. miles). – Population: 22,900.

TRANSPORTATION. – Air service from Athens and bus from Áktion airfield; bus from Athens.

HOTEL. – *Santa Mavra*, C, 38 b.

Lefkás, one of the Ionian Islands, is only just an island: it abuts on to the mainland, separated from it only by a canal which was cut in ancient times and re-cut in 1905. The chief town, Lefkás (pop. 7000), lies near the canal. Opposite it, amid the lagoons on the mainland, is the castle of Santa Mavra, the name by which the island was known during the Middle Ages.

HISTORY. – Human settlement on the island dates back to about 2000 B.C. In the 7th c. B.C. Corinth founded a colony here. In 197 B.C. the island passed into Roman hands. From 1204 it belonged to the Despotate of Epirus, from 1331 to Venice, from 1362 to the Palatine County of Cefalonia (Kefallinía). Between 1467 and 1684 it was held by the Turks, after which it returned to Venetian rule. Thereafter it shared the destinies of the other Ionian Islands.

SIGHTS. – From Lefkás a road runs SW via Lazaráta and Áyios Pétros to **Vasilikí Bay**. To the W of this is the **Leucadian Rock**, from which, according to an ancient tradition, the poetess Sappho sprang to her death in despair at her unrequited love. – On a hill 3 km (2 miles) S of Lefkás is the site of ancient *Leukas* (remains of acropolis, town walls and theatre).

To the S of Lefkás **Nídri** has a beautiful situation at the mouth of Vlíkho Bay.

Opposite it is a peninsula with the chapel of *Ayía Kyriakí* and the grave of the German archaeologist Wilhelm Dörpfeld (1853–1940), who died here. There is a monument to him on the quay at Nídri. Dörpfeld, who worked at Troy with Schliemann and later at Olympia and Pergamon, directed excavations at Nídri from 1901 to 1913 but failed to find any evidence supporting his theory that Lefkás and not Ithaca was the island of Odysseus. He brought to light circular structures, graves and walls dating from the Early Bronze Age (*c*. 2000 B.C.) but nothing belonging to the Mycenaean period, the right period for Odysseus.

Lemnos
ΛΗΜΝΟΣ
(Límnos)

Nomos: Lésbos.
Area: 476 sq. km (296 sq. miles). – Population: 17,400.

TRANSPORTATION. – Air service from Athens; and boats on the Piraeus–Lemnos–Samothrace–Alexandroúpolis route.

HOTELS. – MÝRINA: *Akti Myrina Bungalows*, L, 250 b.; *Lemnos*, C, 58 b.; *Sevdalis*, C, 63 b.

Lemnos is a hilly island in the northern Aegean, though its highest peak rises to no more than 470 m (1542 feet). It is fertile and almost treeless, growing corn and, increasingly, cotton. The island's coastline is much indented, and two inlets, Pourniás Bay in the N and the Gulf of Moúdros in the S, cut so deeply inland that the E and W halves of the island are connected only by an isthmus 4 km (2 miles) wide. The volcanic rocks in the eastern half recall the ancient tradition that after his fall from Olympus Hephaistos set up his smithy and married Aphrodite here. Lemnos was also notorious in antiquity for the acts of ruthless cruelty committed by its people, as recorded by Herodotus, which provided the Athenian leader Miltiades with a pretext for his conquest of the island.

HISTORY. – The walled city of Poliókhni had a history dating back to the beginning of the 3rd millennium B.C. and belonged to the same pre-Greek culture as

Troy and Thermí on Lésbos (see below). The first Greeks arrived on Lemnos around 800 B.C., but about 700 B.C. gave place to the Tyrsenoi from Asia Minor, whose language, on the evidence of the inscriptions found at Kamínia, was closely related to Etruscan – providing some support for Herodotus' belief that the Etruscans originally came from Asia Minor (Lydia). The island was finally settled by Greeks after its conquest by Athens at the end of the 6th c. B.C. The island was noted as a centre of the cult of Hephaistos, associated with an "earth fire" near the town of Hephaisteia in the N of the island. In the 4th c. A.D. Hephaisteia became the seat of a bishop, but the see was later transferred to Mýrina on the W coast. After the 4th Crusade the island came under Venetian control for 100 years before reverting to Byzantium, which granted it as a fief to the Gattelusi family of Lésbos in 1414. From 1479 to 1912 it was in Turkish hands. During the Orlov rebellion of 1770 Mýrina was a Russian naval base. In the First World War the Gulf of Moúdros was used as a base by the Royal Navy during the Gallipoli operation.

SIGHTS. – The island's capital and principal port is **Mýrina** (pop. 3400), usually known as *Kástro*, which occupies the site of the ancient city of the same name. It lies on the W coast, below a crag with a Venetian *castle* built on ancient foundations. This crag, from the top of which there is a good view of the town and surrounding area and, on very clear days, a distant prospect of Mt Athos, 60 km (37 miles) away, separates two bays – to the S the **harbour**, to the N a long sandy beach, excellent for bathing, extending almost to the Akti Myrina Hotel. In this bay too is the *Museum, with a well-arranged collection of material from prehistoric Poliókhni, Hephaisteia and the Kabeirion of Chloe.

10 km (6 miles) E of Mýrina is **Kondiás**, beautifully situated in a bay with a fine sandy beach.

The island's second port, **Moúdros** (pop. 1200), lies on the E side of the Gulf of Moúdros, 28 km (17 miles) E of Mýrina. From here a road runs SE via *Kamínia*, near which the inscriptions in the Tyrsenian language were found, to **Poliókhni** (34 km – 21 miles), where Italian excavations have brought to light town walls, the remains of houses and a gateway with a ramp similar to the one found in Troy II, belonging to a prehistoric settlement on the E coast which dates from about 3000 B.C.

A road runs NE from Moúdros via **Kontopoúli** (30 km (19 miles): pop. 1100) to the excavations of **Hephaisteia** in Pourniás Bay (necropolis of 8th–6th c.

B.C., Hellenistic theatre) and the ancient port of **Chloe** (*Khlói*), where Italian excavations still in progress have brought to light a *Kabeirion*, with the remains of two cult buildings dating from the 6th and the 5th–4th c. B.C.

Leros
ΛΕΡΟΣ
(Léros)

Nomos: Dodecanese.
Area: 53 sq. km (20 sq. miles). – Population: 8500.

TRANSPORTATION. – Served by boats sailing between Piraeus and Rhodes and between Rhodes and Sámos.

HOTELS. – *Alinda*, B, 40 b.; *Xenon Angelou*, B, 16 b.; *Léros*, C, 36 b.; *Miramare*, C, 22 b.; *Panteli*, B, 48 b.

BATHING BEACHES. – On the E and W coasts.

Léros is a hilly island, rising to 327 m (1073 feet), with deeply indented bays, lying between Pátmos and Kálymnos in the Dodecanese. The inhabitants live by farming and fishing.

From the port of **Lakkí** (pop. 1700; medieval church) in the SW there is a road to the chief place on the island, **Ayía Marína** (3 km (2 miles): pop. 2600), with a Byzantine *castle* restored by the Knights of St John, from which it is 12 km (7 miles) to **Parthénion**, in a beautiful situation in the NW of the island. In the plain S of Lakkí is the village of *Xerokambos*, above which is the ancient site of *Palaiokastro*, with the remains of a fortress of the 4th c. B.C.

Lesbos
ΛΕΣΒΟΣ
(Lésvos)

Nomos: Lésbos. – Telephone dialling code: 0277.
Area: 1630 sq. km (629 sq. miles). – Population: 97,000.

ⓘ **Tourist Police, Mytilíni,**
Platía Teloníou;
tel. 2 37 76.
Olympic Airways,
Hotel Lesvion, Pl. Kountourióti,
Mytilíni.

TRANSPORTATION. – Air service from Athens; boats on Piraeus–Chios–Lésbos(–Lemnos) route.

HOTELS. – MYTILÍNI: Blue Sea, B, 69 b.; *Lesvion*, B, 68 b.; *Lesvos Beach* (6 km (4 miles) away), B, 78 b.; *Xenia* (2 km (1 mile) away), B, 148 b.; *Rex*, C, 34 b.; *Sappho*, C, 56 b.

ÁNTISSA: *Athina*, E, 8 b. – KRÁTIGOS: *Katia*, C, 19 b. – ERESSÓS: *Sappho Eressea*, C, 25 b. – MÍTHYMNA: *Delphinia*, B, 94 b. – PÉTRA: *Petra*, C, 34 b. – PLOMÁRION: *Oceanis*, C, 39 b. – POLÝKHNITOS: *Olympos*, E, 16 b. – SÍGRION: *Nisiopi*, B, 11 b. – THERMÍ: *Blue Beach*, B, 12 b.; *Votsala*, B, 94 b.

SWIMMING. – In the S Áyios Isídoros and Vaterá; in the W Eressós and Sígri; in the N Pétra, Míthymna, etc.

Sappho (Brygos vase, *c.* 475 B.C.)

*Lésbos (popularly known as Myti-líni), the third largest (after Crete and Euboea) of the Greek islands, lies in an angle formed by the Anatolian coast, only 10 km (6 miles) away on the N side of the island and 15 km (9 miles) away on the E side. The town of Mytilíni is capital of the nomos of Lésbos, which is divided into the three eparchies of Mytilíni, Míthymna and Plomárion. An island of great scenic beauty, Lésbos is also one of the most fertile regions in Greece.**

The island is broken up by the gulfs of Kalloní and Iéra, which cut deep inland on the SW and SE sides. Its proximity to the mainland of Asia Minor was a major factor in the vicissitudes of its history.

HISTORY. – At Thermí (12 km (7 miles) N of Mytilíni) excavation has brought to light a pre-Greek settlement established about 2700 B.C. which belonged to a cultural group embracing also the Troad and the offshore islands as far away as Lemnos. About 100 B.C. Aeolian Greeks from Thessaly arrived on the island and founded the towns of Mytilene and Methymna, ruled by aristocratic families which were constantly in a state of strife. About 600 B.C. Pittakos, ruling as a tyrant, put an end to faction and arbitrary government, retired voluntarily after ten years and thereafter was counted among the Seven Sages. From 546 to 479 B.C. Lésbos was ruled by the Persians, and after its liberation became a member of the Attic maritime league. Throughout this period, however, and in Hellenistic and Roman times it was able, like Chios, to maintain its independence.

Lésbos was the home of the poet *Terpandros* (7th c. B.C.), who was credited with the invention of the seven-stringed lyre; about 600 B.C. the singer *Arion* was born in Methymna and the poet *Alkaios* and **Sappho**, the greatest Greek poetess, were born in Mytilene. Another native of Lésbos was the philosopher *Theophrastos* (322–287 B.C.), who became head of Aristotle's Lyceum in Athens.

In 1355 a Genoese named Francesco Gattelusi married a daughter of the Byzantine emperor, who received Lésbos as her dowry, and the Gattelusi family ruled the island as a Byzantine fief until 1462, when they were no longer able to hold out against the Turks. During the period of Turkish rule, which lasted until 1913, many of the inhabitants moved to the mainland, particularly to the nearby town of Kydonia (now Ayvalık). After the catastrophe of 1922–23 their descendants returned to the island, the economy of which suffered from the loss of its Anatolian hinterland.

SIGHTS. – The chief town, **Mytilíni** (pop. 26,850), lies in a bay on the E coast, on the site of ancient Mytilene. A breakwater, which is also a popular promenade, protects the **harbour**, on which the commercial activity of the town is centred. Above the tiled roofs of the low houses, some of them fronted by colonnades, rises the characteristic dome of the **church of Áyios Therapón**, the architecture of which betrays western influences. Between the present S harbour and the ancient harbour to the N is an area of low-lying ground, once traversed by a canal, which separates the main part of the town from the massive *castle* of the Gattelusis, built on a crag projecting eastward into the sea. A path runs up through a pinewood to the entrance in the strongly fortified SE side. Fragments of ancient masonry in the walls and towers are a reminder that the extensive castle ward occupies the area of the ancient *acropolis*. There are a number of *mosques* dating from the Turkish period. Over a side entrance on the NW side are the coats of arms of Francesco I Gattelusi (1355–85) and his Byzantine princess, with an inscription of 1377. From the N end of the castle there is a fine *view of the ancient *N harbour*, with the remains of its breakwater.

To the W, above the harbour, is the ancient **theatre** (3rd c. B.C.), which gave Pompey the idea of building the first stone theatre in Rome.

At the S end of the castle hill is a monument to those who died during fighting with the Turks between 1821 and 1923. Nearby is a swimming pool. – The small ***Archaeological Museum***, housed in an old villa, contains a number of capitals of the rare Aeolian type and mosaics dating from late antiquity.

Other features of interest scattered about the island include the ***petrified forest*** formed by volcanic action at *Sígri*, a variety of ancient remains (a prehistoric settlement at *Thermi*, temples at *Ayía Paraskeví, Ákra Fokás* and *Mésa*, a Roman aqueduct at *Mória*), medieval castles at *Míthymna* and *Arísbi*, monasteries and churches.

Circular tour – the N of the island (125 km – 78 miles). – 12 km (7 miles) NW of Mytilíni is the little health resort of **Paralía Thermís**, near which is the prehistoric settlement of **Thermí**, dating back to 2700 B.C., which has been excavated by British archaeologists. The road continues via **Mantamádos** (38 km – 24 miles) and **Sikaminéa** (50 km – 31 miles), birthplace of the contemporary writer Stratis Myrivillis, to **Míthymna** on the N coast, the ancient Methymna (also known as *Mólyvos*: pop. 1800). Above this little port stands a Gattelusi castle, from which there is a view extending to the coast of Asia Minor. As H. G. Buchholz explains in his monograph on Methymna, the first settlement here was established in the 3rd millennium B.C. in the area known as Palaiá Míthymna; in the latter part of the 2nd millennium it was moved to the present site, and in the 1st millennium the town developed far-flung trading connections, reaching in the Hellenistic period as far afield as Egypt.

Continuing S from Míthymna, we pass the little port of **Pétra** (72 km – 45 miles), at the foot of a tall crag, and come to **Kallóni** (87 km – 54 miles: pop. 2000),

4 km (2 miles) N of the Gulf of Kallóni, which extends 21 km (13 miles) inland. Near the town is the **Límonos monastery**, with a richly carved iconostasis and completely preserved wall paintings in the principal *church* (admission for men only), new buildings containing the monastic library and archives and a museum, and an orphanage and old people's home which reflect the abbot's social concern. – The road now leads SE, leaving the Gulf of Kallóni at **Mésa** (94 km – 58 miles), near which are the remains of a temple, later occupied by a church. At **Lámpou Mílli**, also known as *Mória* (109 km – 68 miles), are the remains of a Roman *aqueduct*. Then back to Mytilíni (125 km – 78 miles).

Circular tour – the W of the island (177 km – 110 miles). – Going W from Mytilíni, we come to **Skalakhorió** (54 km – 34 miles), where a road branches off on the right to the remains of ancient **Ántissa**. Beyond Vatoúsa (61 km – 38 miles), to the right of the road, is the **Perivólis monastery** (frescoes, 17th c.), and beyond the new village of Antissa (69 km – 43 miles) the **Ypsiloú monastery**, on Mt Ordímnos (*view; manuscripts). The road reaches the sea at **Sígri** (84 km (52 miles): pop. 550), a little holiday resort on the W coast. SE of the village is the *petrified forest* of trees buried in volcanic ash between 700,000 and 800,000 years ago. From **Eressós** (98 km (61 miles): museum) it is worth making a detour to **Skála Eressoú** on the S coast (101 km (63 miles): sandy beach), the site of ancient *Eressos*, birthplace of Sappho and Theophrastos. To the W, near the beach, are the remains of an Early Christian *basilica* known as the "Skholí Theofrástou" (School of Theophrastos). – Returning to Eressós, we continue via **Ágra** (118 km – 73 miles) and **Kallóni** (147 km – 91 miles) to Mytilíni (177 km – 110 miles).

An interesting trip in the **S of the island** is to **Ayiásos** (30 km (19 miles): pop. 5000), on the northern slopes of Mt Ólympos (968 m – 3176 feet). Its central feature, the *pilgrimage church* (last restored in 1816), attracts thousands of pilgrims on the Feast of the Dormition (15 August). Fine pottery and hand spinning. – From Ayiásos it is possible to continue to **Polýkhnitos** (pop. 5100), 24 km (15 miles) away, with the little port of *Skála Polykhnítou* and *Damándri monastery* (frescoes of 1580). Beyond Polýkhnitos, on the S coast, **Vaterá**, has a good bathing beach.

For another excursion to the S coast, leave Mytilíni on the road which runs along the N end of the Gulf of léra and then turns down the W side of the gulf to reach the bathing beach of **Áyios Isídoros** and the town of **Plomárion** (42 km (26 miles): pop. 5200).

Levadia
ΛΕΒΑΔΕΙΑ
(Levádhia)

Nomos: Boeotia.
Altitude: 200 m (656 feet). – Population: 15,000.

TRANSPORTATION. – Bus services from Athens and Delphi.

HOTELS. – *Levadia*, B, 97 b.; *Helikon*, C, 36 b.; *Midia*, C, 24 b.

Levádia, capital of Boeotia, is a busy town situated on the south-western edge of the fertile Kopais plain. On the main road through the town is a spacious square laid out in gardens, well supplied with tavernas and coffee-houses.

HISTORY. – In ancient times Levádia was famed for the oracle of Trophonios, which continued to flourish into the Roman Imperial period and was described by Pausanias in the 2nd c. A.D. In the Middle Ages the town was occupied by Catalan mercenaries, who built a castle on the hill (now called Áyios Ilías) on which the sanctuary of the oracle once stood. In 1460 Levádia fell into Turkish hands and became the chief town in Boeotia.

SIGHTS. – In the **Erkina Gorge** at the W end of the town is the *Kria (Cold) Spring*, probably the ancient Spring of Mnemosyne. The Springs of Mnemosyne (Memory) and Lethe (Forgetfulness) played a part in the process of consulting the oracle. Recesses for votive offerings can be seen cut in the rock.

SURROUNDINGS. – **Chaironeia** (14 km (9 miles): see p. 106). – **Orkhomenós** (12 km (7 miles): see p. 201). – **Ósios Loukás** (37 km (23 miles): see p. 202).

Lindos
ΛΙΝΔΟΣ
(Líndhos)

Island: Rhodes. – Nomos: Dodecanese.
Altitude: 15–116 m (49–381 feet). – Population: 650.

TRANSPORTATION. – Bus service from the town of Rhodes (55 km – 34 miles).

HOTELS: see Rhodes.

*Líndos, one of the three ancient cities on the island of Rhodes (the others being Ialysós and Kámiros), is the most attractive and interesting of the three, with its situation on two bays, its sandy beaches and bizarrely shaped limestone rocks, its whitewashed houses, its medieval castle and its ancient acropolis.

HISTORY. – Finds dating from the Neolithic period and from Mycenaean cemeteries bear witness to the long history of settlement here, round the only natural harbour on the island. Lindos, which is mentioned in Homer, controlled more than half the island during the Dorian period, and around 700 B.C. founded a colony at Gela in Sicily. Its heyday was in the 7th and 6th c., under the tyrant *Kleoboulos*, one of the Seven Sages, who built a temple to the goddess of Lindos on the acropolis. The Lindos temple chronicles and the list of priests for the years 375–327 B.C. are important historical sources. The town continued to develop during the Hellenistic period and into late Roman times. The Byzantines built a castle on the acropolis, which the Knights of St John made into a powerful stronghold in the 15th c. During the 15th, 16th and 17th c. the shipowners and shipmasters of Líndos became exceedingly prosperous, as the houses they built still bear witness.

SIGHTS. – The road from the town of Rhodes to Líndos comes, shortly before reaching the town, to a hill saddle from which there is a fascinating *view of the bay, the town and the acropolis. Cars must park at the entrance to the town, which is reserved for pedestrians and those travelling on donkey-back. Walking through the narrow streets, visitors will see, in addition to numerous sellers of craft articles and pottery, the typical square whitewashed houses and, here and there, a number of handsome **shipmasters' houses** with elaborately carved stone façades. On the way up to the acropolis, concealed behind a high wall in a courtyard to the left, stands the beautiful ***church of the Panayía**, built for the Orthodox population of the town by Pierre d'Aubusson, Grand Master of the Order of St John from

Temple of Athena Lindia, Líndos

flight of steps leads up to the *main gate*, which – like the *commandant's house* and the *chapel* – was built by the Knights of St John and left in situ by the excavators.

Continuing up to the ancient sanctuary, we come to a large *terrace* dominated by a **stoa**, 80 m (262 feet) long with projecting wings (partly re-erected), which was built about 200 B.C. in front of the **4th c. sanctuary**. This comprises a *monumental staircase* 21 m (69 feet) wide, *propylaia* with five doorways on the Athenian model and the *temple terrace*. This was surrounded on all four sides by stoas, the foundations of which have been preserved. At the far left-hand corner is the *****Temple of Athena Lindia**, which is small in comparison with the grandiose surrounding structures, measuring 8 by 23 m (26 by 75 feet), with four Doric columns at each end (prostyle tetrastyle). It was built after 330 B.C. on the site of a 6th c. temple erected by Kleoboulos. Its eccentric situation at the edge of the sheer crag indicates that the goddess was originally worshipped in the cave under the temple.

From the point of the crag beyond the temple there are views of this **cult cave** (which can also be seen from the E end of the large stoa), of the little **harbour** in which local tradition has it that the Apostle Paul landed and of a Hellenistic tomb in the rock face beyond the town.

1476 to 1503. It has a rich iconostasis and one of the pebble mosaic pavements which are common in Líndos. The barrel vaulting and the dome have paintings of 1779. – Below the town is the sheltered **harbour**, with a sandy beach which is now lined with tavernas and bathing cabins (cabañas).

On the way up to the acropolis (on foot or donkey-back) there is a fine view on the left of the harbour and, beyond it to the N, a circular *tomb* on a hill, known as the tomb of Kleoboulos (6th c. B.C.).

The *****Acropolis** (excavated by Danish archaeologists) contains both ancient and medieval buildings.

Beyond the outer entrance (sale of tickets) is a terrace laid out over ancient cisterns under a vertical rock face, on which a *carving of a ship* commemorates a Rhodian naval victory (c. 180 B.C.). From here a long

Litokhoro
ΛΙΤΟΧΩΡΟ
(Litókhoro)

Nomos: Piória. – Telephone dialling code: 0352.
Altitude: 240 m (787 feet). – Population: 6000.
ⓘ **Hellenic Alpine Club,**
  in main square.

HOTELS. – IN LITÓKHORO: *Markissia*, C, 41 b.; *Park*, C, 40 b. – ON THE NATIONAL HIGHWAY (3 km – 2 miles): *Leto*, B, 177 b. – IN PLÁKA (on the coast): *Olympios Zeus*, B, 168 b.

CAMPING SITE.

There are numerous attractive holiday places along the coast to the S of the town:
LEPTOKARVÁ (9 km (6 miles) from Litókhoro-Pláka): *Olympias Bay*, B, 433 b.; *Achillion*, C, 34 b.; *Alpis*, C, 10 b.; *Astir*, C, 22 b.; *Daphni*, C, 23 b.; *Erato*, C, 20 b.; *Galaxy*, C, 49 b.; *Hecate*, C, 24 b.; *Matos*, C, 62 b.; *Platanos*, C, 35 b.; *Samara*, C, 46 b. – PARALIA SKOTINAS (14 km (9 miles) from Litókhoro): *Lefkes*, C, 18 b. – PLATAMÓN (21 km (13 miles) from Litókhoro): *Maxim*, B, 141 b.; *Platamon Beach*, B, 332 b.; *Xenia*, B, 8 b.; *Akrogiali*, C, 18 b.; *Alsos*, C, 24 b.; *Anessis*, C, 20 b.; *Apollon*, C, 32 b.; *Artemis*, C, 27 b.; *Helvetia*, C, 18 b.; *Hermes*, C, 24 b.; *Ilios*, C, 18 b.; *Kymata*, C, 16 b.; *Olympos*, C, 42 b.; *Tzavara*, 64 b.

Litókhoro, 5 km (3 miles) W of the Salonica–Lárisa road, is the best starting-point for the ascent of Mt Olympus (see p. 200).

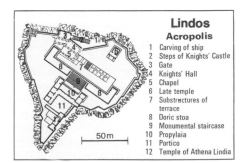

Lindos
Acropolis

1 Carving of ship
2 Steps of Knights' Castle
3 Gate
4 Knights' Hall
5 Chapel
6 Late temple
7 Substructures of terrace
8 Doric stoa
9 Monumental staircase
10 Propylaia
11 Portico
12 Temple of Athena Lindia

50 m

There is a motor road to a mountain hut (skiing area; open in summer) at 2100 m (6890 feet). At 2650 m (8695 feet) is another hut, 100 m (328 feet) below the *Profítis Ilías* peak (2 hours). From there it is a 2½ hours' climb to the summit of **Mitikás**, the highest peak (2917 m – 9571 feet).

Macedonia
ΜΑΚΕΔΟΝΙΑ
(Makedhonía)

Loutraki
ΛΟΥΤΡΑΚΙ
(Lutráki)

Nomos: Corinth. – Telephone dialling code: 0741.
Altitude: 10 m (33 feet).
ⓘ **Tourist Police**,
Yeoryíou Lékka 10;
tel. 4 22 58.

TRANSPORTATION. – Bus service from Athens.

HOTELS. – *Achillion*, A, 115 b.; *Akti*, A, 72 b.; *Apollo*, A, 500 b.; *Bacos*, A, 80 b.; *Karelion*, A, 74 b.; *Palace*, A, 92 b.; *Paolo*, A, 140 b.; *Park*, A, 115 b.; *Pefkaki*, A, 67 b.; *Theoxenia*, A, 50 b.; *Aegli*, B, 48 b.; *Atlantik*, B, 46 b.; *Beau Rivage*, B, 71 b.; *Contis*, B, 70 b.; *Excelsior*, B, 50 b.; *Grand*, B, 58 b.; *Kentrikon*, B, 31 b.; *Marinos*, B, 97 b.; *Palmyra*, B, 74 b.; *Pappas*, B, 153 b.; *Vasilikon*, B, 54 b.; *Acropole*, C, 42 b.; *Alcyones*, C, 51 b.; *Attikon*, C, 32 b.; *Bellevue*, C, 47 b.; *Bretannia*, C, 34 b.; *Ekonomikon*, C, 48 b.; *Elpis*, C, 63 b.; *Galaxy*, C, 72 b.; *Gerania*, C, 33 b.; *Isthmia*, C, 50 b.; *Marrion*, C, 52 b.; *Mitzithra*, C, 83 b.; *Mon Repos*, C, 35 b.; *Olympia*, C, 60 b.; *Pigae*, C, 67 b.; *Plaza*, C, 50 b.; *Posidonion*, C, 72 b.; *Ritz*, C, 59 b.

Large BEACH.

Loutráki is a well-known seaside and health resort at the E end of the Gulf of Corinth. To the NW is the beautiful and archaeologically interesting peninsula of Perakhóra with the sanctuary of Hera (see p. 212).

Macedonian costume

Extending from the Albanian frontier in the W to the River Néstos in the E and from the Yugoslav frontier in the N to Mt Olympus in the S, Macedonia is the largest region in Greece, with an area of 30,000 sq. km (11,583 sq. miles). Its extensive plains, including considerable areas won by the drainage of marshland, make it Greece's most productive agricultural region. Its industrial and commercial centre is Salonica, the capital, and an industrial area has also grown up round Ptolemáis.

HISTORY. – In early times Macedonia lay on the margin of the Greek world. Then in the 4th c. B.C., after achieving internal unity, it rose under Philip II to become the dominant power in Greece and the basis of the world empire of Alexander the Great (356–323 B.C.). Alexander's teacher Aristotle came from Stageira (Stayíra) in Macedonia.

Although Macedonia became part of Greece only in 1913, it has few remains of the Turkish period. It has, however, important ancient sites like **Pélla**, once its capital (see p. 210), and **Vérgina**, with its recent sensational discoveries (p. 253),

Loutráki

and numerous monuments of the Christian period – the basilicas of **Philippi** (p. 214), the monasteries of **Athos** (p. 99), the churches of **Salonica** (p. 228) and **Kastoriá** (p. 153). In the past Macedonia was little visited by tourists except as an area of passage to somewhere else, but in recent years the **Chalcidice** peninsula (p. 106) has developed into a large and well-equipped holiday region.

courtyard, in which is a small structure set at an angle to the main layout, dating from the post-Minoan (Mycenaean) period, possibly a shrine. Continuing S past this, we enter the *Central Court*. To the right of the entrance is the **archive room**, to the left a *hall* with six columns. In front of this hall, along the N end of the court, was a balustrade. Along the E side of the court ran a portico with alternate columns and pillars, and behind this are *kitchens and **store-rooms**, in which finds from the palace are displayed.

We now return to the Central Court. The *altar in the centre is the only one known of its kind. At the SW corner, still in situ, is a *kernos, a circular altar with 34 round cavities, probably for offerings of first fruits. To the N of this are a *grand staircase*, a *pillar crypt*, other staircase leading to the upper floor and a small *one-room* opening into the court. Going through s room, we come to the store-rooms and residential arters which lie to the rear, including a spacious lythyron with a **bathroom** adjoining it. Finally e enter the *W courtyard*, in which are a number of rcular pits* (cisterns or granaries).

From the *entrance hall* we turn right to enter the ...

Gold pendant from Mália

Mani
MANH
(Máni)

Region: Peloponnese. – Nomos: Laconia.

TRANSPORTATION. – Bus service between Gýthion and Areópolis

HOTELS. – AREÓPOLIS: *Mani*, C, 30 b. – ÁYIOS NIKÓLAOS: *Mani*, E, 13 b. – YEROLIMIN: *Akroyiali*, E, 12 b.; *Akrotainaritis*, E, 10 b. – KARDAMYLI: *Dioskouri*, C, 8 b.

The Máni is the middle one of the three peninsulas reaching out from the S of the Peloponnese, traversed by the tail of the Taýgetos range. This remote, hilly and barren area was able, throughout all Greece's periods of foreign rule, to preserve a degree of independence. For centuries the Máni was racked by feuds between different clans, who built the defensive towers still to be seen in many of the little towns and villages. This unproductive land, however, is now increasingly being abandoned by its inhabitants. Its great attraction lies in its beautiful mountain scenery, rising to 1215 m (3986 feet), its picturesque villages and its numerous old chapels, many of them in a state of ruin but still of interest for their wall paintings. Much of the Máni can be seen only on foot or from the sea.

Tower houses at Kítta in the Máni

Going SW from Gýthion, we pass the ruined Frankish castle of *Passava* (10 km – 6 miles) and cut across the peninsula to **Areópolis** (26 km – 16 miles) on the W coast. From here a mediocre road runs N along the coast to **Kalamáta** or *Kalámai* (82 km – 51 miles), passing **Ítylos**, with the Turkish fortress of *Kélefa*, **Áyios Nikólaos** with the Frankish castle of *Léfktron*, and * **Kardamýli**, which Patrick Leigh Fermor describes as "Byzantium restored". – 8 km (5 miles) S of Areópolis is **Pýrgos Dírou**, with the *stalactitic caves* of Díros (5 km (3 miles): restaurant, bathing). Farther S is **Kítta**, with a number of *tower houses*. The road continues to *Yerolimín*, beyond which are the villages of *Alíka* and *Kyparissós*. At the southernmost tip of the peninsula is **Cape Taínaron** (*Matapán*). In ancient times this was thought to be one of the entrances to the underworld, where Herakles descended in quest of the dog Kerberos (Cerberus). More recently Cape Matapán is remembered as the scene of a naval action in the Second World War. – On the E coast 5 km (3 miles) N of the cape is the 16th c. Turkish fortress of **Pórto Káyio**.

Mantineia
MANTINEIA
(Mandinía)

Region: Peloponnese. – Nomos: Arcadia.

The ancient city of **Mantineia**, formed about 500 B.C. by the amalgamation of five villages, lies 15 km (9 miles) N of Trípolis in the Peloponnese. It is reached by taking the road which runs N from Trípolis and in 8 km (5 miles), where the main road bends NW towards Vytína and Olympia, bearing right into a side road to Kakoúri.

HISTORY. – Mantineia was destroyed by Sparta in 385 B.C. but rebuilt in 371 after the Theban victory over Sparta. The battle of Mantineia in 362 B.C. put an end to Theban predominance in the Peloponnese.

The surviving remains date from the rebuilding of 371 B.C. There are considerable remains of the elliptical circuit of **town walls** (total length almost 4 km (2 miles)), particularly on the N and E sides. The walls, faced inside and outside with dressed stone, are between 4·20 and 4·70 m (14 and 15 feet) thick, with ten gates and 120 towers. The River Ophis was diverted to encircle the walls. – Within the town French excavations between 1869 and 1898 uncovered the *Agora*, with the Bouleuterion on the S side, a *theatre* on the W side and scanty remains of *temples*.

Marathon
ΜΑΡΑΘΩΝ
(Marathón)

Region and nomos: Attica.
Altitude: 52 m (171 feet).

TRANSPORTATION. – Bus service from Athens; local boats from Rafína to the islands of Euboea, Ándros, Tínos and Kéa.

HOTELS. – MARATHÓN: *Marathón Golden Coast*, B, 455 b.; *Marathón*, C, 46 b.

NÉA MÁKRI (8 km (5 miles) from Marathón): *Marathon Beach*, B, 296 b.; *Zuberi*, B, 238 b.; *Aphrodite*, C, 54 b.; *Nereus*, C, 245 b.

CAMPING SITE.

MÁTI (12 km – 7 miles): *Costa Rica*, A, 117 b.; *Mati*, A, 130 b.; *Attica Beach*, B, 178 b.; *Myrto*, C, 60 b.

YOUTH HOSTEL.

RAFÍNA (16 km – 10 miles): *Avra*, C, 184 b.; *Bravo*, C, 38 b.; and hotels in category D.

CAMPING SITE.

Marathón was celebrated in antiquity as the place where Theseus killed the bull of Marathón and as the scene of the first great battle between Greeks and Persians in 490 B.C. It was the home of Herodes Atticus (A.D. 101–177), famous in his day as a rhetor but better known for

his munificence in financing such buildings as the Odeon and Stadion in Athens, the Stadion at Delphi and the Nymphaeum at Olympia.

The large village of Marathón lies near the E coast of Attica, 5 km (3 miles) N of the *battlefield of Marathón*, on which stands the 12 m (39 feet) high *burial mound (sorós) erected over the remains of the 192 Athenians who fell in the battle. At the foot of the mound is a replica of the funerary stele of Aristion (*c.* 510 B.C.: original in the National Archaeological Museum, Athens). From the top of the mound there is a view of the battlefield, with the wide arch of the bay in which the Persians landed to the NW and the site of the Athenian camp to the W, at the foot of Mt Agrielíki.

Athenian burial mound, Marathón

SURROUNDINGS. – 8 km (5 miles) W of the village is Lake Marathón, a reservoir which supplies Athens with drinking water.

The road from Athens to Marathón along the N side of Pentélikon passes Diónysos, the home of Thespis, who performed the first tragedy at Athens in 534 B.C. There is a small and secluded sanctuary of Dionysos.

The extensive beaches S of Marathón offer excellent swimming and recreational facilities.

Megalopolis
ΜΕΓΑΛΟΠΟΛΙΣ
(Megalópolis)

Region: Peloponnese. – Nomos: Arcadia.
Altitude: 427 m (1401 feet). – Population: 3000

TRANSPORTATION. – Megalópolis is a station on the Peloponnese railway line from Corinth to Kalamáta.

HOTELS: in category D.

The little town of Megalópolis lies in the centre of the Peloponnese, a short distance S of the River Elisson.

It suffered severe earthquake damage in 1965.

HISTORY. – Megalópolis was founded after the Theban general Epameinondas' victory over Sparta at Leuktra (371 B.C.), and was intended, together with Mantineia (see p. 178) and Messene on Mt Ithómi (p. 149) to prevent any resurgence of Spartan power. In 353, 331 and 234 B.C. the town, peopled with settlers from the surrounding area, successfully withstood attacks by Sparta, but in 223 B.C. it was conquered and destroyed. Although it was rebuilt in 194 B.C. Pausanias, visiting the site in the 2nd c. A.D., found only ruins. Megalópolis was the birthplace of the historian Polybios (200–120 B.C.). The site of the ancient city, which lies astride the River Elisson, a tributary of the Alfios (Alpheios), was excavated by British archaeologists.

SIGHTS. – The remains of the ancient city, which was surrounded by walls with a total extent of almost 9 km (6 miles), lie near the present-day town on the road to Pýrgos. Immediately S of the river is the **Theatre**, which could accommodate 50,000 spectators. The 59 tiers of seats in the semicircular auditorium are divided into wedges by two horizontal gangways and ten staircases. The stage buildings were of wood, and could be stored in the *skenotheke or property room on the W side of the stage; only in the Roman period were they replaced by stone structures.

Immediately N of the Theatre is the **Thersileion** (so named after its donor), a rectangular hall measuring 66 by 52 m (217 by 171 feet) in which the Arcadian federal assembly met. The interior probably had the form of an odeon, with radially disposed Doric columns supporting the roof. On either side of the Thersileion were *altars*. To the W was the Stadion, to the E a sanctuary of Asklepios.

On the other side of the river, opposite the Thersileion, is a large sanctuary of Zeus Soter, and beyond this the Agora, bounded on the N by a stoa erected by Philip II of Macedon.

SURROUNDINGS. – 16 km (10 miles) NW, in the Alpheios (Alfíos) gorge, is Karýtaina (see p. 153). – W of Karýtaina, 60 km (37 miles) from Megalópolis, is the Temple of Apollo at Bassai (p. 104).

12 km (7 miles) SW of Megalópolis on a country road is the **sanctuary of Despoina** (the Mistress) at *Lykosoúra*, with remains of a 4th c. temple. In the cella can be seen the large base of the cult image. In front of a Doric stoa (only foundations preserved) are altars to the goddesses Demeter, Despoina and Ge, and in the small *museum* cult statues by Damophon of Demeter, Despoina and Artemis.

Melos
ΜΗΛΟΣ
(Mílos)

Nomos: Cyclades.
Area: 151 sq. km (58 sq. miles). – Population: 4500.

TRANSPORTATION. – Boat service from Piraeus; buses between Adámas and Trypití, Adámas and Zefyriá, and Trypití and Apollónia.

HOTELS. – ADÁMAS: *Adamas*, B, 22 b.; *Venus Village*, B, 60 b.; *Chronis*, C, 16 b.; *Coral*, C, 31 b.

Melos, the most southerly island in the western Cyclades, offers the attractions of archaeological sites, beautiful scenery and good beaches. It achieved wide fame with the discovery in 1820 of the Aphrodite of Melos (the Venus de Milo), now one of the principal treasures of the Louvre.

The island is almost divided into two by a gulf which cuts deep inland from the NW and contains the port of Adámas. The S of the island, with the hill of **Profítis Ilías** (773 m – 2536 feet), is almost uninhabited. Unlike most of the other islands in the Cyclades, Melos is of volcanic origin – a fact reflected in the bizarre rock formations and fantastic colourings to be seen when entering the gulf. Sulphur, quartzite, barytes and kaolin are worked on the island.

HISTORY. – Melos owes to its volcanic origin the rich deposits of obsidian found here. This glass-like rock formed by the rapid solidification of lava can be knapped like flint to make sharp-edged implements and weapons – knives, arrowheads, spear-tips – and it was the foundation of the island's prosperity from the Neolithic period into classical times. Obsidian was exported as far afield as Egypt, and Pheidias used it in the carving of his chryselephantine statue of Zeus at Olympia. The settlement of Phylakope (Fylakopí) on the N coast, belonging to the Cycladic culture, was established in the 3rd millennium B.C.; in the 2nd millennium it was under Minoan and after 1500 B.C. under Mycenaean influence, before being destroyed by the Dorians about 1100 B.C. Material recovered by the British excavators, including the famous flying-fish fresco, is now in the National Archaeological Museum in Athens.

About 700 B.C. Dorian incomers founded the town of Melos below the present-day village of Trypití, in the NW of the island, with its harbour at what is now the hamlet of Klíma. During the Peloponnesian War the island came into conflict with Athens, which responded with a brutal punitive expedition (cf. the Melian dialogue in Thucydides, V, 116). After being repopulated Melos flourished under Macedonian rule (from 336 B.C.) and under the Romans (from 146 B.C.).

In the 1st c. A.D. it had a Jewish colony, and in the 2nd a Christian community. In the 13th c. it became part of the duchy of Náxos, and in 1537 it fell to the Turks. During the Crimean War (1852–55) it was a French and British naval base.

SIGHTS. – The port of **Adámas** (alt. 10 m (33 feet), pop. 750), on the N side of the large gulf, is a very typical little Cycladic town. 4 km (2 miles) NW is the chief place on the island, **Mílos** or **Pláka** (alt. 200 m (656 feet), pop. 900; bus), which has an interesting little *museum*. On the way up to the Venetian fortress on the top of the hill is the interesting church of *Panayía Thalassítra*.

1 km (about a ½ mile) below Pláka is the village of **Trypití** (alt. 140 m (459 feet), pop. 700), from which a concrete road leads to the Early Christian *Catacombs* (2nd c.), with a *saint's tomb* in the principal chamber and some 2000 tomb niches. The catacombs are unique in Greece.

Venus de Milo (Paris, Louvre)

From the concrete road a side road branches off to the remains of the Dorian town of **Melos**. A signpost (on left) marks the spot where the Aphrodite of Melos, a Hellenistic work of about 150 B.C., was found in 1820. To the right can be seen remains of the *town walls* and a tower. We then come to a small Roman **theatre**, beautifully situated on the hillside overlooking the gulf.

E of Trypití, above the precipitous N coast, is the site of **Phylakope** (*Fylakopí*), with the foundations of houses of the 3rd and 2nd millennia and Mycenaean walls of about 1500 B.C., and beyond this is the pretty little port of **Apollónia** (11 km (7 miles): alt. 10 m (33 feet), pop. 140), which has a sandy beach.

SE of Adámas are **Zefyriá** (6 km (4 miles): pop. 350) and the ruins of **Palaiokhóra**, founded in the 8th c. and abandoned in 1793.

Three smaller islands can be reached by boat – the rocky islet of **Antímilos** (area 8 sq. km (3 sq. miles), max. alt. 643 m (2110 feet), occupied only by wild goats, from Adámas, **Kímolos** (see p. 160) and *Polýaigos* from Apollónia.

Mesolongi
ΜΕΣΟΛΟΓΓΙ
(Mesolóngi)

Nomos: Aetolia and Acarnania.
Population: 19,000. – Telephone dialling code: 0631
ⓘ **Tourist Police**,
A. Damaskinou 11;
tel. 2 25 55.

HOTELS. – *Liberty*, B, 102 b.; *Theoxenia* (in harbour), B, 40 b.

The town of Mesolóngi, capital of the nomos of Aetolia and Acarnania, lies – as its name indicates – "amid the lagoons" on the N side of the Gulf of Pátras. The poet Kóstis Palamás (1843–1943), who was born and brought up here, depicts the character and history of the town in his poem "The Lament of the Lagoon".

HISTORY. – Mesolóngi's main claim to fame is its heroic defence against the Turks during the war of liberation. The town, in which Alexander Mavrokordátos, President elect of Greece, had set up his headquarters in 1821, was defended by the Suliot leader Markos Bótsaris. On 5 January 1824 *Byron* landed at Mesolóngi, but died of fever on 10 April. In 1825 the Turks laid siege to the town. The Greek defenders tried to break through the Turkish lines in April 1826, but only 1800 out of 9000 were successful in doing so, and those left in the town thereupon set fire to the magazines and blew themselves up.

SIGHTS. – Entering the town through a gate in the *town walls*, we bear right to reach the **Heroon** (mod. Greek *Iróon*), a worthy tomb and memorial for those who fell between 1821 and 1826. Beside it is a mound containing their remains and Byron's heart. To the right, on the axis of the main hall of the Heroon, is a *statue of Byron*. Note also the tomb of Bótsaris and the *monuments* to Philhellenes from Britain, America, France, Germany, Italy,

Poland and Scandinavia. – There is a *museum with mementoes of the war of liberation in the Dimarkhion (Town Hall).

SURROUNDINGS. – From the Theoxenia Hotel a causeway runs far out into the *lagoons*. – 4 km (2 miles) N of Mesolóngi, on the right-hand side of the new road to Agrínion, are the remains of the Hellenistic city of **Pleuron** (small theatre, cistern, walls). 6 km (4 miles) beyond this a causeway on the left leads to the little island town of **Aitolikón**, where visitors can sample a local delicacy, *avgotárakho* (fish-roe wrapped in wax). Continuing W via *Neokhorió*, where the wide River Akhelóos is crossed, and *Katókhi*, we come to the overgrown remains of **Oiniadai**, situated on a low ridge of hills. The ancient city was founded by Alkmaion, son of Amphiaraos, and named after his son Oineus. To the N, on what was formerly the shore of Lake Melite, are remains of the harbour; to the SE is the acropolis, with a polygonal wall of the 6th c. B.C. – To the S of the mouth of the River Akhelóos are the **Oxia Islands**, scene of the battle of Lepanto in 1571 in which the Western fleet commanded by Don John of Austria, a natural son of the Emperor Charles V, defeated the Turkish fleet. – Here and there in this area the reed huts occupied by the nomadic Sarakatsans can still be seen.

Mesopotamos
ΜΕΣΟΠΟΤΑΜΟΣ
(Mesopótamos)

Region: Epirus. – Nomos: Préveza.

The village of Mesopótamos, near the W coast of Epirus, achieved fame when the first-known example of a nekromanteion (oracle of the dead) was discovered just outside it.

The village can be reached on the new road which runs S from Igoumenítsa (51 km – 32 miles) or from the port of Párga (24 km – 15 miles). The road to the *Nekromanteion branches off on the left just before the entrance to the village. The land now occupied by rice-fields was formerly Lake Akherousia, which has been drained and taken into cultivation. Through the lake flowed Acheron, the river of the dead, rising in the Tomaris hills and flowing into the sea to the W. The Acheron and Kokytos flowing down from the N formed a right angle, in which the ancients saw the entrance to the under-world; and the existence of an oracle of the dead here is referred to as early as Homer.

Between 1958 and 1964 this cult site, situated on a conical hill under a chapel of St John, was excavated by Sotir Dakaris. It belonged to the city of *Ephýra*, a short distance N. According to Herodotus this was the setting of the myth of Orpheus and Eurydice. The material found on this site and at Ephýra dates back to the Mycenaean period (14th–13th c. B.C.), but nothing is known of the early period of the oracular cult: the buildings excavated date only from about 300 B.C., and they were destroyed in 198 B.C. They do, however, agree with the description given by Homer much earlier (8th c. B.C.) of Odysseus consulting the dead ("Odyssey", X, 515ff., and XI, 24ff.). The excavator stresses the accuracy of Homer's topographical information (though his reference to the Cimmerians is an error for the Cheimerioi, a local Thesprotian people). – A late satirical description of the consultation of the dead is given by Lucian in his "Menippos".

Approaching the site from the W, we enter a courtyard surrounded by the remains of later (3rd c. B.C.) buildings, at the S end of which, near a medieval **tower house**, is a *Mycenaean cist tomb*. The way into the inner shrine, which was probably windowless, leads along a succession of corridors (originally roofed) at right angles to one another. To the left of the *N corridor* are a number of rooms in which those who wished to consult the oracle prepared themselves by a period of meditation and the use of some kind of stimulant. Then follow the *E corridor* and the *S corridor*, which is broken up by internal walls into a kind of labyrinth or maze. Turning right again, we come into the ***inmost shrine**, which measures 21·80 by 21·65 m (72 by 71 feet). Its polygonal walls,

fitted together with great accuracy, are 3·30 m (11 feet) thick and still stand 3·25 m (11 feet) high. It consists of a central aisle and two lateral aisles, each divided into three parts, which contained pithoi for corn and honey and clay figures of Persephone. Through an opening in the floor of the central aisle offerings of food for the shades were deposited in the vaulted *crypt* below, which was held to be the uppermost part of the underground palace of Hades and Persephone. Wheels found here by the excavators pointed to some kind of mechanism by which the priests could cause figures of the dead to appear before worshippers consulting the oracle.

By climbing up on to the walls of the sanctuary it is possible to look into the *chapel of St John*, under which the excavators inserted concrete supports, and to enjoy an extensive view over the Acherousian plain and the sea, with the *Paxi* group of islands lying offshore.

Meteora
ΜΕΤΕΩΡΑ
(Metéora)

Region: Thessaly. – Nomos: Tríkala.

HOTELS. – see under Kalambáka. – IN KASTRÁKI: *Kastraki*, E, 14 b.

CAMPING SITES. – Metéora and Vrákhos, between Kastráki and Metéora.

In north-western Thessaly there rises out of the plain of the Peneios (modern Greek Piniós) a group of conglomerate *rock formations 300 m (984 feet) high which have been weathered by erosion into a

Kastráki, against the backdrop of the Metéora rocks

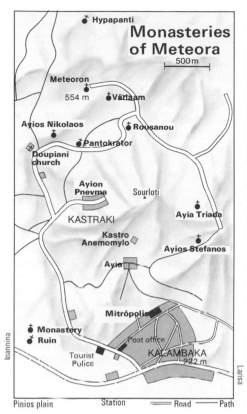

Monasteries of Meteora

500m

Meteoron
554 m   Varlaám
Ayios Nikolaos
         Rousanou
      Pantokrátor
Doupiani
church
   Ayion
   Pnevma   Sourloti
   KASTRAKI
              Ayia Triada
       Kastro
    Anemomylo
              Ayios Stefanos
       Ayia

            Mitrópolis
   Monastery
   Ruin   Post office
       Tourist   KALAMBAKA
       Police   222 m

Pinios plain   Station   ===Road   ——Path

Hypapanti

Ioannina

Larisa

HISTORY. – In the 9th c. the first hermits settled in caves under the rocks of Metéora, and a church of the Panayía was built at Doupianí. The place became known as "stous Ayious" ("at the saints"), which was corrupted into *Stágoi*. In 1340 Thessaly came under Serbian control, and Simeon, an uncle of the young king Stephen Uroš V, was crowned as king of the Serbs and Greeks at Tríkala. During this troubled period the hermits sought safety and tranquillity on the summits of the rocks. Then monasteries were built, beginning with the Great Metéoron, founded by Athanasios the Meteorite between 1356 and 1372 on the Broad Rock (Platýs Lithós) and enlarged from 1388 onwards by his disciple and successor Joasaph, a son of King Simeon. In the heyday of Metéora there were 24 monasteries; but a period of decline began in the 16th c., and only five monasteries are now still occupied. Together with the monasteries of Athos they make an important contribution to our knowledge of the post-Byzantine painting of the 16th c.

TOUR OF THE MONASTERIES. – The road climbs up from Kalambáka to the rocks of Metéora by way of the village of Kastráki. At various places on the way up can be seen the recesses and caves in the rock faces in which the early hermits lived. After passing the little Mitrópolis church of Doupianí we come (on left) to the steep ascent leading up to the monastery of **Áyios Nikólaos Anapafsás**, founded in 1368, painted by the Cretan artist Theophanes in 1527 and enlarged in 1628. Beyond the monastery of **Rousanoú**, perched on a slender pinnacle of rock – the most boldly sited of them all – the road to the Great Metéoron and Varlaám monastery branches off on the left.

Standing below the *Great Metéoron*, we can see on the rock face the traces of the earlier ladders, and at the top the little tower-like building with a timber roof which still houses the windlass formerly used to haul visitors up in a net but now serving only for the hoisting up of provisions. As a result of the increasing numbers of visitors considerable parts of the monastery have been closed to the public.

Visitors are admitted to the **principal church**, dedicated to the Metamórphosis (Transfiguration). The *chapel* built by the founder, Athanasios, is now the chancel of the larger church erected by Joasaph. The *tombs* of the two founders are in the spacious **narthex**, which, like the body of the church (16th c.) and the **apse** (1438), has preserved its *wall paintings* intact. – There is an interesting *collection of icons and books* in the former **refectory** (*trápeza*). Particularly notable is an *icon of the Incredulity of Thomas* (14th c.), which shows Christ and the Apostles along with the cruel Thomas Preljubovič of Ioánnina and his pious wife Angelina Comnena.

variety of bizarre forms. Vertical rock faces, sharply pointed pinnacles and massive crags tower up above Kalambáka and Kastráki, separated by deeply slashed defiles. Perched on these rocks are the ** monasteries of Metéora, which take their name from their situation – ta metéora monastiria, the monasteries hanging in the air.

Originally accessible only by bridle-tracks, ladders and ropes and windlasses, the monasteries have now been brought within the reach of tourists by the construction of modern roads and flights of steps and by signposting; but visitors should be careful to remember that these are places of peace and prayer and meditation and should conduct themselves accordingly.

To get the most out of a visit to this awe-inspiring corner of Greece visitors should avoid hurrying on from one sight to another. The best plan is to allow time to explore the area on foot and to see some of the remoter monasteries, now abandoned, as well as those which are shown to tourists.

The monastery of Varlaám, Metéora

The nearby monastery of **Varlaám**, founded in 1517, has some lively paintings by Frangos Kastellanos of Thebes, including an impressive *Crucifixion* (1548) in the *church of All Saints* (Áyion Pánton). In the narthex is a fine *Last Judgment* (1566). The monastery also has an interesting *museum* and *library*.

On the way back we take the left-hand road at the fork, pass the monastery of **Ayía Triáda** (founded 1438), on the right, and come to the attractive convent of **Áyios Stéfanos**, occupied by nuns. It was founded in 1367 by a Serbian prince, Antony Cantacuzene, and has *frescoes* of 1400 in its chapel. The principal church (St Charálambos) dates only from 1798. From the open space behind the church, on the edge of the crag, there are magnificent *views* of the plain of Thessaly traversed by the River Peneios (Piniós).

Methóni
ΜΕΘΩΝΗ
(Methóni)

Region: Peloponnese. – Nomos: Messenia.
Altitude: 10 m (33 feet). – Population: 1300.

TRANSPORTATION. – Bus service from Pýlos.

HOTELS. – *Methoni Beach*, B, 23 b.; *Alex*, C, 19 b.

BATHING BEACH. – Round the bay.

Methóni is a small village in a sandy bay 12 km (7 miles) S of Pýlos, with an imposing Venetian *fortress*.

HISTORY. – Methóni was held for a brief period after the 4th Crusade by the Villehardouins, who ceded it in 1206 to Venice. The Venetians developed it into a powerful stronghold and naval station, Modon, on the route from the Adriatic to Crete. In 1500 it was captured by the Turks, but in 1686 it was retaken by Morosini and held by Venice until 1715. During the

war of Greek liberation (1825–28) there was violent fighting here between Ibrahim Pasha and a Greek force led by Miaoulis with French support.

SIGHTS. – The castle is entered on a bridge built by French troops in 1828 over the deep castle moat. To the right of the first gate can be seen two strong Venetian **bastions** of the 15th and early 18th c. Inside the gate we turn left through a long **outer ward**, pass through two further gates and enter the spacious inner ward, in which is the **Morosini Column**, with a Byzantine capital. To the right is a gate leading into the **Citadel**, with the remains of Turkish buildings. The wall on the W (seaward) side rises directly above the edge of the rock. On the S side of the fortress we pass through a gate flanked by towers and along a causeway to an octagonal structure of the Turkish period (16th c.), from which there is a view of the islands of *Sapiéntza* and *Skhíza*. Returning along the *wall-walk* on the E side of the castle, we see the remains of a handsome building abutting the wall and beyond this a gate (now walled up) opening on to the bay, with coats of arms on the outside.

View from Methóni towards the island of Sapiéntza

Metsovo
ΜΕΤΣΟΒΟΝ
(Métsovo)

Nomos: Ioánnina.

TRANSPORTATION. – Métsovo lies 2 km (1 mile) below the road from Ioánnina to Kalambáka.

HOTELS. – *Phlokas*, B, 10 b.; *Galaxy*, C, 20 b.; *Olympic*, C, 32 b.

The mountain village of Métsovo, situated in a wooded region in the Pindos range below the Katára pass, is popular both with summer holiday

...ors and winter sports en-
...siasts (ski-lift). During the Tur-
...sh period well-known families like
...he Averofs and the Tositsas built
...hemselves houses in this inaccessible spot. Features of interest
are the Folk Museum in the Tositsa
House, the church of Ayía Paraskeví
and the monastery of Áyios Nikólaos
at the lower end of the village. The
nearby village of Mília is noted for
its trout and its yogurt.

The planned new motorway from Igoumenítsa via
Ioánnina and Kozáni to Salonica is due to pass just S
of the village.

Mistra
ΜΥΣΤΡΑΣ
(Mistrás)

Nomos: Laconia.
Altitude: 380–620 m (1247–2034 feet). – Population:
1500.

HOTEL. – *Vyzantion*, B, 38 b.

RESTAURANTS. – *Xenia* and *Ta Marmára*.

**The village of Mistra, 7 km (4 miles)
from Sparta, lies below the ** ** ruins
of the medieval town of Mistra, built
on an outlying hill of the Taýgetos**
range, and provides the most complete picture we have of a town
of the late Byzantine period (13th–
15th c.).

HISTORY. – The castle of Mistra was built in 1249 by
Guillaume II de Villehardouin, but in 1263, having
been taken prisoner by the Byzantine Emperor
Michael VIII, he was compelled to yield it up to the
emperor, together with the castles of Maina and
Monemvasía. Thereafter, until the Turkish conquest in
1460, Mistra was ruled by Byzantine princes, who
from 1347 bore the title of Despot, the second highest
rank in the Empire (after the Basileus but above
Sebastokrator and Caesar).

Below the Frankish castle on the summit of the hill
there grew up first the upper and then the lower town.
The Despot's palace became the centre of a splendid
court and an active intellectual life, particularly when
Georgios Gemisthos *Plethon* developed his neo-
Platonic philosophy here in the 15th c., contributing
significantly to the development of the Renaissance in
Florence. This, combined with the marriage of one of
the Despots to a Malatesta princess, was the motive
which led Sigismondo Malatesta in 1464 to thrust
down through Turkish-occupied territory to Mistra in
order to bring back Plethon's remains to Rimini, where
they were deposited in the church of San Francesco,
the "Tempio Malatestiano". After the Turkish conquest in 1460 the town declined, particularly
following Turkish reprisals in response to the Orlov
rising of 1770; and when, after the liberation of
Greece, the population moved in 1834 to the newly
founded town of Sparta, Mistra shrank to a small
village below the town walls. The houses and
churches fell into decay: a process which was halted
only by the considerable work of restoration and
conservation carried out by Orlandos and others in the
present century. Thanks to their work we are now able
to get an impression of the life of this town which was
ruled by Greek princes married to wives from western

Mistra – the Pantánassa convent on the hillside below the castle

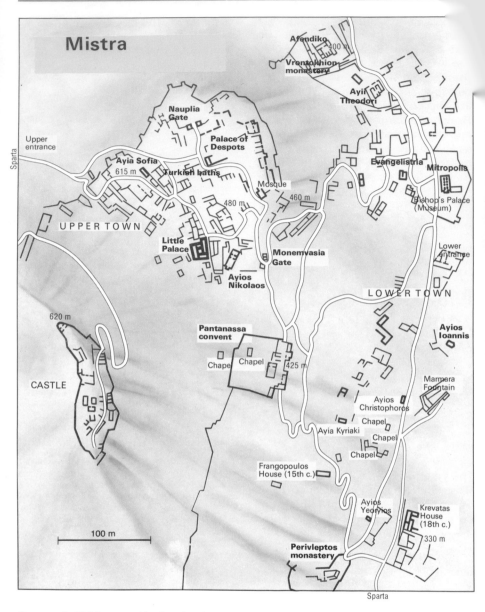

Europe and which became a meeting-place between Byzantine and western culture.

SIGHTS. – Bearing right from the lower entrance, we come to the *Mitrópolis or episcopal church, a three-aisled basilica erected in 1309.

In the 15th c., following the model of other churches subsequently built in the town, the Mitrópolis was given a new upper storey and a cruciform ground-plan. Most of the vigorous *paintings* and the interior furnishings have been preserved. On the floor in front of the *iconostasis* is a *carving of the Byzantine double eagle*, traditionally marking the spot on which Constantine XI Dragases stood to be crowned as emperor on 6 January 1449, relinquishing his authority as ruler of the Peloponnese, after which he made his way to the beleaguered city of Constantinople to rule it as the last Christian monarch and die fighting on the land walls when the Turks captured the city on 29 May 1453. – In the

courtyard, with its open side towards the plain and flanked on two sides by *arcades*, is an ancient *sarcophagus* decorated with Dionysiac themes. The former *Bishop's Palace*, which incorporates some fragments of ancient masonry, now houses a small *museum*. A grille on the outer wall of the church marks the spot where the Turks killed the Metropolitan after the Orlov rising in 1770.

Farther N is the **Vrontókhion monastery**, with the oldest church in Mistra, *Áyii Theódori (1296). This has a large central dome like that of Dafní spanning all three aisles, fine stone and brick masonry in the E end, and the *tomb of a Despot* in the NE chapel. To the same monastery belongs the largest church in Mistra, the **Afendikó**, built shortly before 1311, which has impressive *frescoes* (recently restored). This was the first example of a type of structure characteristic of Mistra, with a basilican lower storey and an upper storey in the form of a domed cruciform church – a synthesis of the Early Christian and Byzantine basilica with later Byzantine traditions.

Retracing our steps, we now walk up past the *Evangelístria*, a mortuary chapel of about 1400, towards the upper town, pass through the *Monemvasía Gate* and come to the *Palace (13th–15th c.), with its large *hall* (10 by 36 m (33 by 118 feet)), its beautiful *loggia* looking out on the Eurotas plain, and its imposing façade, on which the projecting throne recess and remains of Flamboyant window decoration can still be seen. To the W of the palace is the *Nauplia Gate*, and higher up the church of **Ayía Sofía** (1350), from which the **castle** can be reached (fine *views). Near Ayía Sofiá is the upper entrance to the site.

Fresco in the Perívleptos monastery, Mistra

Returning to the Monemvasía Gate and keeping straight ahead, we come to the **Pantánassa convent**, occupied by nuns – the only monastic house in Mistra which is still occupied. (Pantánassa is the feminine equivalent of Pantokrator, "ruler of all".) The Pantánassa church, the last major building to be erected in Mistra (1428), contains notable *paintings. – Continuing down the hill —towards the S, we come to the **Perívleptos monastery** (second half of 14th c.), with very fine *paintings* of the "Palaeologue Renaissance" – masterpieces of this late Byzantine style, full of vigour, life and expressive force. – From here it is a short distance N to the exit.

Monemvasia
MONEMBAΣIA
(Monemvasía)

Nomos: Laconia.
Altitude: 5–300 m (16–984 feet). – Population: 5000.

TRANSPORTATION. – Boat services from Piraeus, Kýthira and Gýthion. – By land Monemvasía can be reached from Sparta (98 km – 61 miles) or Gýthion (64 km – 40 miles).

HOTELS. – ON MAINLAND: *Monemvasia*, B, 18 b.; *Minoa*, C, 30 b.

SWIMMING: at the new village and on the coast to the N. – YACHT SUPPLY STATION.

This little walled town situated at the foot of a 300 m (984 feet) high crag projecting into the sea on the E side of the Peloponnese takes its name from its single entrance (moni embasis). For centuries an almost impregnable stronghold, it is now almost deserted, most of the inhabitants having moved to the new village on the mainland. But even in its abandonment it preserves its magnificent *situation.

HISTORY. – The ancient name of the town, *Minoa*, points to a Cretan settlement. 6 km (4 miles) N are the remains (town walls and a number of temples of the 1st millennium B.C.) of the Mycenaean settlement of *Epidauros Limera*. Monemvasía first appeared on the stage of history, however, in the 8th c., when it became a place of refuge for Greeks fleeing before the Slav invasion of Laconia. It soon developed into a flourishing port, which was able to repel a Norman attack in 1149 and was taken by Guillaume de Villehardouin in 1249 only after a three years' siege. Only 14 years later, however, in 1263, he was compelled to return Monemvasía, together with Mistra and Maina, to the Byzantine emperor, by whom he had been taken prisoner. In 1460, faced with the threat of Turkish attack, the town submitted to the authority of the Pope. Later it passed under Venetian rule, but in 1540 fell into the hands of the Turks, who held it (with another Venetian interlude between 1690 and 1715) until 1821. – The name of Monemvasía survives in garbled form in the wine called Malmsey, which was originally produced here and exported in large quantities.

SIGHTS. – The LOWER TOWN is entered on the S side through the only gate in the *walls*, built by the Turks in the 16th c. on earlier Byzantine foundations. Through picturesque lanes and past a friendly little taverna we come to the *main square*, in which stands a Turkish cannon. Here too is the **Elkómenos church** (14th c., restored 1697). Above the doorway is a broken *carved panel* depicting two pea-cocks, from the iconostasis of an earlier church. The church originally possessed a famous icon of Christ in chains; it now has a fine icon of the *Crucifixion*. Higher up is the 14th c. domed church of **Myrti-diótissa**, in severer style (iconostasis). In another square to the N of the town is the 17th c. **Khrysafiótissa** church, with a large dome, and near this are the chapel of **Ayios Nikólaos** (1703) and the *sea wall* with its gun embrasures.

A zigzag paved street leads up to the strongly fortified UPPER TOWN. Here, on the edge of a precipitous crag, is the church of **Ayía Sofía**, built in the time of Andronikos II (1287–1328) on the model of the church at Dafní, with a large central dome spanning both the central and lateral aisles. Notable features of the exterior are the fine *capitals* and a *carving of Salome's dance* on one of the windows. – On the summit of the crag is a **castle**, from which there are superb *views*.

farthest corner of Argolis, nourisher of horses". Thereafter they mingled with the indigenous population and a hybrid culture evolved. In religion Greek and pre-Greek elements interpenetrated one another; linguistically the newcomers soon established their predominance, but the pre-Indo-European name of Mycenae was retained. Shaft graves dating from the 17th c. B.C. give evidence of this period. Then, around 1580 B.C., a radical change began to take place, as influences from Egypt and the refined Minoan culture of Crete made themselves felt. The Early Mycenaean period which now began (1580–1500 B.C.) is notable for the wealth of gold found in the shaft graves, including the famous gold mask laid over the face of some dead prince and wrongly identified by Schliemann as belonging to Agamemnon (who lived at a later period). From the Middle Mycenaean period (1500–1425) date the first-known defensive walls and the early tholos tombs. The Late Mycenaean period (1425–1100 B.C.) yielded a rich harvest of finds. The 14th c. B.C. saw the construction of the later tholos tombs, including the "Treasury of Atreus"; the older Megaron in the Acropolis (*c.* 1350 B.C.), the first palace of some pretension; and the cyclopean walls round the site. The later Megaron, the Lion Gate and the extension at the E end were built about 1250 B.C. After 1230 B.C., when the threat from new invaders coming from the N was felt to be pressing, five different phases of work on strengthening the defences have been identified; and the history of Mycenae finally came to an end about 1100 B.C. as a result of an assault by the "Sea Peoples" who are referred to in Egyptian sources or by the Dorians who followed them.

Mycenae
MYKHNAI
(Mikínai)

Gold mask from a Mycenaean tomb

Region: Peloponnese. – Nomos: Argolid.
Altitude: 120–278 m (394–912 feet).

TRANSPORTATION. – Mycenae is a station on the Corinth–Tripolis railway line; bus services from Corinth and Argos.

HOTELS. – *Agamemnon*, C, 16 b.; *Petite Planète*, C, 26 b.; *Xenia*, C, 6 b.

CAMPING SITE.

The fortified city of **Mycenae and the Mycenaean civilisation to which it gave its name were first introduced to the world by Heinrich Schliemann's excavations from 1874 onwards, which carried the history of Europe far back into the Bronze Age of the 2nd millennium B.C.; and although many other strongholds and settlements of the same period have since been discovered Mycenae still retains its pre-eminence.**

HISTORY. – When the first Greeks came to this region around 2000 B.C. they would no doubt establish themselves on the 278 m (912 feet) high hill "in the

TOUR OF THE SITE. – On the left of the road which runs up from the village to the site is the most famous *tholos tomb*, known (without any historical warrant) as the "Treasury of Atreus" or the "Tomb of Agamemnon".

A *dromos* 36 m (118 feet) long leads to a *doorway* 10·50 m (34 feet) high, with a massive lintel 8·50 m (28 feet) long, 5 m (16 feet) wide and 1·20 m (4 feet) thick which is estimated to weigh 120 tons. On either side of the doorway were half-columns of greenish stone, remains of which are displayed in the National Archaeological Museum in Athens; traces of the column bases and sockets for fixing them in place can still be seen. Above the door is a relieving triangle, originally covered with a carved stone slab. The *interior* is circular, with a diameter of 14·50 m (48 feet) and a height of 13·20 m (43 feet). It is roofed with a false vault formed of overlapping courses of stone and originally decorated with bronze rosettes. The main chamber was designed for cult purposes; the actual *tomb chamber* is to the right. The tomb is an impressive example of Mycenaean architectural skill: its dimensions were only exceeded by the Pantheon in Rome, built in the 2nd c. A.D.

From the "Treasury of Atreus" there is an excellent view of the *Citadel of Mycenae and its enclosing *walls* (considerable sections of which have been re-erected in recent decades). On the way

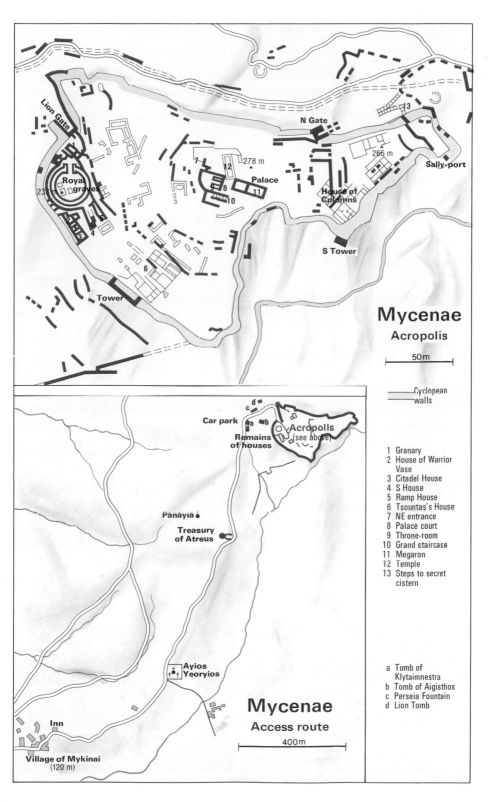

Mycenae

Acropolis

50m

Cyclopean walls

1 Granary
2 House of Warrior Vase
3 Citadel House
4 S House
5 Ramp House
6 Tsountas's House
7 NE entrance
8 Palace court
9 Throne-room
10 Grand staircase
11 Megaron
12 Temple
13 Steps to secret cistern

a Tomb of Klytaimnestra
b Tomb of Aigisthos
c Perseia Fountain
d Lion Tomb

Mycenae

Access route

400m

Grave Circle, Mycenae

to the Citadel a number of Mycenaean *houses* can be seen to the right of the road. Just inside the enclosure are *Grave Circle B*, discovered in 1951, and a number of tholos tombs.

We then enter the Citadel through the ****Lion Gate**, flanked on both sides by bastions. In the relieving triangle is the famous carving of two lions, one on either side of a central column; the heads, which were carved separately and fastened with dowels, are missing. This symbol of religiously based royal authority is a theme found on Cretan seals but here enlarged to monumental proportions.

Inside the gate is the **Grave Circle** found by Schliemann, which originally lay outside the walls. It was only during the extension of the walls in the 13th c. B.C. that the tombs were enclosed within a double ring of stone slabs; the funerary stelae were then set up again on a higher level, and the grave circle became a shrine devoted to the cult of the dead. In the six *shaft graves* to be seen in the excavated area there were found with rich gold grave goods the remains of nine men, eight women and two children. The recently discovered Grave Circle B was dated to the late 17th c. B.C.; this Grave Circle A found by Schliemann dates from some time after 1580 B.C. The fact that no more shaft graves were built and that tholos tombs then came into favour points to a change of dynasty; and indeed ancient traditions spoke of the descendants of the original founder, Perseus (the Perseids), being succeeded by the descendants of Pelops (the Pelopids or Atreids). The Heraclids, who also featured in the traditions, represented the Dorians, who arrived only at the time of, or after, the fall of Mycenae.

Beyond Grave Circle A are a number of other buildings, including the *South House*, the *House of the Warrior Vase* and *Tsountas' House* (named after the Greek archaeologist who excavated it).

From the ramp beyond the Lion Gate a path runs uphill on the left to the badly ruined **Palace**, over which a Greek temple of Athena was built in the 7th c. B.C. The most important parts of the palace lie on the S side – a *courtyard* approached by a stone *staircase* of Mycenaean date which has been preserved, and the *Throne-room* and *Megaron* of the rulers of Mycenae. In the middle of the megaron is the circular sacred hearth. From here there are fine views of the Argolid.

Going downhill towards the E, we see on the right, built against the walls, the "**House of Columns**". Beyond this is the **E Bastion**, with a *sally-port* and the entrance to a secret *cistern* underground. This area of the Citadel is part of the extensions carried out in the 13th c. B.C. – On the way back to the entrance

along the N side of the walls the **N Gate** is passed, and lower down the hill can be seen a number of *store-rooms* with pottery jars for provisions.

Mykonos
ΜΥΚΟΝΟΣ
(Míkonos)

Nomos: Cyclades. – Telephone dialling code: 0289.
Area: 85 sq. km (33 sq. miles). – Population: 3400.

 Tourist Police,
Platía Apováthros;
tel. 2 24 32.

TRANSPORTATION. – Air service from Athens. – Mýkonos is served by boats sailing between Piraeus and Rhodes and between Piraeus and Sámos. – Boat service to Delos.

HOTELS. – MÝKONOS: *Leto*, A, 48 b.; *Kouneni*, B, 36 b.; *Rhenia*, B, 70 b.; *Theoxenia*, B, 93 b.; *Bellou*, C, 14 b.; *Mangas*, C, 37 b.; *Manto*, C, 26 b.; *Marios*, C, 20 b.; *Mykonos*, C, 28 b.; *Mykonos Beach*, C, 32 b. – ÁYIOS STÉFANOS (3 km – 2 miles): *Alkistis*, B, 182 b.; *Artemis*, C, 41 b. – PLATÝS YIALÓS (4 km – 2 miles): *Petinos*, C, 22 b. – KALAFÁTI (10 km – 6 miles): *Aphrodite Beach*, B, 180 b. – ÓRNOS: *Paralos Beach*, C, 76 b. – ANÓ MERÁ: *Anó Merá*, A, 124 b.

Paraportianí church, Mýkonos

Windmills on Mýkonos

The town of Mýkonos

YOUTH HOSTEL.

BEACHES. – Ámmos, at the Xenia Hotel immediately S of the town. – On the Diákofto isthmus, 3 km (2 miles) SW. – At Áyios Stéfanos, 3 km (2 miles) N. – In the Gulf of Pánormos.

Easily accessible from Athens, the island of *Mýkonos in the Cyclades has long been one of Greece's major holiday centres. The Gulf of Pánormos forms a deep indentation on the N coast, and at the W end of the island two smaller bays encroach on the land to form a peninsula. Mýkonos is built up of gneisses and granites and is poorly supplied with water, having no natural springs. The houses, freshly lime-washed every year, stand out in dazzling whiteness against the tawny brown of the earth.

In antiquity Mýkonos was a place of no importance. During the Frankish period it belonged to the duchy of Náxos; later it passed to Venice; and it was held by the Turks for only a relatively brief period (1718–1830).

The chief town, Mýkonos (pop. 2790), is a picturesque little place, with cube-shaped whitewashed houses, churches and chapels with red and blue domes, windmills and pigeon-cotes, shady lanes and a constant bustle of life round the harbour. The best known of the churches – many of them founded by private donors

– is the picturesque *Paraportianí church, with a domed upper church, the chapel of Panayía Paraportianí, and a lower storey (entered from the opposite side) which is known as the "tésseres ekklisíes" ("four churches") because of the four tiny chapels built next to one another, dedicated respectively (from left to right) to Áyios Sóstis, Áyios Efstátios, the Áyii Anáryiri and Ayía Anastasía. The little *Museum in the N of the town contains archaeological material from Mýkonos and the neighbouring island of Rínia, including an early Archaic pithos with relief decoration (scenes from the conquest of Troy). Near the Paraportianí church is a small Folk Museum.

In the interior of the island, 10 km (6 miles) E of Mýkonos, is Anó Merá (pop. 700), with the Tourlianí monastery. From here it is possible to continue to Anna Bay on Cape Kalafáta, to the SE, or to Cape Evros, to the E.

*Delos: see p. 119.

Nafpaktos
ΝΑΥΠΑΚΤΟΣ
(Náfpaktos)

Nomos: Aetolia and Acarnania.
Altitude: 10 m (33 feet). – Population: 8200.

TRANSPORTATION. – Bus service from Antirrion.

HOTELS. – *Amaryllis*, B, 28 b.; *Akti*, C, 70 b.; *Nea Hellas*, C, 20 b.; *Rex*, C, 23 b.

YACHT SUPPLY STATION.

Náfpaktos (Naupaktos) is a charming little port on the N side of the Gulf of Corinth, 9 km (6 miles) E of the Strait of Ríon. It was known to the Venetians as Lepanto, and became famous through the naval battle of Lepanto in 1571.

HISTORY. – The ancient town of Naupaktos, which belonged to Western Lokris, was captured by Athens in 455 B.C. and was used by the Athenians to house the Messenians who had been expelled from their city by Sparta. At the end of the Peloponnesian War, however, the Messenians were once again expelled. During that war, in which Naupaktos played an important part as a base for the Athenian expedition to Sicily, Phormion defeated a numerically superior Spartan fleet (429 B.C. – the year in which Perikles died). – From 1407 to 1499 and from 1687 to 1700 Náfpaktos was a Venetian naval base, which along with the fortresses of Ríon (see p. 227) and Antírrion controlled the entrance to the Gulf of Corinth. From 1499 to 1687 and from 1700 to 1821 the town was held by the Turks, whose fleet sailed from here to fight the battle which marked the first naval victory by the allied powers of Europe over the hitherto undefeated Turks (6 October 1571). This historic battle took place off the Oxia Islands to the W. The commander of the "Holy League" formed by the Pope, Spain, Venice, Genoa and the Order of St John was Don John of Austria, a natural son of the Emperor Charles V. Among those who took part in the battle was Cervantes, author of "Don Quixote", who lost an arm in the encounter.

SIGHTS. – The **Harbour** is protected by a Venetian *wall*, in which many fragments of ancient masonry can be seen. From the harbour the town's powerful **fortifications** climb up in several successive rings to the castle on top of the hill. A walk through the town, passing the main square just off the harbour with its coffee-houses and tavernas, will give some impression of the skill displayed by the military engineers in taking full advantage of the town's excellent strategic situation.

Nafplion
ΝΑΥΠΛΙΟΝ
(Náfplion)

Nomos: Argolid. – Telephone dialling code: 0752.
Altitude: 5–85 m (16–279 feet). – Population: 9000.

ⓘ **Tourist Police,**
Sidéras Merarkhías;
tel. 2 77 76.

TRANSPORTATION. – Náfplion is the terminus of the branch railway line from Argos. Bus services from Argos, Corinth and Athens. Boats to the island of Boúrdzi.

HOTELS. – *Xenia's Palace*, L, 108 b.; *Amphitryon*, A, 86 b.; *Xenia*, A, 98 b.; *Agamemnon*, B, 74 b.; *Alcyon*, C, 35 b.; *Amalia*, C, 16 b.; *Amymoni*, C, 32 b.; *Asklepios*, C, 20 b.; *Athina*, C, 26 b.; *Dioskouri*, C, 93 b.; *Galini*, C, 72 b.; *Hotel des Roses*, C, 24 b.; *Nafplia*, C, 74 b.; *Parartima*, C, 46 b.; *Park*, C, 131 b.; *Rex*, C, 94 b.; *Victoria*, C, 69 b.

YACHT SUPPLY STATION.

CAMPING SITE. – On the S side of the peninsula.

SWIMMING. – From numerous RESTAURANTS round the harbour.

Náfplion (Nauplia) has a magnificent *situation in the Gulf of Argolis under the rocky promontory of Akrónafplia (85 m – 279 feet) and the fortified hill of Palamídi (216 m – 709 feet). The beauty of this situation, the many places of archaeological interest in the surrounding area and the town's numerous hotels have made Náfplion a popular and flourishing tourist centre.

HISTORY. – According to an ancient tradition the town was founded by Nauplios, son of the sea god Poseidon, and his son Palamedes, who was said to have invented dice and various board games to amuse his fellow Greeks during the battle for Troy, after Poseidon had been victorious in a contest with Hera for possession of this territory – a legend which points to a foundation by settlers arriving by sea. From 628 Nauplia was the port of Argos. In Roman times the town was abandoned, but during the Byzantine period it was repopulated and fortified. After the 4th Crusade (1203–04) Leon Sgouros, who had used the town as a base for his conquest of Corinth in 1202, was able to hold it against the Crusaders, who did not take it until 1246. In 1387 Nauplia fell into the hands of the Venetians, who made it one of the most powerful strongholds of the time under the name of Napoli di Levante. The fortifications were still further strengthened by the Turks (1540–1686, 1715–1822), and during a further period of Venetian occupation under Francesco Morosini between 1686 and 1715 the fortress on Palamídi was built. The town was captured by the Greeks in 1822, and in 1828 Nauplia became capital of Greece. The first President of united Greece, Count Kapodistrias, was murdered in an act of private revenge outside the church of St Spyridon on 8 November 1831. On 25 January 1833 the 18-year-old King Otto, son of Ludwig I of Bavaria, landed here to take up his new kingdom, but a year later moved his capital to the newly liberated Athens. The king's arrival is depicted in two large pictures by Peter von Hess in the Neue Pinakothek in Munich.

SIGHTS. – The town has remained largely unspoiled, in spite of land reclamation

The islet of Boúrdzi, off Náfplion

from the sea to the N and E of Akrónafplia and much recent building. It preserves a number of Venetian buildings, two Turkish mosques and neo-classical houses dating from the time of King Otto. In *Sýntagma (Constitution) Square* is a former *mosque* now known as Bouleftikó from its use as the meeting-place of the Greek Parliament. The *Museum, housed in a Venetian building in the square, contains archaeological material from Náfplion and the surrounding area. The oldest items are pieces of Neolithic pottery from Asíni and Berbati, while the Mycenaean period is represented by fragments of frescoes and terracotta idols from Mycenae, a suit of armour from Dendra (15th c. B.C.) and a helmet of the same period.

In the district of **Prónia** is the square in which the Greek National Assembly approved the selection of King Otto in 1832. Here too, on a rock on the right-hand side of the road to Epidauros, is a carved figure of a recumbent *lion* (by a German sculptor, Siegel) commemorating the Bavarians killed in 1833–34. Also in Prónia is the *Ayía Moní*, a nunnery with a church dating from 1149 and a luxuriant garden containing the *spring of Kánathos* in which the goddess Hera annually renewed her virginity.

The town's *fortifications* are still impressive – e.g. the entrance to **Akrónafplia**, on the E side, with a gate built of Roman bricks, a Byzantine gatehouse containing fine *frescoes of 1291 and Venetian bastions. Akrónafplia itself, whose building history can be traced back to the 4th c. B.C., is now a prison.

The mightiest of Náfplion's fortifications is the Venetian stronghold on **Palamídi** (1711–14). It can be reached from the ridge between the two hills on a flight of 857 steps (partly roofed over) or, less

strenuously, by the 3 km (2 miles) long motor road which runs through Prónia. From the top there are panoramic views of the town and the Gulf of Argolis. – 500 m (547 yards) offshore is the little islet of **Boúrdzi**, which is also fortified.

SURROUNDINGS. – The Mycenaean stronghold of **Tiryns** (see p. 251) and other sites in the **Argolid** (p. 62); **Asine** (Asíni), near the village of Tolón (see p. 252); the sanctuary of Asklepios at **Epidauros** (p. 130).

Náxos
ΝΑΞΟΣ
(Náxos)

Nomos: Cyclades.
Area: 428 sq. km (165 sq. miles). – Population: 14,200.

TRANSPORTATION. – Náxos is served by the Cyclades boats (Piraeus–Sýros–Páros–Náxos–Íos–Santorin). – Island bus (Náxos–Apóllona).

HOTELS. – *Ariadne*, B, 48 b.; *Akroyiali*, C, 27 b.; *Aegeon*, C, 40 b.; *Anessis*, C, 27 b.; *Apollon*, C, 34 b.; *Barbouni*, C, 15 b.; *Chelmos*, C, 17 b.; *Coronis*, C, 62 b.; *Hermes*, C, 32 b.; *Naxos Beach*, C, 50 b.; *Nissaki*, C, 30 b.; *Panorama*, C, 33 b.; *Renetta*, C, 23 b.; *Zeus*, C, 29 b.

BATHING BEACHES. – There is a small beach S of the town (15 minutes). On the S side of the Prokópios peninsula is the long sandy beach of Ayía Ánna. There is also good swimming in the harbour of Apóllona, on the N side of the island.

Náxos is the largest of the Cyclades, and has the highest summit in the whole group (Oxiá, 1003 m (3291 feet)). The land, which slopes down gradually from the high ground to the W coast, is well watered and fertile, giving Náxos a relatively luxuriant growth of vegetation. With its limited hotel resources, the island is not equipped to cope with mass tourism, but it has much to offer visitors – an equable climate, a wide variety of scenery, from the sandy beaches of the W coast by way of the green fields of the interior to the austere landscape of the hills, and monuments of antiquity and the medieval period.

HISTORY. – The myth tells us that Theseus abandoned the Cretan princess Ariadne, who had sailed with him on his return voyage from Crete to Athens, on the island of Náxos, where the god Dionysos made her his wife. This myth, like the worship of Zeus on

Náxos, points to a connection with Crete: just as there is a Cave of Zeus on Mt Ida, so there is a Cave of Zeus on Mt Oxiá, which is also known as Ziá (=Zeus).

In the 3rd millennium B.C. the island belonged to the Cycladic culture (cf. the material displayed in the Náxos Museum); in the 2nd millennium it was under Minoan and later Mycenaean influence. The present town of Náxos is on or near the site of a Mycenaean settlement. After the Dorian migration the island was occupied by Ionian Greeks, and enjoyed a period of prosperity in the 7th and 6th c. B.C., when it developed an active maritime trade and produced an important school of sculptors, notable for such works as the colossal statue of Apollo on Delos, the stele of Nikandre (National Archaeological Museum, Athens) and the Sphinx at Delphi. – During the Middle Ages the island increased in importance when it became the residence of the Venetian duke of the Archipelago, Marco Sanudo, in 1207. The Roman Catholic element in the population of the island dates from this period. In 1566 Náxos fell into the hands of the Turks, who granted it as a fief to a Jew of Portuguese origin named Nasi, and thereafter it contrived to retain a measure of independence.

SIGHTS. – The chief town and principal port is **Náxos** (pop. 2640) on the NW coast, which is the seat of a Greek Orthodox metropolitan and also of a Roman Catholic archbishop. In the harbour, which has been enlarged in recent years, is the terminus of the island buses, and the front is lined with tavernas, coffee-houses and shops. The main part of the town lies on a hill which is crowned by the Venetian **Kastro**. From the square picturesque little lanes climb up to the Kastro, in which are a convent of Roman Catholic Ursulines and a girls' school run by the nuns. Other relics of the Venetian

The town of Náxos

period are the Roman Catholic **church of St Mary** and the remains of the *town walls* and the *Sommaripa Palace*. Stoas of the Hellenistic period were brought to light near the principal Orthodox church.

The interesting * **Museum** contains material from all periods of the island's history, including a fine collection of *stone vessels* and *Cycladic idols* of the 3rd millennium B.C., *pottery* of the Geometric, Archaic and later periods, *statues* and *capitals*. In the courtyard are stones carved with *Venetian coats of arms* and a large *mosaic* of Europa and the bull.

The main feature of archaeological interest is the 6 m (20 feet) high marble * **temple doorway** on the little peninsula of Sto Paláti to the N of the harbour. This monumental structure belonged to an Archaic temple begun about 540 B.C. during the reign of the tyrant Lygdamis and left unfinished after his fall. The threshold stone was cut when the temple was converted for use as a Christian basilica in the 5th–6th c.

The most interesting excursion on the island – which is still poorly supplied with roads – is to **Apóllona** on the N coast. The trip gives an excellent impression of the varying scenery of the island at different altitudes. The village of **Sángri** (12 km – 7 miles) has churches containing frescoes. **Khalkí** (17 km – 11 miles) has several churches, including the Áyii Apóstoli, as well as a *castle* of the Sanudo family and number of *towers* in which the population took refuge during pirate raids. **Filóti** (19 km – 12 miles) is the starting-point for the ascent to the *Cave of Zeus* on Mt Oxiá. Then comes the charming hill village of **Apíranthos** (26 km – 16 miles), 12 km (7 miles) E of which is the little port of *Moutsoúna*, with a beautiful beach. Beyond **Koronís** the road winds down into a valley which leads to the port of **Apóllona** (42 km – 26 miles). A few hundred metres before Apóllona, on the left of the road, is an ancient quarry, the seclusion of which has recently been destroyed by the removal of a wall of rock and the construction of a flight of marble steps. In the quarry can be seen a *colossal statue*, 10·45 m (34 feet) long, probably left unfinished because of a fault in the stone of the head. This gigantic figure, dating from the Archaic period, is clothed and bearded: it is, therefore, neither Apollo, as it is usually said to be, nor a kouros, but probably Dionysos, patron of the island of Náxos.

The return journey can be on the new road which traverses the NW of the island and gives an opportunity of visiting the ancient *marble quarries* between **Mélanes** and **Potamiá**, 12 km (7 miles) E of the town. Here, at the edge of a luxuriant garden, can be seen other unfinished statues, this time unclothed kouroi. – On a hillside 3 km (2 miles) from the town is the convent of *Ayios Khrysóstomos*.

To the E of Náxos is the island of **Donoúsa**, to the S and SE the **Erimonísia** group (Koufonísia, Kéros, Skhinoúsa and Iráklia). The regular weekly boat from Piraeus via Náxos to Amorgós and Íos calls in at the islands of this group (except Kéros).

Nemea
NEMEA
(Neméa)

Region: Peloponnese. – Nomos: Corinth.
Altitude: 320 m (1050 feet).

TRANSPORTATION. – The ancient site lies 4 km (2 miles) W of the Neméa railway station on the Corinth–Argos line and the main road which runs parallel with the railway.

The name of Neméa, near the modern village of Iráklion in the north-western Argolid, is linked with one of the labours of Herakles, the killing of the Nemean lion, and with an ancient sanctuary of Zeus. It is also the place where according to an ancient tradition the seer Amphiaraos founded the Nemean Games in 1251 B.C., during the expedition of the Seven against Thebes. This took place on the occasion of the funeral ceremony for the king's son Opheltes, who was left alone by his nurse when she went to show the Seven a spring, and who was fatally bitten by a snake. The Nemean Games were revived in 573 B.C. and thereafter were held in alternate years until the 2nd C. B.C., when they were transferred to Argos.

SIGHTS. – The main feature of the site is a Doric *temple which had 6×12 very slender columns: three of the columns still stand, forming a prominent landmark. The

temple was built in the 4th c. B.C. on the site of an Archaic temple (of which the crypt survives). Outside the E end can be seen the tufa substructure of an altar. To the S of the temple were a long *hostel* (20 by 86 m (66 by 282 feet)), over which a three-aisled Christian **basilica** was built in the 5th c., a *palaistra* and *baths* of the Hellenistic period, near the remains of which is a new **museum**. Recent American excavations have revealed the *stadion*.

SURROUNDINGS. – Beyond the turning for Neméa the Corinth–Argos road comes to the **Dervenáki pass**. In a gorge near here Greek forces led by Kolokotrónis defeated a much larger Turkish army under Dramali Pasha in August 1822.

Going W from the Neméa site, we come in 15 km (9 miles) to the site of ancient **Phlious** (remains of polygonal wa.* of acropolis on right of road). 26 km (16 miles) beyond this is **Kaliáni**, on the N side of the Stymphalian Lake.

Nikopolis
ΝΙΚΟΠΟΛΙΣ
(Nikópolis)

Region: Epirus. – Nomos: Préveza.

The extensive remains of ancient Nikópolis, the "city of victory" founded by Octavian, the future Emperor Augustus, after his victory at Áktion (Actium) in 31 B.C., lies 6 km (4 miles) N of the port of Préveza (see p. 220) on the road to Arta, on the peninsula between the Ionian Sea and the Gulf of Amvrakia.

HISTORY. – After the defeat of Caesar's murderers, Brutus and Cassius, by Octavian and Antony at Philippi in 42 B.C. Antony contrived with the help of the Egyptian queen, Cleopatra, to make himself master of the eastern half of the Roman Empire. The decisive engagement in the conflict between Octavian and Antony took place on 2 September 31 B.C., when Octavian's fleet, under the command of Agrippa, annihilated the fleet of Antony and Cleopatra as it attempted to break out of the Ambracian Gulf. Octavian thus became sole ruler of the Empire, and four years later took the style of Augustus. The town of Nikópolis was founded on the site of his camp and populated with settlers from the surrounding area, from as far afield as Árta. The 13th Pope, Eleutherius (174–189), was a native of Nikópolis. After being destroyed by the Visigoths (397) and the Vandals (474) the town was rebuilt by Justinian on a smaller scale.

TOUR OF THE SITE. – Coming from Árta, we see on the right of the road the massive

Roman **theatre** and, some distance farther on, the **Stadion**, overgrown by scrub. We then cross the (barely visible) line of the *Augustan town walls* and see on the right, parallel with the road, the inner side of **Justinian's walls**, reminiscent of the land walls of Constantinople with their towers and gates and their alternation of stone and brick in the masonry. Then come, immediately left of the road, the considerable remains of the **Basilica of Alkyson**, named after the 6th c. bishop of that name (d. 516). After a bend in the road, where a path to the Roman *Odeon* goes off on the right, we see on the right, on rather higher ground, the three-aisled *Basilica of Doumetios*, with fine *mosaics* and *inscriptions* in the name of Bishop Doumetios (=Demetrius) dating from about 540. Near here is the **Museum**; notable among the exhibits are a good *portrait head* of Agrippa and a circular pedestal of the Roman period, with a relief of Amazons partly covered by Christian mosaics, which was re-used as an ambo in the basilica of Alkyson.

SURROUNDINGS. – 6 km (4 miles) S is the port of **Préveza** (see p. 220), with **Áktion** opposite it on the other side of the Gulf of Amvrakia. – 29 km (18 miles) from Nikópolis, on the right of the road to **Árta** (44 km – 27 miles), the fortress of **Rógoi**, built on ancient foundations by the Despots of Árta (13th c.), rears out of the plain. – The road to Igoumenítsa comes in 18 km (11 miles) to **Kamarína**, with the remains of ancient *Kassope* (small theatre, stoa). Beyond this are the nekromanteion of **Mesopótamos** (see p. 181) and the port of **Párga** (51 km – 32 miles: see p. 203).

Nisyros
ΝΙΣΥΡΟΣ
(Nísiros)

Nomos: Dodecanese.
Area: 41 sq. km (16 sq. miles). – Population: 1250.
ⓘ **Police Station**,
on harbour.

TRANSPORTATION. – Nísyros is served by boats sailing between Piraeus, Pátmos, Kálymnos, Nísyros, Tílos, Sými and Rhodes and between Rhodes and Sámos.

Nísyros is one of the Dodecanese, lying S of Kos, with which it is linked by myth. It is said to be part of Kos which Poseidon hurled at the Titan Polybotes.

HISTORY. – Nísyros was populated by Dorian settlers from Kos and Kameiros. In 1312 it passed into the hands of the Knights of St John, and later became a fief held by the Assanti family. It was occupied by the Turks in 1533.

SIGHTS. – The island has good natural water resources and is fertile. On the N coast is the port of **Mandráki**, with a *cave monastery* on a crag which rears above the village. A little way inland (½ hour: some signposts) is the "**Kastro**", the long walls of the ancient acropolis, 3·60 m (12 feet) thick and still standing fully 6 m (20 feet) high, built of dressed stone. To the right of the gate, which has survived intact, is an ancient flight of steps leading up to the wall-walk (fine views). – 2 km (1 mile) E of the Mandráki is the little spa of **Loutrá**. – The centre of the island is occupied by a *volcanic crater* 4 km (2 miles) in diameter, which is reached from Mandráki by way of **Emborió** (pop. 260). A narrow track leads to the fumaroles and sulphur deposits inside the crater. The outer slopes of the volcano are covered with carefully terraced fields.

Northern and Eastern Aegean Islands

The islands of Chios, Lésbos, Lemnos, Samothrace and Thásos, scattered in the northern and eastern Aegean, do not form a group in any real sense. Each has an individuality of its own.

The history of this region reaches far back into the past. The site of Thermí on Lésbos was occupied about 2700 B.C., and Poliókhni on Lemnos is older than its neighbour Troy. During the Greek colonising movement Aeolians came to Lésbos about 1100 B.C., Ionians to Chios about 1000 and to Lemnos about 800. About 700 B.C. colonies were established on Thásos (from Páros) and Samothrace. The islands enjoyed a period of prosperity in the 7th and 6th c. B.C., when Lésbos produced the singers Terpandros and Arion and the poets Sappho and Alkaios, and Chios a fine school of sculptors. After a period of Persian rule (546–479 B.C.) the islands became members of the first Attic maritime league; then from the 4th c. onwards they came successively under Macedonian, Ptolemaic and Roman influence. – After the 4th Crusade (1204) they belonged to Venice and later to Genoa. Then came the Turkish period, which lasted until 1912. In 1922–23 Lésbos and Chios took in many refugees from Asia Minor, and after the Second World War many Greeks from Egypt settled on Lemnos.

In recent years Turkey has put forward claims to the Anatolian continental shelf, of which Chios and Lésbos are claimed to form part.

Olympia
ΟΛΥΜΠΙΑ
(Olímbia)

Region: Peloponnese. – Nomos: Elis.
Altitude: 60 m (197 feet). – Population: 300.
Telephone dialling code: 0624.

ⓘ Tourist Police,
Douma 13;
tel. 2 25 50.

TRANSPORTATION. – Branch railway line Pýrgos – Olympia.

HOTELS. – Spap, A, 97 b.; Apollon, B, 54 b.; Neda, B, 75 b.; Neon Olympia, B, 59 b.; Xenia, B, 72 b.; Xenios Zeus, B, 72 b.; Ilis, C, 106 b.; Kronion, C, 41 b.

YOUTH HOSTEL.

CAMPING SITE.

**Olympia, lying in the angle between the rivers Alpheios and Kladeos, was a great Panhellenic sanctuary, the venue of the Olympic Games. German excavations from 1875 onwards, which led to the growth of the present village of Olympia, brought to light the sacred precinct which was known in an-

tiquity as the Altis (i.e. sacred grove) and is now again planted with trees. Situated at the foot of the wooded Mt Kronos in an area of gentle hills, Olympia – one of the great achievements of archaeological excavation – makes an impact on the present-day visitor which is fully commensurate with its importance in ancient times. A direct consequence of the excavation was the revival of the Olympic Games by Baron Pierre de Coubertin, the first modern Games being held in Athens in 1896.

HISTORY. – Potsherds of the 3rd and apsidal houses of the 2nd millennium B.C. bear witness to the early settlement of the site. Later the houses gave place to a sanctuary of Zeus which was associated with the older cult of Hera. Olympia lay within the territory of King Oinomaos of Pisa in Elis, who was succeeded by Pelops after his victory in a chariot race and his marriage to Pelops' daughter Hippodameia. A column from the palace of Oinomaos and the grave mound of Pelops (who gave his name to the Peloponnese) were still being shown to visitors when Pausanias visited the site in the 2nd c. A.D.

The Olympic Games probably began as a local funerary celebration in honour of Pelops. The Greeks believed that Herakles had laid down the regulations for the Games and had specified the length of the stadion as 600 feet (183 m). The first historical reference to the Games is in 776 B.C., when a treaty between kings Iphitos of Elis and Lykourgos of Sparta provided for an Olympic truce (ekecheiria) during the summer Games.

From 776 B.C. onwards lists were kept of the winners in the foot-race round the Stadion, giving rise to the Greek method of chronological reckoning by olym-

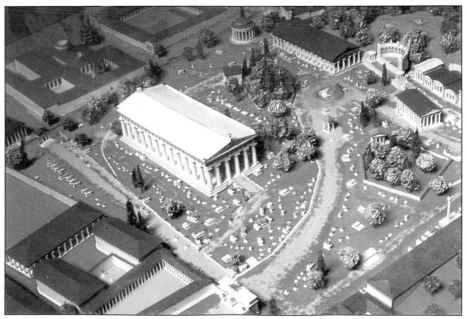

Olympia – model of the Sacred Precinct (Altis)

piads (i.e. periods of four years). Other events were added later – in the 8th c. the two-stade race, the long-distance race and the pentathlon, in the 7th c. boxing, chariot-racing and the pankration, in the 6th c. a race with weapons. The winners received a branch of the sacred olive-tree, but could also expect substantial material rewards (for example meals at public expense) on their return to their native city. The finishing line of the race round the Stadion was originally near the Temple of Zeus, in front of which, looking towards the runners, was Paionios' statue of Nike (Victory) – underlining the religious significance of the race, victory in which was granted by Zeus, the supreme god of the Greeks. Only in the 4th c. was the Stadion moved 80 m (88 yards) E and separated from the Altis. After their heyday in the 5th c. the Games gradually declined: the religious element became increasingly less prominent, and eventually they were contested by professional athletes. They were finally banned by the Emperor Theodosius, and came to an end in A.D. 393 after an existence of more than a thousand years.

TOUR OF THE SITE. – The road from the village crosses the Kladeos on the modern bridge and comes to the large car park. On entering the site we see on the left the **Prytaneion**, in which the victors were entertained with a banquet, and on the left the **Gymnasion**, with the propylon at the SE corner (2nd c. B.C.: only E side preserved) and the **Palaistra** (3rd c. B.C.), the columns of which have been re-erected. Beyond this, on a site originally occupied by 5th c. baths, is the **Work-shop of Pheidias**, which was later converted into a Byzantine church. In this workshop, which was exactly the same

size as the cella of the Temple of Zeus, Pheidias created (438 B.C. onwards) the huge chryselephantine cult statue of Zeus. Continuing S, we come to the *Leonidaion*, at the SW corner of the excavations. Originally built by Leonidas of Náxos in the second half of the 4th c. B.C. as a large hostel for the accom-modation of visitors to the sanctuary, this was altered in Roman times to a new layout in which the living quarters were set round an inner court with a garden and fountains and surrounded externally by Ionic colonnades. To the E are the **S Baths** (2nd c. A.D.), the **S Hall** (4th c. B.C.) and the **Bouleuterion** with its two apses (6th–5th c. B.C.). All these buildings lie outside the walls of the Altis.

We now enter the **Sacred Precinct** through a *Roman gateway* on the S side and see, beyond the re-erected **triangular pillar* which bore Paionios' figure of Victory (*c*. 425 B.C.) and the bases of numerous votive monuments, the ***Temple of Zeus**, built by Libon of Elis between 470 and 456 B.C., which has been called "the finest expression of the Doric canon" (Gruben).

Although the temple collapsed in an earthquake in the 6th c. A.D. the massive remains still allow us to gain some idea of what it was like. On the three-stepped **crepidoma** (52 m – 171 feet), which has been com-pletely preserved, supported on foundations 2·50 m

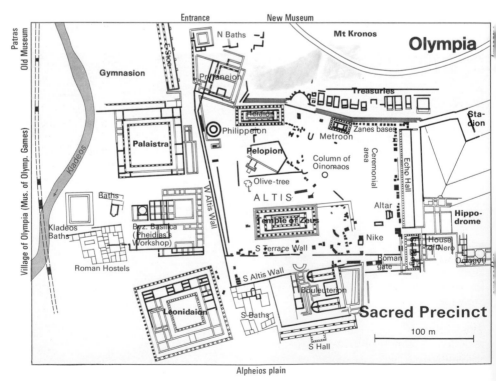

Remains of the Heraion, Olympia

(8 feet) high, stood 6×13 columns each of 10·53 m (35 feet) high and 2·23 m (7 feet) in diameter at the base. The total height of the temple was about 20 m (66 feet). While the main structure was of muschel-kalk limestone faced with stucco, Parian marble was used for the roof with its 102 lion's-head water-spouts and for the *sculpture* on the metopes and the pediments. The sculpture (*c.* 460 B.C.) is masterly work in the Severe style. On the ***E pediment** Zeus stands in the middle, flanked by King Oinomaos, his wife Sterope, his daughter Hippodameia and Hippodameia's future husband Pelops, before the decisive chariot race in which Oinomaos lost both his throne and his life. The ***W pediment** shows Zeus' son Apollo in the middle, intervening imperiously in the battle between Lapiths and centaurs which flared up at the marriage of Theseus' friend Peirithoos with Deidameia. Here the sculptor has broken the scene up into groups of two and three, whose violent movement is in sharp contrast to the tense tranquillity of the E pediment. The **metopes** above the pronaos and opisthodomos depict the 12 labours of Herakles. Particularly fine are the metopes of *Atlas* and *Augeias*; some of the others are much restored or are casts of the originals (which were carried off by the French Expédition de Morée and are now in the Louvre).

The **cella** of the temple, in the pronaos of which is a *mosaic* of the 4th or 3rd c. B.C., had two rows of columns and contained the cult image by Pheidias (after 438 B.C.). This huge chryselephantine statue, which showed Zeus sitting on a richly decorated throne, was counted among the seven wonders of the world

To the N of the temple was the mythical tomb of Pelops, the Pelopion (foundations of Propylon preserved). Beyond this, parallel to the Temple of Zeus, is the oldest temple of Olympia, the **Heraion** (*c.* 600 B.C.). This Doric temple of Hera had 6×16 columns 5·21 m (17 feet) high, four of which have been re-erected. The shafts and capitals of the columns show considerable variety, since the original wooden columns were replaced by stone columns at different times as the need arose, so that the luxuriant Archaic types

of echinus can be seen side by side with the severer forms of a later period. The cella walls were built of the limestone orthostats which have been preserved, with upper courses of mud brick. Along each side were four short cross-walls or buttresses, in each of which a column was engaged. In one of the niches so formed the Hermes of Praxiteles was found.

Going E from the Heraion, we see on the left the **Nymphaeum** (fountain-house) built by Herodes Atticus about A.D. 160 in memory of his wife Regilla, a priestess of Demeter, and in honour of the Roman Imperial house. Beyond this is a terrace at the foot of Mt Kronos with a row of **treasuries**, mostly in the form of small temples in antis, built by various Greek cities between the early 6th and the 5th c. to contain their votive offerings. Pausanias mentions ten. It is a striking fact that of the ten only two (those of Sikyon and Megara) were built by cities in Greece proper. Six belonged to cities of western Greece – Syracuse, Selinus and Gela in Sicily, Sybaris and Metapontion in southern Italy and Epidamnos (Dürres) in Albania – and the remaining two to Kyrene in North Africa and Byzantium.

Base of the Philippeion, Olympia

At the W end of the terrace, immediately adjoining the Nymphaeum of Herodes Atticus, is a small *naiskos* (3·88 by 3·55 m (13 by 12 feet)), with an altar in front of it. Then follow the *treasuries, beginning with that of *Sikyon*, the last to be erected (first half of 5th c. B.C.), which has recently been partly rebuilt. Beyond this come the treasuries of *Syracuse, Epidamnos, Byzantium, Sybaris* and *Kyrene*, a structure which is probably an altar of Herakles, and finally the treasuries of *Selinus, Metapontion, Megara* and *Gela*.

Immediately below the terrace with the treasuries is the site of the badly ruined *Metroon* (c. 300 B.C.), a shrine of the Mother of the Gods which in Roman times was re-dedicated to the Imperial cult. Beside it are a series of bases for the "Zanes" – statues of Zeus which were financed out of fines levied for offences against the rules of the games. Immediately beyond them is the entrance to the Stadion (c. 200 B.C.), the vaulting of which, still visible, was concealed by a propylon.

The **Stadion**, which after the erection of the Echo Hall (330–320 B.C.) was separated from the Altis, was completely excavated by German archaeologists in 1958–62 and restored to its 4th c. form. On the track can be seen the *starting line* for the two-stade race (to W) and the Stadion race (to E). The spectators sat on earth embankments: there were no tiers of stone seating, and only the judges had their tribune on the S side and priestess of Demeter – the only woman who was allowed to be present – on the N side.

On the way back we can see, near the W wall of the Altis, the **Philippeion**, a circular structure begun by Philip II of Macedon in 338 B.C. and completed by his son Alexander, for which Leochares carved five chryselephantine statues of the Macedonian royal family.

The new *Museum** contains a large collection of bronzes, pottery and sculpture. The new excavations of the Stadion were extraordinarily productive, yielding many works which had originally been set up along the embankments. The forecourt of the museum, surrounded by concrete colonnades, gives a foretaste of what is to be seen inside.

The rooms are laid out round the *Central Hall*, designed to house the metopes and figures from the pediments of the Temple of Zeus. In the *entrance hall* (sale of tickets, literature, postcards and slides) is an interesting model of ancient Olympia. – The rooms are arranged in clockwise order, starting from the left. – *Room I*: bronzes of the Geometric and Archaic periods (9th–6th c. B.C.), including parts of *tripods, figures of horses, weapons* and *small bronzes*. – *Room II* contains more bronzes – *helmets* and *weapons, griffins' heads* (c. 600 B.C.), a *bronze relief of a female griffin suckling a young one (c. 620 B.C.), a *relief of the Lapith Kaineus between two centaurs (c. 630 B.C.) and a *bronze breastplate with figures of Zeus and Apollo (c. 650 B.C.). This last piece was originally set up as a trophy on the S side of the Stadion. It was made known by Adolf Furtwängler in 1890 but later disappeared; then in 1969 in turned up in Basle and was bought by Marinatos for 200,000 francs. Other interesting items in this room are a limestone *head of the goddess Hera (?) of about 600 B.C. and a terracotta *disc acroterion* from the pediment of the Heraion. – *Room III* shows the *treasuries* of Gela, with the painted terracotta facing of the geison (c. 560 B.C.), and Megara (510 B.C.). – *Room IV* contains a *terracotta group of Zeus and Ganymede (c. 470 B.C.), an early classical *bronze horse from a four-horse chariot and two *helmets*, one with an inscription recording that it was dedicated at Olympia in 490 B.C. by Miltiades, the victor of Marathón, the other a trophy of the Persian wars. – In *Room V* is the statue of **Hermes with the boy Dionysos**, which is generally agreed to be an original work by Praxiteles (c. 350 B.C.). – *Room VI* contains the *bull of Regilla, priestess of Demeter and wife of Herodes Atticus, which originally stood in the Nymphaeum built by Herodes Atticus. – In the last room are, among much else, items of sporting equipment.

Mt Olympus
ΟΛΥΜΠΟΣ
(Ólimbos)

Regions: Thessaly and Macedonia.
Nomos: Lárisa. – Altitude: 2917 m (9571 feet).

The highest mountain in Greece, lying near the sea on the borders of Macedonia and Thessaly, is the most famous of a number of mountains bearing the pre-Greek name of Olympus in Greece, Asia Minor and Cyprus. It already features in Homer ("Iliad", V, 361) as the home of the gods, who are accordingly known as the Olympians.

This mighty massif, covering an area some 20 km (12 miles) across, climbs steeply up towards the summit, reaching its highest point in **Mítikas** (2917 m – 9571 feet). The highest ridges are difficult to climb: more easily accessible is the most northerly peak (2787 m – 9144 feet), on which there is a *chapel of the Prophet Elijah*. On the **Áyios Antónios** peak (2817 m – 9243 feet), to the S of Mítikas, a *shrine of Zeus* was excavated, yielding remains of sacrifices, pottery, inscriptions and coins. A *shrine of Apollo* was found on the W side of the mountain at an altitude of 700 m (2297 feet). – The best starting-point for the ascent of Mt Olympus is **Litókhoro** (see p. 175), at the foot of the eastern slopes.

Separated from Olympus by the *Vale of Tempe* (see p. 246) is **Mt Ossa** (1978 m – 6490 feet), part of the range which cuts Thessaly off from the sea. On the summit is a mountain hut. The best starting-points for the ascent of Ossa are the hill villages of *Ambelákia*, above the W end of the valley of Tempe (on the NW side of the hill) and *Ayiá* (on the SE side).

Olynthos
ΟΛΥΝΘΟΣ
(Ólinthos)

Region and nomos: Chalcidice.

The ancient city of **Ólynthos** lay on the S coast of Chalcidice at the head of the long gulf between the Kassándra and Lóngos peninsulas. The remains can be seen 8 km (5 miles) W of the little resort of **Gerakíni**.

HISTORY. – Evidence of human occupation in this area dates back to 2500 B.C. Later, about 800 B.C., the site was occupied by Macedonians. After the destruction of the town in the Persian wars (480 B.C.) it was repopulated by settlers from Chalkis on Euboea (see p. 132) and developed into the most important town in Chalcidice. In 348 B.C. Ólynthos, then allied with Athens, was totally destroyed by Philip II of Macedon, and the site has remained uninhabited ever since.

American excavations in 1928–34 revealed a rectangular street layout, public buildings and houses and produced valuable evidence of regular Greek town planning before 348 B.C. Notable among the finds made here were early *pebble mosaics* (5th c. B.C.). The site is now largely overgrown.

Orkhomenos
ΟΡΧΟΜΕΝΟΣ
(Orkhomenós)

Nomos: Boeotia.
Altitude: 360 m (1181 feet). – Population: 1800.

HOTEL. – *Elli*, D, 15 b.

The village of Orkhomenós, on the NE margin of the Kopais plain in Boeotia, is of interest for its ancient remains and for the 9th c. church of Skrípou.

6 km (4 miles) NW of Levádia on the road to Lamía a side road goes off on the right to Orkhomenós, continuing to Kástro on the national highway.

HISTORY. – Orkhomenós was the capital of a Minyan principality which belonged to the Mycenaean cultural sphere, although the site had been occupied much earlier by a Neolithic people. Homer refers to the wealth of the Minyans, evidence of which is provided by a large tholos tomb dating from the heyday of the city (14th c. B.C.). In the 7th c. Orkhomenós was overshadowed and finally conquered by Thebes. The site was refortified during the Macedonian period and was occupied into Byzantine times, when it was abandoned.

SIGHTS. – From the village of **Skrípou** there is a road to the E side of the Akóntion ridge. In the lower part of the site of ancient **Orkhomenós**, near the modern cemetery, the excavators found early circular structures, the *tholos tomb* already mentioned and two *temples*. The long triangular area of the site is divided up by two cross-walls. At the western tip is the *acropolis* (alt. 228 m (748 feet)).

Immediately E of the ancient site is the **Church of the Panayía** of Skrípou, which according to an inscription in the apse was built on the site of an earlier (5th c.) church by the Imperial *protospatharius* Leon in 873–874. This church is important as being the earliest example of a domed cruciform church in Greece. The walls contain many architectural fragments from ancient buildings. – 5 km (3 miles) NE of Skrípou is the church of **Áyios Nikólaos sta Kámpia** (in the Fields). Built about 1040 by the architect of the principal church at Ósios Loukás, it has a simplified version of the same ground-plan.

Oropos

ΩΡΩΠΟΣ

(Oropós)

Altitude: 5 m (16 feet).

TRANSPORTATION. – 50 km (31 miles) from Athens by road; ferry service to Erétria on Euboea.

Oropós, or Skála Oropoú, is an attractive little fishing port on the N coast of Attica, with pleasant tavernas along the front.

SURROUNDINGS. – 6 km (4 miles) SE, in a quiet wooded valley, is the **Amphiareion** (see p. 59), home of an ancient oracular cult.

Osios Loukas

ΟΣΙΟΣ ΛΟΥΚΑΣ

(Ósios Lukás)

Region and nomos: Boeotia.

The monastery of *Ósios Loukás occupies an isolated situation in the Helikon range near the Gulf of Corinth. It is reached by a road (13 km – 8 miles) which runs S from the Levádia–Delphi road via the village of Dístomo (rebuilt after destruction during the Second World War). Its mosaics rank along with those of Dafní, near Athens, and the Néa Moní on Chios as the finest examples of 11th c. mosaic work.

HISTORY. – St Luke of Stiri – the style *osios*, "holy", indicating that he was a monk – was born about 898 in Kastoriá, the village now known as Kastrí on the site of Delphi, and lived from about 910 as a hermit in Phocis, where he died, much revered, on 7 February 953. Between 941 and 944, during his lifetime, the Byzantine governor of the region built a chapel

The monastery of Ósios Loukás

dedicated to St Barbara at his hermitage. Round this the monastery developed, and now dominates its lonely surroundings with its two magnificent churches standing side by side.

THE MONASTERY. – The **chapel of St Barbara** has been preserved as the crypt of the principal church. It contains the *sarcophagus of St Luke* and two other sarcophagi, traditionally believed to contain the remains of the Byzantine Emperor Romanos II (959–963) and Empress Theophano. There are a number of *wall paintings*, including a Last Supper (on the S side of the E wing).

The two **churches**, the principal church dedicated to St Luke and the other to the Theotókos (Mother of God), both

Principal church   **Osios Loukas**

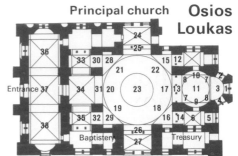

ICONOGRAPHY

1 Christ
2 Theotokos
3 Theotokos
4 John the Baptist
5 Theodore Tyro, Cyprian, Achillius, Spyridon, Silvester
6 Anthimus, Polycarp, Daniel Eleutherus
7 Nations
8 Languages
9 Athanasius
10 Gregory the Theologian
11 Pentecost
12 Ignatius, Gregory of Armenia, Clement (?), Cyril of Alexandria, Theophorus
13 Archangel, Christ, Gabriel, Michael
14 Gregory, Philotheus, Hierotheus, Dionysius
15 Basil, Annunciation
16 Nativity, John
17 Theotokos
18 Archangel Gabriel
19 Archangel Uriel
20 John the Baptist
21 Archangel Raphael
22 Archangel Michael
23 Christ
24 Theotokos, Christ, Michael, James, Luke of Stiri, Gabriel, Prochorus, Stephen the Martyr, Barnabas
25 Nicanor, Timothy, Silas, Theodore Stratiotes, Nicholas the Yr, George
26 Theodore Tyro, Nestor, Demetrius, Cleophas, Raphael, Ananias
27 Theotokos, Christ, Jason, Uriel, Sosipater, Zacharias (?)
28 Gregory the Wonderworker, Agathangelus, Baptism
29 Victor, Presentation of Virgin, Tryphon
30 Antony, Ephraim, Hilarion, Arsenius
31 Mercurius, Christopher, Procopius
32 Theodosius, Euthymius, Sabbas, Pachomius
33 Sisoes, Joannicius, Nilus, Dorotheus, Theoctistus, Maximus, Theodore the Studite, Daniel
34 Acacius, Cimon, Basiliacus, Nicetas, Neophytus, Agathangelus
35 John Climacus, John Colobus, Macarius, Magnesius, Abramius, Poimen, Nicon, Martinianus, John Calybites, Stephen the Yr
36 Washing of the Feet, Matthew, Cimon, Luke, Crucifixion, Cosmas, Cyrus, Irene, Mary, Euphemia, Catherine, Damian, Barbara, Julia
37 Christ, Theotokos, Gabriel, Pegasius, Anempodistes, John the Baptist, Acindynus, Aphthonius, Elpidophorus
38 Paul, James, John the Theologian, Resurrection, Panteleimon, Thomas, Thallelaeus, Bartholomew, Incredulity of Thomas, Philip, Thecla, Constantine, Anastasia, Tryphon, Helena, Agatha, Eugenia, Febronia

Mosaic of St Luke of Stiri

follow the Middle Byzantine pattern of the domed cruciform church. The deep exonarthex (*lití*) of the church of the Theotókos is characteristic of a monastic church.

The monastery was damaged during the Second World War but was thoroughly restored between 1953 and 1962, particular attention being given to the splendid * *mosaics dating from the first half of the 11th c. During the restoration a number of windows which had previously been walled up were reopened, making the principal church lighter and enhancing the spatial effect.

Three factors contribute to the powerful effect of the principal church. As at Dafní and the Néa Moní, the large central dome is borne on eight piers and spans both the central and lateral aisles; the *marble facing* of the walls – missing at Dafní – has been preserved; and most of the *mosaics, which were the work of artists from Constantinople and are of the highest quality, have been preserved or restored.

The subjects of the mosaics, which are notable for their dramatic vigour, are arranged according to the hierarchical rules which had been established by the 9th c. In the narthex are a number of scenes from the Passion, together with angels, saints and the Evangelists. Above the doorway leading into the church is a figure of Christ as the Light of the World. The mosaic of Christ in the central dome was destroyed when the dome collapsed in 1593.

In the squinches under the dome are the Nativity (SE), the Presentation in the Temple (SW) and the Baptism of Christ (NW). In the dome over the sanctuary are the Etimasia (the Preparation of the Throne) and Pentecost, in the apse Mary as Panayía Platytéra.

In the N aisle, to the left, is a portrait-like *figure of*

Ósios Loukás, who is given the style of saint, though he was never officially canonised. Opposite is the *tumba* containing the saint's relics, directly above his sarcophagus in the crypt.

In addition to St Luke other saints of the period of only local importance are included in the iconographic scheme, among them St Nikon Metanoeite, who evangelised Sparta (W end of S aisle), and St Luke the Gournikiote (W end of N aisle).

In the **monastic buildings**, which include the monks' refectory (trápeza), there is a small café (near the entrance, on left).

Parga
ΠΑΡΓΑ
(Párga)

Nomos: Préveza.
Altitude: 10 m (33 feet). – Population: 5000.

TRANSPORTATION. – Bus service from Athens.

HOTELS. – *Hellas*, B, 20 b.; *Lichnos Beach*, B, 164 b.; *Parga Beach*, B, 152 b.; *Avra*, C, 35 b.; and five hotels in categories D and E.

YACHT SUPPLY STATION.

Beautifully situated at the foot of a 16th c. castle in a bay on the W coast of Greece between Igoumenítsa and Préveza – a stretch of coast with few harbours – *Párga is an ideal place for a seaside holiday. There are sandy beaches round the bay and beyond the crag on which the castle

Beach at Párga

Mt *Parnassus, a limestone massif near Delphi rising to a height of 2457 m (8061 feet), was sacred to the cult of Apollo and Dionysos, and in Roman times was regarded as the home of the Muses. The area, with large coniferous forests, is still largely rugged and inhospitable.

From the W end of the village of Arákhova an asphalted road winds its way up into the mountains. At the end of the road is a chair-lift going up to 1900 m (6234 feet), and from there a further lift to the skiing area below the summit plateau.

stands, and rocky coasts on the little offshore islands.

Párga (50 km (31 miles) from Igoumenítsa) is reached from the new Igoumenítsa–Préveza road, turning off at Morfí (38 km – 24 miles).

SURROUNDINGS. – 24 km (15 miles) SE, rising out of the Akheron plain, is the Nekromanteion of **Mesopótamos** (see p. 181). – 14 km (9 miles) N of Morfí is the village of **Paramythiá**, dominated by a Turkish fortress.

Mt Parnassus
ΠΑΡΝΑΣΣΟΣ
(Parnassós)

Region and nomos: Phocis.
Altitude: 2457 m (8061 feet).

Mt Parnis
ΠΑΡΝΗΣ
(Párnis)

Region and nomos: Attica.
Altitude: 1413 m (4636 feet).

HOTELS. – *Casino Mont Parnis*, L, 212 b.; *Xenia*, B, 300 b.; *Kyklamina* (in Ayía Triás), C, 30 b.

CASINO in Mont Parnis Hotel.

Mt Párnis is a limestone mountain (1413 m – 4636 feet) in Attica, to the N of Athens, with large areas of coniferous forest. It is frequently covered with snow well into spring. On the summit there was an ancient shrine of Zeus, the Rain-Bringer. The mountain is now a popular resort, thanks to its climate and the views which it affords.

Parnassus – a distant view from the S

Mt Parnon

ΠΑΡΝΩΝ

(Párnon)

Region: Peloponnese.
Nomoi: Laconia and Arcadia.

HOTELS. – ÁSTROS KYNOURIÁS: *Anthini*, D, 23 b. – PARALÍA TÝROU: *Apollon*, C, 23 b. – LEONÍDI: *Neon*, E, 17 b.

The Párnon range extends along the E side of the Peloponnese for a distance of some 90 km (56 miles) from N to S, separating the Laconian plain around Sparta from the Gulf of Argolis. The northern part of the range consists of schists, the southern part of limestone and marble. Only at Ástros is there a small alluvial plain, the plain of Kynouriá, between the high ground and the sea. The range ends at Cape Maléa in the SE.

This isolated region is still occupied by Tzakonians, a race who claim an ancient origin and preserve some relics of the old Dorian dialect. Along the E coast are a number of small places, beginning in the N with Kivéri, where some years ago a fresh water spring was discovered in the sea; then follow *Ástros* with the coastal resort of *Paralía Týrou* 4 km (2 miles) away, the little ports of *Leonídi* and *Kyparíssi*, and finally the village and castle of **Monemvasía** (see p. 187). The coastal boats sailing between Piraeus and Gýthion call at Kyparíssi and Monemvasía.

Páros

ΠΑΡΟΣ

(Páros)

Nomos: Cyclades. – Telephone dialling code: 0284.
Area: 194 sq. km (75 sq. miles). – Population: 7500.
ⓘ **Tourist Police**,
Apovatna;
tel. 2 16 73 (summer only).

TRANSPORTATION. – Páros is served by the Cyclades boats sailing between Piraeus, Sýros, Páros, Náxos and Santorin. – Boats to Antíparos. – Island buses.

HOTELS. – PÁROS: *Xenia*, B, 44 b.; *Alkyon*, C, 26 b.; *Argonaftis*, C, 27 b.; *Asterias*, C, 50 b.; *Georgy*, C, 43 b.; *Hermes*, C, 36 b.; *Páros*, C, 22 b.; *Stella*, C,

38 b. – ALYKÍ: *Angeliki*, C, 26 b. – DRYÓS: *Annezina*, C, 26 b.; *Avra*, C, 18 b.; *Julia*, C, 23 b.; *Ivi* (*Hebe*), C, 23 b. – MÁRPISSA: *Logaras*, C, 16 b. – NÁOUSA: *Naousa*, B, 19 b.; *Ambelas*, C, 32 b.; *Atlantis*, C, 40 b.; *Galini*, C, 22 b.; *Hippocambus Bungalows*, C, 94 b.; *Mary*, C, 24 b.; *Minoa*, C, 48 b.; *Piperi*, C, 16 b. – PÍSO LIVÁDI: *Marpissa*, 218 b.; *Leto*, C, 28 b.; *Lodos*, C, 20 b.; *Piso Livadi*, C, 24 b.; *Vicky*, C, 28 b.

BATHING BEACHES. – At Páros, Drýos, Náousa and Píso Livádi.

Páros, famed in antiquity for its Parian marble, is one of the most beautiful of the Cyclades, the gentler sister of the larger neighbouring island of Náxos. The Ekatontapyliní church is the finest in the Cyclades. From the central height of Profítis Ilías (750 m – 2461 feet) fertile hilly country slopes down gradually on all sides to the coast.

HISTORY. – On the hill now occupied by the town of Páros evidence of occupation since the Cycladic culture of the 3rd millennium B.C. has been found. In the 2nd millennium the island was settled by Mycenaean Greeks, in the early 1st millennium by Ionians. Its most flourishing period was in the 8th–6th c. B.C. In the 7th c. Páros established a colony on the island of Thásos, one of the founders being the poet Archilochos (*c.* 680–640 B.C.), later revered as a hero. The rich supply of gold on Thásos increased still further the prosperity of the mother island, based on the working of Parian marble. With the Persian wars the political importance of Páros declined, but it was still able to found the colony of Pharos (Hvar) in the Adriatic in 385 B.C. In the Roman period the working of marble became an Imperial monopoly. During the early Byzantine period Páros was sufficiently prosperous to build large churches, but in the 9th and 10th c. the island was plundered and the population decimated by Saracen pirates. In 1207 Páros became part of the duchy of Náxos, and from 1389 to 1537 it was held as a fief of the duchy by the Sommaripa family. Thereafter, until its liberation in the 19th c., it was under Turkish rule.

SIGHTS. – The chief town, **Páros** (pop. 2000), commonly known as **Paríkia**, occupies the site of the ancient capital in a flat bay of the W coast. From the **Harbour** we go past a *windmill* (departure point of the island buses) to reach a spacious square, with several tavernas, and the main street, lined with shops, shipping offices and banks. At a fountain of 1777 a street branches off on the right to the medieval **castle**, built in 1266 on the ancient acropolis, largely of fragments of ancient masonry. The apse of the castle chapel incorporates part of a handsome circular structure of the 4th c. B.C., and architectural elements from an archaic *temple* can be seen in the neighbouring lanes. They date from the time of the Naxian tyrant Lygdamis (*c.* 540 B.C.) and

The fishing harbour, Páros

church too has a synthronon behind the iconostasis, which dates from 1611. – From the S transept of the principal church a door leads into the **Baptistery** (6th c.), also a three-aisled basilica. In the chancel is the original cruciform *immersion font*.

A street immediately S of the church goes past a school to the **Museum** (signpost), with material ranging from early Cycladic idols to late antiquity.

have the same dimensions as the contemporary temple on the Sto Paláti peninsula on Náxos (see p. 193). – From here we continue through narrow lanes to the church of *Áyios Konstantínos* (picturesque arcades) on the highest point of the hill. This was the centre of the ancient settlement: the remains of the prehistoric period have been covered over, but part of the foundations of the archaic temple can be seen immediately N of the church.

The main feature of interest in the town is the *church of Panayía Ekatontapylianí*, the architectural history of which was elucidated by restoration work carried out in the 1960s to restore the church to its original form. The white rendering and various additions which gave it the aspect of a typical Cycladic church were removed, and we can now see the masonry of the original structure (5th–6th c.) and a 10th c. renovation. The name Ekatontapyliani ("with a hundred gates") comes from a wonder-working *icon of the Mother of God*, and has been applied to the church itself only since the 18th c.; it is derived from the older name Katapoliani ("close to the town").

Outside the church, on the left, are ancient **sarcophagi** which have been re-used and decorated with later reliefs. Passing through the *atrium* with its whitewashed arcades, we enter the **principal church**, a three-aisled galleried basilica with a central dome, which dates from the time of Justinian (6th c.). Under the floor were found columns belonging to an earlier Christian building, and below this again remains of a large Roman house with a mosaic of Herakles (now in the museum). A striking feature of the spacious interior is the use of stones of different colours in the *choir vaulting*. This is part of the original structure, as are the *cherubim* in two of the pendentives supporting the dome. Behind the more recent *iconostasis* are a *canopied altar* borne on ancient columns; a *side altar* also incorporating ancient material and a *synthronon* in the apse such as is commonly found in churches of the early Byzantine period.

From the N transept we enter the three-aisled **parekklisia**, which appears to date from the 5th c., with barrel vaulting of the time of Justinian. This

In the *courtyard* are (to left) the *Herakles mosaic* (*c.* A.D. 300) found under the Ekatontapyliani church, *funerary reliefs* and *sarcophagi*. – In the long *entrance hall*, to the left, is an *Ionic capital* which originally bore the figure of a sphinx; as the inscription indicates, it came from the tomb of the poet Archilochos (7th c. B.C.). Near it are two other *inscriptions* relating to Archilochos (3rd and 1st c. B.C.). – The two rooms to the left of the entrance hall contain *pottery* and *small sculpture*. – In the room to the right of the entrance hall is a *fragment of the "Marmor Parium"* or "Parian Chronicle", the major portion of which is in Oxford. This is a chronology of Greek history from the first Attic king, Kekrops, whose date is given as 1582 B.C., to the year 264/263 B.C. – In the *Archaic Hall*, to the right, are a *relief of Apollo and Artemis* and two stone panels from the tomb of Archilochos showing the poet lying on a kline and the lyre and weapons which represent the main activities of his life. – In the last room is a figure of *Artemis* found by Emil Kunze at the Delion.

N of the island (11 km (7 miles): bus). – 2 km (1 mile) E of the town of Páros are the **Tris Ekklisíes**, the ruins of a Christian basilica of the early 7th c., incorporating architectural elements from ancient buildings. An inscripiton found here indicated that the tomb of Archilochos was in this area. Finds from the site are in the museum. – Beyond this, on a hill to the right of the road, is the **Langovárdas monastery** (founded 1657, restored in the 19th c.), one of the few monasteries on the island which are still open, with a school of painting. – **Náousa**, situated in a wide and much indented bay, is a typical little Cycladic town of whitewashed houses.

E and S of the island (20 km – 12 miles). – 3·5 km (2 miles) SE of Páros a footpath goes off on the right to the **ancient marble quarries** (signpost on main road). After passing some abandoned factory buildings the path comes to two entrances to the quarries. To the left of the second entrance is the figure of a *nymph* carved from the rock face. Parian marble was noted for its translucency, particularly the type called Lychnites ("lamp-lit"), which was hewn in underground shafts. – The road continues via the very beautiful hill village of **Léfkes**

(10 km – 6 miles), with the modern *Ayía Triáda* church, and **Márpissa** (15 km – 9 miles) to the little port and seaside resort of **Piso Livádi** and **Dryós** (20 km – 12 miles), which has a fine sandy beach. The return route can be via Márpissa and Náousa.

Walk to the Delion (1 hour). – Walking round the bay from Páros, we come to a small chapel, and from there follow a stony path which climbs N. The **excavations of the Delion** are on a hill, enclosed by a wall. The remains include an ancient *rock-cut altar* within the foundations of a *temenos* and the foundations of a *temple* of the 6th c. B.C. dedicated to the divinities of Delos (Leto and her children Apollo and Artemis). From the site there is a far-ranging view of the northern Cyclades. Nearby are the remains of a *sanctuary of Aphrodite*.

To the island of Antiparos. – It is a short trip by motorboat across the narrow channel to the village of **Antíparos** at the N end of the island of Antíparos (area 34 sq. km (13 sq. miles)). From there a road runs S down the E coast of the island to the bay of **Ákra Akakós**, from which it is a 20 minutes' walk to an interesting stalactitic cave.

Patmos
ΠΑΤΜΟΣ
(Pátmos)

Nomos: Dodecanese
Area: 34 sq. km (13 sq. miles). – Population: 2430.

TRANSPORTATION. – Pátmos is served by boats sailing between Piraeus and Rhodes and between Rhodes and Sámos. – Boats to the neighbouring islands of Lípsi and Arkí.

HOTELS. – *Patmion*, B, 42 b.; *Xenia*, B, 62 b.; *Astoria*, C, 26 b.; *Chris*, C, 48 b.

BATHING BEACHES. – In Kámbos Bay, at the N end of the island, and at other places on the coast.

Pátmos, the most northerly island of the Dodecanese, is of volcanic origin and has a much indented coastline. An isthmus only a few hundred metres wide, on which the island's harbour lies, separates the N end of the island from the southern half, with the famous monastery of St John, who wrote the Book of Revelation here in the latter part of the 1st c.

St John's Monastery, Pátmos

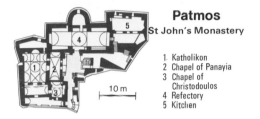

Patmos
St John's Monastery

1. Katholikon
2. Chapel of Panayia
3. Chapel of Christodoulos
4. Refectory
5. Kitchen

HISTORY. – In ancient times there was an acropolis, of which there are traces on the flat-topped hill above the port of Skála. During the Roman period Pátmos was a place of exile, to which John was sent in the reign of Domitian (81–96). According to Irenaeus, a native of Smyrna who died about 200 as bishop of Vienne in southern France, this John was Christ's favourite disciple, author of the Gospel of St John and of the Book of Revelation. He wrote his Revelation while in exile on Pátmos (Rev. 1, 9), and later, during the reign of Nerva, went to Ephesus, where he taught. He died at a great age in the reign of Trajan (98–117) and was buried on the spot where the church of St John was later built. He is known to the Eastern Church as John the Theologian (Ioánnis o Theo lógos), as distinct from John the Forerunner (o Pródromos), the Baptist.

The island first appears in history in the year 1088, when the Byzantine Emperor Alexios Komnenos (1081–1118) granted it to Christodoulos ("Servant of Christ"), who came from the Latmos hills near Miletus in western Asia Minor. Christodoulos founded the monastery of St John, and later a settlement grew up round the fortified monastery, largely populated by refugees from Constantinople (1453) and Crete (1669). During the Turkish period Pátmos suffered little disturbance, and from the 18th c. until 1853 it had one of the few monastic schools in Greece.

SIGHTS. – The boats land their passengers at **Skála**, in a bay on the E side of the island. Above the port can be seen the hill on which the ancient **acropolis** was built. From Skála the chief place on the island, **Pátmos** or *Khóra*, can be reached either on a new road or on the old mule-track. Half way there, on the left, is the **Monastery of the Apocalypse** (*Moní Apokalýpseos*), with the *cave* in which tradition has it that John wrote the Book of Revelation. The **iconostasis* of the right-hand chapel, which is built into the cave, depicts John's visions, and on

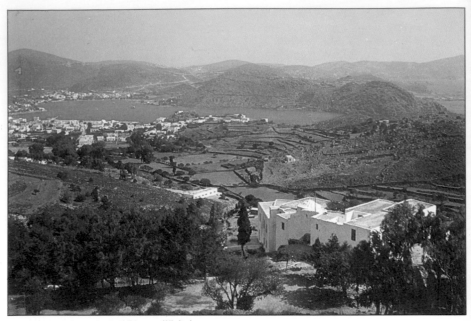

General view of the town of Pátmos (Khóra)

the floor and the wall are marked the spots where he rested, where he heard "a great voice, as of a trumpet", and where he wrote down his visions. Immediately above the monastery can be seen the ruins of the 18th c. *Patmiás School*, and above this again the terraced buildings of the modern Theological College which continues the tradition.

The main centre of tourist interest on the island is the quiet little town of **Khóra** (3 km (2 miles): alt. 130 m (427 feet), pop. 1000), with its whitewashed houses, its monasteries, churches and chapels and above all the ***Monastery of St John the Theologian** (Ioánnou Theológou), a house directly subordinate to the Oecumenical Patriarchate in Constantinople, which looms over the town with its massive 15th c. walls and 17th c. battlements.

A ramp leads up through the entrance gateway into a courtyard surrounded by loggias. On the left is the **Katholikón** or principal church, with an open exonarthex containing four ancient columns and some mediocre 18th and 19th c. paintings. The church itself was decorated and furnished in the 19th c. at the expense of the Tsars of Russia (iconostasis of 1820 with rich carving). The paintings include many representations of St John and his apocalyptic visions. In the first chapel on the right-hand side is the silver-plated *sarcophagus of Osios Christodoulos*, founder of the monastery. In the second chapel, dedicated to the Panayía, are *frescoes* of 1745, under which older paintings were discovered, including the Mother of God enthroned, Abraham entertaining the three angels and Christ and the woman of Samaria

(12th c.). *Frescoes* of the 14th c. have been preserved in the old **refectory** (trápeza).

The ***Treasury** (open 8.30 to 12 and 2 to 4, Sundays 8 to 12) contains mitres, vestments, chalices, crosses, etc., as well as a number of valuable *icons*. There is a very rich ***Library**, with 890 manuscript codices and 35 parchment rolls, 2000 early printed books and the monastic **archives**, containing over 13,000 documents. Some of the finest items are displayed, including the *charter of 1088 (1·42 m (5 feet) long) granting Pátmos to Christodoulos, 33 pages of a 6th c. manuscript of St Mark's Gospel, an 8th c. *manuscript of the Book of Job with 42 miniatures and a *collection of sermons by St Gregory of Nazianzus, written in 941. Of the rich collection of ancient literature once possessed by the monastery there remains a manuscript of the "History" of Diodorus

Fresco of the Mother of God Eleousa, Pátmos

Siculus. Together the Treasury and the Library of St John's Monastery constitute what is surely the richest collection of its kind apart from those of the monasteries on Athos.

After seeing all these treasures visitors should not miss going up on to the *roof terraces* of the monastery to enjoy the superb *views of Pátmos and the surrounding islands.

Patras
ΠΑΤΡΑΙ
(Pátrai)

Nomos: Achaia. – Telephoning dialling code: 061.
Altitude: 5–103 m (16–338 feet). – Population: 112,000.
(i) Greek National Tourist Organisation (EOT),
Iróon Polytekhníou;
tel. 42 03 04.

TRANSPORTATION. – Ferry service from Ancona and Brindisi in Italy; boat connections with the islands of Kefallinía, Páxi and Corfu; station on the Athens–Corinth–Pýrgos railway line; bus connections with Athens and Pýrgos.

HOTELS. – PÁTRAS: *Acropole*, Ayíou Andréou 32, A, 64 b.; *Astir*, Ayíou Andréou 16, A, 222 b.; *Moreas*, Iróon Polytekhníou, A, 180 b.; *Galaxy*, Ayíou Nikoláou 9, B, 98 b.; *Majestic*, Ayíou Andréou 67, B, 103 b.; *Delphini*, Iróon Polytekhníou 102, C, 135 b.; *El Greco*, Ayíou Andréou 145, C, 43 b.; *Esperia*, Zaimi 10, C, 39 b.; *Méditerranée*, Ayíou Nikoláou 18, C, 166 b.

WEST OF PÁTRAS. – PARALÍA PROSTÍOU (3 km – 2 miles): *Achaia Beach*, B, 165 b. – LAKÓPETRA (31 km – 19 miles): *Ionian Beach*, B, 150 b. – METOKHÍ (35 km – 22 miles): *Kalorgia Beach*, B, 182 b. – EAST OF PÁTRAS: see under Ríon.

CAMPING SITES. – Ayía Pátron (5 km (3 miles) NE); Kamínia (13 km (8 miles) SW).

Pátras is the largest town and the principal port of the Peloponnese, chief town of the nomos of Achaia, the see of an archbishop and a university town.

HISTORY. – The town was founded about 1100 B.C., but only became of importance as a port in Roman times (from 146 B.C. onwards). – After the 4th Crusade it became the seat of a Roman Catholic archbishop. In 1408 it came under the control of Venice and in 1430 of Mistra. In 1430 it fell into the hands of the Turks, by whom it was destroyed in 1821, at the beginning of the war of liberation. Thereafter it was rebuilt in neo-classical style on a rectangular street layout.

SIGHTS. – From the busy **Harbour** a broad flight of steps leads to the **Kastro** (alt. 103 m (338 feet)), built by the Byzantines in the 6th c. and rebuilt by the Crusaders in the 13th. To the W of the Kastro are a Roman **Odeon** (Sotiriádis 22) and the **Museum** (Mésonos Street), which contains *grave goods* from Mycenaean tombs and Greek and Roman *sculpture, mosaics* and *pottery*. In Platía Ayíou Andréou, at the W end of the harbour, is the **church of Áyios Andréas** (1836), with the *reliquary containing St Andrew's skull*, which was returned to Pátras by Pope Paul VI in 1964. (According to tradition St Andrew was martyred at Pátras in A.D. 60.)

Paxi and Antipaxi
ΠΑΞΟΙ καὶ ΑΝΤΙΠΑΞΟΙ
(Paxí kai Andípaxi)

Nomos: Corfu.
Area: 2 sq. km (1 sq. mile). – Population: 2200.

TRANSPORTATION. – Boat connections with Kérkyra and Pátras.

HOTEL. – PAXOS: *Paxos Beach*, B, 54 b.

This quiet little group of islands lies immediately S of Kérkyra in the Ionian Sea. The villages of Paxi (pop. 350) in the SE of the main island and Lákka (pop. 60) in the N are linked by a road. In the SE are sulphur springs.

Mt Pelion
ΠΗΛΙΟΝ
(Pílion)

Region: Thessaly. – Nomos: Magnesia.
Altitude: 1618 m (5309 feet).

HOTELS. – ÁYIOS IOÁNNIS: *Aloe*, B, 84 b.; *Galini*, C, 30 b. – AFYSSOS: *Alexandros*, B, 18 b.; *Pharos*, C, 21 b.; *Katia*, C, 24 b. – MAKRÝNITSA: *Archontikon Musli*, A, 13 b. – PORTARIÁ: *Xenia*, B, 152 b.; *Alkistis*, C, 87 b.; *Kentrikon*, C, 22 b. – TSANGARÁDA: *Kentavros*, B, 46 b.; *Xenia*, B, 86 b.; *San Stefano*, C, 71 b.

CAMPING SITES. – Kalá Nerá, Míllina.

The Pelion range extends to the S of Mt Ossa along the E coast of Thessaly as far as the peninsula of Magnesia which encloses the Gulf of Vólos. Rising to a height of 1054 m

(3458 feet) in the peak of Mavrovoúni to the N and to 1618 m (5309 feet) in Mt Pelion itself, above Vólos, it falls steeply down to the E coast, a rugged stretch with no natural harbours.

Pelion was renowned in antiquity for its healing herbs and as the home of the centaurs, one of whom, Chiron, noted for his wisdom and his skill in medicine, was the teacher of Asklepios and Achilles. Under the peak of Pliasídi (1548 m – 5079 feet), which can be climbed from Portariá in 3½ hours, are the Cave of Chiron and a sanctuary of Zeus Akraios.

There are large areas of deciduous forest in this region. The 24 villages which grew up here, well supplied with wood and water, prospered and during the Turkish period were able to retain a measure of independence. Some of these villages can be seen in a round trip from **Vólos**, which in addition to the charm of the villages themselves and the magnificent scenery will take in the sandy bays on the E coast.

Going NE from Vólos, we come in 14 km (9 miles) to **Portariá** (alt. 600 m (1969 feet)). 2 km (1 mile) from here, on a road to the left, is **Makrýnitsa** (alt. 600 m (1969 feet)), with a folk museum. Continuing from Portariá, we reach **Khaniá** (12 km (7 miles): alt. 1100 m (3609 feet)) and **Zagorá** (21 km (13 miles): alt. 500 m (1641 feet)), from which it is 3 km (2 miles) down to **Khorefthó** (beach). Going S from Zagorá we arrive at the coastal villages of **Áyios Ioánnis** (22 km (14 miles)) and **Tsangaráda** (11 km (7 miles): alt. 420 m (1378 feet)), and from there return via **Neokhóri** (15 km – 9 miles), **Kalá Nerá** (14 km – 9 miles) and **Agria** (15 km – 9 miles) to Vólos. From **Áfyssos** a road descends to **Míllina** and **Plataniá** (29 km – 18 miles), at the southern tip of the *peninsula of Magnesia*.

Pella

ΠΕΛΛΑ

(Pélla)

Region: Macedonia. – Nomos: Pélla.

Pélla, once the capital of the kingdom of Macedon, lies 40 km (25

Pélla

miles) W of Salonica on the road to Édessa.

HISTORY. – About 410 B.C. King Achelaos of Macedon transferred his capital from Aigai (see under Édessa and Vérgina), then situated on the N shore of the Gulf of Thermai, to the new city of Pélla, in which the Attic tragedian Euripides spent the last years of his life and Alexander the Great was born in 356 B.C. The city seems to have had two acropolises, one on the site of the present-day village of Palaiá Pélla (1 km (about a ½ mile) N of the national highway) and the other to the W of this, where walls probably belonging to the palace were found (Site II). From there the town extended S to the former island of Phakos, to the S of the road. Following its destruction by the Romans after the battle of Pydna (196 B.C.), of which Pliny gives an account, the town disappeared from sight and was rediscovered only in 1957 by Makaronas and Petsas. The excavations carried out since then have been highly productive.

TOUR OF THE SITE. – Coming from Salonica, we see on the right of the road, immediately after the turning for Palaiá Pélla (bus stop), a number of large **houses**, laid out along streets which intersect at right angles. Dating from

Detail from the Lion-Hunt mosaic, Pélla

about 300 B.C., these are built round colonnaded courtyards and apparently served some public function. Particularly fine is the right-hand house (*Block 1), with an Ionic *peristyle* and fine *mosaics*, which have been left in situ. A number of such mosaics, composed of black, white and yellow pebbles, were found on the site. One of them, the Lion-Hunt, shows Alexander being saved by Krateros; others include Dionysos riding on a panther, another hunting scene, Deianeira fleeing from Theseus, a fight with Amazons, a pair of centaurs, etc. Some of these can be seen in situ; others are in the *Museum, on the other side of the road, which also contains *architectural fragments* and *sculpture*.

Parallel to the road to Salonica is a row of *grave mounds* of the Hellenistic period.

Mountain landscape in the Peloponnese

The myth tells us that Pelops, a descendant of Tantalos, came into this land, defeated King Oinomaos of Pisa in a chariot race, married his daughter and took over his kingdom. The Olympic Games were later founded at his funeral to honour his memory. His descendants, the Pelopids or Atreids, ruled in Mycenae and Sparta.

Peloponnese
ΠΕΛΟΠΟΝΝΗΣΟΣ
(Pelopónnisos)

The most southerly part of the Greek mainland, with which it is linked only by the Isthmus of Corinth, is a peninsula, but it has been known since ancient times as an island – the island of Pelops or Peloponnese.

The peninsula, with an area of 21,440 sq. km (8278 sq. miles), is much broken up by hills and the sea and shows great variety of landscape pattern. In the centre is the thinly populated upland region of Arcadia (see p. 61), bordered on the N by a range of hills with Erýmanthos (2223 m – 7294 feet), Khelmós (2355 m – 7727 feet) and Kyllíni (2376 m – 7796 feet) as its highest peaks. Beyond this the region of Achaia extends N to the Gulf of Corinth. On the E side of the peninsula is the Argolid (see p. 62), with the Gulf of Argolis and the strongholds of Mycenae

A country scene in the Peloponnese, with Taýgetos in the background

and Tiryns. To the S of Arcadia is Laconia with its chief town Sparta (see p. 241), open to the sea in the S and separated from Messenia to the W by the Taýgetos range, which ends in the Máni peninsula (see p. 177). Finally there is the region of Elis in the NW of the Peloponnese, an area of low-lying land with Olympia as its best-known place.

HISTORY. – Originally occupied by a pre-Greek population, in the 2nd millennium B.C. the centre of the Mycenaean world, in the 1st millennium largely under the domination of the Dorian state of Sparta, the Peloponnese is a region rich in myth as well as history; and later centuries have also made their contribution to its story. During the Middle Ages there was an influx of Slavs, though the town remained entirely Greek. After the 4th Crusade (1204) the whole of the Peloponnese passed into the hands of Frankish knights; but Mistra (see p. 185) soon became the starting-point of the Byzantine reconquest. In 1453 the Turks arrived, and in 1821 it was from the Peloponnese that the war of liberation from Turkish rule began.

All the various phases of this long history have left their mark on the Peloponnese, from the strongholds of the Mycenaeans and Greek sites like Olympia, Messene and Neméa to the castles of the Crusaders and Byzantine Mistra. In addition the long sandy beaches on the W coast, in the Gulf of Corinth, at Náfplion and on the peninsula to the E make the Peloponnese a popular holiday region which offers every facility for relaxation and recreation, ideally combined with an encounter with the past.

Mt Pentelikon
ΠΕΝΤΕΛΙΚΩΝ
(Pendelikón)

Region and nomos: Attica.
Altitude: 1109 m (3639 feet).

HOTELS. – PENTÉLI: Achillion, C, 21 b. – KASTRI (3 km (2 miles) NE of Kifissiá): Kastri, A, 122 b. – EKÁLI (5 km (3 miles) NE of Kifissiá): Ariadne, B, 12 b.; Neon Ariadne, C, 33 b. – DROSIÁ (9 km – 6 miles): Dionysos, C, 26 b.; Galini, C, b.; Pefkakia, C, 93 b.; Zorbas, 23 b. – DIONYSÓS (12 km – 7 miles): Hera, C, 10 b.

The Pentelikón or Pentéli range bounds the plain of Attica on the NE. Pentelic marble was used in the great classical buildings on the Acropolis in Athens and in the famous "Moschophoros" in the Acropolis Museum, and it is still worked today.

In a hollow below the summit, surrounded by poplars, is the **Pentéli monastery** (alt. 430 m (1411 feet)), which was founded in 1578. It can be reached from Athens by way of the suburb of Khalándri (8 km (5 miles) from Khalándri). The road continues to just under the summit. From the monastery the ancient **marble quarries**, worked from 570 B.C. onwards, can be reached (alt. 700 m (2297 feet)).

On the eastern slopes of the hill, above the road from Athens to Stavrós and Marathón, is the *Daou Pentéli monastery, founded in the 12th c. and rebuilt in the 16th, which has been called "the only example of a large monastic establishment in Greece outside Athos" (Kirsten-Kraiker). Near the monastery is a sanatorium.

On the N side of Pentelikón, on the road from Athens via Kifissiá and Drosiá to Néa Mákri on the E coast, is **Dionysós** (alt. 460 m (1509 feet)), where there are tavernas popular with the citizens of Athens. Near here is a *sanctuary of Dionysos*, which belonged to Ikaría (see p. 139), home of Thespis, who produced the first tragedy in Athens in 534 B.C.

Perachora
ΠΕΡΑΧΩΡΑ
(Perakhóra)

Region: Megaris. – Nomos: Corinth.

The ancient shrine of Hera at Perachora lies on the shores of a sharply pointed peninsula which separates the Halcyonic Gulf from the Gulf of Corinth.

The road from Corinth, running NW via Loutráki, passes the village of Perachora (on right), skirts a lake (bathing beach, taverna) and ends near a lighthouse (20 km – 12 miles). Below, to the left in the little bay is the ancient site; straight ahead, on the S side of the gulf, stands the prominent bulk of Acrocorinth. It is well worth while making the trip to Perachora both for the historical importance of the scanty remains, dating from the early period of Greek temple-building, and for the magnificent setting; and there is, too, the additional attraction of a swim in the ancient harbour.

HISTORY. – In the Mycenaean period the sanctuary belonged to Megara, later to Corinth. The oracle here, sacred to the goddess Hera, flourished particularly in the Geometric period (9th and 8th c.), although nothing is known of the cult practices. In 390 B.C. the sanctuary was seized by the Spartan Agesilaos. During the Roman period it was abandoned. The site was excavated by British archaeologists in 1930–33.

TOUR OF THE SITE. – On the shores of the bay stands an *altar* with Doric triglyphs (*c*. 500 B.C.), and to the N of this are traces of the *Temple of Hera Akraia*. A stretch of *wall* 6·80 m (22 feet) long running from E to W, with the remains of an apse at the W end, belonged to a temple of the Geometric period (*c*. 850 B.C.), which was only 5–6 m (16–20 feet) wide and 8 m (26 feet) long. About 530 B.C. a considerably larger Archaic *temple* (9·50 by 30 m (31 by 98 feet)), the W end of which has been preserved, was built to the W of the first one. This temple was flanked by an L-shaped stoa (5th–4th c. B.C.) and the Agora (*c*. 500 B.C.).

In a small valley higher up to the E are other ancient buildings, approached by a stepped path. The most striking feature is a large Hellenistic **cistern**. Nearby is the **Temple of Hera Limenaia**, which dates from about 750 B.C. (i.e. the time of Homer). Facing the S, it measures 5·60 by 9·50 m (18 by 31 feet) and contains a number of stone slabs which formed part of the sacrificial altar. While the normal Greek temple was merely designed to house the cult image and the cult ceremonies took place outside the temple, this temple was an assembly hall in which the sacred ceremonies were performed. It thus marks the beginning of a development which ended in the Telesterion of the Eleusinian mystery cult (see p. 129). – Near the temple were found a **sacrificial pit** with many thousands of votive potsherds and a *sacred pond* which was presumably the seat of an oracle.

Part of the palace of Phaistós

HOTELS. – PHAISTÓS: *Xenia Pavilion*, D, 11 b. – AYÍA GALÍNI: *Galini*, 16 b.; *Acropolis*, C, 34 b.; *Astoria*, C, 42 b.; *Candia*, C, 22 b.; *Cristof*, C, 27 b.; *Daidalos*, C, 24 b.; *Miramare*, C, 13 b.; *Selena*, C, 18 b.; *Soulia*, C, 24 b.; and hotels in categories D and E.

Phaistós, one of the largest of the Minoan palaces, lies in the S of Crete 60 km (37 miles) from Iráklion, on a site which was traditionally associated with Rhadamanthys, brother of Minos. There were two palaces here, one dating from 2000 to 1650 B.C. and the other from 1600 to 1400 B.C. Parts of the older palace, more clearly visible here than on other sites, can be seen to the W and NW of the site; elsewhere the earlier palace is covered by the later one. The site was reoccupied in post-Minoan times, as is shown by the remains of a Greek temple dedicated to Rhea, mother of Zeus, in the SW part of the site. In later periods the town was overshadowed by Górtys. The SE part of the palace has fallen away.

Phaistos

ΦΑΙΣΤΟΣ

(Festós)

Island: Crete. – Nomos: Iráklion.
Altitude: 100 m (328 feet).

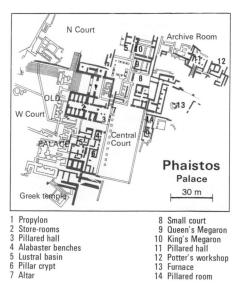

Phaistos
Palace
⊢——— 30 m ———⊣

1 Propylon
2 Store-rooms
3 Pillared hall
4 Alabaster benches
5 Lustral basin
6 Pillar crypt
7 Altar
8 Small court
9 Queen's Megaron
10 King's Megaron
11 Pillared hall
12 Potter's workshop
13 Furnace
14 Pillared room

The Phaistós Disc (Iráklion Museum)

The *Palace of Phaistós, smaller than the one at Knossos, is splendidly situated, with views of Mt Ida and the Mesará plain. It is built round a central court, and there is also – as at Knossos – a west court. The royal apartments here lie to the N.

From the Tourist Pavilion we cross the *N Court* and descend a flight of steps, from which we have a view of both the old and the new palace. The *W Court*, to the right, and the *Grand Staircase* which bounds it on the N belong to the **Old Palace**, as does the *terrace* at the foot of the steps, which is in fact the W front of the earlier palace, still standing 1 m (3 feet) high. When the New Palace was built the W front was moved 7 m (23 feet) and all the rest, including the courtyard, was covered over and brought to light again only when the site was excavated.

Going S along the terrace, on which there are remains of a small **sanctuary**, we come to the entrance to the Old Palace, at the point where the paved road from the grand staircase turns to enter the palace complex. The *column base* of coloured stone, 1·25 m (4 feet) in diameter, once bore a massive timber column.

We now retrace our steps and enter the **New Palace** by the *Grand Staircase*, with 12 steps some 13·60 m (45 feet) wide, which leads up to *propylon* at the W entrance. Beyond this are a number of small rooms and a *pillared hall*, with *store-rooms* to the right and the Central Court to the left. Immediately S of this are *offices* and *servants' quarters*. The *Central Court*, like the one at Knossos, is a rectangular area aligned from N to S. Along its E side were *living quarters* with a *peristyle courtyard*. From the court there is a fine *view northward over the clearly articulated façade of the N range of buildings to the majestic peak of Mt Ida.

In the *N range* of buildings we go along the N–S corridor and across a courtyard to reach two *royal apartments*. The first has benches along the walls, the second is a *polythyron* with four doors on the N side and four on the E side opening into colonnades. Adjoining is a *lustral basin* under a modern protective roof. To the NE are walls of the older palace, a metal-working *furnace* and other remains. In the long rooms which meet at an angle at the N end of the palace the famous Phaistós Disc was found. – From here we return to the terrace beside the Tourist Pavilion.

SURROUNDINGS. – From Phaistós a new road leads to the royal villa of **Ayía Triáda** (see p. 102). – 10 km (6 miles) SW of Phaistós via *Áyios Ioánnis* and *Pitsidiá* is **Mátala**, in ancient times the port of Górtys, with a sandy bay edged by cliffs containing caves which in the past were used as tombs and as dwellings.

The main road continues to **Tymbáki** (pop. 2800), 67 km (42 miles) from Iráklion, and the coastal villages of **Kókkinos Pýrgos** (74 km (46 miles) from Iráklion) and **Ayía Galíni** (79 km (49 miles): pop. 450), both of which have tavernas and excellent facilities for swimming.

From here it is possible to continue to **Réthymnon** on the N coast (67 km (42 miles): see p. 221).

Philippi

ΦΙΛΙΠΠΟΙ

(Fílippi)

Region: Macedonia. – Nomos: Kavála.

Although the Apostle Paul first set foot in Europe at Neapolis (Kavála: see p. 155) on his second missionary journey, it was at Philippi, 15 km (9 miles) NW of Kavála on the road to Drama, that he established the first Christian community in Europe. Here are to be seen impressive remains of both the ancient and the Christian period.

HISTORY. – The rich deposits of gold in the Pangaion hills led settlers from the island of Thásos to establish a

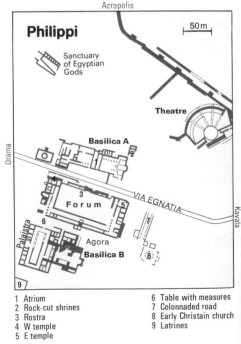

1   Atrium
2   Rock-cut shrines
3   Rostra
4   W temple
5   E temple
6   Table with measures
7   Colonnaded road
8   Early Christain church
9   Latrines

town here which they called Krenides because of the springs in the area. The old name is perpetuated in the present-day village of Krínides. In 361 B.C. new settlers established themselves on the site, but only five years later the town was taken by *Philip II* of Macedon, who named it Philippoi. The place is best known for the battle of Philippi in 42 B.C., in which *Octavian* (later the Emperor Augustus) and *Antony* defeated Caesar's murderers, *Brutus* and *Cassius*. The victors then established a colony of veterans in the town. Philippi grew in importance as a result of its situation on the Via Egnatia, which ran from the Adriatic to Constantinople, and at the beginning of the 4th c. it became the seat of a bishop. The town's decline began with the Slav and Bulgar invasions of the 9th c.

TOUR OF THE SITE. – Approaching the site from Kavála, we see on the hillside on the right the **Theatre**, built in the 4th c. B.C. and (like the one at Dodóna: see p. 128) altered by the Romans in the 3rd c. A.D. to make it suitable for wild beast fights. It is now used for dramatic performances in summer. Following the line of the old **town walls** (well preserved for most of their length) up the hill, we come to the site of the **Acropolis**, on which there are remains dating from Macedonian, Roman and Byzantine times.

From the theatre there is a view of the plain below, with the excavations carried out by French and Greek archaeologists on both sides of the modern road, which here follows the line of the Via Egnatia. On the near side of the road is **Basilica A** (*c.* A.D. 500), a three-aisled building with a flight of steps leading up to the atrium and a synthronon in the apse. To the W of this another three-aisled basilica has recently been excavated. From here we can climb up to the *Sanctuary of the Egyptian Gods* half way up the hill.

Most of the excavated area lies to the S of the road. Immediately adjoining the road is the large rectangular Roman **Forum** (70 by 148 m (230 by 486 feet)), which dates from the time of Marcus Aurelius (A.D. 161–180). This had colonnades round three sides and temples at each end. A Roman *cistern* between the western temple and Basilica A is identified by local tradition with the prison in which the Apostle Paul was confined. At the SW corner of the forum is a marble *table marked with standard measures*. Immediately S is the largest church in Philippi, **Basilica B**, also known by the Turkish name of "Direkler" ("Pillars") from the massive masonry piers which form a prominent landmark. Built about 560 by an architect from Constantinople over an ancient *palaistra* (remains of which can be seen to the W), it was designed as a domed basilica on the model of St Sophia in Constantinople, but the dome collapsed and the church was never completed. In addition to the massive piers there are extensive remains of the building, including some fine early Byzantine *capitals*.

SW of Basilica B are well-preserved *latrines*. To the E, approached by a colonnaded road, is the oldest church in Philippi, an octagonal structure built about 400.

Basilica B, Philippi

Pindos
ΠΙΝΔΟΣ
(Píndhos)

This massive mountain range traverses Greece from N to S, extending in a series of chains of hills, for the most part over 2000 m (6562 feet) high, from Mts Grámmos (2529 m – 8297 feet) and Smólikas (2637 m – 8652 feet) on the Albanian frontier to Vardoúsia (2437 m – 8055 feet), Gióna (2510 m – 8235 feet) and Mt Parnassus (2457 m – 8061 feet) near the Gulf of Corinth. This region of forest-covered hills, with summer grazings above the tree line, is thinly populated, much of it occupied solely by shepherds, and with only two roads of any consequence passing through it – between Ioánnina and Kalambáka and between Karpenísi and Lamía. The Pindos range forms the watershed between the rivers flowing into the Ionian Sea (Thyámis, Akheron, Árakhthos and Akhelóos) and those flowing into the Aegean (Piniós and Sperkhiós).

Piraeus
ΠΕΙΡΑΙΕΥΣ
(Pireéfs)

Nomos: Attica. – Telephone dialling code: 01.
Altitude: 15 m (49 feet). – Population: 200,000.
(i) Greek National Tourist Organisation (EOT),
Vasílissis Sofías 105;
tel. 4 12 94 92.
(Information also available from shipping offices round harbour.)

TRANSPORTATION. – From Piraeus there are both international shipping services to other ports in Europe and the Middle East and many Greek domestic services. There are frequent sailings to the islands in the Argo-Saronic Gulf (Aegina to Spétsai). – Fast electric trains to Athens (Omónia) and Kifissiá. – Terminus of State Railways line to Salonica and of Peloponnesian Railway. – Town buses.

HOTELS. – *Cavo d'Oro*, Vasiléos Pávlou 19, B, 138 b.; *Diogenis*, Vasiléos Yeoryiou A 27, B, 146 b.;

Homeridion, Kharíláou Trikoúpi 32, B, 112 b.; *Noufara*, Vasiléos Konstantínou 45, B, 84 b.; *Triton*, Tsamádou 8, B, 104 b.; *Acropole*, Gounári 7, C, 42 b.; *Anita*, Notará 25, C, 47 b.; *Argo*, Notará 23, C, 47 b.; *Arion*, Vasiléos Pávlou 109, C, 69 b.; *Atlantis*, Notará 138, C, 93 b.; *Capitol*, Kharíláou Trikoúpi, C, 91 b.; *Castella*, Vasiléos Pávlou 75, C, 57 b.; *Cavo*, Filonos 79–18, C, 89 b.; *Delphini*, Leokhárous 7, C, 93 b.; *Diana*, Filellínon 11, C, 79 b.; *Eri*, Pétrou Rálli 54, C, 90 b.; *Glaros*, Kharíláou Trikoúpi, C, 72 b.; *Ionion*, Kapodistríou 10, C, 41 b.; *Leriotis*, Akto Themistokléous 294, C, 85 b.; *Lilia*, Pasalimáni 131, C, 21 b.; *Louis*, Notará 2, C, 38 b.; *Niki*, Iannakíou Tzelépi 5, C, 27 b.; *Park*, Kolokotróni 103, C, 152 b.; *Phidias*, Koundourióti 189, C, 44 b.; *Santorini*, Kharíláou Trikoúpi 6, C, 63 b.; *Skorpios*, Aktí Themistokléous 156, C, 44 b.; *Seriphos*, Kharíláou Trikoúpi 5, C, 59 b.

YOUTH HOSTEL.

Many RESTAURANTS, particularly fish restaurants, round the Pasalimáni (Zéa) and Mikrolimáno harbours.

Piraeus, the port of Athens since the 5th c. B.C., is now the largest port in Greece. In addition to the principal harbour, Kántharos, the two smaller ancient harbours on the E coast are still in use – Pasalimáni (the ancient Zea), and Tourkolimáno, now known as Mikrolimáno (the ancient Mounychia). New port installations to relieve the pressure on the main harbour are under construction at Fáliron.

HISTORY. – From 482 B.C. onwards Piraeus was developed by Themistokles into a commercial harbour and naval base for Athens. It was connected with Athens by the "Long Walls" and laid out in the time of Perikles on a rectangular street pattern according to

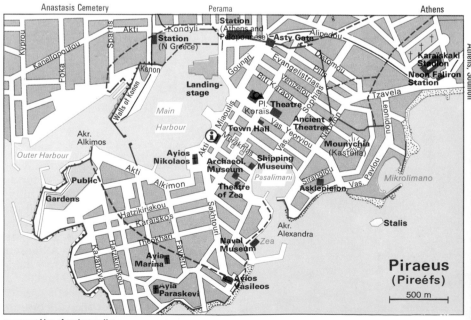

Line of ancient walls

Pasalimáni harbour, Piraeus

the system evolved by Hippodamos of Miletus. The town was destroyed by Sulla in 86 B.C. and thereafter was a place of no importance. In the Middle Ages it was known as Porto Leone after an ancient marble figure of a lion which stood at the entrance to the harbour but was removed to Venice in 1682 and now stands outside the Arsenal there. Piraeus recovered its importance after the liberation of Greece in the 19th c., when the modern town was laid out on a rectangular plan (by Schaubert) as the ancient one had been.

SIGHTS. – The remains of ancient **boatsheds** can be seen under water in Pasalimáni harbour, the ancient harbour of Zea, and behind the Archaeological Museum (at present in course of reconstruction) are remains of a Hellenistic **theatre**. Round the W and S sides of the peninsula (Akti) between the Kántharos and Pasalimáni harbours are considerable stretches of the **walls** built by Konon in 394–391 B.C.; the older walls of Themistokles are now built over. – There is an interesting *Shipping Museum on the quay of Pasalimáni harbour, covering the history of shipping from antiquity to modern times. – The most characteristic parts of the modern town, combining the atmosphere of a large port with the amenities of a city, are round the principal harbour, in Koráis Square between that harbour and Mikrolimáno, and round Mikrolimáno with its tavernas.

Plataiai
ΠΛΑΤΑΙΑΙ
(Plateé)

Region and nomos: Boeotia.

Plataiai (Plataea) was the scene of the last battle on Greek soil during the Persian wars.

HISTORY. – The battle, in which the Persian commander Mardonios was killed, finally ended the

Persian threat to Greece. To commemorate their victory the allied Greek cities set up in the sanctuary of Apollo at Delphi the bronze column of intertwined snakes, originally bearing a tripod, which now stands in the Hippodrome in Istanbul, and established the Eleutheria (Freedom Games) which were held every four years.

Plataiai is reached from Thebes by the old road to Athens. 2 km (1 mile) from Thebes a road goes off on the left to the battlefield of **Leuktra**, where Epameinondas defeated the Spartans in 371 B.C. (fragments of a trophy erected by the Thebans at km 16). – 11 km (7 miles) from Thebes is *Erythrai*, where the road to **Plataiai** (5 km – 3 miles) branches off on the right.

The ancient city lay on the northern slopes of Mt Kithairon, at the modern village of *Kókla*. Excavations by an American expedition (1890) and by the Greek archaeologist Skias (1899) established the line of the walls surrounding the oval *acropolis* on the level top of the hill and of other associated walls. To the S of this central point were the **agora** and a **temple**. – Plataiai sent 1000 men to take part in the battle of Marathón. Destroyed and rebuilt on a number of occasions, it survived into Roman and Byzantine times. – The battle of Plataiai took place to the NE of the town in the plain of the River Asopos.

Poros
ΠΟΡΟΣ
(Póros)

Nomos: Attica. – Telephone dialling code: 0298.
Area: 23 sq. km (9 sq. miles). – Population: 4500.
(i) **Tourist Police**,
    Demosthénous 32;
    tel. 2 24 62 (only in summer).

TRANSPORTATION. – Póros is linked with Piraeus and the neighbouring islands by the Argosaronikos service. There are boats to Galatás on the mainland, and buses from there to Náfplion.

HOTELS. – PÓROS: *Anessis*, B, 9 b.; *Latsi*, B, 54 b.; *Neon Aegli*, B, 78 b.; *Poros*, B, 146 b.; *Saron*, B, 46 b.; *Sirene*, B, 228 b.; *Aktaeon*, C, 38 b.; *Angyra*, C, 87 b.; *Chrysi Avgi*, C, 145 b.; *Manessi*, C, 39 b. – GALATÁS: *Stella Maris* Nautic Holiday Center, B, 176 b.; *Galatia*, C, 41 b.; *Papasotiriou*, C, 30 b.

BATHING BEACHES. – W of the town of Póros (sandy beach) and in bays on the N coast.

Póros, the ancient Kalaureia, is separated from the NE coast of the

Póros

Peloponnese by a strait only 250 m (820 feet) wide. On a rocky promontory on the strait is the chief town, Póros (pop. 4000). The quiet bay to the W of the town is like an island lake; and indeed the channels on the E and W sides are passable only by small boats.

HISTORY. – There was a town here in Mycenaean times, on the site of the later temple of Poseidon. The temple enjoyed the right of sanctuary; and here in 322 B.C. Demosthenes, the great advocate of resistance to the Macedonian hegemony, poisoned himself while fleeing from Antipatros. The ancient city was abandoned in Roman times; the present town was established only in the later medieval period.

SIGHTS. – The town of **Póros** has a strikingly beautiful setting. The old **Arsenal** built by Kapodistrias now houses a Naval Training School, of which the cruiser "Averof", moored in the bay, forms part.

A road runs past the Naval School to the *Panayía monastery (4 km – 2 miles), which has a richly gilded *iconostasis*. From here a footpath ascends (45 minutes) to the **sanctuary of Poseidon** on the Paláti plateau. There are only scanty remains of the temple (6th c. B.C.), but the climb is worth it for the sake of the view. From the site it is another 45 minutes' walk through a pine forest to the N coast with its beautiful bays.

An interesting trip can be made to **Galatás** on the mainland and from there to the remains of ancient **Troizen** (see p. 253), the setting of the myth of Hippolytos and Phaidra.

Porto Kheli

ΠΟΡΤΟ ΧΕΛΙ

(Pórto Khéli)

Region: Peloponnese. – Nomos: Argolid.

TRANSPORTATION. – Air services from Athens; boats from Piraeus; hydrofoil service from Marína Zéa.

HOTELS. – PÓRTO KHÉLI: *Chinitsa Beach,* A, 385 b.; *PLM Porto Cheli,* A, 404 b.; *Apollo Beach,* B, 282 b.; *Galaxy,* B, 325 b.; *Giuli,* B, 305 b.; *Thermissia,* B, 70 b.; *Ververoda,* B, 463 b.; *Porto,* C, 20 b.; *Rozos,* C, 44 b. – SALÁDI: *Saladi Beach,* B, 776 b. – KÓSTA: *Cap d'Or,* B, 204 b.; *Lido,* B, 72 b. – PETROTHÁLASSA: *Lena Mary,* B, 228 b.; *Scarlet Beach,* B, 785 b. – ERMIÓNI: *Costa Perla,* B, 110 b. – PLÉPI: *Hydra Beach,* A, 516 b.; *Porto Hydra,* A, 456 b. – GALATÁS: *Stella Maris* Nautic Holiday Center, B, 176 b.; *Galatia,* C, 41 b.; *Papasotiriou,* C, 30 b.

The little port of Pórto Khéli lies in a large seaside holiday area near the southern tip of the Argolid peninsula, opposite the island of Spétsai.

Pórto Khéli

The holiday area begins at Sáladi, to the NW, continues with Pórto Khéli, Kósta, Petrothálassa, Ermióni and Plépi (opposite the island of Hýdra) and extends round to Galatás on the N coast (opposite the island of Póros).

Porto Rafti

ΠΟΡΤΟ ΡΑΦΤΗ

(Pórto Ráfti)

Nomos: Attica.
Altitude: 5 m (16 feet).

HOTELS. – PÓRTO RÁFTI: *Korali,* C, 28 b.; *Kyani Akti,* C, 47 b. – KAKÍ THÁLASSA (Keratéa): *Galini Bungalows,* A, 11 b.

Pórto Ráfti, a picturesque little port in a bay on the E coast of Attica, is

named after the large marble statue of the Roman period, popularly known as the "Tailor" (*raftis*) on a rocky islet outside the harbour.

HISTORY. – The predecessor of the present town in ancient times was *Prasiai*, on the hill of Koroni at the SE end of the bay, which played an important part in the shipping trade between Attica and the islands during the 7th and 6th c. B.C. The ancient town walls which can still be seen, however, date only from the 3rd c. B.C.

Pórto Yermenó

SURROUNDINGS. – There are a number of other ancient sites along the neighbouring coast. To the N of Pórto Ráfti bay was **Steiria**, to which a necropolis of the Mycenaean period in the Peráti district belonged (finds in museum at Brauron: see p. 105). Inland, at **Merénda**, a later cemetery (8th–4th c. B.C.) was found, together with a kouros and kore which are now in the National Archaeological Museum in Athens.

9 km (6 miles) N of Pórto Ráfti is **Brauron** (p. 105), with its sanctuary of Artemis.

9 km (6 miles) farther N is **Loútsa**, where, behind the dunes, a Doric temple of the 4th c. B.C. was discovered. It was probably the Temple of Artemis Tauropolos which according to Euripides was erected by Orestes after returning from Tauris with his sister Iphigeneia and landing at Brauron. Loútsa occupied the site of ancient *Halai Araphenides*, which is known from inscriptions to have been the scene of a festival of Artemis (the Tauropolia) and a festival of Dionysos.

9 km (6 miles) N of Loútsa is the port of **Rafína**, which preserves the name of ancient *Araphen*. Rafína is connected by local boats with *Marmári* and *Krýstos* on Euboea and with the islands of Ándros, Tínos, Kéa, Mýkonos and Sýros.

25 km (16 miles) S of Pórto Ráfti is **Kerátea** or *Kakí Thálassa*. To the left of the road to Lávrion is the site of ancient **Thorikós** (28 km – 17 miles), on a hill on the N side of Lávrion Bay, which was fortified in 490 B.C., during the Persian wars. There are the remains of two tholos tombs (between the two summits of the hill and on its eastern slope) belonging to the Mycenaean settlement. The most striking feature of the site is the *theatre* (5th–4th c. B.C.) associated with a sanctuary of Dionysos. It has a rather archaic air, since the orchestra is neither circular nor semicircular but almost rectangular and the auditorium also departs from the usual circular form. In front of the auditorium, to the left, is the site of a small *temple of Dionysos*; to the right are two earlier rock-cut chambers.

Porto Yermeno
ΠΟΡΤΟ ΓΕΡΜΕΝΟ
(Pórto Yermenó)

Nomos: Attica.
Altitude: 10 m (33 feet).

TRANSPORTATION. – Bus service from Athens.

HOTEL. – *Aegosthenion*, C, 154 b.

Pórto Yermenó is a village on the southern slopes of the Kithairon range at the NE corner of the Gulf of Corinth, with a broad sandy beach. It occupies the site of ancient Aigosthena, with fortifications which are a magnificent example of Greek defensive architecture of about 300 B.C.

Pórto Yermenó is reached from the Eleusis–Thebes road. 3 km (2 miles) beyond Inói, at the fortress of **Panakton** on the frontiers of Attica – whose walls of dressed stone, still standing to the height of the wall-walk, with towers and seven gates (after 346 B.C.), are impressive even when seen at some distance from the road – a side road branches off on the left and runs via Vília to **Pórto Yermenó** (23 km – 14 miles).

There are substantial remains of the ancient town – founded by Mégara to counter the Attic frontier fortress of Panakton – to the E of the village. The **acropolis** is surrounded by a double *wall* with towers at intervals of 48 m (157 feet), and a long stretch of defensive wall runs down from the NW corner to the sea. Within this wall are the remains of a five-aisled Early Christian *basilica*, over which a monastic church was later built. The walls are mostly constructed of polygonal blocks. The gateway of the acropolis is on the W side. Diagonally uphill from this, to the right, is the imposing *SE tower*, which rises 9 m (30 feet) above the acropolis walls.

Preveza
ΠΡΕΒΕΖΑ
(Préveza)

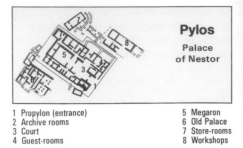

Pylos

Palace
of Nestor

1 Propylon (entrance)	5 Megaron
2 Archive rooms	6 Old Palace
3 Court	7 Store-rooms
4 Guest-rooms	8 Workshops

Nomos: Préveza.
Altitude: 10 m (33 feet). – Population: 13,000.

TRANSPORTATION. – Ferry to Áktion (35 times daily: tel. 22 22 6), where there is an airfield; boats to Lefkás.

HOTELS. – *Aktaeon*, C, 30 b.; *Dioni*, C, 57 b.; *Metropolis*, C, 23 b.; *Minos*, C, 36 b.

CAMPING SITE.

YACHT SUPPLY STATION.

SWIMMING. – S of the ferry station (sandy beach, backed by a small wood).

The port of Préveza is attractively situated on the N side of the entrance, only 350 m (1148 feet) wide, into the Gulf of Amvrakia (or of Árta).

HISTORY. – A town was founded on this site about 290 B.C. by King Pyrrhos of Epirus, who named it Berenikia after his mother-in-law Berenike, wife of the Egyptian ruler Ptolemy I. In 31 B.C. the battle of Aktion (Actium) was fought in the waters S of the town, and Octavian founded the town of Nikópolis (see p. 195) to commemorate the victory. In the late medieval period a new town was founded under the present name of Préveza, and in 1499 this town passed into the hands of Venice. From this period dates the castle which is the only substantial remnant of the town's former fortifications, and which affords an excellent general view of the gulf. In 1797, under the treaty of Campo Formio, the town passed from the Venetians to the French, but in the following year the French forces were driven out by Ali Pasha of Ioánnina. Préveza became part of Greece in 1912.

SURROUNDINGS. – 6 km (4 miles) N is **Nikópolis** (see p. 195), and 15 km (9 miles) away on the S side of the gulf **Vónitsa** (p. 225). – 20 km (12 miles) away is the island of **Lefkás** (p. 170).

Pylos
ΠΥΛΟΣ
(Pílos)

Nomos: Messenia.
Altitude: 20 m (66 feet). – Population: 4000.

TRANSPORTATION. – Buses from Kalamáta and Athens.

HOTELS. – *Nestor*, B, 30 b.; *Kastor*, B, 19 b.

The name of Pýlos summons up associations with the Mycenaean

hero Nestor, and the more recent memory of the naval battle of Navarino; but it also offers the attraction of some of the most fascinating scenery in Greece, in Navarino Bay.

Navarino Bay – the name is a corruption of the Byzantine phrase "ton Avarinon" ("of the Avars" – referring to the Slav invaders of Greece) – is the only large natural harbour on the W coast of the Peloponnese. It is enclosed on the seaward side by the island of **Sfaktiría**, a huge rocky barrier 4·6 km (3 miles) long and rising to a height of 135 m (443 feet). The main entrance to the bay, at the S end, is 1200 m (3937 feet) wide, but is constricted by the islet of **Pýlos** and a number of small reefs. The entrance at the N end is the Sykia Channel, only 100 m (328 feet) wide and much silted up, which runs between Sfaktiría and the 250 m (820 feet) high hill of Koryfásion, below which is the Osman Aga lagoon.

HISTORY. – The Mycenaean kingdom of Pylos was conquered by Neleus, and thereafter was ruled by his youngest son, Nestor. In 1939 Carl Blegen discovered at Epáno Englianós a site belonging to that period. – In the 7th–6th c. B.C. a Dorian settlement named Pýlos was established on Mt Koryfásion at the N end of the bay. In 425 B.C., during the Peloponnesian War, the town was occupied by the Athenians, who also captured the island of Sphakteria (Sfaktiría) and took its Spartan defenders prisoner. – In the 13th c. A.D. the Crusader Nicolas de Saint-Omer built a castle here (Palaiókastro, the "Old Castle"), which was later successively held by Venetians and Turks. In 1573 the Turks built a new castle (Neókastro) on the hill of Áyios Nikólaos at the S end of the bay, and in 1825 Ibrahim Pasha made this his headquarters during the war of liberation.

The present-day town of **Pýlos** grew up at the foot of the hill, on a site which had not been occupied in ancient times. Its most notable features are the *arcaded houses* in the Platía and the old *plane-tree* which gives shade to the square and the patrons of its coffee-houses and tavernas. The square is called the Platía Trión Navárkhon after the three commanders of the victorious allied fleet in the battle of

Navarino – the British Admiral Sir Edward Codrington, the French Admiral de Rigny and the Russian Count von Heyden – who are also commemorated by a monument on one side of the square. There are relics of the battle in the small *Museum* (on the way up to the castle), which also contains some very fine antiquities (pottery, gold jewellery).

The allied fleet sailed into Navarino Bay on 20 October 1827 to make a show of strength, but a shot fired by the Turkish and Egyptian fleet unleashed a battle which had not been intended by the allied governments and which ended in the destruction of 58 out of the 87 Turkish vessels. Their remains can be seen lying on the bottom of the bay when the sea is calm. The battle gave a decisive new impulse to the Greek war of liberation.

There are three *monuments* to those who fell in the battle – a British one on Khelonáki ("Tortoise Island") in the middle of the bay, a Russian one on the island of Sfaktiría and a French one on the little island of Pýlos.

SURROUNDINGS. – A motorboat can be taken to the island of **Sfaktiría**, on which, a short distance from the landing-stage at Panagoúla, is a chapel which was restored some years ago by the Soviet Union. – 12 km (7 miles) S is the Venetian fortress of **Methóni** (see p. 184). – The remains of a medieval castle built on ancient foundations can be seen on **Mt Koryfásion** (9 km (6 miles): ½ hour's climb; view). On the N side of the hill is the "Cave of Neleus"; at the foot is the site of the Mycenaean harbour.

The *Mycenaean palace at Epáno Englianós (18 km – 11 miles) is not so imposing as Mycenae or Tiryns, since it lacks their massive cyclopean walls – it is the only unfortified Mycenaean palace; but the layout is so clear and easy to follow that the site is a very rewarding one to visit. The whereabouts of Nestor's stronghold were the subject of dispute even in ancient times; but the American excavations in 1939 and since 1952 have suggested very strongly that the palace found here was indeed the home of the Homeric hero. The excavations brought to light some early remains dating from before 1300 B.C., an Old Palace (1280 B.C.) and a New Palace (1250 B.C.); destroyed between 1200 and 1190 – dates which fit in with the traditions about Neleus' conquest of the land, his palace and the palace of his son Nestor.

Parts of the **Old Palace** can be seen on the W side of the site. The plan of the **New Palace** is completely preserved, and the remains are now covered with a protective roof and labelled. The *Propylon*, beside which were archive rooms, leads into a court, beyond which is the central element in the palace, the *Megaron*, with two antechambers preceding the main hall (11·20 by 12·90 m (37 by 42 feet). In the centre of the hall is the circular hearth, 4 m (13 feet) in diameter, with painted stucco decoration; on the right-hand wall the position of the throne can be identified. A depression in the floor beside the throne was probably for libations. – On the right-hand side of the court is a propylon giving access to a corridor, in which are a staircase leading to the upper floor and *apartments for*

the queen, or possibly for guests. In one of the rooms is a small circular hearth, in another a terracotta *bathtub*. Other rooms alongside or beyond the megaron served as store-rooms (*pithoi for oil still in situ). – To the NE of the palace is a **tholos tomb**. At the foot of the palace hill the excavators found remains of the lower town and numbers of tombs. From in front of the palace there is a good view of the gentle green countryside extending to Navarino Bay.

Finds from the Palace of Nestor (tablets with inscriptions in Linear B, gold jewellery, fragments of fine wall paintings, pottery, etc.) can be seen in the village of **Khóra**, 3 km (2 miles) N.

Pýrgos
ΠΥΡΓΟΣ
(Pírghos)

Nomos: Elis.
Altitude: 23 m (75 feet). – Population: 23,000.

TRANSPORTATION. – Pýrgos is on the Peloponnese Railway line from Athens via Pátras to Kalamáta and on the branch line to Olympia and Katákolo. – Bus connections with Athens and Pátras.

HOTELS. – *Alkistis*, C, 55 b.; *Letrina*, C, 96 b.; *Olympos*, C, 71 b.

The busy commercial town of Pýrgos in the western Peloponnese is believed to occupy the site of ancient Letrinoi. Most visitors see it only on the way to Olympia, 21 km (13 miles) E.

The port of Pýrgos is **Katákolo**, 13 km (8 miles) W (sand and pebble beach), the site of the ancient port of *Pheia*, on the acropolis of which the Villehardouins built the castle known as Póndiko Kástro in the 13th c. There is good swimming N of Pýrgos in the direction of Kyllíni (see p. 166).

Rethymnon
PEΘYMNON
(Réthimnon)

Island: Crete. – Nomos: Réthimnon.
Telephone dialling code: 0831.
Altitude: 10 m (33 feet). – Population: 15,000.
(i) Tourist Police,
    Vas. Yeoryíou B 7;
    tel. 2 25 89.

TRANSPORTATION. – Bus connections with Iráklion and Khaniá.

HOTELS. – *El Greco*, A, 515 b.; *Rithymna*, A, 657 b.; *Ideon*, B, 193 b.; *Xenia*, B, 50 b.; *Brascos*, C, 151 b.; *Ionia*, C, 24 b.; *Minos*, C, 54 b.; *Park*, C, 18 b.; *Valari*, C, 55 b.

Réthymnon, lying on the N coast of Crete between Iráklion and Khaniá, is the island's third largest town and the centre of the nomos of Réthymnon.

The town's status as provincial capital during the Venetian period and (from 1645) under the Turks is reflected in its fortifications, various Venetian buildings, mosques and Turkish houses. The main features of interest are the *Loggia of the former Governor's Palace (museum), the *Arimondi Fountain* (1623), the Venetian church of **San Francesco** and a small *mosque* (18th c.) in the public gardens.

SURROUNDINGS. – 23 km (14 miles) SE, situated at an altitude of 500 m (1641 feet), is **Arkádi**, the most famous of all Cretan monasteries and a kind of national monument. When the monastery was under attack by Turkish troops on 8 November 1866 the Cretans who had taken refuge there, together with their wives and children, blew themselves up rather than face massacre and slavery. – The monastery church has a fine *Renaissance doorway* (1517).

A road runs S from Réthymnon via Spíli to **Ayía Galíni** on the S coast (61 km – 38 miles), from which it is possible to continue via Phaistós and Górtys to Iráklion (79 km (49 miles) from Ayía Galíni).

An interesting excursion can be made from this road. At **Melámpes**, 23 km (14 miles) S of Réthymnon, where the main road turns E, take a side road which runs S via **Koxaraí** and the **Kourtaliótiko Gorge** to Asómatos, and continue on a little country road to **Préveli monastery**, standing high above the S coast (40 km – 25 miles). The monastery, which was founded in the 17th c., can also be reached by bus (Réthymnon to Lefkóyia).

Rhamnous
ΡΑΜΝΟΥΣ
(Ramnús)

Region and nomos: Attica.

Rhamnoús is an ancient town and coastal stronghold on the NE coast of Attica, opposite the island of Euboea.

Rhamnoús is reached from Marathón by way of Káto Soúli (8 km – 5 miles), continuing past the turning for Ayía Marína (on right, 5 km – 3 miles) for another 2 km (1 mile).

TOUR OF THE SITE. – Approaching from the S, we come to the terrace of the **Sanctuary of Themis and Nemesis**, the goddesses of the legal order of things and of retribution. Immediately adjoining a **temple in antis** dedicated to Themis and built of polygonal limestone masonry (*c.* 500 B.C.), which housed a cult statue by Agorakritos, is the larger **Temple of Nemesis**, built in marble, a Doric peripteral temple with 6×12 columns which was begun about 430 B.C. but – as can be seen from the unfinished state of some of the columns – never completed. In front of this temple can be seen the *altar.* – From the temple terrace there are beautiful wide-ranging *views over the site of the ancient town, now largely overgrown by macchia, and across the gulf to the hills of Euboea.

Temple of Themis, Rhamnoús

A footpath flanked by *tombs* descends to the sea, above which rises the hill on which the **acropolis** was built. Remains of the *walls* can be seen on the E side, of a *theatre* on the seaward side.

Rhodes
ΡΟΔΟΣ
(Ródhos)

Nomos: Dodecanese. – Telephone dialling code: 0241.
Area: 1398 sq. km (540 sq. miles). – Population: 67,000.
ⓘ **Greek National Tourist Organisation (EOT)**,
  Makaríou/Papágou;
  tel. 2 36 35.
  KTEL (buses),
  Papágou 1.
  Olympic Airways,
  Ieroú Lókhou 9.

HEAD POST OFFICE. – Ieroú Lókhou/Eleftherías.

TRANSPORTATION. – Air connections with Athens, Iráklion, Kárpathos and Kos. – Served by boats on the

Piraeus–Cyclades–Rhodes, Piraeus–Crete–Rhodes and Rhodes–Sámos routes. – Boats to Kastellorízo, the most easterly Greek island.

HOTELS. – RHODES TOWN: *Grand Hotel Astir Palace, L, 698 b.; Belvedere, A, 322 b.; Blue Sky, A, 332 b.; Chairon Palace, A, 201 b.; Chevaliers' Palace, A, 284 b.; Ibiscus, A, 313 b.; Imperial, A, 151 b.; Kamiros, A, 90 b.; Mediterranean, A, 252 b.; Metropolitan Capsis, A, 1198 b.; Oceanis, A, 423 b.; Park, A, 153 b.; Regina, A, 144 b.; Riviera, A, 116 b.; Acandia, B, 150 b.; Aglaia, B, 206 b.; Alexia, B, 257 b.; Amphitryon, B, 188 b.; Angela, B, 118 b.; Athina, B, 267 b.; Cactus, B, 336 b.; Constantinos, B, 120 b.; Corali, B, 217 b.; Delphini, B, 135 b.; Despo, B, 122 b.; Esperia, B, 462 b.; Europa, B, 147 b.; Manusos, B, 204 b.; Olympic, B, 86 b.; Phoenix, B, 94 b.; Plaza, B, 244 b.; Poseidon, B, 63 b.; Spartalis, B, 141 b.; Thermai, B, 210 b.; Achillion, C, 94 b.; Adonis, C, 28 b.; Aegli, C, 69 b.; Africa, C, 144 b.; Als, C, 97 b.; Amaryllis, C, 75 b.; Ambassadeurs, C, 80 b.; Aphrodite, C, 77 b.; Arion, C, 72 b.; Astron, C, 82 b.; Atlantis, C, 26 b.; Caracas, C, 99 b.; Carina, C, 108 b.; Colossos, C, 99 b.; Diana, C, 52 b.; Diethnes, C, 78 b.; Egeon, C, 28 b.; El Greco, C, 140 b.; Elite, C, 86 b.; Embona, C, 30 b.; Flora, C, 148 b.; Florida, C, 36 b.; Galaxy, C, 71 b.; Helena, C, 163 b.; Hermes, C, 64 b.; Irene, C, 97 b.; Isabella, C, 76 b.; Laokoon, C, 63 b.; Lydia, C, 111 b.; Majestic, C, 147 b.; Mandraki, C, 20 b.; Marie, C, 109 b.; Mimosa, C, 129 b.; Minos, C, 135 b.; Moschos, C, 46 b.; New York, C, 43 b.; Nufara, C, 61 b.; Parthenon, C, 150 b.; Pavlidis, C, 96 b.; Perle, C, 70 b.; Petalouda, C, 75 b.; Phaedra, C, 98 b.; Royal, C, 80 b.; Saronis, C, 54 b.; Savoy, C, 87 b.; Semiramis, C, 230 b.; Soleil, C, 160 b.; Sylvia, C, 67 b.; Tilos, C, 39 b.; Vassillia, C, 77 b.; Vellois, C, 92 b.; Victoria, C, 70 b.; Villa Rhodos, C, 52 b.

NW COAST. – IXÍA (5 km – 3 miles): *Miramare Beach, L, 306 b.; *Rhodos Palace, L, 782 b.; Apollonia, A, 34 b.; Avra Beach, A, 353 b.; Bel Air, A, 293 b.; Dionysos, A, 507 b.; Elisabeth, A, 144 b.; Rhodos Bay, A, 611 b.; Leto, B, 184 b.; Solemar, B, 194 b. – TRIÁNDA (8 km – 5 miles): Electra Palace, A, 400 b.; Golden Beach, A, 431 b. – THEÓLOGOS (20 km – 12 miles): Iliovasilema, C, 18 b.

EAST COAST. – KALLITHÉA (4 km – 2 miles): Sunwing, A, 444 b. – RÉNI KOSKINI (6 km – 4 miles): Eden Roc, A, 712 b.; Paradisos, A, 355 b. – FALIRÁKI (13 km – 8 miles): Apollo Beach, A, 539 b.; Phaliraki Beach, A, 550 b.; Siravast, A, 170 b.; Blue Sea, B, 300 b.; Esperides, B, 578 b.; Dimitra, C, 50 b.; Lido, C, 38 b.; Sophia, C, 56 b. – AFÁNTOU (19 km – 12 miles): Xenia, B, 52 b.

ON MT PROFÍTIS ILÍAS: Elafos–Elafina, A, 127 b.

RESTAURANTS and coffee-houses are to be found in various places in the town of Rhodes – restaurants, for example, in the New Agora, coffee-houses in the tree-shaded square between the museum and Socrates Street.

ENTERTAINMENT. – Rhodes is well equipped to cater for tourists, with such events as the "Son et Lumière" shows given in summer in the gardens of the Grand Master's Palace and the wine festival at Rodíni in July and August.

The juxtaposition of remains and monuments dating from antiquity, the Byzantine period, the European Middle Ages and the centuries of Turkish rule, combined with beautiful scenery, a mild climate and a well-developed infrastructure of hotels and other facilities have made **Rhodes, the "Island of Roses", one of the great modern holiday and tourist centres. Within the town of Rhodes (between the town of the Knights and the northern tip of the island) and in the surrounding area one of Greece's largest concentration of hotels has grown up, and there are a total of over 23,300 beds for visitors on the island as a whole, some 13,500 of them in the town of Rhodes. Away from the main tourist attractions and the main built-up areas, however, the island is still relatively unspoiled, particularly in the S.

Rhodes – the largest of the Dodecanese and the fourth largest island in Greece after Crete, Euboea and Lésbos – is part of the island bridge which extends from the Peloponnese by way of Crete and Kárpathos to Asia Minor. It is only 20 km (12 miles) from the mainland of Asia Minor at its nearest point. 78 km (48 miles) long and up to 30 km (19 miles) wide, it is traversed by a long ridge of hills, with Mt Atávyros (1215 m – 3986 feet) as their highest point. The land falling gradually away to the coasts is fertile.

HISTORY. – About 1400 B.C. Mycenaean Greeks settled on the island, and about 1100 B.C. they were followed by Dorians, who established major centres at Kámeiros, Lindos and Ialysós. In 408 B.C. a unified state was established on the island, with the town of Rhodes as its capital. When the Rhodians successfully withstood an attack by the Macedonian king Demetrios Poliorketes in 305 B.C. they erected at the entrance to the harbour of Rhodes a 30 m (98 feet) high statue of the sun god by Chares, a pupil of Lysippos – the shortest-lived of the seven wonders of the world, which collapsed in an earthquake in 227 B.C. (It is certain that this statue did not stand – as it invariably does on souvenirs offered for sale in Rhodes – with its legs straddling the entrance to Mandráki harbour.) In the 2nd c. B.C. Rhodes became a centre of intellectual life, with a university which was attended in the following century by such Romans as Cicero, Caesar and Pompey. The Rhodian school of sculptors flourished in the 1st c. B.C., its best-known work being the Laokoon group (now in the Vatican) by Agesandros, Athenodoros and Polydoros.

A new era began for Rhodes in 1309, when the Order of St John established itself on the island after the loss of the Holy Land and made it a staging point on the pilgrim and trade route between Europe and the Levant. In 1522 the Knights were compelled to surrender to the Turks, and the 180 surviving knights, led by Grand Master Villiers de l'Isle-Adam, moved from Rhodes to Malta. Thus after a period of 200 years of European rule the island was under Turkish rule for

Entrance to the Mandráki Harbour, Rhodes, with the stag and the hind

390 years. It returned to European hands in 1912, when it passed to Italy. In 1947, together with the rest of the Dodecanese, it became part of Greece.

SIGHTS. – The main places of interest are the old town and acropolis of Rhodes, Líndos and its acropolis, the site of ancient Kámeiros and the acropolis of Ialysós, together with the numerous castles of the Knights and Orthodox chapels to be seen all over the island.

At the northernmost tip of the island is the town of **Rhodes** (pop. 33,000), capital of the island since 408 B.C. and now also chief town of the nomos of the Dodecanese. The ancient city, laid out on a rectangular grid in accordance with the principles developed by Hippodamos of Miletus, extended from the acropolis hill in the W to the E coast. The considerably smaller medieval town had many streets following the ancient layout (e.g. the Street of the Knights, and Homer, Hippodamos and Pythagoras streets). The Collachium (walled enclosure) of the Knights occupied the NW corner of the old town, the rest of which was occupied by Greeks. During the period of Ottoman rule the Greeks were expelled from the walled town; the western part was then occupied by Turks and the smaller eastern

part became the Jewish quarter, which survived until the Second World War.

Our tour of the town starts from *Freedom Square* (Platía Eleftherías), which lies between the town of the Knights and the hotel district. From the square we pass through a modern breach in the walls to see the remains of a **temple of Aphrodite** (3rd c. B.C.). Continuing straight ahead, we see on the right the large **Hospital of the Knights** (1440–89), a two-storied building laid out round a central courtyard which now houses the *Archaeological Museum.

From the courtyard we go up an outside staircase to the first floor, on which is the large *Infirmary Ward* (small chapel recess immediately opposite entrance; tombstones of knights). To the right is a room

Freedom Square, Rhodes

...taining finds from Ialysós, Kámeiros and other ...s, including two archaic *kouroi* (6th c. B.C.), and ...e *funerary stele of Krito and Tamariste* (end of 5th c. ...C.). In other rooms are a life-size *Aphrodite*, an expressive Hellenistic *head of Helios* and the well-known little *Kneeling Aphrodite* (1st c. B.C.). There is also a rich collection of *pottery* in the small rooms opening off the gallery round the central courtyard, covering all periods from Mycenaean times onwards and including some particularly fine examples of Rhodian ware.

From the museum we return to the *Street of the Knights* (Odos Ippotón), which since the removal of Turkish additions during the period of Italian occupation presents the picture of a *late Gothic street* such as can be seen nowhere else in Europe. The Order of St John was divided into national units or "Tongues", each with its own "Inn", and in the Street of the Knights can be seen the 15th and early 16th c. *Inns* of *Italy*, *France*, *Provence* (all on the right) and *Spain* (on left), just before an arch which spans the street. Just beyond the E end of the street is the Inn of *England*. To the N of the Street of the Knights the massive **Grand Master's Palace** was the Citadel of the town of the Knights. The present building is an Italian reconstruction. It now houses a collection of antiquities.

To the W of the palace stands the **Amboise Gate** (1512), an impressive demonstration of the Order's mastery of the art of fortification. Retracing our steps and turning S inside the walls, we come to a number of Turkish buildings – the *Clock Tower* (1852) of the **Suleyman Mosque** (built 1522, rebuilt 1808), the **Medresse Mosque** (with an interesting Turkish *library*) and the **Suleyman Baths**. In Socrates Street (Sokrátous), with its innumerable souvenir shops, we pass the *Aga Mosque*, projecting at an angle into the street. Bearing right at the end of the street, we see the 15th c. **Archbishop's Palace**, with the *Sea-horse Fountain* in front of it, the remains of a Gothic *church of Our Lady* and the imposing Gothic vaulting of the **Hospice of St Catherine** (1516).

From here we can return to Freedom Square either by the street which runs alongside the harbour outside the walls, passing the Marine Gate, or by the longer route through the old town and up Pythagoras Street (Pythagórou).

The district N of the old town, with many buildings dating from the period of Italian rule, is also of interest. Among its main features are the E breakwater of **Mandráki Harbour**, with its *windmills* and *Fort St Nicholas* (Áyios Nikólaos), the new *Market* with its tavernas, the Law Courts, the Post Office and the **church of St John**, transferred here from the Grand Master's Palace, which is now the Orthodox *Evangelismós church*. Beyond this are the **Governor's Palace**, in Venetian Gothic style, the **Turkish Cemetery**, with the elegant *funerary mosque of Murad Reis*, and the northern tip of the island, where the **Aquarium** is situated. – Every visitor should *walk round the walls* (guided walks daily in summer, usually about 3 p.m., starting from the Grand Master's Palace).

The ancient **Acropolis** lies SW of the old town (reached on foot or by bus). On the top of the hill, from which there are magnificent *views of the town, the island and the sea, one corner of the *Temple of Apollo* has been re-erected. Lower down, to the E, is an interesting group of structures comprising a small *"theatre"* (probably in fact an auditorium of some kind), largely rebuilt, and a *stadion*, both dating from the 2nd c. B.C.

EXCURSIONS ON THE ISLAND. – A road runs SE from the town of Rhodes to **Rodíni** (2 km – 1 mile), where a number of ancient tombs can be seen, including the so-called *Tomb of the Ptolemies*, a rock-cut chamber tomb of the Hellenistic period. Near the village is the little valley of Rodíni, which offers a pleasant walk. The road continues to **Kallithéa** (10 km – 6 miles), a popular spa and seaside resort, with attractive gardens laid out in 1935 (town buses).

Another road, of excellent quality, runs S to **Kolýmbia** (26 km – 16 miles). Beyond this, on a steep-sided hill overlooking the sea (off the road to the left), is

Governor's Palace, Rhodes

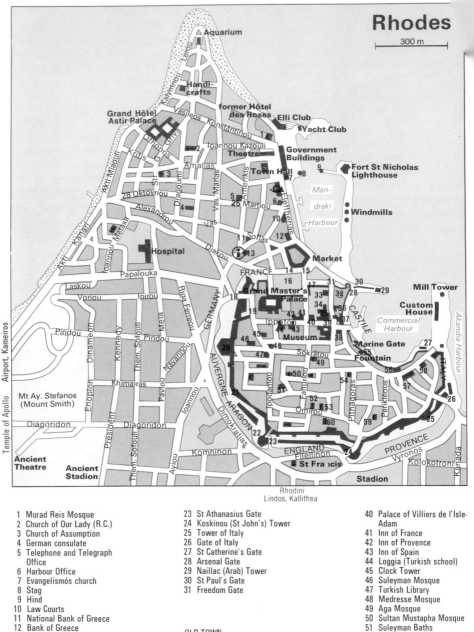

Rhodes

300 m

Key to numbered locations:

1 Murad Reis Mosque
2 Church of Our Lady (R.C.)
3 Church of Assumption
4 German consulate
5 Telephone and Telegraph Office
6 Harbour Office
7 Evangelismós church
8 Stag
9 Hind
10 Law Courts
11 National Bank of Greece
12 Bank of Greece
13 EOT, Tourist Police
14 Bus Station
15 Taxi stance
16 Son et Lumière
17 St Peter's Tower
18 Amboise Gate
19 Artillery Gate
20 St George's Tower
21 Tower of Spain
22 St Mary's Tower

23 St Athanasius Gate
24 Koskinou (St John's) Tower
25 Tower of Italy
26 Gate of Italy
27 St Catherine's Gate
28 Arsenal Gate
29 Naillac (Arab) Tower
30 St Paul's Gate
31 Freedom Gate

OLD TOWN

32 Temple of Aphrodite
33 Municipal Picture Gallery
34 Archaeological Institute
35 Museum of Decorative Art
36 Inn of Auvergne
37 Church of the Order of St John (museum)
38 Inn of England
39 Inn of Italy

40 Palace of Villiers de l'Isle-Adam
41 Inn of France
42 Inn of Provence
43 Inn of Spain
44 Loggia (Turkish school)
45 Clock Tower
46 Suleyman Mosque
47 Turkish Library
48 Medresse Mosque
49 Aga Mosque
50 Sultan Mustapha Mosque
51 Suleyman Baths
52 Church of Áyios Fanoúrios
53 Redjeb Pasha Mosque
54 Ibrahim Pasha Mosque
55 Commercial Tribunal
56 Archbishop's Palace
57 Church of Our Lady of the City
58 Hospice of St Catherine
59 Dolapli Mosque
60 Bourouzan Mosque

Tsambíkas monastery. At **Malóna** (39 km – 24 miles) a road goes off on the left to **Férakos Castle**, a stronghold of the Knights standing above the seashore. Beyond **Kálathos** (50 km – 31 miles) the road forks: the branch to the right runs down to the S end of the island, the one to the left leads to *Líndos (see p. 174), climbing to a saddle beyond which there is a superb view of the town and its acropolis lying across the bay.

The road which continues S from Kálathos comes in 16 km (10 miles) to a turning on the right which leads to **Asklipió** (5 km – 3 miles), which has a *church with notable frescoes, and beyond this to **Yennádi** (20 km – 12 miles),

View towards the Acropolis of Líndos

Lakhaniá (29 km – 18 miles) and Kattaviá (41 km – 25 miles).

A road follows the W coast from the town of Rhodes, coming in 8 km (5 miles) to Triánda, where the road to Ialysós (p. 139) branches off on the left. Beyond Paradísi (17 km – 11 miles) another road goes off on the left to the famous Valley of Butterflies (Petaloúdes). At Kalavárda (30 km – 19 miles) a road on the right leads to the site (on left, above the road) of Kámiros (34 km (21 miles): see p. 151), the third of the ancient cities on Rhodes.

From Kalavárda a road leads inland to Mt Profítis Ilías (52 km (32 miles): 798 m (2618 feet)), a summer resort, from which it is possible to continue E to Eleoúsa and Dimiliá, where the *Foundouklí Chapel, with frescoes of the 13th–14th c., can be visited. – Another road runs S to Mt Atávyros (1215 m – 3986 feet), with the typical Rhodian village of Embónas (alt. 430 m (1411 feet), pop. 1200), and Monólithos (50 km (31 miles): alt. 290 m (951 feet), pop. 500), with an imposing castle of the Knights SW of the village. The road then continues to Apolakiá (62 km – 39 miles) and Kattaviá (79 km – 49 miles), in the extreme S of the island, where it joins the road which runs N via Kálathos to the town of Rhodes.

From Rhodes there is a weekly boat to Meyísti (Kastellorízo), Greece's most easterly island (pop. 500), lying off the S coast of Asia Minor. It has a medieval castle which was rebuilt by the Knights of St John.

Rion
PION
(Ríon)

Region: Peloponnese. – Nomos: Achaea.

HOTELS. – ALONG THE GULF COAST. – RÍON: Averof Grand Hotel, A, 493 b.; Rhion Beach (1 km – about a ½ mile), C, 164 b.

CAMPING SITE. – ARAKHOVITIKÁ (3 km (2 miles) E): Alexander Beach, B, 212 b. – PSATHÓPYRGOS (9 km (6 miles) E): Florida, B, 156 b.

Ríon, 6 km (4 miles) NE of Pátras, owes its importance to its situation at the narrowest point of the Gulf of Corinth, the "Little Dardanelles", opposite Antírrion, only 2 km (1 mile) away on the N side of the gulf. It is a busy ferry station linking the Peloponnese with the mainland of Greece (96 crossings daily).

Beside the landing-stage is the Kástro Moréas (16th c.), which along with the Kástro Roumélis at Antírrion controlled the entrance to the gulf.

Salamis
ΣΑΛΑΜΙΣ
(Salamís)

Nomos: Attica. – Telephone dialling code: 01. Area: 95 sq. km (37 sq. miles). – Population: 23,700.

TRANSPORTATION. – Ferries from Pérama (50 services daily), 13 km (8 miles) from the centre of Athens, and from Néa Péramos, E of Mégara.

HOTELS. – EÁNTION: Gabriel, C, 40 b. – SELINIÁ: Selinia, C, 92 b.

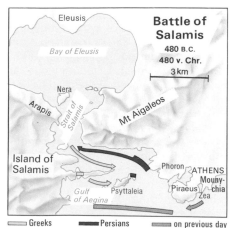

The island of Salamís, lying close to the mainland of Attica, shuts off the Bay of Eleusis, which can be entered only through two narrow channels. The famous naval battle of Salamis (480 B.C.) took place in the more easterly of these channels. This limestone island, with hills rising to 404 m (1326 feet) and a deeply indented gulf on the W side, has little arable land. It is now involved in the rapid growth of the Athens region.

Salamís

HISTORY. – Probably first settled by Phoenicians, Salamis took part in the Trojan War under its king Aias (Ajax), son of Telamon. Another of Telamon's sons, Teukros, was believed to be the founder of the town of Salamis at the E end of Cyprus, which he named after his native island. The island was conquered by Athens in the time of Solon or Peisistratos. The naval battle fought in September 480 B.C. in the narrow strait, in which the large Persian vessels were unable to manoeuvre, was a powerful vindication of Themistokles' strategy and heralded the splendid flowering of classical culture in the 5th c. Aeschylus took the battle as the theme of his topical tragedy "The Persians", which was performed in Athens for the first time eight years later, in 472 B.C.

SIGHTS. – The ferry from Pérama passes through the waters in which the battle took place, with Xerxes watching from a throne set up on the mainland. 3 km (2 miles) from the landing-stage at Paloukiá, at the head of the deep bay on the W side of the island, is the chief town, Salamís (pop. 12,000), with the church of Panayía tou Katharoú. 6 km (4 miles) W of the town is the Faneroméni monastery, founded in 1661, in the building of which material from an ancient sanctuary was used. The church contains frescoes of 1735. – The road continues to the NW tip of the island, where the ferry from Néa Péramos puts in.

Salonica
ΘΕΣΣΑΛΟΝΙΚΗ
(Thessaloníki)

Nomos: Salonica. – Telephone dialling code: 031.
Altitude: 15 m (49 feet). – Population: 500,000.

ⓘ Greek National Tourist Organisation (EOT),
Aristotélous 8;
tel. 27 18 88.
Tourist Police,
Egnatías 10.

British CONSULATE: Vas. Konstantínou 11.

HEAD POST OFFICE: Megálou Alexándrou 8.

TRANSPORTATION. – Salonica has a direct air connection with London, and with Athens, Alexandroúpolis, Ioánnina and Lemnos; it is a station on the (Belgrade–)Évzoni–Athens and Salonica–Alexandroúpolis(–Istanbul) railway lines; and it has bus connections with Athens, Ierissós (Athos), Kavála, Édessa and other towns in the surrounding area.

HOTELS. – *Makedonia Palace, Leofóros Megálou Alexándrou, L, 542 b.; Capitol, Monastiríou 8, A, 353 b.; Electra Palace, Pl. Aristotélous 6A, A, 230 b.; Astor, Tsimiskí 20, B, 159 b.; Capsis, Monastiríou 28, B, 823 b.; City, Komnínon 11, B, 178 b.; Egnatia, Leóntos Sófou, B, 277 b.; El Greco, Egnatía 23, B, 162 b.; Elisabeth, Monastiríou 292, B, 40 b.; Metropolitan, Vasílissis Olgas 65, B, 224 b.; Olympic, Egnatía 25, B, 104 b.; Palace, Tsimiskí 12, B, 83 b.; Philippion, Antheón, B, 174 b.; Queen Olga, Vas. Olgas 44, B, 261 b.; Rotonda, Monastiríou 97, B, 142 b.; Victoria, Langadá, B, 127 b.; A.B.C., Angeláki 41, C, 208 b.; Aegeon, Egnatía 19, C, 112 b.; Amalia, Ermoú 33, C, 124 b.; Anessis, 20 Oktovríou 20, C, 72 b.; Ariston, Diikitiríou 5, C, 61 b.; Continental, Komnínon 5, C, 59 b.; Delta, Egnatía 13, C, 217 b.; Emborikon, Sýngrou 14, C, 63 b.; Esperia, Olýmpou 58, C, 132 b.; Grande Bretagne, Egnatía 46, C, 77 b.; Mandrino, Antigonídon 2, C, 136 b.; Minerva, Sýngrou 12, C, 74 b.; Olympia, Olympou 65, C, 177 b.; Park, Ionos Dragoúmi 81, C, 105 b.; Pella, Ionos Dragoúmi 61, C, 118 b.; Rea, Komnínon 6, C, 55 b.; Rex, Monastiríou 39, C, 111 b.; Teloni, Ayíou Dimitríou 16, C, 120 b.; Thessalikon, Egnatía 66, C, 53 b.

YOUTH HOSTELS: Platía X.A.N. and Ayía Sofía 11.

CAMPING SITE.

YACHT SUPPLY STATION.

ON THE THERMAIC GULF. – ARÉTSOU (3 km – 2 miles): Aceanis, C, 30 b. – NÉA EPIVÁTai (10 km – 6 miles): Europa House, C, 36 b. – MIKRÁ (13 km – 8 miles): Haris, B, 30 b. – PERÉA (18 km – 11 miles): Lena, B, 80 b.; Aegli, C, 18 b. – AYÍA TRIÁS (25 km – 16 miles): Sun Beach, B, 200 b.; Aegeon, C, 14 b.; Galaxy, C, 152 b.; Riviera, C, 12 b.

CAMPING SITE. – PANÓRAMA (10 km (6 miles) away in the hills E of Arétsou, alt. 340 m (1116 feet)): Nephele, A, 130 b.; Panorama, A, 85 b.; Pefka, C, 104 b.

Salonica, situated on the Thermaic Gulf, is Greece's second largest city, the capital of Macedonia, a university town and the see of a metropolitan. It is an important port and commercial city, noted for its international trade fair, and is also of great historical and artistic interest with its many Byzantine churches.

HISTORY. – The town was founded by Kassandros in 315 B.C. near the old settlement of Thermai and named after his wife Thessalonike, sister of Alexander the Great. During the Middle Ages it was the second city of the Byzantine Empire, but suffered a succession of heavy blows when it was taken by the Saracens (904), who carried off 20,000 Greeks into slavery, by the Normans (1085) and by the Turks (1430), who expelled or exterminated the Greek population. About 1600 some 20,000 Spanish Jews established themselves in the town. During the 18th c. Greeks began to return to the town, which was finally liberated from the Turks on 8 November 1912, when Greek forces led by Crown Prince Constantine marched in. In 1913 King George I was assassinated in Salonica. In 1915 an Allied expedition occupied the town, in which Venizelos set up a government pledged to carry on the war against Germany. In 1917 there was a disastrous fire in which the lower town, extending uphill to the church of St Demetrius, was destroyed. After the First World War the city began to take on its present-day aspect, following its rebuilding in modern style to the designs of Hébrard, the expulsion of the Turkish population and a great influx of refugees from Asia Minor. During the Second World War the city was under German occupation, and few of its Jews of Spanish origin survived. After the war the economy of Salonica was damaged by the closing of the frontiers to the N, but later the success of the autumn trade fair brought a considerable economic upswing. In 1978 an earthquake caused substantial damage.

In spite of the vicissitudes of history Salonica has preserved many ancient and historic buildings, covering the development of church architecture from the 5th c. onwards. To the 1st–3rd c. belong the forum, the Roman baths, and a nymphaeum; to the period around A.D. 300 the Rotunda, the Arch of Galerius and the palace of Galerius; about 400 the conversion of the Rotunda into the church of St George; to the 5th c. the churches of Áyios Dimítrios, Ayía Paraskeví and Ósios David; to the 7th the rebuilding of Áyios Dimítrios; to the 8th

White Tower, Salonica

Ayía Sofía; to the 11th Panayía Khalkéon; to the 13th Ayía Ekateríni; to the 14th the Áyii Apóstoli, Áyios Nikólaos, Áyios Ilías, the monastery of Vlatádon and the church of the Metamórphosis.

SIGHTS. – In *Egnatía Street* is the *Arch of Galerius, with carvings depicting the emperor's campaigns against the Persians (A.D. 297). It originally consisted of two rows of four piers, the four central piers being covered with a dome. To the S were the Imperial Palace and the Hippodrome (the scene of a great massacre in A.D. 391 for which the Emperor Theodosius I was taken to task by Ambrose, bishop of Milan). From the arch a colonnaded street ran N for 100 m (328 feet) to the Rotunda, built as a mausoleum for Galerius. About 400 it was converted into a Christian church dedicated to St George, with mosaic decoration; during the Turkish period it became a mosque; and it is now a museum. The building, 24 m (79 feet) in diameter, still preserves the remains of fine *mosaics* in the dome and the recesses in the walls. The mosaic in the centre of the dome is missing, but below it can be seen the figures of angels, and below these again architectural façades on a gold ground.

Egnatía Street runs into Queen Sophia Avenue (Leofóros Vasílissis Sofías), which leads down to the White Tower (Turkish, 16th c.) on the seafront. In the adjoining gardens is the *Archaeological Museum, with a varied collection of material from Salonica itself, Macedonia and Thrace.

Arch of Galerius and Rotunda, Salonica

Among items of particular interest are an **arch** from the Octagon of Galerius; a *kouros* and the *torso of a kore* from Thrace (6th c. B.C.); a *vase from Pélla (4th c. B.C.) with *figures of Amazons*; a **bronze krater** from Dervéni (end of 4th c. B.C.); Roman *statues and portraits of Emperors* (Augustus, Vespasian, Septimius Severus); and a *bronze hand* (with pine-cones, snakes and lizards) from a figure of the Phrygo-Thracian vegetation god Sabazios. A particular attraction since 1978 has been the collection of **finds from the Macedonian royal tombs* at Vérgina (see p. 253).

From the White Tower Pávlou Méla Street leads to the church of **Ayía Sofía**, an early form of domed cruciform church (8th c.) which in the 9th c., after the end of the conflict over the worship of icons, was decorated with new figural *mosaics*. They include a figure of the Mother of God Platytéra in the apse, replacing an earlier cross, and a magnificent representation of the Ascension in the dome.

To the N of this church, on the far side of Egnatía Street, is the Early Christian basilica of **Ayía Paraskeví** (5th c.), occupying the site of an earlier Roman villa, a *mosaic pavement* from which can be seen the N aisle. Going W along Egnatía Street, we come to the church of **Panayía Khalkéon** (1028; restored in recent years), the church of the Mother of

God of the Coppersmiths, which stands in the old coppersmiths' quarter. From here we turn uphill past the *Agora* of the Roman period to reach the town's principal church, ***Áyios Dimítrios**. This five-aisled basilica is built over a Roman *bath-house*, remains of which can be seen to the N of the church, and a stretch of Roman road which is visible in the crypt. The church was known until the 9th c. as the "church by the Stadion" (which lay close by). Investigations from 1917 onwards confirmed the tradition that the Emperor Galerius caused an officer named Demetrius to be confined in the baths and subsequently killed (306). Thereafter St Demetrius quickly became the town's principal saint and patron. The basilica was originally built in the 5th c., and the general plan of this first church was preserved in a 7th c. rebuilding after a fire and in the reconstruction carried out from 1917 onwards. At the SE corner is the chapel of *Áyios Efthymios* (St Euthymius), added in 1303.

Passing through the narthex, we enter the nave. Immediately on the left is a chapel marking the supposed position of the saint's tomb. The church is of impressive spatial effect, even though little of the original material was used in the 20th c. rebuilding (e.g. some of the capitals). Fortunately some of the

Salonica
(Thessaloniki)

|— 400 m —|

old *mosaics* have been preserved. At the W end of the inner lateral aisle on the S side is a 5th c. *head of St Demetrius*, and there are a number of * *7th c. figures* – on the NE pier Demetrius with two children, on the SE pier St Sergius (martyred in Syria in 307), St Demetrius between Bishop John and Leontios (the governor responsible for the 7th c. rebuilding), and Demetrius with a deacon. – In the chapel of St Euthymius are * *wall paintings* dating from the original building (1303), probably by Manuel Panselinos, the leading representative of the "Macedonian school" of painting. – The **Crypt** is built on the Roman ground level. Here can be seen part of a fountain which dispensed holy water to pilgrims.

There are more churches in the picturesque maze of narrow streets and alleys of the *upper town* which also contains the *birthplace of Atatürk*. Among them are **Ayía Ekateríni** (13th c.); **Profítis Ilías** (14th c.); the small square domed church of **Ósios David** (5th c.), with a * *mosaic* of the vision of Ezekiel; and **Vlatádon monastery**, immediately adjoining the Citadel (views of the town and the Thermaic Gulf). The **Citadel**, with seven towers which earned it the Greek name of Eptapýrgion and the Turkish name of Yedikule, is an imposing stronghold, with walls standing 10·50 m (34 feet) high. The highest tower, in the centre, was built by the Turks in 1431, a year after their capture of the town. – Considerable stretches of the *town walls*, which abut the Citadel at both ends, have been preserved, and a walk along these walls will take the visitor into some interesting old parts of the town.

SURROUNDINGS. – There are many attractive holiday resorts around the Thermaic Gulf within easy reach of Salonica, and also on the higher ground a little way inland (e.g. *Panórama*). There are other resorts on the W coast of the Thermaic Gulf (see p. 248).

Samaria Gorge

ΦΑΡΑΓΓΙ ΤΗΣ ΣΑΜΑΡΙΑΣ

(Farángi tis Samariás)

Island: Crete. – Nomos: Khaniá.

The ****Samariá Gorge is the best known and the most impressive of the many gorges which slash the limestone mountains of Crete.**

18 km (11 miles) long and at its narrowest point no more than 4 m (13 feet) wide, the

Samariá Gorge

gorge extends between rock faces up to 600 m (1969 feet) high from the Ómalos plateau in the N to the sea in the S. It is possible to travel by road (bus services) from Khaniá to Khóra Sfakíon, take a boat from there to Ayía Roúmeli, walk up into the gorge and then return by the same route. The following circular tour, however, is recommended.

From **Khaniá** a road runs SW via **Fournés** (15 km – 9 miles) and **Lákki** (9 km (6 miles): but service as far as here) to the *Ómalos plateau* (15 km (9 miles): 1050 m (3445 feet)). 7 km (4 miles) S of the village of Ómalos (Xenia tourist pavilion, B, 7 b.), at a height of 1200 m (3937 feet), a path zigzags its way down into the gorge. The walk through the gorge to the S end takes something like 6 hours, and those who undertake it must be properly shod and equipped. After reaching the bottom of the gorge the track follows a small stream, which must be frequently crossed. At the abandoned village of Samariá the narrowest part of the gorge begins, as the rock faces come increasingly close together. The gorge ends at the village of **Ayía Roúmeli**, with a 16th c. church of the Panayía on the site of a temple of Apollo belonging to the Dorian town of *Tarrha* (of which remains dating from the Hellenistic period have been found). On the beach, a quarter of an hour's walk below the village, are a number of other houses and a taverna (bathing).

From Ayía Roúmeli it is 2 hours by boat to **Khóra Sfakíon** (Xenia Hotel, B, 23 b.). There is also a footpath (for tough and fit walkers only!) by way of the churches of **Áyios Pávlos** and **Áyios Ioánnis** (near which is the "Dragon s Cave"), the village and gorge of Arádena and the village of **Anópolis**, above the ancient port of *Phoenix*. From Khóra Sfakíon the return to Khaniá is by road (service bus).

Two or three days should be allowed for the complete round trip, though the travel agencies offer a "package" covering the whole trip in a very long day.

Samos
ΣΑΜΟΣ
(Sámos)

Nomos: Samós. – Telephone dialling code: 0273.
Area: 476 sq. km (184 sq. miles). – Population:
32,600.
ⓘ **Olympic Airways,**
Odós Sofoúli
(beside the Xenia Hotel).

TRANSPORTATION. – Air connections with Athens;
boats between Piraeus–Sámos and Sámos–Rhodes.

HOTELS. – SÁMOS: *Xenia*, B, 46 b.; *Sámos*, C, 160 b.;
Surf Side, C, 56 b.

NORTH COAST. – KOKKÁRI (10 km – 6 miles): *Kokkari
Beach*, C, 90 b.; *Tsamadou*, C, 34 b.; *Venus*, C, 88 b. –
AVLÁKIA (18 km – 11 miles): *Avlakia*, C, 18 b. –
KARLÓVASI: (36 km – 22 miles): *Merope*, B, 152 b.

SOUTH COAST. – PYTHAGÓRION: *Doryssa Bay*, B, 334 b.;
Damo, C, 19 b.; *Dolphin*, C, 18 b.; *Polykrates*, C, 16 b.;
Pythagoras, C, 55 b. – There are also hotels of
category D at Iraíon, Marathókambos and Pýrgos.

BATHING BEACHES. – In Iangou Bay 1·5 km (1 mile)
E of the town of Sámos (town bus); on the N coast at
Áyios Konstantínos (sand) and Karlóvasi (pebble); on
the S coast at Pythagórion, near the Heraion (Iraíon)
and at Marathókambos.

The island of *Sámos has other
attractions as well as the wines for
which it is famed. It is a green, well-
wooded island, still little affected by
mass tourism, and it possesses the
site of one of the most important
sanctuaries and cultural centres of
the ancient world, the Heraion.
Geographically an outlier of Asia
Minor, from which it is separated by
a strait only 2 km (1 mile) wide,
Sámos rises in the centre to 1140 m
(3740 feet) (Mt Ámpelos) and in the
W to 1440 m (4725 feet) (Mt Kérkis).**

HISTORY. – Traces of human habitation on Sámos go
back to the 3rd millennium B.C. In the 11th c. B.C. it was
occupied by incomers from Ionia. The period of rule of
the tyrant Polykrates (538 or 532 to 522 B.C.) is
memorable not only for the great Temple of Hera and
the aqueduct constructed by Eupalinos but also for
the poet Anakreon and the philosopher Pythagoras.
The island became a member of the Attic maritime
league in 477 B.C., but having rebelled against Athens
it was conquered by Perikles in 439 B.C. and the town
razed to the ground. Thereafter it was a place of no
importance. In 190 B.C. Sámos became part of the
kingdom of Pergamon; in 133 B.C. it passed under
Roman rule. It belonged to Rome and subsequently to
Byzantium until 1207, when it passed to Venice. Later
it fell to Genoa, and from 1453 to 1912 was under
Turkish rule. During the last 80 years of this period,
however, Turkish control was purely nominal, for from
1832 onwards the island enjoyed autonomy under

Greek Princes of Sámos. A rising organised by
Themistoklis Sofoúlis led to its reunion with Greece in
1912.

SIGHTS. – The capital of the island since
1832 has been the town of **Sámos**, which
was founded in that year and later
amalgamated with the older town of
Vathý. It now has a population of 8000. It
has an attractive square and picturesque
little streets climbing the slopes of the hill.
The ***Museum** contains material recovered by the German excavators of the
Heraion from 1910 onwards.

In the room to the left are the base and three of the
original six figures of a group by the Archaic sculptor
Geneleos (*c.* 560 B.C.). To the right is sculpture of the
Hellenistic and Roman periods. On the upper floor are
prehistoric material, pottery ranging from the Geometric to the classical period and some very fine
ivories and bronzes.

The friendly little port of **Pythagórion** or
Tigáni (11 km (7 miles) from Sámos: bus
service) occupies the site of the ancient
city of *Sámos*. There are remains of *town
walls* of the 4th c. B.C., and the foundations of the breakwater are also ancient.
On the site of the ancient *acropolis*, near
the cemetery, are the **Metamórfosis
church** and a **castle** built by Lykoúrgos
Logothetis (1822–24). Nearby is the site
of a Hellenistic villa, over which a
Christian basilica was built in the 5th c.
No structures belonging to the ancient
acropolis have been found. In the eastern
part of the site of the ancient city is the
monastery of **Panayía Spilianí**, below
which, reached on a signposted path, is a
depression marking the site of a theatre.
Farther W is the entrance to a ***tunnel**
1 km long carrying a water channel,
constructed by Eupalinos in the 6th c. B.C.
It is 1·75 m (6 feet) high and wide and has
been made passable for visitors. 425 m
(465 yards) from the S entrance can be
seen the spot where the two shafts, one
driven from each side, met one another,
making an almost perfect join.

On the island of Sámos

To the W is the Heraion (8 km (5 miles) from Pythagórion, 19 km (12 miles) from Sámos). Here, according to an ancient tradition, the Ionian settlers led by Prokles found at the mouth of the River Imbrasos a wooden image concealed among the branches of a willow tree. Recognising it as a cult image of the goddess Hera, they erected an altar beside the tree, and this was followed by others. The seventh was the *Altar of Rhoikos (c. 550 B.C.: partly rebuilt), which in size and magnificence was to be surpassed only by the Great Altar of Pergamon. – To the W of the altar is the **Temple of Hera**. The modest wooden Temple I (first half of 8th c. B.C.) and Temple II (after 670 B.C.) were succeeded by a colossal stone structure, Temple III, built by Rhoikos and Theodoros in 570–550 B.C. This covered an area of 105 by 52·5 m (345 by 172 feet) and had a double row of Ionic columns 18 m (59 feet) high, 104 in all. Soon afterwards this temple was destroyed by fire, and Polykrates thereupon commissioned a replacement, Temple IV. With an area of 112·20 by 55·16 m (368 by 181 feet), this was the largest temple ever designed by Greek architects, but – like other gigantic Ionic temples – it remained unfinished. Nothing of this temple now survives but its massive foundations and a single column. Finally a small peripteral temple of 4×6 columns was built close to the altar to house the cult image (Temple V).

The high water table made excavation difficult, but the work of E. Buschor and his successors has made it possible to follow the development of the sanctuary in detail. In 1963 the excavators even brought to light the remains of the ancient willow-tree. Near the site of the temples can be seen the apse of an Early Christian church. To see some of the other remains in the area, however – such as the basin in which the image of Hera was annually bathed – it is necessary to have either a knowledgeable guide or a good plan of the site.

The return to Sámos is either via Pythagórion or by way of the medieval capital of **Khóra** (7·5 km (5 miles) from the Heraion) and **Mytilíni** (10·5 km (7 miles): pop. 5000).

The road from the town of Sámos along the N coast, which is mostly fringed by cliffs, comes in 10·5 km (7 miles) to the little port of **Kokkári**. About half way there, near a *chapel of Ayía Paraskeví* to the right of the road, is a modest Early Christian *baptistery*. Beyond Avlákia (20 km – 12 miles) a road goes off on the left to **Vourliótes** (3 km – 2 miles), from which it is 2 km (1 mile) to the **Vrontianí monastery** (founded 1566), on the northern slopes of Mt Ámpelos. The coast road continues to **Áyios Konstantínos** (26 km – 16 miles) and **Karlóvasi** (32 km (19 miles): pop. 5000), a port at which the regular boats call (as well as Vathý). From here there is an attractive return route to Sámos through the beautiful hilly country in the interior of the island, passing through *Pýrgos*, *Koumaradéi* and *Khóra*.

There are a number of other monasteries on the island, including **Zoodókhos Piyí**, 8 km (5 miles) E of Sámos (founded 1756: wide views), **Profítis Ilías**, 4 km (2 miles) S of Karlóvasi (founded 1625) and **Stavrós**, 3 km (2 miles) E of Khóra (founded 1586).

Samothrace
ΣΑΜΟΘΡΑΚΗ
(Samothráki)

Nomos: Évros.
Area: 178 sq. km (69 sq. miles). – Population: 3000.

TRANSPORTATION. – Boats from Piraeus to Lemnos, Samothrace and Alexandroúpolis; ferry from Alexandroúpolis.

HOTELS. – KAMARIÓTISSA: *Akrophiali*, C, 26 b.; *Ilios*, E, 7 b. – PALAIÓPOLIS: *Xenia*, B, 12 b.

*Samothrace, lying 40 km (25 miles) off the Thracian coast, is the most northerly outpost of the Greek archipelago. From its highest peak (Mt Fengári, 1600 m (5250 feet)), according to Homer, Poseidon watched the fighting at Troy. Lying by itself in a sea without any neighbouring islands, it is an island of great scenic beauty which is noted particularly for its sanctuary of the Great Gods, the home of a mystery cult, and for the "Victory of Samothrace" which was found here and is now in the Louvre.

HISTORY. – As its name ("Thracian Sámos") indicates, Samothrace was originally populated by Thracians, who founded the sanctuary of the Great Gods here. About 700 B.C. the first Greeks arrived on the island, and thereafter the sanctuary grew and developed: until the 1st c. B.C., however, Thracian remained the cult language. In the 4th c. B.C. Philip II of Macedon was initiated into the mysteries, and it is said that he met his wife Olympias here. From the early 3rd c., when Ptolemy II and his sister Arsinoe erected splendid new buildings in the sanctuary, the cult spread widely through the Hellenistic world. Under the Romans (168 B.C. onwards) the cult of Cybele which had originated in Asia Minor became associated with that of the Great Gods. Only the spread of Christianity put an end to the cult, about A.D. 400; but the town of Palaiópolis, immediately W of the sanctuary, was inhabited until the 15th c.

Excavations by French and Austrian archaeologists in the 19th c. and more recent American excavations (Karl and Phyllis Lehmann, 1948 onwards) have brought to light impressive remains of the sanctuary and have thrown some light on the mysteries practised there; but our knowledge of the cult remains imperfect, partly because of the secrecy maintained by the adepts and partly because the remains have been overlaid by the deposits left by many subsequent centuries.

The Kabeiroi, formerly thought to be the deities to whom the sanctuary was dedicated, were not the only objects of worship there. A central position among the Great Gods, who are referred to in inscriptions, was occupied by the Thracian mother goddess Axieros as mistress of nature. Associated with her were Axiersos and Axiersa, two divinities of the underworld who were identified by the Greeks with Pluto and Persephone, the youthful vegetation god Kadmilos and the two Kabeiroi. They were revered as the protectors of nature, and later increasingly as patrons of shipping and rescuers of those in peril on the sea. Initiation into the mysteries, which took place in two stages, was open to both Greeks and non-Greeks, men and women, free men and slaves – a factor which no doubt facilitated the later diffusion of the cult.

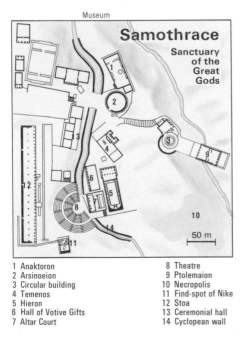

1 Anaktoron
2 Arsinoeion
3 Circular building
4 Temenos
5 Hieron
6 Hall of Votive Gifts
7 Altar Court
8 Theatre
9 Ptolemaion
10 Necropolis
11 Find-spot of Nike
12 Stoa
13 Ceremonial hall
14 Cyclopean wall

SIGHTS. – The main feature of interest on the island is the Sanctuary of the Great Gods. The *town walls* of **Palaiópolis** are also well worth seeing, and **Mt Fengári** offers a rewarding *climb. The chief place on the island, **Khóra** (pop. 1500), a picturesque little medieval village, lies in a fold in the hills 5 km (3 miles) SE of the tiny port of **Kamariótissa** (pop. 280), where there are eating places and coffee-houses.

The ***Sanctuary of the Great Gods** lies on the N coast 6 km (4 miles) E of Kamariótissa. A chapel dedicated to Ayía Paraskeví and the towers of a castle of the Gattelusi family on the slopes of the hill mark the site of the ancient *harbour* (shingle beach).

The *excavations* lie 500 m (547 yards) inland. From the museum (behind the Xenia hotel and restaurant) a signposted path runs SE, passes through a wooden gate, crosses the middle one of three streams which traverse the hilly terrain and after passing a viewpoint comes to the first large structure on the site, the **Anaktoron** or "House of the Masters" (i.e. the gods), which dates from about 550 B.C. Here the worshippers received the first degree of initiation (*myesis*). The northern part of the building, the holy of holies, was closed off; in the SE corner was a walled *libation pit*. Immediately S, on a higher level, is the "**Sacristy**" in which registers of the initiates were maintained. Then comes the *Arsinoeion, the largest roofed rotunda of Greek antiquity, built by Arsinoe (later Queen Arsinoe II of Egypt) between 289 and 281 B.C. It occupies the site of an earlier cult building, now represented by walls and a *rock altar* dating from Greek and pre-Greek (Thracian) times which were found within the Arsinoeion. On the hillside above the Arsinoeion are remains of an ancient road and a circular building. Other altars dating from the early period of the cult lie between the Arsinoeion and the next building to the S, the **Temenos**. Built between 350 and 340 B.C., this was the first marble building on the site, with an Ionic propylon which had a frieze of female dancers in archaicising style (fragments in museum). Going along the middle terrace past an archaic altar, we come to the re-erected façade of the **Hieron**, built in the late 4th c. B.C., with a portico added in the 2nd c. With an apse at the S end (under which a crypt was constructed during the Roman period), it is reminiscent of the plan of a Christian church. Here the adepts were admitted to the second degree of initiation (*epopteia*), probably after they had confessed their sins at two blocks of marble outside the E side of the building (Lehmann). Parallel to the Hieron are the **Hall of Votive Gifts** (6th c. B.C.) and the **Altar Court**, the colonnade of which probably served as the stage wall of the (badly ruined) *Theatre* built about 200 B.C.

From the Hieron a path runs E, past a *necropolis* dating from the 6th c. B.C., to the **Ptolemaion**, built in 285–280 B.C. by the Egyptian king Ptolemy II as a ceremonial entrance from the town into the sacred precinct. All that survives is the *substructure*, with a vaulted drainage channel. Blocks of marble from the building lie nearby. Higher up the hill is the polygonal **W wall** of the ancient town.

Returning to the Hieron, we bear left over a modern concrete bridge and up the hill to the building in which the Victory of Samothrace was found. This winged figure of Nike, goddess of victory, carved from Parian marble (c. 190 B.C.), stood in the upper of two fountain basins on a base in the form of a ship's prow made of marble from the island of Thásos. From here, or from the 103 m (338 feet) long *Stoa* to the W, there is a general view of the central area of the sanctuary. From the N end of the stoa we descend into the valley and return to the * **Museum**.

Room A of the museum contains the partly restored *circular gallery* of the Arsinoeion and parts of the roof, Room B fragments of the *frieze of dancing girls*, Room C a *Nike* by Hieron and various *grave goods*, Room D other grave goods of the 7th c. B.C. and a cast of the Nike.

Santorin/Thera

ΣΑΝΤΟΡΙΝΗ / ΘΗΡΑ

(Santoríni/Thíra)

Nomos: Cyclades. – Telephone dialling code: 0286.
Area: 76 sq. km (29 sq. miles). – Population: 6200.
(i) **Tourist Police,**
in Firá

HOTELS. – FIRÁ: *Atlantis*, B, 47 b.; *Kavalari*, C, 29 b.; *Panorama*, C, 34 b.; *Tataki*, D, 14 b. – EMBORIÓ: *Archea Elefsina*, D, 24 b. – KAMÁRI: *Kamari*, C, 104 b.; *Sigallas*, C, 24 b. – MESARIA: *Artemidoros*, C, 26 b. – PÉRISSA: *Christina*, C, 16 b. – FIROSTÉFANO: *Kafieris*, C, 20 b.

Accommodation can also be had in *Atlantic Villas* (old island houses, restored) at Ia (Oia).

BATHING BEACHES. – Kamári and Monólithos on the E coast, Périssa on the S coast (buses from Firá).

BOAT TRIPS. – From Skála to Mikrá Kaiméni in the caldera, with the 1925 crater; to the adjoining island of Thirasía; in good weather to the island of **Anáfi** (see p. 60), 20 km (12 miles) E.

****Santorin, the most southerly of the Cyclades, lying only 140 km (87 miles) from Crete, is an island of striking beauty which is unique among Greek islands. The main island, a semicircle open to the W, and the smaller islands of Thirasía (area 9 sq. km (3 sq. miles), pop. 400) and Aspronísi (2 sq. km (1 sq. mile), uninhabited) are the relics of a larger island of some 150 sq. km (58 sq. miles) which was blown apart by a volcanic explosion.**

Visitors sailing into the drowned crater of the volcano (area 84 sq. km (32 sq. miles), depth 390 m (1280 feet)) are confronted with a fascinating and dramatic spectacle: rising from the sea to a height of some 300 m (984 feet) are the almost vertical walls of the crater, formed of the red tufa and black basalt which originally constituted a mountain some 1500 m (4922 feet) high and topped by a layer of yellowish-white pumice deposited during the great explosion, with the dazzlingly white houses of the islanders lining the top of the cliff. – On the outer slopes the land falls gradually away towards the sea, and large numbers of vines and many kinds of fruit are grown in terraced fields. The pumice of Santorin was used in the construction of the Suez Canal and is still an important export. – Santorin came into the news when the excavations carried on by Spyridon Marinatos from 1967 onwards at Akrotíri in the S of the island brought to light a town – a "second Pompeii", as it was called – which had been engulfed by the volcanic catastrophe about 1500 B.C.

HISTORY. – The excavations at Akrotíri have shown that Santorin was a flourishing and prosperous place in the first half of the 2nd millennium B.C. The archaeological evidence makes it clear that it was in contact with Minoan Crete but nevertheless developed a distinctive culture of its own. The excavators found no palace, but a number of large houses, suggesting that the island was not ruled by a king or governor but by a plutocracy of merchants and shipowners who had trading links with Libya. This trade, and perhaps also an ethnic connection with this part of North Africa, can be deduced from the wall paintings, of astonishingly high artistic quality, which were found at Akrotíri and are now in the National Archaeological Museum in Athens.

The golden age ended with the eruption of the volcano, which was originally dated to the 16th c. B.C. but now seems likely to have taken place in the mid 15th c. It must have been many times more violent than the Krakatoa eruption of 1883. Marinatos suggested that it had also led to the destruction of the Minoan settlements on Crete.

The island was not reoccupied until many centuries later, at the beginning of the 1st millennium B.C., when Dorian incomers established settlements on a limestone ridge to the S of Mt Profítis Ilías and elsewhere on the island. Their king, Grinos, founded the colony of Kyrene, the largest Greek colony in North Africa, in

Wall of the crater, Santorin

Firá (Santorin)

630 B.C. From 275 to 146 B.C. Santorin was occupied by an Egyptian garrison, which held it on behalf of the Ptolemies; thereafter it came under Roman rule. – In 1207, after the 4th Crusade, Santorin was conquered by Marco Sanudo, the ruler of Náxos, and remained in Italian hands for three centuries. From this period date the name Santorin (=Santa Irene), the ruined castle of Skáros and the Roman Catholic element in the population. In 1539 the island was taken by the Turks. It was finally reunited with Greece in 1830.

The volcanic force which originally built up the island round the older limestone cone of Mt Profítis Ilías (584 m – 1916 feet) and then destroyed it shortly after 1500 B.C. continued to manifest itself in later centuries. In 197 B.C. the islet of Palaiá Kaiméni (the "old burnt-up" island) rose out of the drowned crater, followed in A.D. 1570 by Mikrá Kaiméni and in 1707–11 by Néa Kaiméni, which in 1925–26 joined up with Mikrá Kaiméni and is still active. The last violent volcanic phenomena, combined with earth tremors which caused considerable damage, took place in 1956.

SIGHTS. – The chief place on the island, **Firá** or *Thíra* (pop. 1480), is reached from the landing-place in the little port of **Skála** by riding up a steep and winding mule-track (587 steps) on the edge of the crater. Some boats also put in at the more southerly port of **Athiniós**, from which there is a road to Firá.

Now that the damage caused by the 1956 earthquake has been made good Firá is an attractive little town with its whitewashed houses and chapels. The *Archaeological Museum* in the N of the town contains material of the Cycladic and Minoan periods (i.e. before the explosion of the volcano) and also later material of Dorian, Hellenistic and Roman date. It

is planned to open a new museum for the Akrotíri finds beside the Mitrópolis church. The present museum was built after the earthquake.

Near the village of **Akrotíri**, 12 km (7 miles) SW of Firá, Spyridon Marinatos excavated between 1967 and his death in 1974 considerable areas of a large town destroyed in the great eruption. The buildings date from the 16th c. B.C. and show evidence of the earthquake damage which preceded the final catastrophe, e.g. in the form of bulging walls which were held in place by the pumice sand deposited by the erupting volcano. Combined with the fact that some of the houses were of two or three storeys, this created problems of excavation and conservation: indeed Marinatos himself was killed during the excavation work and is buried in a house opposite the place where the accident occurred.

Entering the site (which is roofed over for protection from the weather) on the S side, we pass between houses which have been preserved to first or even second floor level. Going N along *Odos Telkhinon*, we come to a triangular space, on the far side of which is the "**W House**". This contained many frescoes, including the picture of a naval expedition and a naked youth carrying bunches of fish. In the most northerly house were found numbers of *pithoi* containing provisions. Returning S, we pass a house with a staircase leading up to the first floor, with steps broken by an earth tremor, and a large complex with the small room (Room 2) in which the "Spring Fresco" was found.

The principal building in this "second Pompeii", which is 1600 years older than the Roman Pompeii and will keep the archaeologists busy for many years to come, have plans and explanations posted up to help visitors.

On the way back from Akrotíri we can take a road to the right (2 km (1 mile) from Akrotíri) which leads to the chapel of *Áyios Stéfanos Marmarítis*, set among trees on a site once occupied by an ancient temple, and beyond this to the little coastal village of **Périssa** (bathing beach).

In the SE of the island, above the coastal village of **Kamári**, is the rocky hill of Mesávouno, with the site of *ancient **Thera** (excavated by Baron Hiller von Gaertringen in 1895–1902). A roughly paved road, with many bends, runs up to the *Selláda saddle* (264 m – 866 feet), from which there is a footpath to the top of the ridge (370 m – 1214 feet).

After passing a chapel dedicated to St Stephen, we come to a **temenos** built by Artemidoros of Perge, an admiral in the service of Ptolemaic Egypt (altar of Concord, rock carvings of divine emblems). To the right, uphill, are the *remains of temples* and a rock-cut *cult niche* for Demeter and Kore. This is near the highest point on the site, with the headquarters of the Ptolemaic garrison (Governor's Palace, Gymnasion). To the S are the residential districts, with numerous *cisterns*, a *house with a colonnaded courtyard* and a **temple of Apollo Pythios**. Going down to the left, we come to a *temple of Dionysos*, which in Roman times served the Imperial cult (high base of dressed stone), and then to the centre of the town's public life, the **Agora**, a narrow open space 100 m (328 feet) long. On the uphill side is the two-aisled *Royal Stoa* (Stoa Basilike). Beyond this, below the road on the left, is the *Theatre*. – The principal cult buildings of the Dorian period are towards the S end of the ridge, which becomes steadily narrower and more rugged: the ***Temple of Apollo Karneios** (6th c. B.C.), dedicated to the ancestral god of the Dorians, with the *terrace* on which ceremonial dances in honour of the god were performed; the ***Column of Artemis**, hewn from the rock; and the **Gymnasion of the Ephebes**. In this area can be seen many of the famous ***rock-cut inscriptions** in the ancient Theran script, erotic in content, by admirers of the boys who performed the sacred dances.

The highest hill on Santorin, Mt Profítis Ilías (584 m – 1916 feet), can be climbed from the village of **Pýrgos**, 6 km (4 miles) from Firá. It is a rewarding trip, both for the extensive views to be had from the hill and for the interesting *monastery of Profítis Ilías*. The principal church has a richly carved iconostasis and a 15th c. Cretan "crown of Elijah". In the monastery museum are the mitre and staff of Patriarch Gregorios V, who was hanged in Constantinople in 1821. Other features of interest are the library, the archives and the kitchen. During the Turkish period the monastery ran one of Greece's many "secret schools".

From the monastery it is possible to find your way down on narrow footpaths to the **Selláda** saddle (264 m – 866 feet) and continue on foot to ancient Thera or to Périssa or Kamári. – From Firá a very attractive path (*views) runs N along the cliffs. 3 km (2 miles) along this, on a dauntingly rugged promontory, is the Venetian castle of **Skáros** and at the very tip of the island (11 km – 7 miles) the pretty little village of **Ia** (Oia).

Saronic Gulf
ΣΑΡΩΝΙΚΟΣ ΚΟΛΠΟΣ
(Saronikós Kólpos)

HOTELS. – LOUTRÓYRGOS (30·5 km (19 miles) from central Athens): *Akti*, C, 46 b. – NÉA PÉRAMOS (Megálo Péfko, 40 km (25 miles)): *Hellas*, C, 32 b.; *Megalo Pefko*, C, 136 b. – KINÉTTA (50–57 km – 31–35 miles): *Kinetta Beach*, A, 380 b.; *Sun*, B, 96 b.; *Hotel 50*, C, 19 b. – ÁYII THEÓDORI (67 km – 42 miles): *Chanikian Beach*, A, 416 b.; *Margarita*, B, 22 b.; *Siagas Beach*, B, 190 b.

The Saronic Gulf lies to the E of the Gulf of Corinth, separating Attica from the Peloponnese. It is named after Saron, a king of Troizen about whom nothing is known except that he was drowned in the gulf.

Along the shores of the gulf are numerous tourist resorts, from **Méthana** (see p. 64), **Palaiá** and **Néa Epídavros** (p. 132) in the S, by way of **Loutró Elénis** and **Isthmía** (p. 147) in the W, to the resorts on the W coast of Attica.

Serifos
ΣΕΡΙΦΟΣ
(Sérifos)

Nomos: Cyclades.
Area: 71 sq. km (44 sq. miles). – Population: 1100.

TRANSPORTATION. – Served by boats on the Piraeus–Melos route; taxis from Livádi to Khóra.

HOTELS. – IN LIVÁDI BAY: *Perseus*, B, 20 b.; *Maistrali*, C, 49 b.; *Seriphos Beach*, C, 45 b.

Sérifos is one of the western Cyclades. Its iron ore was already being worked in ancient times.

On the island of Sérifos

The port, **Livádi**, lies in a sandy bay below the chief place on the island, **Sérifos** or *Khóra* (3 km (2 miles): pop. 800), an unspoiled little Cycladic village with its trim little lanes densely packed with houses, its chapels and its tiny gardens. Two hours' walk away is the village of **Panayía**, with a **church of the Panayía* dating from 950, the oldest on the island. Near the village stands the **monastery of the Taxiarchs** (Archangels), built in the 16th c. (18th c. frescoes, library).

Serrai/Serres

ΣΕΡΡΑΙ / ΣΕΡΡΕΣ

(Sérrai, Sérres)

Nomos: Sérrai.
Altitude: 50 m (164 feet). – Population: 40,000.

TRANSPORTATION. – Station on the Salonica–Alexandroúpolis railway line.

HOTELS. – *Xenia*, B, 56 b.; *Galaxy*, C, 67 b.; *Metropolitan*, C, 56 b.; *Pan*, C, 144 b.

Sérrai, 100 km (62 miles) NE of Salonica, is a commercial town which was rebuilt in modern style after its destruction by the Bulgarians in 1913.

Its main features of interest are the **Mitrópolis church**, a three-aisled basilica with a *synthronon* and remains of *mosaics*, and the ruined **castle** which crowns the hill formerly occupied by the ancient acropolis (view).

Servia

ΣΕΡΒΙΑ

(Sérvia)

Nomos: Kozáni.
Altitude: 430 m (1411 feet). – Population: 4000.

The Macedonian town of Sérvia lies on a pass between two ranges of hills to the W of Mt Olympus. As the name indicates, it was founded by Serbs during the Middle Ages.

Its main tourist attraction is not so much its ruined 11th c. *episcopal church* as **Lake Aliakmón**, an artificial lake 6 km (4 miles) NW.

Continuing from there, we come in 20 km (12 miles) to **Kozáni** (alt. 710 m (2330 feet), pop. 23,000), with a bell-tower of 1855 in the Platía Níkis and a small museum housed in a former mosque. 28 km (17 miles) beyond Kozáni is the industrial town of **Ptolemáis** (alt. 600 m (1969 feet), pop. 17,000).

Sifnos

ΣΙΦΝΟΣ

(Sífnos)

Nomos: Cyclades.
Area: 73 sq. km (28 sq. miles). – Population: 2100.

TRANSPORTATIONS. – On the route of the Piraeus–Melos boats; bus from the port, Kamáres, to Apollonía.

HOTELS. – APOLLONÍA: *Apollonia*, B, 18 b.; *Anthousa*, C, 12 b.; *Siphnos*, C, 14 b.; *Sophia*, C, 22 b. – ARTEMÓN: *Artemon*, C, 46 b. – KAMÁRES: *Stavros*, C, 34 b. – PLATÝS YIALÓS: *Platys Yialos*, B, 38 b.

Sífnos, one of the western Cyclades, has many sandy bays on its E and W coasts. In ancient times the wealth of the island, which was populated by Ionians, rested on its silver and lead, which enabled it in 525 B.C. to build one of the handsomest treasuries at Delphi (see p. 122).

The island's port, **Kamáres**, is on the W coast. From Kamáres a road runs through a verdant valley to the chief place on the island, **Apollonía** (5 km (3 miles): pop. 940), in the fertile eastern half of the island, with a *Folk Museum* in the tree-shaded square. Most of the settlements (and numerous pigeon-cotes) are in this part. Among them are **Artemón**, immediately N of Apollonía – twin villages which preserve the names of the divine twins Apollo and Artemis – and **Kástro**, on the coast 5 km (3 miles) E at the foot of a medieval castle.

Church on the island of Sífnos

Scattered about the island are a number of Hellenistic *watch-towers* and numerous *chapels*, mostly of the 16th and 17th c. On Mt Profítis Ilías (694 m – 2277 feet) is the **Profítis Ilías monastery**, in Vathý Bay the *Church of the Taxiarchs* and, in the beautiful southern part of the island, the **monastery of Panayía tou Vounoú** (Mother of God on the Hill), from which there is a charming view of **Platýs Yialós**, the longest beach in the Cyclades (15 km (9 miles) from Apollonía: tavernas, potter's workshop).

Sítia is a port on the N coast of Crete, 68 km (42 miles) E of Áyios Nikólaos, on the site of ancient Eteia. The town rises in a semicircle from the harbour to the Venetian castle. Sitía is a good base for excursions to the E end of the island.

SURROUNDINGS. – 14 km (9 miles) E of the town a road branches off on the left to the fortified **Toploú monastery** (3 km – 2 miles). The main road continues for another 7 km (4 miles) to **Palaíkastro**, 2 km (1 mile) E of which, by the sea, were found remains of the Minoan settlement of `Heleia`. 6 km (4 miles) N of Palaíkastro is the palm-grove of **Vái**, with a good beach.

Sikinos
ΣΙΚΙΝΟΣ
(Síkinos)

Nomos: Cyclades.
Area: 41 sq. km (16 sq. miles). – Population: 420.

TRANSPORTATION. – Served by boats doing the round trip Piraeus–Páros–Santorin–Folégandros–Síkinos Íos–Náxos–Piraeus.

This bare little Cycladic island lies between Melos and Íos.

Passengers arriving in Síkinos are landed by small boats in Aloprónia Bay on the S coast (sandy beach). The only village on the island, 3 km (2 miles) from the landing-place, is **Síkinos**, a typical Cycladic village situated at an altitude of 280 m (919 feet) above the steeply scarped N coast, with a medieval **castle**. 1½ hours' walk W of the village is the **Episkopí chapel**, built on the site of an ancient mausoleum and also known as Naós Apóllonos ("Temple of Apollo").

Sitia
ΣΗΤΕΙΑ
(Sitía)

Island: Crete. – Nomos: Lasíthi.
Altitude: 2–40 m (7–131 feet). – Population: 5300.

TRANSPORTATION. – Boat connections with Piraeus and Rhodes; bus connections with Iráklion, Palaíkastro and Anó Zákros.

HOTELS. – *Sitian Beach*, A, 238 b.; *Alice*, C, 87 b.; *Crystal*, C, 75 b.; *Itanos*, C, 138 b.; *Sitia*, C, 70 b.; and hotels in category D.

Skiathos
ΣΚΙΑΘΟΣ
(Skiáthos)

Nomos: Magnesia. – Telephone dialling code: 0424.
Area: 48 sq. km (19 sq. miles). – Population: 3900.
ⓘ **Tourist Police.**
Antoníou Riga;
tel. 4 23 92
(only in summer).

TRANSPORTATION. – Air service from Athens; ferry service from Vólos, the other Sporades and Kými on Euboea; bus and boat connections with the beaches on the S coast.

HOTELS (some of them outside the town of Skiáthos). – **Skiathos Palace* (13 km – 8 miles), L, 367 b.; *Esperides* (4 km – 2 miles), A, 300 b.; *Nostos* (4·5 km – 3 miles), A, 208 b.; *Xenia* (13 km – 8 miles), B, 64 b.; *Agnandema*, C, 27 b.; *Akti*, C, 22 b.; *Belvedere/Kali Thea* (4 km – 2 miles), C, 60 b.; *Koukounaries*, C, 32 b.

TAVERNAS. – In the square at Skiáthos harbour, and elsewhere.

BATHING BEACHES. – On the S coast, from W of the harbour to Koukounariés; also isolated beaches on the N coast.

Skiáthos is one of the northern Sporades (see p. 244), the closest to the mainland, lying only 4 km (2 miles) from the peninsula of Magnesia. It has no ancient monuments, but the delightful scenery of this green, wooded island has made it a popular holiday resort.

The attractive chief town, **Skiáthos** (pop. 3000), lies in a bay on the SE coast which is picturesquely dotted with a number of small islets. At the E end of the little town the rocky **Boúrdzi** peninsula projects into the sea. At the base of the peninsula is a *monument* to the short-story writer Alexandros Papadiamantis (1851–1912), whose house can be seen in the street just beyond the harbour. From the little hill on which stand a *clock-tower* and the *chapel of St Nicholas* there are panoramic views. Another good viewpoint is the **church of Áyios Fanoúrios**, reached on a road which branches off on the W side of the town (30 minutes).

A road runs W from Skiáthos to the beaches of **Akhládes** (4 km – 2 miles), **Tzaneriá** (4·5 km – 3 miles) and **Koukounariés** (13 km – 8 miles). The beach of Koukounariés, backed by a pinewood, is one of the most beautiful in the Aegean.

The medieval capital of **Kástro**, abandoned only in 1825, lies on an impregnable crag on the N coast (accessible by boat or by a walk of some 3 hours).

Skopelos
ΣΚΟΠΕΛΟΣ
(Skópelos)

Nomos: Magnesia.
Area: 96 sq. km (37 sq. miles). – Population: 4500.

TRANSPORTATION. – Skópelos is served by boats sailing between Vólos, the Sporades and Kými (Euboea).

HOTELS. – *Xenia*, B, 8 b.; *Aeolos*, C, 79 b.; *Avra*, C, 51 b.

Skópelos, known in antiquity as Peparethos, is, like its neighbour in the Sporades Skiáthos, a green and fertile island.

The chief town, **Skópelos** (pop. 3000), is beautifully situated on the slopes of a north-facing bay, along the E side of which are gardens and a sandy beach. The houses have characteristic roofs of tiles and slate. Among the numerous churches *St Michaèl's* is of particular interest. The

Skópelos

medieval *castle* is built on part of the site of ancient *Peparethos*. The other ancient settlements on the island were *Selinous* (present-day *Glóssa*) and *Pánormos* (present-day *Klima*).

SURROUNDINGS. – Near the town are the **monasteries** of *Episkopí, Ayía Evangelistría* and *Ayía Varvára*. There is a road from the town to the bay of **Stáfilos** (5 km (3 miles): sandy beach), **Agnóndas** (9 km – 6 miles) and **Glóssa** (alt. 240 m (787 feet)), situated in the W of the island above the landing-place at **Skála Glóssas**.

Skyros
ΣΚΥΡΟΣ
(Skíros)

Nomos: Euboea.
Area: 209 sq. km (81 sq. miles). – Population: 3000.

TRANSPORTATION. – Ferry services link the island with Kými (Euboea) and the other islands in the Sporades.

HOTEL. – *Xenia* (on the E coast near the town of Skíros), B, 38 b.

Skíros is the farthest from the mainland of the northern Sporades. 36 km (22 miles) long and up to 14 km (9 miles) wide, it is barer and less fertile than the other islands in the group, the cultivated areas being mainly in the valleys·in the northern half of the island. The coast is much indented, with pleasant beaches in its numerous bays.

HISTORY. – Homer tells us that Thetis hid her son Achilles among the daughters of King Lykomedes of Skyros in order to preserve him from an early death, but that he was discovered by the wiles of Odysseus. Lykomedes treacherously killed Theseus, who had taken refuge on Skyros, by casting him down from the castle rock; and this later provided Kimon with a pretext for his conquest of the island in 476–475 B.C. Thereafter Skyros remained under Athenian control until the Roman period. Kimon took Theseus' remains to Athens, where he built a Theseion – not yet discovered – in the hero's honour.

Skíros is now noted for its handicrafts, particularly hand-weaving and furniture (low chairs), with characteristic carved decoration in the Byzantine tradition.

From the port of **Linariá** (pop. 250), on the W coast, a road runs across the island to the chief town, **Skíros** (pop. 2500; bus), on the E coast. This little town of white cube-shaped houses lies on the

Fishermen on the beach, Skýros

slopes of the imposing crag once occupied by the ancient *acropolis* and now crowned by a Venetian castle, with remains of ancient masonry incorporated into its walls. Below the summit plateau is a **monastery** dedicated to St George. In Platía Kýprou is a *monument to Rupert Brooke*, who died on his way to the Dardanelles in 1915 and is buried in the bay of Tris Boukes. There is a small local **museum** in the town.

From both Linariá and Skýros boat trips can be arranged to the island's many bays. There are also pleasant walks from Skýros, for example to *Mt Olympos* (368 m – 1207 feet), at the foot of which is the *Olympianí monastery* (8 km (5 miles) W).

Sounion
ΣΟΥΝΙΟΝ
(Súnion)

Region and nomos: Attica. – Altitude: 60 m (197 feet).

TRANSPORTATION. – Buses from Athens (60 km – 37 miles).

HOTELS. – *Belvedere Park*, A, 90 b.; *Cape Soúnion Beach*, A, 126 b.; *Aegeon*, A, 89 b.; *Sun*, B, 521 b.; *Triton*, B, 78 b.; *Saron*, C, 30 b

SWIMMING. – In the bay (sandy beach).

Cape Soúnion, at the south-eastern tip of Attica, is famous for its **Temple of Poseidon, magnificently situated on the edge of a precipitous crag.

HISTORY. – Homer refers in the "Odyssey" (III, 278) to the "sacred cape" of Sounion. In the 7th c. B.C. there was probably a simple altar here; about 600 B.C. the large figures of kouroi now in the National Archaeological Museum in Athens were set up beside it; and about 500 B.C. work began on the construction of a temple in poros limestone which was still unfinished when the Persians destroyed it in 480 B.C.

On the substructure of the earlier temple the architect responsible for the Temple of Hephaistos in Athens erected in 449 B.C. the present marble *Temple of Poseidon, with 6 × 13 exceptionally slender Doric columns. It stands on a terrace, artificially enlarged, to which a propylon gave access. In the bay below were *boathouses*, of which some remains can be seen.

On a flat-topped hill NE of the temple (beyond the modern road) is a **sanctuary of Athena** of the 6th c. B.C. Beside a small building measuring only 5 by 6·80 m (16 by 22 feet), of which the lower courses of the walls and the base of a cult statue are preserved, are the foundations of a similar but larger **temple** (11·60 by 16·40 m – 38 by 54 feet), with the *base* of a cult statue. The roof was borne on four columns, in the fashion of a Mycenaean megaron. After suffering damage during the Persian wars the temple was rebuilt with two colonnades, not at the E and W ends as was the normal arrangement but at the E end and along the S side. The reason for this departure can only be guessed at.

SURROUNDINGS. – 9 km (6 miles) N is **Lávrion**, noted in antiquity for its silver-mines. 2 km (1 mile) beyond Lávrion is **Thorikós**, with a theatre of rather archaic type.

Temple of Poseidon, Cape Soúnion

Sparta
ΣΠΑΡΤΗ
(Spárti)

Nomos: Laconia. – Telephone dialling code: 0731.
Altitude: 211 m (692 feet). – Population: 11,000.
ⓘ **Tourist Police**,
Khílonos 8;
tel. 2 87 01.

HOTELS. – *Xenia*, A, 61 b.; *Lida*, B, 75 b.; *Menelaion*,

Spartan warrior (bronze, 4th c. B.C.)

who like his brother Agamemnon, belonged to the Trojan War generation, was later revered in the Menelaion. The last Mycenaean king was Tisamenos, son of Orestes.

A new epoch began when the Dorians arrived, established the four villages of Pitane, Limnai, Mesoa and Kynosoura about 950 B.C. and divided up the conquered territory among the Spartiates. When Amyklai, which had remained a Mycenaean stronghold, also fell to Sparta about 800 B.C. the characteristic dual monarchy came into being, with one king continuing the line of Dorian tribal leaders, the other that of the kings of Amyklai. In addition to the two kings Sparta had a Council of Elders (Gerousia) and five ephors, who were elected annually. It developed into a military state, in which art was not entirely disregarded (as the finds made at Olympia and Dodóna show) but played a less important role than in Athens. Thus Thucydides could write: "If Sparta became desolate and only the temples and the foundations of its public buildings were left, posterity would be unable to accept its fame as the true measure of its power." The Spartan ideal was incarnated in the lawgiver *Lykourgos* (8th c. B.C.) and *Leonidas* and his 300 Spartans who fell at Thermopylai in 480 B.C.

In a succession of wars (740–720, 660, 464–459 B.C.) Sparta subjugated Messenia, to the W of Taýgetos. Its decline began with a severe earthquake in 464 B.C. which killed all its young men, and it received a further blow in the defeat of a Spartan army by the Thebans under Epameinondas at Leuktra in 371 B.C. The first defensive walls were built round the town about 200

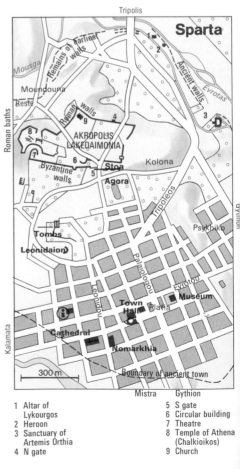

B, 88 b.; *Apollo*, C, 82 b.; *Dioscuri*, C, 60 b.; *Lakonia*, C, 52 b.; *Maniatis*, C, 150 b.; *Mystras*, C, 48 b.

RESTAURANTS. – Around the Platía.

Sparta, capital of Laconia, lies in the fertile Evrotas plain, which is enclosed between the Taýgetos (2404 m – 7888 feet) and Párnon (1937 m – 6355 feet) ranges and bounded on the S by the sea. The town was refounded on the ancient site in 1834 by King Otto, with streets laid out at right angles around a large central square.

HISTORY. – The subjugation of the original pre-Greek population of this area by Mycenaean Greeks is reflected in the myth of Hyakinthos, who was killed by Apollo during a discus-throwing contest. The story of the Mycenaean period also finds expression in the myths of Leda, the Dioskouroi (Kastor and Polydeukes), and Menelaos and Helen. King Menelaos,

1 Altar of Lykourgos
2 Heroon
3 Sanctuary of Artemis Orthia
4 N gate

5 S gate
6 Circular building
7 Theatre
8 Temple of Athena (Chalkioikos)
9 Church

B.C. Under the Roman Empire Sparta enjoyed a revival of prosperity, but it was devastated by the Heruli in A.D. 267 and by Alaric's Visigoths in 395. In the 7th c. Slavs established themselves in the region. In the 10th c. it was evangelised by St Nikon, who was buried on the acropolis hill at Sparta. In the 13th c. Sparta was replaced by the newly founded town of Mistra (see p. 185).

SIGHTS. – In Evrotas Street, E of the Platía, is the *Archaeological Museum, set in attractive gardens.

In the entrance hall are sickle stelae associated with the cult of Artemis. In the rooms to the right of the entrance are an archaic *stele depicting Helen and Menelaos, finds from the *Menelaion* and the *"Throne of Apollo"* at Amyklai, the *Dioskouroi* and an early classical *torso of a warrior (Leonidas?) of remarkable vigour and power. To the left of the entrance are *lead figurines* and *terracotta masks* from the sanctuary of Artemis. There are a number of Roman mosaics in the town (keys from the museum).

Just off Leonidas Street, in the N of the town, is the Leonidaion, a building of unknown function: the tomb of Leonidas was elsewhere, to the W of the acropolis. 500 m (547 yards) N of this building is the low *acropolis hill*, on the S side of which is the Hellenistic Theatre (altered in Roman times), which had a movable stage wall. On top of the hill are the foundations of a temple of Athena built by Gitiadas in the 6th c. B.C. This was a timber-framed mud-brick building on a stone base, known as the Chalkioikos from its facing of bronze plates. – To the E is the 10th c. Basilica of St Nikon, in which the saint was buried. – The Agora, which lay S of the acropolis, has not been excavated, and most of the buildings and monuments mentioned by Pausanias cannot be identified.

Between the road to Trípolis and the Evrotas, just outside the town (on right), is the Sanctuary of Artemis Orthia, so named because the cult image was found standing upright. According to Pausanias it was brought from Tauris by Iphigeneia and Orestes. In this sanctuary Spartan boys were flogged as part of their initiation into manhood. There was a 6th c. temple (foundations preserved) built over an earlier 8th c. structure, with altars for burnt offerings. During the Roman period tiers of seats in amphitheatre formation were built to accommodate spectators of the ritual flogging.

SURROUNDINGS. – The ruined medieval town of Mistra (see p. 185) is 7 km (4 miles) W of Sparta.

To reach the Menelaion, leave Sparta on the Geráki road, which crosses the Evrotas; then in 4·5 km (3 miles) turn into a footpath which goes past a *chapel of Áyios Ilías* and up Mt Therapne (500 m – 1641 feet). On top of the hill are the remains of the *Menelaion, a Heroon built in the 5th c. B.C. It stands on the site of a complex of Mycenaean buildings (excavated in 1973) which it has been suggested was the palace of Menelaos.

11 km (7 miles) S of Sparta is Amyklai, on the hill of *Ayía Paraskeví*, with the site of the Sanctuary of Apollo Amyklaios and the 13 m (8 miles) high *"Throne of Apollo" built over the grave of Hyakinthos.

48 km (30 miles) S is the castle of Geráki (see p. 136). – 18 km (11 miles) E of Sparta is Khrysáfa, with four churches containing frescoes – *Khrysafiótissa* (1290:), *Áyii Pántes* (All Saints, 1367), *Kímisis* (Dormition) and *St Demetrius* (17th c.) – and the monastery of the Pródromos (St John the Baptist), with a church of 1625.

Spetsai/Spetses

ΣΠΕΤΣΑΙ / ΣΠΕΤΣΕΣ

(Spétsai, Spétses)

Nomos: Attica.
Area: 22 sq. km (8 sq. miles). – Population: 3500.

TRANSPORTATION. – The Argosaronikos service links Spétsai with the neighbouring islands and with Piraeus, and there are motorboat services linking it with Kósta and Pórto Khéli on the mainland.

HOTELS. – *Kastelli*, A, 139 b.; *Posidonion*, A, 83 b.; *Spetses*, A, 125 b.; *Ilios*, B, 51 b.; *Myrtoon*, B, 74 h.; *Roumanis*, B, 65 b.; *Pharos*, B, 64 b.; *Star*, B, 68 b.

Boats in Spétsai harbour

BATHING BEACHES. – W of the town (rocky); at Ayía Paraskeví on the S coast; at Kósta, on the mainland.

With its gentle landscape and its mild climate, the little island of *Spétsai or Spétses, at the mouth of the Gulf of Argolis, is a popular holiday resort. Around the harbour are numerous tavernas, and in the town itself are attractive old houses, including some substantial mansions, and a small museum. There are many features of interest on the island, including the remains of two Early Christian basilicas on the SE coast and a stalactitic cave on the S coast.

Sporades
ΣΠΟΡΑΔΕΣ
(Sporádhes)

The Sporades are, etymologically, the "scattered" islands. The northern Sporades, lying off the peninsula of Magnesia, runs SE from Skiáthos by way of Skópelos and Alónissos to Skýros, with the smaller islands of Pélagos, Ghioúra and Pipéri to the N.

HISTORY. – The Sporades played no great part in history or in art, either in antiquity or in later centuries. In the 5th c. B.C. Athens gained control of the whole group; in 338 B.C. the islands became Macedonian and in 168 B.C. Roman; thereafter they belonged to Byzantium. From 1207 to 1263 they were ruled by the (Venetian) Ghisi family, whose seat was on Skýros; and later they returned to Byzantium and then again to Venice before falling under Turkish rule. They were united with Greece in 1828–29.

The main islands in the group have recently become popular as holiday resorts offering peace and quiet, beautiful scenery and numerous bathing beaches. The two islands nearest to the mainland, Skiáthos (see p. 239) and Skópelos (p. 240), are particularly well equipped with holiday facilities. The others are attractive to those who prefer the simple life. The southern Sporades include the Dodecanese (p. 127) and the group around Sámos (p. 232).

Symi
ΣΥΜΗ
(Sími)

Nomos: Dodecanese.
Area: 58 sq. km (22 sq. miles). – Population: 2480.

TRANSPORTATION. – On the route of the Piraeus–Kálymnos–Nísyros–Sými–Rhodes and Rhodes–Sámos boats.

HOTEL. – *Nirefs*, B, 12 b.

The island of Sými, in the Dodecanese, lies between two long promontories projecting from the Anatolian coast. It is a bare island which in the 19th c. was relatively prosperous with its sponge fisheries and boatbuilding but has since then lost much of its population by emigration.

The chief town and port, Sými, lies in a beautiful bay on the N coast, with its houses rising in a semicircle on the slopes of the hill. In a house on the harbour (commemorative tablet) the surrender of the Dodecanese to the Allies was signed on 8 May 1945. There are numerous tavernas around the little harbour.

Sými

SIGHTS. – On the hill above the town of Sými is a castle of the Knights of St John, built on the foundations of the ashlar walls of the ancient *acropolis*. From the castle there is a view of the "Windmill Hill", on which, above the windmills, is an ancient *circular tomb*, and (to the E) of the next bay, with the village of Pédion and the only stretch of flat fruit-growing land on the island. – In a bay at the S end of the island, 4 km (2 miles) from Sými, is the monastery and pilgrimage centre of *Áyios Panormítis*.

Syros
ΣΥΡΟΣ
(Síros)

Nomos: Cyclades.
Area: 84 sq. km (32 sq. miles). – Population: 18,600.

TRANSPORTATION. – On the Piraeus–Páros–Santorin boat route.

HOTELS. – ERMOUPOLIS. *Hermes*, B, 47 b.; *Europe*, C, 51 b.; *Nissaki*, C, 78 b. – FÍNIKAS (12 km – 7 miles): *Olympia*, C, 30 b. – POSIDONIA (15 km – 9 miles): *Delagrazia*, B, 21 b.; *Posidonion*, C, 51 b. – VÁRY (8 km – 5 miles): *Achladi*, C, 25 b.; *Domenica*, C, 26 b.; *Kamelo*, C, 45 b.; *Romantica*, C, 58 b. – MÉGAS YIALÓS (11 km – 7 miles): *Alexandra*, C, 58 b.

Sýros is an island in the central Cyclades.

HISTORY. – From the time of the 4th Crusade until 1566 the island belonged to the duchy of Náxos. Since then it has had a strong Roman Catholic minority, which during the Turkish period was under the protection of France. During the Greek struggle for freedom Sýros remained neutral, and thus provided a refuge for Greeks fleeing from the massacres of Chios and Psará. The new arrivals founded the town of Ermoúpolis around the harbour, which developed during the 19th c. into the largest Greek port, before being overtaken by Piraeus. – The town of Anó Sýros, predominantly Roman Catholic, was founded in the 13th c.

SIGHTS. – To the visitor arriving at Sýros **Ermoúpolis**, capital of the island and of the Cyclades as a whole, combines with **Anó Sýros**, 4 km (2 miles) inland, to present a striking and distinctive sight – the neo-classical town (with a local *museum* in the town hall) rising above the harbour, to the rear the hill (105 m – 345 feet) on which stands the principal **Orthodox church**, and to the left of this the hill of Anó Sýros (180 m – 591 feet) with its stepped lanes and the **Roman Catholic Cathedral** on the summit. The boatyards and boathouses round the harbour bay are a reminder of the island's importance (not yet lost) in the shipping trade. Everywhere visitors will find loukoumi (Turkish delight) offered for sale.

There is ample scope for EXCURSIONS, particularly in the fertile southern part of the island. There are bathing beaches at **Episkopí** and the fishing village of **Kíni** (7 km (4 miles) W of Ermoúpolis), **Fínikas** (12 km (7 miles) SW), **Posidonia** (15 km (9 miles) SW), **Váry** (8 km (5 miles) S in a sheltered bay) and **Mégas Yialós** (11 km – 7 miles), at the southern tip of the island.

Taygetos
ΤΑΥΓΕΤΟΣ
(Taíyetos)

Region: Peloponnese.
Nomoi: Messenia and Laconia.

The Taýgetos range, fully 100 km (62 miles) long and rising to a height of 2407 m (7897 feet) in Mt Profítis Ilías, traverses the Peloponnese from N to S, separating the regions of Laconia and Messenia. The range, built up of limestones and marbles, comes to an end at Cape Tainaron or Matapán in the Máni peninsula. The main ridge, 18 km (11 miles) long and 2100 m (6890 feet) high, to the W of Sparta is snow-covered for most of the year. The only route through the range is the recently built and well-engineered road, largely following the old mule-track through the Langáda gorge, which links Sparta with Kalamáta.

The Taýgetos range

Tegea
ΤΕΓΕΑ
(Teyéa)

Region: Peloponnese. – Nomos: Arcadia.

At the little village of Tegéa, 8 km (5 miles) SE of Trípolis, is a sanctuary of Athena Alea.

On the site of an earlier Archaic building, destroyed by fire in 395 B.C., Skopas erected between 350 and 340 B.C. a new *temple, which was decorated with his own sculpture. In this temple, the first temple in the Peloponnese entirely built of marble, Skopas preserved the rather old-fashioned elongated ground-plan with 6×14 columns. In the cella he did not follow the regular practice of dividing it into three aisles by rows of columns but set Corinthian half-columns against the interior walls, so as to achieve an effect of space and magnificence. He thus carried a stage further the trend towards giving increased emphasis to the interior which Iktinos had begun in the Parthenon and continued at Bassai (see p. 104). – *Ramps* at the E end and also on the N side show that the temple could be entered either from the E or from the N. The only surviving remains of the temple are the foundations and a number of columns and capitals.

Tempe
TEMΠH
(Témbi)

Region: Thessaly. – Nomos: Lárisa.

The River Piniós (Peneios), coming from Thessaly, flows through the gorge-like *Vale of Tempe between Mt Olympos and Mt Óssa, 8 km (5 miles) long, to reach the sea. Celebrated in antiquity for its abundance of water and luxuriant vegetation and as the place where Apollo came to purify himself after slaying Python, the valley – long the principal route into central Greece from the N – has lost much of its original character through the construction of a modern road.

It is still worth while, however, to pause at a parking place, visit the *Spring of Daphne* in its shady setting and cross a suspension bridge to the much-frequented cave chapel of *Ayía Paraskeví*. Just beyond this, going S, is the narrowest point of the gorge, **Lykóstomo**, the Wolf's Jaws. At the S end of the Vale, on a hill opposite the village of **Témpi**, is the site of the fortress of **Gonnos**, built by Philip II of Macedon to control the valley (Greek excavations). Beyond Témpi a road goes off on the left and climbs, with many bends, to **Ambelákia** (5 km (3 miles): alt. 600 m (1969 feet), pop. 1500), on **Mt Óssa** (see p. 201).

Thasos
ΘΑΣΟΣ
(Thásos)

Nomos: Kavála. – Telephone dialling code: 0593. Area: 379 sq. km (146 sq. miles). – Population: 13,500.
ⓘ **Tourist Police,** tel. 2 15 00 (only in summer).

TRANSPORTATION. – Ferries from Kavála and Keramotí; island buses from Thásos harbour.

HOTELS. – THÁSOS: *Timoleon*, B, 54 b.; *Xenia*, B, 50 b.; *Angelika*, C, 50 b.; *Glyphada*, C, 92 b.; *Laios*, C, 32 b.; *Lido*, C, 30 b.; *Panorama*, C, 16 b.; *Theano*, C, 18 b.

EAST COAST. – MAKRYÁMMOS (3 km – 2 miles): *Makryammos Bungalows*, A, 402 b. – POTAMIÁ (12 km – 7 miles): *Arion*, C, 11 b.; *Atlantis*, C, 12 b.; *Blue Sea*, C, 23 b.; *Helen*, C, 24 b.; *Maria*, C, 8 b. – KÍNYRA: *Gerda*, C, 20 b.

WEST COAST. – RAKHÓNI (10 km – 6 miles): *Argyro*, C, 58 b. – *Prinos* (14 km – 9 miles): *Crystal*, C, 12 b. – LIMENARIÁ (42 km – 26 miles): *Menel*, C, 30 b.; *Sgouridis*, C, 25 b. – PEFKÁRI (44 km – 27 miles): *Esperia*, C, 15 b. – POTÓS (47 km – 29 miles): *Potos*, C, 17 b.; *Thomi*, C, 21 b.

CAMPING SITE. – Rakhóni.

BATHING BEACHES. – At Makryámmos, SE of the town of Thásos; in the bays of Potamiá Skála and Kínyra on the E coast; between Limenariá and Potós, and elsewhere on the W coast.

Thásos, the most northerly of the Aegean islands, lying only 6 km (4 miles) from the mainland, is a fertile island of undramatic scenery. The marble ridge of Mt Ypsári rises out of the surrounding uplands to a height of 1003 m (3291 feet).

HISTORY. – The island achieved importance in ancient times with its gold, silver, copper and lead. According to Herodotus the minerals were first worked by the Phoenicians. Between 710 and 680 B.C. Thásos was occupied by settlers from the island of Páros (see p. 205), the commander of the Parian fleet being Telesikles, father of the poet Archilochos.

SIGHTS. – The chief town, **Thásos** or **Limín** (pop. 2000), with its jumble of modern buildings and ancient remains, has a small **harbour**. From the landing-stage it is a short distance to the fishing harbour, the ancient naval harbour, inland from which are the **Museum** and the Agora.

The central hall of the museum is dominated by a *colossal marble statue*, found on the Acropolis, of a *kouros carrying a ram, an unfinished 7th c. work.

Other items of particular interest are a **protome of Pegasos** (late 6th c. B.C.), an ivory ***lion's head**, *pottery*, Thasian *coins*, ***Aphrodite on a dolphin** and a **statue of Dionysos** from the Dionysion (3rd c. B.C.).

The **Agora**, rhomboid in shape, has some buildings dating from the beginnings of Greek settlement, but most of the remains belong to the Hellenistic period. In front of the *NW Stoa* (to left) are the precinct of Zeus Agoraios and a circular structure. To the NE a building, later overlaid by a Christian basilica, has been interpreted as a lawcourt. The *SE Stoa* (1st c. A.D.) is built over a monument to Glaukos, a friend of Archilochos' (7th c. B.C.). Outside the *SW Stoa* is the substructure of a monumental altar. In the centre of the agora are altars, statue bases, etc.

Returning to the fishing harbour and going NE from there, we come to a stretch of the 5th c. **town walls**, with the *Chariot Gate* and the *Gate of Hermes*, both opening off the harbour. From the Chariot Gate a path (on right) runs between the *sanctuaries of Poseidon and Dionysos* to the *Theatre* (4th c. B.C.), in which performances are given in summer. The path then continues up to the *Acropolis*. The first hill is occupied by a Genoese **castle**, which has at the SW corner an ancient ***relief of a funeral banquet. On the second hill are the foundations of the 5th c. *Temple of Athena*. On the slopes of the third is the triangular niche of a *sanctuary of Pan*. From here we can return downhill either by retracing our steps or by going down a flight of ancient rock-cut steps (difficult going) alongside the walls.

In the walls along the SW side of the town are the large **Gate of Zeus**, the **Gate of Herakles** and the **Gate of Silenos**, all named after the *reliefs* on the uprights. In the village square, between the pier and the post office, are the remains of an Early Christian *basilica*.

ROUND THE ISLAND. – An attractive road encircles the island, keeping close to the coast all the way. Going S from Thásos, we pass through **Panayía** (9 km – 6 miles) and come to **Potamiá** (12 km – 7 miles), on the E side of **Mt Ypsári**, from which there is a very fine view over the wooded valley to the sea and the 4 km long beach of *Khrysoammoúdio*, with the little port of **Potamiá Skála** (4 km – 2 miles) and its tavernas. The road continues via **Kínyra** (23 km – 14 miles) and the **Aliki** peninsula (40 km (25 miles): remains of a sanctuary of the Dioskouroi and two Early Christian basilicas) to **Potós** (45 km – 28 miles), where a road branches off on the right and ascends through a romantic valley to the hill village of

Theológos (8 km (5 miles): alt. 240 m (787 feet)). The main road continues to the little mining town of **Limenariá** (50 km (31 miles): pop. 2000), with offices once occupied by the firm of Krupp just above the harbour, and then returns via **Prínos** (78 km – 48 miles) and **Rakhóni** (82 km – 51 miles) to Thásos (92 km – 57 miles).

Thebes
ΘΗΒΑΙ
(Thívai)

Nomos: Boeotia.
Altitude: 218 m (715 feet). – Population: 16,000.

TRANSPORTATION. – Station on the Salonica–Athens railway line; bus services from Athens. The exit from the Salonica–Athens highway is 5 km N of the town.

HOTELS. – *Dionysion Melathron*, B, 42 b.; *Meletiou*, C, 65 b.; *Niobe*, C, 51 b.

Thebes, capital of the nomos of Boeotia in central Greece, occupies the site of the ancient city of the same name, "seven-gated Thebes".

HISTORY. – On the site of a stone apsidal building of the Early Helladic period (second half of the 3rd millennium B.C.) similar to the one of the same date at Lérna, near Argos, a Mycenaean stronghold was built. The myth relates that Kadmos came from Phoenicia to Boeotia in search of his sister Europa who had been carried off by Zeus, and about 1500 B.C. founded the fortress which was named Kadmeia after him. Round his royal dynasty there grew up the great cycle of tragic myths centred on such figures as Oidipous (Oedipus), his mother Iokaste (Jocasta), their daughters Antigone and Ismene and their sons Eteokles and Polyneikes, whose rights were fought for by the Seven against Thebes. – The site of Kadmos' palace, which was destroyed in the 13th c. B.C., was later occupied by the agora and, according to Pausanias, a sanctuary of Demeter Thesmophoros. In the 4th c. B.C. Thebes, under the leadership of Pelopidas and Epameinondas, became for a brief period the dominant power in Greece, but after a rising against Macedonian rule it was razed to the ground by Alexander the Great in 335 B.C., with the exception of the house occupied by the great lyric poet Pindar (c. 520–445 B.C.). Thereafter Thebes, which was destroyed on a number of later occasions, was a place of no importance until the 19th c., when it began to recover a measure of prosperity.

SIGHTS. – The *Acropolis* is now covered with modern building, which inevitably hampers archaeological investigation. Recent excavations, however, have brought to light *walls* belonging to Mycenaean Kadmeia. In buildings to the S of the excavated area were found not only jewelry, ivory and tablets written in Linear

B but also cuneiform texts which provided support for the ancient tradition of connections between the city of Kadmos and the Middle East. Tombs were found on the hill of Kastélla, to the E of the town, and a *sanctuary of Apollo Ismenios* near the cemetery, to the SE. The positions of the seven gates are known, but the only visible remains are the foundations of a round tower at the Elektra Gate on the SE of the ancient city.

In the N of the town, beside a 13th c. Frankish tower dating from the time when Thebes was subject to the de la Rue family who were masters of Athens, is the *Museum.

Room I: *kouros (No. 3: *c.* 550 B.C.) from the Ptoion (sanctuary of Ptoan Apollo). – Room II: *lapis lazuli seals* from the East. – Room III: painted *funerary stelae* from Thespiai and Tanagra. – Room IV: *Mycenaean sarcophagi* from Tanagra (13th c. B.C.).

SURROUNDINGS. – 20 km (12 miles) S is the site of the battle of **Plataiai** (see p. 217), which ended the Persian wars. – 19 km (12 miles) SW is the battlefield of **Leuktra** (see p. 217), where Thebes broke the power of Sparta in 371 B.C. – 8 km (5 miles) W in the direction of Théspiai an interesting cult site has been excavated – the *Kabeirion of Thebes, with the remains of a temple and the orchestra of a theatre.

Thermaic Gulf
ΘΕΡΜΑΙΚΟΣ ΚΟΛΠΟΣ
(Thermaikós Kólpos)

HOTELS. – METHÓNI (43 km (27 miles) from Salonica): *Agiannis*, C, 56 b.; *Arion*, C, 74 b.

CAMPING SITE.

KÓRINOS (58 km (36 miles) from Salonica): *Europa*, C, 40 b.

KATERÍNI (68 km – 42 miles): *Olympion*, C, 54 b.; *Park*, C, 38 b.; *Pieria*, C, 18 b.; *Zephyros*, C, 26 b.

PARALÍA KATERÍNIS (74 km – 46 miles): *Alkyone*, B, 64 b.; *Acropole*, C, 26 b.; *Aktaeon*, C, 69 b.; *Argo*, C, 26 b.; *Athina*, C, 20 b.; *Avra*, C, 35 b.; *Dion*, C, 29 b.; *Emilios*, C, 20 b.; *Galini*, C, 36 b.; *Hamvourgo*, C, 36 b.; *Hellas*, C, 44 b.; *Kastoria*, C, 64 b.; *Katerina*, C, 20 b.; *Leftheria*, C, 22 b.; *Lido*, C, 43 b.; *Muses' Beach*, C, 72 b.; *Posidon*, C, 31 b.; *Sonia*, C, 28 b.; *Vienni*, C, 38 b.; *Zorbas*, C, 37 b.

There are other resorts farther S round Litókhoro (see p. 175). – For holiday and bathing resorts on the E side of the gulf, see under Salonica, Surroundings.

The Thermaic Gulf, lying between the mainland of Macedonia and the Chalcidice peninsula, is named after the ancient city of Thérmai near present-day Salonica.

The present coastline has Ieen formed by alluvial deposits from three rivers, the Axiós (Vardar), the Loúdias and the Aliakmón, flowing respectively from the N, the NW and the SW. As a result the inlet giving access to the port of Salonica is now only 6 km (4 miles) wide. Originally the gulf extended far to the W, reaching almost to Édessa in the NW and to Véria (ancient Beroia) in the S, joining up with the present coastline at Methóni. When the Macedonian capital of Pélla (see p. 210) was established about 400 B.C. it lay on the N shore of the gulf: it is now 30 km (19 miles) from the sea. In the lowest-lying part of this area the lake of Yianitsá (now drained) survived into modern times. The new alluvial land is now under cultivation.

Round the Thermaic Gulf is a long string of holiday and seaside resorts.

Thermopylai
ΘΕΡΜΟΠΥΛΑΙ
(Thermopílai)

Nomos: Phthiotis.

HOTEL. – *Aegli*, C, 81 b.

*Thermopýlai ("Warm Gates") takes its name from the hot sulphur springs round which a small spa has grown up (recommended for rheumatism, arthritis, gynaecological and skin conditions).

Here the mountains approach so close to the coast that in ancient times there was only the breadth of a single waggon at the narrowest point in the pass. The extension of the land by alluvial deposition has completely altered its character, and the modern highway now approximately follows the ancient coastline. In the little museum on the S side of the hill is a model showing the lie of the land in antiquity.

Here Leonidas and his 300 Spartans sacrificed themselves in 480 B.C. and thus covered the retreat of the Greek army after the treachery of Ephialtes had revealed to the Persians the alternative route by a mountain path called the Anopaia. There is a modern *monument* on the hill on which the Spartans made their last stand, and also a tablet with the famous epitaph, "Go tell the Spartans, thou who passest by, That here, obedient to their laws, we lie."

Thessaly
ΘΕΣΣΑΛΙΑ
(Thessalía)

Thessaly, in central Greece, is bounded on the W by the Pindos mountains, on the N by Macedonia, on the E by the Aegean and on the S by Boeotia.

Thessaly, with an area of 14,000 sq. km (5405 sq. miles), is a fertile agricultural region which was famed in ancient times for its horses and is now Greece's principal producer of cereals. The wide expanses of cultivable land available here, in contrast to the regions farther S, led in classical and Turkish times to the development of large estates and in more recent times has favoured the establishment of agricultural co-operatives. The mountain barriers which enclose the region – Pindos, Olympus, Óssa, Pélion, Óthrys – give it a continental climate, with hot summers and cold winters, so that the olive does not flourish in Thessaly.

The capital of Thessaly is **Lárisa** (see p. 169), near which recent excavations have brought to light traces of very early settlement. From the 4th millennium onwards the land around the Gulf of Vólos saw a continuous succession of settlements – Sesklo (4th millennium), Dimini (3rd millennium), Iolkos (2nd millennium), in the 1st millennium B.C. Pherai, Pagasai and Demetrias, and finally Vólos, the only port in Thessaly, which is cut off from the sea by Mt Pélion.

MYTH and HISTORY. – The importance of this region in the Mycenaean period is reflected in the numerous myths which have Thessaly as their setting. This was the home of the centaurs, including the wise Cheiron who initiated Asklepios into the art of healing and brought up Peleus and his son Achilles; Admetos and Alkestis lived in Pherai; and the Argonauts set out in quest of the Golden Fleece from Iolkos.

Apart from the ****monasteries of Metéora** (see p. 182), the touristic interest of Thessaly is confined to the mountain villages in the **Pélion** massif (see p. 209) and the coastal resorts on the peninsula of **Magnesia**.

Thrace
ΘΡΑΚΙΑ
(Thrakía)

Thrace, the most north-easterly province of Greece, of which it became part only in 1913, is named after the Thracians who settled here in the 2nd millennium B.C. It extends in a long narrow strip, between the northern Aegean and Bulgaria, from Néstos in the W to the River Évros which forms the frontier with Turkey. Like Macedonia, Thrace is a region of fertile plains, an agricultural region which is addition to corn, wine and in recent years rice also produces tobacco. The capital is Komotiní.

Tilos
ΤΗΛΟΣ
(Tílos)

Nomos: Dodecanese.
Area: 60 sq. km (23 sq. miles). – Population: 600.

TRANSPORTATION. – On the Piraeus–Astypálaia–Rhodes boat route.

The little Dodecanese island of Tílos, with hills rising to a height of 650 m (2133 feet), lies between Rhodes and Kos.

Two large bays cut into the island on the N and one on the S side. The landing-place

The rocks of Metéora in Thessaly

at *Livádia* lies in the north-eastern bay, the principal settlement, **Megalokhorió** (pop. 300), 12 km (7 miles) away in the north-western bay, under a *castle of the Knights of St John*. In the interior of the island is the little village of *Mikrokhorió*.

Tinos
ΤΗΝΟΣ
(Tínos)

Nomos: Cyclades. – Telephone dialling code: 0283.
Area: 194 sq. km (75 sq. miles). – Population: 8230.
ⓘ **Tourist Police,**
  Platía Eleftherías;
  tel. 2 22 55
  (only in summer).

TRANSPORTATION. – Boat connections with Piraeus and with Mýkonos, Rafína and Ándros.

HOTELS. – *Tínos Beach*, A, 339 b.; *Favie Souzane*, B, 63 b.; *Theoxenia*, B, 59 b.; *Tinion*, B, 49 b.; *Argo*, C, 20 b.;

Pilgrimage church of Panayía Evangelistría

Asteria, C, 72 b.; *Avra*, C, 31 b.; *Delphinia*, C, 73 b.; *Flisvos*, C, 66 b.; *Galini*, C, 15 b.; *Leto*, C, 36 b.; *Meltemi*, C, 66 b.; *Oasis*, C, 18 b.; *Oceanis*, C, 91 b.; *Poseidonion*, C, 73 b.

BATHING BEACHES. – Stávros (2 km (1 mile) NW of Tínos), Kiónia (4 km (2 miles) NW), Áyios Fokás (2 km (1 mile) SE), Pánormos Bay (in the N of the island).

The island of Tínos, in the Cyclades, is a continuation of the mountain chain which extends SE from Euboea by way of Ándros.

On the island of Tínos

HISTORY. – In ancient times, from the 3rd c. B.C. onwards, the sanctuary of Poseidon and Amphitrite on Tínos was a major religious centre; and in our own day, since the early 19th c., the island has possessed a leading shrine of the Orthodox Church. – Held from 1207 to 1712 by Venice, Tínos had the longest "Frankish period" of any part of Greece, and its population includes a considerable proportion of Roman Catholics. The Orthodox population began to increase from 1822, when – during the war of liberation – a nun named Pelagia, guided by a vision, found a wonderworking icon of the Panayía, which soon became the object of annual pilgrimages on the feasts of the Annunciation (25 March) and Dormition (15 August), so that Tínos developed into a kind of Greek Lourdes. The island came into international prominence when on 15 August 1940 – two months before Mussolini's declaration of war – an Italian submarine torpedoed the Greek cruiser "Elli", which was lying in Tínos harbour for the Feast of the Dormition.

SIGHTS. – The chief town, **Tínos** (pop. 2900), lies on the S coast. Around the harbour, now enlarged, are numerous tavernas and coffee-houses, the rendez-vous of both local people and tourists.

Pigeon-cotes, Tínos

From here a broad processional avenue leads to the gleaming white complex, built from 1822 onwards using stone from the sanctuary of Poseidon, of the **monastery** and the *pilgrimage church of Panayía Evangelistría* or Tiniótissa. Within the church, under a stone canopy, is the wonderworking *icon*, spangled with pearls and precious stones and surrounded by large numbers of ex-votos. – On the lower floor of the building are a room commemorating those who were killed in the Italian attack on the "Elli" in 1940 and an impressive little *chapel*.

The small *Archaeological Museum* some distance below the church contains finds from the sanctuary of Poseidon and Amphitrite, including architectural elements (in the courtyard) and, on the upper floor, large pottery vessels, among them a *pithos with relief decoration* depicting the birth of Athena from the head of a winged Zeus (7th c. B.C.).

4 km (2 miles) NW of Tínos is **Kiónia**, where the foundations of the Hellenistic **Sanctuary of Poseidon** have been excavated (propylaia, Doric stoa, court containing an altar, Doric temple).

A road runs NW from Tínos to **Istérnia** (22 km (14 miles): church with ceramic-faced dome), the picturesque village of **Pýrgos**, with a school of fine art, and its harbour at **Pánormos** (29 km – 18 miles). At Xinara a road goes off on the right to *Loutrá*, one of the island's most attractive villages.

13 km (8 miles) N of Tínos (bus to Falatádos) is the large **convent of Kekhrovoúni**, founded in the 12th c. and at present occupied by some 70 nuns. In addition to a number of interesting *icons* visitors are shown the quarters occupied by Pelagia, the nun who found the wonderworking icon in 1822. From the convent there are fine *views* of the harbour of Tínos and **Mt Exóbourgo** (533 m – 1749 feet), the site of the island's chief town in medieval times, with the ruins of a Venetian castle.

Characteristic of Tínos are the handsome Venetian *pigeon-cotes* which are encountered all over the island.

Tiryns
ΤΙΡΥΝΣ
(Tírins)

Region: Peloponnese. – Nomos: Argolid.

The mighty **Mycenaean citadel of Tiryns stands on a rocky hill which is only 25 m (82 feet) high but commands the coastal plain extending to the Gulf of Argolis. The site was occupied from the 3rd millennium B.C., and excavation has revealed the remains of a large circular structure.

The site was excavated by Schliemann and Dörpfeld from 1884 onwards, and some sections of the massive cyclopean walls were re-erected.

HISTORY. – Tiryns was associated in ancient legend with Perseus and with Eurystheus, in whose service Herakles performed his 12 labours. It shows many

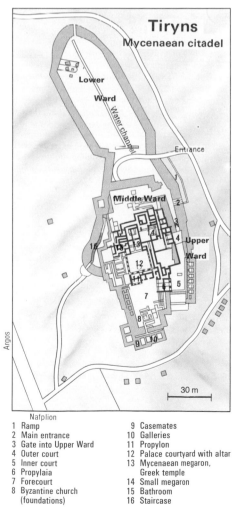

Tiryns
Mycenaean citadel

Lower Ward

Water channel

Entrance

Middle Ward

Upper Ward

Argos

Nafplion

30 m

1 Ramp	9 Casemates
2 Main entrance	10 Galleries
3 Gate into Upper Ward	11 Propylon
4 Outer court	12 Palace courtyard with altar
5 Inner court	13 Mycenaean megaron,
6 Propylaia	Greek temple
7 Forecourt	14 Small megaron
8 Byzantine church	15 Bathroom
(foundations)	16 Staircase

parallels with Mycenae (see p. 188). The first fortress was erected in the 16th c. B.C.; then in the 14th and 13th c. the walls and bastions on the S and E sides were built in their present form, and the old E gate was buried under the new propylaia. The ramp on the E side, the flight of steps on the W side and the new palace also date from this Late Mycenaean period, when there was evidently a threat from bands of invaders. Recent excavations have shown that the lower part of the Citadel to the N was not, as had long been supposed, merely a place of refuge for the population of the surrounding area but was densely built up and remained inhabited after the fall of Tiryns (*c.* 1125 B.C.) and into the 11th c. B.C.

The entrance to the site is at the SE corner. The ramp on the E side leads up to the **entrance gate**, guarded by two towers. Turning left, we pass through another gate, originally of the same dimensions as the Lion Gate at Mycenae. We then turn right and pass through the **propylaia** into the *Forecourt.* From here we can descend to the **E Bastion**. The *corridor* (which was originally roofed) has been preserved, but the six chambers in the thickness of the outer wall are badly ruined. There are other casemates at the southern tip of the Citadel.

From the forecourt we enter the *Inner Court*, in which, immediately on the right, is a circular *altar*. The far side of the court was occupied by the dominating bulk of the principal Megaron (remains of a 7th c. temple of Hera built over its ruins). Adjoining it on the right is a smaller megaron. These formed the central element of the palace, with a series of smaller rooms grouped around them. To the W can be seen the large stone slab which was the floor of a *bathroom* (with drain). Near this is the massive **W Bastion**, a 13th c. addition to the Citadel's defences. Within the bastion is a staircase leading down to a postern gate. Outside this can be seen an area of the town which has recently been excavated.

Tolon
ΤΟΛΟΝ
(Tolón)

Region: Peloponnese. – Nomos: Argolid.
Altitude: 5 m (16 feet).

HOTELS. – *Dolphin*, B, 42 b.; *Solon*, B, 56 b.; *Aktaeon*, C, 43 b.; *Aris*, C, 58 b.; *Artemis*, C, 28 b.; *Coronis*, C, 36 b.; *Electra*, C; *Epidavria*, C, 70 b.; *Phlisvos*, C, 54 b.; *Minoa*, C, 83 b.; *Phryne*, C, 26 b.; *Posidonion*, C, 69 b.; *Romvi*, C, 33 b.; *Spartakos*, C, 18 b.; *Thetis*, C, 24 b.; *Tolo*, C, 72 b.

CAMPING SITE.

The little fishing village of Tolón, 12 km (7 miles) SE of Náfplion in a bay on the Gulf of Argolis, has developed into a popular holiday resort, thanks to its beautiful situation and its sandy beach.

SURROUNDINGS. – Near the village of *Asíni*, NW of the town, are the remains of ancient **Asine**, on a site which was occupied from the 3rd millennium onwards. The remains include the massive walls of the acropolis, on which there are traces of other buildings (Swedish excavations).

Trikala
ΤΡΙΚΑΛΑ
(Trikala)

Nomos: Trikala.
Altitude: 115 m (377 feet). – Population: 35,000.

TRANSPORTATION. – Station on the Palaiofársalos-Kalambáka railway line; bus connections with Athens, Kalambáka and Lárisa.

HOTELS. – *Achillion*, B, 122 b.; *Divani*, B, 121 b.; *Dina*, C, 96 b.; *Palladion*, C, 34 b.; *Rex*, C, 104 b.

Trikala, on the western edge of the plain of Thessaly, famed in ancient times for its horses, is the market town and centre of this agricultural region.

Ancient *Trikka* was the home of the hero Asklepios, who became the god of healing. In the Middle Ages it was the capital of a Serbian prince. It has a lively *bazaar*, with excellent tavernas, and pleasant walks along the banks of the River Lithaios. There are fine views from the Byzantine **castle** which occupies the site of the ancient acropolis.

SURROUNDINGS. – A road runs SW via **Piyí** (7 km – 4 miles) to the *Pórta pass* (21 km – 13 miles) and the church of *Panayía Pórtas*, founded in 1283 (mosaics of that period and 15th c. frescoes). – On a hill 14 km (9 miles) E, to the left of the road to Lárisa, are the walls of ancient **Pelinnaion**, on a site later occupied by the Byzantine episcopal town of *Gardiki*.

Tripolis
ΤΡΙΠΟΛΙΣ
(Trípolis)

Nomos: Arcadia. – Telephone dialling code: 071.
Altitude: 660 m (2165 feet). – Population: 20,000.
ⓘ **Tourist Police,**
   Platía Yeoryíou B 7;
   tel. 2 30 39.

TRANSPORTATION. – Station on the Corinth–Kalamáta railway line; bus connections with Athens, Corinth and Sparta.

HOTELS. – *Menalon*, A, 66 b.; *Arcadia*, B, 85 b.; *Semiramis*, B, 68 b.; *Alex*, C, 59 b.; *Anaktorikon*, C, 60 b.; *Artemis*, C, 114 b.; *Galaxy*, C, 150 b.; *Palladion*, C, 35 b.

CAMPING SITE.

Trípolis, capital of Arcadia, on the central Arcadian plateau, was founded by settlers from Albania in the 14th c. During the Turkish period, under the name of Tripolitsa, it was the seat of the Pasha of the Morea. The town was captured by Kolokotrónis in 1821, but destroyed by Ibrahim Pasha in 1828. It is now the centre of the surrounding agricultural region, situated at the intersection of the principal roads traversing the Peloponnese.

SURROUNDINGS. – Within easy reach of Trípolis are the sites of three ancient cities – **Mantineia** (15 km (9 miles)), **Tegea** (8 km (5 miles) SE) and **Megalopolis** (34 km (21 miles) SW). See the entries for these places.

and then taking a road to the left (3 km – 2 miles).

TOUR OF THE SITE. – From the village a footpath leads in 25 minutes to the scattered remains. After passing over the line of the *town walls* and crossing the River Yefírion we come to the **Sanctuary of Hippolytos**, with the remains of buildings of the 4th and 3rd c. B.C. The late 4th c. Temple of Hippolytos had 6×11 columns. To the NW are a *peristyle building* of some size which is interpreted as an Asklepieion or a sacred refectory, a small *temple* of Aphrodite Kataskopia (?) and the Byzantine **Episkopí church** (11th c.), with the *Bishop's Palace* adjoining. To the SW are some foundations which may belong to the tomb of Phaidra.

The central area of the town, with the *Agora*, the remains of Roman *baths* and *chapels* on the site of an Early Christian basilica, is some distance away to the SE, the Acropolis, with a *temple of Athena*, to the S.

Troizen
ΤΡΟΙΖΗΝΑ
(Trizína)

Region: Peloponnese. – Nomos: Argolid.

The ancient city of Troizen, on the N coast of the Argolid peninsula opposite the island of Póros, had close links with Athens.

HISTORY. – Troizen was believed to be the birthplace of the Attic hero Theseus. Here too Hippolytos, son of Theseus and the Amazon Hippolyte, was dragged to death by his horses when he rejected the love of his stepmother Phaidra (cf. Euripides' "Hippolytos"). When Athens was evacuated in 480 B.C. in face of the Persian threat many refugees, particularly women, fled to Troizen. The town continued to exist into Christian times. The site was excavated in 1890 and 1932 by French and German archaeologists respectively.

The village of *Trizín* (commonly known as *Damalá*) can be reached from Náfplion via Ligourió, Trakhiá and the coastal villages of Fanári and Kalóni, turning right 9 km (6 miles) beyond Kalóni into a side road (3 km – 2 miles); or from Galatás (opposite Póros), going 7 km (4 miles) W

Vergina
ΒΕΡΓΙΝΑ
(Véryina)

Region: Macedonia. – Nomos: Imathia.

HOTELS. – In Véria, 15 km (9 miles) W (see below).

The village of Vérgina, 75 km (47 miles) SW of Salonica on the southern edge of the Aliakmón plain, has long been known for the palace and tombs of Palátitsa, but has recently come into the news again with the sensational finds made here by Manolis Andronikos, an archaeologist who has made a special study of this region.

Palátitsa, situated on a terrace above the River Aliakmón, was settled about 1000 B.C., but its rise to importance began in the 4th c. B.C. The discovery of a *domed tomb* of the Hellenistic period in 1855 was followed after a long interval by the excavation in 1939 of a *chamber tomb with four Ionic half-columns and a temple-like pediment on the façade and a *marble throne* in the tomb chamber (*c*. 250 B.C.). The tomb lies 500 m (547 yards) from the E end of Vérgina, on the right of the road. The occupant of this tomb must have been a member of the same aristocratic caste to which the *palace situated above the village must be ascribed.

From the E end of the palace, which is rectangular in plan, an entrance corridor 10 m (33 feet) wide leads into a large *central courtyard*, 44·80 m (147 feet) square, surrounded by four **colonnades** of 16 columns each, off which the various rooms of the palace open. A circular room on the left, beyond the entrance corridor, was probably a *Heroon* for the cult of ancestors. At a subsidiary entrance on the S side are two rooms with *mosaic floors*, probably used for the reception of guests. On the W side are large *banqueting rooms*, on the N a hall 104 m (341 feet) long. The living quarters were no doubt on the upper floor, of which no trace remains.

Both the chamber tomb and the palace date from the first half of the 3rd c. B.C. In the autumn of 1977, however, Andronikos discovered a completely intact **royal tomb** which was confidently dated to the 4th c. (350–320 B.C.) by the coins and pottery it contained.

Under a burial mound 12 m (39 feet) high and 100 m (328 feet) in diameter was found a stone-built tomb chamber with a sealed marble door, above which was a painting of a lion-hunt (5·50 by 1·20 m – 18 by 4 feet) – the first original Greek painting of this period so far discovered. In the antechamber was a marble sarcophagus, within which was a casket of solid gold weighing 8·5 kg (19 lb) containing human remains and fragments of a cloak of deep blue material embroidered with gold. In the main chamber was a larger gold casket (11 kg – 24 lb) with the Macedonian royal emblem of a 16-pointed star on the lid, which contained human remains, a diadem and sceptre, and parts of a costly suit of armour.

The excavator concluded from the contents of the tomb that it was the **tomb of King Philip II of Macedon** (383–336 B.C.), father of Alexander the Great. The armour found in the main tomb chamber included two greaves of unequal length, and it is known from the sources that Philip had a limp. Five small ivory heads found in the tomb were identified by Andronikos as Philip, his parents, his last wife Kleopatra and his son Alexander. All this suggests that the Macedonian capital of Aigai, where members of the royal family would be buried, lay not at Édessa (see p. 129) but at Vérgina. At any rate it is certain that the tomb was a royal one, and its furnishings – first shown to the public in Salonica in 1978 – were of astonishing quality.

In August 1978 Andronikos found a second richly furnished tomb, also intact, in the same mound, only a few metres away from the first. It was dated rather earlier, between 375 and 350 B.C. Further finds and further additions to knowledge are to be anticipated.

Veria
BEPOIA
(Véria)

Nomos: Imathia.
Altitude: 180 m (591 feet). – Population: 3000.

HOTELS. – *Polytimi*, C, 50 b.; *Vasilissa Vergina*, C, 46 b.; *Villa Elia*, C, 65 b.

The Macedonian town of Véria, the ancient Beroia, lies N of the River Aliakmón, 75 km (47 miles) SW of Salonica on the road to Kozáni.

HISTORY. – First recorded in 500 B.C., Beroia belonged to the kingdom of Macedon, and became Roman in 168 B.C. along with the rest of Macedonia. In A.D. 54 the Apostle Paul preached the new faith to the Jewish community of the town (Acts 17, 10–13 and 20, 4). In the 14th c. the town was occupied by the Serbs, in the 15th by the Turks.

SIGHTS. – Véria has a number of churches, the most interesting of which are **Áyios Khristós** (paintings of 1315), **Ayía Fotiní** (also with paintings) and **Áyios Kýrikos**, all in Odós Makariótissa. In the main square can be seen remains of the ancient *town walls* and a Turkish **mosque**, and there are other ancient remains, including a **town gate** excavated in 1960, at the junction of the roads from Salonica and Náousa. The **Museum** (on the N side of the road to Vérgina) contains local finds dating from Hellenistic and Roman times.

SURROUNDINGS. – 15 km (9 miles) away are the **Vérgina** excavations (see p. 253). – Véria is a good base from which to climb **Mt Vermíon** (2016 m – 6614 feet), a popular winter sports area (ski-lifts).

Volos
ΒΟΛΟΣ
(Vólos)

Nomos: Magnesia. – Telephone dialling code: 0421.
Altitude: 10–30 m (33–98 feet). – Population: 67,500.

(i) Greek National Tourist Organisation (EOT),
Ríga Feraíou;
tel. 2 35 00.
Tourist Police,
Khatziárgyri 87;
tel. 2 70 94.

TRANSPORTATION. – Air and bus connections with Athens; boat connections with Piraeus, the Sporades and Kými (Euboea); station on the Lárisa–Vólos–Palaiofársalos railway line.

HOTELS. – *Pallas*, A, 80 b.; *Aegli*, B, 80 b.; *Alexandros*, B, 134 b.; *Argo*, B, 40 b.; *Nepheli*, B, 100 b.; *Park*, B, 225 b.; *Xenia*, B, 88 b.; *Admitos*, C, 53 b.; *Avra*, C, 42 b.; *Philoxenia*, C, 34 b.; *Galaxy*, C, 102 b.; *Iolkos*, C, 25 b.; *Kypseli*, C, 100 b.; *Sandi*, C, 67 b.

Vólos

Vólos, in the much-indented Gulf of Vólos (mod. Greek Pagasitikós Kólpos), rebuilt after earthquake damage in 1955, is Greece's third largest port and the principal port for the shipment of the agricultural produce of Thessaly. It has weaving mills, cement works and tobacco factories.

HISTORY. – The town was founded only in the 14th c., although it lies in an area which has been occupied by man since the Neolithic age. The oldest settlements were found at the villages of Sésklo (4th millennium) and Dímini (3rd millennium), to the W of the town. The 2nd millennium saw the establishment, within the area of the present-day town, of the Mycenaean Iolkos, seat of King Pelias and home of his nephew Jason, who sailed from Iolkos with the Argonauts. To the same period belongs Pherai, situated near Lake Boibeis (Karla), now almost completely drained, the seat of Admetos and Alkestis; the site is at Velestíno, 20 km (12 miles) NW of Vólos, to the right of the Vólos–Lárisa road. The port of Pherai was Pagasai, after which the gulf is named. Immediately N of Pagasai is the site of Demetrias, founded by Demetrios Poliorketes in 293 B.C.

SIGHTS. – On the way up from the busy new town around the harbour to the eastern outskirts on the slopes of Mt Pelion an extensive view opens up. – On the NW side of the town, to the right of the Lárisa road between the railway and the river-bed, remains of *Mycenaean buildings* have been excavated. Here an earlier

palace built about 1400 B.C. was succeeded by a later one, which was destroyed by fire in about 1200 B.C. – There is an interesting *Archaeological Museum in the W of the town. Since reorganisation in 1976 the exhibits are presented in the most modern way.

The material begins with the Neolithic period (Sésklo, Dímini, Pýrasos), but the great feature of the museum is its unique collection of more than 200 painted *grave stelae of the 3rd c. B.C. from Demetrias. Other items of particular interest are a *torso of Aphrodite* from Skópelos and a Hellenistic *head of Asklepios* from Trikka.

SURROUNDINGS. – Sésklo (18 km (11 miles) W) and Dímini (6 km (4 miles) W) are recommended only for those with a special interest in the prehistoric and early historical periods.

3 km (2 miles) S of Vólos the road crosses the site of Demetrias and the older town of Pagasai. To the right of the road can be seen the *Theatre* (restored 1960) and the hill (84 m – 276 feet) on which Demetrios Poliorketes built his palace. The chapel of *Áyios Ilías* on a hill to the left of the road marks the most southerly point of the walls of Demetrias and the most easterly point of Pagasai (some remains of walls still to be seen).

The road continues to **Néa Ankhialòs** (22 km – 14 miles), founded by refugees from the Black Sea coast of Anatolia in 1907. It occupies the site of ancient *Pýrasos*, which had known human occupation since Neolithic times. Four Early Christian basilicas have been found here. The small museum contains material from Pýrasos, which was the port of the ancient town of Thebai Phthiotides.

Within easy reach of Vólos is the beautiful scenery of **Mt Pélion** (see p. 209).

Vonitsa
BONITΣA
(Vónitsa)

Nomos: Aetolia and Acarnania.
Altitude: 10 m (33 feet). – Population: 2500.

TRANSPORTATION. – Bus connections with Amfilokhía and Lefkás.

HOTELS. – *Avra*, C, 27 b.; *Leto*, D, 16 b.; *Anaktorion*, E, 12 b.

The little village of Vónitsa, on the S side of the Ambracian Gulf, is dominated by a massive Venetian castle.

Vónitsa can be reached either from the pretty little fishing village of **Amfilokhía**, at the SE corner of the gulf (tavernas on the shore: fish a speciality), on a narrow but quiet little asphalted road which runs through beautiful hilly country (40 km – 25 miles); or by taking the ferry from **Préveza** (see p. 220) and driving 15 km (9 miles) E.

HISTORY. – The castle was originally built in the Byzantine period, and in 1084 withstood an attack by Robert Guiscard. From 1362 it was held by Leonardo Tocco and his successors, who gloried in the titles of duke of Leucadia, count of Cefalonia and lord of Vónitsa. They developed the castle into such a formidable fortress that it was able to hold out until 1479, although surrounded by Turkish territory.

The **castle** has well-preserved walls, bastions and gates, and contains within the ramparts several towers, a chapel, a cistern and other buildings.

SURROUNDINGS. – From Vónitsa a road goes SW, past the airport, to the island of **Lefkás** (19 km (12 miles): see p. 170). – A recently improved road runs S to the three fishing villages of **Páleros** (15 km – 9 miles), **Mítikas** (18 km – 11 miles: boats to the offshore island of Kálamos) and **Astakós** (33 km – 21 miles).

Xylokastro
ΞΥΛΟΚΑΣΤΡΟ
(Xilókastro)

Nomos: Corinth.
Altitude: 10 m (33 feet). – Population: 4000.

TRANSPORTATION. – On the highway and railway between Corinth and Pátras; bus connections with both towns.

HOTELS. – *Arion*, A, 120 b.; *Apollo*, B, 48 b.; *Phaidra*, B, 51 b.; *Miramare*, B, 42 b.; *Rallis*, B, 132 b.; *Periandros*, C, 45 b.

CAMPING SITE. – BEACH BUNGALOWS.

W OF XYLÓKASTRO. – LYKOPORÍA (12 km – 7 miles): *Alcyon*, C, 26 b.

E OF XYLÓKASTRO. – MELISSA (3 km – 2 miles): *Xylokastron Beach*, C, 154 b. – KIÁTON (13 km – 8 miles): *Triton*, B, 56 b.; *Galini*, C, 48 b.; *Pefkias*, C, 26 b.; *Sikyon*, C, 46 b. – KOKÓNI (16 km – 10 miles): *Angela*, C, 260 b.

Xylókastro is a popular holiday resort 33 km (21 miles) W of Corinth on the S side of the Gulf of Corinth.

SURROUNDINGS. – Driving 13 km (8 miles) SE to Kiáton and then turning right, we come to the village of *Vasilikó* (6 km – 4 miles) and the site of ancient **Sikyon**, home of the sculptor Lysippos. There are remains of a theatre, a stadion, a gymnasion, the bouleuterion, a temple and the stoa of the agora; small museum.

Turning sharp right (W) from Kiáton, we come in 35 km (22 miles) to the village of **Stymphalia**, on the **Stymphalian Lake** (alt. 740 m (2428 feet)), which is subject to sharp seasonal variations in level. Strabo believed that the spring at Kefalári, S of Argos, was the outflow from the lake. This was the home of the fearsome Stymphalian birds which Herakles destroyed.

31 km (19 miles) SW is the village of **Tríkala** (alt. 1100 m (3609 feet)), from which **Mt Kyllíni** (2376 m – 7796 feet) can be climbed.

Near Xylókastro are a number of other coastal resorts which also offer good bathing.

Zakynthos
ΖΑΚΥΝΘΟΣ
(Zákinthos)

Nomos: Zákynthos. – Telephone dialling code: 0695.
Area: 402 sq. km (155 sq. miles). – Population: 30,200.
ⓘ **Tourist Police**,
Eleftheríou Venizélou,
Zákynthos town;
tel. 2 25 50.

TRANSPORTATION. – Air connections with Athens; ferry from Kyllíni; bus from Athens.

HOTELS. – ZÁKYNTHOS: *Strada Marina*, B, 91 b.; *Xenia*, B, 78 b.; *Adriana*, C, 18 b.; *Aegli*, C, 16 b.; *Angelika*, C, 32 b.; *Apollon*, C, 18 b.; *Astoria*, C, 15 b.; *Diana*, C, 69 b.; *Phoenix*, C, 70 b.; *Zenith*, C, 14 b. – ALYKÁ (16 km (10 miles) NW): *Asteria*, C, 16 b.; *Montreal*, C, 16 b. – ARGÁSI (4 km (2 miles) SE): *Mimosa Beach*, B, 60 b.; *Argassi Beach*, C, 14 b.; *Chryssi Akti*, C, 76 b. – LAGANÁS (8 km (5 miles) SW): *Galaxy*, B, 84 b.; *Zante Beach Bungalows*, B, 360 b.; *Asteria*, C, 23 b.; *Atlantis*, C, 20 b.; *Eugenia*, C, 20 b.; *Hellinis*, C, 18 b.; *Ilios*, C, 16 b.; *Ionis*, C, 42 b.; *Blue Coast*, C, 20 b.; *Medikas*, C, 20 b.; *Panorama*, C, 18 b.; *Selini*, C, 16 b.; *Vezal*, C, 18 b.; *Victoria*, C, 18 b.; *Vyzantion*, C, 16 b.; *Zephyros*, C, 22 b. – PLÁNOS (4 km (2 miles) NW): *Anessis*, C, 14 b.; *Cosmopolit*, C, 27 b.; *Orea Eleni*, C, 28 b.

Zákynthos is the most southerly of the Ionian Islands in the main group, lying off the Peloponnese opposite Kyllíni and Olympia. During the period of Venetian rule between 1479 and 1797 (and under the British protectorate) it was known as Zante, and its mild climate earned it the name of "Zante – fior di Levante". The W coast is steep and rugged, the E coast hilly, between the coasts the lower land resembles one large garden.

The chief town, **Zákynthos** or *Zante* (pop. 10,000), lies on the E coast below a Venetian **castle** occupying the site of the ancient acropolis (panoramic views). Many of the town's old churches were destroyed in the 1953 earthquake: notable among those that survived or have been restored are **Kýra ton Ángelon** and **Áyios Dionýsios** (which is dedicated to the patron saint of the island and preserves his relics). By the harbour is the church of **Áyios Nikólaos**, on the N side of *Solomós Square*. In the centre of this spacious square stands a **monument to Dionýsios Solomós**. On the W side of the square is the *****Museum**, with a very fine collection of icons, wall paintings and iconostases which illustrates the development of *icon-painting* on Zákynthos in the 16th and 18th c. under Italian influence. Of particular interest are the *frescoes* in popular style from the church of Áyios

Andréas at Vólimes and works by Michael Damaskinos and two other refugees from Crete, Angelos and Emmanuel Lombardos.

NW of the museum is the **Mausoleum** of Dionýsios Zákynthos (1798–1857), who together with Ugo Fóscolo and Andréas Kálvos represents the island's contribution to modern Greek literature and is honoured as the author of the national anthem.

SURROUNDINGS. – Near the town is the beach of **Tsiliví**. There is also a long beach at **Laganás**, 9 km (6 miles) from Zákynthos in the wide bay at the S end of the island. The road to Laganás continues to the pitch springs of *Kerí* (20 km – 12 miles), which have been known since ancient times.

Practical Information

Corinth Canal

the higher upland regions the climate shows some continental features, with marked temperature differences between day and night and between summer and winter. Elsewhere in mainland Greece and on the islands the climate is of Mediterranean type, with high winter and summer temperatures. The rain falls mainly in winter.

For a more detailed account of the climate in the different parts of Greece, see p. 13.

When to Go

The best times of year for a visit to Greece are the spring and autumn – from the second half of March to the end of May or beginning of June and during the months of September and October and sometimes also the beginning of November. The summer months (mid June to the beginning of September) are very hot, particularly in the large towns, though the *meltemi*, the N wind which blows throughout the year, brings a measure of coolness in the Aegean area. At this time of the year the numerous insects, particularly mosquitoes, can be troublesome. September is still warm, but may bring the first showers of rain.

Even in summer it is advisable to take a warm jacket or pullover, for on the coast and in the hills it is often cool in the evening.

Weather

In northern Greece, in some enclosed areas in the interior of the country and in

Time

During the winter Greece is on Eastern European Time, which is 2 hours ahead of GMT, 7 hours ahead of New York time. From April to September *Greek summer time* is in force – 3 hours ahead of GMT, 2 hours ahead of British summer time and 8 hours ahead of New York time.

Travel Documents

Visitors from the United Kingdom, the United States of America, Australia, Canada and New Zealand (among other countries) require only a valid **passport**, without visa, for a stay of up to 3 months provided that they do not take up any employment in Greece during that period. If they wish to stay longer than 3 months they must apply for an extension, at least 20 days before the end of the period, to the Aliens Police in Athens (Astynomia Allodapon, Khalkokondyli 9) or, outside Athens, to the local police authorities.

US and British **driving licences** and car **registration documents** are accepted

Temperatures and Rainfall in Greece

Temperatures in °C (°F)

Area	Air					Sea		Ann. av. rainfall in mm (in.)
	Ann. av.	Jan.	Jul./Aug.	Ann. min.	Ann. max.	Jan.	Jul./Aug.	
Athens	17·8 (64)	9·3 (49)	27·5/27·5 (81/81)	−5·5 (22)	43·0 (109)	14·8 (59)	24·9/25·6 (77/78)	401 (16)
Salonica	16·4 (62)	5·0 (41)	26·6/26·3 (80/79)	−9·5 (15)	41·6 (107)	11·5 (53)	24·5/24·8 (76/77)	477 (19)
Corfu	17·4 (63)	10·0 (50)	26·7/26·6 (80/80)	−2·8 (27)	41·0 (106)	15·5 (60)	25·7/26·8 (78/80)	1137 (45)
Crete	19·0 (66)	12·3 (54)	25·9/25·6 (79/78)	+0·1 (32)	45·7 (114)	15·2 (59)	25·9/25·6 (79/78)	539 (21)

Average hours of sunshine: 2500–3000 annually

in Greece but holders of a licence issued in the Republic of Ireland must have an International Driving Permit. Foreign cars must display an oval international distinguishing sign of the approved type and design. Failure to comply with this regulation is punishable by a fine. A "green card" (international insurance certificate) must be carried. – Pleasure craft (small motorboats and sailing boats without sleeping accommodation) are admitted with either a carnet or a "free use" card issued by the customs authorities.

Medical cover. – Now that Greece is a member of the EEC British visitors, like other EEC citizens, are entitled to receive health care on the same basis as the Greeks. You should apply to the Department of Health and Social Security, well before your date of departure, for leaflet SA30 which gives details of reciprocal arrangements for medical treatment and contains an application form for a certificate of entitlement (Form E111). Fuller cover may be obtained by insuring privately. Visitors from non-EEC countries should certainly take out such insurance.

Customs Regulations

Visitors to Greece can take in without payment of duty items required for their personal use, including a camera and films, and sports and camping equipment, together with small quantities of provisions for the journey (including a bottle of spirits and 200 cigarettes or 50 cigars or 200 grams of tobacco). They can also take in new articles up to a value of 150 U.S. dollars provided that they are intended for their personal use or as gifts but not for sale (excluding electrical apparatus and photographic and film equipment). The import of flowers and plants, and also of radio transmitters is prohibited.

Items brought in for the visitor's personal use must be taken out again. Provisions up to the value of 50 U.S. dollars and souvenirs to the value of 150 dollars may be taken out free of export duty. The export of *antiquities* and *works of art* is prohibited except in special cases with the authorisation of the State Archaeological Service (Polygnotou 13, Athens).

Currency

The unit of currency is the **drachma**, which is divided into 100 *lepta*.

There are *banknotes* for 50, 100, 500 and 1000 dr. and *coins* in denominations of 5, 10, 20 and 50 lepta and 1, 2, 5, 10 and 20 dr.

Visitors may take into or bring out of Greece a maximum of 1500 dr. in Greek currency. There are no restrictions on the import of foreign currency either in the form of cash or travellers' checks. Foreign currency up to 500 U.S. dollars may be taken out again within a year; larger amounts may be taken out if they have been declared on entry. – It is advisable to take money in the form of travellers' checks or to use a credit card. The principal credit cards are widely accepted.

Postal Rates

Letters within Greece cost 8 dr. (up to 20 grams); to Western Europe by air mail 14 dr. (20 g); to the U.S.A. and Canada by air mail 18 dr. (10 g) or 22 dr. (20 g).

Postcards cost 6 dr. within Greece, 10 dr. to Western Europe and 12 dr. to the U.S.A. and Canada (all by surface mail).

Travel to Greece

The main access routes to Greece from Northern and Western Europe are through Yugoslavia or by way of Italy and by ferry from one of the Italian Adriatic ports to Igoumenítsa, Pátras or Piraeus.

The quickest and easiest way to get to Greece is *by air*. There are regular services from London to Athens (daily), Salonica and Corfu, and charter flights, particularly during the holiday season, to these and other Greek airports. From New York TWA and Olympic fly non-stop to Athens.

The shortest route to Greece *by road* is through Yugoslavia via Zagreb and Belgrade, reaching the Greek frontier at either Evzoni (approx. 550 km (342 miles) from Athens) or Niki (approx. 600 km (373 miles) from Athens). The distance through Yugoslavia from the Austrian or

Italian frontier is between 1100 and 1200 km (684 and 746 miles). Long sections of the route through Yugoslavia have been rebuilt and are good, but stretches of the road are in poor condition. This route is overloaded with heavy trucks in transit to the Middle East and, during the season, with holiday traffic. Drivers using this road, therefore, should exercise particular care. It should be avoided at night, in view of the numerous vehicles driving with inadequate lights, or no lights at all.

Much pleasanter, and not much longer, is the Adriatic coast road, which runs down the beautiful Adriatic coast of Yugoslavia from the Italian frontier via Rijeka, Split, Dubrovnik and the Bay of Kotor to Petrovac. From there a road runs inland to Titograd, Priština and Skopje to join the inland route into Greece.

The journey via either of these routes can be shortened by using one of the motorail services from either 's-Hertogenbosch in The Netherlands or Brussels (Belgium) to Villach in Austria or Ljubljana in northern Yugoslavia.

The alternative route by road is down through Italy and then across to Greece on one of the numerous car ferries from the Italian Adriatic coast (see table on p. 265). Here again the journey can be shortened by using the motorail services.

Travel in Greece

Greece is well served by domestic air, bus and rail services and by boat services to its numerous islands.

Travel by road

The Greek *road system* has been considerably improved in recent years, and the visiting motorist will now find asphalted roads almost everywhere – though in the remoter parts of the country they will often be narrow and winding. – When driving at night it is necessary to keep a good lookout for animals and unlit vehicles.

Salonica and Pátras are connected with Athens by new **national highways** (single carriageway motorways) on which tolls are charged.

Highway code. – As in the rest of continental Europe traffic travels on the right, with overtaking on the left. *Seat belts* must be worn when driving. It is an offence to drive when under the influence of *alcohol*. The use of a *warning triangle* is compulsory for all vehicles.
WARNING
Parking in Athens can be difficult and expensive. The police there are empowered to confiscate and detain the number plates from visitors' cars which are illegally parked. A heavy fine will also be imposed upon offenders and visitors are reminded that it is illegal to drive a vehicle without number plates.

The **speed limit** on national highways is 100 km p.h., on other roads 80 km p.h., in built-up areas 50 km p.h.

The main tourist routes are patrolled from April to September by the breakdown service of the Greek Automobile and Touring Club (ELPA). Drivers in need of assistance should indicate this by raising the hood or bonnet of their car or displaying a yellow cloth. ELPA assistance is free to foreign motorists.

Car ferries: see table on next page.

Car Ferries

SERVICE	FREQUENCY	COMPANY
Italy–Greece		
Ancona–Corfu/Pátras	Several times weekly	Karageorgis
Ancona–Corfu/Katakolon/Piraeus/Mýkonos[1]	Weekly	Med. Sun Lines
Ancona–Igoumenitsa	Twice weekly	Strintzis Lines
Ancona–Pátras	Weekly	Chandris
Ancona–Piraeus	Weekly 16 June–18 Oct.	Libra Maritime
Ancona–Piraeus	Weekly	Med. Sun Lines
Bari–Corfu/Igoumenitsa/Pátras	Daily	Epirus Line
Brindisi–Corfu/Igoumenitsa/Pátras	Daily	Hellenic Med. Lines
Brindisi–Corfu/Igoumenitsa/Pátras	5 times weekly	Fragoudakis Line
Brindisi–Corfu/Igoumenitsa	Daily	Libra Maritime
Otranto–Corfu/Igoumenitsa	5 times weekly	R Line
Venice–Pátras	Weekly	Chandris
Venice–Piraeus/Rhodes	Weekly	Adriatica
Venice–Piraeus/Rhodes	Weekly	Hellenic Med. Lines
Pátmos/Iráklion/Corfu–Ancona[1]	Weekly	Med. Sun Lines
Rhodes/Iráklion/Santorin/Piraeus–Ancona[1]	Weekly	Med. Sun Lines
Yugoslavia–Greece		
Bar–Igoumenitsa/Corfu	Twice weekly	Jadrolinija
Turkey–Greece		
Bodrum–Rhodes/Iráklion/Santorin/Piraeus[1]	Weekly	Med. Sun Lines
Kuşadası–Pátmos/Iráklion/Corfu[1]	Weekly	Med. Sun Lines
Piraeus–Bodrum[1]	Weekly	Med. Sun Lines
Istanbul–Piraeus	Twice monthly	Black Sea Steamships, Odessa
Piraeus/Mýkonos–Kuşadası[1]	Weekly	Med. Sun Lines
Israel–Greece		
Haifa–Piraeus	Weekly 18 June–18 Oct.	Libra Maritime
Egypt–Greece		
Alexandria–Piraeus	Weekly	Adriatica
Greece–Cyprus		
Piraeus–Larnaca	Twice monthly	Black Sea Steamships, Odessa
Piraeus/Rhodes–Limassol	Weekly	Adriatica
Piraeus–Limassol	Weekly	Sol Maritimo Services
Piraeus/Rhodes–Limassol	Weekly 15 June–26 Sept.	Hellenic Med. Lines
Piraeus/Rhodes–Limassol	Weekly	Lesvos Maritime Lines, Piraeus
Greece: mainland–islands		
Piraeus–Chios/Mytilíni/Salonica	Daily	Lesvos Maritime Lines, Piraeus
Piraeus–Iráklion (Crete)	Daily	Minoan Lines
Piraeus–Sámos	3 times weekly	Shipping & Tourist Co., Athens

[1] Service only in direction indicated

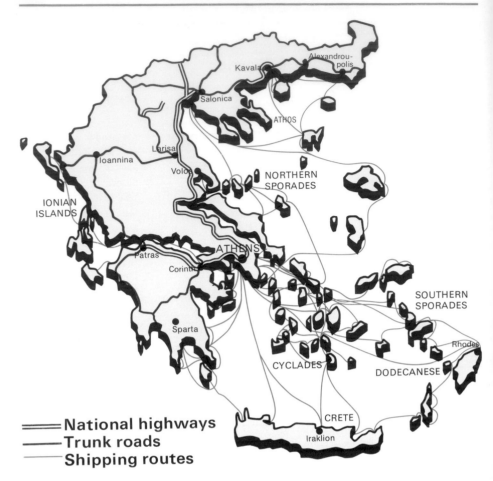

=== National highways
——— Trunk roads
——— Shipping routes

Local Ferry Services

Perama–Salamís	60–70 times daily	Pátras–Corfu	Twice weekly
Ríon–Antirrion	96 times daily	Préveza–Aktion	35 times daily
Aidipsos–Arkitsa	7–12 times daily	Igoumenitsa–Corfu	13 times daily
Eretria–Oropós	35 times daily	Corfu–Paxi	13 times daily
Glyfa–Ayiokampos	6–8 times daily	Kyllíni–Zákynthos	4 times daily
Pátras–Sami	4 times daily	Kavála–Thásos	7–18 times daily
Pátras–Sami–Ithaka	Daily	Keramoti–Thásos	10–12 times daily
Pátras–Paxi	Once or twice weekly	Alexandroúpolis–Samothrace	Daily

Caravan owners should note that there may be restrictions on the size of vehicles on some of these services. Check with the shipping line or travel agency before booking!

Information and Reservations

Adriatica,
158 Fenchurch Street,
London EC3;
tel. (01) 626 6961

437 Madison Avenue,
New York, N.Y.;
tel. 212 838 2113

Chandris,
66 Haymarket,
London SW1;
tel. (01) 930 0691

666 Fifth Avenue,
New York, N.Y.;
tel. 212 586 8370

Hellenic Mediterranean Lines,
18 Hanover Street,
London W1;
tel. (01) 499 0076

200 Park Avenue,
New York, N.Y.;
tel. 212 697 4220

Jadrolinija,
24 Charles II Street,
London SW1;
tel. (01) 839 7611

Karageorgis,
36 King Street,
London WC2;
tel. (01) 240 2695

1350 Avenue of the Americas,
New York, N.Y.;
tel. 212 582 3007

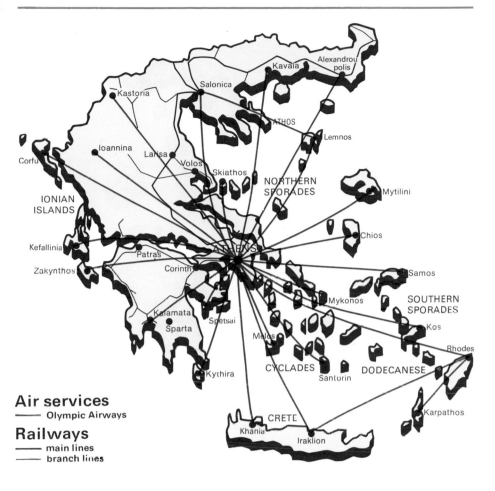

Air services
—— Olympic Airways
Railways
—— main lines
—— branch lines

Travel by Air

Greece is linked with the international air service network by the national airline **Olympic Airways**, and many foreign airlines. The country's principal airport is Athens-Ellinikó (with separate terminals for Olympic Airways and for other airlines); there are also international flights to and from Salonica and Corfu, in addition to numerous charter flights using these and other airports.

Greece also has a dense network of domestic air services. Thus Athens has air connections with all the larger Aegean islands and with Alexandroúpolis, Corfu, Ioánnina, Iráklion, Kalamáta, Kastoriá, Kavála, Kefallinía, Khaniá, Kos, Lemnos, Mýkonos, Mytilíni, Rhodes, Salonica, Sámos, Skiáthos and Santorin. There are also flights between other Greek airports, e.g. between Iráklion and Rhodes and between Salonica and Lemnos. – It should be noted that Greek domestic air timetables cannot always be implicitly relied on: it is advisable, therefore, to check in advance that your particular flight is actually operating at the time shown in the published timetables.

In addition to the many charter flights, particularly during the main holiday season, there are a variety of special flights, e.g. for students.

Travel by Rail

The Greek railway system – not surprisingly in view of the nature of the terrain – is much more restricted in its coverage than the systems of most other European countries. The only main line operated by **Greek Railways** (*Organismós Sidirodromón Elládos*, OSE) runs from Athens to Salonica and Alexandroúpolis, with connecting services to Yugoslavia, Bulgaria and Turkey and branch lines to Vólos, Kalambáka and Stylis. – There are also services (narrow-gauge) from

Greek Ports

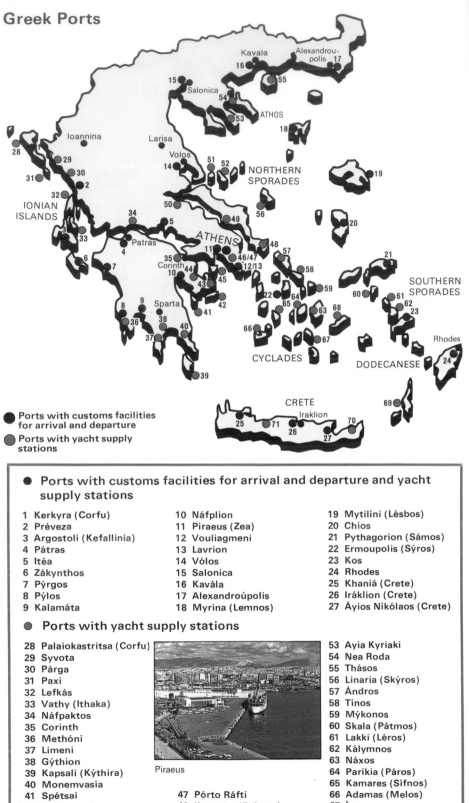

Ports with customs facilities for arrival and departure

Ports with yacht supply stations

Ports with customs facilities for arrival and departure and yacht supply stations

1 Kerkyra (Corfu)	10 Náfplion	19 Mytilíni (Lésbos)
2 Préveza	11 Piraeus (Zea)	20 Chios
3 Argostoli (Kefallinía)	12 Vouliagmeni	21 Pythagorion (Sámos)
4 Pátras	13 Lavrion	22 Ermoupolis (Sýros)
5 Itéa	14 Vólos	23 Kos
6 Zákynthos	15 Salonica	24 Rhodes
7 Pýrgos	16 Kavála	25 Khaniá (Crete)
8 Pýlos	17 Alexandroúpolis	26 Iráklion (Crete)
9 Kalamáta	18 Myrina (Lemnos)	27 Áyios Nikólaos (Crete)

Ports with yacht supply stations

28 Palaiokastritsa (Corfu)	53 Ayia Kyriaki
29 Syvota	54 Nea Roda
30 Párga	55 Thásos
31 Paxi	56 Linaria (Skýros)
32 Lefkás	57 Ándros
33 Vathy (Ithaka)	58 Tínos
34 Náfpaktos	59 Mýkonos
35 Corinth	60 Skala (Pátmos)
36 Methóni	61 Lakki (Léros)
37 Limeni	62 Kálymnos
38 Gýthion	63 Náxos
39 Kapsali (Kýthira)	64 Parikia (Páros)
40 Monemvasía	65 Kamares (Sífnos)
41 Spétsai	66 Adamas (Melos)
42 Hýdra	67 Íos
43 Póros	68 Katapola (Amorgós)
44 Palaia Epidauros	69 Kárpathos
45 Aegina	70 Sitía (Crete)
46 Glyfada	71 Réthymnon (Crete)

Piraeus

47 Pórto Ráfti
48 Karystos (Euboea)
49 Khalkis (Euboea)
50 Kaména Voúrla
51 Skiáthos
52 Skópelos

Athens to Corinth and the Peloponnese, one line going to Mycenae, Argos and Messíni, another to Pátras, Pýrgos and Kyparissía. – The system is not electrified, and in comparison with Western Europe the trains are slow.

Reduced fares. – There are reductions for parties of more than ten, schoolchildren and students at Greek universities. For tourists there are rail cards at cheap rates covering unlimited travel within a stated period. Children under 4 travel free; between 4 and 12 they pay half fare. – There is a reduction of some 20% on return tickets.

Bus Services

There is a dense network of bus services covering the whole country – both long-distance services and local services between towns and the surrounding area. For journeys starting from bus stations tickets are usually issued at the ticket office before departure. Local services are designed to meet the needs of the rural population, and tend to travel into town in the morning and return to the country in the afternoon.

Shopping, Souvenirs

Greece offers the visitor a wide choice of attractive souvenirs. But articles of this kind are now produced on a mass scale, and it may be necessary to look round a little to find items of good quality and taste.

The best place in Athens to find Greek **handicrafts** is in the vicinity of Monastiraki Square and in the adjoining Pandrosou Street. Metal articles (copper, brass, etc.) are to be found in this area, in nearby Adrianou Street and in many other places.

Pottery is offered for sale in all price ranges, from poor imitations of ancient vases, through good copies, to the beautiful products of the island of Páros. Líndos on the island of Rhodes is famous for its plates and Arkhangelos, also on Rhodes, for its vases. Among other distinctive local products is the ware made on the island of Sífnos.

Hand-weaving in a style derived from Byzantine traditions is to be found in the Pindos mountains (Métsovo), and fine work is also produced on the islands of Skýros, Kárpathos and Rhodes. The kelims of the Delphi region (Arákhova) also carry on ancient traditions. Articles with classical motifs (meander decoration, the Parthenon) are produced exclusively for tourist consumption.

Flokáti carpets, knotted woollen carpets which look rather like long-fleeced sheepskins, are another popular buy. They are made in natural wool or in a rich variety of colours.

Also popular with visitors are Greek traditional *costumes, embroidery, lace, leather goods* (particularly handbags) and *olive-wood carvings*.

Goldsmiths' work can be bought in the larger towns. Ioánnina is renowned for its *silver articles*.

Those who have sufficient room in their luggage may be attracted by the elaborately carved *child-sized furniture* made on the island of Skýros.

Finally many visitors may be tempted by the rich assortment of *sweets* and other delicacies on offer – aromatic honey, fig cakes soaked in ouzo, chocolate, nougat, etc. – and the variety of *nuts* (walnuts, almonds and above all pistachios).

A very interesting **exhibition of Greek handicrafts** can be seen in the showrooms of the National Organisation of Greek Handicrafts in Athens (Mitropoleos 9; tel. 3 22 10 17). The articles displayed are not for sale, but prospective purchasers can be put in direct touch with the craftsmen concerned. There are similar exhibitions in Alexandroúpolis, Ioánnina, Salonica, Pátras, Vólos, Kerkyra (Corfu), Trípolis and other towns. – Handicrafts are also displayed, and can be purchased, at the showrooms of the Hellenic Artisan Trades Cooperative in Athens (Leoforos Amalias 56; tel. 3 23 34 58).

Replicas of ancient works of art in museums all over Greece can be bought in the **National Archaeological Museum** in Athens, and can be exported without formality.

Warning: The export of antiquities and works of art (e.g. icons) is prohibited.

In exceptional cases an authorisation to export such items may be granted by the State Archaeological Service (Polygnotou 13, Athens). There are heavy penalties for contravention of the regulations.

Language

In most parts of Greece visitors are likely to come across local people with some knowledge of English of another European language; but in the remoter areas and on the islands it is helpful to have at least a smattering of modern Greek.

Modern Greek is considerably different from ancient Greek, though it is surprising to find how many words are still spelled the same way as in classical times. Even in such cases, however, the pronunciation is likely to be very different (cf. the table on p. 271). This difference in pronunciation is found in both the main forms of modern Greek, **dimotikí** (demotic or popular Greek) and **katharévousa** (the "purer" official or literary language). All official announcements, signs, timetables, etc., and the political pages in newspapers are written in katharévousa, which approximates more closely to classical Greek and may be deciphered, with some effort perhaps, by those who learned Greek at school. – The ordinary spoken language is demotic. This form, the result of a long process of organic development, has now also established itself in modern Greek literature, and is used in the lighter sections of newspapers. The differences between katharévousa and demotic are differences of both grammar and vocabulary. In addition there are various local, and particularly insular, dialects.

The Greek **alphabet** is shown in the table on p. 271. There is no recognised standard system for the transliteration of the Greek into the Latin alphabet, and many variant spellings are found. – The position of the *stress* in a word is very variable, but is always shown in the Greek alphabet by an accent, either acute ('), grave (`) or circumflex (˜); since there is no difference in modern Greek between the three types of accent, the acute is used in this Guide to indicate stress. – The *"breathings"* over a vowel or diphthong at the beginning of a word, whether rough (') or smooth ('), are not pronounced. – The *diaeresis* (¨) over a vowel indicates that it is to be pronounced separately, and not as part of a diphthong. – **Punctuation marks** are the same as in English, except that the semicolon (;) is used in place of the question-mark (?) and a point above the line (·) in place of the semicolon.

Numbers

0	midhén
1	énas, miá, éna
2	dhió, dhío
3	tris, tría
4	tésseris, téssera
5	pénde
6	éksi
7	eftá
8	okhtó
9	enneá
10	dhéka
11	éndheka
12	dhódheka
13	dhekatrís, dhekatría
14	dhekatésseris, dhekatéssera
15	dhekapénde
16	dhekaéksi, dhekáksi
17	dhekaëftá, dhekaëptá
18	dhekaokhtó, dhekaoktó
19	dhekaënneá, dhekaënnéa
20	íkosi,
21	íkosi énas, miá, éna
22	íkosi dhió, dhío
30	triánda
31	triánda énas, miá, éna
40	saránda
50	penínda
60	eksínda
70	evdhomínda
80	oghdhónda, oghdhoínda
90	enenínda
100	ekató(n)
101	ekatón énas, miá, éna
153	ekatón penínda tris, tría
200	dhiakósi, dhiakósies, dhiakósia
300	triakósi, -ies, -ia
400	tetrakósi, -ies, -ia
500	pendakósi, -ies, -ia
600	eksakósi, -ies, -ia
700	eftakósi, -ies, -ia
800	okhtakósi, -ies, -ia
900	enneakósi, -ies, -ia
1000	khíli, khílies, khília
5000	pénde khiliádes
1,000,000	éna ekatommírio

Ordinals

1st	prótos, próti, próto(n)
2nd	dhéfteros, -i, -o(n)
3rd	trítos, -i, -o(n)
4th	tétartos, tetárti, tétarto(n)
5th	pémptos
6th	éktos
7th	évdhomos, evdhómi
8th	óghdhoos
9th	énnatos, ennáti
10th	dhékatos, dhekáti
11th	endhékatos, endhekáti
20th	ikostós, -i, -ó(n)
30th	triakostós, -i, -ó(n)
100th	ekatostós, -i, -ó(n)
101st	ekatostós prótos
124th	ekatostós ikostós tétartos
1000th	khiliostós

Fractions

$\frac{1}{2}$	misós, -i, -ó(n), ímisis
$\frac{1}{3}$	tríton
$\frac{1}{4}$	tétarton
$\frac{1}{10}$	dhékaton

The Greek Alphabet

Single letters

Greek letter	Anc. Gk name	Mod. Gk pron.	Pronunciation of letter
A α	alpha	álfa	a	semi-long
B β	beta	víta	v
Γ γ	gamma	gháma	gh, y	see on right
Δ δ	delta	dhélta	dh	as in English "the"
E ϵ	epsilon	épsilon	e	open, semi-long
Z ζ	zeta	zíta	z
H η	eta	íta	ee	semi-long
Θ ϑ	theta	thíta	th	as in English "thin"
I ι	iota	ióta	i, y	see on right
K $\varkappa$	kappa	kápa	k, ky	see on right
Λ λ	lambda	lámdha	l
M μ	mu	mi	m	see on right
N ν	nu	ni	n	see on right
Ξ ξ	xi	ksi	x
O o	omicron	ómikron	o	open, semi-long
Π π	pi	pi	p
P ϱ	rho	ro	r	lightly rolled
Σ σ^1	sigma	síghma	s	see on right
T τ	tau	taf	t
Y v	upsilon	ýpsilon	i, y	see on right
Φ φ	phi	fi	f
X χ	chi	khi	ch	see on right
Ψ ψ	psi	psi	ps
Ω ω	omega	oméga	o	open, semi-long

[1] written ς at the end of a word

Combinations of letters

Comb.	Pronunciation		Example	Pronunc.	Meaning
$\alpha\iota^2$	e	open, as in "hen"	$\nu\alpha\iota$	nè	yes
$\alpha\upsilon^2$	av	before vowel before $\beta, \gamma, \delta, \zeta, \lambda, \mu, \nu, \varrho$	$\pi\alpha\acute{\upsilon}\omega$	pávo	cease
	af	before $\vartheta, \varkappa, \xi, \pi, \sigma, \tau, \varphi, \chi, \psi$	$\alpha\grave{\upsilon}\gamma\acute{o}$ $\alpha\grave{\upsilon}\tau\acute{o}\varsigma$	avghó aftós	egg this
γ	gh	before a, o or u sound	$\gamma\acute{\alpha}\lambda\alpha$	ghála	milk
	y	before consonant before e or i sound	$\gamma\varrho\acute{\alpha}\mu\mu\alpha$ $\gamma\acute{\epsilon}\varphi\upsilon\varrho\alpha$	ghrámma yéfira	letter bridge
$\gamma\gamma$	ng	before a, o or u sound before consonant	$\mu\alpha\gamma\gamma\alpha\nu\epsilon\acute{\iota}\alpha$ $\varphi\alpha\gamma\gamma\varrho\acute{\iota}$	mangania fangrí	witchcraft sea-bream
	ngy	before e or i sound	$\acute{\alpha}\gamma\gamma\epsilon\lambda\acute{o}\varsigma$	ángyelos	angel
$\gamma\iota$ $\gamma\varkappa$	y ng	before a, o or u sound before consonant	$\gamma\iota\acute{\alpha}$ $\acute{\epsilon}\gamma\varkappa\omega\pi\acute{\eta}$	ya engopí	for cut
			$\acute{\epsilon}\gamma\varkappa\lambda\eta\mu\alpha$	énglima	crime
	ngy	before e or i sound	$\acute{\alpha}\gamma\varkappa\upsilon\varrho\alpha$	ángyira	anchor
	g	at beginning of word	$\gamma\varkappa\alpha\varrho\acute{\iota}\zeta\omega$	garíso	shout
$\gamma\chi$	ngkh	in foreign words (for χ see below)	$\mu\alpha\gamma\varkappa\alpha\zeta\acute{\iota}$ $\acute{\epsilon}\gamma\chi\acute{\omega}\varrho\iota\sigma\varsigma$	magazi engkhórios	shop native
$\epsilon\iota^2$	i	semi-long	$\epsilon\acute{\iota}\delta\sigma\varsigma$	idhos	kind, sort
	y	unstressed before vowel	$\grave{\alpha}\sigma\varphi\acute{\alpha}\lambda\epsilon\iota\alpha$	asfálya	safety
$\epsilon\upsilon^2$	ev	before vowel before $\beta, \gamma, \delta, \zeta, \lambda, \mu, \nu, \varrho$	$\epsilon\grave{\upsilon}\omega\delta\acute{\iota}\alpha$ $\epsilon\grave{\upsilon}\gamma\epsilon\nu\acute{\eta}\varsigma$	evodhía evyenís	perfume polite
	ef	before $\vartheta, \varkappa, \xi, \pi, \sigma, \tau, \varphi, \chi, \psi$	$\epsilon\grave{\upsilon}\varkappa\sigma\lambda\sigma\varsigma$	éfkolos	easy
ι	i	semi-long	$\grave{\iota}\varrho\iota\varsigma$	iris	rainbow
	y	unstressed before vowel	$\acute{\iota}\delta\iota\sigma\varsigma$	ídhyos	self
$\varkappa$	k		$\varkappa\alpha\lambda\acute{o}\varsigma$	kalós	good
	ky	before e or i sound	$\varkappa\alpha\acute{\iota}$	kyè	and
	yky	between vowel and e or i sound	$\pi\alpha\iota\delta\acute{\alpha}\varkappa\iota$	pedáykyi	small child
$\mu\pi$	b	at beginning of word	$\mu\pi\alpha\acute{\iota}\nu\omega$	béno	go in
		in foreign words	$\mu\pi\acute{\iota}\varrho\alpha$	bira	beer
	mb	between vowels	$\varkappa\sigma\lambda\acute{\upsilon}\mu\pi\iota$	kolímbi	swimming
$\nu\tau$	d	at beginning of word	$\nu\tau\acute{\upsilon}\nu\omega$	díno	dress
		in foreign words	$\grave{\alpha}\nu\tau\acute{\iota}o$	adío	goodbye
	nd	between vowels	$\delta\acute{o}\nu\tau\iota$	dhóndi	tooth

A ν at the end of a word affects the consonant at the beginning of a following word:
..ν $\varkappa$.. =ng; ..ν $\mu\pi$.. =mb; ..ν $\nu\tau$. =nd; ..ν ξ.. =ngs; ..ν π.. =mb; ..ν τ.. =nd; ..ν $\tau\sigma$.. =nds; ..ν ψ.. =mbs

| $\sigma\iota^2$ $\sigma\upsilon^2$ | i u | semi-long semi-long | $\sigma\grave{\iota}\varkappa\sigma\iota$ $\pi\sigma\grave{\upsilon}$ | íkyi pu | at home where |

σ s
A sigma at the end of a word (ς) is voiced (i.e. pronounced like z) when the following word begins with $\beta, \gamma, \delta, \lambda, \mu, \nu$ or ϱ

υ	i	semi-long	$\grave{\upsilon}\pi\nu\sigma\varsigma$	ípnos	sleep
	y	unstressed before vowel	$\gamma\upsilon\alpha\lambda\acute{\iota}$	yialí	glass
χ	ch	before consonant or a, o or u sound, as in Scottish "loch"	$\chi\varrho\grave{\omega}\mu\alpha$	khróma	colour
		before e or i sound, as in German "ich": i.e. somewhere between ch and sh	$\chi\acute{\epsilon}\varrho\iota$	khéri	hand

[2] pronounced separately when there is an accent or diaeresis on one of the vowels

Everyday expressions

Good morning, good day!	Kaliméra!	Excuse me	Me sinkhoríte
Good evening!	Kalispéra!	Yes	Nè, málista (turning head to side)
Good night!	Kalí níkhta!	No	Ókhi (jerking head upwards)
Goodbye!	Kalín andámosi(n)!	Please	Parakaló
Do you speak English?	Omilíte angliká?	Thank you	Efkharistó
French?	ghalliká?	Yesterday	Khthes
German?	yermaniká?	Today	Símera, símeron
I do not understand	Dhen katalamváno	Tomorrow	Ávrio(n)
		Help!	Voíthia!
		Open	Aniktó

Closed	Klistó
When?	Potê?
Single room	Dhomátio
	mè éna kreváti
Double room	Dhomátio
	mé dhío krevátia
Room with bath	Dhomátio mè lutró
What does it cost?	Póso káni?
Waken me at 6 o'clock	Ksipníste me stis eksi
Where is	Pu inè to
the bathroom?	apokhoritírion?
a pharmacy?	éna farmakíon?
a doctor?	énas yatrós?
a dentist?	énas odhondoyatrós?
. . . Street?	i odhós (+ name in
	genitive)
. . . Square?	i platía (+ name in
	genitive)

Travelling

Aerodrome, airfield	Aerodhromíon
Aircraft	Aeropláno(n)
Airport	Aerolimín
All aboard!	Is tas théses sas!
Arrival	Erkhomós
Bank	Trápeza
Boat	Várka, káiki
Bus	Leoforíon, búsi
Change	Alásso
Departure (by air)	Apoyíosis
(by boat)	Apóplus
(by train)	Anakhórisis
Exchange (money)	Saráfiko
Ferry	Férri-bóut, porthmíon
Flight	Ptísis
Hotel	Ksenodhokhíon
Information	Pliroforía
Lavatory/bathroom	Apokhoritírion
Luggage	Aposkevá
Luggage check	Apódhiksis ton
	aposkevón
Non-smoking	
compartment	Dhya mi kapnistás
Porter	Akhthofóros
Railway	Sidhiródhromos
Restaurant car	Vagón-restorán
Ship	Karávi, plíon
Sleeping-car	Vagón-li, klinámaksa
Smoking compartment	Dhya kapnistás
Station (railway)	Stathmós
Stop (bus)	Stásis
Ticket	Bilyétto
Ticket-collector	Ispráktor
Ticket-window	Thíris
Timetable	Dhromolóyion
Train	Tréno
Waiting room	Éthusa anamonis

Months

January	Yanuários, Yennáris
February	Fevruários, Fleváris
March	Mártios, Mártis
April	Aprílios
May	Máyos, Máis
June	Yúnios
July	Yúlios
August	Ávghustos
September	Septémvrios
October	Októvrios, Októvris
November	Noémvrios, Noémvris
December	Dhekémvrios
Month	Min, mínas

Days of the week

Sunday	Kiriakí
Monday	Dheftéra
Tuesday	Tríti
Wednesday	Tetárti
Thursday	Pémpti
Friday	Paraskeví
Saturday	Sávato(n)
Week	Evdhomádha
Day	(I)méra
Weekday	Katheriminí
Holiday	Skholí

Holidays

New Year's Day	Protokhroniá
Easter	Páskha, Lambrá(i)
Whitsun	Pendikostí
Christmas	Khristúyenna

At the post office

Address	Dhiéfthinsis
Air mail	Aeroporikós
Express	Epíghusa
Letter	Epistolí
Letter-box	Çhrammatokivótio(n)
Package	Dhematáki
Postcard	Takhidromikí kárta
Poste restante	Post restánt
Post office	Takhidhromíon
Registered	Sistiméni
Stamp	Ghrammatósimo(n)
Telegram	Tileghráfima
Telephone	Tiléfono(n)
Telex	Tilétipo(n)
Parcel	Dhéma, pakétto

Motoring

Accelerator	Mísa
Accident	Dhistíkhima
Battery	Bataría
Bolt	Vídha
Brake	Fréno
Breakdown	Atíkhima
Car	Aftokínito
Carburettor	Karbiratér
Clutch	Ambrayás
Cylinder	Kílindhros
Engine	Kinitír
Fuse	Asfálya
Garage	Garás
Gear	Takhítites
Gearbox	Kivótion takhitíton
Gear-lever	Mokhlós allayís takhítitos
Grease	Grassáro
Headlight	Fanós
Horn	Klákson
Ignition	Anáfleksis
Insurance	Asfálisis
Jack	Ghrílos
Lamp, light	Lámba
Motorcycle	Motosiklétta
Nut	Paksimádhi
Oil	Mikhanéleo(n)
Oil change	Allayí eléu
Parking place	Stathmós na parkáro

Petrol/gas	Venzíni	Speed	Takhítis
Petrol station/gas station	Venzinádhiko	Speedometer	Takhímetro(n)
Plug	Busí	Starter	Ekkinitís
Pressure	Píesis aéros	Steering wheel	Timóni
Radiator	Psiyíon	Tow away	Rimulkíso
Repair	Epidhiorthóno	Tyre	Lástikho
Screwdriver	Katsavídhi	Valve	Valvídha
Spanner	Klidhí(on)	Wheel	Ródha
Spare part	Andalaktikó	Workshop	Erghastírio(n)

Accommodation

Hotels

Greece possesses some 3500 **hotels**, all affiliated to the Greek Chamber of Commerce. In addition to the hotels there are numerous *bungalow villages* and *holiday houses and apartments*, a list of which can be obtained from the Greek National Tourist Organisation. In country areas accommodation in *private houses*, simple but clean, is available everywhere.

The hotels are officially classified into six categories – L (luxury), A, B, C, D and E – and most visitors will look for accommodation in one of the first four categories. A new hotel in a lower category may well be pleasanter than an old one in a higher category.

The tariffs shown in the following table are inclusive of service and taxes. Given the present trend of inflation, however, increases are to be expected.

Category	Single room per person per night	Double room per person per night
	dr.	dr.
L (luxury)	300 up	500 up
A	200–550	330–750
B	170–410	250–580
C	140–280	180–340
D	120–190	170–280
E	90–170	130–220

Youth Hostels

There are youth hostels providing accommodation at reasonable prices, particularly designed for young people, both on the mainland of Greece and on the islands of Crete and Corfu. Most of them are open throughout the year. In hostels in the mountains and on the coast advance booking is advisable. The stay at any one hostel is limited to not more than 5 nights. Youth hostellers must produce a membership card issued by their national youth hostels association.

Information from the *Organosis Xenonon Neotitos Ellados* (Greek Youth Hostels Association), Dragatsaniou 4, Platia Klafthmonos, Athens, tel. (01) 3 23 41 07 and 3 23 75 90.

Camping and Caravanning

Facilities for camping and caravanning are still in course of development in Greece. Sites are run by the Greek National Tourist Organisation, the Greek Touring Club and private individuals, some of them with bungalows (chalets) available for renting. Most of the sites are in areas of scenic beauty and on the coast. – Camping outside authorised sites is not officially permitted.

Information from information bureaux of the Greek National Tourist Organisation and the local Tourist Police.

Food and Drink

In the larger hotels visitors will usually be offered the standard international cuisine, with some Greek dishes to add an extra touch of colour. In **restaurants** (*estiatórion, tavérna, restorán*), **rotisseries** (*psistariá*) and **inns** (*pandokhion*) the national cuisine predominates, showing strong Eastern (mainly Turkish) influence and making much use of olive oil, garlic and herbs. The menu is often in English or another Western European language as well as in Greek, though in the more modest establishments it is likely to be only in Greek, and usually written by hand. Except in restaurants of the higher classes, however, it is the normal thing for clients to go into the kitchen and choose for themselves what they want to eat.

The **breakfast** (*próyevma*) served in hotels is usually of the normal continental type. **Lunch** (*yévma*) is normally eaten between 12 and 3, **dinner** (*dhípno*) between 8 and 10.

Tipping (*purboár*). – The hotel guide published by the Chamber of Commerce of the Hotel Industry gives the inclusive tariffs which are charged by hotels. Otherwise the normal service charge is 15%, and this applies also in restaurants. It is usual to round up the sum given to a waiter (*garsón*) in a restaurant, and also to leave a small amount on the table for the waiter's boy assistant (*mikrós*); and visitors should, of course, imitate the regular Greek practice in this respect.

An important role is played in the daily life of the Greeks by the **coffee-house** or café (*kafeníon*), which is not merely for drinking coffee but performs a social function as a place for meeting friends, for conversation and for playing cards or other games. Coffee is served with the accompaniment of a glass of water (*neró*), which is usually very good; *ouzo*, the aniseed-flavoured national aperitif, is accompanied by small pieces of cheese, olives, etc. – The *patisseries* (*zakharoplastíon*) serve pastries and sweets as well as beverages.

The Greek Menu
(*katálogos, lísta*)

The *table setting*: plate *piáto*, cup *flitsáni*, spoon *kutáli*, knife *makhéri*, fork *pirúni*, glass *potíri*.

Hors d'œuvre (*orektiká*). – There is a wide choice. In addition to the appetisers (*mesedakía*: pickled olives or cocktail onions, cheese, pieces of squid, etc.) which are served with the aperitif (usually *ouzo*) the range includes prawns, seafood, vine-leaves stuffed with rice (*dolmádhes*) and salads (*salátes*).

Soups (*súpes*). – Greek soups are usually very substantial, and are often made with eggs and lemon juice. *Fasólada* is a popular thick bean soup; others include pepper soup (*pipéri súpa*), with the addition of vegetables and meat, and clear bouillon (*somós kréatos*). *Kakaviá* is a fish soup similar to the bouillabaisse of Marseilles, made of various kinds of fish and seafood with onions, garlic and olive oil. There are also other excellent fish soups (*psárosupes*).

Meat (*kréas*). – The favourite kind of meat is lamb (*arní*), usually roasted or grilled. *Suvlákia* and *döner kebab* (meat grilled on the spit) are also popular. *Kokkorétsi* (lamb entrails roasted on the spit) are a popular dish in country areas. Pork (*khirinó kréas*) is rarely served.

Vegetables and salads (*lakhaniká, salátes*). – Typical Mediterranean vegetables are artichokes (*angináres*), aubergines/eggplants (*melitsánes*), courgettes/zucchini (*kolokithákia*) and peppers (*piperiés*), usually stuffed or cooked in oil. Salads include lettuce (*marúli*), tomato salad (*tomáto saláta*) and asparagus salad (*sparángia saláta*).

Fish (*psári*). – Fish and seafood feature prominently on Greek menus. The commonest species are sea-bream (*sinagrída, tsipúra, ridrinári*), sole (*glóssa*), cod

(*murúna*), red mullet (*barbúni*) and tunny (*tónnos*), together with langoustes (*palinúri*), lobsters (*astakós*), mussels (*mídia*), squid (*kalamári*), octopuses (*oktapódi*) and sea-urchins (*akhinós*).

Desserts (*dessér*). – The commonest desserts are fruit (*frúta*) or an ice (*pagotón*). There is a wide variety of fruit. Locally grown, and usually excellent, are melons (*mulkáiko, pepóni, karpúsi*), peaches (*rodákino*), pears (*akhládi*), apples (*mílo*), oranges (*portokáli*), grapes (*stafília*) and figs (*síka*).

Cheese (*tirí*). – Most Greek cheeses are made from sheep's milk or goat's milk. Among them are *agráfa* (a sheep's-milk cheese reminiscent of Gruyère), *manúri*, *kopanistí* (a highly spiced sheep's- or goat's-milk cheese), *misíthra* (a mild curd cheese) and *anári* (a goat's-milk cheese). Yogurt (*yaúrti*), made from sheep's or goat's milk, is also commonly found.

Miscellaneous. – Bread *psomí*, butter *vútiro*, salt *aláti*, pepper *pipéri*, sugar *zákharis*, milk *gála*, roll *psomáki*.

Drinks (*potá*). – The commonest drink is wine (*krasí, ínos*), either white (*áspro krasí*) or red (*mávro krasí*). The usual table wines are resinated to improve their keeping qualities (*retsína, krasí retsináto*), and have a characteristic sharp taste which has to be got used to. The better quality unresinated wines have already been brought into line with EEC directives; they are identified by the letters VQPRD on the label.

Beer (*bíra*). – The brewing of beer in Greece dates from the reign of King Otto I, a native of Bavaria. Thanks to the good water of Greece, the beers, mostly brewed to Bavarian recipes, are excellent.

Spirits (*pnevmatódi póta*). – The commonest type of spirit is *ouzo*, an aniseed-flavoured schnapps usually drunk as an aperitif with the addition of water. *Ráki* is similar but stronger Greek brandy (*konyák*) has a fruitier aroma than the French variety but less character. *Mastíkha* is a liqueur made from the bark of the mastic tree.

Soft drinks. – These include mineral water (*metallikó neró, sóda*), orangeade and lemonade (*portokaláda, lemonáda*), and freshly pressed fruit juices (orange juice, *portokaláda fréskya*).

Coffee (*kafés*) comes in different strengths and degrees of sweetness – e.g. *kafés glikís vrastós* made with plenty of sugar, *varýs glikós* strong and sweet, *métrios* medium strength with little sugar, *elafrós* light. – *Tea* (*tsái*) is of different kinds – *mávro tsái* black tea, *tsái ménda* peppermint tea, *tsái tu vunú* an infusion of mountain herbs.

Squid (*kalamári*)

Wine-Growing Regions

Red wine
White wine
Red and white wine

The Major Wine-Growing Regions of Greece, *with a selection of their wines*

Thrace

Macedonia
Naussa

Epirus
Sitsa

Corfu
Ropa

Thessaly
Ambelakia
Rapsani

Euboea
Marmari
Kokkineli
Chalkidas
Kymi

Central Greece
Mavrudi (Delphi)

Attica
Attiki
Retsina
Kokkineli
Pendeli

Lefkás
Lefkas

Kefallinía
Rombola
Mavrodaphne

Zákynthos
Verdea

Peloponnese
Mavrodaphne
Demestica
Achaia
Nemea
Mantinia
Castel Danielis

Lemnos
Kalpaki

Ándros
Andros

Ikaría
Ikaria

Sámos
Samos (Muscat)

Páros
Paros

Náxos
Naxos

Íos
Ios

Amorgós
Amorgos

Kos

Santorin (Thera)
Thira
Santorini
Vinsanto

Crete
Creta
Malvasia
Romeiko
Pesa
Gortys

Rhodes
Malvasia (Malmsey)
Lindos

Wine

The Greek liking for resinated wines dates back to ancient times, as is shown by the remains of resin found in the earliest amphoras. The resin is added to the wine during fermentation and gives it a very characteristic taste which may not appeal to everyone at first; but resinated wines, once the taste has been acquired, are very palatable and stimulating to the appetite.

About half the wine produced in Greece is resinated.

There are also some unresinated wines which have been brought into line with EEC directives and bear the letters "VQ-PRD" on the label.

Both dry and sweet wines are produced. The wines best known outside Greece are the white wine of Sámos and Mavro-daphne, a sweet red wine.

The Language of the Wine Label

Ἀφρώδες κρασί (Afródhes krasí)	Sparkling wine	Οἶνος (Ínos)	Wine
Ἐμφιάλωσις (Emfiálosis)	Bottling	Οἶνος ἐρυθρός (Ínos erithrós)	Red wine
Ἐπιτραπέζιο κρασί (Epitrapézio krasí)	Table wine	Οἶνος λευκός (Ínos lefkós)	White wine
Καμπανίτης (Kambanítis)	Sparkling wine	Οἶνος μαῦρος (Ínos mávros)	Red wine
Κρασί (Krasí)	Wine	Παραγογή (Paraghoyí)	Production
Ξηρός (Ksíros)	Dry	Πίνεται δροσερό (Pinetè dhroseró)	To be drunk cold
Μαῦρο κρασί (Mávro krasí)	Red wine	Ρετσίνα (Retsína)	Retsina (resinated wine)
Οἰνοποιεῖον (Inopiyíon)	Wine-making establishment	Ροζέ (Rosé)	Rosé wine
		Σαμπάνια (Sampánya)	Champagne-type wine

Manners and Customs

The people of Greece are courteous to strangers and ever ready to help them, though never over-officious. Belonging as they do to an old seafaring nation, they show a lively interest in world events and international politics; but visitors will do well to observe discretion in discussing political matters and above all to avoid thoughtless criticism of conditions in Greece. – It is pleasant to find a general absence of begging and guides, porters, etc., who do not pester visitors to employ them.

As in many southern countries, importance is attached to *correct dress*, though with the development of

tourism there has been some relaxation in this respect. *Nude bathing* is prohibited everywhere in Greece.

Opening times. – *Shops* are usually open on weekdays from 8 to 2.30, and on Tuesdays, Thursdays and Fridays (food shops on Tuesdays, Fridays and Saturdays) from 5.30 to 8.30. – *Banks* normally open at 8 and close at 1.30. In major tourist centres they are sometimes open also in the afternoon and on Saturdays and Sundays (list from Greek National Tourist Organisation). – *Museums* and archaeological sites have varying opening times. They are usually closed on Tuesdays (exceptions are the National Archaeological Musuem and Benaki Museum in Athens and the Archaeological Museum in Iráklion, which are closed on Mondays, and the National Historical Museum in Athens, which is closed on Sundays), and on 1 January, 25 March, Good Friday, Easter Day and 25 December. On Sundays and public holidays admission for individual visitors (but not for conducted groups) is free. Special permission is required for taking photographs and filming with a tripod.

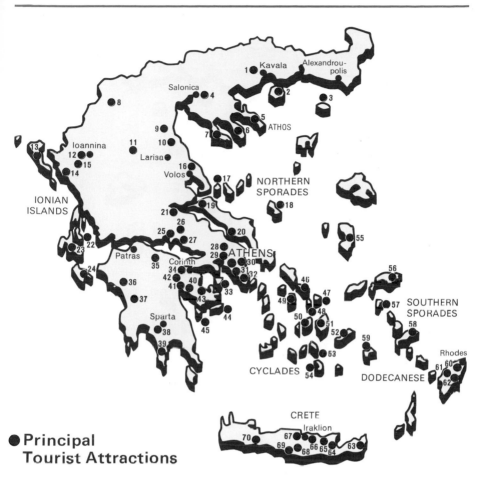

● Principal
Tourist Attractions

1 Philippi	25 Delphi	49 Island of Sýros
2 Island of Thásos	26 Mt Parnassus	50 Island of Páros
3 Island of Samothrace	27 Ósios Loukás	51 Island of Náxos
4 Salonica	monastery	52 Island of Amorgos
	28 Mt Parnes	53 Island of Íos
CHALCIDICE	29 Dafní monastery	54 Island of Santorin
5 Athos peninsula		
6 Sithonia peninsula	30 ATHENS	55 Island of Chios
7 Kassandra peninsula		56 Island of Sámos
	31 Attic Riviera	
8 Kastoriá	32 Cape Soúnion	SOUTHERN
9 Mt Olympus	33 Island of Aegina	SPORADES
10 Vale of Tempe		57 Island of Pátmos
11 Metéora monasteries	PELOPONNESE	58 Island of Kos
12 Ioánnina	34 Corinth	
	35 Megaspileon	59 Island of Astypálaia
13 Island of Corfu	monastery	ISLAND OF RHODES
14 Párga	36 Olympia	60 Town of Rhodes
15 Dodóna	37 Bassai	61 Kámiros
16 Mt Pelion	38 Mistra	62 Líndos
17 Island of Skiáthos	39 Diros caves	
18 Island of Skýros	40 Náfplion	CRETE
	41 Tiryns	63 Káto Zákros
EUBOEA	42 Mycenae	64 Áyios Nikólaos,
19 Loutra Aidipsou	43 Epidauros	Gourniá
20 Khalkis	44 Island of Hýdra	65 Mália
21 Thermopylai	45 Island of Spétsai	66 Knossos
		67 Iráklion
SOUTHERN IONIAN	CYCLADES	68 Górtys
ISLANDS	46 Island of Tínos	69 Phaistós, Ayía Triáda
22 Ithaca	47 Island of Mýkonos	70 Samaria Gorge
23 Kefallinía	48 Island of Delos	
24 Zákynthos		

Bathing and Water Sports

● Bathing Beaches

1 Ayía Triáda
2 Sani
3 Gerakini
4 Paliouri
5 Ay. Kiriaki
6 Stavros
7 Kavala
8 Alexandroúpolis
9 Corfu
10 Párga
11 Vólos
12 Argostoli
13 Pátras
14 Kaména Voúrla
15 Loutra Aidipsou
16 Eretria
17 Skafidia
18 Náfplion
19 Aegina
20 Vouliagmeni
21 Lagonisi

22 Andros
23 Kalamáta
24 Areopolis
25 Sámos
26 Khaniá
27 Amnisos
28 Áyios Nikólaos
29 Rhodes

● Scuba Diving Areas

30 Kassandra
31 Amoliani/Athos
32 Sithonia
33 Corfu
34 Paxos
35 Lefkás
36 Kefallinía
37 Zákynthos
38 Mýkonos

Párga (Epirus) – a sandy beach on the Ionian Sea

Water-Skiing

There are water-skiing schools at Vouliagmeni, Varkitsa, Lagonisi, Gerakini (Chalcidice), Corfu, Khaniá and Elounda (Crete), and Pórto Khéli and on the islands of Póros, Skiáthos and Spétsai.

Information: *Greek Water-Skiing Association,*
Stournara 32,
Athens;
tel. (01) 5 23 18 75.

Scuba Diving

There are facilities for learning scuba diving in Athens, Piraeus and Salonica and on the islands of Rhodes and Corfu.

There are *decompression chambers* at the diving schools in Athens, Salonica and Corfu, in the Naval Hospital in Piraeus and at the naval base in Souda Bay, near Khaniá (Crete).

Information: *Greek Sub-Aqua Diving Club,*
Ayios Kosmas,
Athens-*Elliniko;*
tel. (01) 9 81 99 61.

Sailing

There are sailing schools in Athens, Salonica, Vólos, Kalamáta and Alexandroúpolis and on Corfu and Sýros.

Information: *Greek Sailing Club,*
Xenofontos 15A,
Athens;
tel. (01) 3 23 68 13 and 3 23 55 60.

A caique – the maid-of-all-work of the Aegean

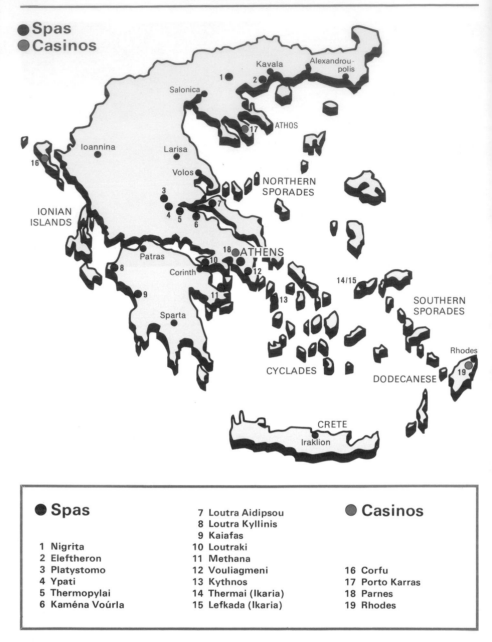

● Spas
● Casinos

● Spas		● Casinos
	7 Loutra Aidipsou	
	8 Loutra Kyllinis	
	9 Kaiafas	
1 Nigrita	10 Loutraki	
2 Eleftheron	11 Methana	
3 Platystomo	12 Vouliagmeni	16 Corfu
4 Ypati	13 Kythnos	17 Porto Karras
5 Thermopylai	14 Thermai (Ikaria)	18 Parnes
6 Kaména Voúrla	15 Lefkada (Ikaria)	19 Rhodes

Golf

Golf was late in coming to Greece, but it is now becoming increasingly popular. There are at present four courses – *Glyfada* Golf Club (18 holes), 16 km (10 miles) from Athens in the direction of Soúnion; the Hellenic Golf Club (9 holes) at *Varibobi*, 21 km (13 miles) N of Athens; the *Corfu* Golf and Country Club (18 holes), 14 km (9 miles) W of Kerkyra; and the Afantou Golf Club (18 holes), 20 km (12 miles) E of the town of *Rhodes*. Courses are planned or under construction on the Chalcidice peninsula, on the island of Skiáthos and at Anavyssos on the coast road to Cape Soúnion.

Golf course at Glyfada, near Athens

● Stalactitic Caves

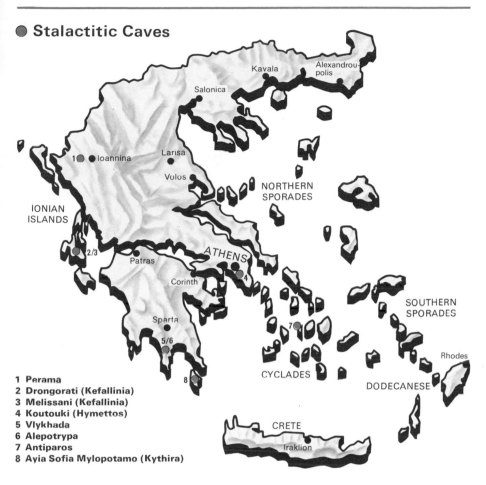

1 Perama
2 Drongorati (Kefallinia)
3 Melissani (Kefallinia)
4 Koutouki (Hymettos)
5 Vlykhada
6 Alepotrypa
7 Antiparos
8 Ayia Sofia Mylopotamo (Kythira)

Climbing

The mountains of Crete, the Peloponnese, central Greece, Thessaly, Macedonia and Epirus offer ample scope for hill walkers and climbers. There are numerous mountain huts, mostly between 1100 and 2000 m (3609 and 6562 feet), run by the Greek climbing clubs.

Information: *Greek Alpine Club,*
Karageorgis Servias 7,
Athens;
tel. (01) 3 23 45 55.

Greek Touring Club,
Polytekhniou 12,
Athens;
tel. (01) 5 24 86 01.

Winter Sports

The mountainous parts of Greece are increasingly being opened up for skiers by the installation of lifts and hoists. At altitudes of around 1800 m (5906 feet) the winter sports season lasts from December to March; on Mt Olympus, Mt Parnassus and the higher levels in the Pindos range it continues until May.

Folk Traditions

In recent years the old Greek **traditional costumes** have become rarer, but in some parts of the country they are still to be seen. Thus on the island of Crete, for example, men can still sometimes be encountered wearing the characteristic breeches (*vraka*) and black head-scarf; and the old costumes can also be seen on Kárpathos, in the southern part of Rhodes, in the Pindos range and on Corfu. The picturesque uniform of the "Evzones" (the former royal bodyguard) who can be seen, for example, at the National Memorial in Athens, is derived from an old Albanian costume.

Many old traditional customs still find expression in the numerous **church festivals** (particularly Easter and patronal festivals) and in family celebrations in country areas.

Within recent years Greek **folk music**, with its characteristic rhythms and its (to Western ears) unusual intervals, has become widely known in the rest of Europe, and it has also been a major influence of Greek light music. In addition to the popular *bouzoúki*, a mandoline-like stringed instrument, the *santoúri* and various woodwind instruments feature prominently in the music.

The best-known Greek **folk dance** is the *sirtáki*, a kind of round dance centred on one leading dancer.

Greek traditional costumes

Calendar of Events

January	
1st	
Everywhere	New Year's Day; St Basil's Day; cutting of the *vasilopitta* (New Year cake)
Island of Ándros, Plateos (Véria)	Popular festivals
6th	
Many places	Three Kings' Day (Epiphany); Blessing of the Waters (immersion of cross in sea, lake or river)
Kozani	Bourbousaria festival
Monoklisia, N. Petra (Serrai)	"Women's Day"
February	
Carnival	
Many places	Carnival celebrations, particularly at Pátras, Athens (Plaka), Zákynthos, Sparta, Chalcidice (Poliyiros), Salonica, Kalambáka, Skýros, Pourno, Ayia Anna (Euboea), Ayiasos (Lésbos), Thimiana (Chios) and Naousa
February/March	
Meliki (Veria)	Mock peasant wedding
March	
Kastoriá	Fur Fair
Beginning of month	
Kozani	Fanos festival (bonfires, folk dances of the Pontos region)
Ash Wednesday	
Everywhere	Kathara Dheftera (Ash Wednesday) celebrations, with picnics, kite-flying and Lenten dishes. Traditional celebrations at Thebes, Ayia Eleni (Serrai), Messina and Nesta (Chios); Carnival at Galaxidi, Ayiasos (Lésbos), Vasilika and Sokho (Salonica)

25th	
Everywhere	National Day; military parades
April	
15th and 21st	
Corfu	Feast of St Spyridon, patron saint of the island
Holy Week	
Everywhere	Procession with lighted candles on Good Friday; midnight mass on Easter Saturday; feast, with lamb on the spit and hard-boiled eggs dyed red, on Easter Day. Particularly picturesque celebrations at Ia, Tripolis, Levádia, Trapeza (Pátras) and Olympos (Karpathos: Wednesday)
23rd	
Many places	St George's Day: particularly on Lemnos (horse-races), at Asi Gonia near Khaniá (sheep-shearing competition) and at Arakhova
May	
Kalymnos	Departure of the sponge-divers
1st	
Everywhere	Labour Day and Feast of Flowers. Particular celebrations at Nea Filadelfia, Nea Khalkidona, Nea Smyrni, Kifissia and Karyes (Florina)
End of month	
Kardítsa	Karaiskakia festival
21st	
Corfu	Anniversary of reunion with Greece
21st	
Northern Greece	Anastenaria: dance with icons on glowing embers at Ayia Eleni and Ayios Petros (Serrai) and Langada (Salonica)

27th–29th	
Khaniá	Dance festival in commemoration of the battle for Crete
End of month	
Kolindros (Pieria)	Cherry Festival
End of May/beginning of June	
Ayia Paraskevi (Lésbos)	Bull Fair: sacrifice of calf, riding events and folk songs and dances
June	
Agrinion	Papastratia festival of cultural and sporting events
21st	
Rhodes	Kalafonon (midsummer bonfires)
End of month	
Lasíthi (Crete)	Klydona folk festival in villages of Piskokefalo and Krousta
June/July	
Port towns	Navy Week (in Vólos a re enactment of the sailing of the Argonauts)
July	
Náfpaktos	Papakharalambia (festival of artistic and sporting events)
Beginning of month	
Lefkimi (Corfu)	Fair, with folk dancing
Second half of month	
Réthymnon (Crete)	Cretan Wine Festival
Sitía (Crete)	Raisin Festival
26th	
Langadia (Tripolis)	Feast of Ayia Paraskevi, with folk-song contest
July/August	
Préveza	Nikopolia festival
August	
Ioánnina	Festival of literature and art
Katerini (Litokhoro)	Olympus Festival
Lefkás	Festival of literature and art
6th	
Anoyia (Crete)	Fair, with traditional celebrations
Middle of month	
Zákynthos	International Festival of Medieval and Popular Drama
Gýthion	Festival, with performances of classical tragedies
15th	
Many places	Festival of the Panayia, celebrated with particular pomp at Tínos, on Corfu and Lésbos, at Neapolis (Crete) and Kymi, on Páros (Fish and Wine Festival), and at Siatista (horse-racing) and Vlastis, near Kozani
Second half of month	
Portaria (Pelion)	Mock wedding in local style
Ithaka	Dramatic festival
Kritsa (Crete)	Cretan Wedding

24th	
Zákynthos	Feast of St Dionysius, patron saint of the island
September	
Salonica	International Trade Fair, with Song Festival and Film Festival
Zákynthos	Festival of art
Mesolóngi	Vyronia (festival of literature and art)
1st–15th	
Ankhialos (Salonica)	Wine Festival
8th–9th	
Spétsai	Naval Festival, commemorating the defeat of the Turks
Middle of month	
Nikiti (Chalcidice)	Folk festival
End of month	
Kýthira	Fair at Myrtidiotissa monastery
Elos Kisamou (Khaniá)	Chestnut Festival
October	
28th	
Everywhere	National Day
November	
4th	
Corfu	Feast of St Spyridon
8th	
Réthymnon (Crete)	Commemoration of Arkadi monastery
December	
24th	Christmas Eve: children go round singing *kalanda* (carols)
31st	New Year's Eve: exchange of gifts, singing of *kalanda*

Seasonal Events

The National Tourist Organisation of Greece organises every year, particularly during the summer, a series of events of tourist interest – the **Athens Festival** (July–September), with performances of classical drama, opera, music and ballet in the Odeon of Herodes Atticus; the **Epidauros Festival** of classical drama in the ancient theatre at Epidauros from July to mid August, followed by similar performances in other ancient theatres (Dodóna, Thásos, Philippi, etc.); performances in the *open-air theatre on Lykabettós*, Athens, during the summer; *operatic performances* by the Lyric Theatre (Skini Lyriki) company of Athens, given in the Odeon of Herodes Atticus in summer and in the Olympia Theatre in winter; the *Demetria Festival* at Salonica during the International Trade Fair in October; *folk-dancing* in the open-air theatre on Philopappos Hill (May–September) and the Aliki Theatre (November–March) in Athens and the theatre of Rhodes from June to October; and Wine Festivals in the Tourist Pavilion at Dafní near Athens (July–September), at Alexandroúpolis (July–August) and at Rodini on the island of Rhodes (July–September).

Statutory Public Holidays

1 January	New Year's Day
6 January	Three Kings' Day (Epiphany)
25 March	National Day
15 August	Dormition of the Mother of God
28 October	National Day
25 and 26 December	Christmas
Movable feasts	Monday before the beginning of the Fast (Lent), Good Friday and Easter Monday (usually on different dates from the Western churches)

Information

National Tourist Organisation of Greece

Ellinikós Organismós Tourismoú (*EOT*)

Head Office
Amerikis 2,
Athens;
tel. (01) 3 22 31 11.

United Kingdom
195–197 Regent Street,
London W1R 8DL;
tel. (01) 734 5997.

United States of America
Olympic Tower,
645 Fifth Avenue,
New York, NY 10022;
tel. (212) 421 5777.

627 West Sixth Street,
Los Angeles, CA 90017;
tel. (213) 626 6696.

168 North Michigan Avenue,
National Bank of Greece Building,
Chicago, IL 60601;
tel. (312) 782 1084.

Canada
Suite 67,
2 Place Ville Marie,
Esso Plaza,
Montreal, Quebec H3B 2C9;
tel. 871 1535.

Australia
51–57 Pitt Street,
Sydney, N.S.W. 2000;
tel. 241 1663–4.

There are EOT tourist information offices in the larger Greek towns. In smaller places information can be obtained from the **Tourist Police** (*Astynomia Allodapon*), who are responsible for helping foreign visitors to Greece.

Automobile and Touring Club of Greece (*ELPA*)

Head Office
Mesoyion 2,
Athens;
tel. (01) 7 79 16 15–19.

Branch offices in Salonica, Vólos, Pátras, Kavála, Kerkyra (Corfu), Lárisa, Khaniá (Crete) and Iráklion (Crete).

Greek Touring Club,
Polytekhniou 12,
Athens;
tel. (01) 5 24 86 01.

Diplomatic and Consular Offices in Greece

United Kingdom
Embassy
Ploutarkhou 1,
Athens;
tel. (01) 73 62 11.

Consulates
Papalexandrou 16,
Iráklion (Crete);
tel. (081) 22 40 12.

Thessalonikis 45,
Kavála;
tel. (051) 22 37 04.

Zambeli 2,
Kerkyra (Corfu);
tel. (0661) 3 00 55 and 3 79 95.

Votsi 2,
Pátras;
tel. (061) 27 73 29.

25 Martiou 23,
Rhodes;
tel. (0241) 2 72 47 and 2 73 06.

Vasileos Konstantinou 11,
Salonica;
tel. (031) 27 80 06 and 27 81 69.

Ayiou Theodorou,
Vathy, **Sámos**;
tel. (0273) 2 73 14.

United States of America
Embassy
Leoforos Vasilissis Sofias,
Athens;
tel. (01) 71 29 51 and 71 84 01

Consulate
Vasileos Konstantinou 59,
Salonica;
tel. (031) 26 61 21

Canada
Embassy
Ioannou Gennadiou,
Athens;
tel. (021) 73 95 11–18.

Airlines

Olympic Airways
Head Office:
Leoforos Syngrou 96,
Athens;
tel. (01) 92 92/1.

Desks at all commercial airports in Greece.

141 New Bond Street,
London W1;
tel. (01) 493 7262.

649 Fifth Avenue,
New York;
tel. (212) 750 7933.

British Airways
Othonos 10;
Athens;
tel. (01) 3 25 06 01.

Kapodistriou 20A,
Kerkyra/Corfu;
tel. (0661) 3 37 95–96.

Plotin of Crete Ltd,
Ieronimaki 1,
Iráklion/Crete;
tel. (081) 28 68 81–82.

Ereta Tours,
Ierou Lokhou 11,
Rhodes;
tel. (0241) 2 67 10–11.

Vas. Konstatinou 3,
Salonica;
tel. (031) 22 52 06–07.

Radio Transmissions in English

The Greek radio transmits a weather forecast in English daily at 6.35 a.m. and a news bulletin in English, French and German between 7.30 and 7.45 a.m. on weekdays and at 7.15 a.m. on Sundays.

There is a television news bulletin in English daily at 6.15 p.m.

International telephone dialling codes

From Britain to Greece	**010 30**	From Greece to Britain	**00 44**
From the United States or		From Greece to the United	
Canada to Greece	**011 30**	States or Canada	**00 1**

Radio Messages for Tourists

In cases of special emergency messages for tourists can be transmitted by the Greek radio. For information apply to motoring organisations or the police.
Messages in English are transmitted by the Greek National Service (medium wave, 728 kHz) in their morning news bulletin (7.15–7.30) and by the Greek Military Radio Service (medium wave, 1142 kHz) at 3 and 11 p.m.

Emergency calls within the Athens area

Police (central area)	**100**
Police (suburban areas)	**109**
Ambulance	**166**
Fire service	**199**
Tourist Police	**171**

In case of emergency outside Athens apply to the local Tourist Police.